9780934490092
AF573890

INDIAN ART OF THE AMERICAS

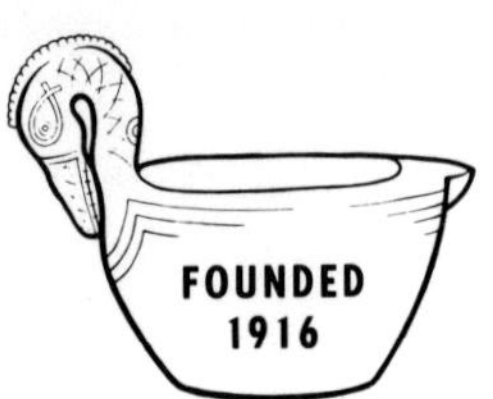
FOUNDED
1916

INDIAN ART OF THE AMERICAS

TEXT BY FREDERICK J. DOCKSTADER

PHOTOGRAPHY BY CARMELO GUADAGNO

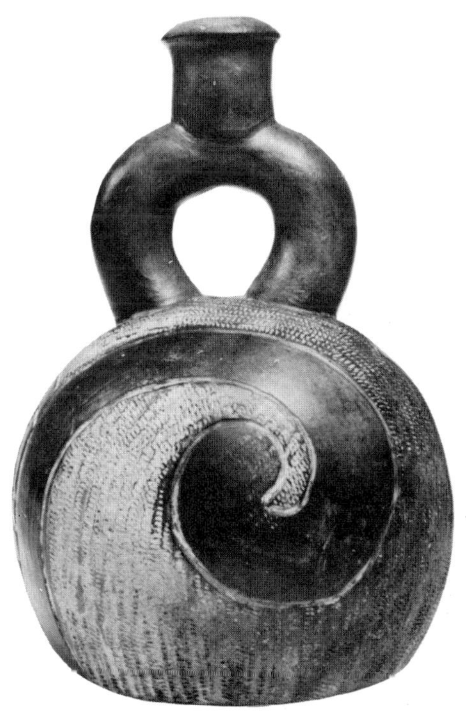

NEW YORK
MUSEUM OF THE AMERICAN INDIAN
HEYE FOUNDATION
1973

INDIAN ART OF THE AMERICAS
A touring exhibition organized by the
Museum of the American Indian, Heye Foundation

Grateful acknowledgement is made to
The National Endowment for the Arts
Washington, D.C.,
and
Philip Morris Incorporated on behalf of Marlboro
for their support in organizing this exhibition
and the publication of this catalog.

A portion of the proceeds from the sale of this catalog is being set aside to provide a scholarship fund for American Indian students interested in pursuing a career in the museum profession.

Library of Congress Catalog Card Number 73-89979.

Printed by LaSalle Litho, Inc., New York City

← *on the overleaf*

198. Stirrup-spout Vessel
Some of the finest pottery in South America is also among the earliest. This gracefully formed Chavín vessel has a swirling design achieved by removing the polished surface, leaving the pattern in bold relief. CUPISNIQUE. Tembladera, Cajamarca, Peru. 700-500 B.C. 6″ x 9″. 24/3517.

TABLE OF CONTENTS

PREFACE

This comprehensive exhibition was selected entirely from the collections of the Museum of the American Indian, Heye Foundation. It reflects the rich cultural heritage of all of the varied and little-known Indian civilizations that once extended down the American continents from the Arctic to Tierra del Fuego. And it offers what we feel is an unprecedented opportunity to compare and contrast, in one place and at one time, the esthetic achievements of Amerindian societies as they have evolved over the last 4,000 years.

Philip Morris is pleased and proud to sponsor such a showing. We are, of course, intrigued by the Indian reverence for tobacco. The beautifully crafted pipes shown here attest to the ceremonial significance of tobacco in the lives of the North American Indians; and in the myths of South American Indians, tobacco was an ethereal and spiritual substance.

Yet it was not solely our particular affinity for the magic of tobacco, nor even just our appreciation of the originality and beauty of Indian art that led us to sponsor this exhibition. More important in our view was the desire that you share with us a deeply felt, almost tangible evocation of Indian thinking and feeling—of a vital way of life that we can only try to re-capture here, through these extraordinary Indian images.

George Weissman
Vice-Chairman
Philip Morris Incorporated

FOREWORD

THE scope of this exhibition is the Indian of the North, Central and South American continents, from the time of the earliest surviving material culture to the expressions of contemporary Indian artists working in various media. It is an effort to expose the viewer to the work of the several Indian tribes throughout America, over a period of approximately 4,000 years, and in so doing, to open the door to the accomplishments of the Indian artist working in all of the resources provided by nature. The selection is esthetic; and while some objects may be more effective in arousing an emotional reaction from the viewer than others, it is our hope that each of the 500 specimens will present some degree of visual pleasure, and perhaps will introduce heretofore unknown art experiences, or else expand the knowledge the viewer already possesses.

The source of these objects is entirely from one institution: the Museum of the American Indian, Heye Foundation, in New York City. While this offers strength in the extraordinary quality and depth of those collections, it is also true that it presents the weakness any single collection must have–that is, the inevitable gaps to be found in any collection. These may or may not be serious. In the present instance it is not felt that the loss to the viewer is a particular concern, since there has been a concentrated effort to select as wide a range of the areas of art expressions as possible. The audience in mind is that of the usual museumgoer who enjoys an experience and exposure to new material and a feeling of relationship with the makers of exotic or unusual art. Some will have a considerable knowledge of Indian art in North America, while others may have experienced the pre-Columbian arts of Middle or South America; but it is the rare viewer who will possess an equal knowledge of the range of art expressions throughout the New World. The goal of the exhibit is simple—to present the native heritage of the Americas throughout the historic period and as far back into the prehistoric as it is possible for us to venture. We hope to indicate the extraordinary wealth of art which was present before the European arrived and then examine what happened to those artistic creations with the arrival of new ideas, new materials and a new audience.

The fact that this is a traveling show affects the content of the selection. In order to cut down or control costs of transportation, it was manifestly impossible to include very heavy or very large material. As a result, the present exhibition does not have the opportunity of showing some of the monumental works of art which the native was so fond of creating. Some of the extraordinarily long or unusually delicate-but-large examples had also to be omitted; fragility had to be considered in view of the number of times the exhibition would be taken down and put up in various museums throughout the country. This meant that delicate objects had to be kept to a minimum.

With these restrictions in mind it is nevertheless our feeling that the objects selected for this exhibition truly represent a cross-section of what one would find throughout the New World in any exploration at any given time. There are few, if any, major areas, types of materials, or technical processes which have not been included in the present exhibit. This is not only a tribute to the excellence of the collection formed by Dr. Heye, but is also a testimonial to the wealth and range of artistic endeavors of the Indian who created them.

Necessarily, the exhibition is basically visual. The great depth of music, drama, dancing, literature and related non-visual arts have had to be eliminated for obvious reasons. It must be borne in mind throughout this exhibit, that one is enjoying solely that which can be seen in the material cultural aspects of Indian life. Remember, too, that many of these objects were accompanied by music, particularly as regards musical instruments; or by pageantry, in the use of some of the costume and mask materials; and religious or political ritual in the instance of those objects which were intended to add prestige, status or religious power to the owner

In considering the New World, we have arbitrarily selected a geographical and chronological organization, beginning for convenience sake with the Arctic area and traveling south, following as best we can the route taken by the prehistoric emigrants into the New World. In each area prehistory is followed by the more recent period. Reference to the maps and charts provided will allow the reader to more clearly understand the sequence of cultures, and the relationship of one to the other. The tribal and regional divisions are those favored by the anthropologist. Although we have elected to simplify these to some extent, it is felt that most viewers will accept the basis upon which the tribal relationship has been presented.

The organization of **Indian Art of the Americas** originally stemmed from the conviction that too few people understand the interrelationship of the various native cultures of the New World, and most tend to talk about a given area as though it were "the Indian." For example, in the United States when one speaks of the American Indian, by and large the reference is to the Indian of the United States and Canada; it rarely applies to people south of the border. To the collector of Pre-Columbian art, then, the term usually refers only to the so-called "high cultures" of Middle and South America, namely the Aztec, Maya, or Inca. To point out that the Maya were Indians often comes as something of a surprise; likewise to offer the relationship between the war bonnet of the Sioux and the feathered headdress of Montezuma is incongruous to many. The present exhibit was organized in an effort to erase some of this lack of perception.

In an effort to more clearly aid in an understanding of Indian art, we have elected to present a general essay on the subject and then give a more specific consideration of items in the extended captions which accompany the specimens on exhibit. It is hoped that this combination will best serve the reader in achieving our goal. For further reference, an extensive bibliography is provided, divided again into the sections as presented in this text.

In developing this exhibition we have not been unmindful of the Indian of today and have been fortunate in securing the advice of many Indian people as to the direction this exhibition should take, the types of materials which should be included and something of the manner in which it should be presented. In order to strengthen the activities of Indian youth throughout the country, we have also allotted a portion of the income from this catalog to provide scholarship funds for those Indians who are interested in museum work to be able to experience such professional activities first hand. Hopefully, they will then graduate into Indian Museums on their own reservation area or in Indian Museums in various parts of the country.

Our acknowledgement and appreciation for support is a most pleasant task. Initially, Dr. Thomas Leavitt of the National Endowment for the Arts was instrumental in assisting us in starting the project, and his enthusiasm was later shared by many others, most particularly the interest of Philip Morris Incorporated on behalf of Marlboro, who generously funded the traveling exhibit, the several première openings, and with matching funds supplied by the National Endowment for the Arts, allowed us a far better catalog than we would originally have been able to provide. The efforts of Mr. George Weissman, Mr. William Ruder, Mr. Frank Saunders, and Mrs. Caroline Goldsmith, are hereby most happily acknowledged. We cannot overlook the opportunity to extend our most sincere appreciation to Miss Nancy Hanks, Dr. John Spencer and Miss Diane Kartalia, of the National Endowment for the Arts, for their assistance in making possible the matching grant which has literally put this show on the road.

From the staff of the Museum of the American Indian, I am particularly grateful for the services of several people who responded far beyond the call of duty in assisting in the organization of this exhibit, and who patiently stood at my elbow while the many decisions were made as to what should be included. In this selection, the counsel of Lewis Krevolin and Lynette Miller were of paramount importance. The curatorial skills of William F. Stiles, Vincent Wilcox and Ellenda Wulfestieg warrant major recognition, and for assistance in researching data on some of the objects, Anna Roosevelt and Marlene Martin were generous with their time and talent. None of this would have been possible without the wholehearted support of all of these individuals, and of those colleagues who, in showing this exhibition in their own museums, will assure the success which we anticipate.

All photographs in this catalog are by Carmelo Guadagno and his assistant, Carlos Castro-Rojas; the manuscript was typed by Sophie Arctander. Arthur Fleisher patiently assisted the printing work which resulted in the excellent graphic display contained herein. Carla O'Rorke and Stephanie Spivey coördinated the various activities connected with the benefit performances for the American Association of Museums, as well as providing the public relations needs for the exhibition.

INTRODUCTION

TO understand American Indian art, the viewer must immediately set aside those preconceptions or judgments which he has earlier formed in examining Western art. To do so will allow him to look with an open mind upon the type of esthetic expression which the Native American established, growing out of an encounter with nature which had lushly and generously provided many materials necessary for the creation of true art.

The Indian artist developed certain ground rules which in time have proven to be quite different from those of the White artist. Since these basic points of view are different, to attempt to evaluate Indian art in terms of Western art is obviously unwise, if not impossible. At best, it is difficult for non-Indians to evaluate Indian art; and surprisingly, not all Indians are able to achieve a satisfactory judgment of their own work, just as all Caucasians are not capable of judging Western art equally. While it may not be accurate to say that one must be an Indian to appreciate Indian art, it is true that the finer subtleties and the depths of significance which are often lost to the non-Indian are quite obvious to the Indian. It should be noted that in judging Indian art, we are necessarily basing our reactions on only a small fragment of that which has gone before. The destruction of Indian cultures has been so thorough that in many areas we are completely without sufficient examples upon which to base adequate evaluation. In examining prehistoric materials we are even less able to judge, since the organic materials have largely disappeared and it is only in a few quite dry areas that any of the textiles, woods and other fragile materials have survived. We are, therefore, judging on the basis of either insufficient or very thin evidence, for the most part.

Along with all of the visual factors discussed above there are psychological and emotional qualities. In judging Indian art the White man is necessarily looking upon a way of life which he has successfully suppressed if not eradicated. It is impossible, therefore, for most non-Indians to accept as equal the esthetic contributions of the Native American. In attempting to translate into contemporary non-Indian terms (which often do not apply, or did not apply earlier) we are taking one racial and cultural expression and transposing it into another. As we do this, we are often guilty of handling this expression as something exotic or so distant from our own point of view that it is extremely difficult to establish a point of reference for clear understanding.

Much of what we know of early Indian cultures stems from studies made about them by non-Indians, or from the journals, diaries and records left by early explorers. These men were all non-Indian and frequently reflected the prejudices, biases, ignorance or insensitivity that any group necessarily will reflect in discussing the culture of another. No matter how sympathetic a person may be, it is impossible for him to really get beneath the skin of another, and share all of his emotional and intellectual attitudes and feelings. If this were not enough, there is a further problem: by and large, Indian history, Indian cultural accounts, records and comments have all been recorded by the enemy of the Indian. While many of the explorers were genuinely interested in and friendly with Indians, and many of the students who lived among Indian people were sympathetic, understanding and often extraordinarily well-informed, still, the accounts of Indian culture have largely been left by his antagonists. We, therefore, are in the unfortunate situation of trying to interpret a culture, however interesting and picturesque it may be, in terms of an alien viewer.

Prior to the Twentieth Century, Indian cultures were considered as essentially savage and hardly meriting Western attention. Only recently has the feeling developed that there is in Indian art something beyond the childish scrawls of the primitive mind.

Furthermore, it should also be realized that not all Indian cultures were equal in esthetic quality. Some apparently were able to develop a far more striking response to the visual needs of the people than others. It is equally true that while all tribes had some form of art, the best of these was not necessarily on a par throughout the New World. The quality and beauty of art vary just as widely in the Indian world as in the Western, for there were good and bad artists and the fact that an Indian turned his hand to a given task in no way guaranteed outstanding esthetic success.

What is Indian art? To use the term "Indian art" is to fall into an all-too-common trap, since there is no "White art," nor, in truth, a "Western art." Indian art is an expression which covers a tremendously wide horizon, not only in terms of materials, but the approach to those materials and the manner in which they are used. Furthermore, it also involves those which are found in some areas and are not included in others. As a matter of fact, the factor of inclusion or non-inclusion very often is one of the means whereby we can identify a given Indian art expression, period or region.

Even the use of the word *art* introduces the problem of basic differences between Western and Indian concepts. Many tribes, for example, lacked a word meaning *art*; art to them was anything that was well done in the technical sense, or in the end result. This effect might be magical, or it might be power (again in the magical sense), and the concept of an *artist* was simply a person who was better at the job than another. Only a few cultures give any special significance to artists; the Northwest Coast and the Maya, Inca, and some others developed a group of professionals who made their living by art. They were sought out by wealthy patrons for the specific purpose of creating such works of art, as objects of prestige and wealth. But this was an unusual situation.

This is certainly not to say Indian people were insensitive to superior artistic creations. The difference between a well woven basket and a sloppy piece of work, or a particularly well designed carving as against a crudely made example, did not go unnoticed by any means. Fine workmanship commanded respect and even in European terms was highly prized.

The Indian was no different than the Westerner in his goals as expressed through his art. He sought to arouse an emotion within his viewer, whether that viewer be another Indian, a person within his own family, or perhaps a supernatural being. Much of his art was expressed in religious terms in an effort to arouse a benign God to good deeds, or to placate a hostile God. The manner in which he successfully communicated with his audience lay largely in the way in which he achieved the end goal of his work. One of the major criteria was the degree to which the artist recognized the force of tradition. The social organization of most of the tribes did not allow much latitude for experimentation, and it often was so rigid as to force the artist to work in strictly limited channels.

Here again, differences existed. It is known that certain individual artists made specific contributions to the culture of their people and some even introduced what came to be tribal traditions simply by the very force of their own talent. In contemporary times, Nampeyó, the Hopi potter (**354**), and Julián and María Martínez, of San Ildefonso Pueblo are examples (**377**). One suspects that prehistorically the same thing occurred. For example, at Mimbres, in southwestern New Mexico, there were individuals of exceptional talent who must have established something like a "school" of art, and it also seems likely that the so-called Temple Mound cultures of the Southeast developed a like attitude toward their work. Contemporary arts and crafts activities in Mexico and Guatemala suggest a similar situation, as do the textile arts in Ecuador and Peru.

The statement, "all Indian art is functional," is frequently heard. There is some truth in this, in that Indians were primarily nomadic, and had to create household goods which provided maximum utilization. Yet it is not true that Indians lacked a sense of the creation of objects intended to beautify their lives. One has only to view some of the examples in this collection to realize that Indian artists frequently created objects simply to "look nice" rather than "do something." Two examples which come to mind are the Weeden Island vessel (**39**), and the bandolier bag (**423**).

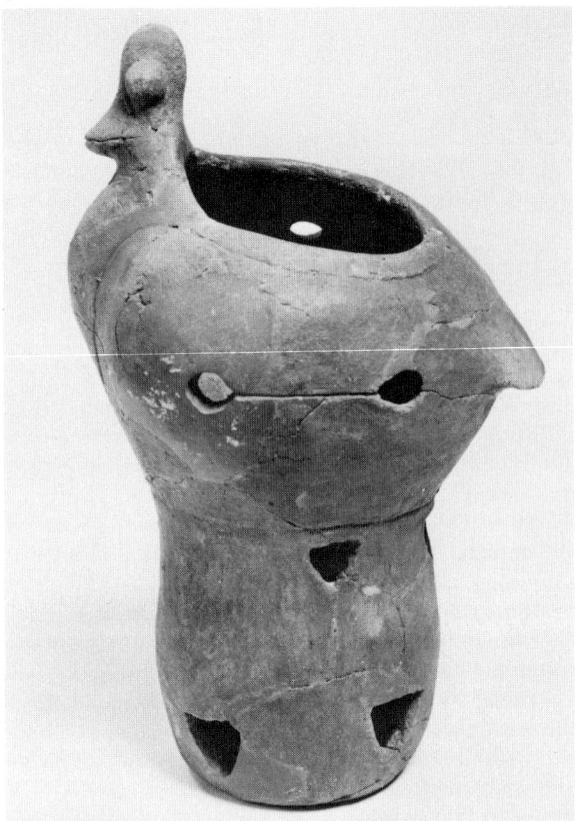

39. Open-work Vessel
With a design representing a bird, this is an example of the ceramics often found with large cut-out perforations, clearly making it impossible for them to be used as containers. Excavated by Clarence B. Moore. WEEDEN ISLAND CULTURE. Wakulla County, Florida. 500-1000. 6" x 10¼". 17/4919.

Each of these undoubtedly started out as something quite different in early days. As time passed, the decoration which is so obvious in the Weeden Island bowl was worked to a point where it could no longer serve as a container and therefore became an *objet d'art*. The bandolier bag was originally a pouch in which the man carried his religious properties. Over a period of time the pocket disappeared and the bag simply became in effect an apron, worn around the shoulders with the large panel displayed prominently to show off the beautiful bead work. The container facility of the pouch was no longer supplied.

Indian tribes vary greatly in their response to art works which are produced. Political and military societies found their major art expressions in the world of weaponry and elaborate costume. This is most profound with the Plains Indians and the military societies of the south, such as the Aztec and Inca. Those cultures in which ceremonialism became the primary expression of life, such as the Pueblo people, or the Maya, expressed their esthetics in terms of pageantry, costuming and ritual arts—most particularly in those which either reflected the dieties involved or were regarded as offerings to such a diety.

Some objects were intended solely for religious use, some reserved strictly for secular function, while not a few combined both needs equally. It is not surprising then, to see a beautifully carved bowl which, when used during a ceremony, becomes a religious object, but when included in everyday life may simply be an attractively carved bowl for foodstuffs or possibly for use as a gift.

The symbolism of Indian art is a much misunderstood subject. The Indian artist was not interested simply in drawing a picture of something, since he realized he could not draw a tree, for example, as perfectly as it could be made by the Creator. Secondly, since so much of his art was religious or spiritual in nature, he sought to involve or incorporate this into his design. Therefore, it can be said that Indian art is not so much drawings, carvings or reproductions *of* an object, but more the representation of the spirit *within* it. In short it embodies the essence of the subject as well as its appearance. This magical character is difficult for the Western mind to understand, and not infrequently the non-Indian will ask, "what does that design mean?" This question makes little sense to the artist, who might reply that it meant just what he wanted it to mean. It is also difficult for an Indian to respond to a question as to "what a design means." Often the Westerner will inquire about a given design on a basket, carving, or bead work. The artist will usually reply something to the effect of it being a leaf or an arrowhead, hoping that this is a sufficient answer. What he actually meant was that the design is "leaf-like" or "leaf-shaped." But his inquirer immediately translates this to mean that the object means "a leaf or an arrowhead," and interprets this as being a *symbol* of the particular object.

Not all Indian art was religious or political. There was an equal amount of mundane work, just as there was a goodly amount of profane, often vulgar art, and there was also far more humor expressed in Indian art than most Western viewers realize. There was likewise a certain quantity of erotic art—perhaps more strongly expressed in some areas than others—but probably not absent from any given region. The wide variety and extensive subject matter of this art form is not generally realized.

The successful achievements of Indian art depended largely upon the environment. People living in the great forest areas, for example, became great sculptors in wood. Those who found themselves living adjacent to major clay deposits became skillful potters, whereas those tribes who roamed grasslands usually became fine basket makers—all of which was simply a response to a generous nature. There is virtually no medium that has not been used at some time or another by Indian artists: various stones, shell, wood, grass and plant fibers, all of them used widely and skillfully. Surprisingly, many unusual materials (unusual to the Western mind) were incorporated into lovely works of art: porcupine quills, moose hair, sea lion whiskers, maidenhair fern, and milkweed fiber—resulting in the natural quality which one finds in the various objects made. Not only does this often give a softer effect visually, but the tendency of the Indian artist to follow the outlines of nature rather than superimpose his own design creates a pleasing freedom. The Western artist usually places his art forms within rigid boundaries; for example, a painter will take a square canvas and then create a curved or linear or rounded landscape within it. The Indian artist will take the irregular shape and fit his design to it, allowing for the vagaries of nature to make of his composition something even more pleasing (*i.e.*, **119**).

Although the differences between Indian art forms throughout the continents are many and varied, similarities do exist, and these can be used to suggest relationships. They can be used as well to indicate contacts between given societies. This matter of contact must not be overlooked: just as early man traveled thousands of miles wandering from one area to another in search of a home, so did the early merchant travel great distances in order to reap the economic rewards. It is not unusual to find a conch shell, for example, from the Gulf Coast of Mexico used in interior Canada—a distance of several thousand miles. Indeed, we know of many trade routes which were established by the itinerant peddler going from one Indian community to another to dispose of his wares. In so doing, he not only picked up new objects, but in the manner of all traveling salesmen everywhere, he brought back to his own people the idle gossip, the latest news of the day, as well as his observations, ideas, concepts and attitudes. These could not help but have a profound effect upon the listeners to whom he reported the results of his latest sojourn abroad. In time, these new ideas or design motifs would become incorporated into the local art forms and pass into tradition.

Furthermore, warfare and intertribal marriages had a great effect upon art styles; the capturing of people for their talent was a by-product of many of the wars of the Northwest coast, and we note in the Spanish chronicles of the capture of fine skilled craftsmen by the Aztecs, who used them for their own purposes. Furthermore, when two people from different tribal backgrounds intermarried—as sometimes happened—one spouse would take craft designs, ideas and concepts to the home of the partner. These in time often became incorporated into the art styles of the new home area, and eventually enjoy the status of "traditional art," particularly if the artist was an important person.

In addition, when any group of people leave an ancient homeland, and journey over tremendous distances, a new culture tends to develop. An example is the Sioux, who left the Carolinas and moved to the Great Lakes, subsequently going out onto the Plains. The several tribes they met along the way each made cultural contributions in varying degrees, out of which emerged a new esthetic expression.

We have no way of knowing how often a migrant culture would bring some new material or idea with them into an area. There, they would find something that to them was different and exciting—and would, in turn, develop the material, motif, or concept in a quite different and unusual manner. This usually provided a wholly new esthetic creation, from which development came the innovation, inventiveness and experience that today we associate with the varieties of Indian art. It is also true that under the same environmental circumstances one quite frequently finds totally disparate cultural expressions. It is easy to identify and separate Hopi work from Navajo, even though both lived in essentially the same area and were not too far distant from each other in point of time. Environment, therefore, is not the whole answer to a variety in art expression.

In speaking of Indian art, very often the term "tourist art" is used. While it is true that this usually is a reference to work that is strictly commercial, or perhaps of limited quality, it need not necessarily be a bad term; for just as there are tourists today who are sensitive and have a keen eye for quality, so were there such tourists in ancient days—Indians who, going from one area to another, knew what they wanted. They were themselves skilled craftspeople and sought only the best from the area in which they were traveling. The fact that they brought with them highly desired material, often raw resources valuable to the craftsmen, or currency of sorts, such as jade, feathers, and foodstuffs—perhaps with magical properties—meant that objects would be created to please them. This latter is the true designation, in my opinion, of tourist art: when the object is made to satisfy the outsider rather than for disposal within the host group. It is when the outsider comes in with wealth but no knowledge that tourist art often becomes bad art.

In order to bring this more closely into focus, let us examine the three major areas of the New World, beginning with North America and traveling slowly into the Central and Southern continents.

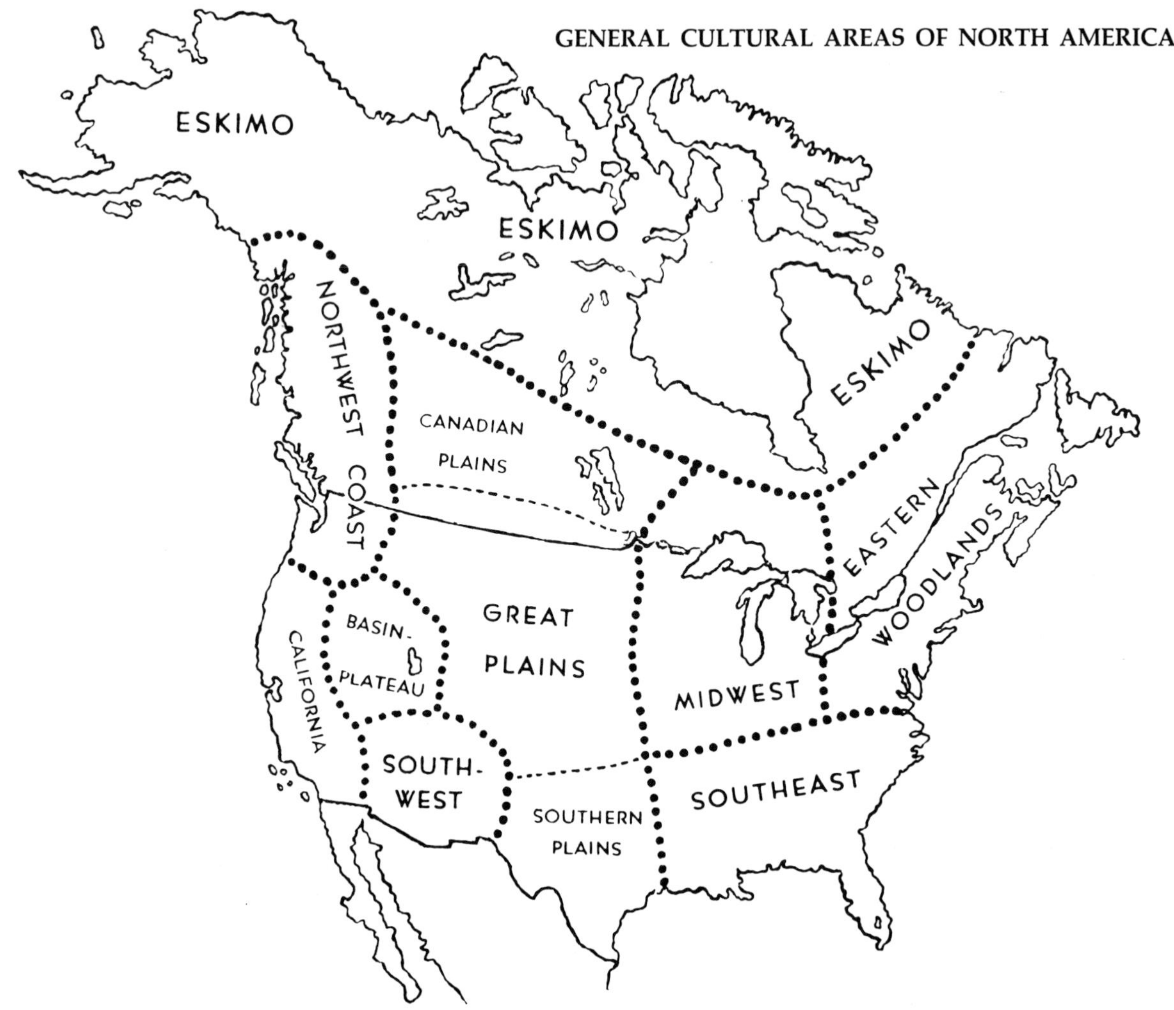

NORTH AMERICA

IT is the prehistoric North American Indian expression that is perhaps least well known to most persons interested in New World art. Part of the reason for this is that there is less of it in existence, other than arrowheads, axes, gouges, hammers, pestles and the like. It can also be said that a certain degree of indifference to North American archeological art is responsible for this lack; these Indians left none of the great architectural monuments that their cousins in Central and South America created. While there were mounds in the central and eastern part of the United States, most of these were relatively small earthworks upon which a structure of wood might or might not be erected. To compare such a mound with the spectacular ruins at Chichén Itzá, or Teotihuacán is unreasonable if one seeks equalization in terms of esthetic appreciation. In point of fact, it is only in the cliff dwellings and Pueblos of Arizona and New Mexico that any measure of architectural achievement can still be seen. These constitute the majority of such surviving structures, in comparison to the ruins of Mexico and Guatemala and Peru. Yet, not all of these cliff dwellings were insignificant: the great structure of Pueblo Bonito at Chaco Canyon in New Mexico was one of the major architectural accomplishments of the Southwesterner, where hundreds of families were sheltered in a single structure containing more than 400 rooms. These apartment houses were well suited for their environment; the earth walls provided excellent insulation in winter and were cool in summer. Their heights reached to seven stories, although most were between two and four levels.

THE ARCTIC

Stretching across the Arctic Circle west from Alaska to Labrador, this region includes literally hundreds of "tribes," often small bands related one to the other by language or culture. The Eskimo are usually sub-divided into the Western, or Alaskan branch; the Central; and the Eastern branch, which includes Greenland. The artistic talents of these people seem most pronounced in the West, with the Eastern area less productive. Within this larger division are the Aleut, related to, but somewhat distinct from their neighbors, plus a number of small Indian groups who have migrated into the Eskimo territory. They have influenced, and been influenced by, the latter. Among these are the Ahtena, Chipewyan, Ingalik, Koyukon, Kutchin, Montagnais, Naskapi, Tainana, and several other Athapascan-speaking tribes. While anthropologists do not classify the Eskimo as Indians, strictly speaking, they are included here due to their settlement in the New World.

This bleak, inhospitable area seems unlikely as a home for aristic accomplishment. There is little raw material available, and the overriding need to secure food supplies allows little time for craft work. Yet, out of this uninviting environment came some of the most imaginative and humorous of Indian art work. During the long winter nights, the Eskimo had plenty of time to work the ivory obtained from the walrus and killer whale. Art styles favored carving in the round, decorated by incising, with a limited amount of inlay. Since the basic materials were of an elongated, tapering shape, this dictated the forms of the final carving (247). This might be embellished by incising, engraving, or sculptural forms into which black pigment from charcoal fires was rubbed. We know of work from the Eskimo going back several thousand years; such fossil ivory carvings, which were highly prized then, are even more eagerly sought out today. They eventually developed a beautiful patina, and attained extreme value because of the scarce, richly colored material.

An eminent characteristic of Eskimo art is the degree of humor which one finds expressed as a caricature, or cartoon, perhaps in one of the many driftwood masks which are known throughout the area (253). These masks, which are the Eskimo's most famous art product, have enjoyed popularity throughout the world. Many tribes made wooden masks and decorated them colorfully; no North American aboriginal people ever developed the art of imaginative characterizations to such an extreme. These are surrealism *par excellence,* and demonstrate a combination of realism, imagination and supernatural qualities which are uniquely Eskimo. The mechanical skill with which they are put together is a further testimonial to the ingenuity of the artists.

More recently, a stone art form which uses the deposits of gray and green steatite found around Hudson Bay has become quite popular with art collectors. These are usually given an artificial coloring and are popular because of the view of everyday life which they reflect (255). While they do carry on the inherent sculptural skills of the Eskimo, they owe their origin and their commercial promotion to non-Indian agents who worked closely with several of the crafts groups to make this a successful source of income. The inception of this art around 1950 is testimony to the latent talent which is embodied in most Indian groups and that with proper encouragement can readily be revived. More recently a form of graphic art, derived from Japanese print-making techniques, has also become popular.

Other forms of artwork are expanding in a healthy manner today, most particularly in Alaska, where Native Craft Guilds have been active in producing contemporary work in wood, ivory and metal.

THE NORTHWEST COAST

It is difficult to define this area with precise accuracy, since it encompasses such a large and varied culture. By and large, for our purposes it includes Coastal Alaska and western British Columbia, including Vancouver Island. The dominant tribes are the Haida, Kitksan, Tlingit and Tsimshian in the central-northern section, with the Bella Bella, Bella Coola, Kwakiutl, Makah and Nootka to the south. There are also peripheral peoples who have taken on some of the cultural traits of the Northwest Coast, but these do not fall quite within the range of this section.

This is the area so richly endowed with tremendous forests of spruce and cedar where the American Indian sculptor achieved his finest expression. The influence of tools is also exemplified here, for with the introduction of steel knives obtained from traders on the ships which came up the coast, the artist was free to demonstrate his talent in esthetically superb sculpture rivaled by no other Indian people in North America—the great totem poles, the huge wooden dwellings decorated by carved posts (**299**), the smaller figures which enriched many of these structures, and the masks, rattles and other carved objects which were so much admired by the Northwest Coast Indian. These were often painted and inlaid with abalone shell, taking on a quality which was so distinctive that they are not only eagerly sought by collectors, but are readily identifiable (**264**).

Another remarkable quality of Northwest Coast art is the ability of the carver to fit his designs into forms. He excels at taking a given shape, area or prescribed form and adapting a design into it without sacrificing the integrity of the original form, or distorting his design.

Perhaps the most impressive art form from this area is the great totem poles, often 60 to 70 feet high, which have been widely misinterpreted. These are not religious, nor were they ever intended to be worshipped. Actually, they are historical documents which recorded the wealth, social position or relative importance of the person who paid for the pole. Some could be regarded as personal milestones, thus serving as a memorial to a successful act or the establishment of the position of a given individual or individuals. Upon entering a village, the great poles standing in front of a dwelling allowed the visitor to not only assess the wealth, political importance and the lineage of the owner, but also to gain an "introduction" to the village chief by simply examining the designs on the pole.

The goal of all of this art was to add luster to the power of the individual. Wealth was the primary criterion, created for the sole purpose of impressing the villager, the visitor, or the rival. Since most of this period coincided with the coming of the White man and his desire for the rich furs of the area, as well as the control of great fishing areas, the strategic position of the Northwest Coast tribes allowed them to acquire tremendous wealth in a very brief space of time. No other single group, with the possible exception of the Plains people, came up so fast from basic subsistence patterns to a position of extreme wealth and leisure, and then declined as rapidly to a position where today they are tragically low on the totem pole, in social, economic and political terms, as compared with their situation a century ago.

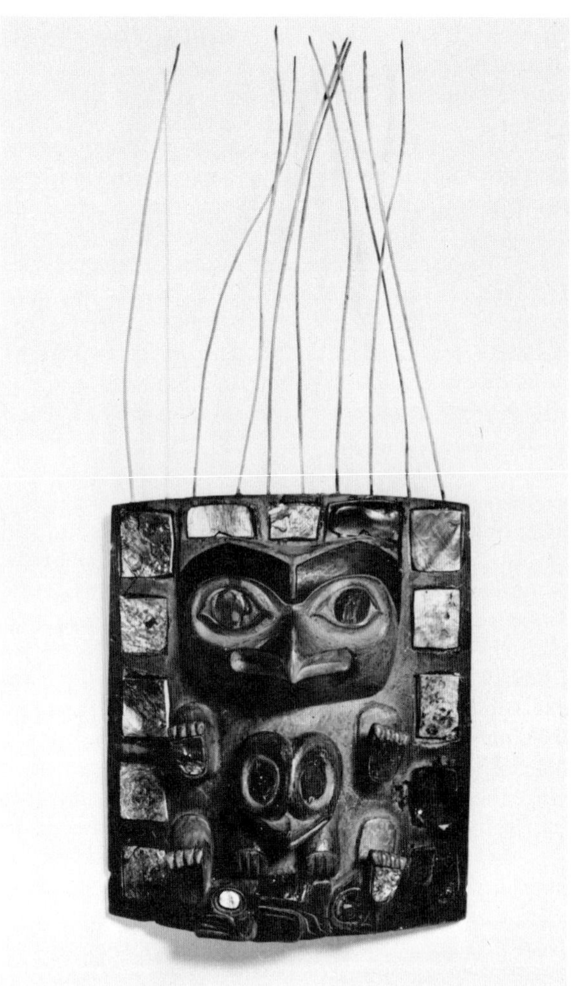

259. Forehead Ornament
Thin, carefully-carved wooden placques, commonly called "frontlets," were an important part of the costume of many wealthy individuals. This example, portraying a hawk holding a fish in its talons, is painted and inlaid with abalone shell; sea lion whiskers project from the top. TLINGIT. Sitka, Alaska. 1875-1880. 6¾" x 16". 18/9007.

It may be surprising, if not disheartening, to learn that most of the work which was commissioned was destined to be destroyed, given away or otherwise neglected. The life goal of many of these tribes involved the belief that the greatest value was to give away all of one's possessions. This may seem paradoxical, but the more one gave away, the greater was one's prestige. The custom of the *potlatch* was a system tending to impoverish from time to time simply by giving away all of one's possessions. In turn, the rival had to give back the same or more material wealth than he had received, to show even greater contempt for material possessions. Frequently these were burned, broken up, or cast into the sea. Slaves were sometimes killed, or families were even sold into slavery. From all of this came the surviving esthetic masterpieces which we value so highly today. One is irresistibly reminded of the parallel in Western religious art, when the great artistic creations came at the expense of those folk least able to pay, yet who were entirely willing to sacrifice for social aggrandizement, if not religious satisfaction.

These people were also capable of developing metal work to its highest degree. While some copper was obtained locally, most of it came from whaling ships, either as cargo brought in for trade or peeled from the hulls of wrecked ships. This was worked with great skill, especially by the Tlingit and Haida artists, into knives, masks, overlays and great shield-shaped "coppers" which were highly prized (**258**).

But the most remarkable art form to be found in this region—indeed, among all of the North American tribes—were the magnificent carved wooden masks used in the many religious and social ceremonials. Some of these were portraits, caricatures or representations of religious deities; others were spirits. But all were carefully designed, carved and decorated—often with paint and *haliotis* shell inlays. The tremendous quantity of these masks, together with their unending variety, make them among the most highly sought-after Indian work (**282**).

The Kwakiutl created a particularly intriguing dance mask, often called 'movable,' 'mechanical,' or 'transformation masks,' since they provide a two-in-one function. Upon initial viewing, these show the Being intended; the performer in the dance, by pulling strings attached to the several parts of the mask, opens it out, revealing an inner design, often the spirit of the outer personification. These masks were used in dramatic performances in which puppets, elaborate costumes, and colorful pageantry provided a spectacular presentation of Indian art sophistication.

These people worked on a large scale; their dugout canoes often carried up to 40 men several hundred miles out to sea in pursuit of the great whales. Dwellings which held many families were constructed from cedar planks and featured colorfully painted sides. Weaving was no mystery; the Chilkat blankets for which the coastal area is famous were woven from the wool of mountain goats and cedar bark fibers, and some tribes even raised small herds of white dogs for their hair which was subsequently spun into yarn for weaving (**269**).

In addition to weaving hair and fur textiles, woven basketry was commonplace. The use of cedar bark, shredded and spun into fibers, was highly developed; flattened strips were also made into mats for sitting, sleeping, and as wrappers, and a wide variety of garments was produced for ordinary wear. Containers of many sizes were made for storage of foodstuffs, fish, and berries, and as baskets to hold personal possessions. These were often dyed in brilliant colors (**260**).

The ivory carvings so widely used in the Northwest Coast are among the most valued and esthetically pleasing of art objects. The basic material was obtained from walrus tusks, seal and killer whale teeth, and then carved into an unending variety of designs (**264**). Northwest Coast ivory carving differs from Eskimo work in the same medium in that it tends to be more intricate and involved in design, whereas the Eskimo product is usually simpler and less detailed, while equally effective esthetically.

It is difficult to compare the several tribes from the Northwest Coast, since each had its own particular skill. Probably the Tlingit of Alaska are most versatile, and yet the Niska or Kitksan prove equally skilled and sensitive; the Tsimshian offer their own particular genius. The Kwakiutl find themselves at home with wood and offer the most dramatic or bizarre art motifs, usually outlined in strong, bold color. The Haida are the people responsible for the familiar black "slate carvings" which are actually argillite, a variety of clay-like stone found only in the Queen Charlotte Islands (**278**).

With the coming of the White man to the Northwest Coast, a brief period followed during which the economic and esthetic levels of art production enjoyed a vast increase. Carvings were turned out in great quantities, primarily for the tourist trade which followed the purchase of Alaska. Unfortunately, this quality approach soon degenerated into curio-shop goods. One of the first products to suffer this ignominous decline were the Chilkat blankets. These are rarely produced any longer, and it is not unlikely that they will disappear completely as a regular craft, other than for the occasional weaver working to preserve the skill. Only a few craft objects are carved and painted today, such as rattles and masks; unfortunately, these are largely replicas of older examples—and this is, in essence, a copying process which is largely mechanical, lacking the creativity of the original. Argillite carving is enjoying a modest renaissance, but most of this is in the form of small ornamental accessories. In general, the exuberance and power of the earlier objects is yet to be fully realized.

BASIN and PLATEAU

This region, into which the inhabitants entered relatively late, is an area completely surrounded by many other tribes. From each has come something to meld into the whole, and each strongly reflects those influences. Embracing the present-day states of Idaho, Nevada, Utah and parts of Oregon and Montana, the major tribes are Bannock, Kutenai, Nez Percé, Paiute, Shoshoni and Ute, as well as some smaller groups.

Their culture is marked by great variations in esthetic accomplishment; these were the people called "Diggers" by the first explorers, from their custom of digging camass roots, and the lack of spectacular costuming which was at that time something of a cultural index in the minds of the Whites. That this was not an accurate index is well demonstrated by the fine basketry produced by some of the least impressive peoples of the region, as well as by the complex cosmology and linguistic patterns which they developed. (**311**).

These Indians regularly wandered out onto the Great Plains for the buffalo which served as supplemental diet to their more usual subsistance fare of roots, nuts and berries. From this Plains contact came many cultural influences in art as well as in social organization—it is difficult to distinguish Shoshoni beadwork from Crow beadwork, for example, and much of the Nez Percé product is similar in appearance to Blackfoot. Raiding Ute parties brought back materials, motifs and ideas from surrounding tribes, resulting in cultural adaptations which often provide considerable confusion in the identification of their material products. The mobility of Ute culture probably accounts for the lack of pottery in a significant degree, and the absence of wood in the region was another deciding factor in their choice of basic materials; one does not find sculpture a primary outlet for the artist of the area. On the other hand, painting was a completely successful development, with most of this expressed on animal hides, similar in form to that of the Plains tribes (**410**). Indeed, some of the most effective painted hide artistry comes from the Plateau tribes.

These people were among the earliest Western tribes to be assimilated, and they accepted Christianity more willingly than many of their neighbors. From this fact can be traced the rapidity with which much of their culture disappeared. In the relationship of Indian and White, one of the hallmarks of the quality of "Indianness" has been the degree of receptivity of non-Indian culture; with those tribes who have resisted acculturation most strongly, among the least culturally impoverished. On the other hand, those who welcomed the European are among the most far adrift as far as personal identity is concerned.

CALIFORNIA

In the Pacific Coast region, the greatest art contribution has been in the field of basketry. Not only did they excell in comparison with the other New World tribes, but no other areas of the world have proven as adept at the basketry arts as have these people (**317**). Once numerous, their numbers are few today, due largely to the brutal slaughter which reached its height during the Gold Rush period, when Indians were hunted for sport, or were killed off *en masse* to clear the lands for settlement.

To list all of the tribes would require several paragraphs. Suffice it to say that their number was legion, and the linguistic diversity as great as existed in any region of North America. Primarily, one should include in the *North:* the Hupa, Karok, Klamath, Shasta, Tolowa and Yurok. In the more *Central* region were the Maidu, Miwok, Pomo, Yokuts and Wintun. Farther *South* were the homelands of the Chumash, Diegueño, Luiseño, Kawia, Mohave and Yuma.

In spite of such savage suppression, these craftsworkers executed delicate basketry, often embellished with bird feathers, shells and other ornaments, which are among the greatest esthetic expressions of the New World (**325**). Among these the Pomo surpassed all others; their tiny baskets, some no larger than the head of a match, or tremendous containers measuring three or four feet in diameter, equally attest to their skill in working grass into lovely objects (**326**).

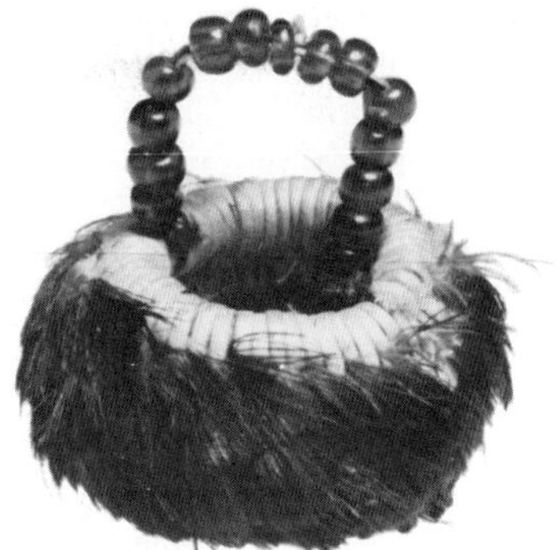

326. Miniature Feather Basket
A further demonstration of the basketry art is this object, into which feathers have been inserted during the weaving process. Presented by Mrs. Thyra Maxwell. Pomo. California. 1890-1910. 1/2" x 3/4". 24/6919.

But artistic mastery in one medium does not necessarily dictate equal skill in others. Although the California tribes were gifted basket weavers, none produced really outstanding ceramics, and very little wood work of unusual artistry has been found. They were not remarkable sculptors, even though they did execute some unusual work in stone; and so far as is known, they never turned out quantities of textiles, as did their Southwestern neighbors. It was only in basketry that they made the most of the undeniable artistic talents with which they were endowed.

THE SOUTHWEST

The early Pueblo Southwesterners are usually called *Anasazi*, a term which includes a great number of people throughout Arizona and New Mexico. Perhaps distantly related to them were the *Mogollón* of central Arizona-New Mexico, and the *Hohokám* peoples of southern Arizona, the ancestors of today's Pima and Papago tribes. In the southwestern part of New Mexico were the *Mimbreño,* who either wholly disappeared, or may have melded into a contemporary tribe—most likely one of the Pueblo groups.

Not only does this include the largest Indian tribe today, the Navajo, but it was apparently always fairly well populated. In addition to the twenty-one Río Grande Pueblos, one finds here the homeland of the several Apache sub-tribes, the Havasupai, Hopi, Huálapai, Pápago, Pima and several smaller groups.

The people in the Southwest were some of the most successful decorative artists of the continent. Their use of color and the many materials around them, particularly the clay and brilliant mineral pigments, resulted in an art form which is highly regarded even today. There was a native cotton which antedated the arrival of Spanish sheep that provided an excellent fiber for the intricate weaves and colorful dyestuff in which these people gloried. It was upon this Pueblo basis that the Navajo later established a textile art which matured to a point where today Navajo weaving excels that of their Pueblo teachers (**348**). Clay was abundant in the area, and pottery, therefore, prospered.

And yet, in the midst of all of the stone in the Southwest, the Pueblo artist was never a truly outstanding sculptor. For what reason, we cannot say—but it is true, even in wood. A closely-knit communal structure and social organization of the Southwest dictated a strongly conventionalized art which adhered to rigid forms. It has fine technical competence and control of line and form, but with little tendency to experiment; patterns were reworked in many intricate designs, but remained basically the same. This conservatism in art reflected the traditional culture of the Pueblos.

The ability to work grass into containers was once important in the Southwest, and a skillful technology did develop in the region (**357**). But the time required to obtain, prepare and weave the various basketry forms is increasing every year, as land use encroaches upon previously unsettled areas. It seems certain that basketry will eventually disappear as a major craft. There will always be those determined persons who continue to weave; but by and large these will be few in number, supplying a specialized market.

Pottery, the greatest of all the prehistoric arts in terms of quantity and variety, is still a major activity in the Southwest, but the audience has changed. Whereas earlier, pottery vessels were intended for regular use, today their forms have become more self-consciously esthetic, and are directed toward the outside market as a specific work of art, and relatively high priced (**368**). The quality has also improved, with far greater care taken in the forming and firing of the clay. Little is made for native use.

This factor introduces the element of specialization which has long been an aspect of Southwestern art and in recent years has become more widespread. There is considerable evidence to suggest that the small drilled shell and stone beads found in immense quantity in prehistoric sites were produced by "specialists" who then traded them widely for raw materials or objects which they, in turn, needed. This custom continues today, where one finds such tribes as Santo Domingo and Zuni executing a favorite product or technique which is then sold to other craftsmen. Certain Navajo smiths specialize in making silver beads which they trade to Indians who then mount the beads on necklaces or other jewelry, selling them in turn as a completed set.

Indeed, silversmithing, an art in which the Navajo excel, is actually far more recent than generally recognized; it was only in 1853 that the first Navajo smiths became generally active. But in the century of activity since that time the craft has developed into an art which enjoys world-wide appreciation. It has been established fairly conclusively that this effort owes its introduction to Mexican leather and iron workers; but as with weaving, the Navajo have taken the art far beyond the original forms in which it was received (**351**). Settings of turquoise were introduced around 1890, and more recently, variations have been introduced in the form of "cluster turquoise" jewelry, overelaborated and highly affected by the fashion market. Some tribal differences have become popular: Zuni fascination with mosaic and "needlepoint" turquoise settings, or the extensive Hopi use of overlay, are completely successful.

Wooden sculpture is limited in the Southwest, largely due to the absence of suitable basic materials. The varieties of pine, cedar and spruce which are common to the area do not lend themselves to artistic sculpture. The most common carvings are the small painted and decorated Kachina dolls made by the Hopi and the Zuni (**361**). These enjoy a wide popularity, and have become tremendously influenced by non-Indians. Once intended mostly as an educational gift, they are now primarily directed towards the tourist and art market.

Sand painting, today regarded as a Navajo expression, in all probability was adapted by that tribe from the Pueblo people who had known the art from prehistoric times. As with weaving, the Navajo took over the art and developed a more complex expression far beyond the original Pueblo form. Not only did it become an exciting design concept, but it was incorporated into and became basic to Navajo religious ritual to such an extent that it can be said that these ceremonies no longer operate effectively without the extensive use of sand paintings. Many of the Pueblo tribes still employ dry paintings in their religious ceremonies, but less extensively.

In short, there are few materials which were not used in the Southwest; with some the people proved themselves both technically and esthetically expert. Of the others, either the lack of basic raw materials or the avenue of approach has not allowed the greatest degree of success.

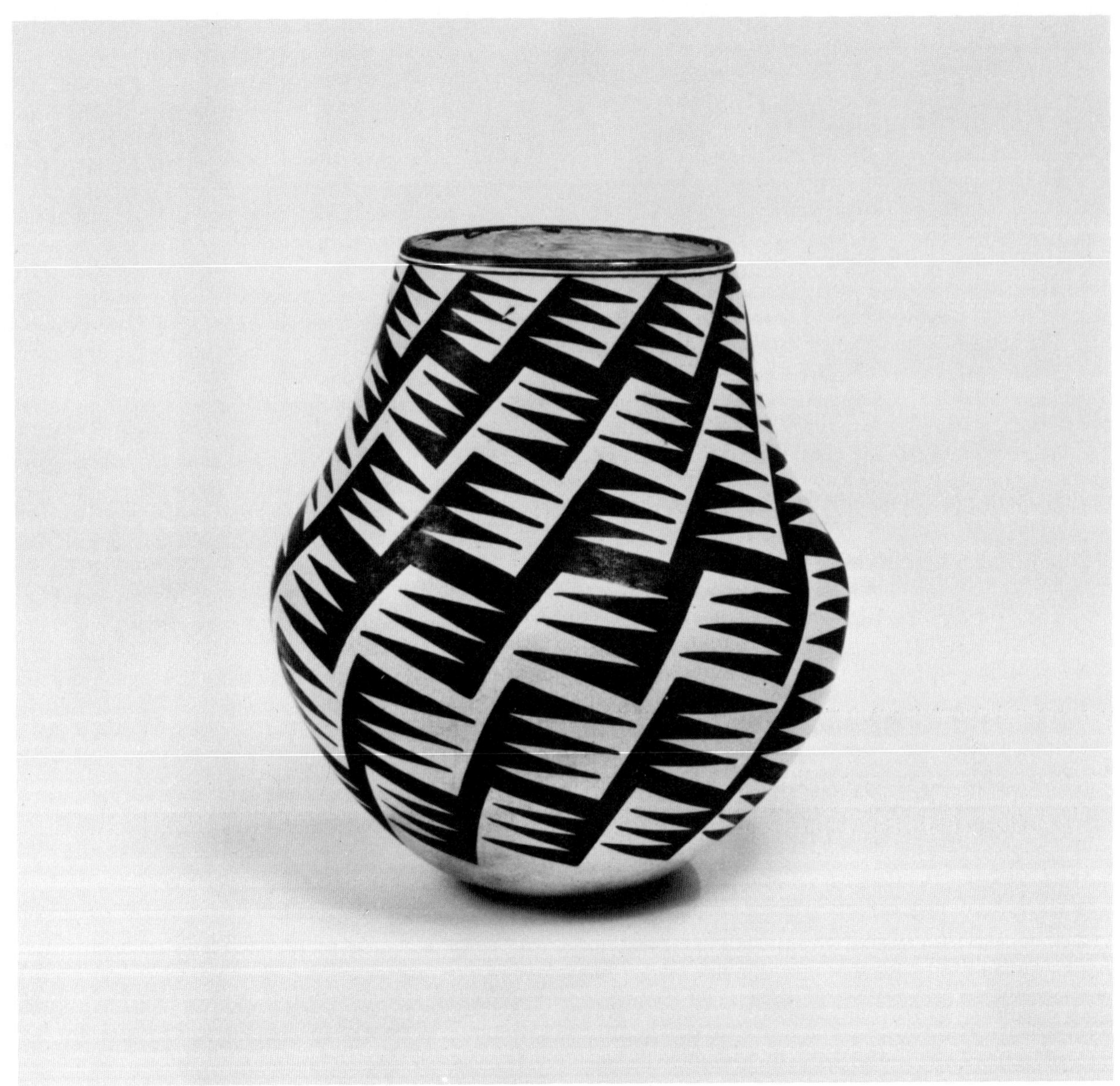

368. Modern Clay Bowl
An example of the contemporary ware produced by one of the more outstanding potters, Lucy Lewis, this is an excellent demonstration of a healthy continuum in Pueblo arts. ACOMA. New Mexico. 1969. 7″ x 8″. 24/7772.

THE PLAINS

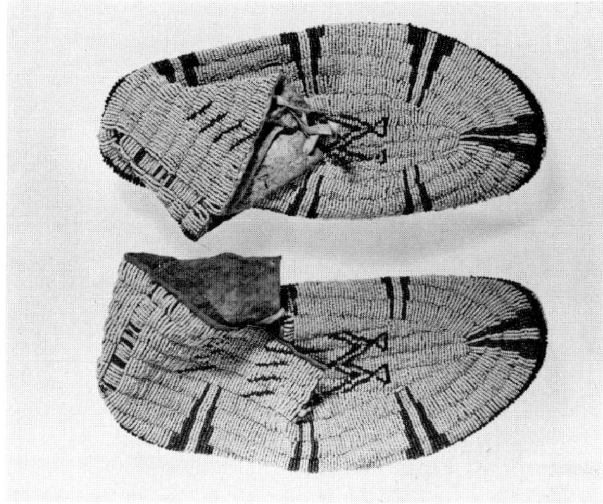

389. Beaded Moccasins
Footwear was usually made of deer hide, and had a colorful decoration applied by quilling or beadwork. Even the soles of this pair are fully beaded. These are often termed "wedding moccasins," or "burial moccasins," but their use was not restricted to such purposes. Crow. Montana. 1875-1890. L: 10½". 22/457.

Prehistorically, the Indians of the Plains did not numerically dominate the region, nor did their esthetics seem to have developed beyond the basically functional forms. It was only in later years that the wealth which resulted from the acquisition of the horse allowed the Plains people to develop the colorful porcupine-quill decoration, dramatic buckskin-and-beadwork costuming, the magnificent feathered bonnets, and painted buffalo hides that so personify the American Indian to most people today. Yet, this was not a monolithic culture; the arts of these various tribes varied as much as did the locale. Some Indian groups seem to have had superior esthetic taste, with sensitive and inventive artistic expressions; while others seem not to have been as careful, or as experimental, and their crafts accomplishments suffer by comparison.

The tribal groupings of this region include some of the most familiar names in American history. For convenience they are usually divided into three geographical sections: *Northern Plains,* the Arapaho, Arikara, Blackfoot, Cheyenne, Crow, Mandan, and the several Dakota (Sioux) groups. *Central Plains,* the Kansa, Omaha, Oto, Pawnee, and Ponca. *Southern Plains,* the Comanche, Kiowa, Missouri, Osage and Wichita.

Color in the Plains, as in almost all other areas, was achieved by mineral pigments or vegetable dyes. In time, these were supplanted by commercial aniline dye and trade colors supplied by the peddlers who brought them to the Indians in return for furs or other objects of value. Paint was important, and was applied by the women in geometric designs to animal hides, particularly the great buffalo robes, by means of bone "paint brushes." The realistic designs which portrayed war exploits were reserved for men to paint (**410**).

Two arts were particularly outstanding among the Plains people. One involves the use of porcupine quills, in which the small quills of the American porcupine were flattened, dyed and then applied to the surface of animal hides or textiles—an art produced nowhere else in the world. With the introduction of glass trade beads obtained from traders, quillwork declined; today the art is executed by only a very few people, primarily in the Northern Plains area (**390**). The other, bead work, is found in several forms, most commonly applied to the surface of hides or textiles. The technique allows the individual bead, or a group of perhaps five to ten looped on a strand of sinew or thread, to be attached to give the ridged or smooth design favored by the individual worker. The beads, which were brought in by traders, were primarily made in Venice and other Italian cities or Czechoslovakia. They were introduced as early as the 18th Century and by the middle of the 19th Century had almost entirely supplanted other forms of decoration (**406**).

Not only did the Plains Indian decorate his home, he also embellished himself, doing up his hair, face and clothing with painted and colored ornaments directed toward the aggrandizement of his person. He also devoted the same attention to his horse, including beautifully decorated gear for special occasions. To see an exhibit of such finery in a static museum case is to lose much of the beauty which one sees when the costuming and gear are worn by the person and his horse. The motion of the wearer and the colorful beading give the feathered bonnet and fringed buckskin shirt a brilliance, vitality and graceful flair (**398**).

Very little woodworking occurs in proportion to some of the other arts. There was a respectable skill in carving bowls, fetishes, effigies, figurines and the like, but these never attained the competence of the great totem pole carvers of the Northwest Coast. While some pottery was made, it was minimal and of functional quality only, without the esthetic overtones which would be required to give it any rating as a major art form. Basketry was also a secondary art among these people.

Most of their esthetic expression was in the use of animal hides, a great deal of which was decorative or spiritual in purpose. A given design might appear to us today as a secular decoration; but to the owner, it had magical or religious content which often embodied the spirit of his guardian ancestor who was expected to protect him from harm (**403**). One other art was the use of various feathers, in many combinations and forms, to give beauty, color, and dramatic accents to costumes and ritual paraphernalia. Much of this feather decoration was done not only out of respect to the bird spirits, but also as a form of appreciation for the graceful, swooping flight of these creatures.

MIDWEST

The people of this vast area were related to the Indians who built the great Serpent Mound and similar effigy mounds, which were tremendous piles of earth fashioned into various zoömorphic forms. This "Mound Culture," which extended from the Great Lakes south to Alabama, and from Oklahoma east as far as eastern Tennessee and Georgia, developed around 1000 AD and lasted until the arrival of the Spaniards. Accompanying it were remarkable esthetic accomplishments in shell, bone, stone and wood. One large mound, Cahokia, near St. Louis, Illinois, was the largest earthworks in existence before it was bull-dozed to make way for modern buildings. These people were not afraid to tackle large-scale construction.

Yet with all of this building, they have left little to mark their passage. The so-called 'temple mounds,' which may have had wooden structures at the summit, have either been levelled for agricultural use, or have been so torn up as to show little of their earlier majesty. Prehistorically, these were the Hopewell and Adena cultures; in time they gave way to several major tribes, primarily the Chippewa, Menomini, Potawatomi, Winnebago, Kickapoo, Sauk-Fox, Miami and Ottawa. Later, the Sioux came in from the South, but were forced out onto the Plains in wars with the Chippewa.

In both the Great Lakes and Midwestern regions, we find similar cultural expressions, although none have survived from prehistoric periods in sufficient number to allow us to judge the esthetic quality accurately. We do know that textiles were woven in the Midwest, as well as basketry. However, were it not for the survival of stone, shell and some bone objects, we would have little basis for an appreciation of prehistoric Great Lakes craftwork. Pottery is average, but was apparently never a major craft activity, and although worked copper has been found in large quantities, it was primarily made into functional objects such as projectile points and axe heads, rather than ornaments and decorations, although these were also fabricated from sheets pounded out of nuggets.

Basketry continues its earlier tradition, most particularly in splint work, and in the use of reeds and fibers common to the area. Sleeping mats, which are found throughout the Great Lakes area, have interesting colored patterns woven into them, and the use of reed, basswood, and similar fibers allowed a wide variety of designs (**425**). Bark objects were important, and were fashioned into a variety of containers; the ubiquitous *mokcock* appeared in many forms, often decorated by incised or surface-scraped designs.

Textiles were less common until the introduction of European yarns and cordage helped satisfy the need for small medicine pouches and bags. When traders brought in brightly-colored silk, satin and trade cloth, a new art was born, based upon prehistoric motifs. This silk-ribbon appliqué work provided one of the most colorful costume and decorative techniques to be found among Indian peoples (**416**).

Wood was important, both for functional objects, and in artistic creations. Clubs, effigies, implements, and particularly burl bowls for food, ritual medicines, and similar purposes, were carved and lovingly polished until they shone. Often these were inlaid or incised with decorative patterns which added to their beauty (**394**).

Trade beads were used singly, or woven in strips on wooden looms. This latter technique was more popular, and can be found throughout the Midwest and Great Lakes region. With it, long strips are possible, for necklaces, belts, panels, headbands and hair ornaments (**424**). Porcupine quillwork was equally popular in this region—it is probable that the Plains people took the art with them into their new homes when they left the Great Lakes area in the mid-17th century.

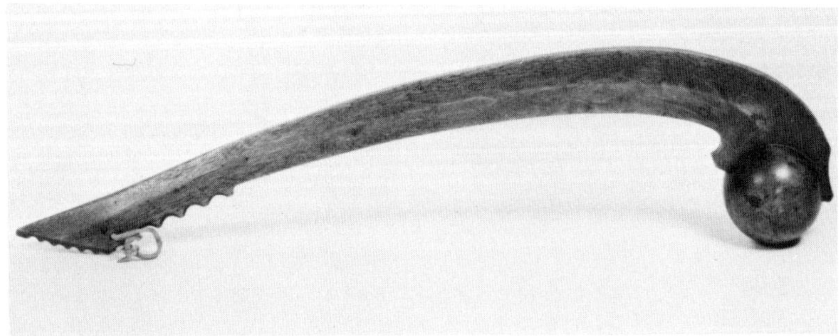

433. Wooden War Club

One of the most characteristic weapons of the Midwest Woodlands people were these ball-headed clubs. Carved from one piece of hardwood, they often included a small animal effigy at one end; in this instance, the otter is depicted. This was collected in 1850. Presented by the Mattatuck Historical Society. OTTAWA. Mackinac Island, Michigan. 6½" x 25". 24/1959.

THE SOUTHEAST

In prehistoric times this area was part of the most artistically exciting region of the North American continent. Here were the temples, mounds and monuments which show the existence of an amazing civilization. We can readily understand the legends that grew up around this vital culture that was still evident when the Spanish arrived. Much of the art work of this area suggested considerable interchange with ancient Mexico; the use of incised shell and bone, intricately decorated with inlay, and more particularly the pipes carved in bird and animal forms, leads one inevitably to compare the art with the Teotihuacán, Maya, Toltec and Aztec people of Central Mexico. This leaves little doubt that at one time there was either sporadic or regular contact between the two regions.

Early Spanish accounts record the colorful ceremonies which they witnessed, reflecting the glories of the Natchez, Creek and Timucua peoples. Other tribes include the Alabama, Catawba, Cherokee, Chitimacha, Choctaw, Huma, Koasati, Mobile, and literally dozens of smaller groups. The Tuscarora traveled north to join the Iroquois, the Sioux migrated to the Great Lakes, and much later, the Seminole separated from the Creek and established themselves as a major group in Florida.

In the realm of carving and sculpture, wood was widely used, although little of this has survived. Those examples still existing indicate the quality of this art; unfortunately, the condition of most of them offer frustrating hints of greater sculptural skills. We must accordingly fall back on stone or clay in order to view the greatest vitality of the art work from the Southeast. By far the most impressive art form is the rich stone sculpture. Carved heads, effigies, and figurines in human forms were widely distributed. Whether these were of deities, ancestral memorials, or offerings to honor the deceased, is not known. But they are competently carved and designed, and were still in use at the time of the entry of the Spanish explorers in 1540. The extent of this skill in working stone can readily be demonstrated. An examination of the finely-carved human effigy figurine from Tennessee leaves little doubt that this is the product of a master sculptor (**50**). The carved stone pipe bowls, often in bird or animal form, also offer testimony to the skill of the artist; these were distributed widely throughout the region (**47**).

The most exuberant, and in many ways the more exciting, art form from the Southeast is the diversity of ceramic artistry executed in a tremendous variety of designs. Bowls, highly polished water bottles, huge burial urns, food dishes—all decorated with geometric incised lines, appliqué ornaments, or manipulation of the clay itself—provide ample evidence of the imagination, skill and the sheer love of clay for its own sake that these early potters must have felt. Unfortunately, with the coming of the White man, most of these great creative talents were destroyed.

Most of the arts and crafts of the Southeast have been completely lost today, or are less actively pursued. Stone sculpture is continued in a more modest proportion than formerly; and while there are individual sculptors who have achieved remarkable success in wood, they are numerically fewer than in some of the other fields. Pottery has changed considerably—the vitality of the earlier work is rarely seen today, and the styles are less imaginative, tending to be somewhat repetitive; most of this is carried on by Cherokee and Catawba potters (**452**). The most active technique, and economically the most rewarding, is basketry, in which the present-day artists are in every way equal to, if not better than, their tribal predecessors (**446**). One of the most familiar arts of this region, although a relatively recent development, are the cloth appliqué textiles of the Seminole. Dating from the introduction of cotton cloth by White settlers in the mid-19th Century, this has become a traditional art form which provides a variety of brilliantly-colored garments in complex designs (**455**).

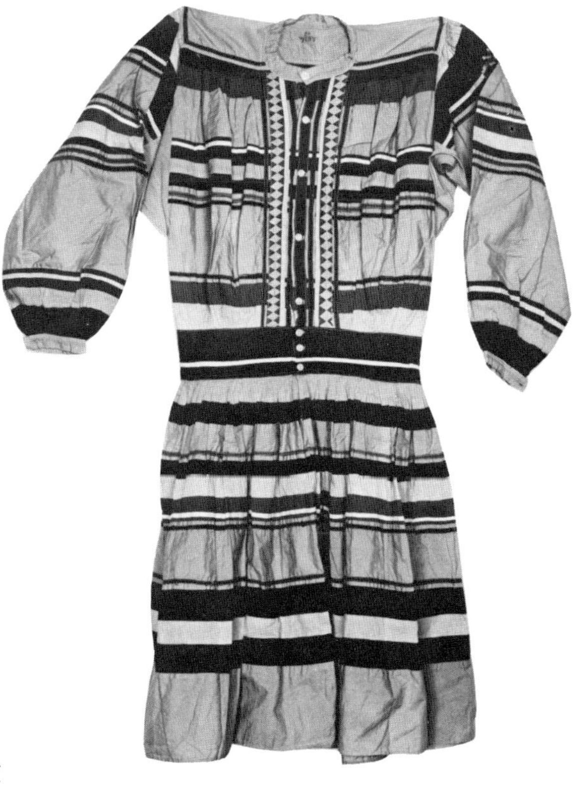

455. Cloth Appliqué Costume

The use of scraps of cloth, usually gingham or cambric, became an art form when it was adopted by the Florida Indians. This Councillor's Coat has the band design of the older forms; later, elaborately pieced patterns became common, and today, rickrack is universally incorporated into the sewing. Presented by Frank L. Humphries. SEMINOLE. Florida. 1900-1910. 19" x 43". 20/7193.

THE NORTHEAST

Inhabited by two major groups with a similar-but-different art style, this was the land of the Iroquoian and Algonquian peoples. The Iroquois were a federation of warrior-diplomats which included the Cayuga, Mohawk, Oneida, Onondaga and the Seneca; in the early 18th Century the Tuscarora migrated from the Southeast to form the last of the Six Nations Confederacy occupying New York, Pennsylvania and lower Canada. It was this group whose political organization so impressed the colonists during the formation of the United States. The vitality of their culture seized the imagination of the Whites, so that a great deal was written about them, and they have become a well-known group today. Their numbers still make them an important political factor in New York State.

The Algonquian-speaking tribes included the Abnaki, Passamaquoddy and Penobscot of Maine, and the Malecite, Micmac, Montagnais and Naskapi of neighboring Labrador. A host of sub-tribes or bands occupied Massachusetts, Connecticut, Rhode Island, and Long Island, New York; the Lenni Lenape (or Delaware) also ranged through this lower corridor. The Algonquian people formerly occupied a far larger area, but the coming of the White man and the resultant economic rivalry saw their decline at the hands of the more aggressive Iroquois, who eventually gained dominance over the Northeast.

These Indians, most notably the Iroquois, have enjoyed a wide variety of art work, and are best known for their carved False Face Society masks, for their shell wampum belts, and for the use of porcupine quilling, wooden burl bowls and ladles (**444**). Another interesting art is the use of cornhusks from which masks, dolls and costuming are made. Basketry was primarily of the splint-weave type, rarely ornamented except for the application of a stamped or painted vegetable dye design.

Wood enjoys maximum interest, and is particularly effective when carved into graceful but effective canes, clubs, staffs, and other ritual objects often enhanced by incised designs. Unique expressions are the use of moosehair, the black dyed deerskin, and milkweed fiber which were employed in Iroquois artistry (**438**).

One intriguing art now entirely lost was the beautifully painted and tattooed designs applied to the body by the early Woodlands people. The many engravings which survive leave little doubt as to the importance of this decorative art during the period.

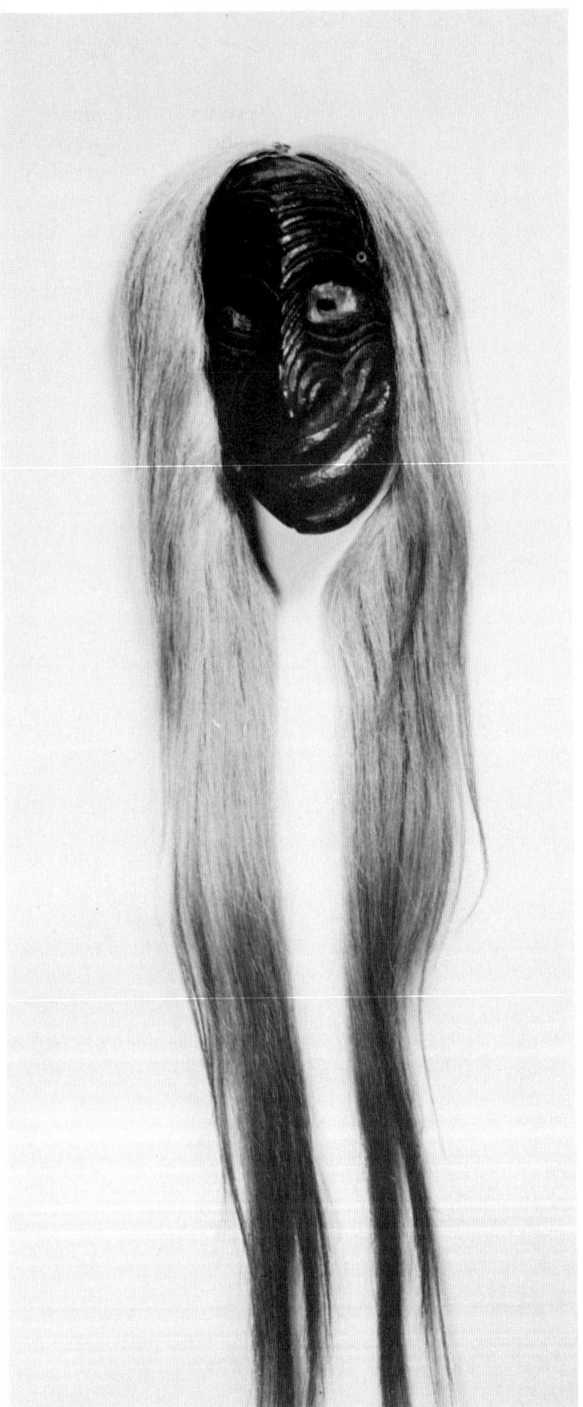

441. False Face Mask
The False Face Society is a curing group, whose religious importance extends throughout all of the Iroquoian people of New York State and southern Ontario. This mask of butternut wood is an example of the "Crooked Nose" being. Collected by G. F. Fuerst about 1880. CAYUGA. Grand River Reservation, Ontario, Canada. 6½" x 10½". 8/1206.

INDIAN TRIBES OF MIDDLE AMERICA

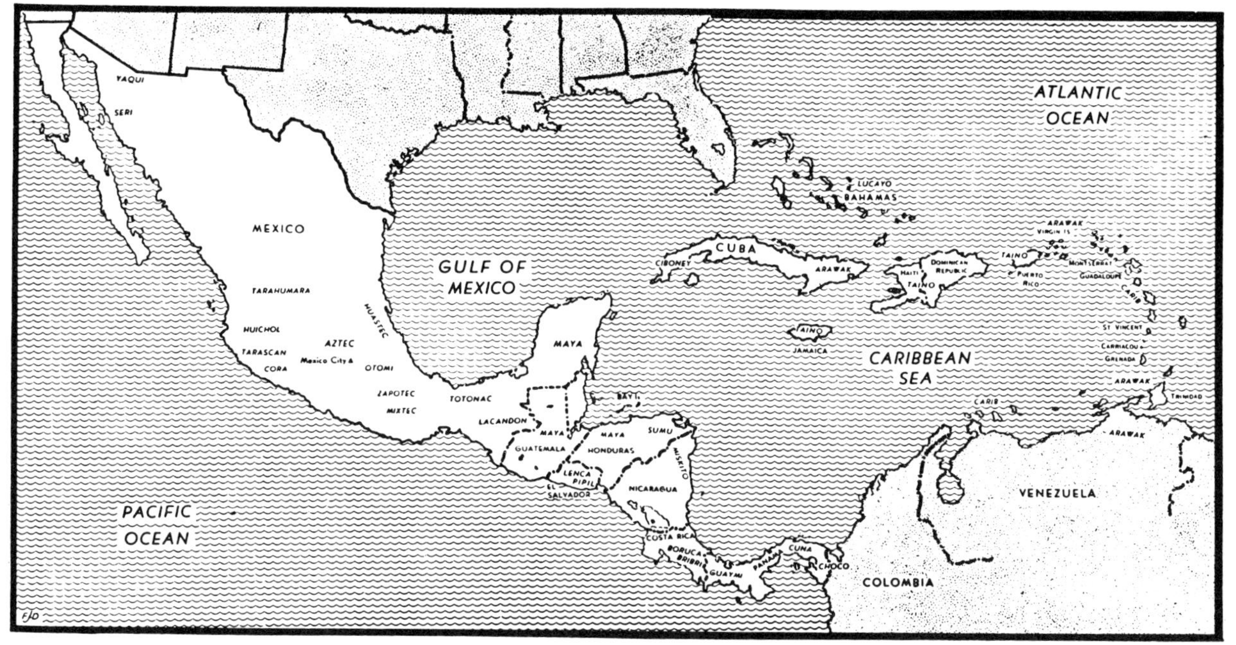

ARCHAEOLOGICAL SITES IN MEXICO

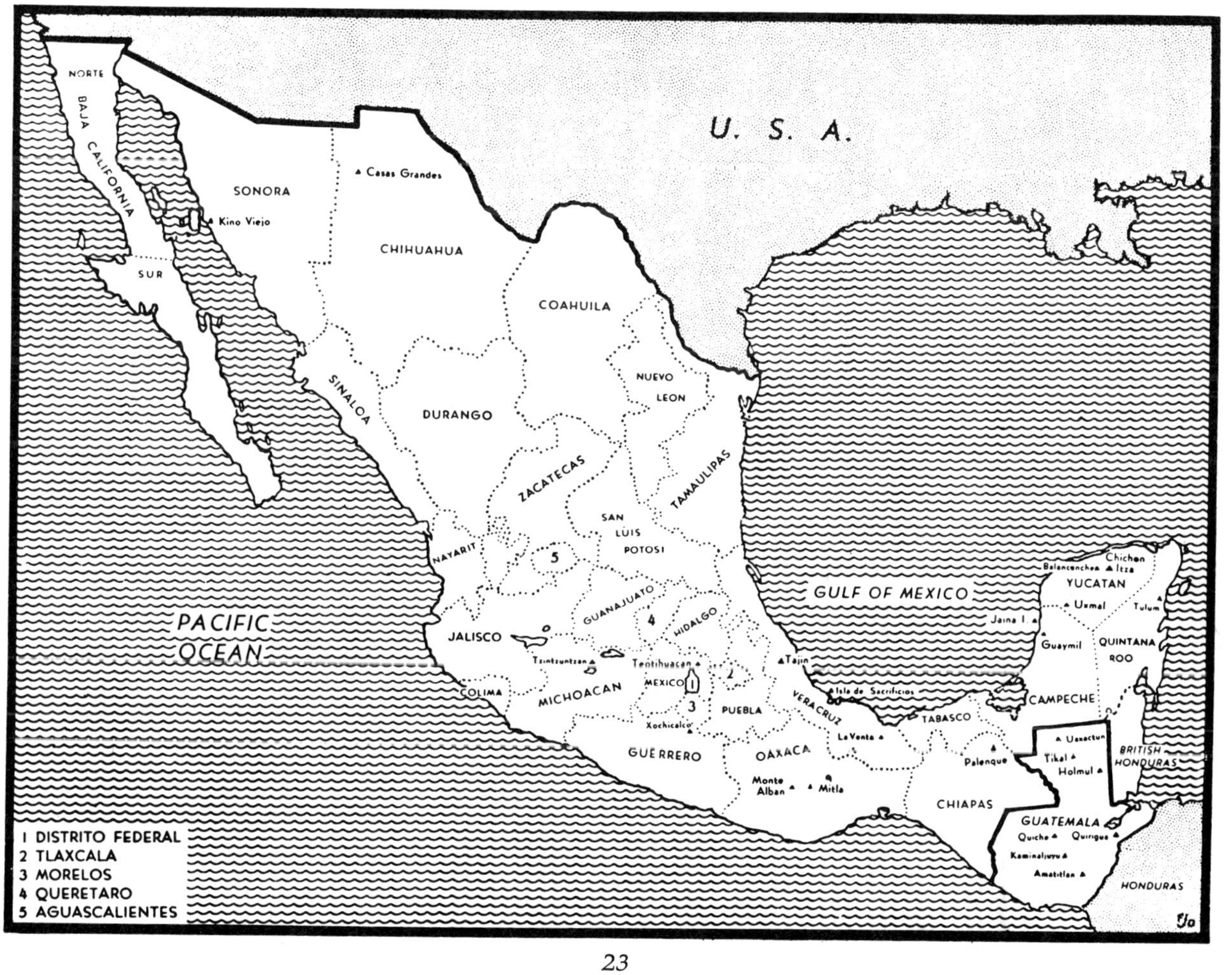

U. S. A.
GULF OF MEXICO
PACIFIC OCEAN
NORTE
BAJA CALIFORNIA
SUR
SONORA
Kino Viejo
CHIHUAHUA
Casas Grandes
COAHUILA
NUEVO LEON
SINALOA
DURANGO
ZACATECAS
TAMAULIPAS
SAN LUIS POTOSI
NAYARIT
JALISCO
GUANAJUATO
HIDALGO
COLIMA
MICHOACAN
Tzintzuntzan
Teotihuacan
MEXICO
Tajin
Isla de Sacrificios
VERACRUZ
PUEBLA
Xochicalco
GUERRERO
OAXACA
Monte Alban
Mitla
La Venta
TABASCO
Palenque
CHIAPAS
CAMPECHE
YUCATAN
Chichen Itza
Balancanchen
Uxmal
Jaina I
Guaymil
Tulum
QUINTANA ROO
Uaxactun
Tikal
Holmul
BRITISH HONDURAS
GUATEMALA
Quiche
Quirigua
Kaminaljuyu
Amatitlan
HONDURAS

1 DISTRITO FEDERAL
2 TLAXCALA
3 MORELOS
4 QUERETARO
5 AGUASCALIENTES

MEXICO AND CENTRAL AMERICA

MEXICO has been separated from North America for the purposes of this text because its culture and art form are so different that it is more convenient to consider it as part of Central America—although geographically, of course, it is part of North America. The Indians inhabiting the region are also more influenced by Spanish traditions—an effect largely absent from the North American aboriginal peoples. But it is also true that pre-Columbian contacts between these people and the Indians of North America in prehistoric times and influence can be traced by the historian.

In order to successfully unravel this story, one need only consider their arts. The earliest identifiable art form in Mexico is that of the Olmec—the mysterious "rubber people" whose culture flourished as early as about 1000 BC from Guerrero to Veracruz and as far south as Guatemala and Honduras. These were the people who carved the colossal heads found at La Venta, the delicate baby-face figures, the turned-down mouth which we refer to as the were-jaguar (**73**). Closely associated with them, but later, were the people who inhabited Tlatilco, Chupícuaro and the related early sites which have become so well known for their lovely clay figurines of nude women with fantastic coiffures (**64**). About the same time another group of people in western Mexico developed, notably in Colima, Jalisco and Nayarit. Far less is known about these areas, because very little archeological work has been undertaken on a professional scale. So much of this area has been looted by *huaqueros* that we have almost lost hope of unraveling the complete story of these people. Recent tomb finds, made under controlled archeological conditions, have revealed a far earlier dating and greater cultural complexity than had been previously assumed.

Coincidental with the Christian era, a major architectural construction in ancient America was evolving which reached its height around 600 A D. This was the city of Teotihuacán—the 'Home of the Gods', which exercised such a tremendous influence from Central Mexico as far south as Central America. It was these people who carved the great stone masks which seem impossible to have been worn, and probably were intended to be placed upon stone or wood statues (**80**).

By far their greatest accomplishment was in the construction of the huge pyramids located today not far from Mexico City. The Pyramid of the Sun, one of the largest man-made structures known, has no rival in ancient architecture, measuring some 738 feet at the base, and 212 feet in height. This was only one of perhaps a dozen or so major structures, many of which have disappeared today. But there is ample evidence of a tremendous city-state complex which was already in ruins by the time the Aztecs came into the Valley. Where this culture went is not clear today; it seemingly became absorbed by other, later groups.

Widely separated from one another, the Toltec and the Mixtec peoples also left their mark. The Toltec, whose home was in Tula, eventually traveled as far east as the Yucatán Peninsula where they mingled with the Itzá, to develop the great site of Chichén Itzá near Mérida. Mixtec peoples who lived around Mitla and Monte Albán became famed for their own art, particularly gold work. These master craftsmen who traded their work far and wide were often pursued during the warfare frequently carried on solely to obtain captives for sacrifice, or to capture precisely such talented artists for the later creation of art work destined to enrich their captors.

Along the east coast in Veracruz, Tamaulipas, and San Luís Potosí, a band of Mayan people became separated who are known today as the Huástec. They developed a new cultural expression by 250 BC, which today is definitive for this group. Other Tarascan folk in the area who were active in Veracruz promoted the innumerable "smiling face" effigies and related works to give us a feeling of an exuberant people (**92**). This is particularly true when one considers the great number of clay whistles and small happy figurines that are found in the area.

But in time, even they yielded to the Aztec, who by 1200 had come from the northwest and established themselves in the Central Valley which they called *Méxica;* hence the name Mexico. Their cultural expression featured a powerful and even brutal art world in which stone was a favorite medium. The rounded muscular figures which they produced were originally painted very much as in Greek sculpture. They were far less skillful in pottery, gold work and some of the other media that we commonly associate with prehistory. The most skillful arts seem to have been the products of neighboring people such as the Mixtec, either introduced by trade or possibly by capture; the strength of the Aztec Empire was such that the great works which were incorporated into their culture became milestones in the progress of the Indian in Middle America (**109**).

It is also around Veracruz that one finds the strange triad of carved stone objects whose use is such a mystery. The first of these, the *palma,* is so called because of its likeness to a hand, which was once thought to have had a religious significance (**94**). The *hacha* with a thin blade is so termed because of its resemblance to an axe, and thought to also have a

ARCHAEOLOGICAL SITES IN CENTRAL AMERICA

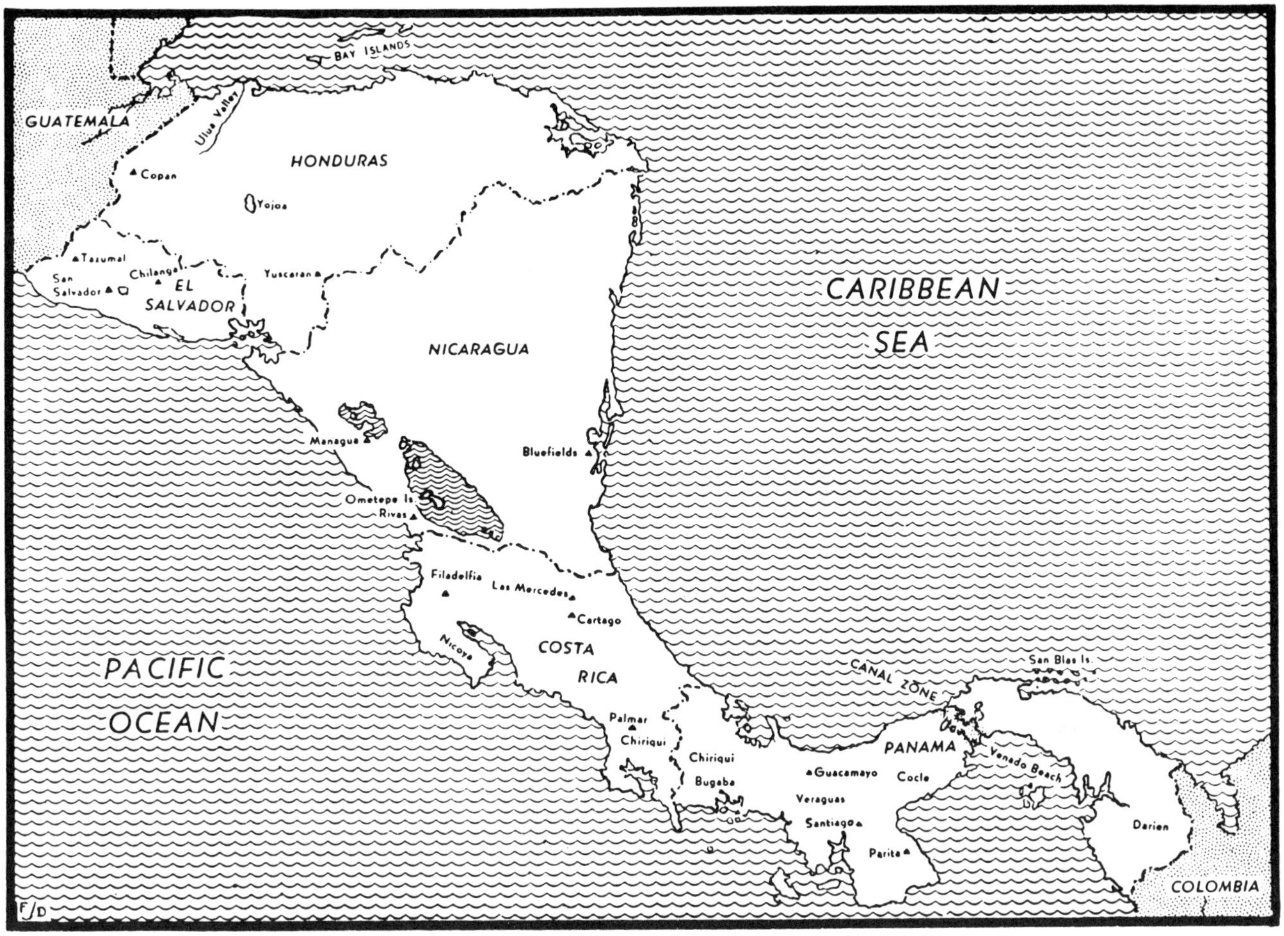

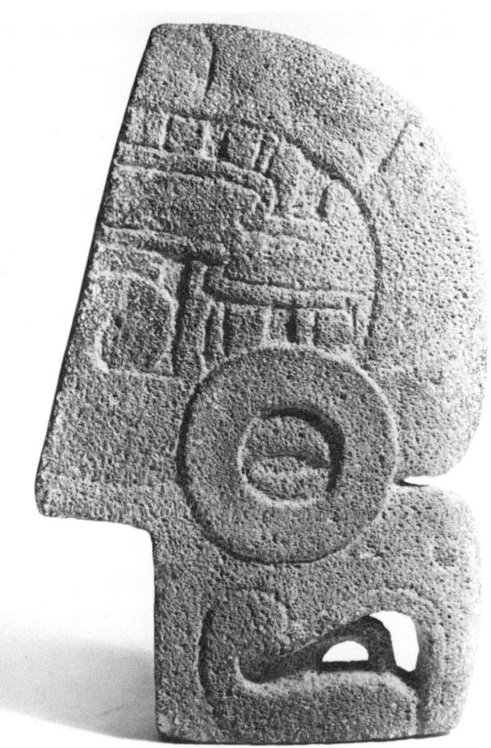

ceremonial function (**95**). The third, the *yugo* (or yoke) was once believed to have been used to hold down the head or neck of a sacrificial victim (**96**).

We now feel that these are no longer supportable theories. It is more likely that the *hacha* was an architectural decoration of some sort, possibly inserted into the wall of a building; the *palma* was probably used along with the *yugo* as an accessory to *tlatchtli*, the ball game somewhat similar to soccer. Indeed, many small clay figures have been found with such decorations fastened to the yoke-like belt of the ball player. *Tlachtli*, whose purpose was to propel a gutta-percha ball through the air without touching it with the hands and strike a disk on the wall, was the major sport of the ancient peoples. It was not unlike the World Series ball games of today, and tremendous exchanges of personal property usually resulted from such a victory. In fact, sometimes one's life was at stake in an important contest.

95. Carved Scoria Hacha
Designed in the form of a bird head, possibly a mask, this is tenoned for placement on a ledge or base. The knife-like edge of these objects forms the basis for the name. EL TAJÍN. Veracruz, Mexico. 300-1200. 8¼" x 13¾". 22/5853.

In Central America a completely different world appeared, which we call today the Maya, centered in Guatemala and Honduras where the twin capitols of Quiriguá and Copán are still well-known sites. They spread into El Salvador, British Honduras and over one-half of Mexico, where tremendous numbers of Mayan sites have been found. Of these, undoubtedly the most famous monuments are Chichén Itzá, Uxmal, Palenque, and Uaxactún. Off the coast of Campeche is the island cemetery of Jaina, on which we have found magnificently modeled and delicately-worked figurines of clay (**104**). The importance of these, aside from their esthetic merit, is the amount which they can tell us of the costumery and other attributes of the ancient people; they seem to be faithful reproductions of costumed personages, often elaborately decorated, and with coiffure or headdress indicating rank and position. While the Mayan were the most art-conscious people of the ancient Americas, and were competent in the use of many raw materials such as shell, bone, stone, etc., it is surprising that they never seemed to take to metal work; gold, silver and copper objects are exceedingly rare in Maya culture. Their great art as far as skill, rarity and value is concerned was in carving, especially in jade, the most highly-prized treasure of the Mayan people. This gem was worked into pendants, inlays, ornaments and figurines, all made with the thought of embellishing the many deities, statues and art objects, as well as the persons of the nobles and priests who were so prominent in the Mayan world (**119**).

Painting was important, as is evidenced by the dramatic murals at Bonampak, as well as on the lovely polychrome vases, where the fluid brush line and rich coloring of their art form is well used in the portrayal of important personages in ceremonial or ritual poses (**125**). Writing, an accomplishment developed to its highest ancient level by these people, is also an art form, for the glyphs represent a pictorial calligraphy which is not only meaningful, but assures it of a place in any consideration of art (**121**).

From an early beginning in Guatemala around 250 AD, the Mayan civilization reached its crest *circa* 750, and by 900 had almost disappeared. A few remnant groups kept the culture active until about 1200, but by then they could no longer be regarded as having a close relationship to the original Maya peoples.

Farther south in Nicaragua, Costa Rica and Panama a quite different expression appears. We believe this to be the result of influences coming up from the south and spreading into the Isthmus area, mingling with what may have been remnant Maya folk, giving rise in turn to an art form which was similar to but not specifically Mayan—nor was it specifically that of any other people. The Chorotega, Nicarao, and Gueter developed superb polychrome pottery and a strong sense of stone carving, and above all a magnificence in gold casting which was responsible for a greater bulk of work in gold than any of the other peoples of Middle America. An examination of any collection of ancient gold will reveal the extraordinarily large quantities which were present at the time the Spaniards arrived, and which are still found today as excavation continues throughout Panama and Costa Rica (**148**).

Unfortunately, we know too little about these people, nor do we know very much of their architectural work. Some large stone sculptures have survived from Penonomé in Panama, which suggest that the use of large stone was not unknown; but most of the surviving structural walls have been re-used in the years following the Spanish Conquest by non-Indians who employed the stones for building their own structures. Indeed, the eradication of native culture in Central America has been so rigorous that south of Guatemala very little has survived to indicate the artistic heights which were to be seen at the time of the arrival of the European.

THE CARIBBEAN ISLANDS

The native inhabitants of this region included several language groups, primarily the Arawak, Carib and Ciboney, who settled in Puerto Rico, Española, Cuba and Jamaica, and neighboring smaller islands. The Taíno, a division of the Arawak, seem to have

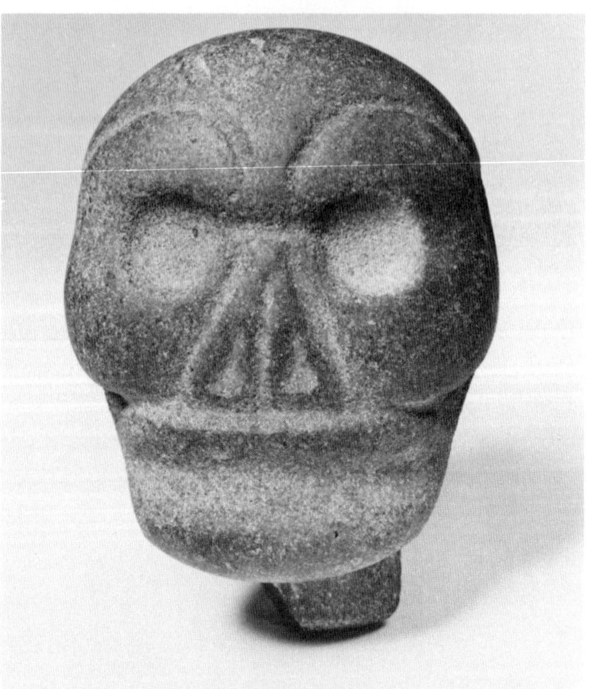

164. Sculptured Death's Head
An ever-present sense of death seems to have haunted the Taíno people. Grotesque masks, or death's heads, are found everywhere in the islands; many of them have tenons, suggesting that they were lashed to something. Presented by V. T. Hammer. TAÍNO. Mayagüez, Puerto Rico. 1200-1500. 4¾" x 6¾". 9/3779.

been the most artistically skilled, and their work commands respect in any display of the sculptural arts.

This is one of the most tragic areas of the New World, for it has undoubtedly lost more of its aboriginal character than any other region, and under particularly brutal circumstances. The total decimation of the native population of the Islands so shortly after the Conquest and its replacement by Negro slaves ruled out any possible continuum of Indian cultural expression. The residents of these Islands today feel little sense of relationship to the ancient inhabitants, and the average non-Indian has no understanding of the wealth of arts which were to be found there in the past. Most of the evidence we have as to the strength of this culture is to be found in stone; very little perishable material has survived. A few wood carvings plus a small amount of shell and bone have been found.

The sophisticated, powerful work found in the carved tri-pointed *zemi,* often human or zoömorphic in form, indicate the wealth that was once prevalent (**162**). These have been unearthed throughout Puerto Rico and Española, as were carved stone pestles, and the strange stone collars—oval carvings that may be related to the yokes found in Mexico and Guatemala (**163**). But the most common art motif is the human head, often a death's head, suggesting a culture preoccupied with mortality (**164**). The peoples of these insular regions were also intrigued by odd shapes in stone. The unusual "comma stones" whose meaning is lost in antiquity, have been found scattered throughout the Antilles; the extreme number of these and the skill with which they were worked suggests an important role in the culture.

Pottery was a major art. Although the clay of the islands was poor in quality, the Taíno produced a wide variety of smoothly-proportioned forms, with grotesque modeled decorations (**159**). The great quantity of clay work is indicated by the tremendous number of *adornos*—the ornate modeled heads or lugs which ornamented the vessels—which are found in prehistoric sites.

The fact of considerable traffic traveling in canoes back and forth between South America and the Islands, and even up into southern North America and the mainland of Central America, indicates something of the wide knowledge of the trans-Caribbean area which the prehistoric Taíno peoples enjoyed.

162. Tri-point Stone

The so-called *zemi,* or tri-pointed stone, is unique to the Caribbean region. Although we do not know their actual use, it is theorized that they were lashed to a wooden staff or implement. Collected by H. P. McCormick. TAÍNO. Aguas Buenas, Puerto Rico. 1200-1500. 4½" x 9". 1/2300.

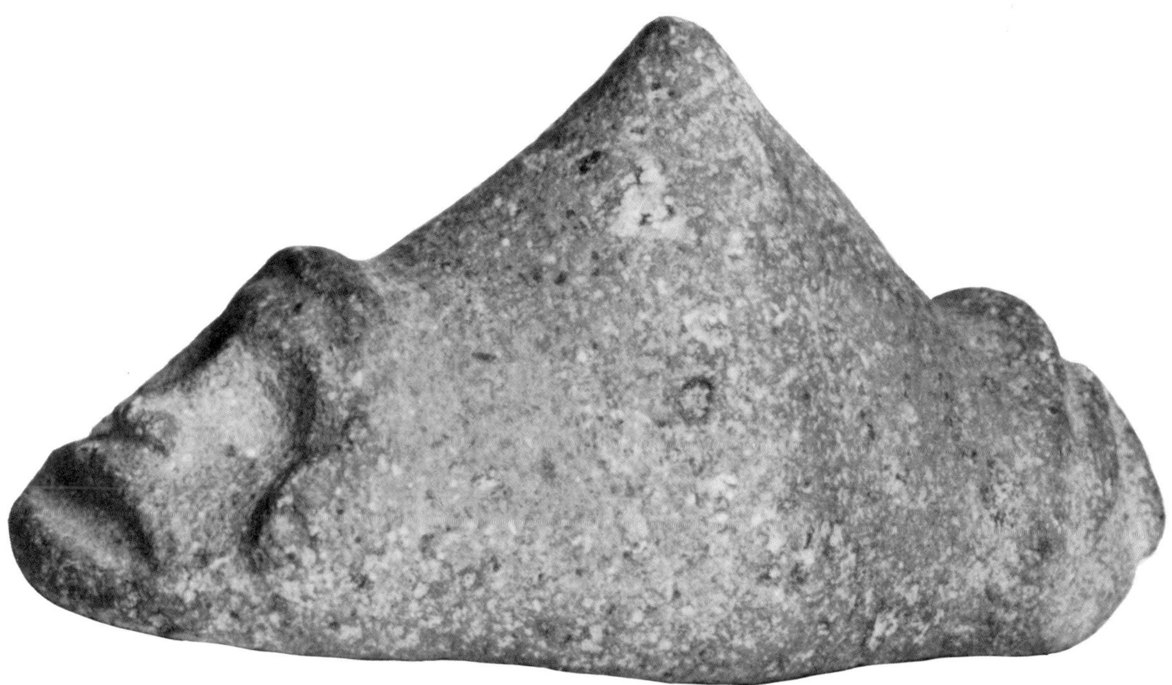

ARCHAEOLOGICAL SITES IN SOUTH AMERICA

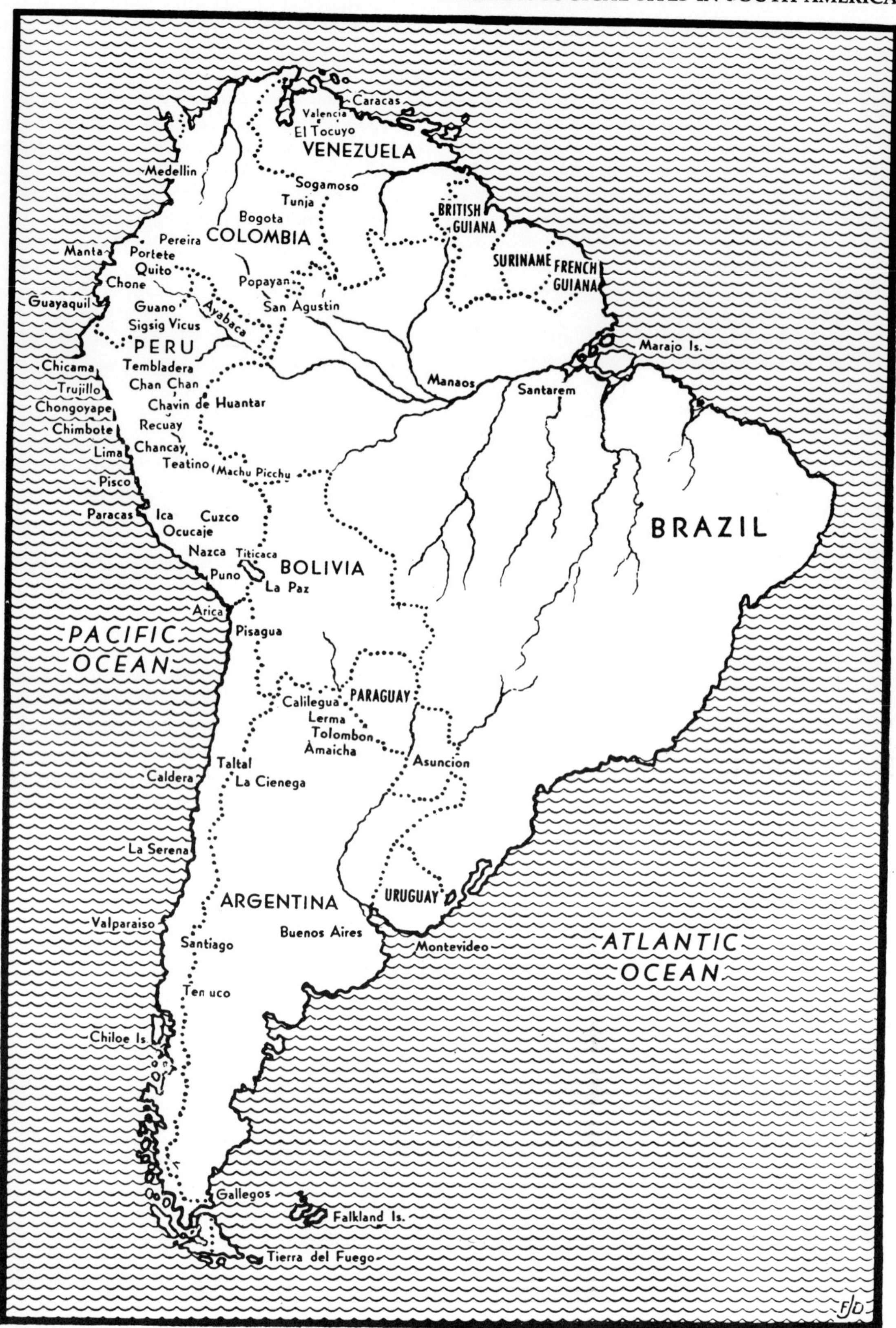

SOUTH AMERICA

HERE again the tendency to lump disparate cultures together is seen in the habit of speaking of the "Inca" as representing all of Peru. In fact, when we examine the evidence critically, we find that the Inca were perhaps the least esthetically remarkable of the people in South America, most of whom attained artistic levels only occasionally equalled by those later comers. It was only in the architectural use of stone, and perhaps in the textile skills, that the Inca held his own in comparison with the other, earlier, people of Peru. There were the very same widespread differences to be found between cultural groups in South America as we have seen obtained in Central or North America.

Weaving is admittedly one of the three great arts in South America. The Peruvian weaver probably excelled all other prehistoric peoples of the world in variety and color and quantity. One can imagine the astonishment of the early Spaniards when they saw this radiant clothing for the first time. Sadly, it had far less importance to them as compared with the gold which they really coveted.

Metalsmithing was certainly at its zenith in Peru, Colombia and Ecuador; each of these cultural regions were equal to the working of the raw material. It is invidious to try to compare Tairona gold with Quimbaya or Sinú; each of these people mastered the lost-wax process, hammered out sheets of gold into various forms and readily executed gold works weighing many pounds. The delicate granulation found at La Tolita is legendary, and the overlaying, which they enjoyed, seems not to have existed elsewhere. That goldwork was well-advanced is demonstrated by major discoveries at Chongoyape, where the Chavín had worked gold earlier than any other peoples in the New World, having mastered this art as early as 900-500 BC.

Perhaps the most widespread art enjoying the greatest variety of form is that of pottery. In an exciting range of imaginative forms are included the delicate thin-walled pottery of the Chavín peoples, the negative-ware vessels from Vicús in northern Peru, the painted ware from Ecuador or the carving skills of the Tairona potters. This was an art which was alive all along the western coast of South America (**198**). Stone was popular, but apparently never in the great quantity or quality that one finds in Middle America. The Inca, as has been mentioned, used the huge intricately-cut stone blocks found at Cuzco, Sacsahuamán and Machu Picchu, while an equally interesting sculptural form of architecture is known at San Agustín in Colombia. Blocks of stone were carved into thrones or seats for Ecuadorean noblemen, but none attained the skill of the sculptors of Guatemala and Mexico.

Goldsmithing was a major art form; large pieces, as well as tiny miniatures, have been discovered. There are great quantities still found, and in some sites, such as La Tolita, literally hundreds of thousands of tiny gold beads—each cast individually—have been uncovered. Furthermore, platinum has been found worked into jewelry; these remarkable people knew how to cast this metal, whose melting point is so tremendously high that our own technology mastered the art only a century or so ago.

Colombia was among the earliest South American regions to become settled. Pre-pottery sites have been discovered which we know to have been inhabited as early as 10,000 BC, but with the exception of El Falcón, where radiocarbon dating has revealed habitation as far back as 14,920 BC, little else has been recovered. Carved shells were used, as were bone, and, presumably, wood. This was a contact point with many of the Antillean peoples, who traveled back and forth developing an inter-tribal trade which became an important factor in the dissemination of ideas and materials.

We must turn to Ecuador for an examination of some of our earliest art forms, for this is one of the most intriguing as well as the most puzzling areas of South America. The area had long been ignored by scholars until surprising radiocarbon dates began to emerge, and many students now believe that ancient man may well have established his first foothold in this region. It is presently believed to harbor the earliest datable pottery, perhaps as early as *circa* 3200 BC, when pottery is known to have been developed at Valdiva, following which comes a long, steady period of development (**181**). After 3200 BC, the ability to work clay spread rapidly, and several major regional styles developed; that this was accomplished in great quantity is revealed not only by archeological excavation, but also by early Spanish accounts.

Little is known of Brazil in prehistoric times; only around the Amazon area do we find evidence of the cultures which were in existence at the time of Columbus. Much of the surviving material has been lost because of dense jungle growth and weather conditions. Probably the most esthetically exciting material is the pottery found on Marajó Island, which incorporates modeling and painting with relief carving (**193**). This is not a plentiful pottery; fragments are commonly found, but complete vessels are extremely rare. Curiously, this dynamic and powerful style seems not to have influenced any other cultures which surrounded it. Exciting forms have survived today in some of the Indian groups of the Amazon area, most particularly in their clay work, and in some of the woven and

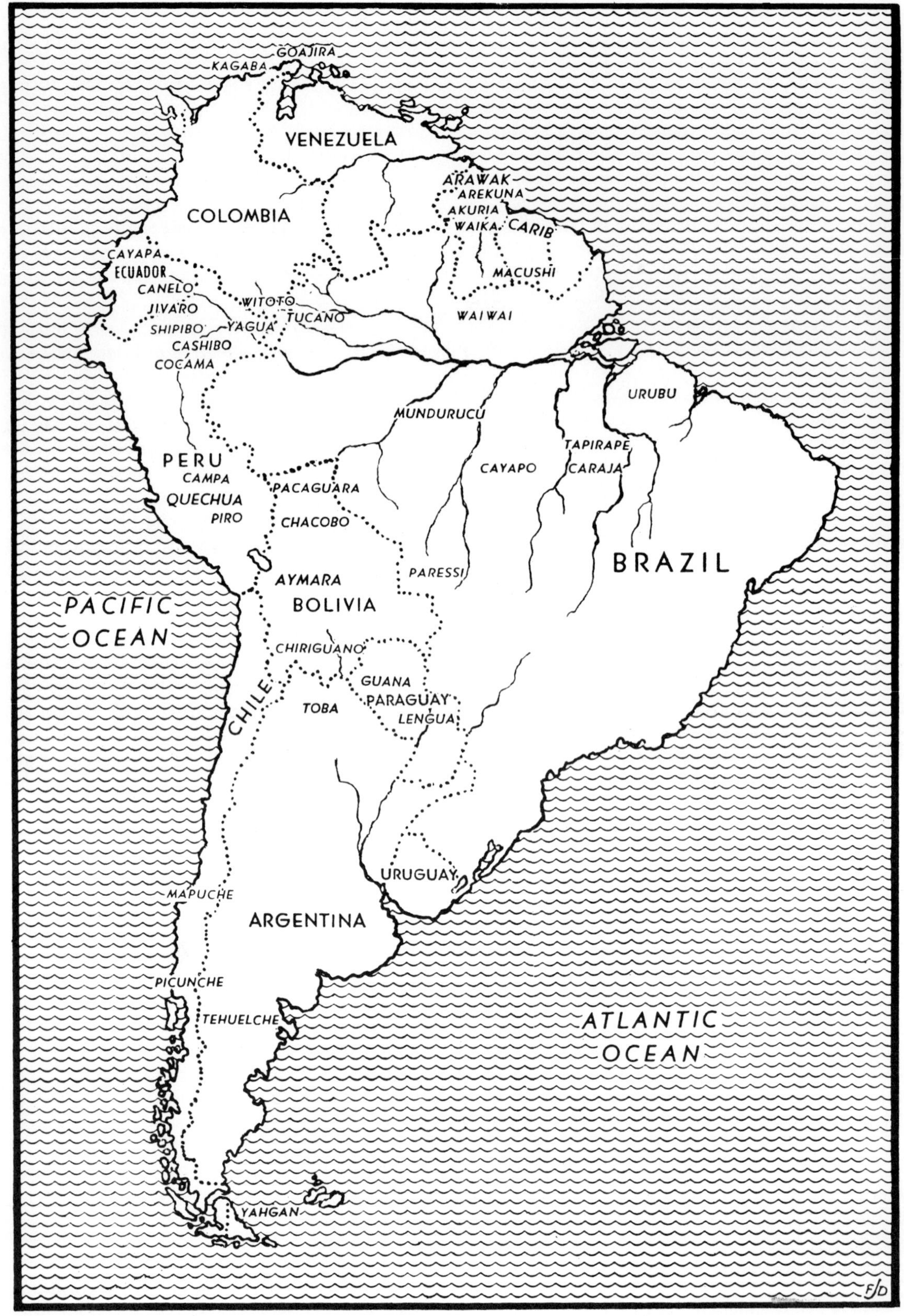
GOAJIRA
KAGABA
VENEZUELA
ARAWAK
AREKUNA
AKURIA
WAIKA
CARIB
COLOMBIA
CAYAPA
ECUADOR
CANELO
MACUSHI
WITOTO
JIVARO
TUCANO
WAIWAI
SHIPIBO
YAGUA
CASHIBO
COCAMA
URUBU
MUNDURUCU
TAPIRAPE
PERU
CAYAPO
CARAJA
CAMPA
PACAGUARA
QUECHUA
PIRO
CHACOBO
BRAZIL
PARESSI
AYMARA
PACIFIC
OCEAN
BOLIVIA
CHIRIGUANO
GUANA
CHILE
PARAGUAY
TOBA
LENGUA
URUGUAY
MAPUCHE
ARGENTINA
PICUNCHE
TEHUELCHE
ATLANTIC
OCEAN
YAHGAN
F/D

painted art styles found in textiles (**491**).

The great civilizations of Peru have long attracted the attention of layman and scholar alike. Much of this interest is due to the accounts of the Spaniards, and to the great architectural monuments which have survived. The ruins of Machu Picchu, Tiahuanaco, and Sacsahuamán attest to the achievement of highly skilled people. Pottery has been found throughout the area, although it is not as early as that in Ecuador and Colombia; the oldest we have been able to date thus far is no earlier than 1200 BC. Vessels which have survived are notable for what they tell us of the cultures of these early people; the Mochica reflect the costumes and customs of the region which make these some of the most interesting of the early pottery forms (**208**).

The ruins around Chavín de Huantar have given the name *Chavín* to one of the earliest and most remarkable civilizations in South America. Carved stone and shell objects, pottery reflecting advanced skills, the evidence of stone construction, and a remarkably sophisticated gold work all bear witness to a truly magnificent era in ancient history (**199**). Also in Peru, recent discovery has brought to light evidences of another civilization as early as the Chavín, named *Vicús* after the valley in which it was uncovered. This dates between 250 BC and 500 AD, where pottery was produced resembling the wares of nearby Ecuador, and goldwork similar to other early forms (**205**). The importance of this discovery is that it indicates there is much yet to be uncovered in the vast South American continent.

South of the Chavín region another high culture developed on the Paracas peninsula. Featuring a thin-walled ware which has some of the most extraordinary incised designs and resin-base color, this must have been a colorful region (**201**). The great woven mantles, ponchos and tapestries that were created between 1000 and 250 BC also attest to a remarkable populace.

As people from the Chavín civilization filtered south to influence Paracas, in the north they also influenced the Moche peoples. Commonly termed *Mochica,* from 250 BC to about 750 AD, these folk developed a *genre* art form that includes some of the finest plastic sculpture in the history of pottery (**209**). The extensive number of objects produced suggests a populous civilization, replete with power and wealth. Gradually, as has been true with all civilizations throughout the world, the Mochica were succeeded by the *Chimú,* who established one of the great urban centers of ancient Peru at their capital, Chan Chan, from AD 1000 to 1500. This huge city, which is still visible today, was one of the great wonders of the ancient world of South America. The bounty of gold, textiles, pottery, and carvings which these people developed and left behind them, together with the great walls which were carved, worked and painted, attested to one of the great civilizations of which we know far too little (**229**). Fortunately, the arid climate of Peru has preserved many of the more perishable materials from this capital city which once housed approximately 100,000 persons.

In the south, a great ceramic development was under way in the Nazca Valley, which started about 250 BC and endured for approximately 1000 years or so. Perhaps among the most technically-advanced pottery in South America, the wares from this region were extremely thin-walled, produced both individually and in molds, and then finished off—often being painted in brilliant colors. The firing point is very high, and the decoration, in general, is quite remarkable (**210**). Although Nazca pottery is static in design and tends to be very repetitive, the quality of the ceramics is among the highest in the New World.

Nazca weavers, however, certainly surpassed anything any other group had done since the time of the magnificent Paracas weaving, and turned out literally miles and miles of hand-woven textiles in myriads of designs and colors. Their skill was such that the repetition did not destroy the beauty, and the overall patterns often provided harmony rarely seen elsewhere (**240**). Surprisingly, with all this wealth of artistry, Nazca goldwork was rather poor in comparison to that of other areas; it would seem almost as if the goldsmith decided his product was no longer as exciting as it had once been. Thin sheets of gold were hammered out and tooled with low-relief embossing, undoubtedly in large quantity. Whether the thin sheet was due to a lack of gold, or an effort to supply a huge market with a rare material, we do not know.

Closely related to and extended from Nazca is the work of the *Ica* civilization, which lasted from about 1000-1500 AD. While the pottery was of very high quality, though not as finely finished as that of the Nazca, their textiles were every bit as good (**216**). This was apparently a numerically smaller group, and in comparison to the Nazca never reached the ramifications of the earlier group. In Central Peru the *Chancay* peoples were in existence when the Spaniards arrived. Their pottery, which started around 1000 AD, is a simple black-and-white ware painted in soft, very fugitive colors; it is rare to find a Chancay piece in perfect condition. Much of it is crude in appearance, but often humorous in design (**218**). Many such pieces show a lively sense of the absurd and the designs remind one of a prehistoric comic strip. Chancay weaving, on the other hand, is excellent; along with Inca, Nazca, and Chimú, it represents the fine work for which Peru is famous.

Erotic art was at its height in Peru, particularly among the Mochica. Why this particular culture should have become such an exponent of sexual esthetics is not clear; although erotica is not absent from most Indian groups, it is far more commonplace and graphically elaborated among these ancient people. While some students suggest that this primarily reflects religious practices, one feels it far more likely that it expressed much the same general attitude then as does today's explicit sexual honesty, with the same overtones of humor, sensuality and passion.

In neighboring Bolivia, another major civilization began developing from about 250-750 AD; known as the Tiahuanaco, its origin is not completely apparent nor do we truly understand where it went. It is a rather sterile, angular art, where walled cities, huge doorways with intricately carved panels, and paved roads used more stone than any other culture save perhaps the later Inca peoples. Tiahuanaco pottery is a secondary ware compared to that of some of the neighboring peoples. At its best it is perhaps significant work, but tends not to have the excitement one normally associates with early pottery from Peru. Again, the great art of this civilization is their weaving—second only to the stone work, it gives us the impression of a very rich and colorful culture (**196**).

Inca, the best known of all of the Peruvian cultures, of course, is the latest; for it was this which the Spaniards reported on in such detail. It had begun around 1200 although the Empire itself was not established until 1438. When the Spaniards arrived approximately 100 years later, in 1532, the Inca Empire was at its height, and extended from Argentina and Chile in the south to Ecuador in the north. The influence of the Inca civilization is readily identified by a characteristic pottery shape called the aryballus; wherever the Inca went, the aryballus is sure to be found (**190**). There were several important emperors, all of whom carried on extensive conquests over the Andean region, and the Inca were involved in a bitter factionalism at the time of the Spanish invasion, which proved fatal in the face of the European assault.

That this attack was brutal is indicated by the fact that at the time of Spanish contact the Inca Empire numbered some six million individuals. There was a political hierarchy which controlled the entire Empire, looked after the welfare of the people, and developed a great civilization for those who were within its boundaries. In a period of 30 years this huge population had been decimated to something around 1,500,000. Part of the terrible legacy is that less art survives from the Inca period than from the older or far smaller Peruvian worlds. For example: there are more Tiahuanaco ponchos than there are from the Inca period; there is more Chimú gold; and Inca pottery is far less common than Mochica or Nazca.

However, metals were well-known; silver and gold were worked, and gold was claimed in the form of tribute from the subject peoples and treated as a gift to the Sun God. Sadly, it was this richness of the Inca Empire which proved its undoing—for it attracted the Spaniard and aroused his lust for gold. Cast copper was even more widely used, both for implements and tools, and for *objets d'art* (**227**).

Thus, very shortly after the Spanish Conquest the Inca Empire declined to a point where it was nothing more than an existant shell, much as it is today. Weaving, pottery, woodwork, stone carving, gold work—all of these have passed over into the hands of the invaders or disappeared, and the Inca almost became a memory. Were it not for the records and the surviving Inca peoples today, we would know very little of this early culture.

Passing to the south in Chile and Argentina, man continued on his long trek, crossing the great Atacama Desert and going into the Andean Highlands of the southern part of the continent. Here several civilizations developed, among them the Diaguita, Calchaquí and the Atacameño groups. Each of these in time developed their own cultures, became individual and, of course, warred back and forth with one another. But out of this group of newly-developed civilizations several distinct pottery, stone and textile arts developed. Some were unique, some were quite ordinary and less or equal in quality than those which were found farther north. Although gold was never a major product, copper became one of the most important metal arts of this region. Cast gongs, embossed shields, plaques and elaborate casting are known, and attest to the skill of the metalsmith (**189**). The origins of these people took place not much before 500 BC and the strength of their civilization lasted from about the time of Christ to the conquest by the Inca in the middle 1400's.

If there seems an overemphasis on pottery in this and related discussions, it is only because far more clay work survives than any other material. The tremendous amounts of wood, featherwork and textiles have largely disappeared; even metals corrode and lose their designs, so that we must judge by what we have at hand. Fortunately, pottery tells us a great deal, combining as it does the visual evidence with the physical. Today, with thermoluminescence, we have added the opportunity to fairly accurately establish relative chronologies. Ceramics therefore remains not only quantitively available, but one of our most valuable allies in tracing antiquity and the range of prehistoric cultures.

COLONIAL PERIOD

With the arrival of the Europeans and the introduction of Western motifs, technologies and tools, a tremendous impact was made upon indigenous arts. While this change falls more properly into the realm of Colonial Art, and therefore is alien to our basic subject matter, it should be mentioned that the clergy brought Indian craftsmen into the Church, taught them European designs and technology, and used their skills to produce the tremendous amount of art works which were required in the churches and cathedrals which were being constructed throughout the continent. These introduced many unusual design combinations, for often the native artist was faced with the problem of executing a design whose significance was wholly unknown to him, in techniques and artistic expressions of which he was a master. From these have come some of the more bizarre Indian or Colonial art creations to be seen throughout Latin America.

The Colonial period in the Americas differed radically. In the north, the transition was less religious than political, and was accompanied by wars for land, with traumatic results for the Indian. Forced to leave their home and remove to new, unknown areas, often far less suited to human habitation, the Indians of North America were either killed off by warfare, starvation, or disease, or overcome by assimilation or suicide (the latter was and remains far more prevalent than generally realized).

In Middle America, the contact between Indian and White was accompanied by initial annihilation, then Church contest, with priests often standing between the native and the soldier. In time, of course, this failed, and the Indian was either removed from what became Church or Crown lands, or became an integral part of the new culture, eventually establishing almost a new "race."

The meeting between Indian and White in South America was accompanied by a far more brutal conflict. The initial shock of Spanish contact was savage, with hundreds of thousands of natives killed off in the drive to conquer, and the search for gold. The land rush involved an area so vast and so difficult of settlement that it tended to affect large, isolated regions. With expansion, the Indian was forced into assimilation, isolation in the remote regions, or extinction. This latter was often accomplished by barbaric cruelty; indeed, even hunts where organized as late as 1840 for the specific purpose of killing off the Indian occupants of the area. And, even more recently, in 1970 Indians have been slaughtered *en masse* in efforts directed towards "clearing the land" to make way for *mestizo* settlers migrating from the large cities in Brazil.

It is rarely understood what a tremendous effect the Conquest of the New World had, for one must realize that the result was the acquisition of an area several hundred times the size of the colonizing countries. Even more dramatically, this was shortly followed by an attempt to weld this vast, tremendously complex region into a single major unit. Earlier, of course, there had been aboriginal efforts at conquest and empire building, but these were never quite the same as the European venture. Furthermore, this came at the same time as a socio-cultural revival in Europe. The Renaissance was an individual movement towards universality which, hand-in-hand with the Church morality of the period, resulted in a complacent feeling of righteousness about Christianity which even today remains a problem in our efforts to establish a tolerance of differences.

The major art expressions in Europe, such as Baroque and Rococo, were not only art forms, but were also ways of life, which required an over-blown, ornate quality satisfied only by the opulence and wealth which came from the New World. Indian efforts to imitate this European original did not come off, and most of them reflect this quality of a copy of a misunderstood original.

The ensuing conflict between righteous Christian, greedy European, and the proud but over-powered Indian was the annihilation of a population whose total civilization is not realized even today. Suffice it to say that, almost overnight, the labor force disappeared, and hundreds of thousands of Negro slaves were brought into the New World to work in the mines, plantations and industries. From this introduction has come many unusual blood mixtures, and in some areas, has almost resulted in a new "race." Surprisingly, this intermixture has had little effect upon the arts.

In the Middle Americas, the contemporary Indian situation is mixed. In some sections, such as El Salvador and Costa Rica, the Indian presence is minimal; indeed, many citizens of those countries do not realize there is any surviving aboriginal population. In Honduras, Nicaragua and Panama, the population is heavily intermixed with Negro blood; the latter country has some smaller enclaves of Indian populations, most notably the Cuna, whose appliqué textile arts have gained considerable popularity in the current market, as have their wood carvings used in curing ceremonies.

Little has been done in the way of formal schooling for the development of these arts; there are some small craft shops in the cities, and individual sponsors have undertaken the problem of encouraging craft production, often with very satisfactory results, although this is often pursued in a manner primarily to serve the White market, rather than to meet indigenous needs. The *Indigenista* movement in these countries is more of an academic trend, stressing social and economic goals, rather than the esthetic.

In Mexico, on the other hand, a significant contemporary Indian arts and crafts activity has shown remarkable results. The range of designs has expanded, and generally in a favorable direction. There has been some decline in quality, particularly in those crafts which enjoy mass acceptance; this often results in garish or over-blown design. However, quality work has not disappeared, and experimentation is often healthy, accompanied in many instances by work in new media. The presence of established craft outlets, such as the excellent Regional Museums, and the Arte Popular organizations, have combined to give a broad base of support, and sense of dignity, to this effort.

Much of this mastery is still to be seen today, with the return to older, more traditional forms which have come from the encouragement on the part of outside influences seeking to work towards the re-establishment of older motifs; nowhere is this more evident than in Mexico. And, with the strengthening of native pride, a great degree of esthetic excitement is to be found. The degree to which this will become a dominant force, if ever, cannot yet be judged. It is more likely that a harmonious plateau will evolve which will, hopefully, result in a melding of the best of the two worlds.

The arts reflected these attitudes, as well as other colonial activities. Church art introduced a quite different approach, both as regards the object, the technique and the material. Priests incorporated Indian craftsworkers into the cultural development of the regions under their control, teaching them Christian ideas, attitudes and goals, which resulted in a variety of strange, non-European motifs, produced by excellent artists for Church and home architecture. There is little of the earlier indigenous sensitivity of form; rather, one finds a more mechanical approach to art, lacking any inspiration, and with a very stylized format.

INDIAN ART TODAY

And what of Indian art today? In the contemporary art marketplace, Amerindian arts and crafts occupy a peripheral role. Only recently has there been any genuine interest in the esthetic product of the Native American. In those instances where it has been expressed, it is largely as souvenir or exotic curiosity products rather than a truly developed appreciation of the esthetic quality which one normally assigns to art when seen in an exhibition. Even in those specialized institutions devoted to Indian materials or interested in the American West, the treatment is largely sentimental or romantic, frequently reflecting the advance of the frontier in terms of the so-called "conquest" of the Western area. This was certainly the case in North America. It is regrettable that in many Latin American countries where the Indian was still a vibrant force and where the population is largely Indian, even those well-to-do citizens who are of Indian extraction fail to regard this as a prideful quality.

It is not surprising to find this the case, since the displacement of the Indian by the Westerner was accompanied by a rejection of his product, other than as curiosities of a defeated people. Only in the last 20-30 years has there been anything like a willingness to regard Indian art in terms of viable and respectable intellectual products. Even here, most of the active interest tends to be more in the so-called pre-Columbian field, which means in this context, the Mayan, Aztec, Inca and related civilizations of Latin America rather than the equally prehistoric cultures of North America.

The most active efforts to preserve Indian art and make of it something of consequence have taken place in the United States. During the 1920's a group of White artists located in Santa Fe and Taos, New Mexico, found the work of the Indians of the Southwest an exciting, visual experience. They united to make possible the development of some of the qualities they saw in these arts and by exhibits and encouragement of the younger Indian people, these influential artists succeeded in bringing the values of Indian art to the attention of the outside world. Meantime, this group saw to the establishment of the School of Indian Art in Santa Fe, which operated until the Depression. Out of that school came some of the more familiar names of painters, potters and weavers (**498**).

Another surge of interest came with the enactment of the Indian Reorganization Act of 1934, which among other things, was responsible for the establishment of the Indian Arts and Crafts Board. This body, operating under the authority of the Interior Department, was charged by Congress with the promotion, encouragement and revival of native arts and crafts. The credit for the establishment of the Board was due largely to the work of John Collier, Oliver LaFarge and Frederic H. Douglas. The effort was for the most part an economic one, originally to develop Indian income, but it rapidly grew as more and more of the older people were found who still remembered the technology of the past, were delighted to see their work appreciated, and were willing to teach the younger people how to create the arts which they valued. Out of this program came a renaissance which continues today, although the work of the Board was seriously curtailed during World War II.

Among all of the North American tribes, painting is probably the one art that has taken the strongest, positive direction, and it is here that there has been a willingness not only to experiment, but a receptivity on the part of the Indian and non-Indian alike to view the new steps in a sympathetic way. Some of the younger Indian people today have developed successful careers not only economically, but also in the form of social recognition.

In more recent times the hopeful signs of progress are to be seen in such institutions as the newly-established Institute of American Indian Art in Santa Fe. This school reflects the efforts of the Indian Arts and Crafts Board to establish an on-going educational institution for young Indian people. Today, it has perhaps a greater opportunity for developing what can be a viable esthetic and economic product than any one other single device, unless it might be some of the native schools which are slowly developing on the reservations. As the native artist finds himself more and more in a contemporary world, it may be that there will be little need for governmentally-operated institutions; at present this seems doubtful, but the future will provide the answer.

The greatest problem the younger Indian artist has today is that of being able to select from his Indian background those qualities which are important to him, express them through his art work in a manner which will be acceptable to the Western World, and in so doing not sacrifice the very quality of Indianness that gives him expression and identity.

Possibly the most encouraging, and in the long run influential, development of the past decade has been the many cultural centers which are springing up on reservations throughout the country. Many of these incorporate teaching facilities in arts and crafts, along with museums for the exhibition of the products of the schools, as well as the traditional arts which can be used as an inspiration to the younger people. If these multiply and become viable, it is hoped that they will answer many of the needs of younger Indian people today, for they will also increase the respect which the outside world will give to the Indian artist.

It must be recognized that with so many years of cultural denial, the renaissance of Indian art is difficult to establish. It cannot be done magically; it must be done coöperatively with the artist, the patron, and the entrepreneur working together to assure a quality product. As long as the Indian is relegated to the production of knick-knacks and tourist souvenirs, his art will never be other than a curiosity occupying a minimal role in the art world. If, however, he is able to achieve recognition through talent and through the willingness of the outside world to look carefully rather than hastily, he has every opportunity of occupying the place that he should in that world.

In Latin America, organizations similar to those in the United States have slowly developed. Most of these are more involved with the political world than they are with the art world. They give lip service to arts and crafts as produced within their boundaries, all too often consisting of a relatively passive attitude lacking the serious attention which would enable one to develop pride of creation or accomplishment. Much of the interest lies solely in the proportion of economic return involved, rather than something intended to develop dignity or pride. In the political sphere, since many of the countries involved actually enjoy an Indian majority, the tendency is usually to proceed cautiously—a revolutionary movement could very easily affect the balance of power within the country. For this, and for racial-cultural reasons, Indianism and Indian art are sensitive issues in most of the Latin American countries.

Of these South American countries, Peru, Bolivia and Ecuador retain the greatest degree of Indianness, as does Guatemala in Middle America. The balance have varying degrees of native cultural remnants, but with a considerable degree of European influence, some entirely so.

Mexico remains a case apart; the Indian element is dominant in many regions of the country, and *Indianismo* is a major force in the country. Some large-scale regions of the nation are relatively pure Indian; elsewhere, this is less marked. Yet of the countries enjoying this racial structure, Mexico has probably been more successful in integrating Indian arts than the others. In fact, during the past decade, this integration has threatened the survival of some of the more exotic forms, for these have been adapted to the demands of the urban market, both Indian and non-Indian, to such an extent as to radically change their form and character. It seems doubtful that Indian art, as such, will be able to withstand the pressures of the economic forces involved in the arts and crafts marketplace.

But there is a vitality still to be seen, and it is this which makes much of Mexican Indian art so exciting and greatly in demand. It remains to be seen how successfully the Indian artist will be able to keep his balance in this very challenging situation.

In closing, we trust that the present exhibition will have opened the eyes of the viewer to a new world, if this has not already been familiar to him. If, on the other hand, he had enjoyed previous exposure to these expressions, it is hoped that we may have expanded that consciousness. For both, we sincerely trust that this will give an opportunity to examine in one viewing the general range of the heritage of America as it existed before, during, and after the arrival of Columbus, and thereby demonstrate the strengths of Man's spirit at work in creating beauty from a generous nature.

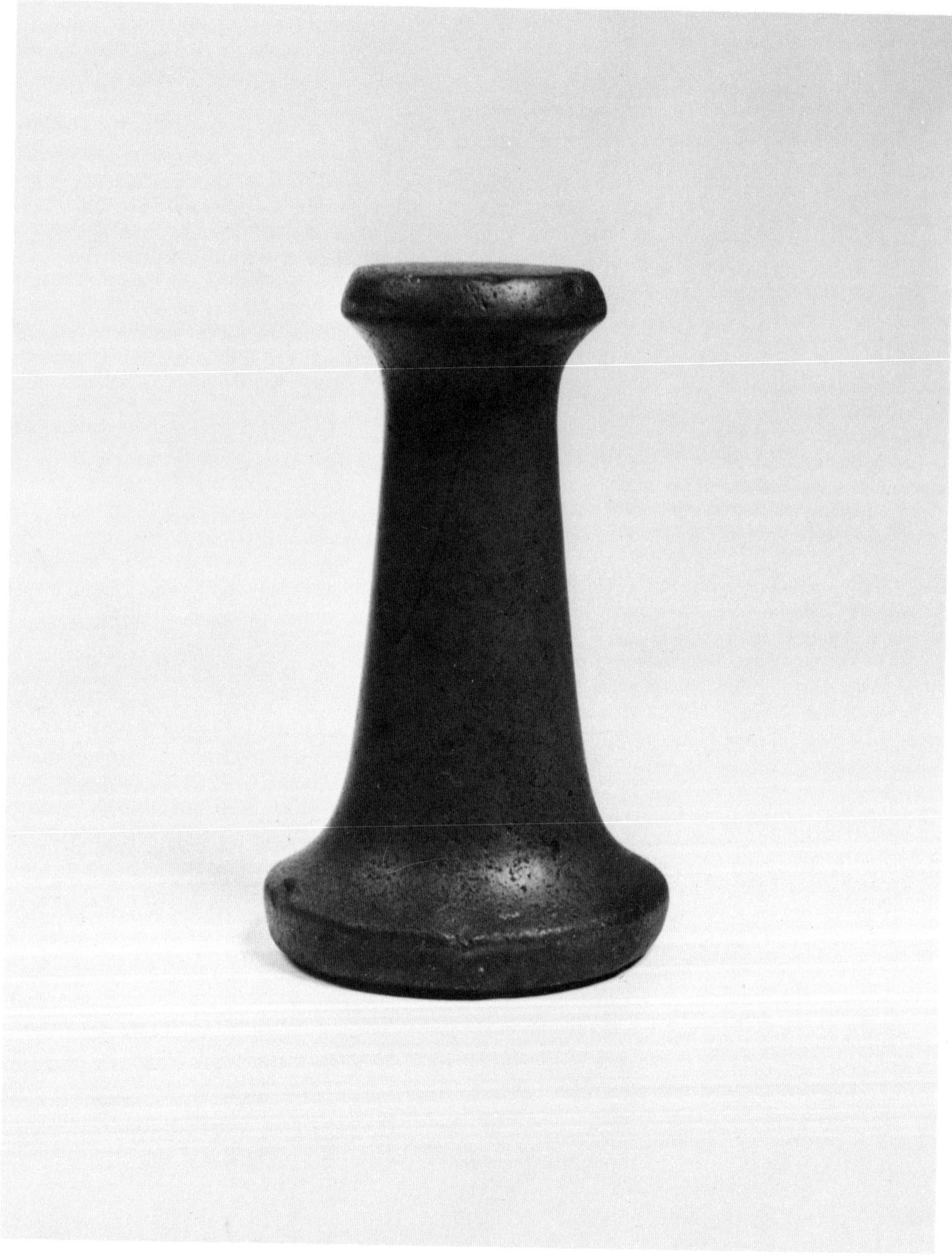

1. Stone Pestle

These finely carved and polished objects were usually combined with a wood or stone mortar, to pound up berries, nuts, meat, and herbs. The form is typical of the Northwest Pacific region. Collected in 1860. KWAKIUTL. Cape Mudge, Vancouver Island, British Columbia. 4″ x 7¼″. 10/278.

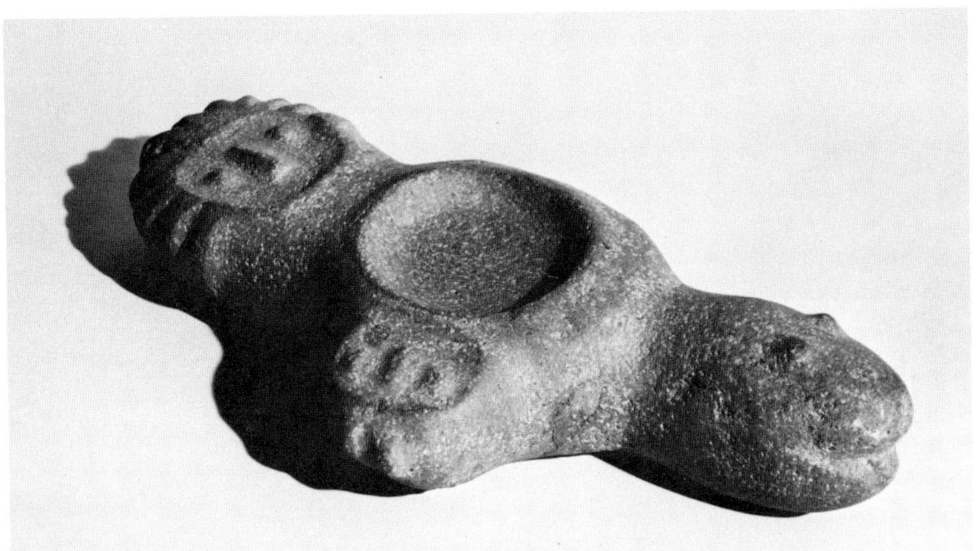

2. Zoömorphic Mortar
Carefully carved and smoothened, this design represents a human, owl, and serpent head combined in a pleasing balance. Dalles Culture. 1000-1200. Wasco County, Oregon. 1¾" x 8¾". 19/339.

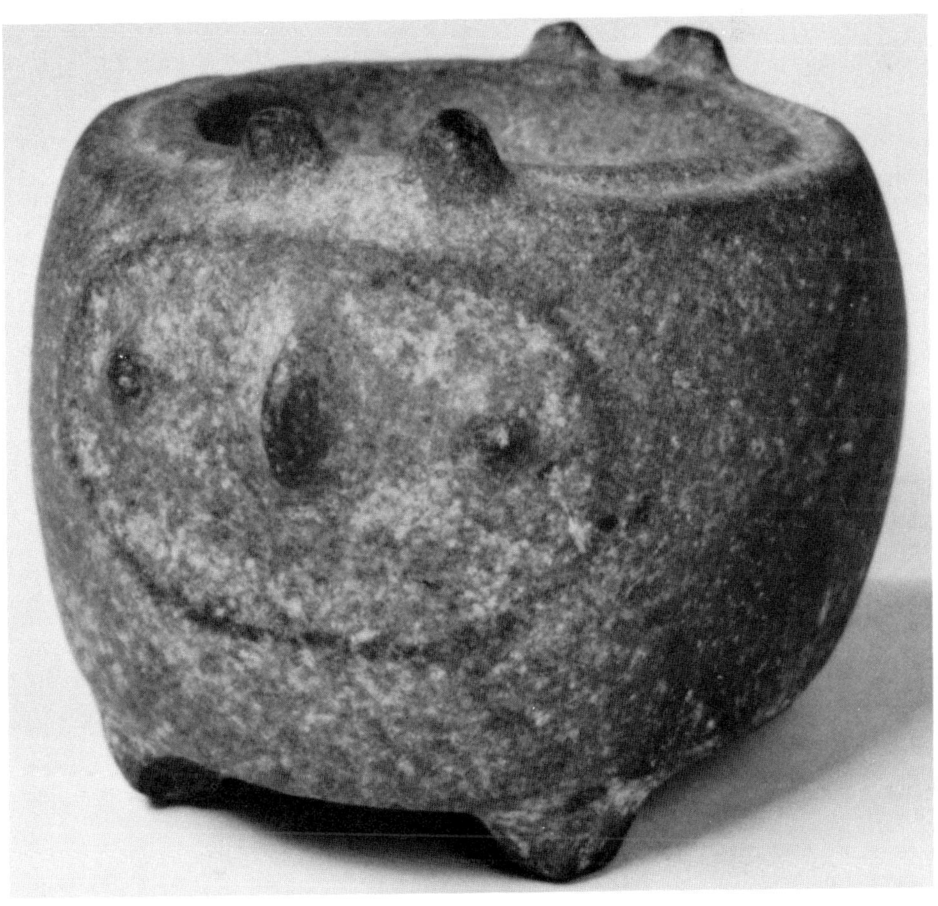

3. Medicine Mortar
Carved to represent the head of an owl, this small granite mortar is of the type used for medicines and herbs. Dalles Culture. 1000-1200. Wasco County, Oregon. 3½" x 4½". 19/336.

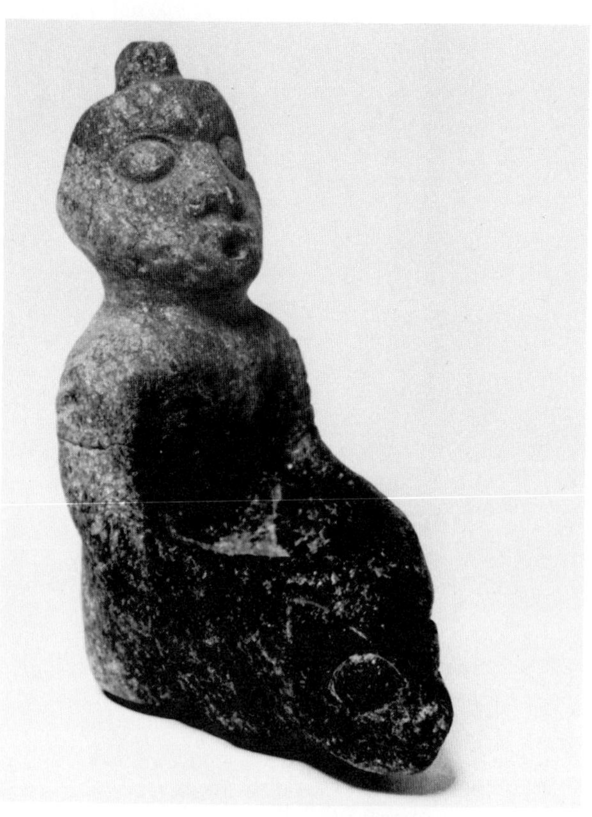

4. Stone Effigy Mortar
The design of a man holding a bowl is a common motif in the Northwest Pacific area; this steatite specimen is typical of a wide variety of such mortars. Collected before 1840. DALLES CULTURE. 1000-1200. Fraser River, British Columbia. 4" x 5¼". 5/563.

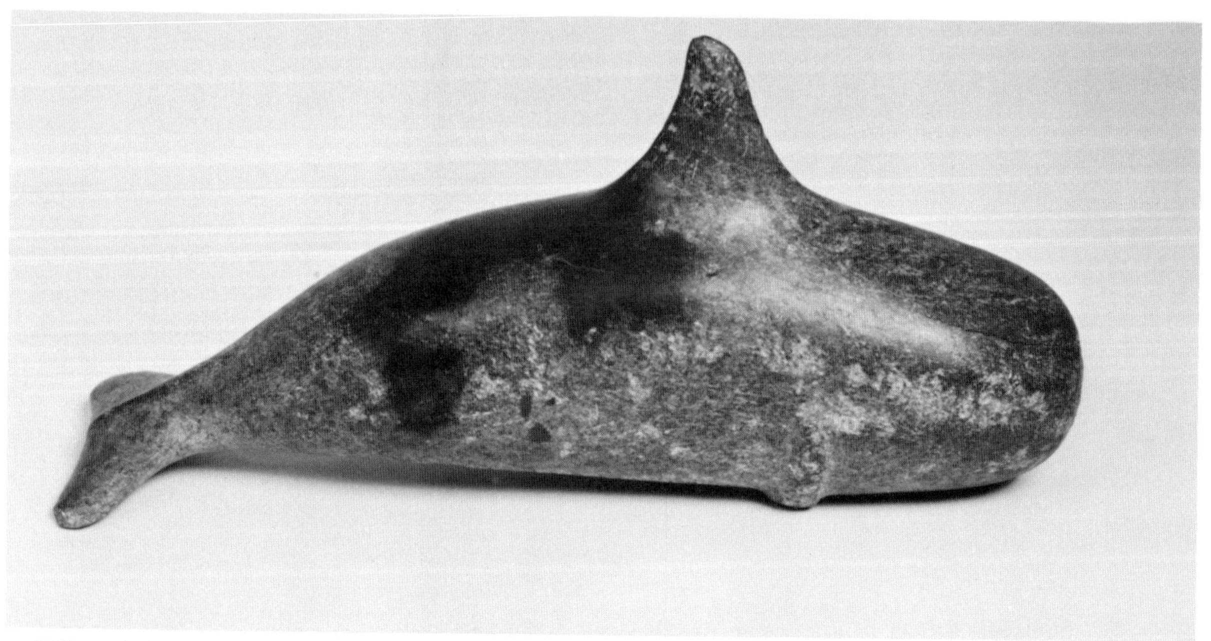

5. Killer Whale Effigy
These graceful, realistic sculptures may have been used as fetishes or charms by the Channel Islands people. CANALIÑO. 1500-1700. San Nicolas Island, California. 6¼" x 13". 19/36.

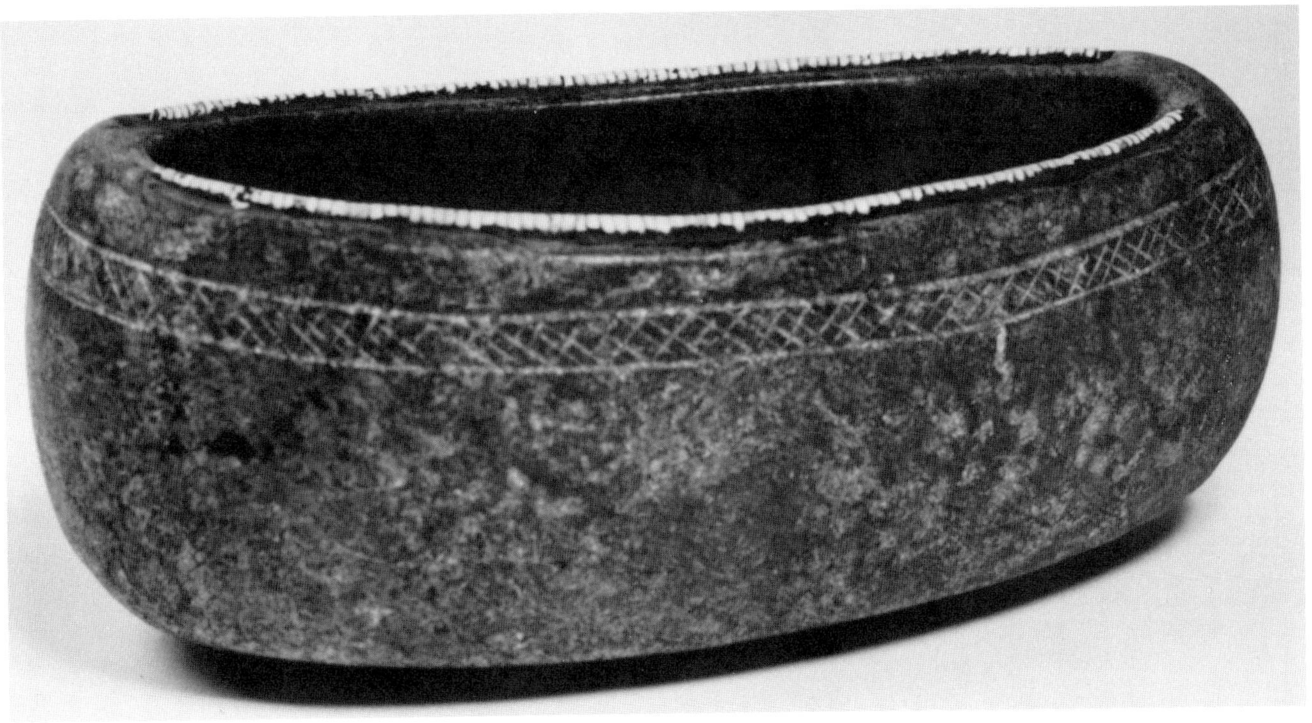

6. Oval Steatite Bowl
These carved bowls, often with incised designs and inlaid shell decorations, are commonly found in the Southern California region. CANALIÑO. 1500-1700. Point Dume, Los Angeles County, California. 3½″ x 4½″ x 9″. 20/1031.

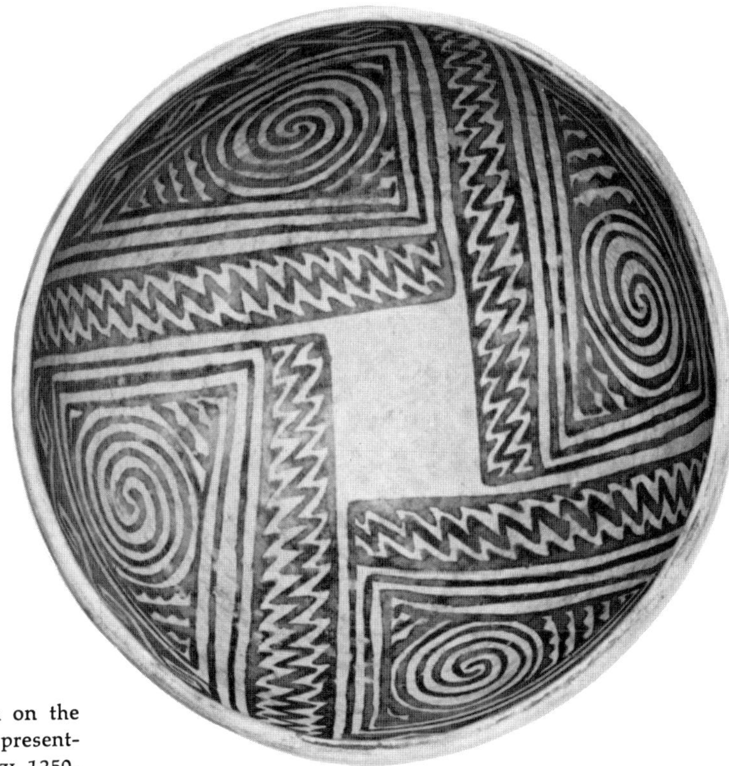

7. Black-on-White Ware Bowl
This has a well-balanced geometric design on the interior. The culture is the ancestor to the present-day Pueblo peoples of the Southwest. ANASAZI. 1250-1300. Flagstaff, Coconino County, Arizona. 4¼″ x 8¼″. 18/9175.

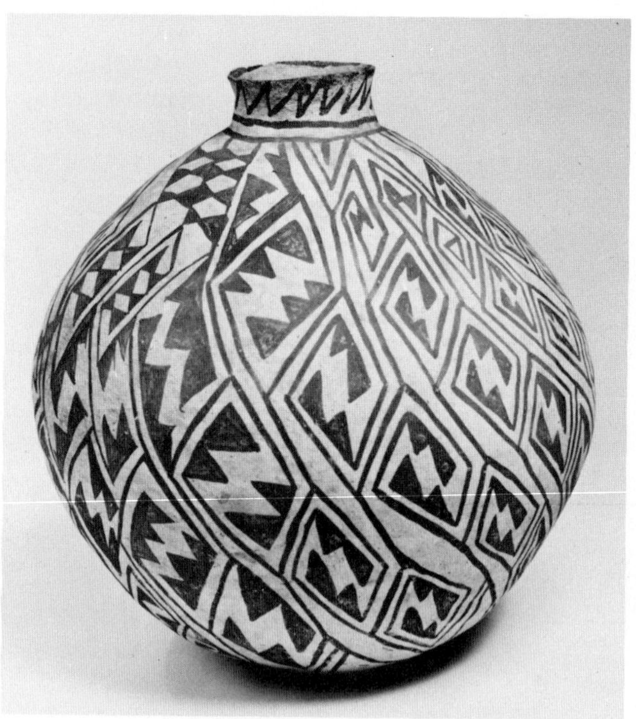

8. Globular Olla

These well-rounded forms were used as containers for liquid; the small orifice retards evaporation. ANASAZI. Canyon de Chelly, Arizona. 1100-1300. 12″ x 13¾″. 14/7150.

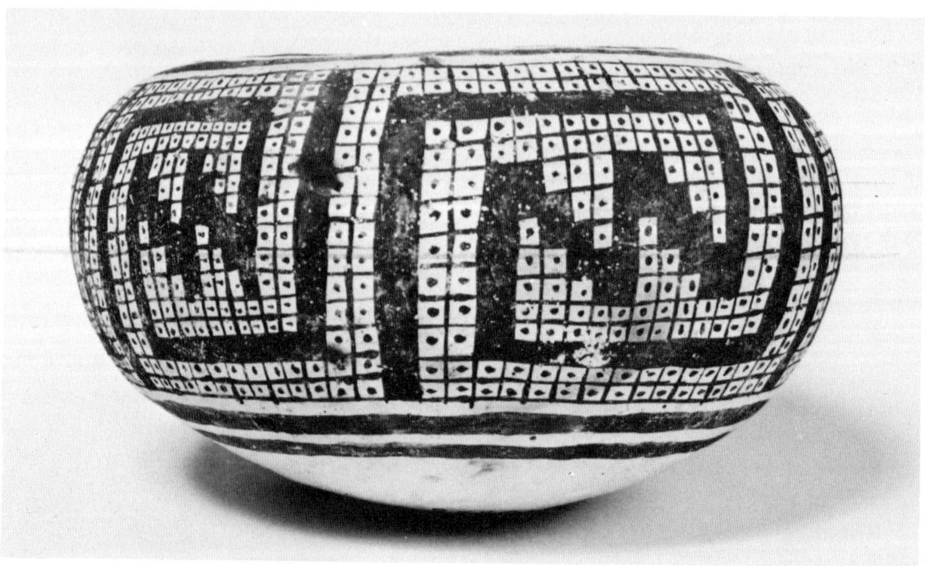

9. Shallow Clay Bowl

The small squares with dots painted on this incurved-rim vessel are often symbolic of a corn design. Collected by Lancelot Ely. ANASAZI. Spring Creek, Gila County, Arizona. 1250-1500. 5″ x 8″. 21/5026.

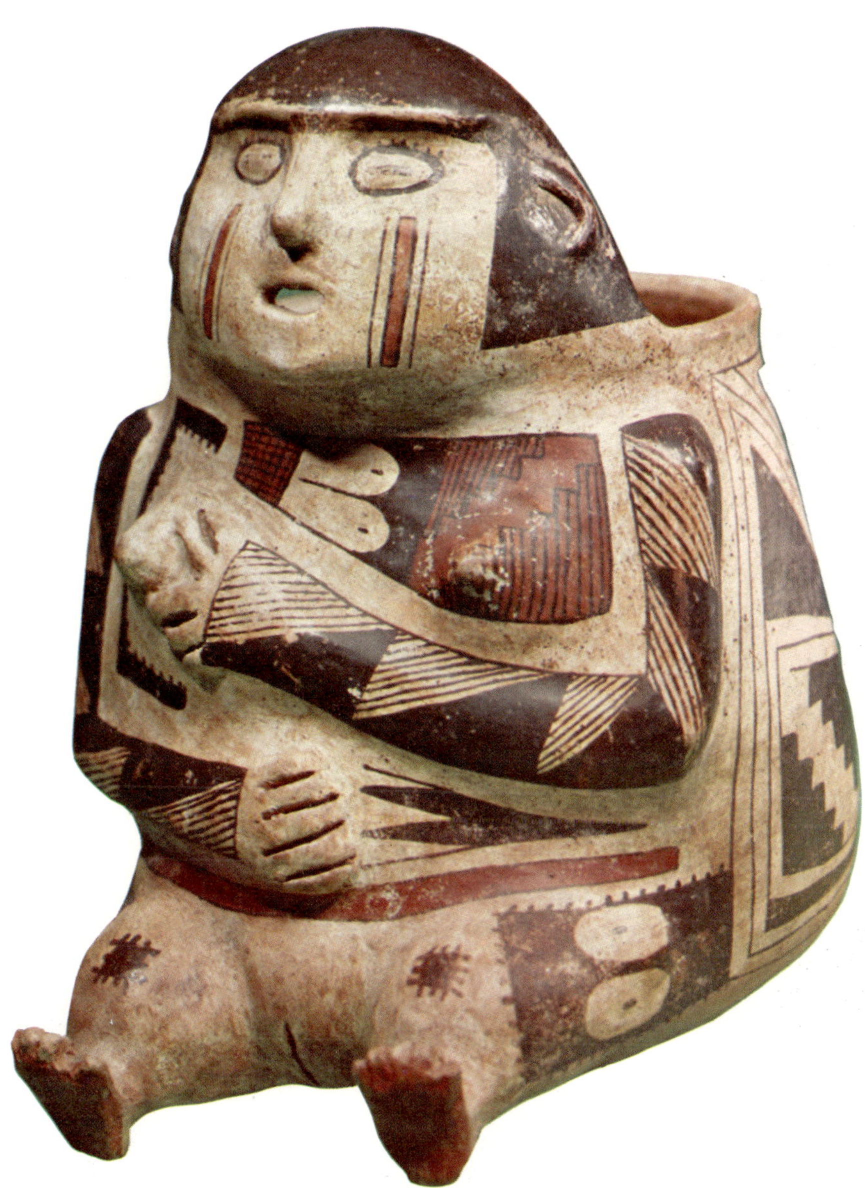

51. Polychrome Effigy Bowl

While primarily a container, this has developed into a definite effigy form. The design portrays a seated female holding her breast; her brightly colored body may represent tattooing, or textile garment motifs. Collected by Edward Ledwidge. CASAS GRANDES. Coahuila, Mexico. 1200-1500. 6¼″ x 10½″. 6/582.

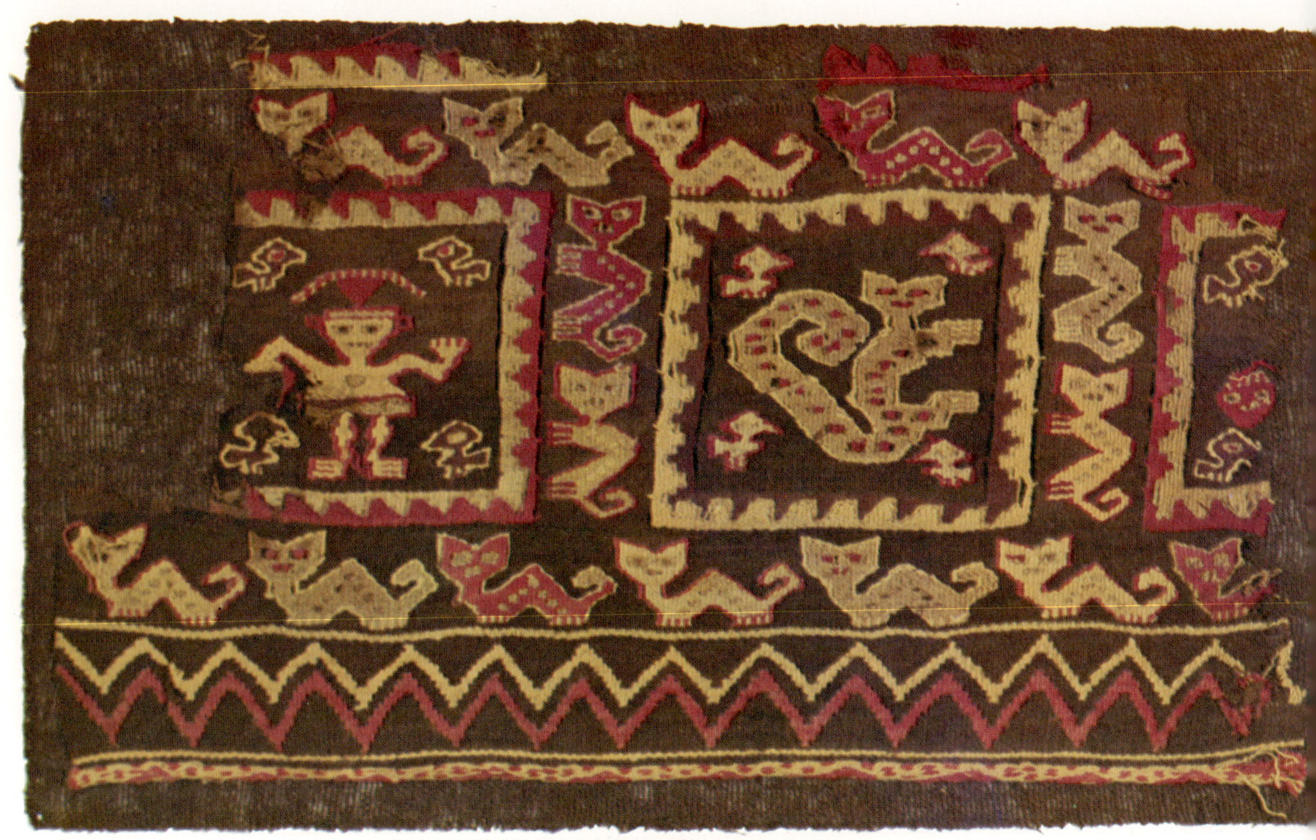

240. Tapestry Weave Fragment

Although only a portion of the original textile has survived, this polychrome slit-weave fabric retains all of the splendour which it earlier displayed. The skill of the ancient weaver in patiently working the small panels of designs into an over-all design is impressive. COASTAL PERU. 1000-1300. 10¼" x 18". 24/8378.

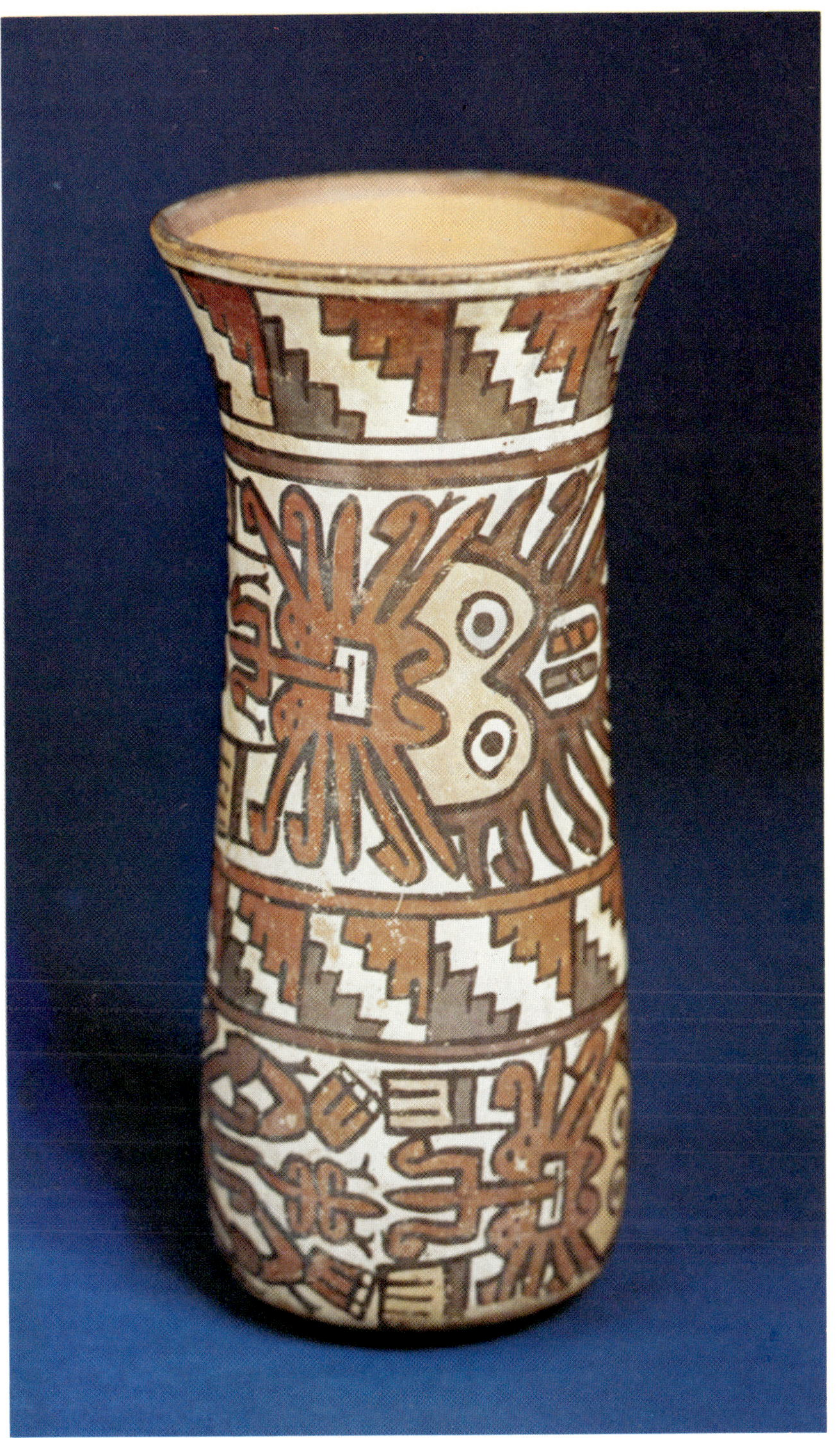

213. Polychrome Vase

The geometric design on this elongated vase is broken by bands of elaborately painted mythological creatures in abstract patterns. NAZCA. Nazca Valley, Peru. 550-650. 4¼″ x 9″. 16/8883.

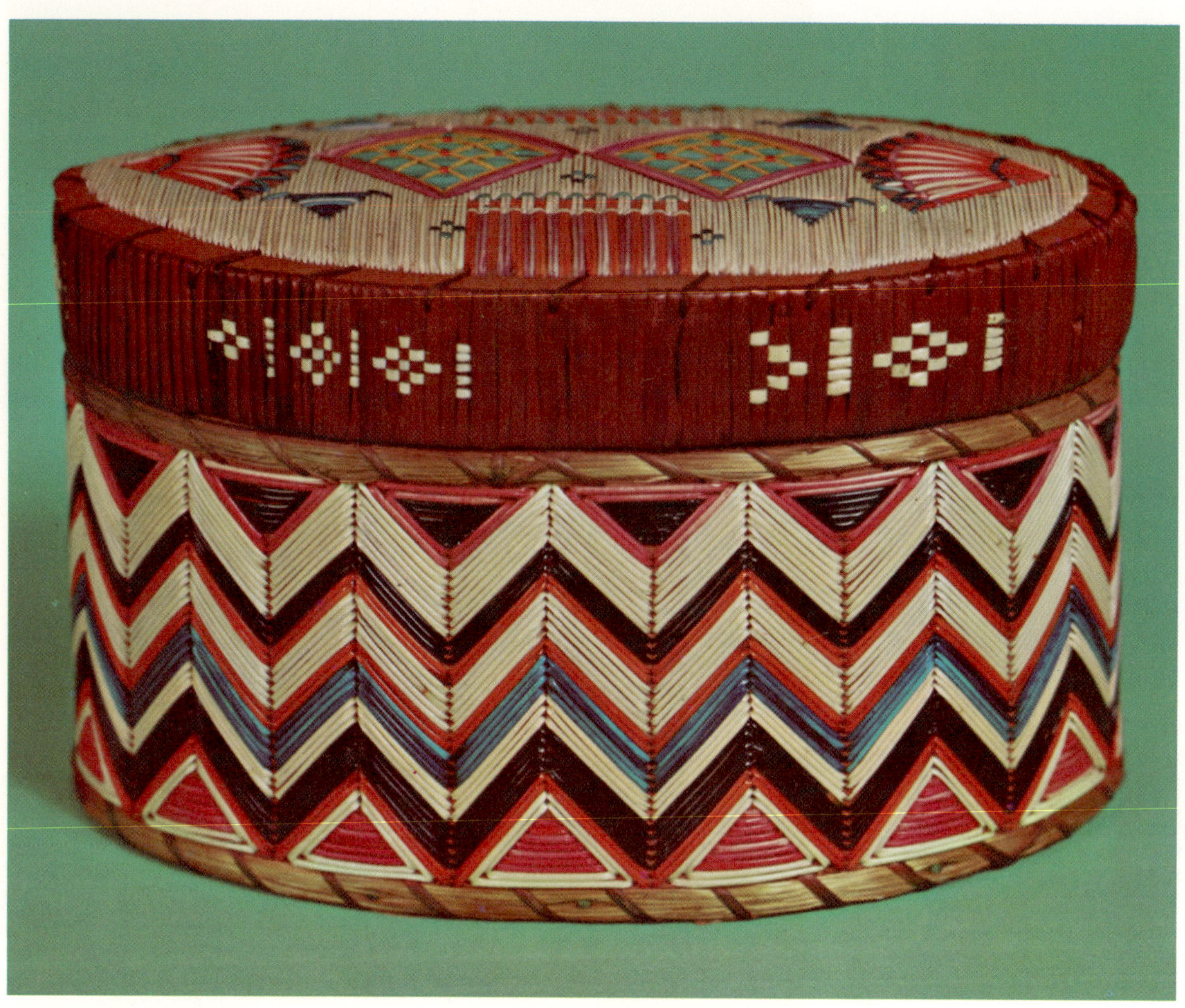

447. Quill-decorated Box
An oval birchbark box, decorated with brilliantly colored quillwork. These have been tinted with aniline dyes, and while intended for the tourist trade, they have lost little of their early technical skill. MICMAC. Nova Scotia, Canada. 1900-1920. 5″ x 5½″ x 9″. 2/5796.

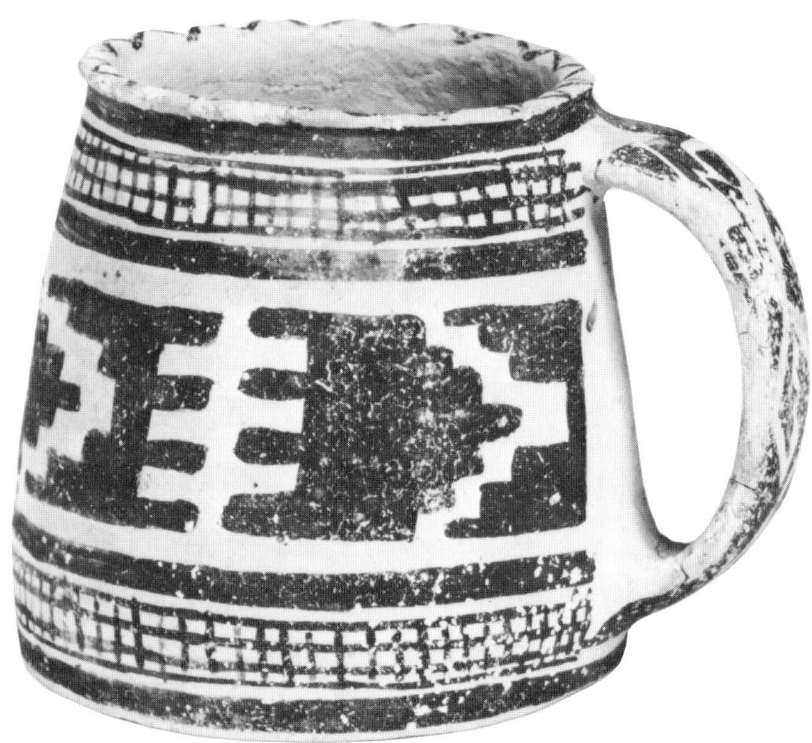

10. Black-on-White Ware Mug
These are very common in the "Four Corners" area of the Southwest. Collected by George H. Pepper. ANASAZI. Mesa Fachada, Chaco Canyon, New Mexico. 1070-1130. 4" x 4". 5/2122.

11. Brown Ware Tinaja
The coils of clay are wound around to form the vessel, and then impressed with a stick to form the corrugated pattern seen in this storage vessel. Collected by William J. Mackay. MOGOLLÓN. Socorro County, New Mexico. 900-1100. 13" x 14". 8/7640.

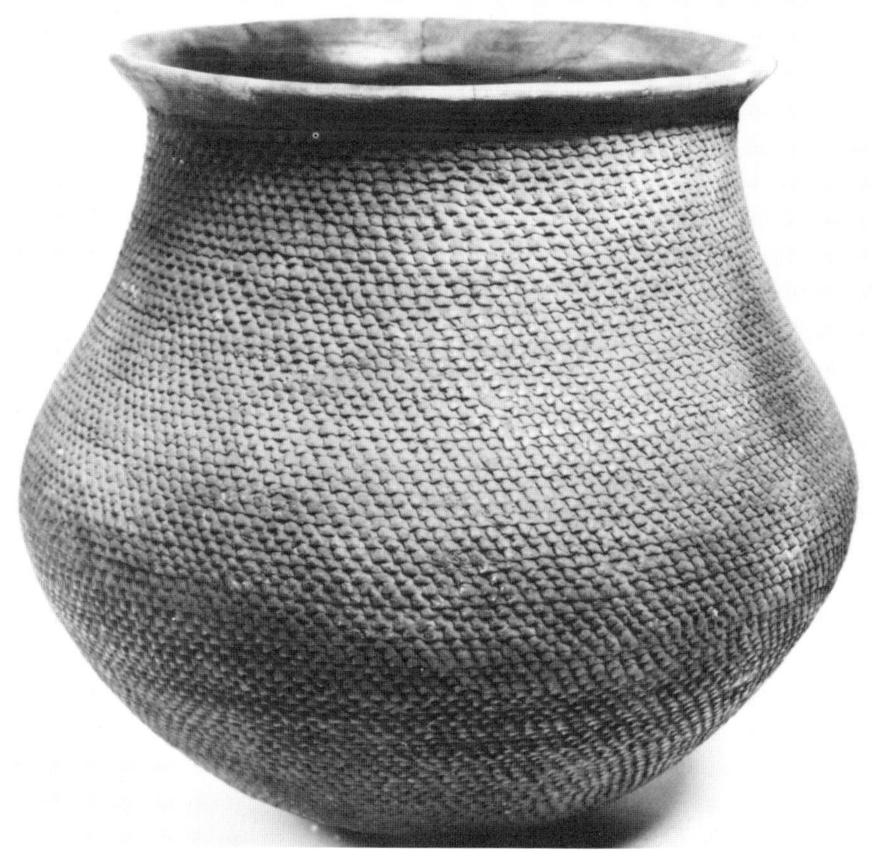

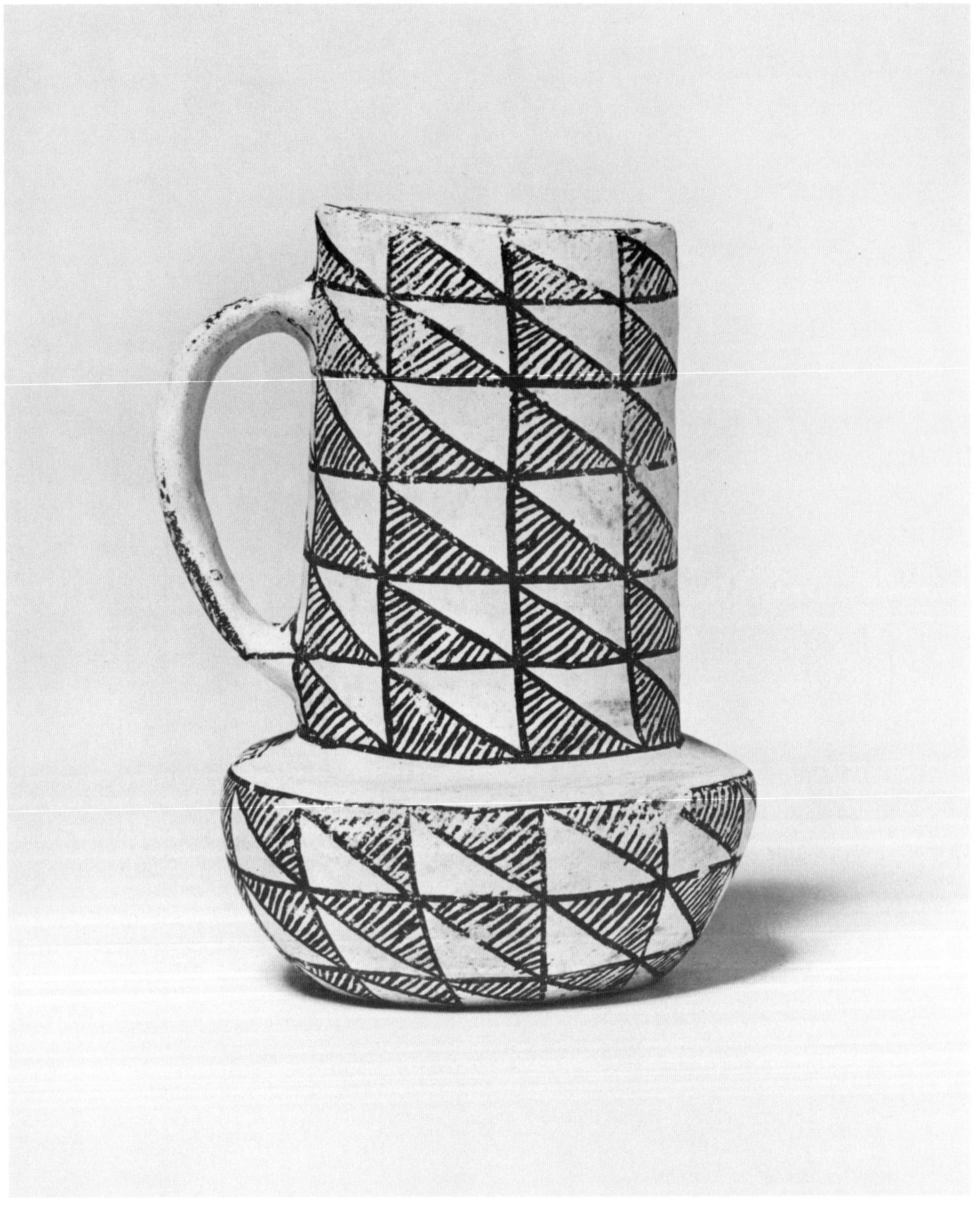

12. Cylindrical Vessel
These slender, delicately-formed vessels are found in the northeastern part of Arizona; they are often equipped with a pouring lip and tiny handle. ANASAZI. Chaco Canyon, New Mexico. 1070-1130. 5″. 5/2873.

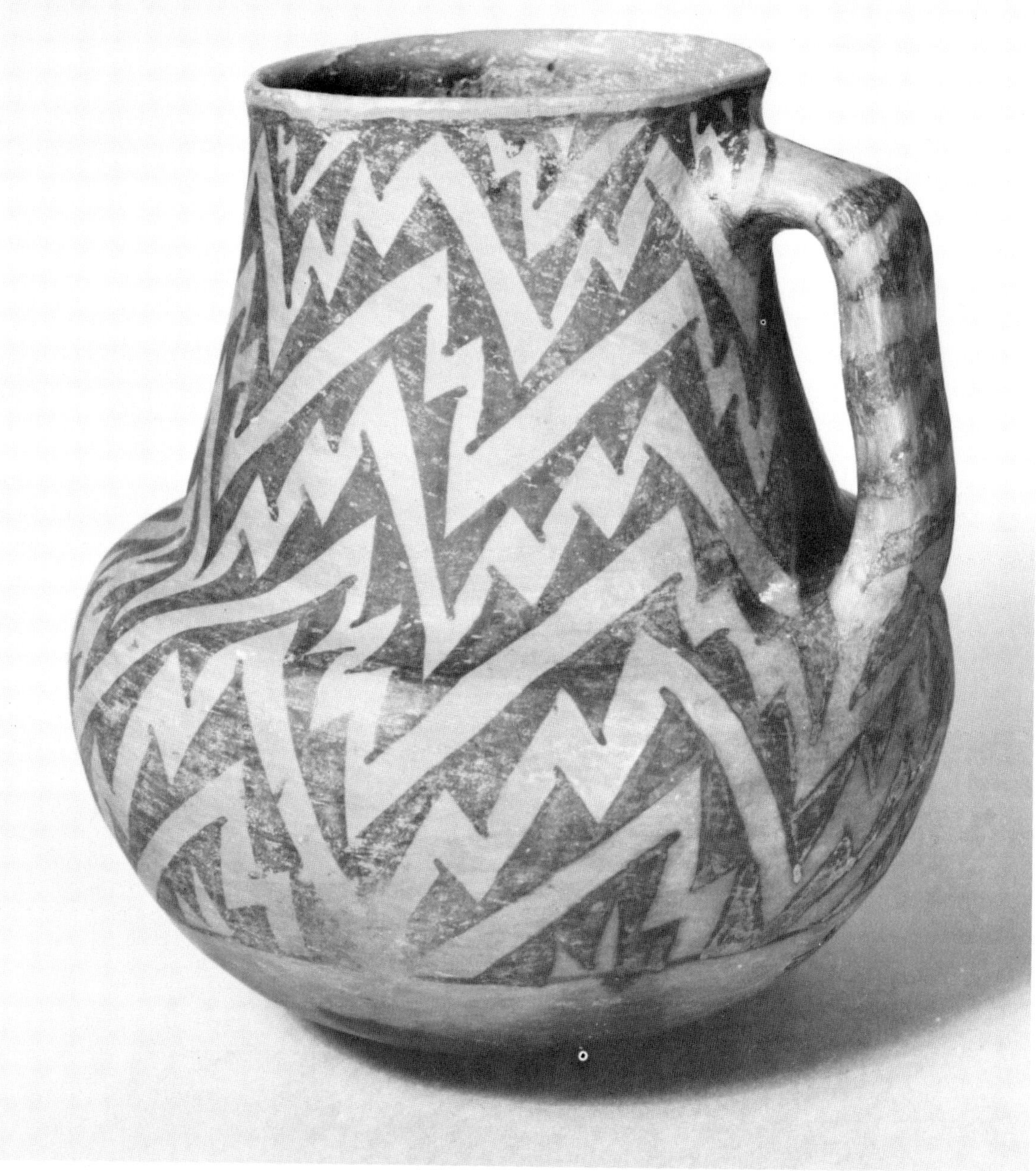

13. Redware Pitcher

This graceful form is further embellished by a geometric design painted in black on the rich terra cotta surface. Collected by George LeMonte Cole. ANASAZI. St. Johns, Apache County, Arizona. 1100-1300. 6¾" x 7½". 4/9615.

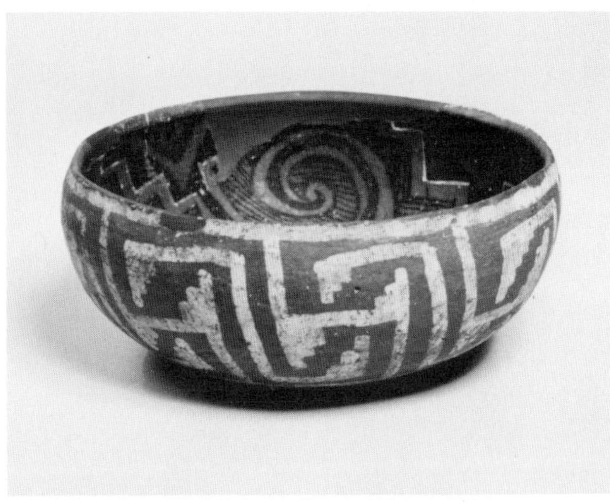

14. Redware Bowl
The interior of this shallow vessel is decorated in black with traces of white; the exterior has a dramatic fret design in white. Collected by Reamer Ling. ANASAZI. St. Johns, Apache County, Arizona. 1175-1300. 3½″ x 8½″. 12/8002.

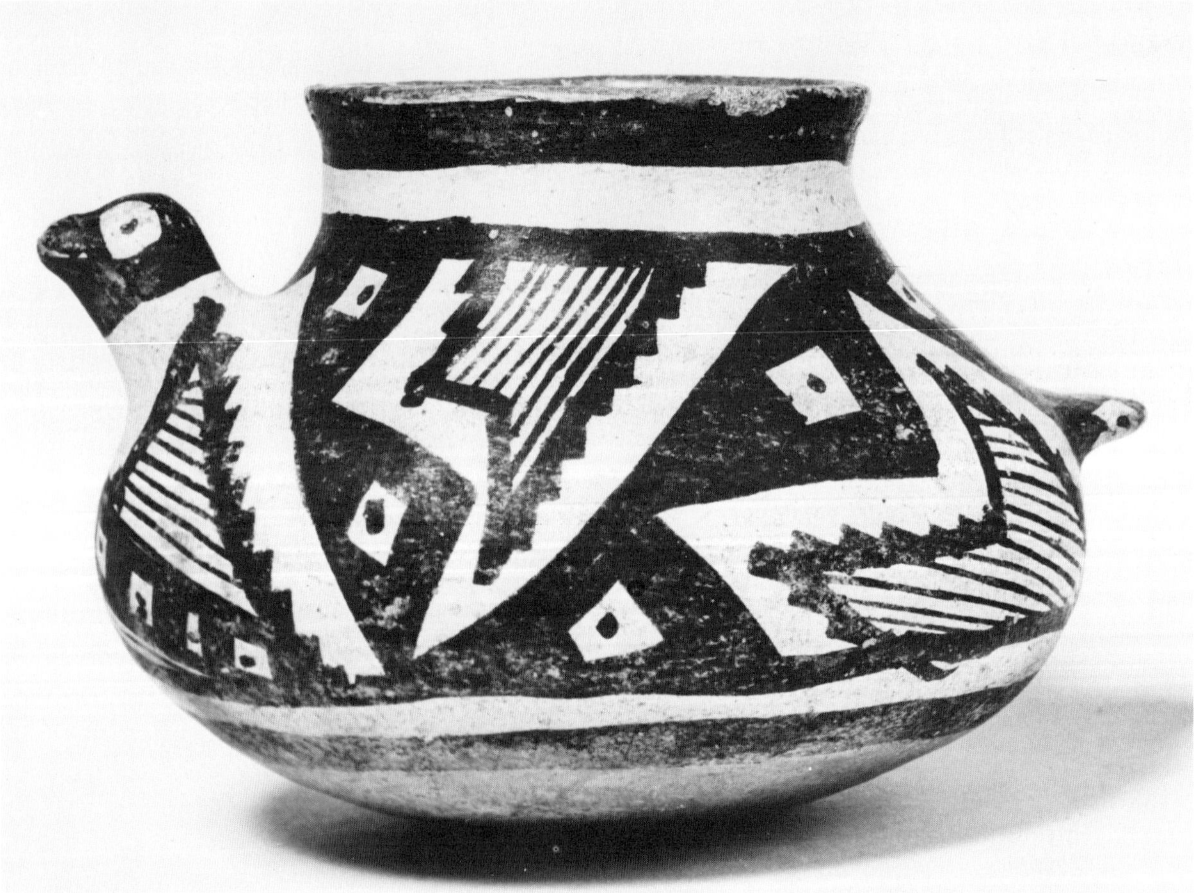

15. Bird Effigy Bowl
One of the small modeled effigy bowls often found in Southwestern ceramics. This redware vessel has been painted with a white and black design depicting the wings and tail of the bird. Collected by James E. Sullivan. SALADO. Gila County, Arizona. 1250-1500. 3¾″ x 6″. 23/1917.

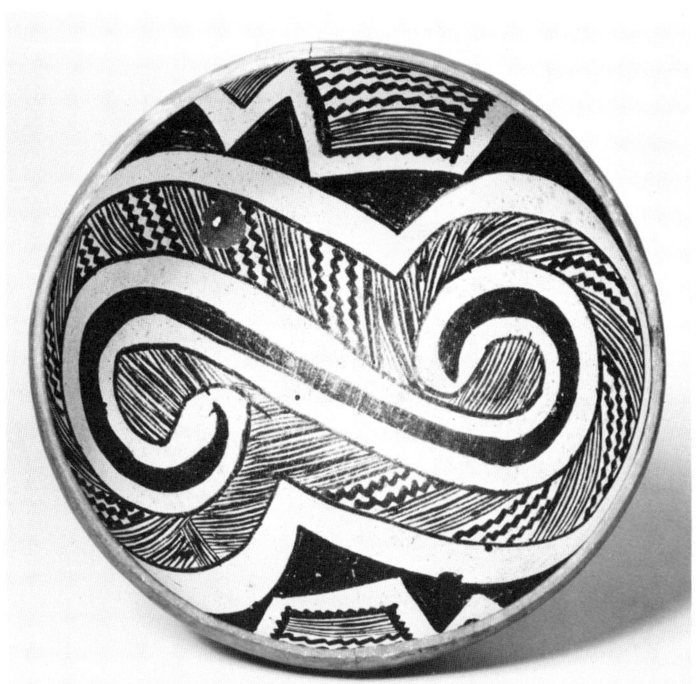

16. Redware Bowl
This large bowl has been painted in a strong swirling pattern on the interior. The hole is the result of deliberately striking the vessel prior to burial, to "kill" the spirit within it. Collected by James E. Sullivan. MOGOLLÓN. Gila County, Arizona. 900-1000. 5½" x 11". 23/1909.

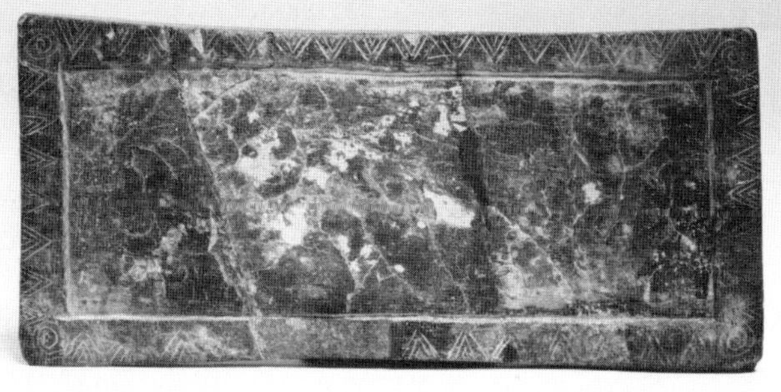

18. Paint Palette
Incised slate palettes are well-known from the southern Arizona region; this rectangular example is a classic form. HOHOKÁM. Maricopa County, Arizona. 900-1100. 3¾" x 8½". 20/3976.

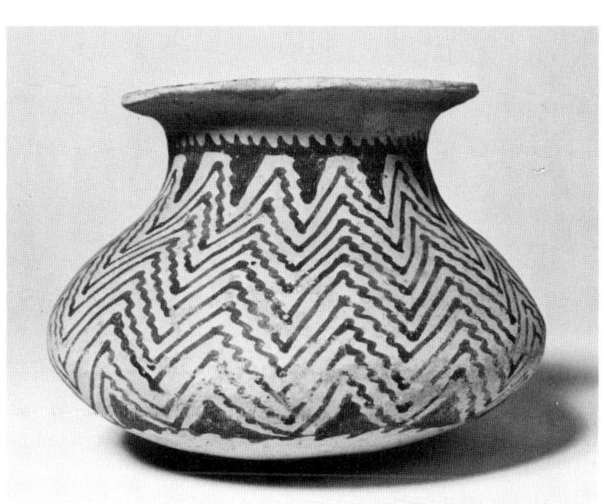

17. Wide-mouthed Bowl
Painted on the exterior in the terra cotta zigzag lines so typical of this early ware, this was produced by the ancestors of the present-day Pima and Papago people. HOHOKÁM. Toltec, Pinal County, Arizona. 900-1100. 5½" x 7¼". 21/1342.

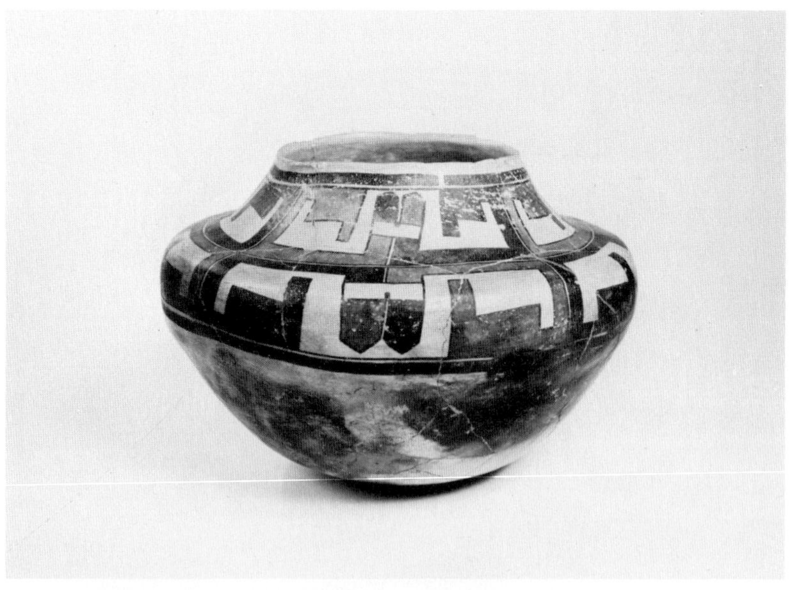

19. Polychrome Olla
This is the early form of what has come to be regarded as the traditional Pueblo *olla.* Excavated by Frederick Webb Hodge. HÁWIKUH, McKinley County, New Mexico. 1500-1680. 8¾″ x 12½″. 8/9088.

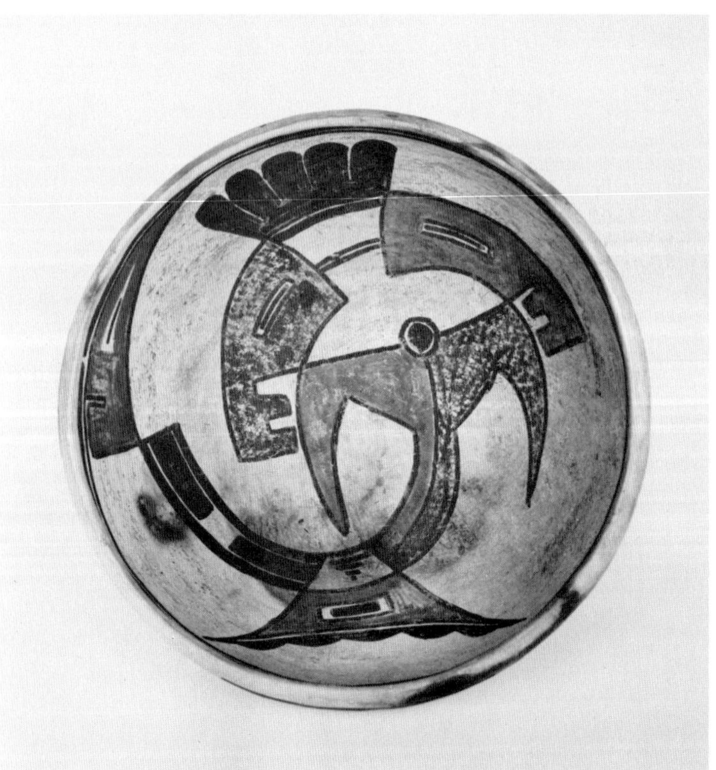

20. Shallow Painted Bowl
Another form of the classic pottery from the Pueblo area first visited by the Spanish explorers in 1540, this design seems to represent an abstracted bird form. KECHIPAUAN, McKinley County, New Mexico. 1375-1475. 5″ x 11½″. 12/3853.

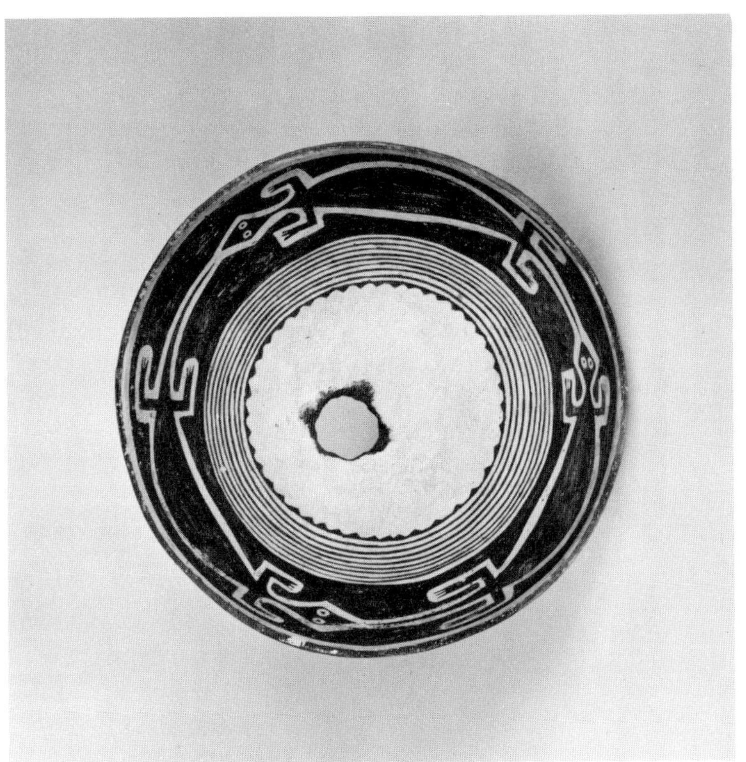

21. Black-on-White Bowl
The design on the inside of this bowl apparently depicts three lizards (or Gila monsters) around the rim. It has been "killed" prior to burial. MIMBRES, Grant County, New Mexico. 900-1100. 5 x 10¼". 24/2959.

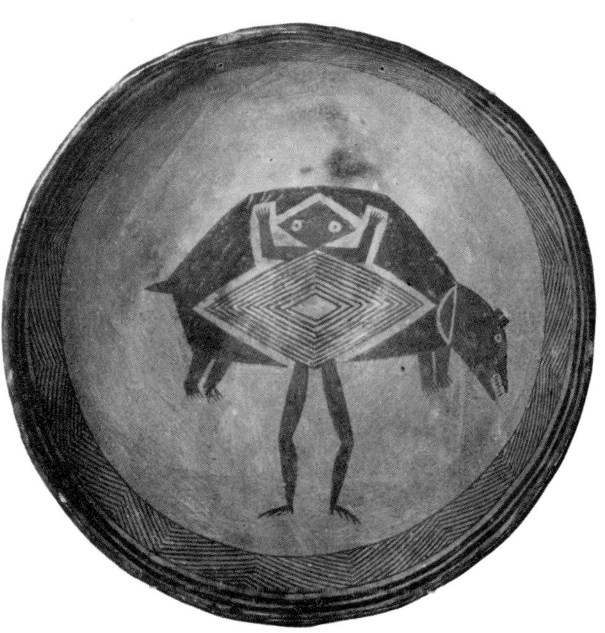

22. Red-on-White Bowl
The difference in color of this paint is due to the firing; normally this carbonizes and turns black. The design shows a combination of a bear and a stylized human or animal form. MIMBRES, Grant County, New Mexico. 900-1100. D: 10½". 24/6890.

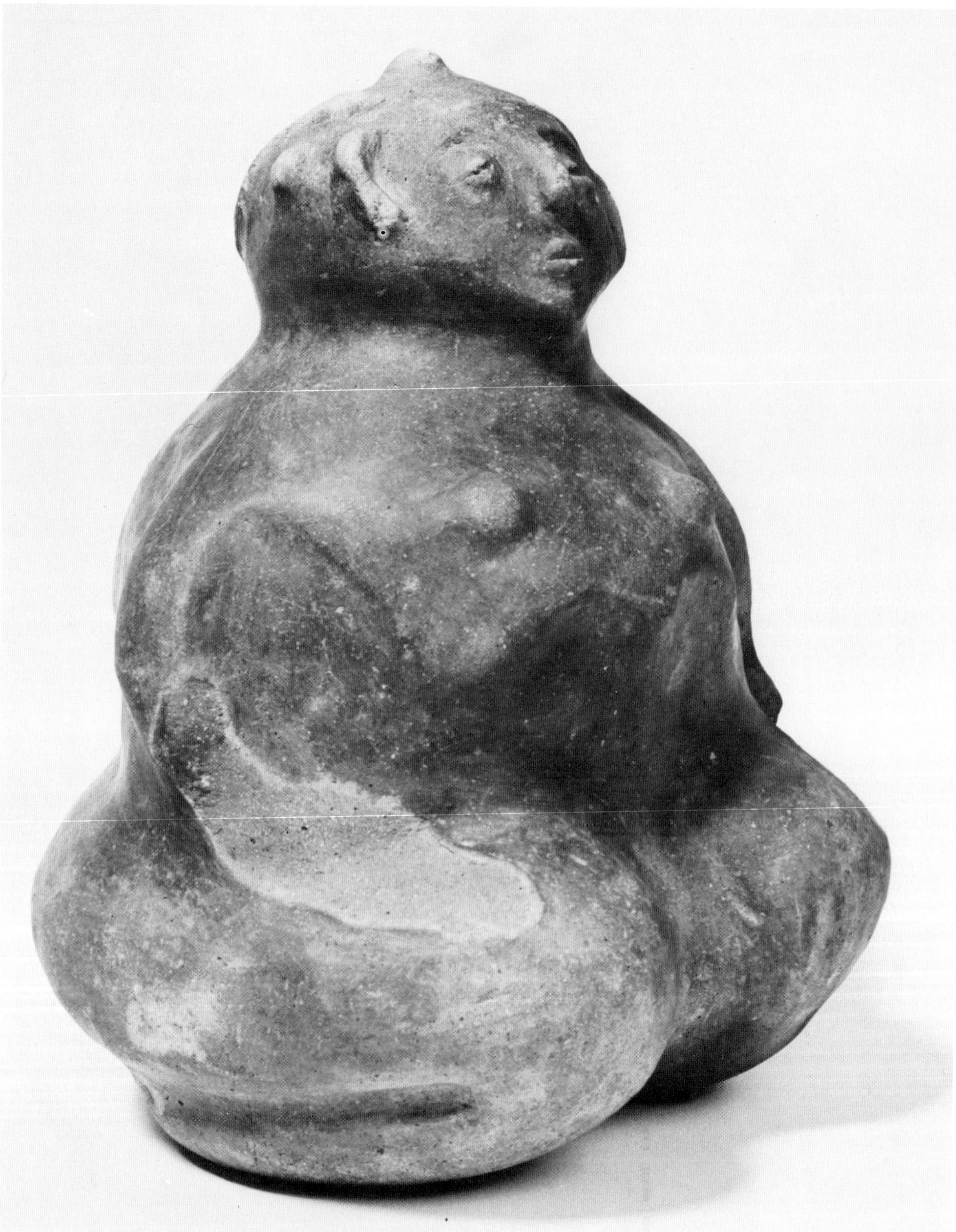

23. Human Effigy Jar

Modeled of shell-tempered grayware in the form of a humpbacked person. The legs are turned under to provide a support. Collected by C. F. Artes. TEMPLE MOUND II. Big Bone Bank, Posey County, Indiana. 1200-1600. 6¼″ x 9″. 5/5668.

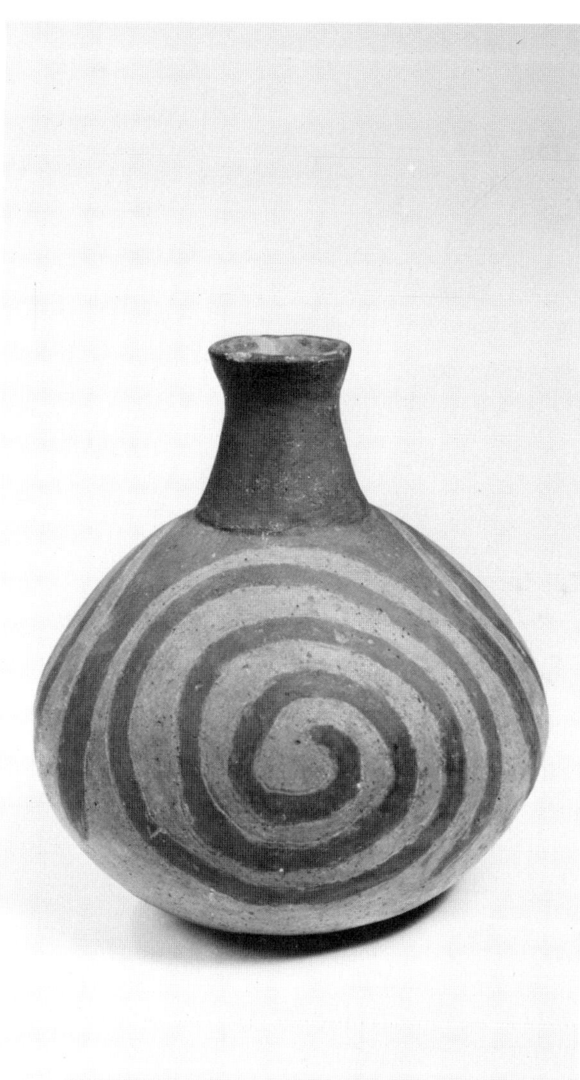

24. Globular Water Jar
The deep red design painted in swirling patterns on the coarse surface, is typical of the Mississippian tradition. Collected by L. F. Branson. Temple Mound II. Carden Bottom, Yell County, Arkansas. 1200-1600. 8″ x 9¼″. 5/6438.

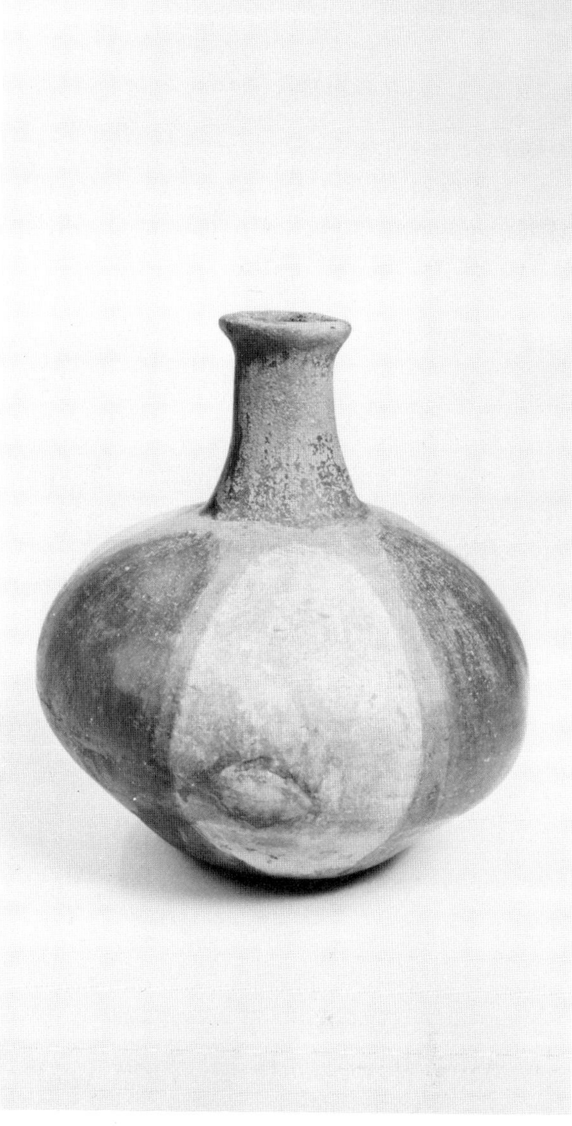

25. Globular Water Vessel
Painted in large circular panels of red and white, on a buff clay base. Collected by H. L. Cruikshank. Temple Mound II. Jackson County, Arkansas. 1200-1600. 8½″ x 9½″. 16/6020.

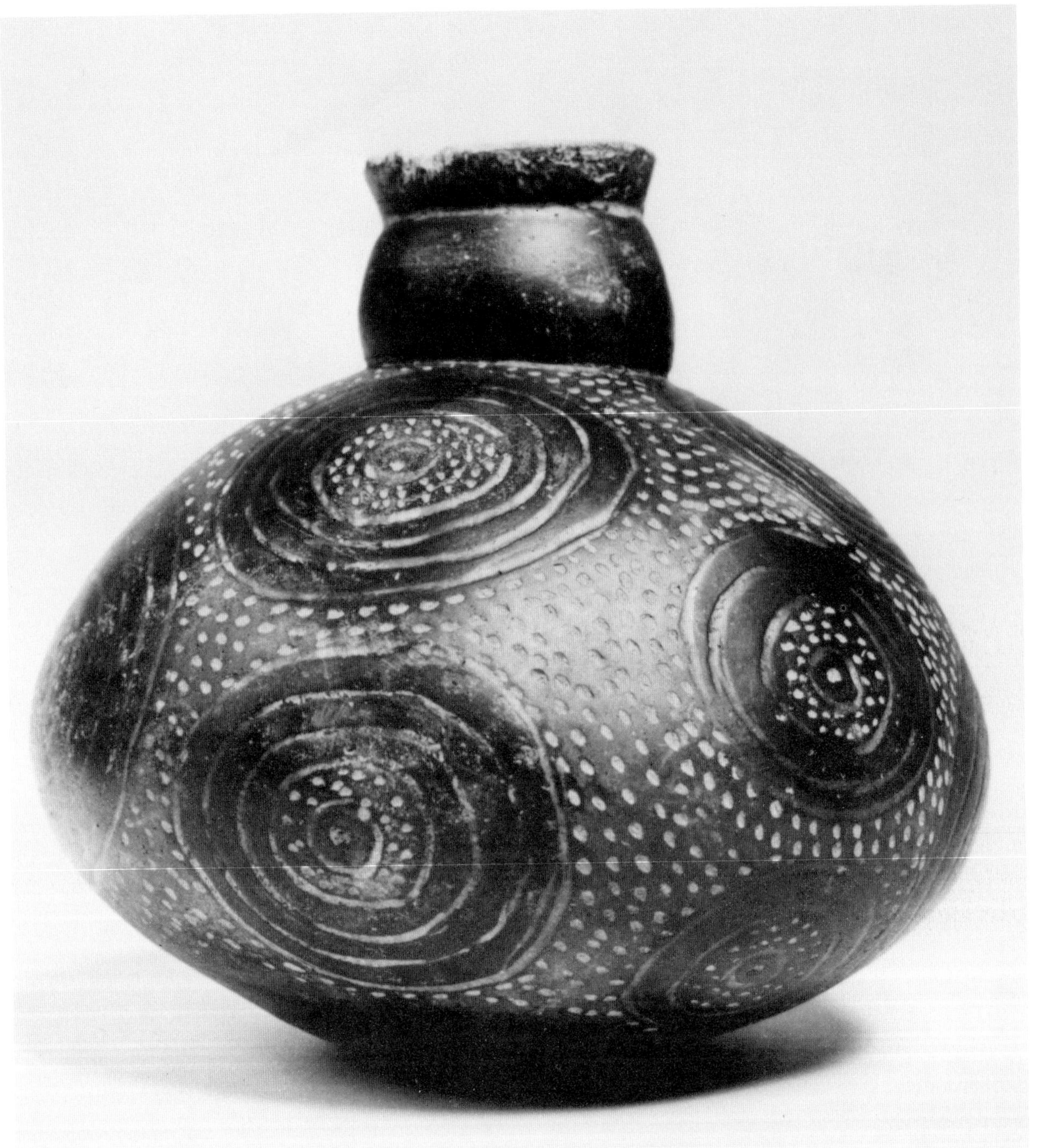

26. Blackware Water Vessel
Beautifully formed and incised with a pecked design, this is a classic example of Mississippian ceramics. Collected by Lancelot Ely. TEMPLE MOUND II. Yell County, Arkansas. 1200-1600. 6″ x 6¼″. 21/4954.

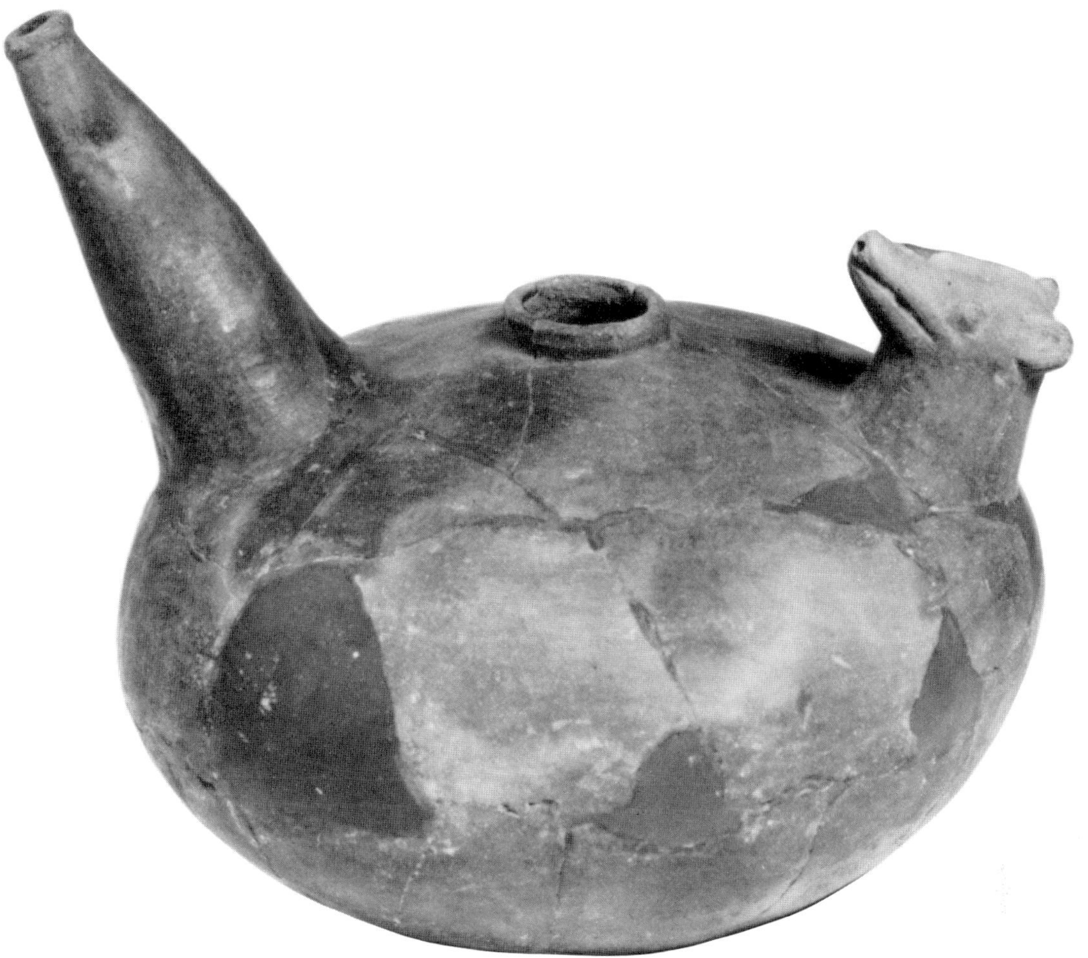

27. Zoömorphic Vessel

Representing an effigy of an opossum on its back, this has a long tapering spout for pouring. Excavated by Clarence B. Moore. TEMPLE MOUND II. Rose Place, Cross County, Arkansas. 1200-1600. 8¼″ x 9″. 17/4234.

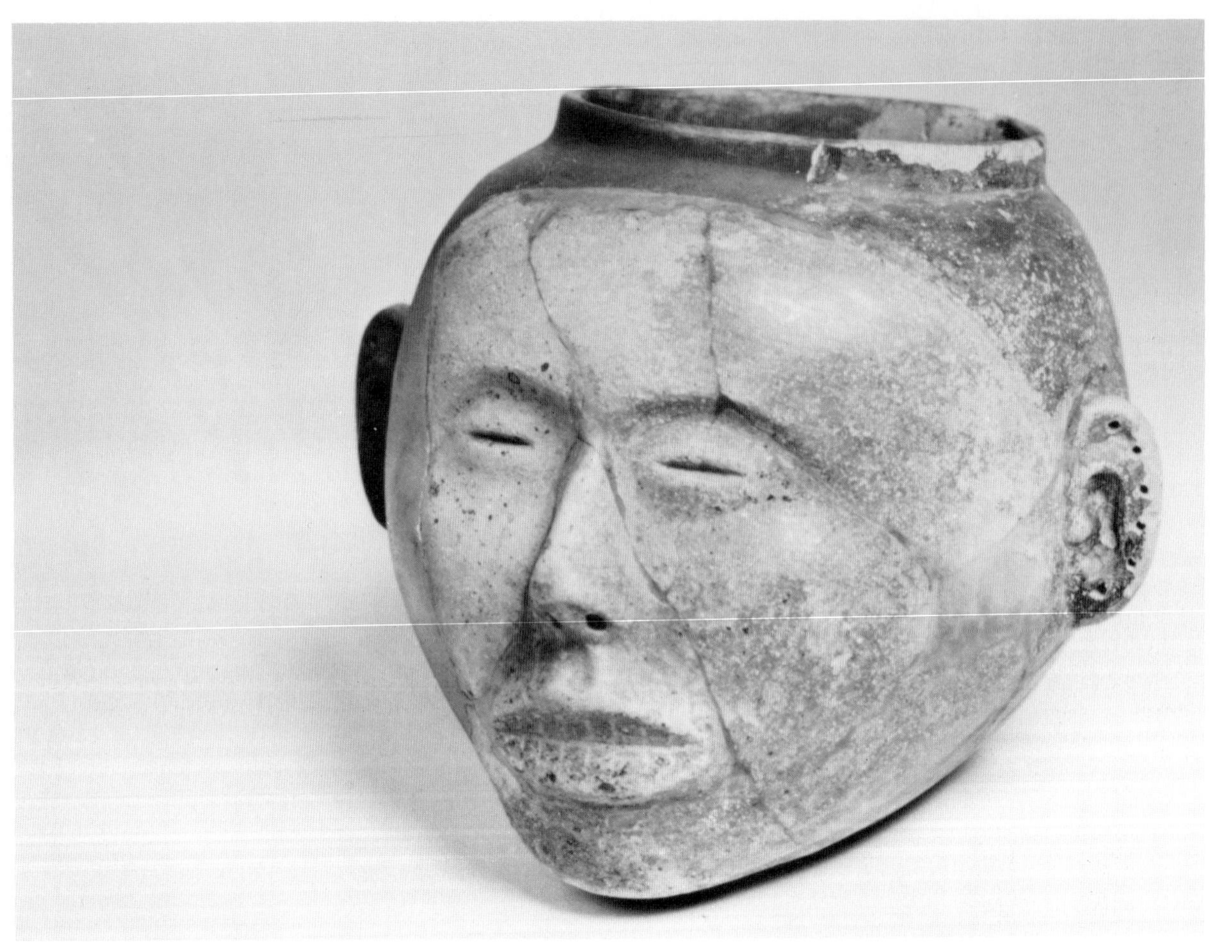

28. Trophy Head Vessel

The taking of human heads as trophies was apparently a common practice in the prehistoric Southeast. The holes in the ears may at one time have contained ornaments. Excavated by Clarence B. Moore. Temple Mound II. Rose Place, Cross County, Arkansas. 1200-1600. 6¼" x 7". 17/3277.

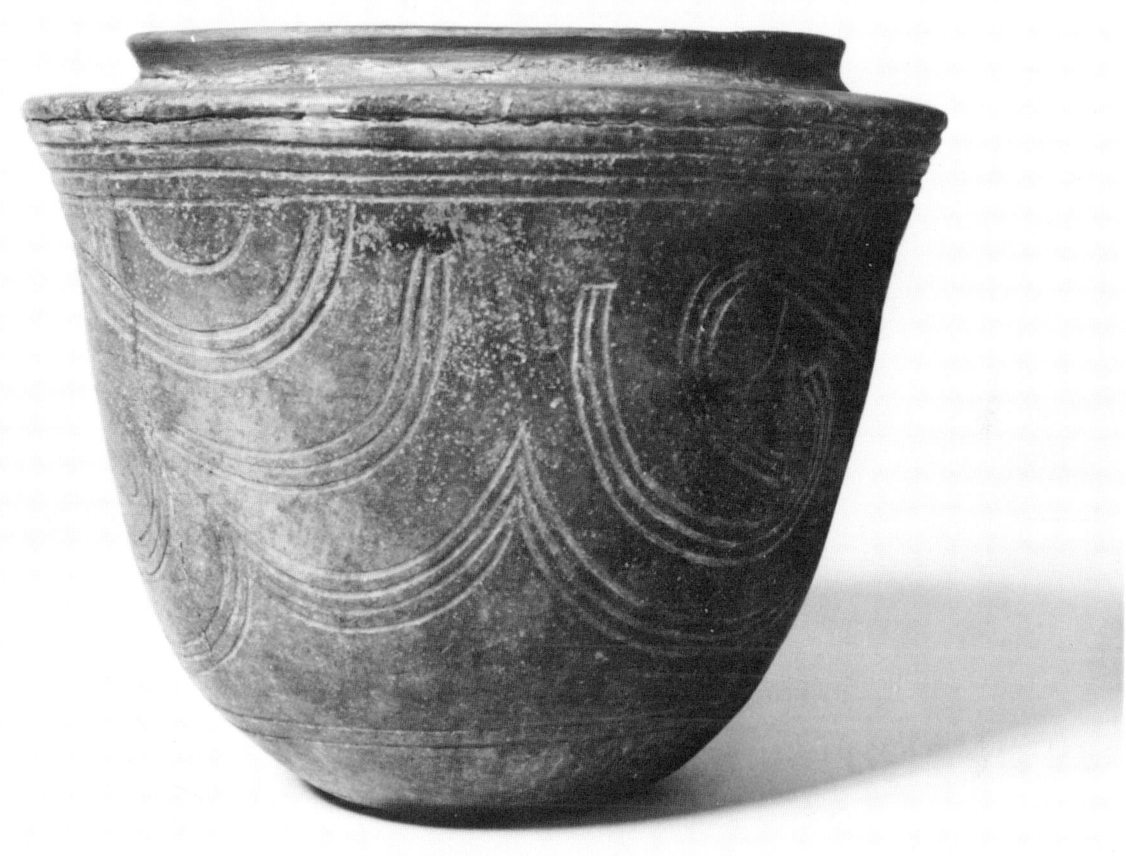

29. Wide-Mouth Bowl

This flat-topped vessel bears the familiar scroll pattern of the Southeast. It may at one time have had a cover, but this has since been lost. Excavated by Clarence B. Moore. Temple Mound II. Glendora Place, Ouachita Parish, Louisiana. 1200-1600. 7″ x 8½″. 17/3729.

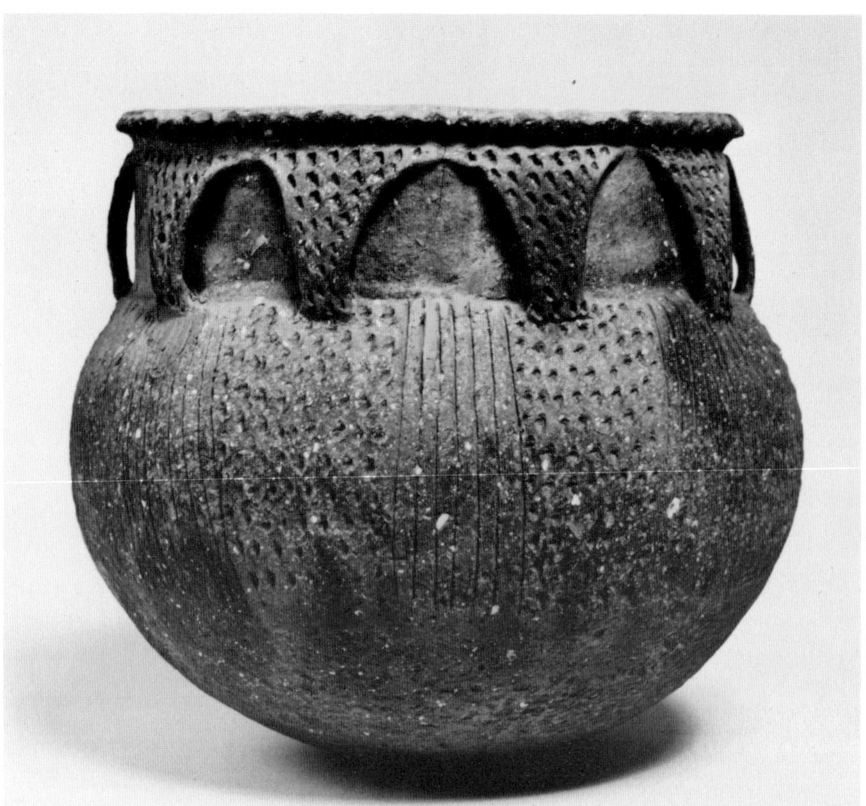

30. Arcaded Rim Bowl
This globular vessel has a serrated, raised layer of clay around the rim; the surface is incised and pecked. Excavated by Clarence B. Moore. TEMPLE MOUND II. Canebrake Mound, Madison Parish, Louisiana. 1200-1600. 8½″ x 10″. 17/3656.

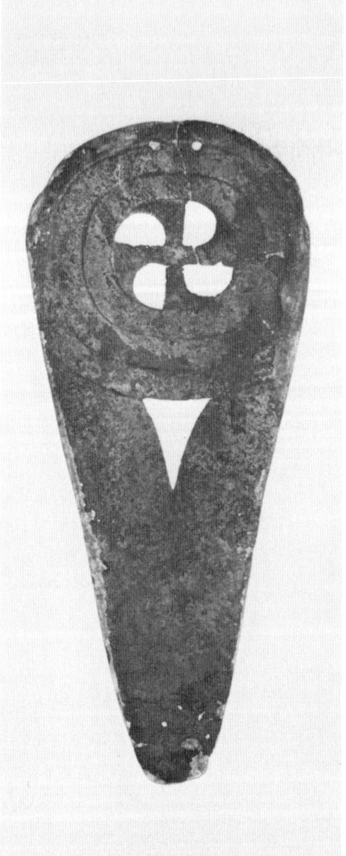

31. Copper Hair Ornament
The use of metal was not common in the Southeast, although copper is known in some areas. This triangular object may have been what is known today as a "roach spreader". Excavated by Clarence B. Moore. TEMPLE MOUND II. Moundville, Hale County, Alabama. 1200-1600. 2¾″ x 6½″. 17/225.

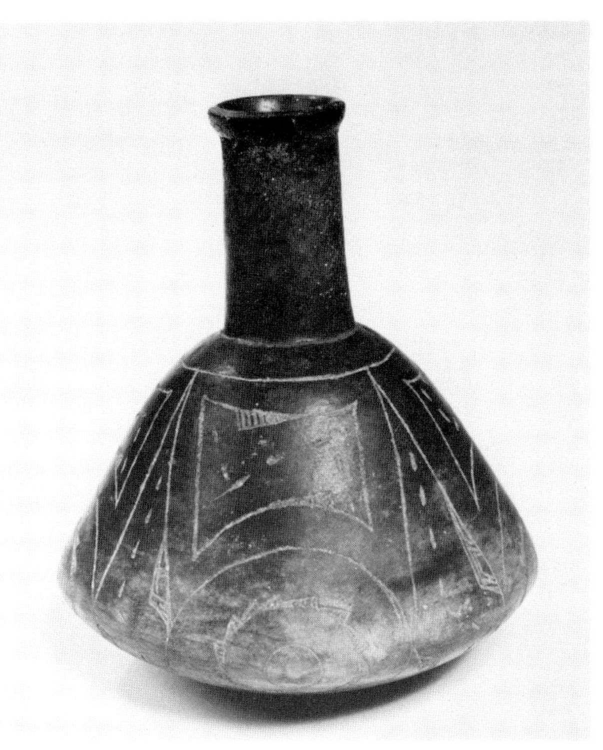

32. Blackware Water Bottle
The squared form of this Caddoan vessel is further enhanced by delicate incising, with traces of red color applied to the lines. Excavated by Clarence B. Moore. TEMPLE MOUND II. Foster Place, LaFayette County, Arkansas. 1200-1400. 5½″ x 7¼″. 17/4139.

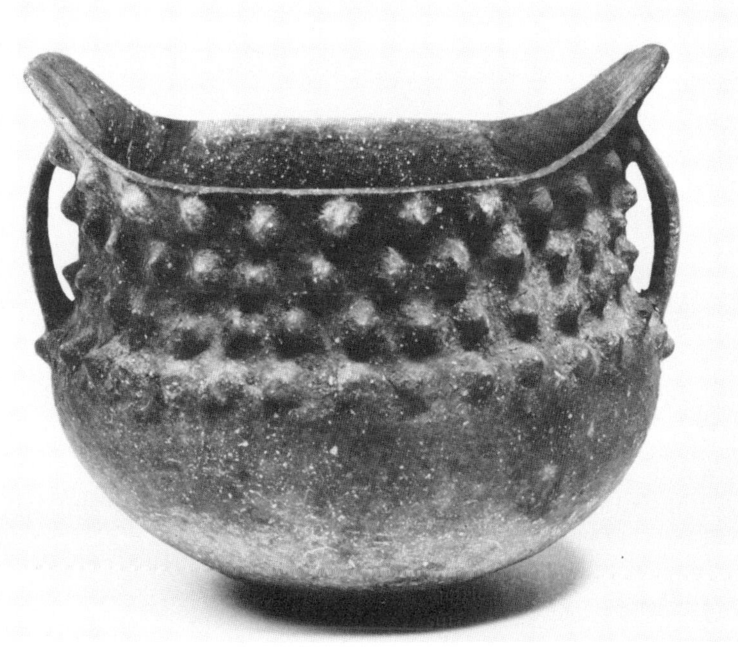

33. Nodule Grayware Bowl
Decorated with rows of raised clay nodules, and two vertical loop handles, the mouth of this bowl is formed in a graceful smoothly-worked oval. Excavated by Clarence B. Moore. TEMPLE MOUND II. Mason Island, Limestone County, Arkansas. 1200-1600. 6½″ x 8″. 17/4416.

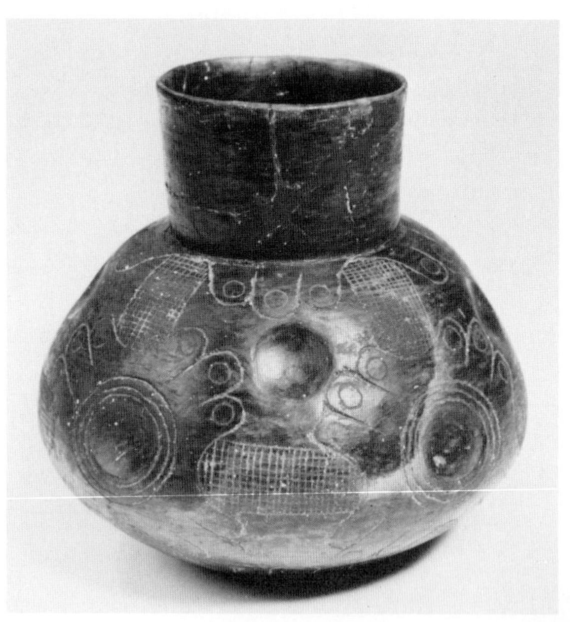

34. Blackware Bowl

The polished surface of this bowl is further decorated by finely-incised lines, and rounded depressions. Excavated by Clarence B. Moore. TEMPLE MOUND II. Moundville, Hale County, Alabama. 1200-1600. 6″ x 6¼″. 17/3375.

35. Monolithic Axe

The sculptural beauty of these spectacular implements is ample evidence of the skill of the early craftsman. This form is found throughout the Southeast. Moundville, Hale County, Alabama. TEMPLE MOUND II. 1200-1600. 7″ x 13¾″. 24/2569.

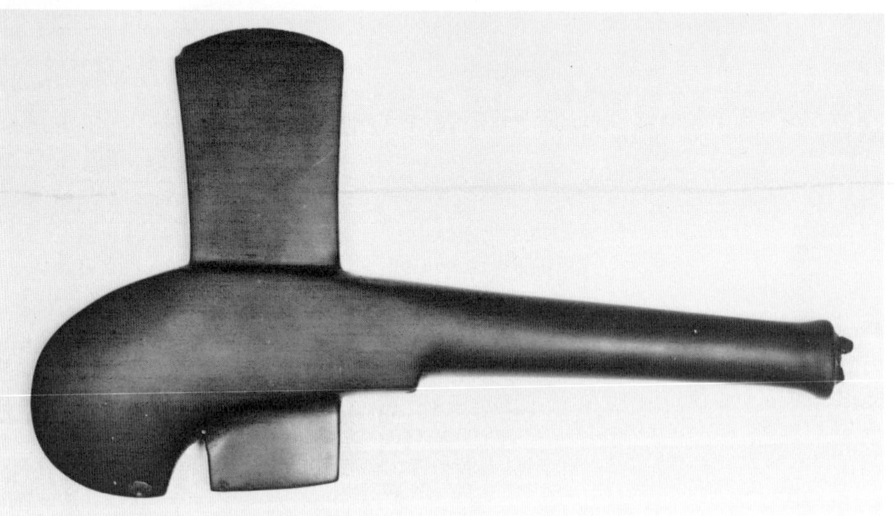

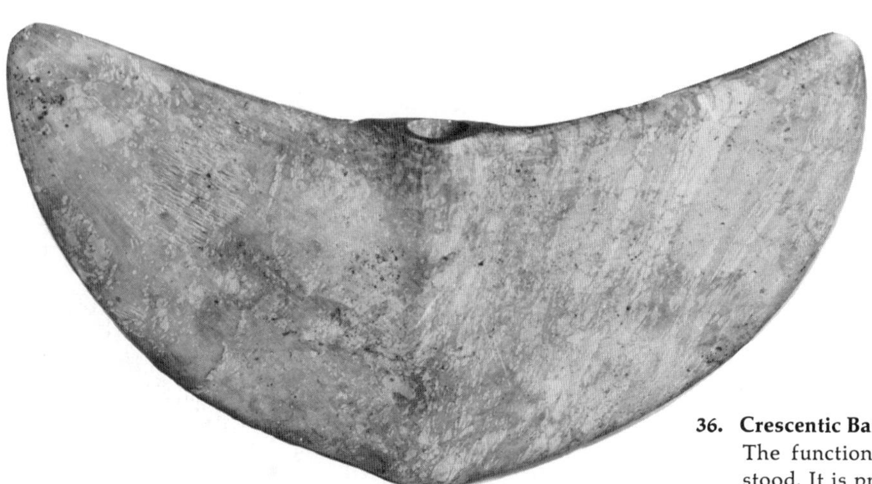

36. Crescentic Bannerstone

The function of these objects is not clearly understood. It is probable that they were insignia of social or political significance; they may have been *atlatl* weights. Presented by James E. Byrd. TEMPLE MOUND II. Gates County, North Carolina. 1200-1600. 3½″ x 6¼″. 21/3424.

37. Shell Gorget

Incised in patterns frequently seen in the Southeast, these gorgets are usually found deposited on the breasts of deceased persons. The designs may indicate membership in a prehistoric society. Collected by Edgar Burke; presented by Mrs. R. H. Schwab and Mrs. F. S. Lee. Temple Mound II. Broadford, Smyth County, Virginia. 1200-1600. 4¾″ x 5¼″. 22/250.

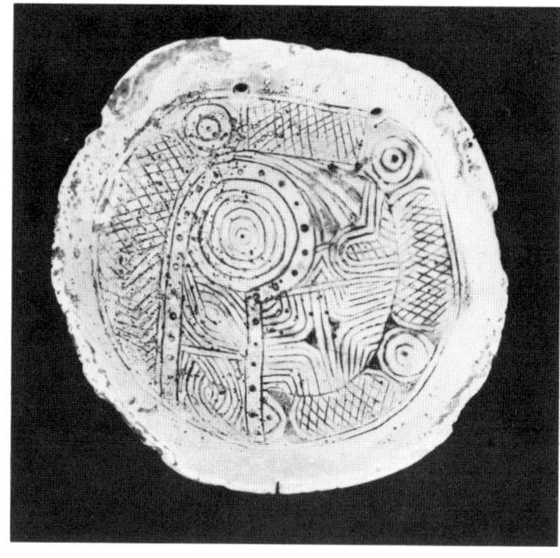

38. Black Slate Birdstone

Several theories have been advanced concerning the probable use of these objects; it is most likely that they were balances and counterweights for the *atlatl* common during this period. Collected by M. F. Savage. Late Archaic. Hardin County, Ohio. 1000-500 B.C. 2″ x 4″. 6825.

39. Open-work Vessel

(See page 10)

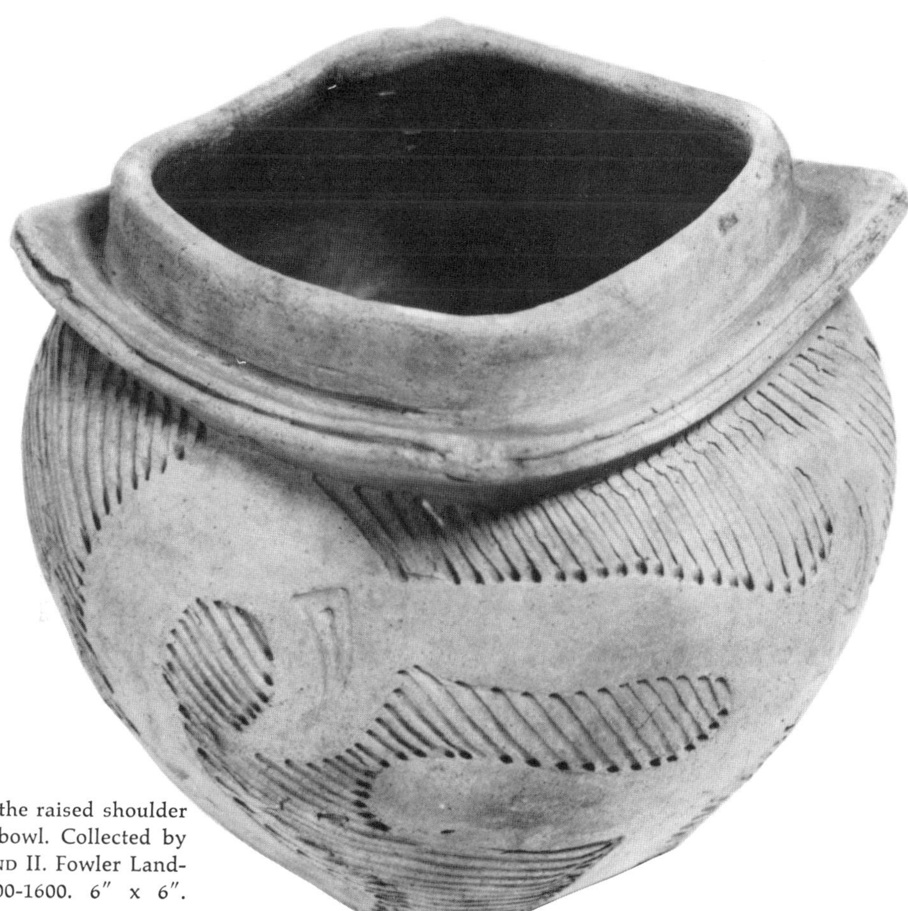

40. Buffware Vessel

The linear pattern incised below the raised shoulder gives a colorful texture to this bowl. Collected by Clarence B. Moore. Temple Mound II. Fowler Landing, Levy County, Florida. 1200-1600. 6″ x 6″. 17/1459.

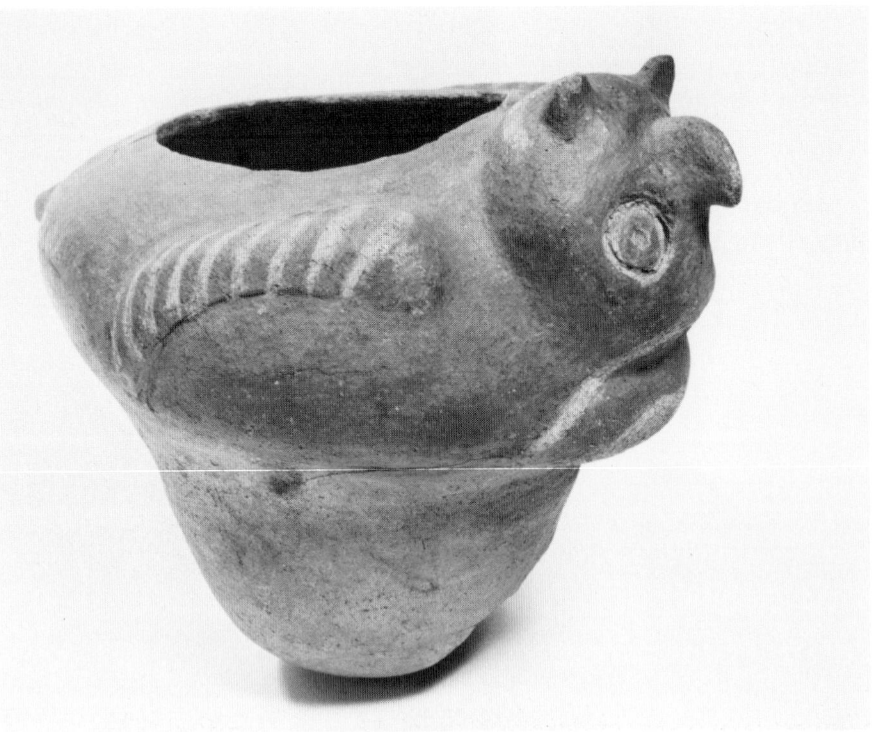

41. Owl Effigy Vessel
The redware vessel retains traces of the original white paint once rubbed into the incising; it was "killed" prior to burial. Weeden Island Culture. Apalachee Bay, Wakulla County, Florida. 500-1000. 8" x 10". 17/4915.

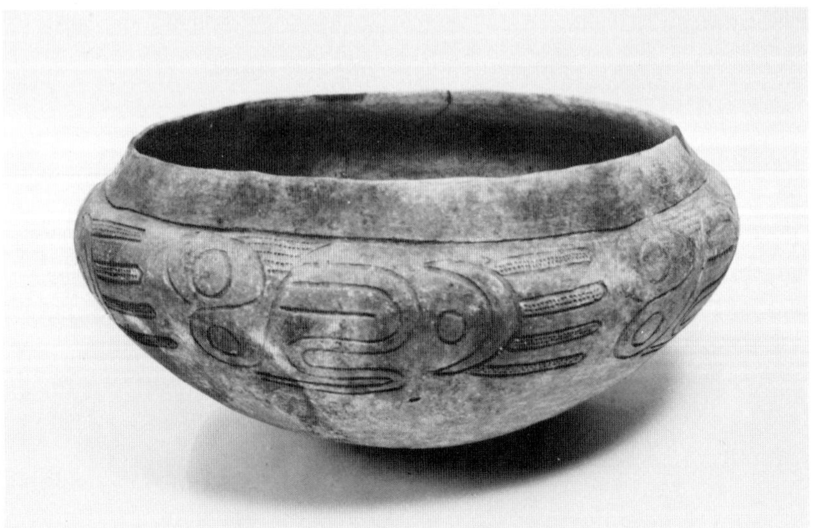

42. Large Grayware Bowl
Decorated by incised and punctate lines, perhaps representing an abstraction of a bird wing. Excavated by Clarence B. Moore. Burial Mound Culture. Santa Rosa County, Florida. 1-500 A.D. 7½" x 15½". 17/4955.

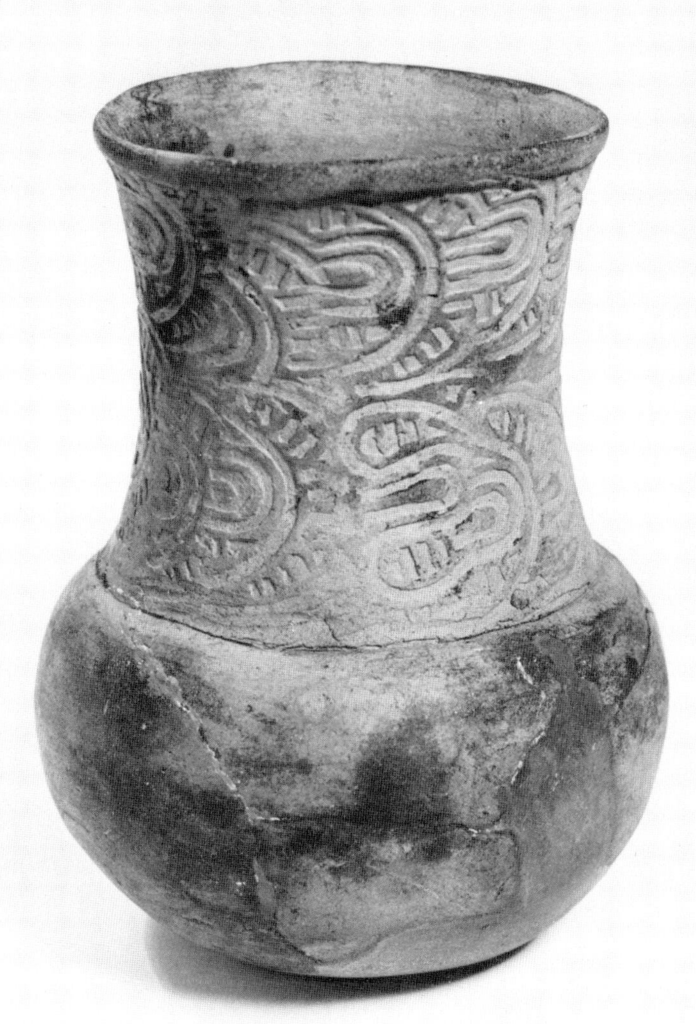

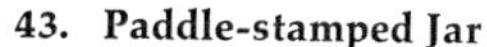

43. Paddle-stamped Jar
Decorated around the neck by means of applying wooden paddles into which designs have been carved, this is a common technique in Southeastern ceramics. Excavated by Clarence B. Moore. Temple Mound II. Horseshoe Point, Lafayette County, Florida. 1200-1600. 5½" x 6¾". 18/364.

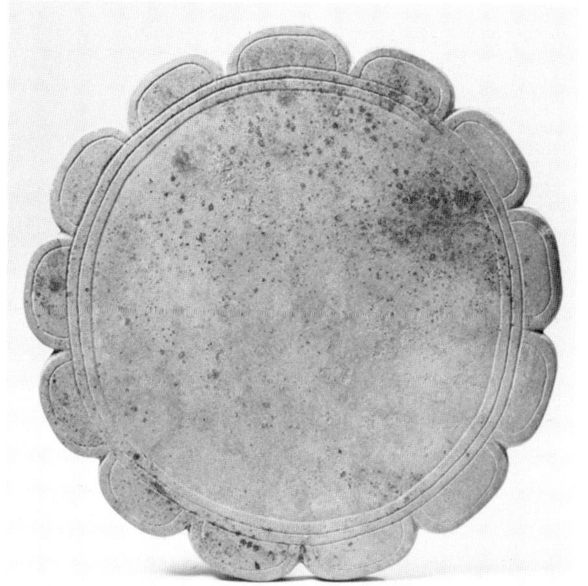

44. Circular Stone Palette
Believed to have been used for grinding pigments, these large palettes occur in circular and rectangular forms in the Southeast. Some are known with elaborately incised designs. Excavated by Clarence B. Moore. Temple Mound II. Moundville, Hale County, Alabama. 1200-1600. D: 10¼". 17/1474.

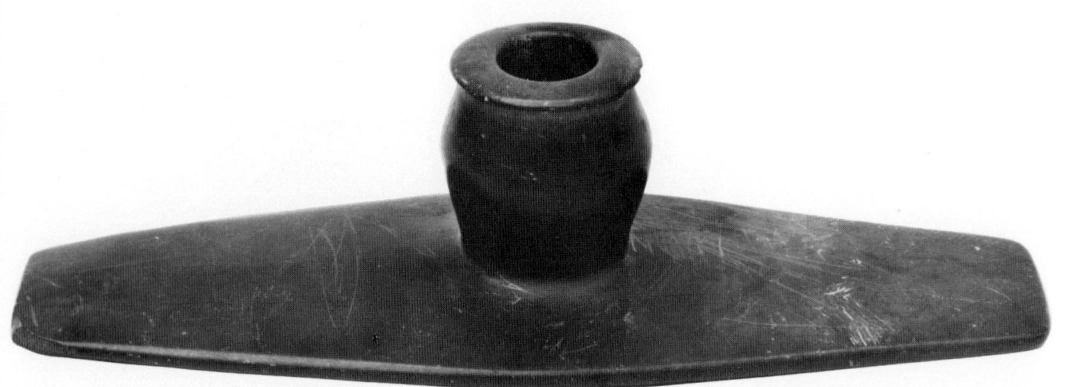

45. Monitor Pipe
Characteristic of a wide-ranging type of stone pipes, this redstone example is unusually large for the style. Collected by Albert L. Addis. HOPEWELL. Allen County, Indiana. 250 B.C.-250 A.D. 2½″ x 2¼″ x 8½″. 4/7220.

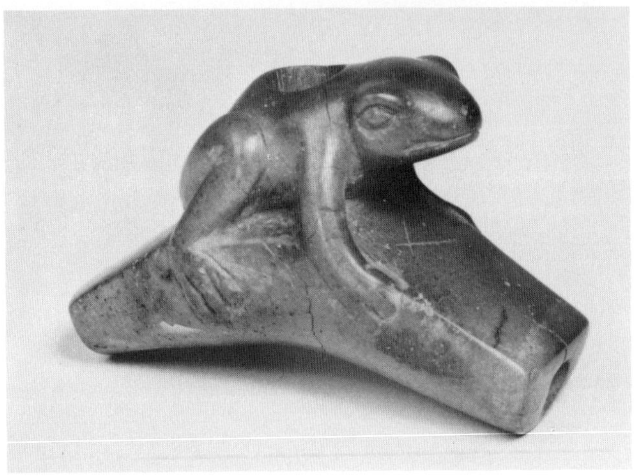

46. Monitor Effigy Pipe
Carved in the form of a frog, this is an excellent example of the Hopewellian style of animal effigy pipes. This is from the classic site in Ohio whence the name of the culture is derived. HOPEWELL. Ross County, Ohio. 250 B.C.-250 A.D. 2″ x 3″. 24/6583.

47. Steatite Effigy Pipe
A great variety of heavy steatite pipes are found throughout the Southeast, carved in the forms of birds of the area. This depicts the crested wood duck, and was intended for use with a reed, inserted in the end of the pipe; tobacco was put into the bowl back of the bird's head. Collected by S. C. Heighway. TEMPLE MOUND II. Peachtree, Cherokee County, North Carolina. 1200-1600. L: 8″. 4/4251.

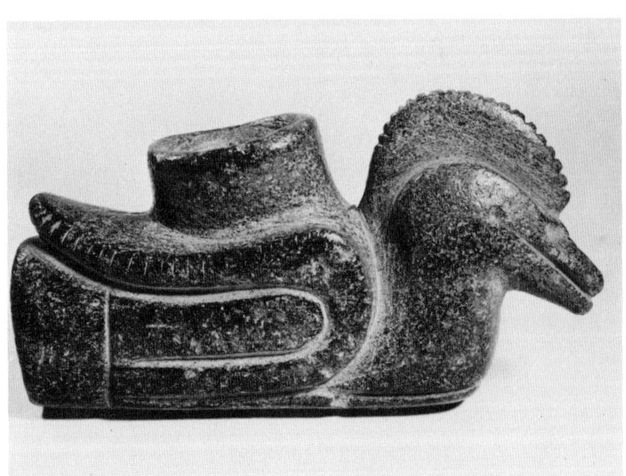

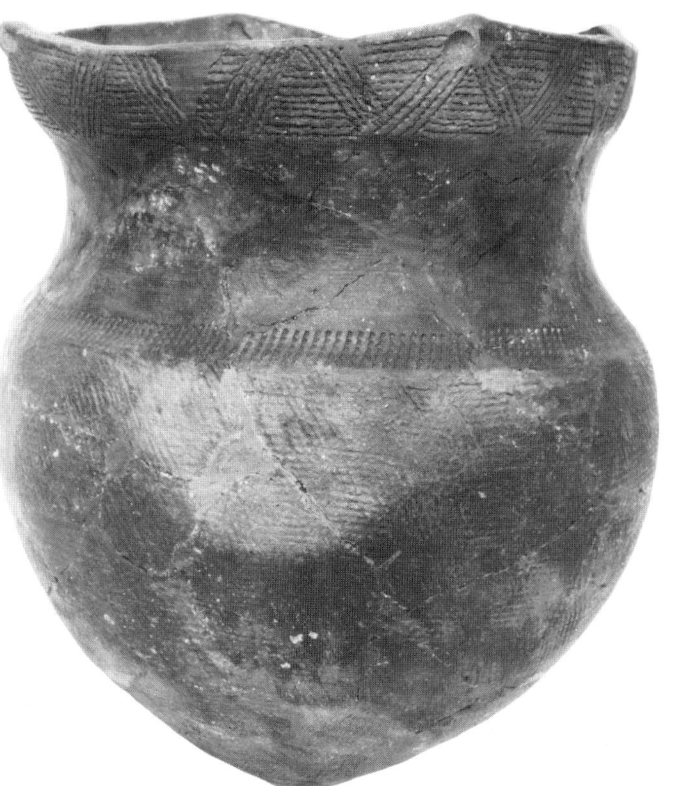

48. Castellated Bowl

The standard shape of the Iroquoian potters was an ovoid bowl, somewhat pointed at the base, and topped by a four-pointed incised, scooped rim in squared-off form. Presented by Harold J. Baker. IROQUOIAN. Fishers Island, New York. 1400-1700. 10¼" x 12½". 18/7403.

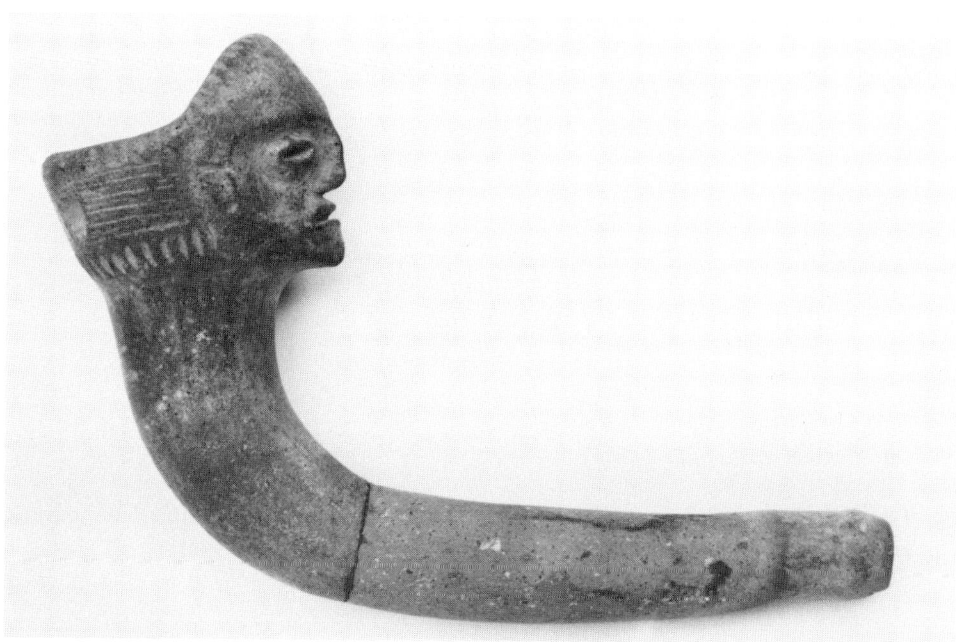

49. Modeled Clay Pipe

The common elbow pipe of the Eastern Woodlands people took on many forms. This, with a head modeled towards the smoker, is the most usual style. Collected by William H. Lewis; presented by Palma Hope Lewis. IROQUOIAN. Seneca Lake, Seneca County, New York. 1400-1700. 2¼" x 5¼". 20/6512.

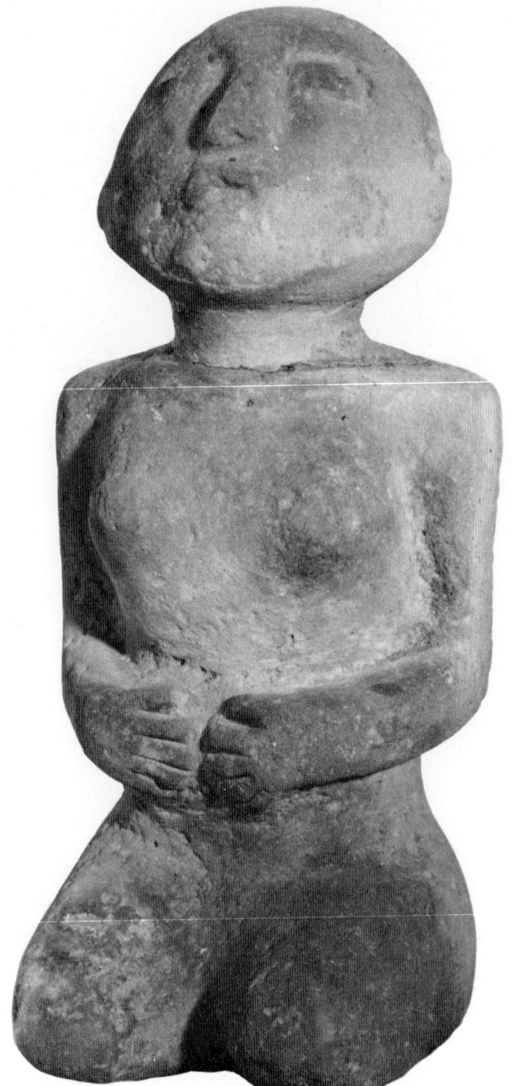

50. Sculptured Stone Effigy
These carefully worked figures were still in use when the Spaniards entered in the Southeast in 1540. We do not know their purpose; they may represent ancestors, important personages, or perhaps were worshiped as idols. Their distribution ranges from the Mississippi to Georgia. Presented by The Viking Fund, Inc. TEMPLE MOUND II. Dayton, Rhea County, Tennessee. 1200-1600. H: 13". 21/965.

51. Polychrome Effigy Bowl

(See color insert facing page 40)

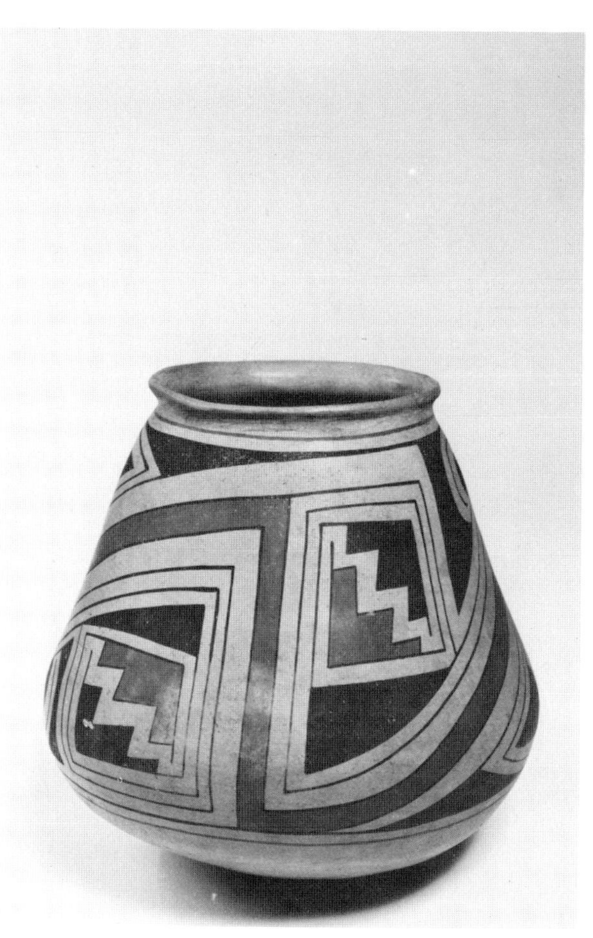

52. Polychrome Bowl

The classic form of ceramics from this site, this example shows something of the motifs which suggest a relationship with the more northerly Pueblo peoples. Collected by Edward Ledwidge. CASAS GRANDES. Coahuila, Mexico. 1200-1500. 9½" x 9½". 6/592.

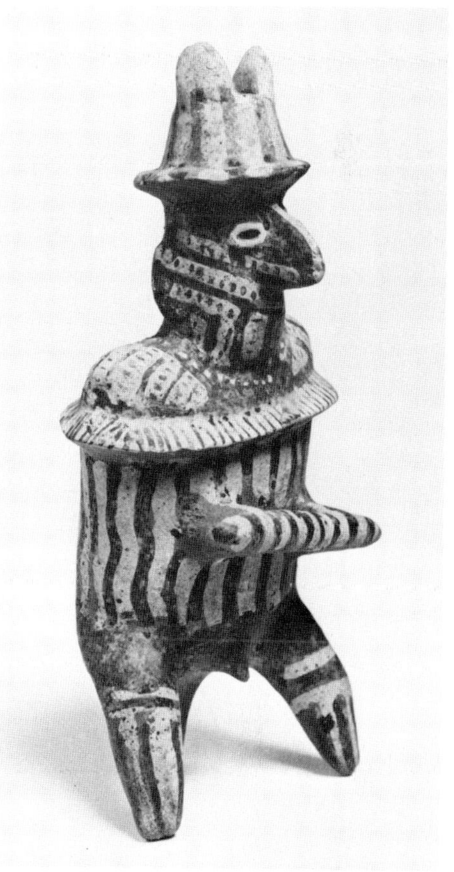

53. Painted Male Effigy

These effigies have aroused considerable controversy; whether they are ball players, or more likely warriors, is uncertain. The designs suggest body tattooing, while the conical hat with "horns" has been given several interpretations. NAYARIT style. Found in Michoacán, Mexico. 100-250. 4½" x 9". 22/1218.

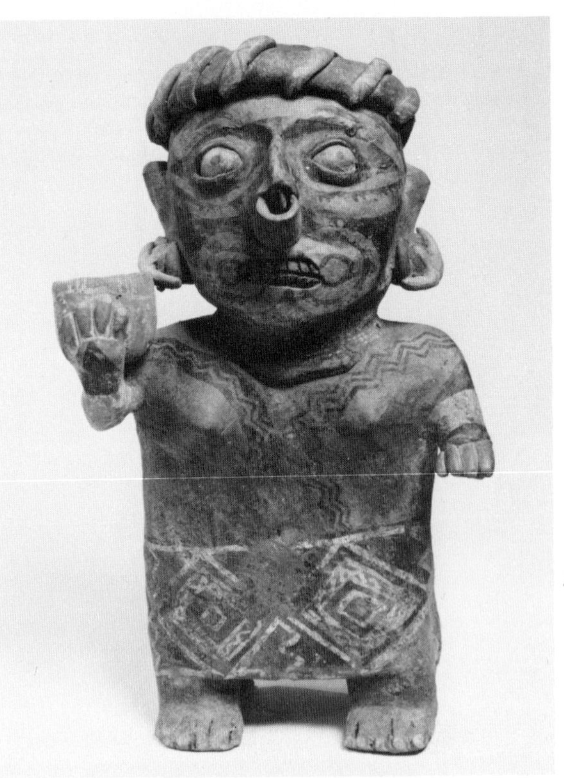

54. Polychrome Female Figurine

This brightly painted modeled clay figurine of a woman holding a bowl on her shoulder is typical of the funerary ware of this region. Her hair is wrapped in a cloth binding similar to the coiffure still favored by Tarascan women of the West Coast. NAYARIT style. Found in Michoacán, Mexico. 100-250. 8" x 14". 21/6887.

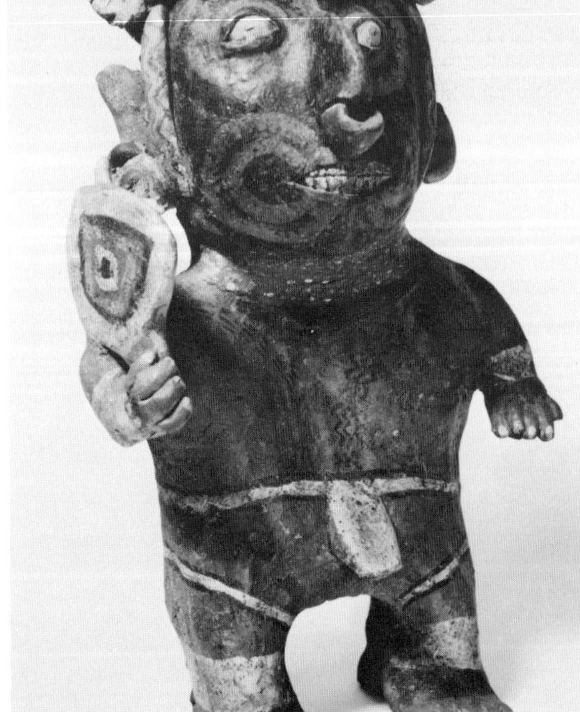

55. Polychrome Male Figurine

The companion to #54, this depicts a male holding a fan. He is wearing the ovoid penis cap, nose rings, and hairdress typical of the region. The facial painting may represent tattooing. NAYARIT style. Found in Michoacán, Mexico, with #54. 8½" x 14". 21/6886.

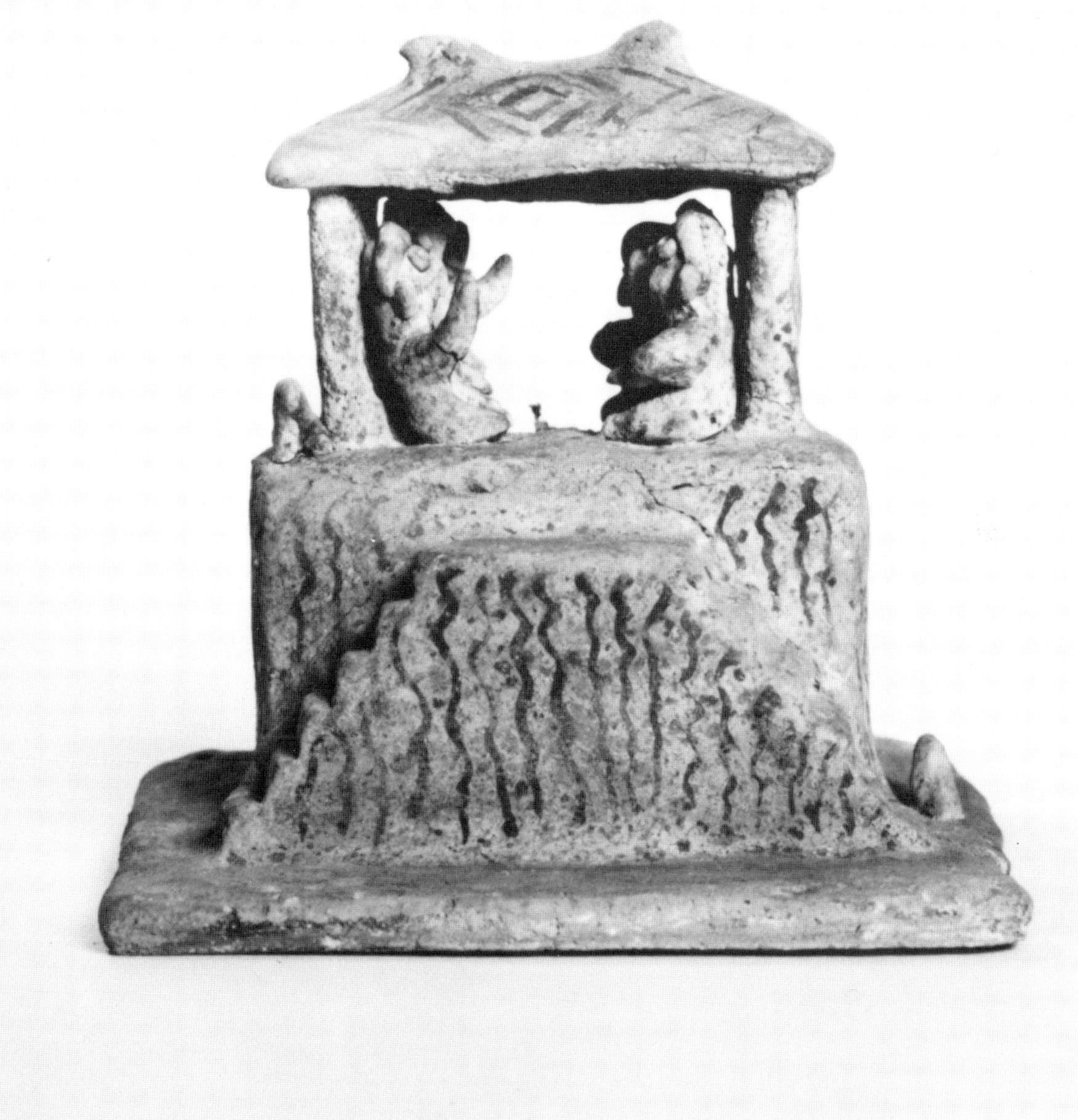

56. Ceramic House Model

These miniature dwelling models are an interesting feature of the prehistoric art of Western Mexico. This example has several occupants, together with architectural details of the structure which reflects a similar house-type used today. Presented by John S. Williams. NAYARIT, Mexico. 100-250. 5½" x 6" x 6". 22/7129.

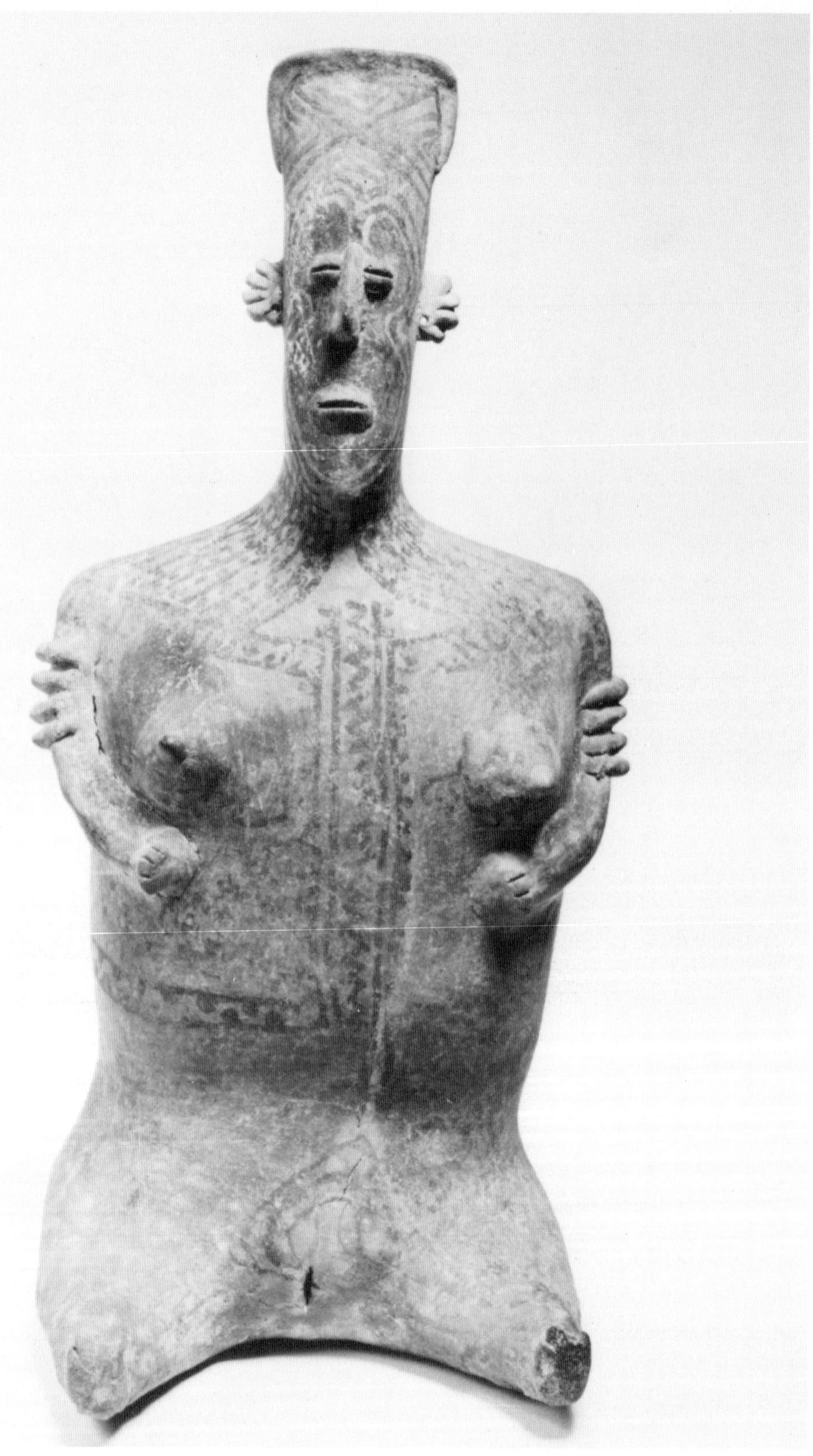

57. Seated Female Effigy
A superbly proportioned effigy of a woman with body tattooing and ornaments is a fine example of the narrow-headed form seen occasionally in work from the Western Mexican area. JALISCO, Mexico. 100-250. 9″ x 19½″. 22/7167.

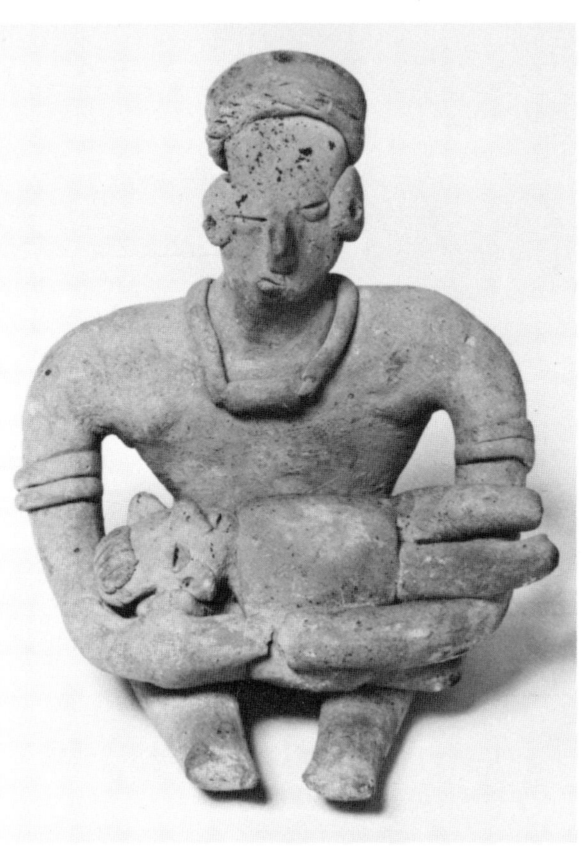

58. Clay Mother and Child
Miniature figurines are found in tremendous profusion in prehistoric Mexican archeology. This carefully modeled effigy of a woman with her baby is an example of the *genre*. We do not know if these were intended as burial offerings, or simply as depictions of everyday life. COLIMA, Mexico. 100-250. 3½″ x 4″. 23/909.

59. Modeled Clay Dog
This is typical of a large variety of beautifully modeled clay dogs which are representations of the actual animals, called *techichi,* which were raised for food in prehistoric Mexico. COLIMA, Mexico. 100-250. 6¾″ x 7″. 7/1382.

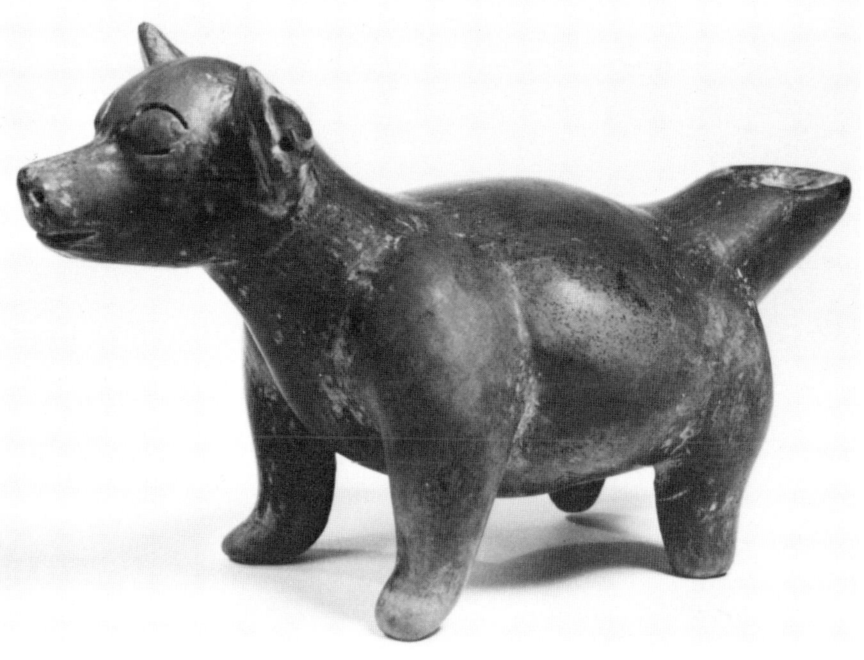

60. Sculptured Clay Drummer

Some of the finest clay sculpture in Middle America is to be found in Western Mexico. This smoothly modeled drummer is a superb example. The redware is burnished with a small stone to reflect a brilliant polish. Colima, Mexico. 100-250. 6″ x 10″. 23/1827.

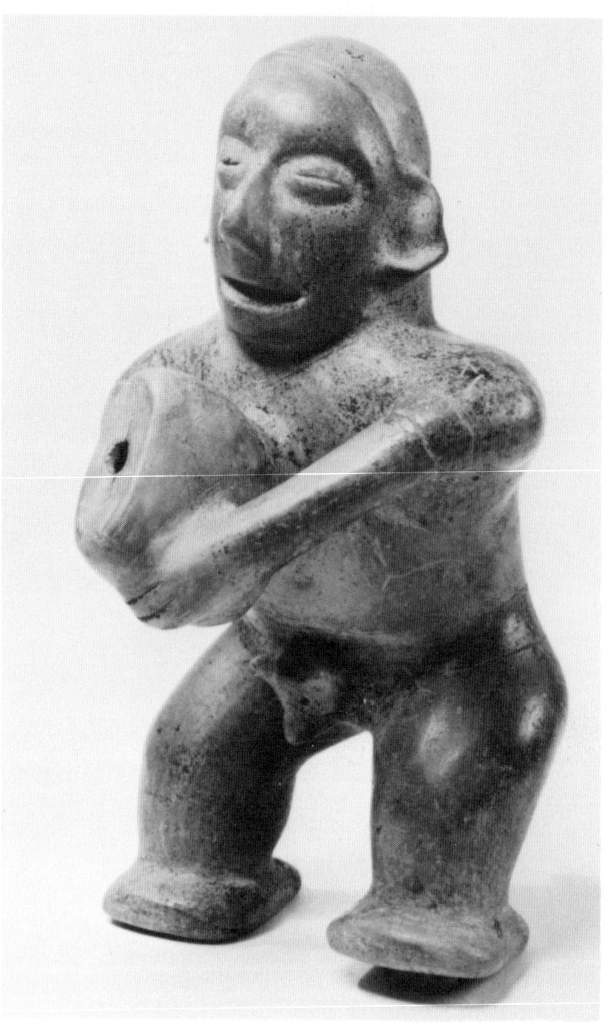

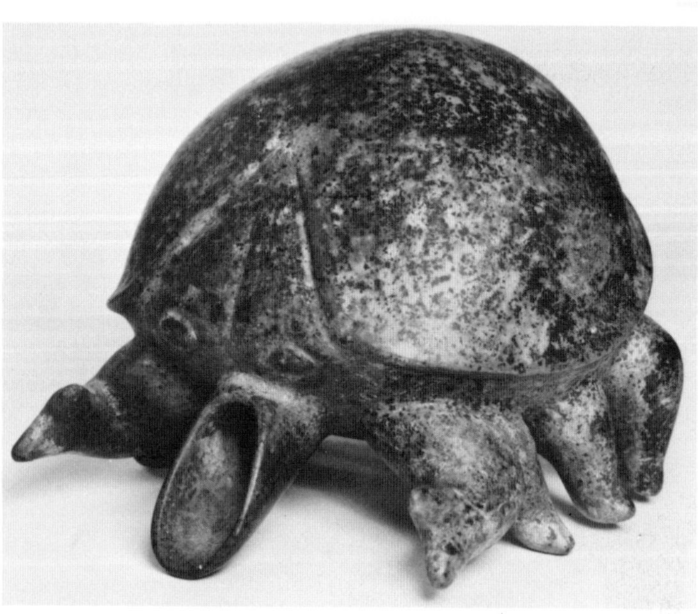

61. Redware Crab Effigy

A veritable zoo can be found among the modeled ceramic effigies from prehistoric America. This well-crafted crab has all of the compact proportions of the original animal. Presented by Mr. Cedric H. Marks. Colima, Mexico. 6½″ x 7¾″. 100-250. 24/4001.

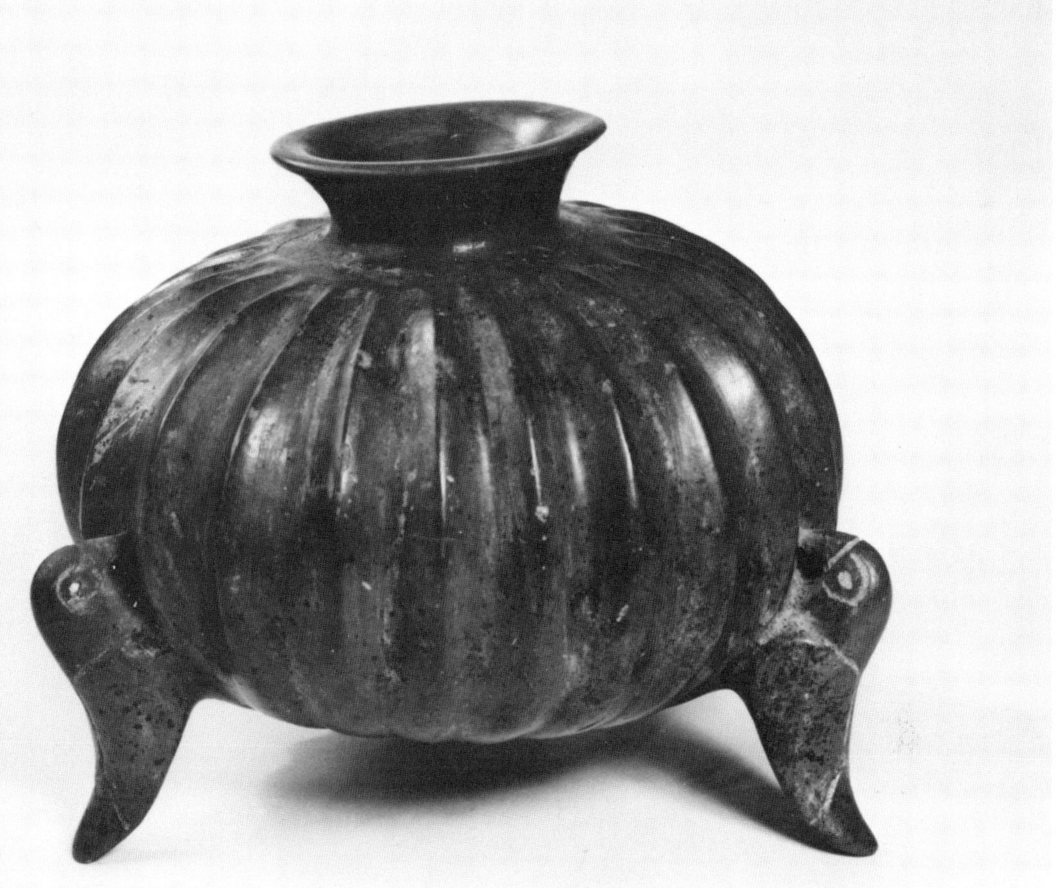

62. Redware Tripodal Bowl

This beautifully proportioned bowl with fluted sides is supported by three parrots. The rich sheen and rotund form of this example makes it a *tour de force* in prehistoric art. COLIMA, Mexico. 100 B.C.-250 A.D. 8½″ x 10″. 24/7346.

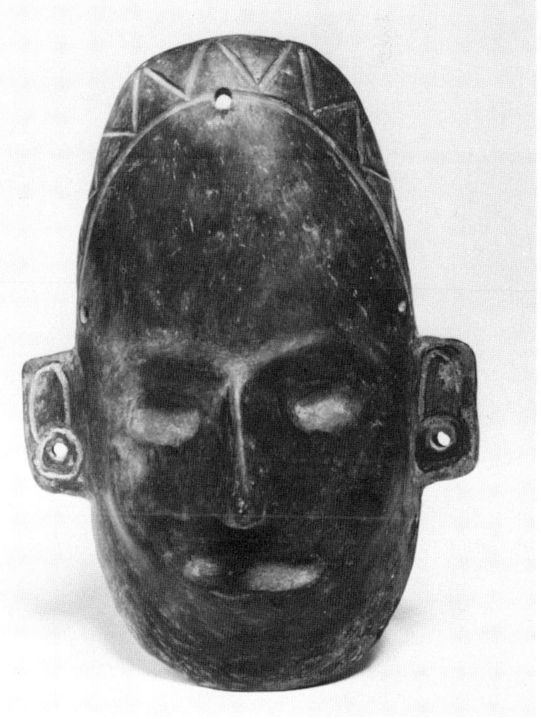

63. Blackware Mask

The use of face masks was an early feature of Middle American life. This burnished and incised example is a classic example. COLIMA, Mexico. 100 B.C.-250 A.D. 6¾″ x 9″. 22/2549.

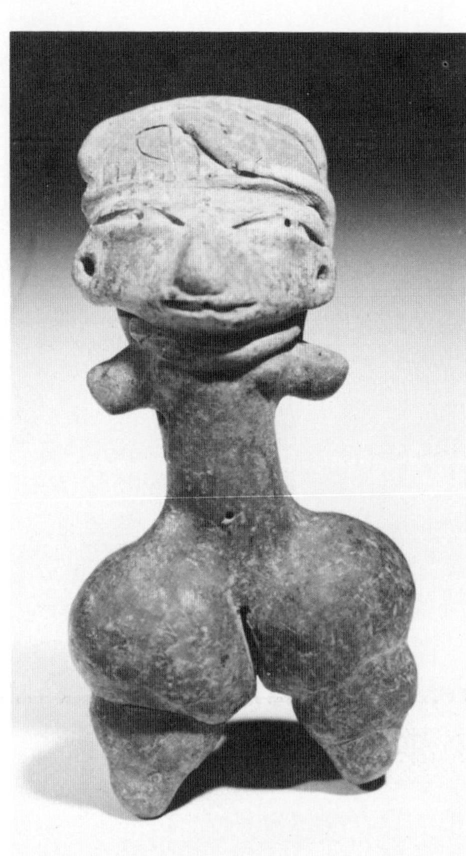

64. Modeled Clay Figurine
The so-called "Pretty Ladies" from Central Mexico are found in a great variety of forms, and in enormous quantity. They are not only remarkable for their charming appeal, but equally for the early dating of their production. Presented by Dr. and Mrs. Arthur M. Sackler. TLATILCO, Mexico. 1000-500 B.C. 2" x 4". 23/8601.

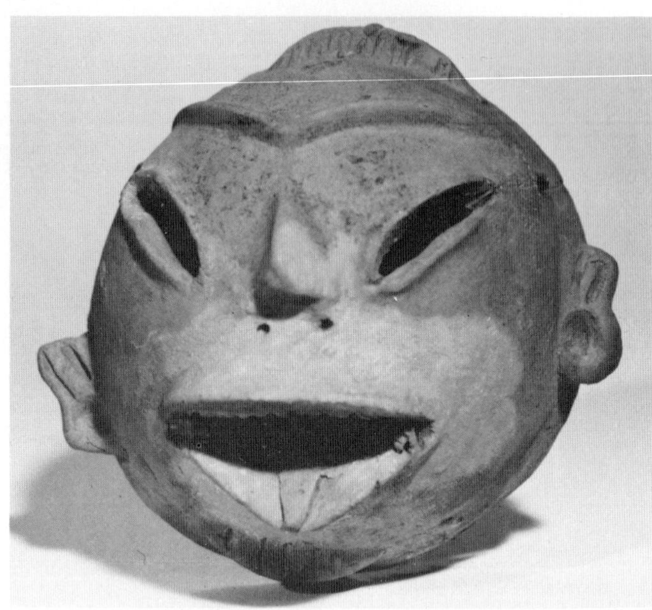

65. Miniature Face Mask
Among the earliest clay masks to be found in Mexico are these rotund examples, often painted with fugitive red and yellow pigment. TLATILCO, Mexico. 1000-500 B.C. 5¼" x 5½". 23/5588.

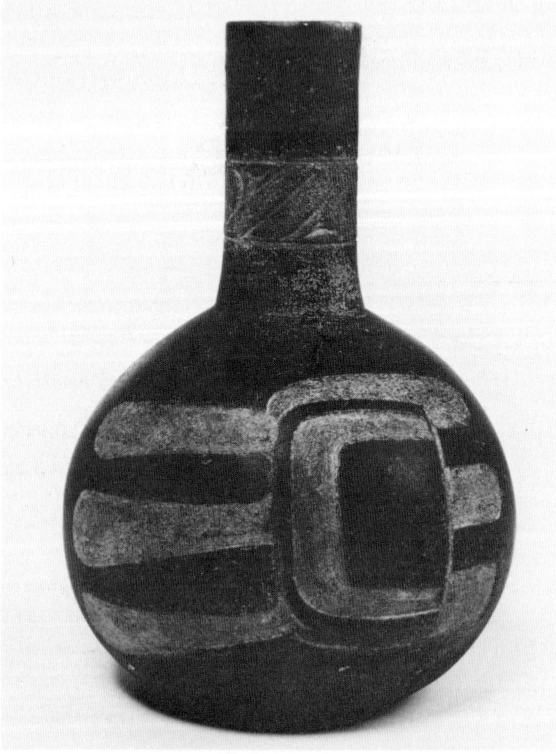

66. Blackware Water Bottle
This globular vessel has been decorated with a design accomplished by carving away the surface, and rubbing red pigment into the design. OLMEC. Las Bocas, Puebla, Mexico. 1250-750 B.C. 5¾" x 8¼". 24/1148.

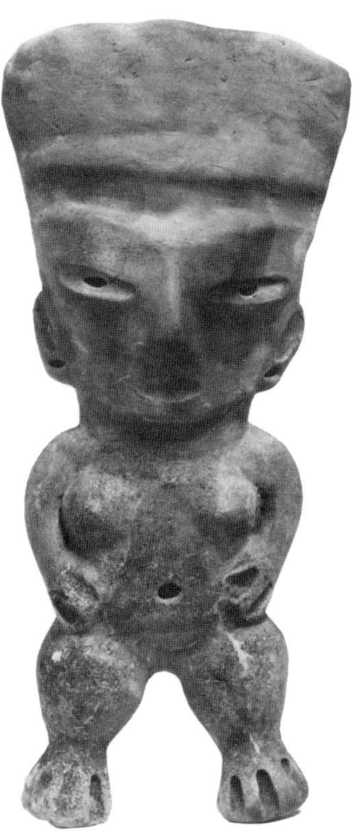

68. Large Clay Figurine
Another area where the production of female figurines was prominent is represented by this wide-headed example. GUALUPITA. Morelos, Mexico. 1000-500 B.C. 5″ x 10¾″. 21/8819.

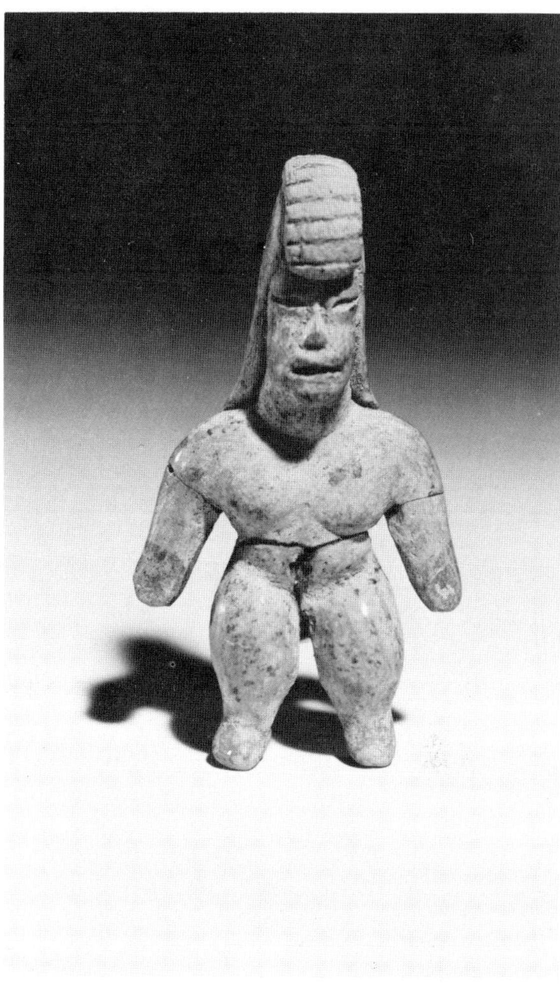

67. Female Figurine
Traces of original red paint are still to be seen on this modeled clay figurine of a nude female wearing a fancy coiffure. Presented by Robert L. Stolper. OLMEC. Las Bocas, Puebla, Mexico. 1250-750 B.C. 2″ x 3½″. 23/6824.

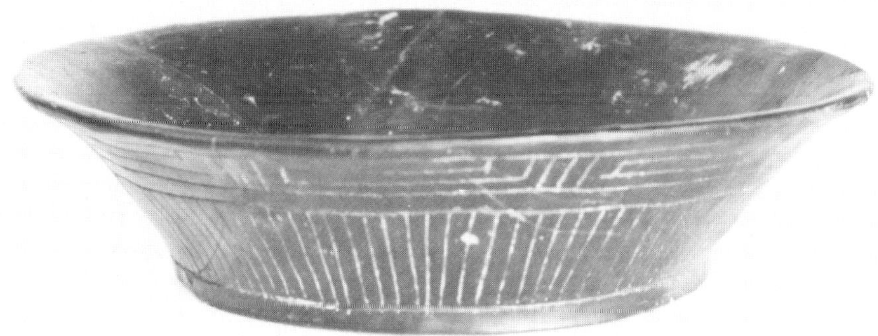

69. Shallow Blackware Dish
A characteristic form of early wares, these flat-bottomed dishes have an incised design on the flaring rim, as well as an occasional interior decoration. Presented by Robert L. Stolper. OLMEC. Tlapacoya, Mexico. 1000-500 B.C. 2″ x 9¼″. 23/4926.

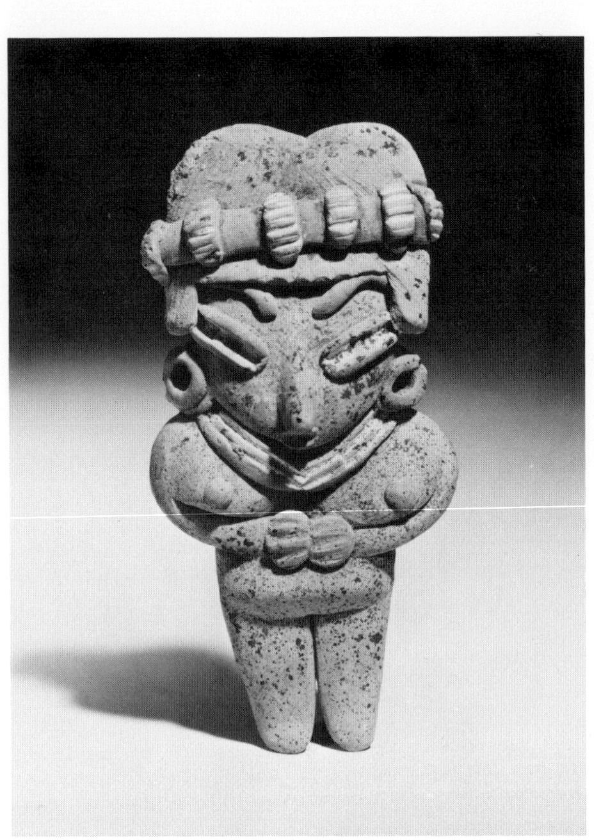

70. Modeled Female Figurine
Another example of the "Pretty Lady" figurines is this voluptuous effigy from the Preclassic period. Her nude body is decorated with paint, an elaborate necklace, and a fancy coiffure. Presented by Dick Cavett. CHUPÍCUARO. Guanajuato, Mexico. 100 B.C.-250 A.D. 2¼" x 4¼". 24/7614.

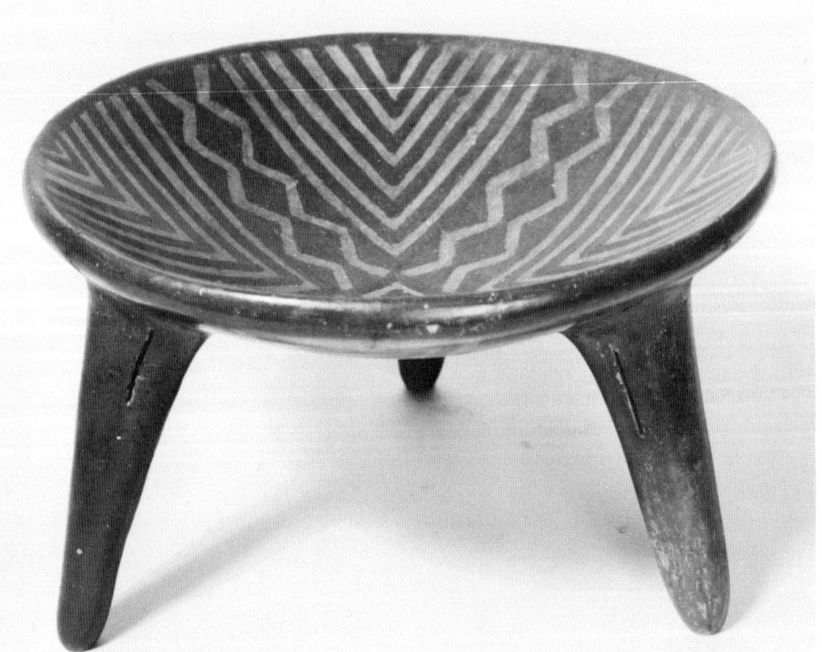

71. Tripodal Redware Dish
A beautifully burnished and painted redware dish, these often have pebbles in the hollow legs, allowing it also to serve as a rattle. CHUPÍCUARO. Guanajuato, Mexico. 100 B.C.-240 A.D. 6¼" x 10¼". 22/5691.

72. Standing Redware Figurine
The polished and burnished redware figurines from this early site are famous throughout Mexico. The designs may represent body paintings or tattooing; possibly they are abstracted costume designs. Presented by Dick Cavett. CHUPÍCUARO. Guanajuato, Mexico. 100 B.C.-250 A.D. 3¼″ x 6¾″. 24/6748.

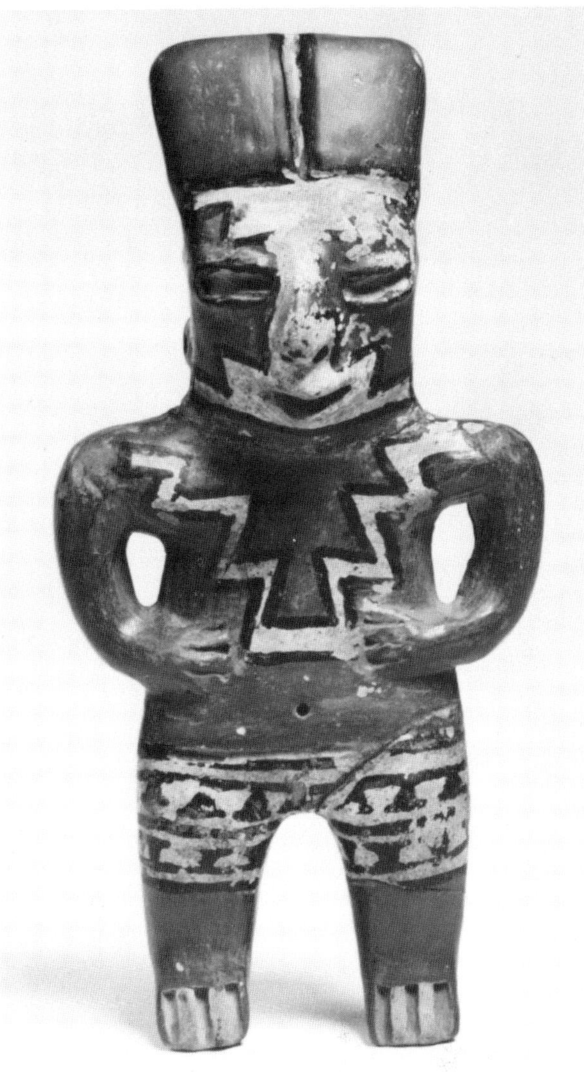

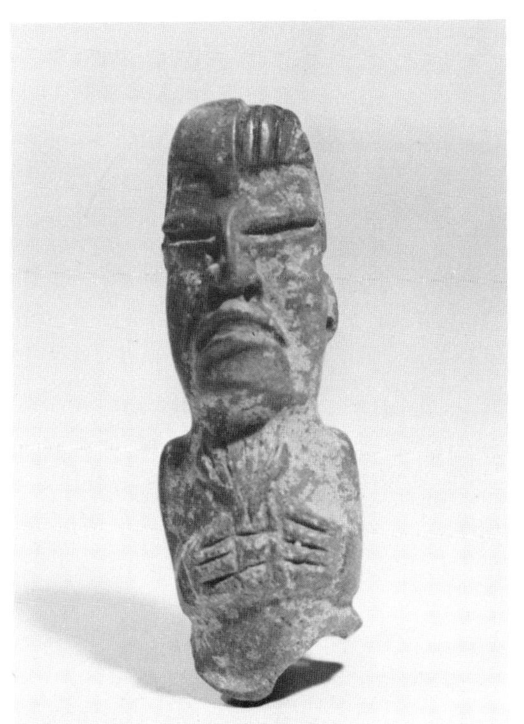

73. Figurine Fragment
Even though much of the body is missing, the carefully sculptured details on this green-gray stone effigy make it a powerful example of Preclassic work. OLMEC. Xochipala, Guerrero, Mexico. 1250-750 B.C. 1″ x 3″. 24/744.

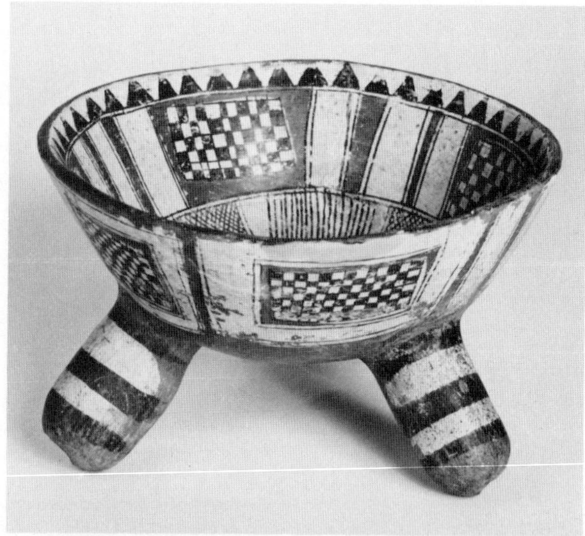

74. Painted Tripodal Bowl
The brilliant designs on this bowl are still fresh, giving a rare example of the beauty of prehistoric ceramic design. The hollow legs are rattles, with small pebbles inserted before firing. Presented by William M. Lannik. GUERRERO, Mexico. 100-250. 5½" x 9½". 23/7051.

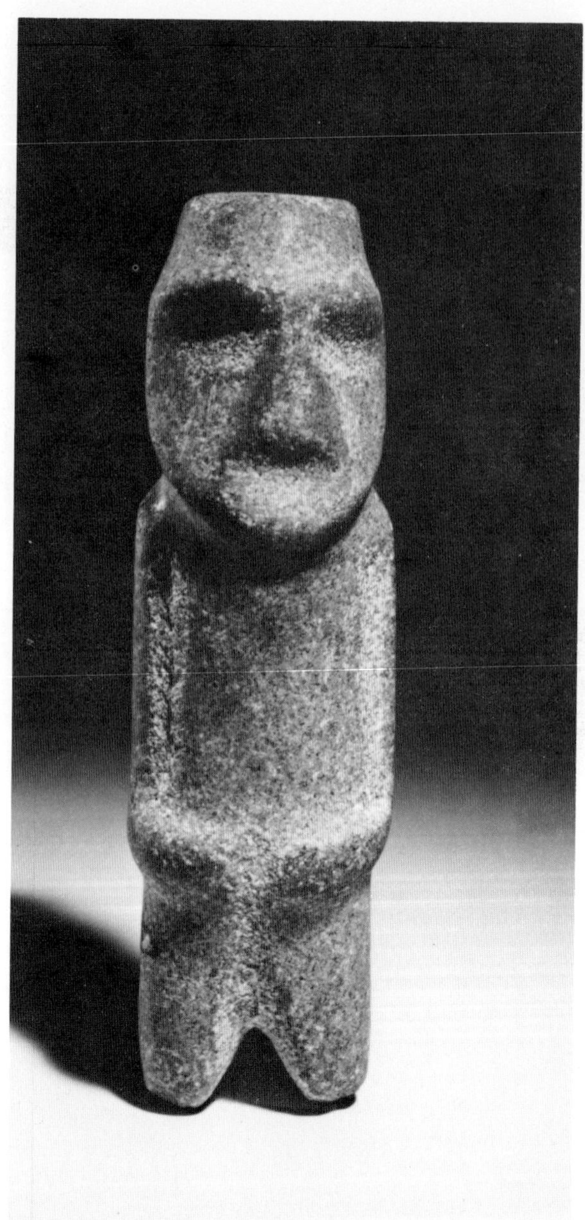

75. Carved Greenstone Effigy
These strange figurines are found in tremendous quantity along the Mezcala River. Almost nothing is known of their dating, relationship to other cultures, or their place in Mexican archeology. MEZCALA. Guerrero, Mexico. 100 B.C.-250 A.D. (?) 2½" x 8". 18/9297.

76. Alabaster Mask

Another form of carving common to the Central Mexican area is this type of "mask" (perhaps more accurately termed a face panel). These are carved from *tecali*, a soft limestone often used in Mexican sculpture. GUERRERO, Mexico. 100 B.C.-250 A.D. (?) 4¾" x 5¼". 14/9034.

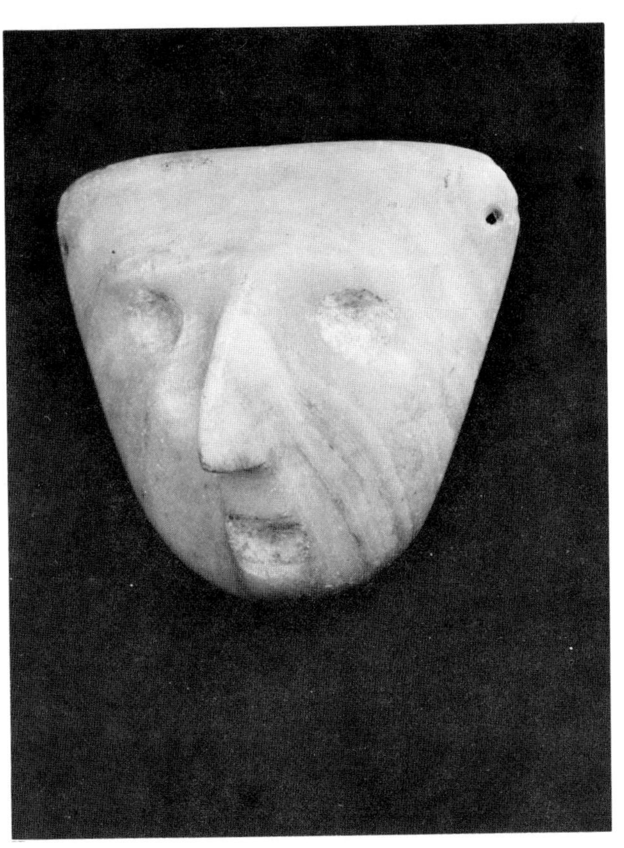

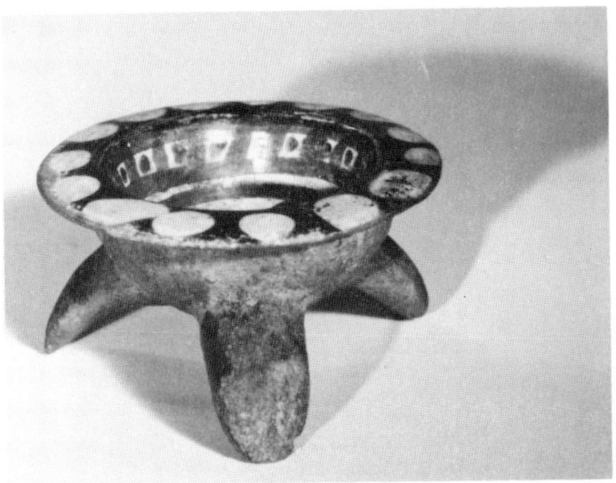

78. Miniature Tripodal Bowl

Faithful to the full-sized original in every way, these tiny ceramic vessels are ancient prototypes of ware still being made today in Mexico. We do not know if these were intended as toys for children, or served as inexpensive burial offerings. Presented by Dr. and Mrs. Arthur M. Sackler. TZINTZUNTZÁN, Michoacán, Mexico. 1370-1522. 1¼" x 2¼". 23/8725.

77. Painted Tripodal Bowl

(See color insert facing page 120)

79. Fresco Painted Bowl

The brilliant paint still surviving on the exterior of this shallow bowl makes it a rare example of prehistoric ceramic painting. The coloring was applied after the vessel was fired. TZINTZUNTZÁN, Michoacán, Mexico. 1370-1522. 3½" x 8½". 23/9894.

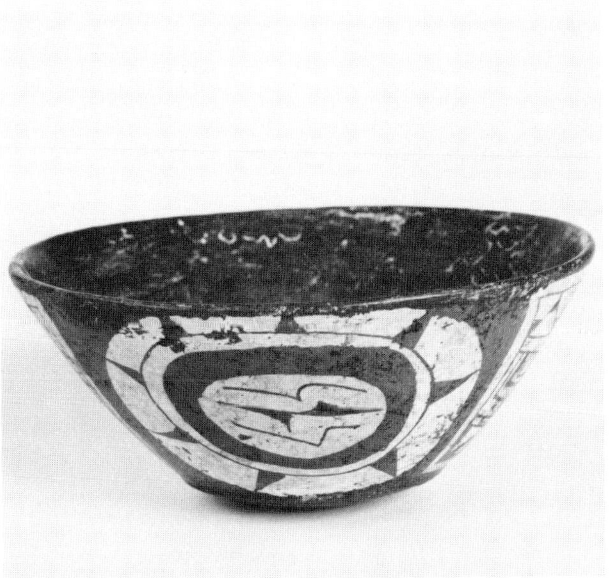

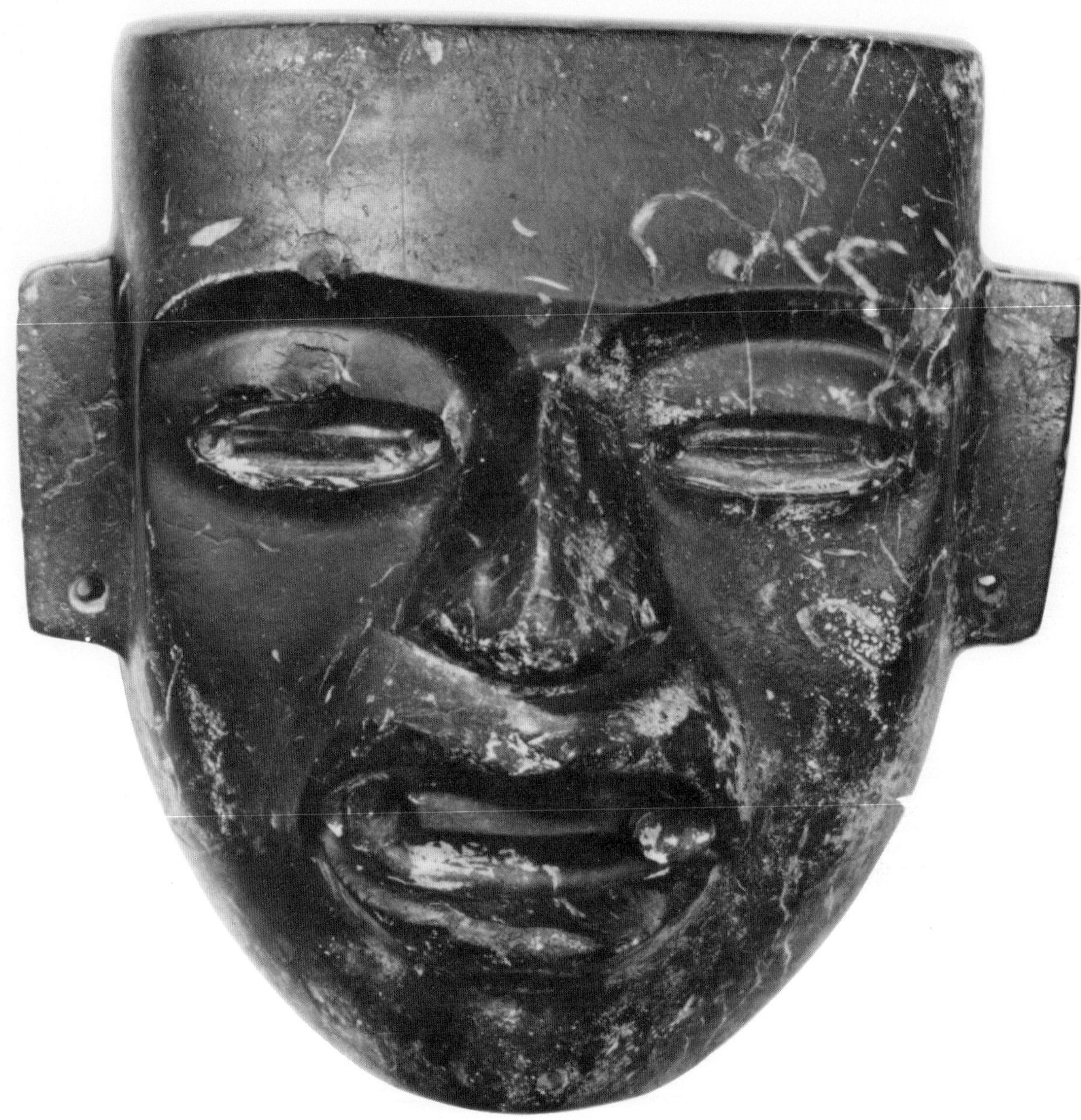

80. Black Stone Mask

The most famous masks in Middle America are undoubtedly those of the Teotihuacán style. Although often seen in collections, they are rarely encountered in actual professionally-excavated archeological sites. Since most are far too heavy to have been actually worn, it is more likely they were decorations on statues or possibly architectural ornaments. TEOTIHUACÁN. Mexico. 500-650. 8″ x 8″. 14/2042.

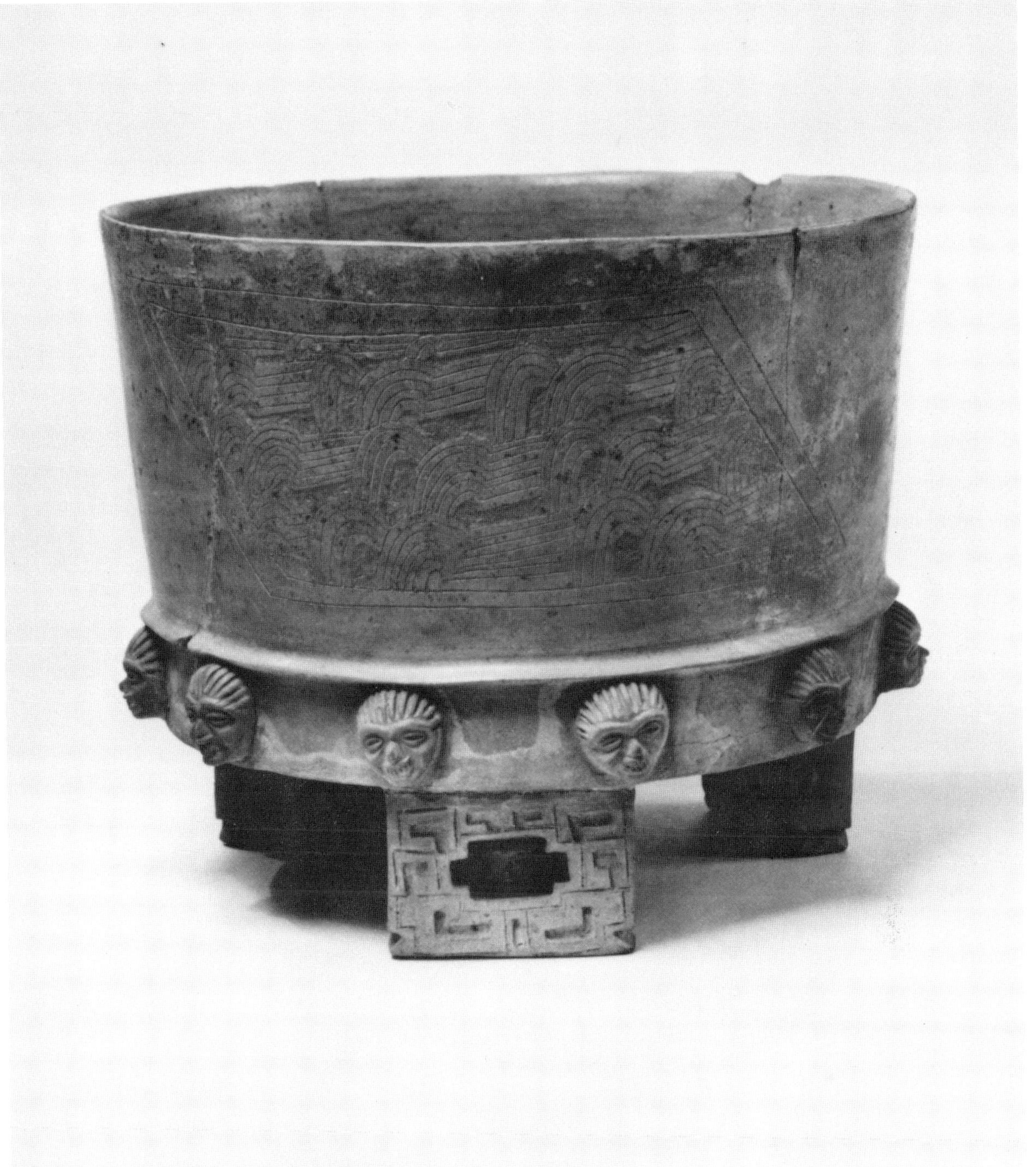

81. Buffware Tripodal Vessel
This thin-walled vessel features appliqué clay heads around the base of the rim. The legs have been made in molds, and attached to the base before firing. Presented by Dr. and Mrs. Arthur M. Sackler. TEOTIHUACÁN. LaVentanilla, Mexico. 250-650. 9″ x 11″. 24/454.

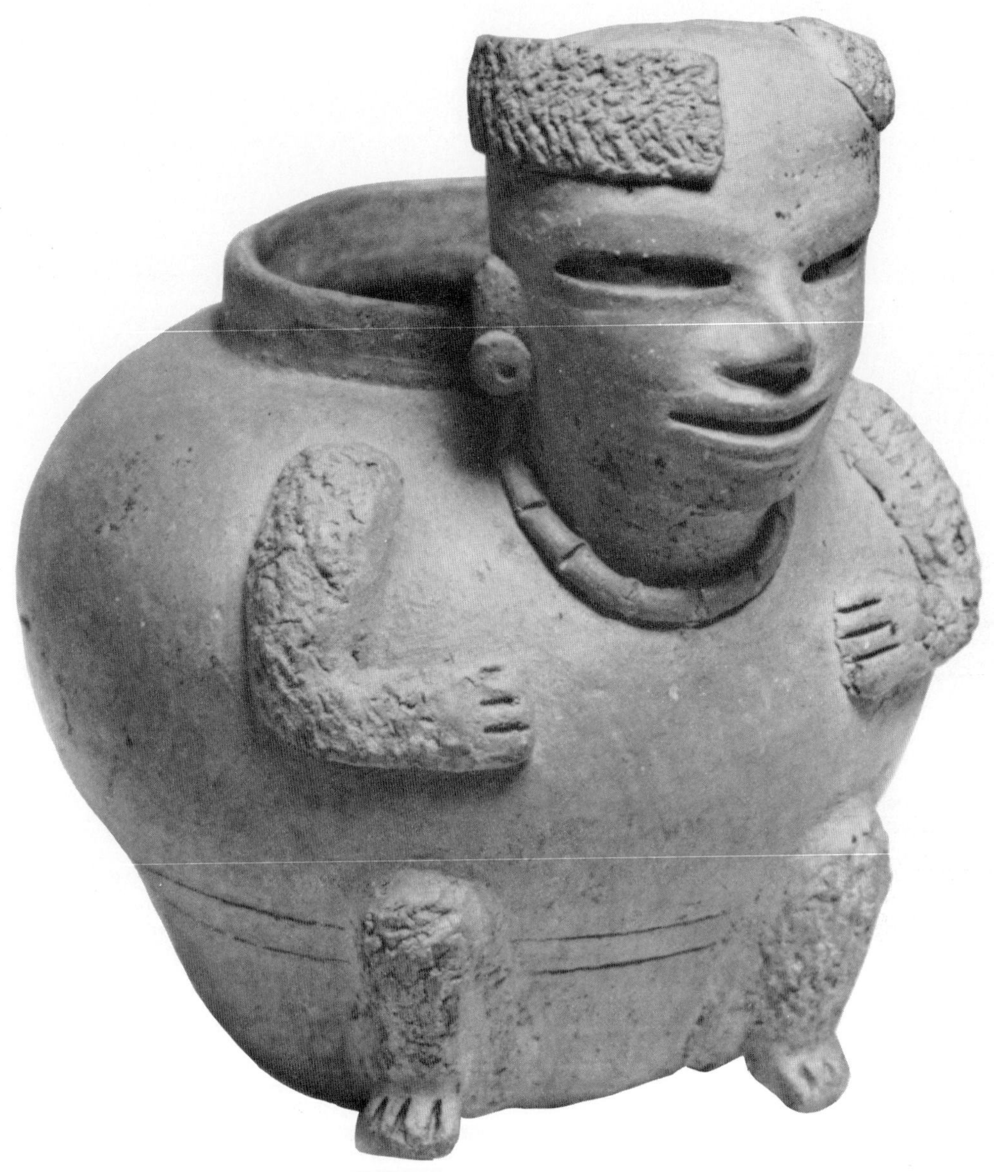

82. Orangeware Effigy Bowl

This modeled bowl has not been completely fired, resulting in a buff color, rather than the more usual "thin orange" hue common to ware from this Central Mexican site. These are known in several sizes, all following a similar pattern. TEOTIHUACAN. Veracruz, Mexico. 250-600. 7¼" x 6¾". 23/3435.

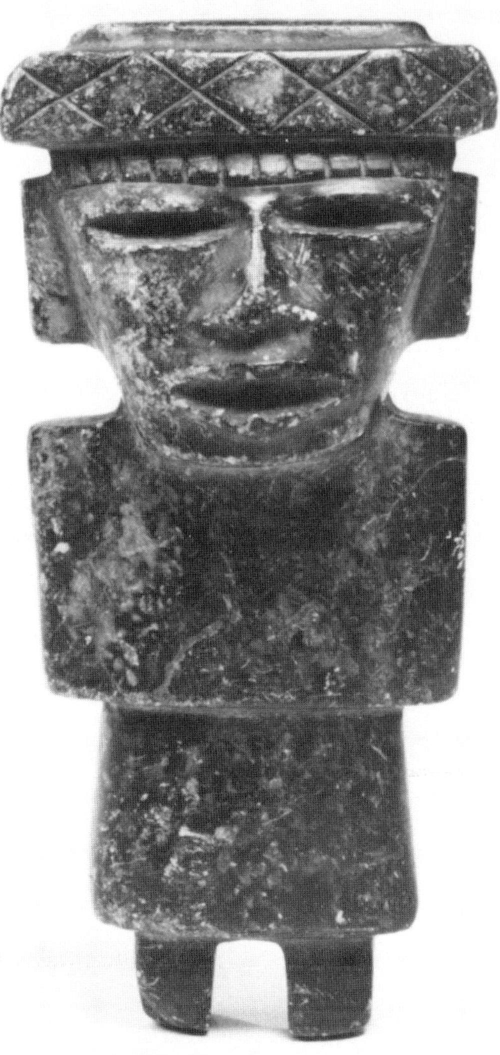

83. Greenstone Figurine

The most typical figurine from Teotihuacán are these small carved greenstone effigies with facial designs very similar to the masks from the same site (*see* #80). They range in size from minute to very large; this is about average. TEOTIHUACÁN. Mexico. 250-650. 2½" x 5¼". 23/1877.

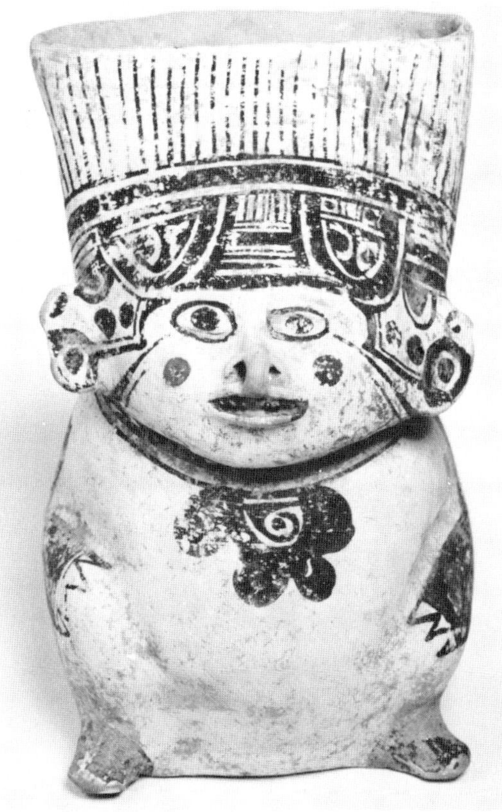

84. Painted Clay Effigy

The soft kaolin of the East Coast region is not conducive to preservation; figurines from this area are rare, particularly those which have retained any degree of paint. The pendant on his breast is the Wind God symbol. HUÁSTEC. Pánuco, Veracruz, Mexico. 900-1200. 5½" x 9". 22/9584.

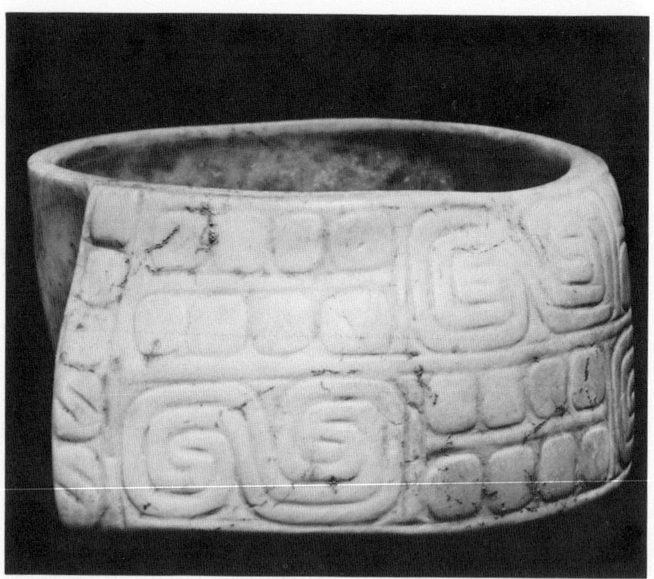

85. Shell Bracelet
Carved from the cross section of a giant conch shell, this has been formed into a lovely bracelet. The use of conch is common to the Huástec region; they were a popular object of inter-tribal trade. HUÁSTEC. Pánuco, Veracruz, Mexico. 900-1200. 1¾″ x 4″. 24/3565.

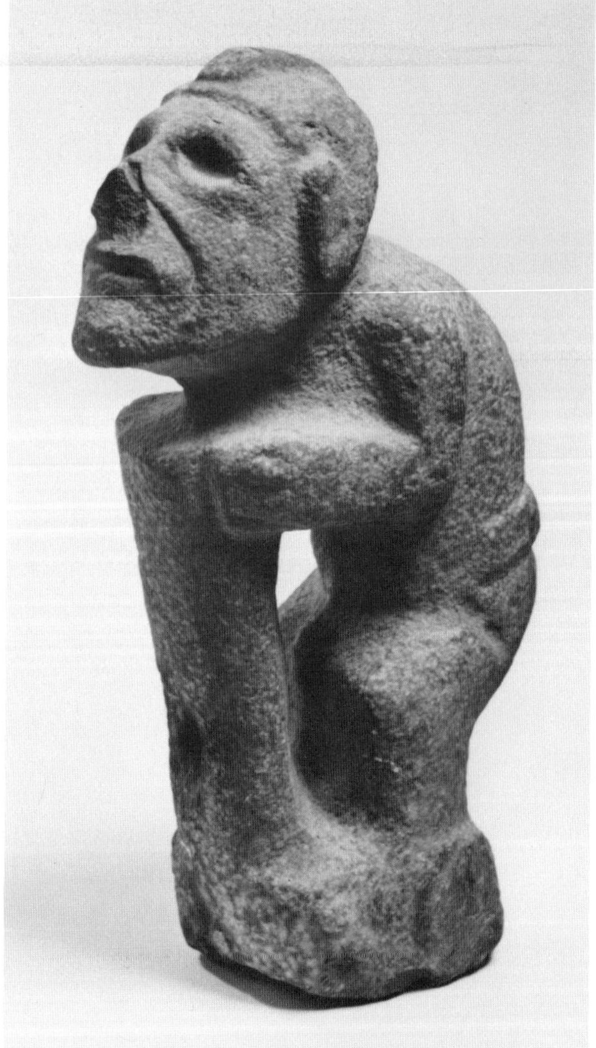

86. Crouching Stone Effigy
This particular design is the most typical form of Huástec sculpture. This example was collected by Joseph Jones before 1850. HUÁSTEC. Tuxpán, Mexico. 900-1200. 6½″ x 13¼″. 8004.

87. Wide Mouth Urn
(See color insert facing page 200)

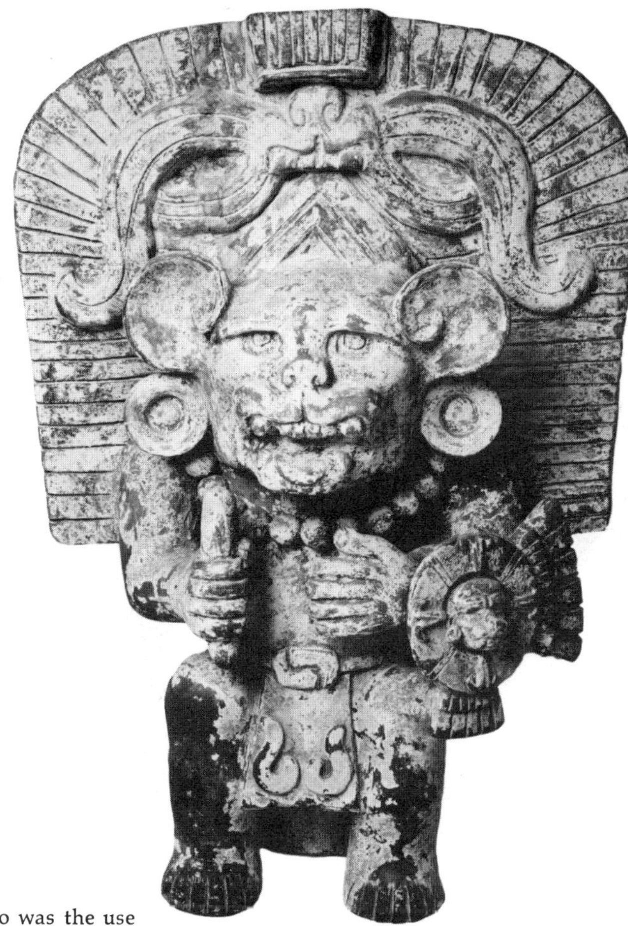

88. Modeled Funerary Urn
A common practice in southern Mexico was the use of elaborately modeled *incensarios*, which often served also as guardians of the deceased. Presented by Mrs. Thea Heye. ZAPOTEC. Etla, Oaxaca, Mexico. 550-750. 13½″ x 18¾″. 16/6073.

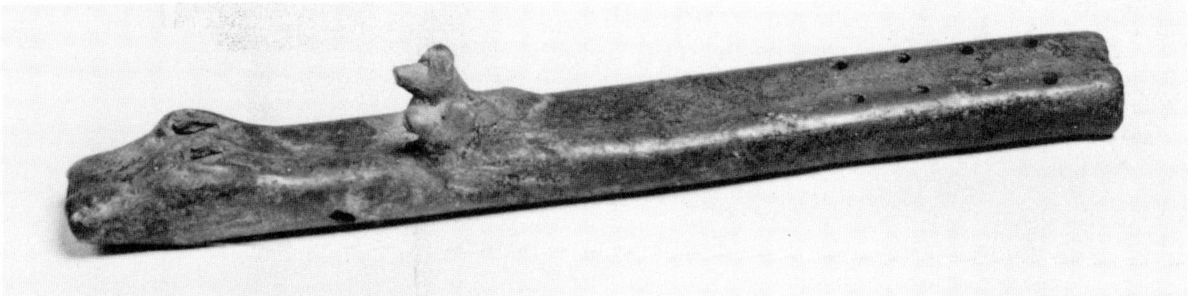

89. Ceramic Double Flute
The variety of musical instruments known to the ancient Indians is incredible. This flute has two tubes, with 8 notes; the birds modeled on the upper part suggest the beauty of the tones. COLIMA. Mexico. 250-500. L: 12″. 20/20.

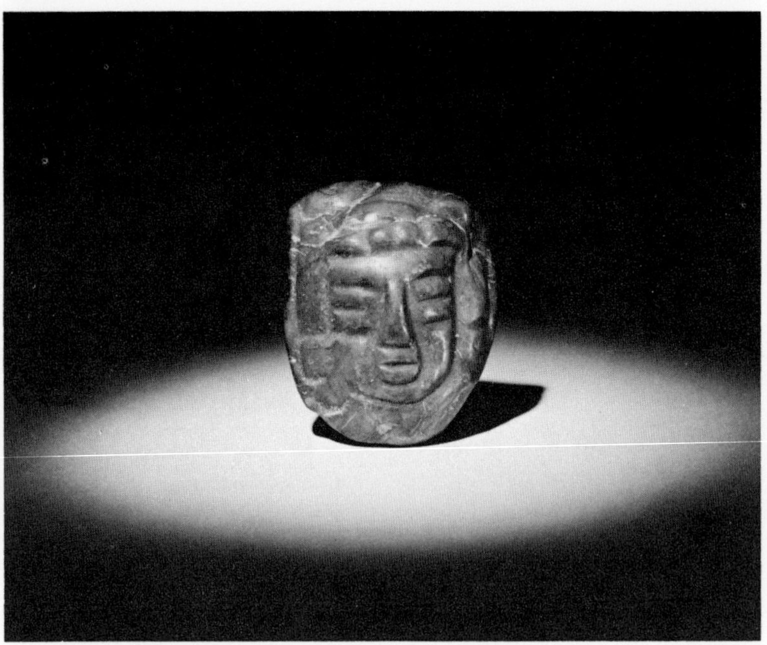

90. Carved Jade Pendant
Small fragments of jadeite were often carved into pendants and body ornaments for various purposes. This was obtained in Europe, where it had been taken over a century ago. Presented by Mrs. Thea Heye. MIXTEC. Oaxaca, Mexico. 1000-1500. 1¼″ x 1½″. 17/7036.

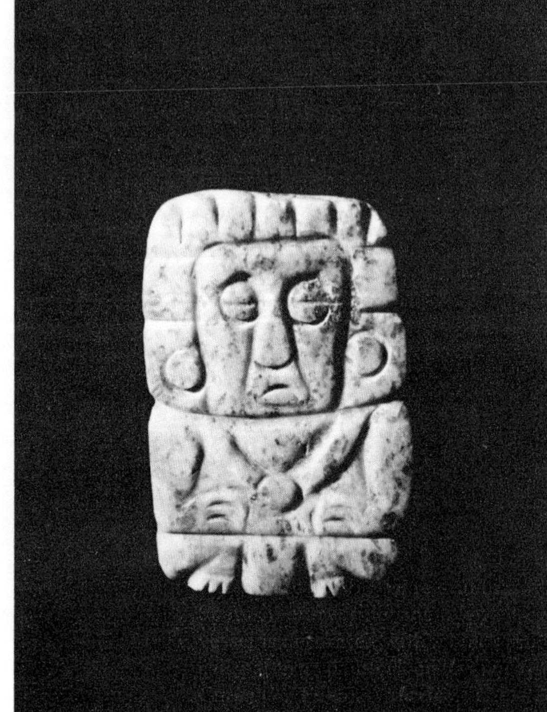

91. Greenstone Pendant
Another form of the numerous small stone pendants found in the Mixteca region. These are still used by Indians of Oaxaca today. Collected by B. T. Gilbert. MIXTEC. Oaxaca, Mexico. 1000-1500. 1½″ x 2½″. 1/2563.

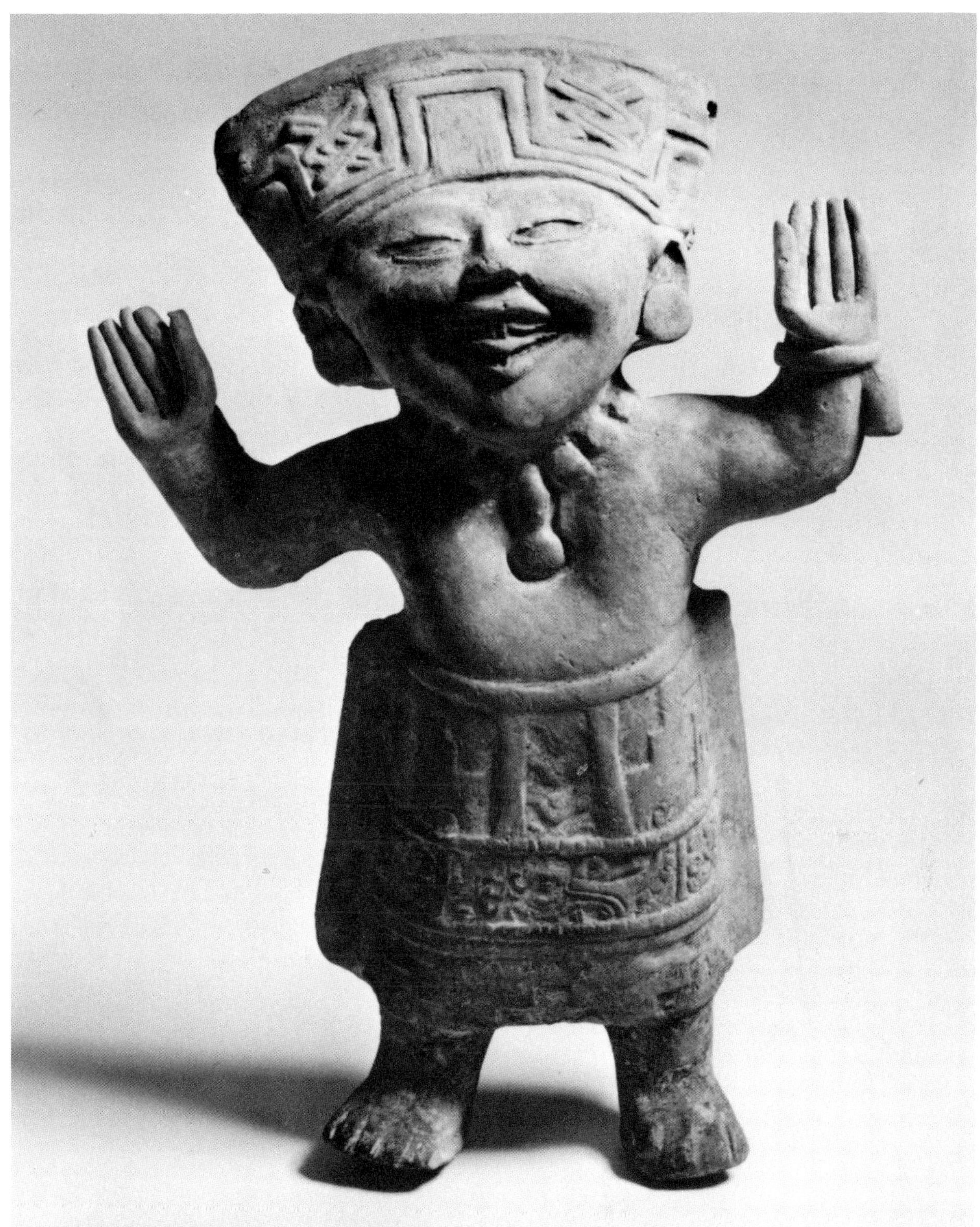

92. Standing Clay Figure

The so-called "Laughing Faces" are common in the southern area of Veracruz; usually they are found minus the bodies. This complete effigy shows the headdress styles common at the time, as well as the textile fashion and design. LAS REMOJADAS. Veracruz, Mexico. 1300-1521. 10″ x 14¼″. 23/3925.

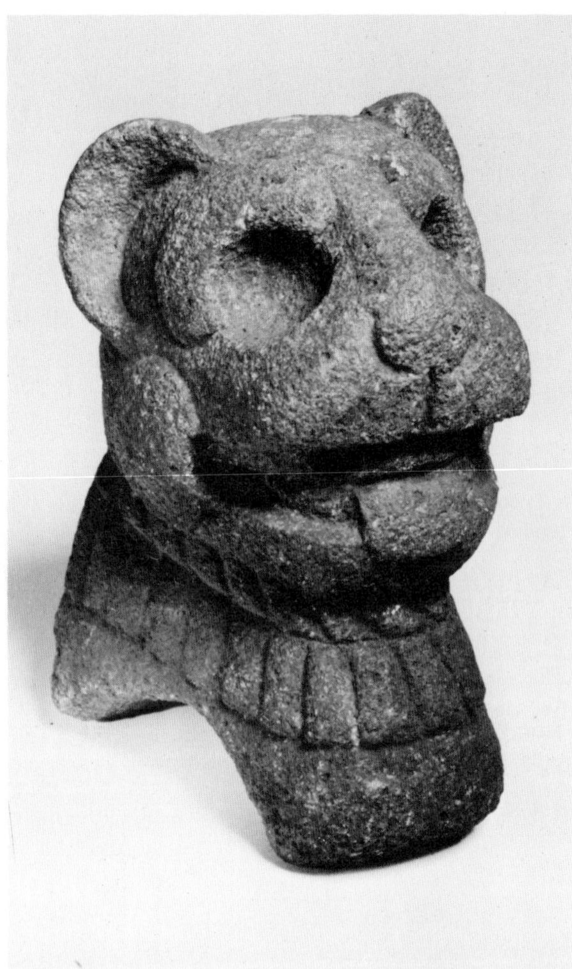

93. Zoömorphic Palma
Sculptured in the form of a jaguar head, this is one of the several styles in which the *palma* is found. El Tajín. Veracruz, Mexico. 300-1200. 5½" x 8". 24/2418.

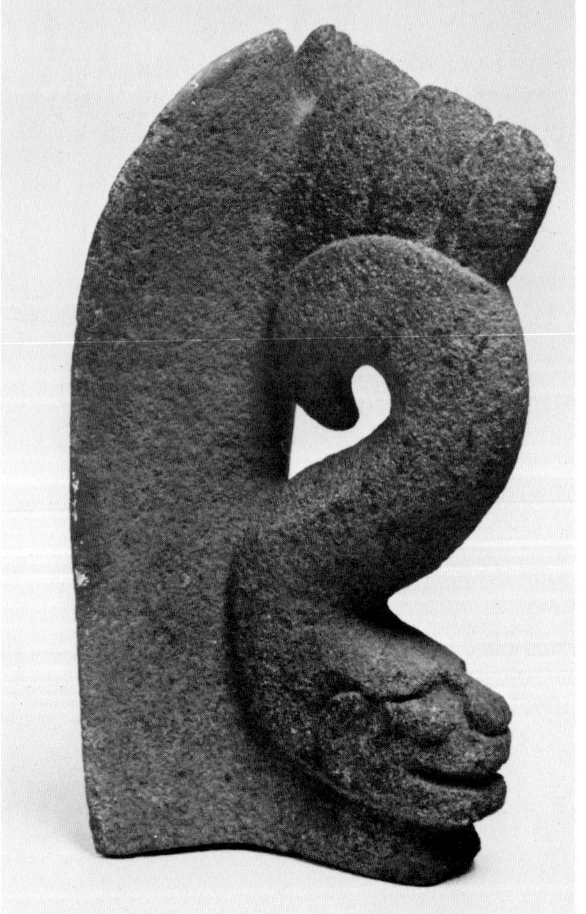

94. "Feathered Serpent" Palma
Perhaps representing the legendary Quetzalcóatl, this is the more elongated form of *palma*. Collected by George G. Heye. El Tajín. Veracruz, Mexico. 300-1200. 6¾" x 13". 19/5811.

95. Carved Scoria Hacha
(*See page 25*)

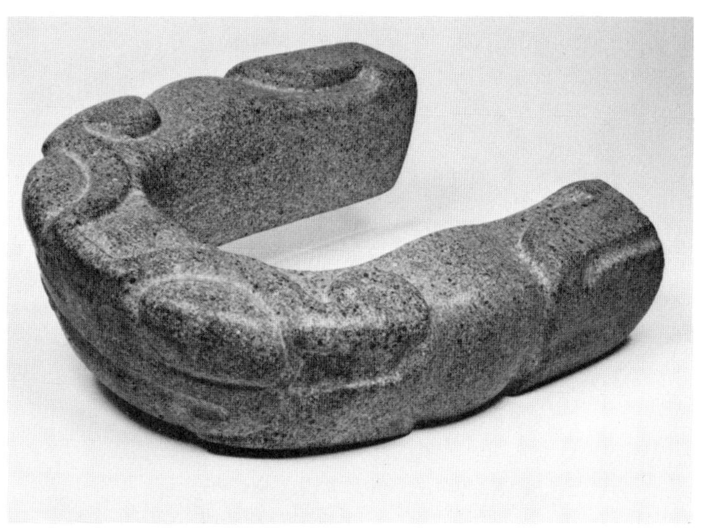

96. Carved Stone "Yoke"
The puzzling *yugo*, found throughout the Mexican area, is well represented by this example, carved in the form of an abstract frog design. The function of these beautiful sculptures is a mystery, although they seem to have been connected with the ball game, *tlachtli*. Zempoala, Hidalgo, Mexico. 300-1000. 4½" x 16½". 20/865.

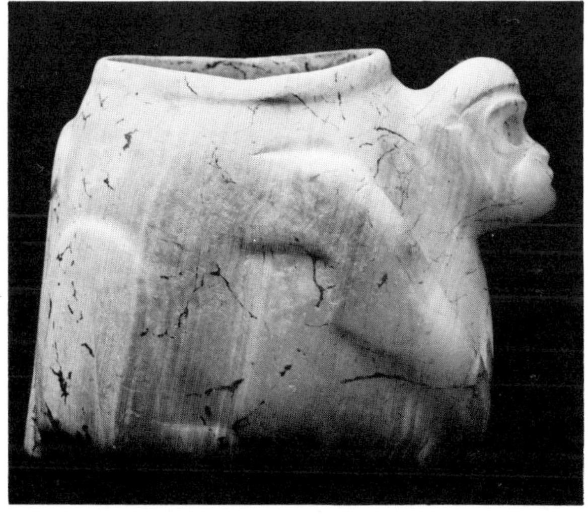

97. Onyx Effigy Jar
Carved from *tecali*, a form of aragonite commonly called alabaster, this has the design of a monkey in relief on the side. These were probably used as funerary offerings; their beauty suggests a major role in Maya culture. MAYA. Isla de Sacrificios, Veracruz, Mexico. 950-1250. 4¾" x 7". 16/3465.

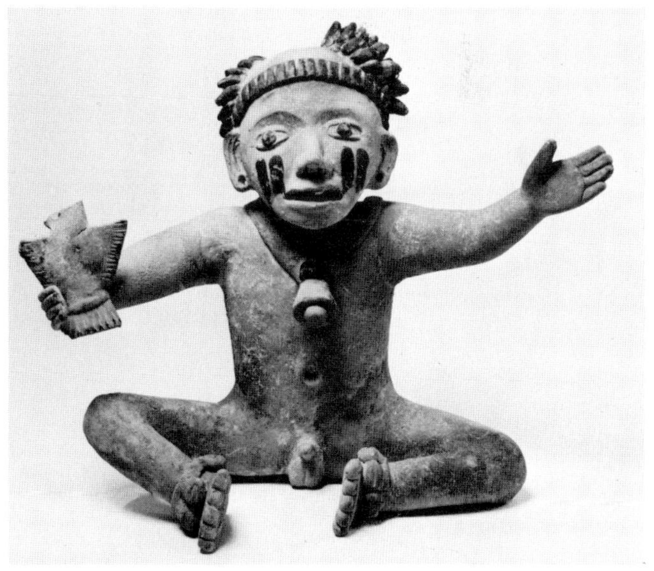

98. Seated Clay Effigy
A realistically modeled representation of a nude young man holding a fan in one hand, this has the remarkably human sensitivity found so often in sculpture from this region. LAS REMOJADAS. Veracruz, Mexico. 1300-1521. 12" x 16". 23/6257.

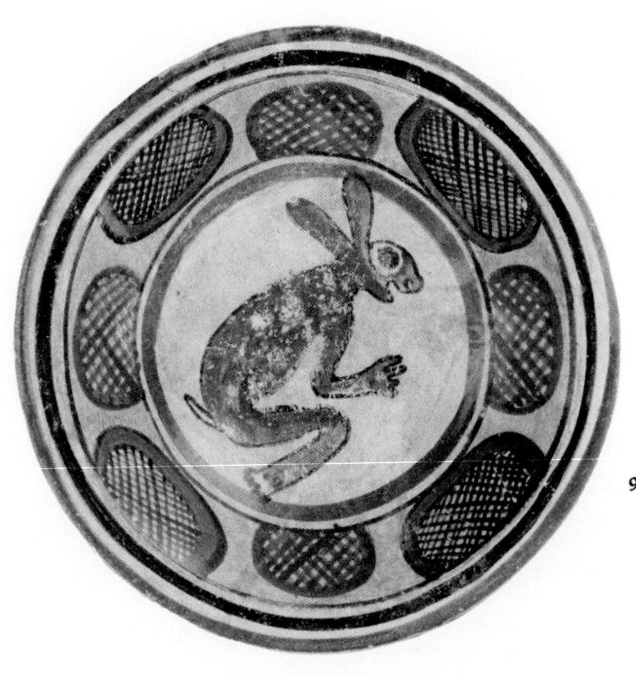

99. Painted Orangeware Bowl
The brilliant orange tone of these vessels provides a strong background for the rich red and black designs painted on the interior. This depicts a crouching rabbit, one of the symbols commonly used in Mayan art. MAYA. Campeche, Mexico. 900-1200. 3″ x 12″. 23/5888.

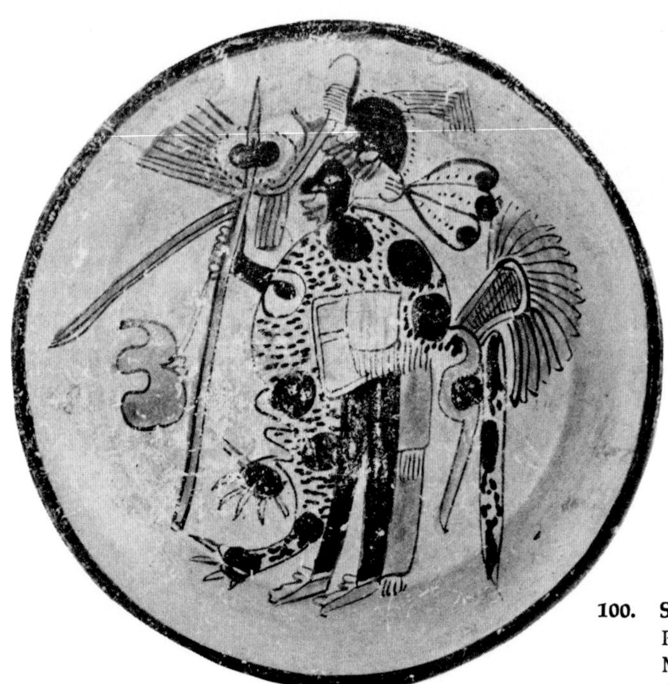

100. Shallow Orangeware Platter
Painted with the elaborately decorated and costumed Mayan nobles so frequently incorporated into the designs of the Mexican area, this is a fine example of the more flamboyant style. These designs are often particularly valuable for what they tell us of the details of costuming and customs of the prehistoric period. MAYA. Yucatán, Mexico. 900-1200. 2¾″ x 13½″. 24/3366.

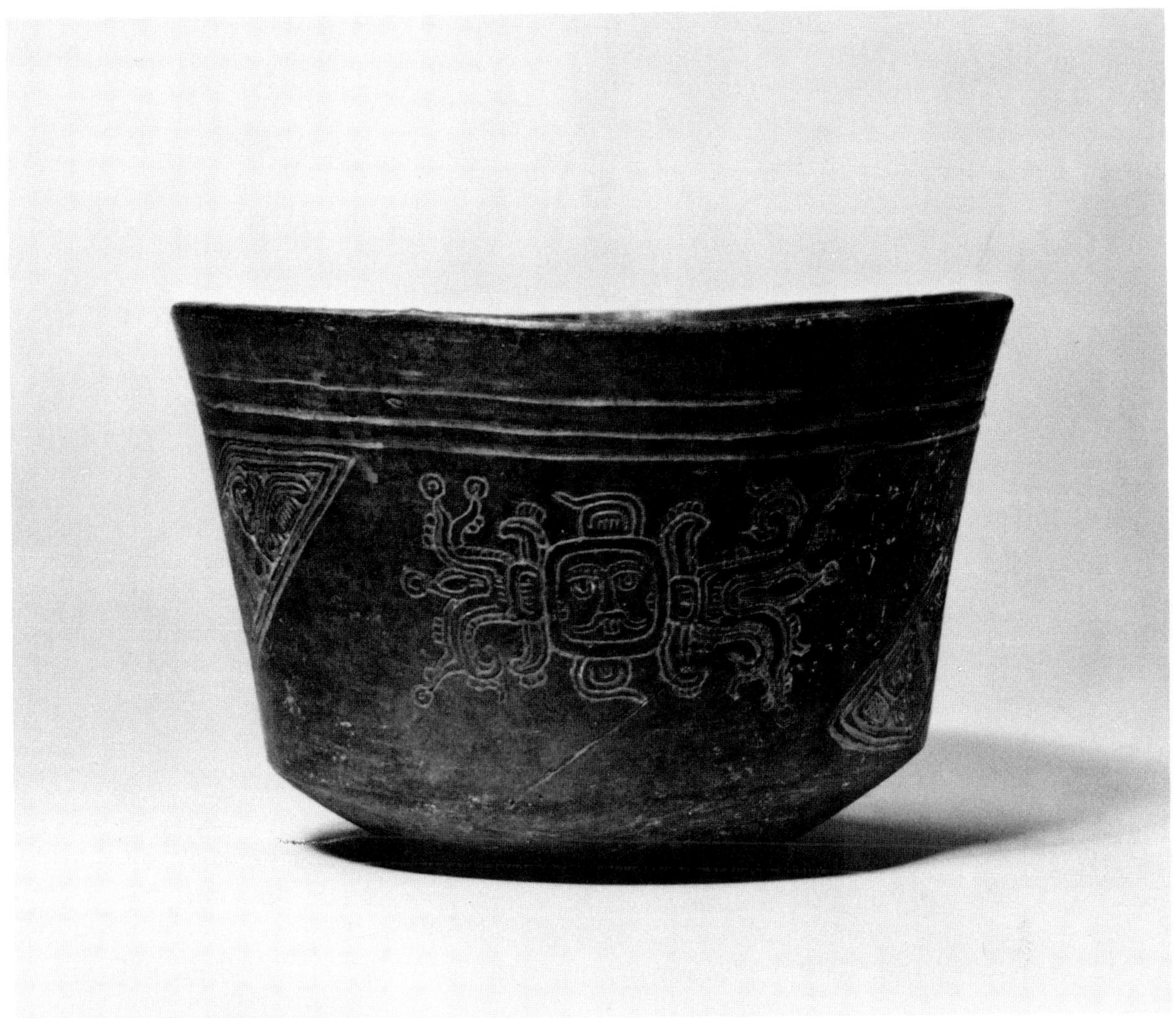

101. Incised Grayware Bowl

This slateware bowl is unusual in that it has two bottoms; pebbles have been inserted into the hollow space prior to firing, to give the vessel the function of a rattle. Glyphs have been incised on the sides. MAYA. Cocha, Campeche, Mexico. 600-900. 4¾" x 7½". 23/2270.

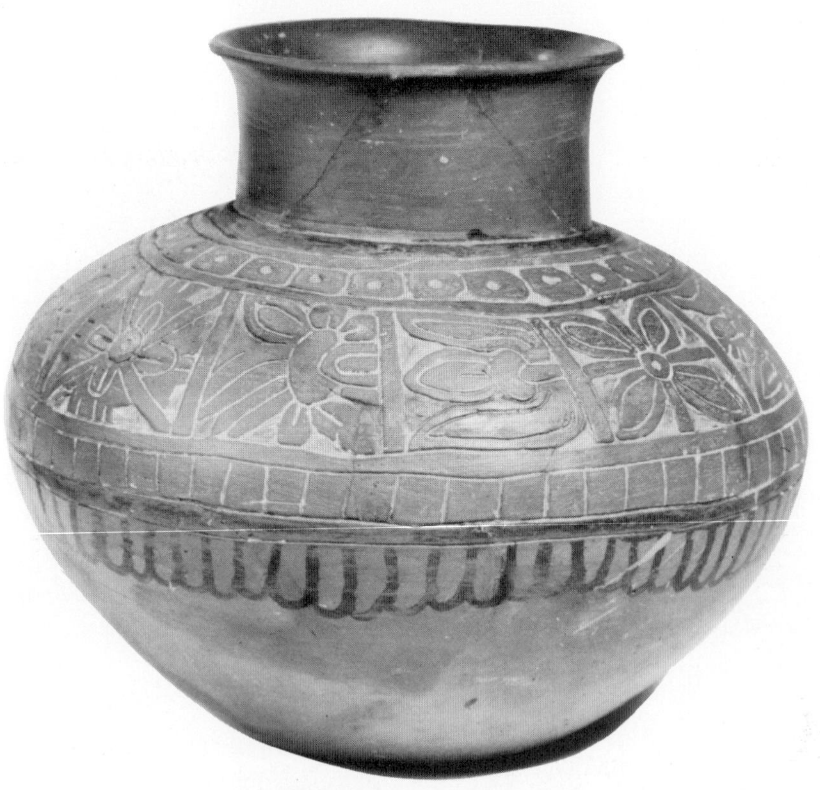

102. Incised Orangeware Bowl
The rich vermilion surface of this smoothly rounded form is decorated by panels of deeply incised designs, and a band of black painted lines. Presented by Mary W. Williams. MAYA. Campeche, Mexico. 900-1200. 8¾" x 10½". 23/3416.

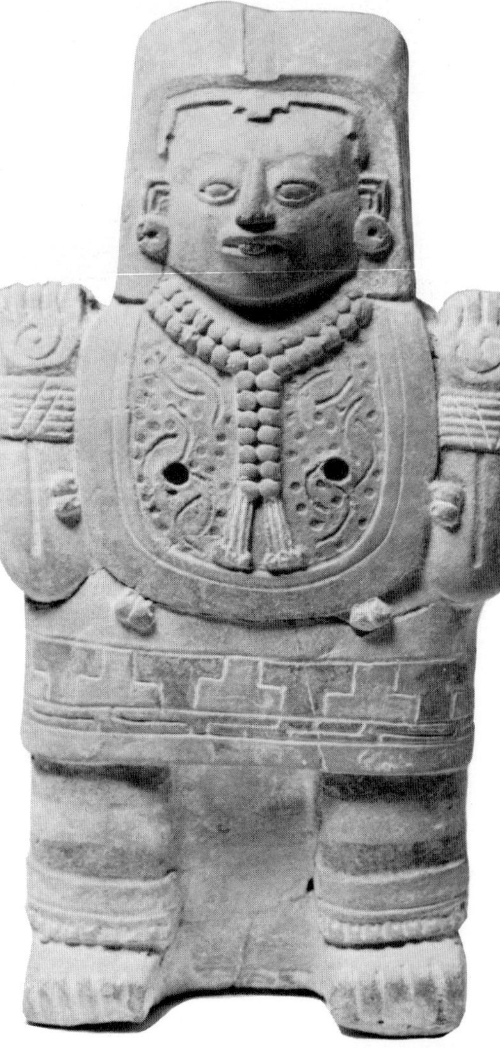

103. Mold-made Effigy Rattle
Made from two clay molds, designed in the form of an elaborately costumed person standing with upraised hands, this retains much of the original paint. The jade beads, textile *huípil,* and teeth formation were critical measures of Maya esthetic standards. MAYA. Jaina Island, Campeche, Mexico. 900-1200. 5" x 9¼". 24/8747.

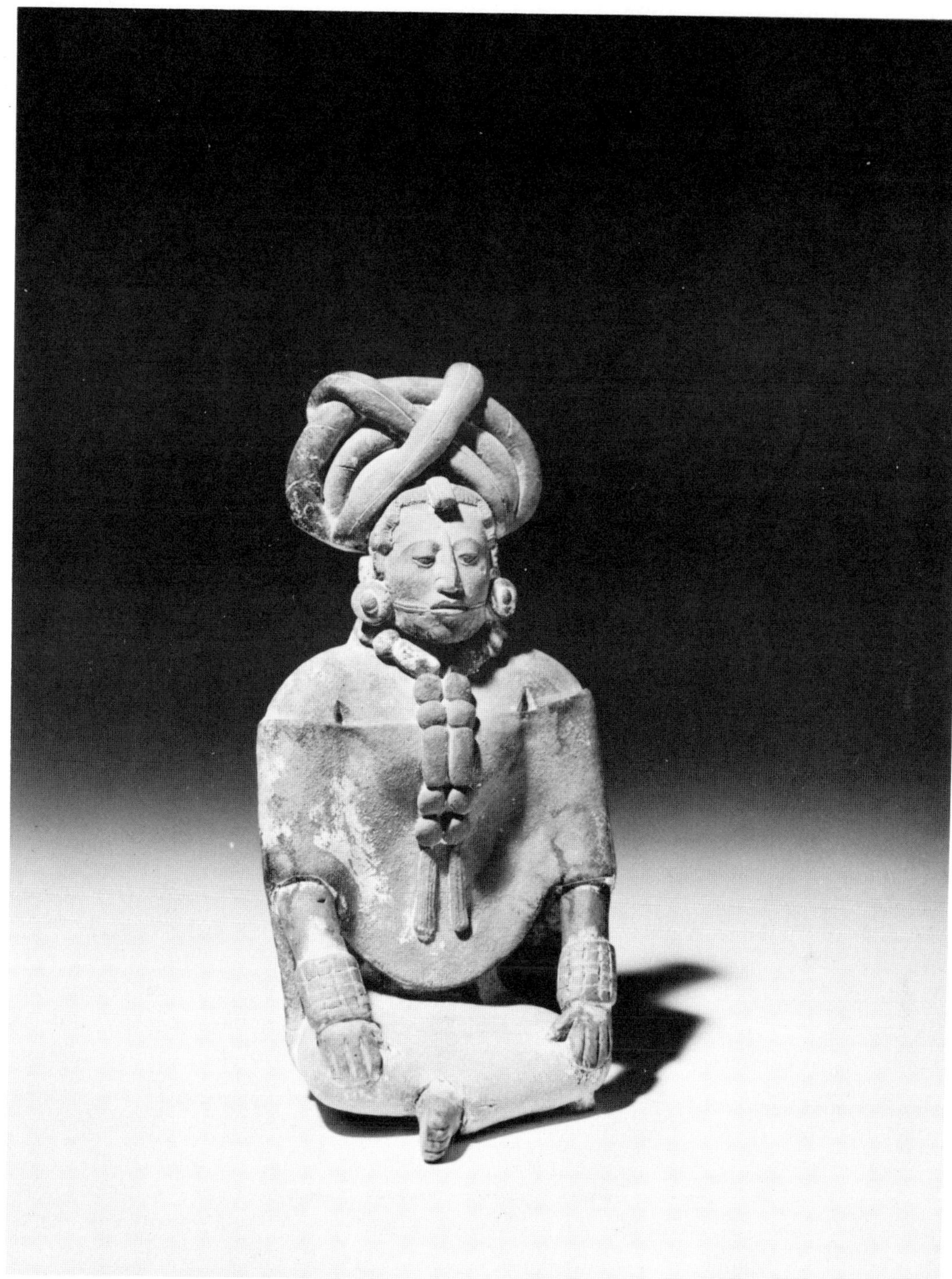

104. Modeled Clay Whistle

This graceful figurine is a fine example of classic Maya ceramic sculpture. The simply modeled form, actually a whistle, still retains a large amount of the original "Maya blue" coloring which was so highly favored by these early artists. The design portrays a person dressed in a large *huipil* similar in shape to the smaller *quexquemitl* with jade necklace and wrist ornaments. MAYA. Jaina Island, Campeche, Mexico. 600-900. 3¼" x 6¾". 24/3929.

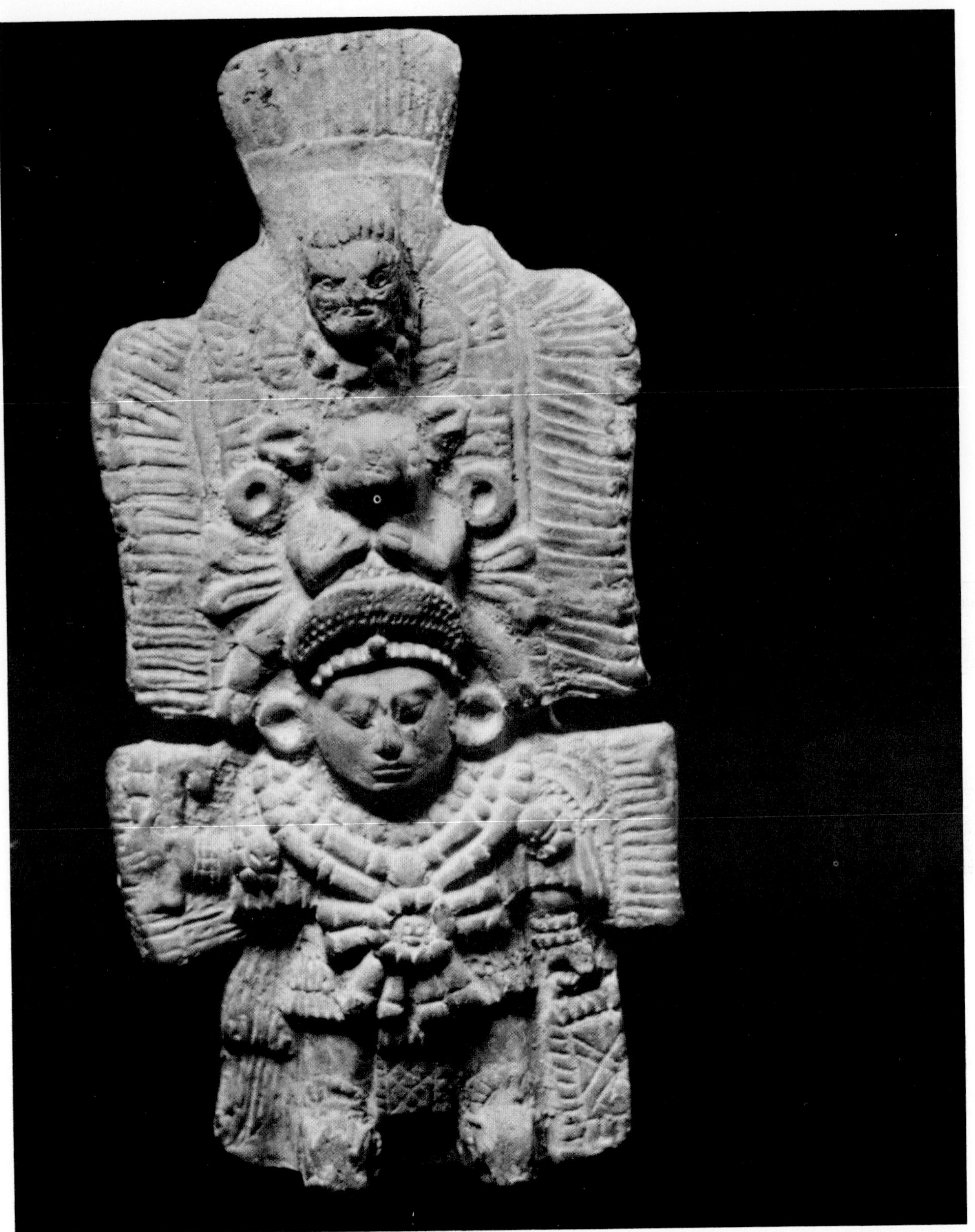

105. Elaborate Clay Figurine
Made from a mold, and further decorated by hand tooling, this ceramic whistle shows a richly-dressed individual, perhaps a priest, holding a sacrificial knife in one hand and a textile pouch in the other. The headdress is ornamented with feathers, and heads of the Bat and the ubiquitous Old Man God symbol. MAYA. Jaina Island, Campeche, Mexico. 900-1200. 4″ x 8″. 24/8749.

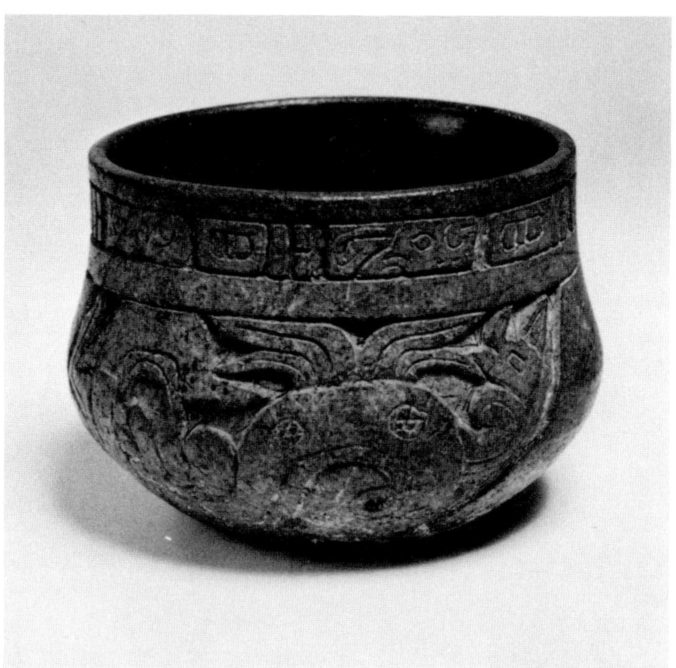

106. Carved Grayware Bowl
The art of carving moist clay before firing was one of the interesting ceramic techniques of the Maya. This small bowl has designs of two serpents around the sides, with glyphs carved along the rim. Presented by Cedric H. Marks. Zacuaba, Campeche, Mexico. 900-1200. 4½″ x 5¾″. 24/4003.

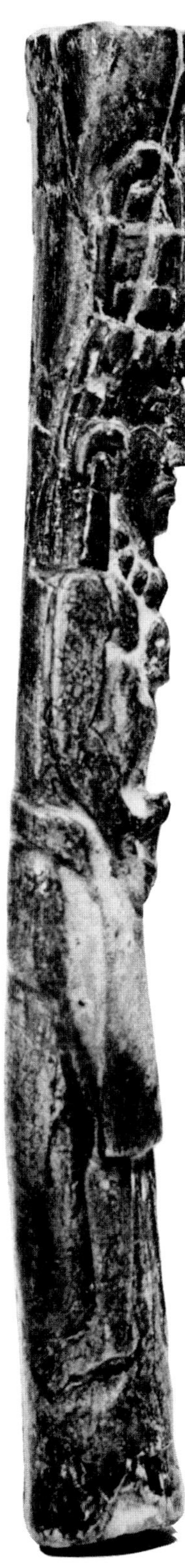

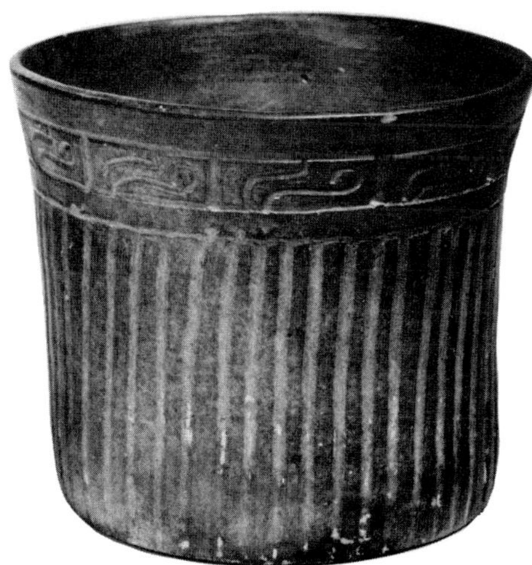

108. Fluted Slateware Bowl
The flat bottom and slender fluted sides mark this a Maya product. While this would have probably been intended as a strictly functional vessel for everyday use, it lacks none of the grace of many of the more ceremonial objects. Presented by Dr. and Mrs. Arthur M. Sackler. MAYA. Yucatán, Mexico. 600-900. 6″ x 7″. 23/6328.

107. Carved Bone Ornament
Bone was a popular art medium among the Maya. This slender object, whose function is unknown, portrays a figure wearing a feathered headdress and holding a vase in his hands. Jaina Island, Campeche, Mexico. 600-900. 1¼″ x 8½″. 24/3672.

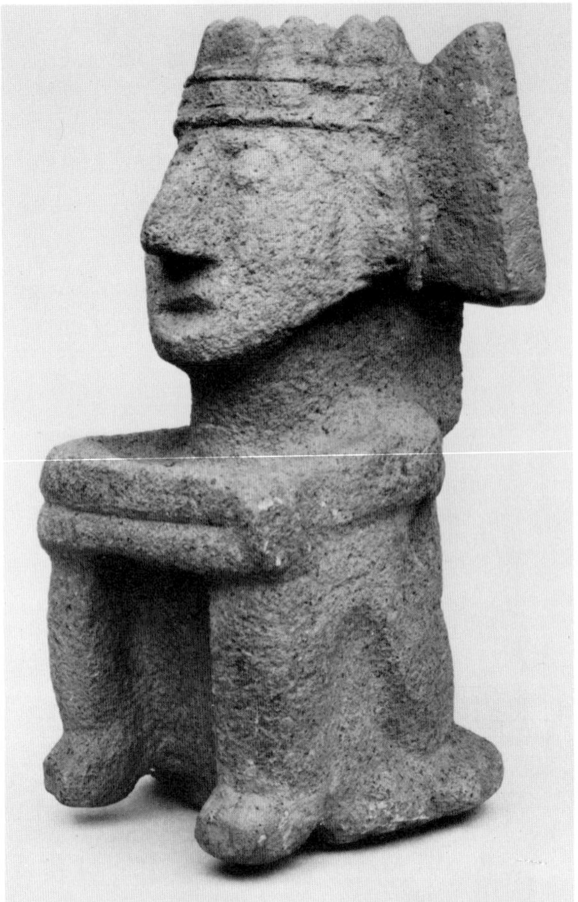

109. Seated Stone Sculpture
These carved effigies are found in a variety of forms representing the many complex deities and rulers of ancient Central Mexico. Their identification usually depends upon the details of iconography in the headdress and costume. This may represent Topiltzin, one of the major rulers of Tollán. Toltec. Tula, Mexico. 950-1200. 7″ x 11¾″. 15/5590.

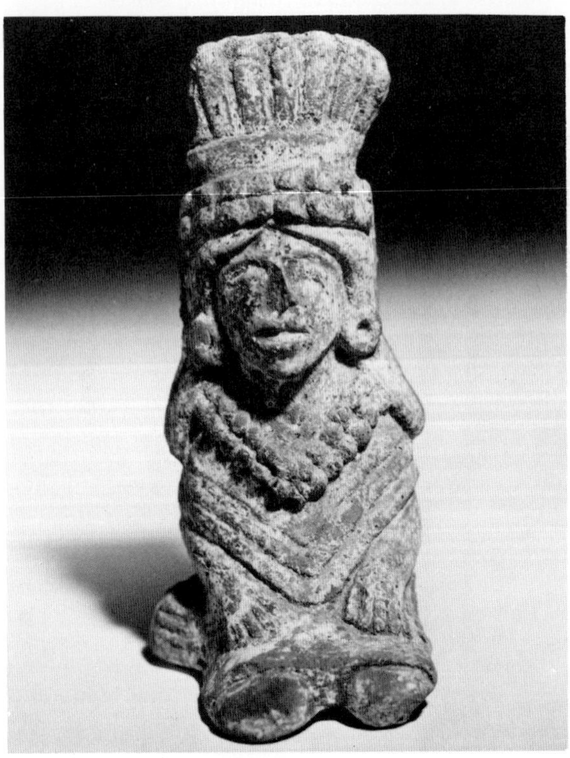

110. Mold-made Clay Figurine
This style of effigy is characteristic of Aztec ceramics, when such objects were turned out *en masse* to satisfy the ever-increasing market. This depicts a personage in a feathered headdress and *quexquemitl*. Aztec. Mexico, D.F., Mexico. 1340-1521. 2″ x 4¾″. 24/1878.

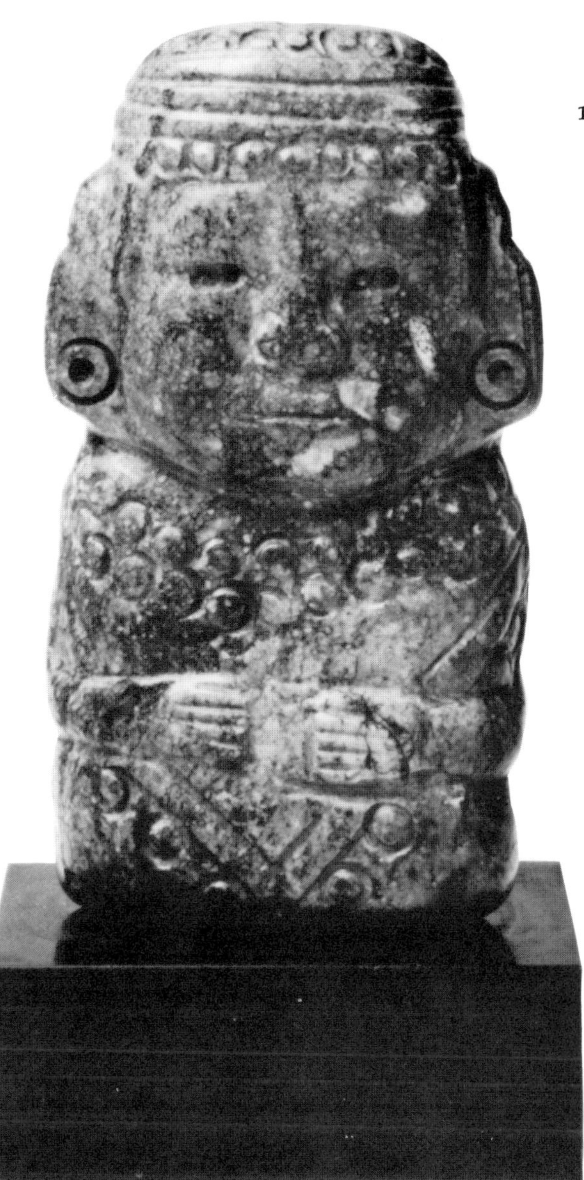

111. Carved Greenstone Figurine
A delicately carved and polished representation of Chalchiuhtlicue, the Water Goddess, one of the major deities of the Méxica. AZTEC. Mexico, D.F., Mexico. 1340-1521. 2½" x 4¾". 24/4221.

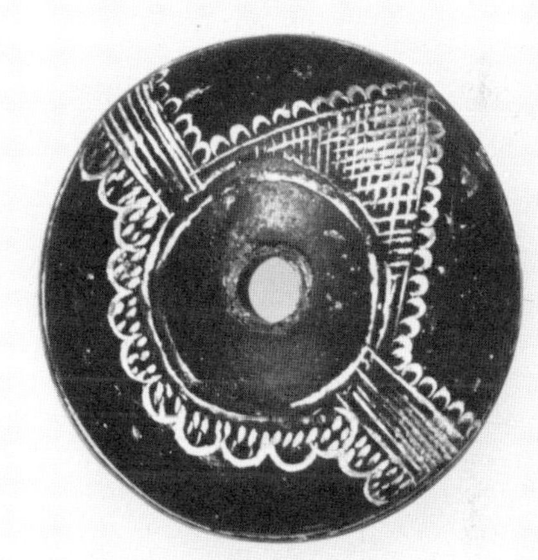

113. Incised Spindle Whorl
The *malacate* was used to balance the shaft of the spindle when used in spinning thread and yarn. Many of these were carefully incised, molded or modeled to embellish their appearance. AZTEC. Mexico, D.F. Mexico. 1340-1521. D: 2". 1937.

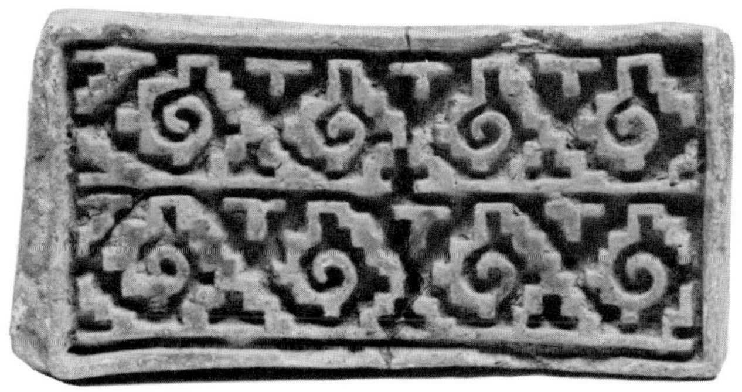

112. Carved Clay Seal
These small deeply worked objects are *sellos*, probably used for some duplicating function, such as stamping designs on the body, on textiles, or perhaps on pottery. AZTEC. Aguila, Guerrero, Mexico, D.F., Mexico. 1340-1521. 2" x 3". 24/6521.

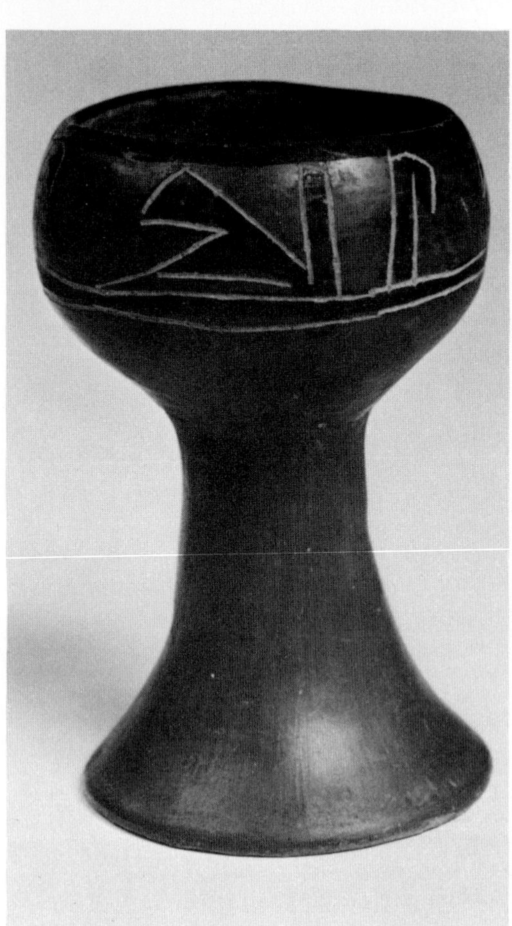

114. Redware Goblet
Primarily used in drinking *pulque*, the beverage made from the mescal plant, this is decorated with a black painted geometric design, and post-fired incising. Collected in 1880 by Gustave Bauer. Aztec. Huexotla, Mexico. 1340-1521. 3¼″ x 5¼″. 1471.

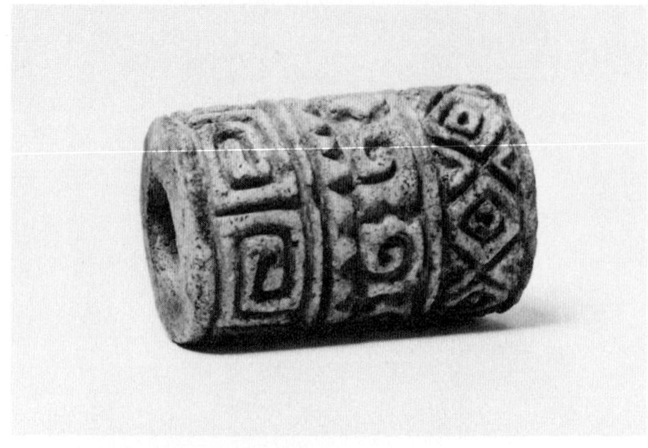

115. Cylindrical Roller Stamp
These deeply carved *sellos* were used somewhat like a printing roller. Presumably dipped in dye or pigment, they were applied to the body, to the surface of textiles, or perhaps to pottery. Aztec? Aguila, Guerrero, Mexico. 1340-1521. 1¾″ x 3″. 24/6506.

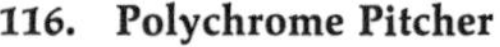

116. Polychrome Pitcher
An example of the ware still in use at the time of the Spanish entry into the New World, this globular vessel is decorated with a black and orange geometrical pattern painted on a burnished red surface. Cholula. Puebla, Mexico. 1200-1521. 3¾″ x 8½″. 2/7184.

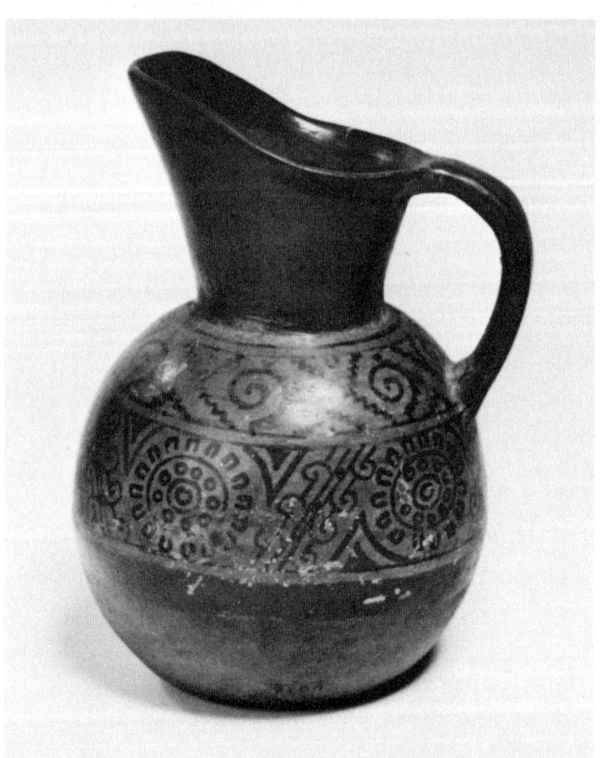

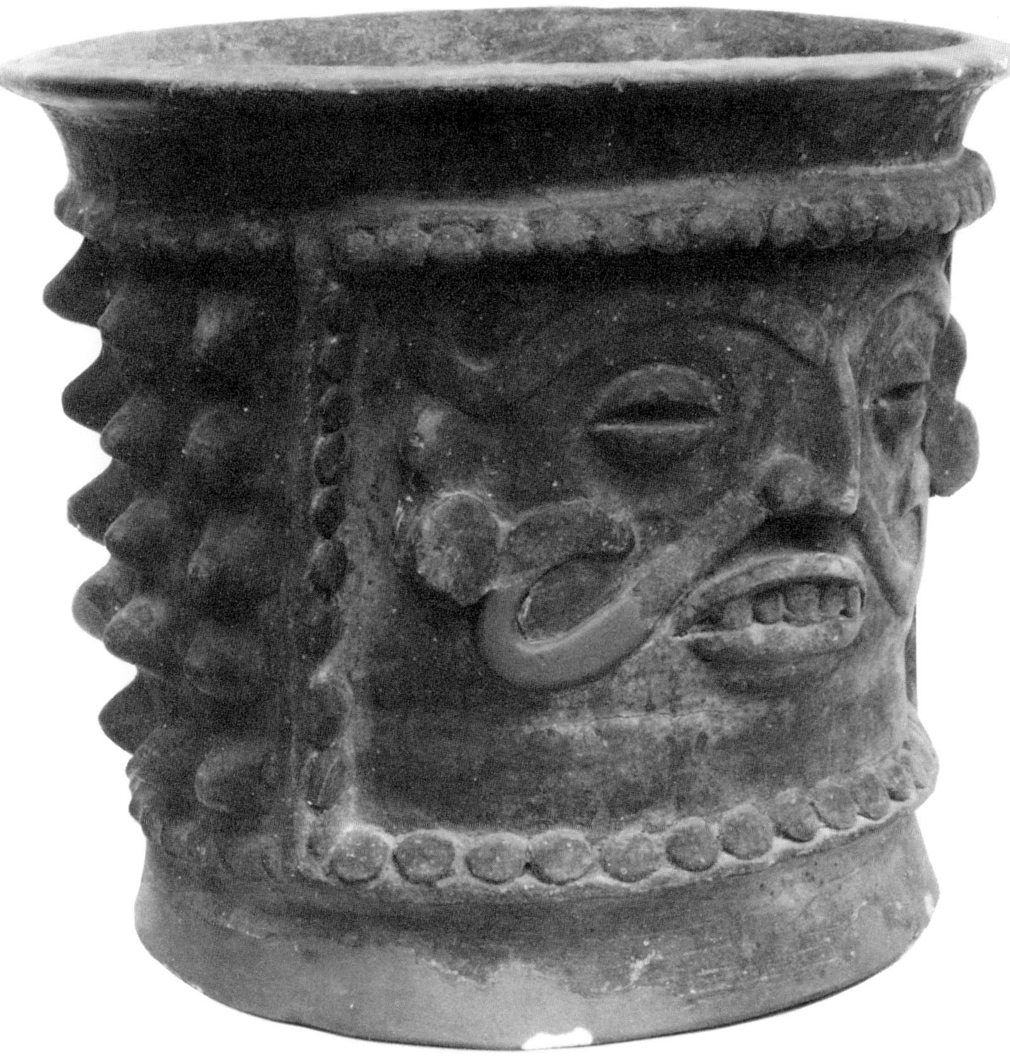

117. Large Blackware Urn
Decorated in high relief by a modeled human head, bordered by appliqué clay knobs, this design shows a definite influence from Central Mexico. Collected by Samuel K. Lothrop. MAYA. Santa Cruz, Quiché, Guatemala. 950-1100. 11″ x 13″. 15/3562.

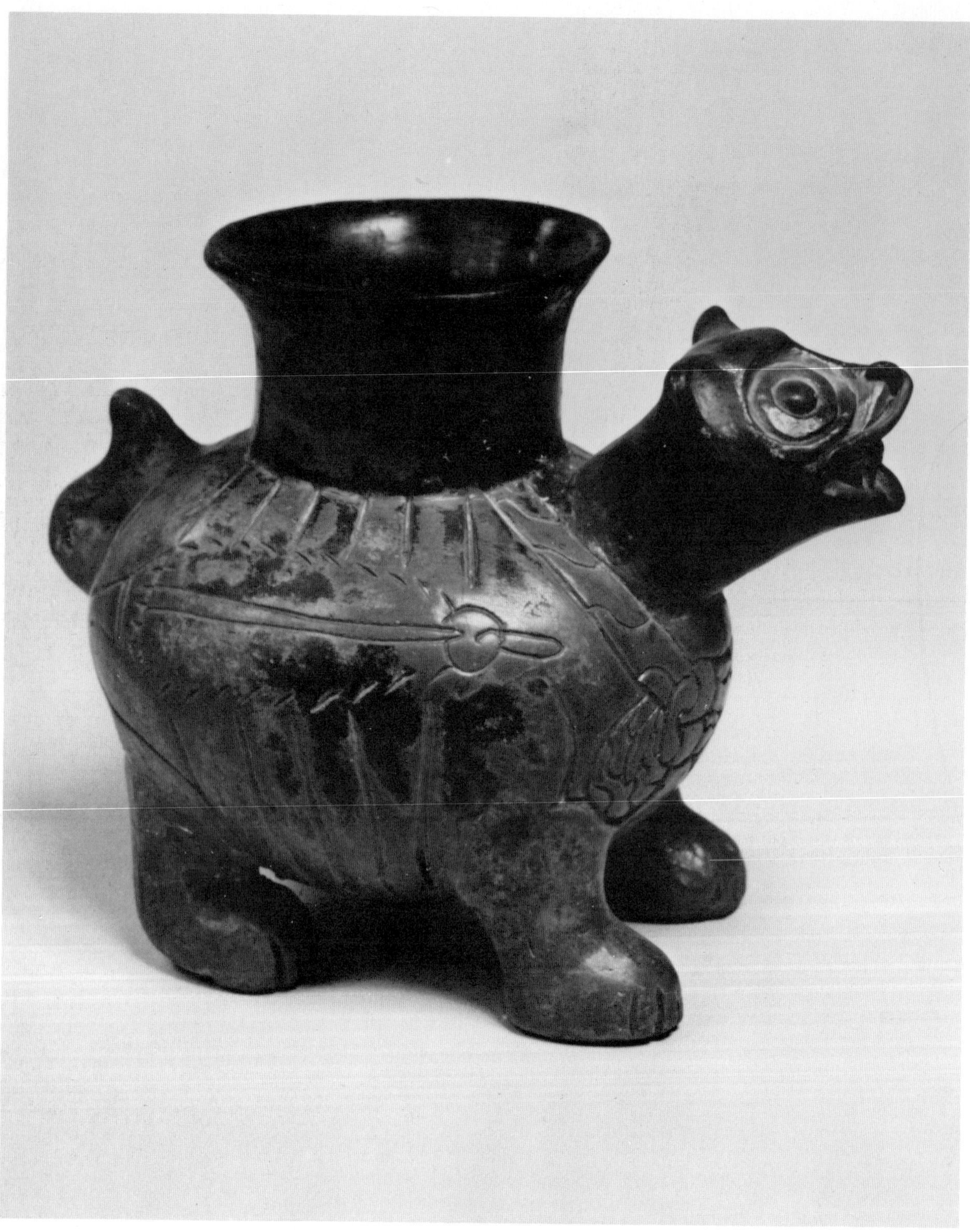

118. Plumbate Animal Effigy

Apparently representing a dog, this is a fine example of plumbate ware, a highly prized pottery developed someplace along the Mexican-Guatemalan border, or perhaps between Guatemala and El Salvador. Plumbate enjoyed a very brief period of manufacture, but was traded widely throughout Central America. MAYA. Antigua, Guatemala. 7½″ x 9″. 950-1200. 23/3436.

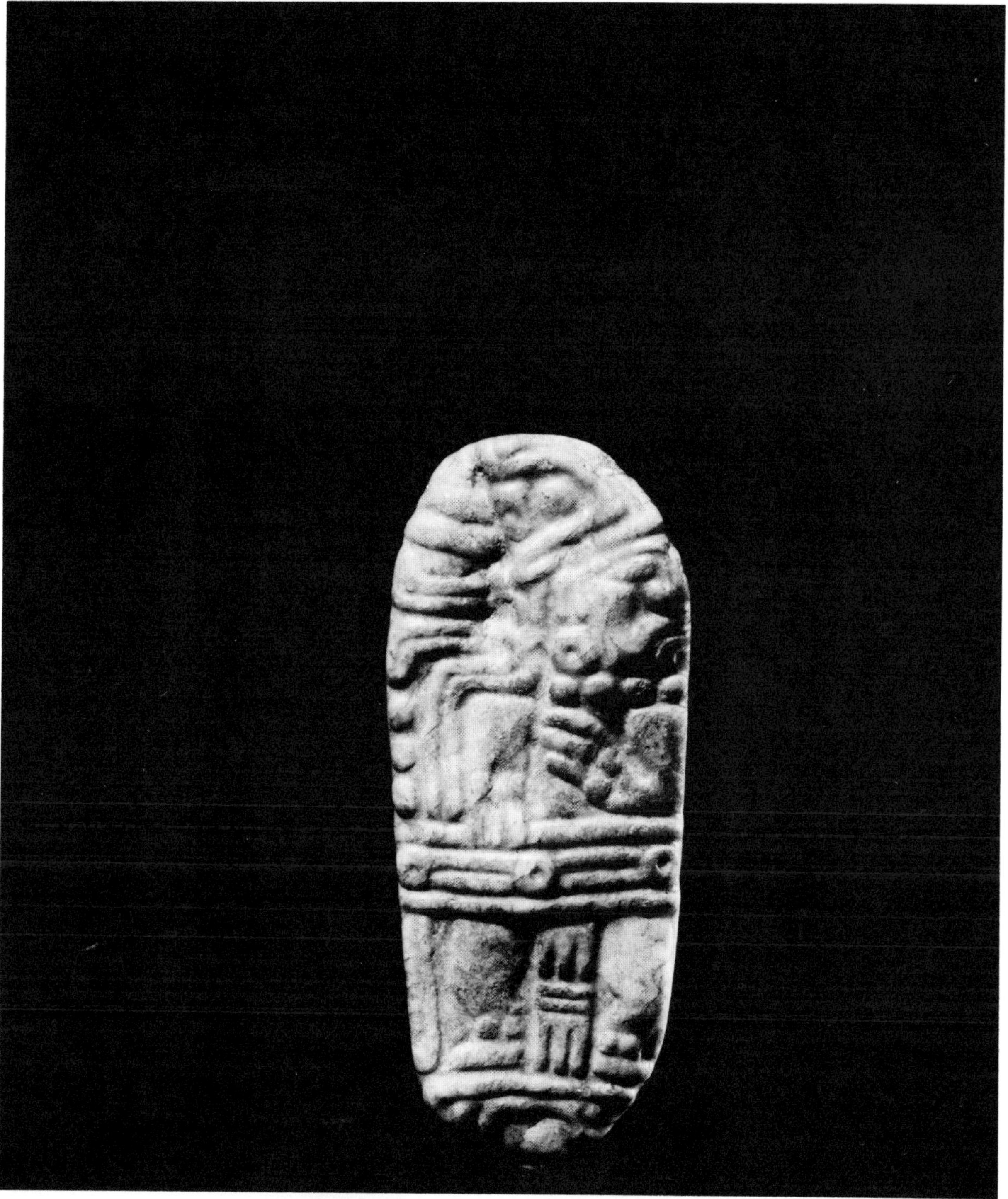

119. Jade Pendant

Jade was one of the most valued possessions of the early Maya people. This pendant shows how the artist fitted his carving to the natural outlines of the stone. This highly abstract design represents a personage in an elaborate headdress and costume, standing in profile. MAYA. Momostenango, Suchitepequez, Guatemala. 550-950. 1¾" x 4½". 24/2961.

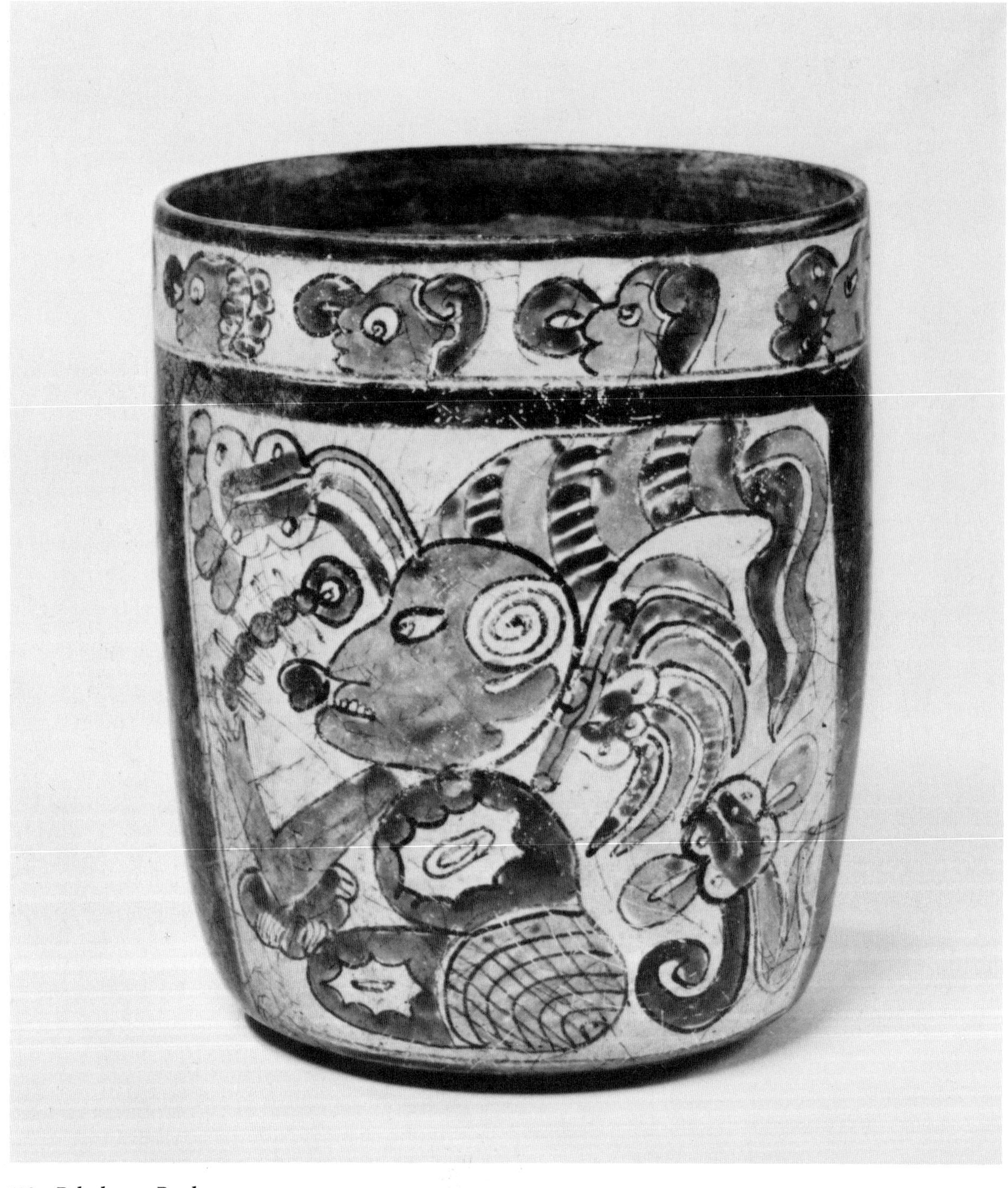

120. Polychrome Bowl
This large, brilliantly painted vessel has the flamboyant quality typical of the Late Classic period. The center panel shows a Maya nobleman with his hair tied in a flaring coiffure, and dressed in colorful textile garments. The designs of a dancer and a musician suggest a relationship of this bowl to a ceremonial pageant. MAYA. El Petén, Guatemala. 550-950. 7¼" x 8½". 24/7491.

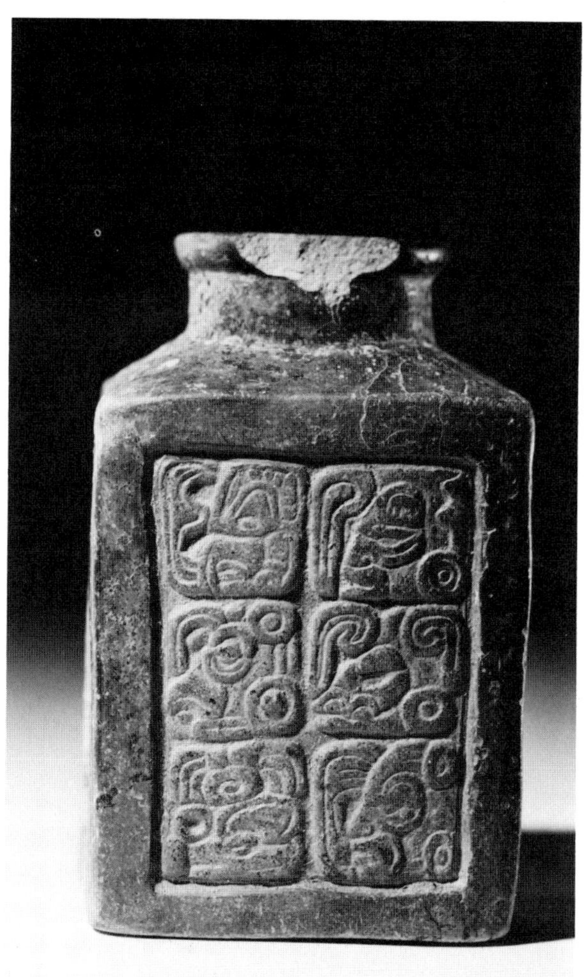

121. Moldmade Glyph Vessel
Unusual for its rectangular shape as well as for the six glyphs impressed into the surface, this grayware container demonstrates the artistic quality of Mayan glyphic writing. Red cinnabar has been rubbed into the surface for contrast. The designs on both sides are identical in detail, confirming the use of a mold. MAYAN. El Petén, Guatemala. 900-1250. 2¼″ x 2¾″ x 4½″. 24/8347.

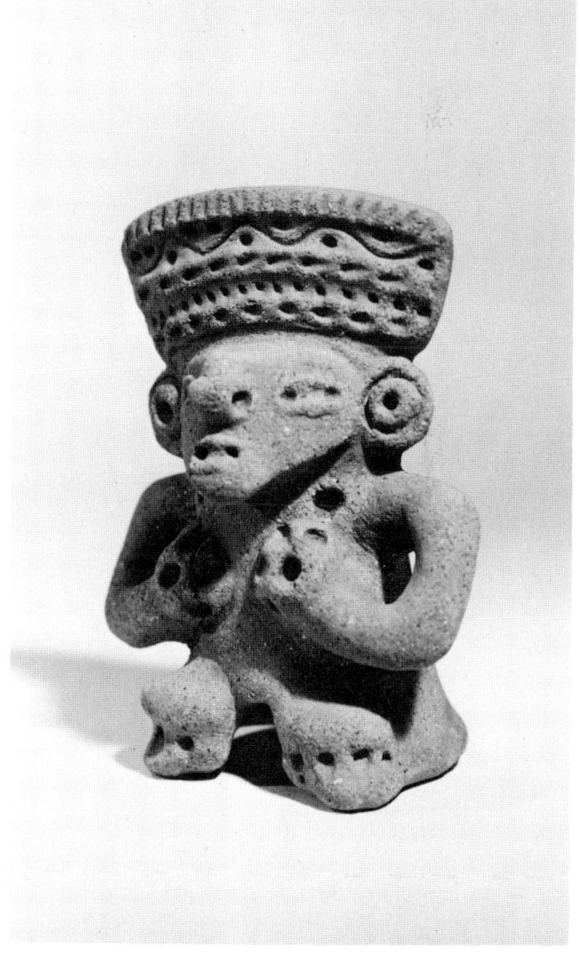

122. Seated Effigy
An example of the unusual ware found on the coastal islands of Honduras, these small figurines are characterized by a combination of linear and punctate decoration. Presented by F. A. Mitchell-Hedges. BAY ISLANDS. Morat, Honduras. 800-1500. 4″ x 5″. 18/7736.

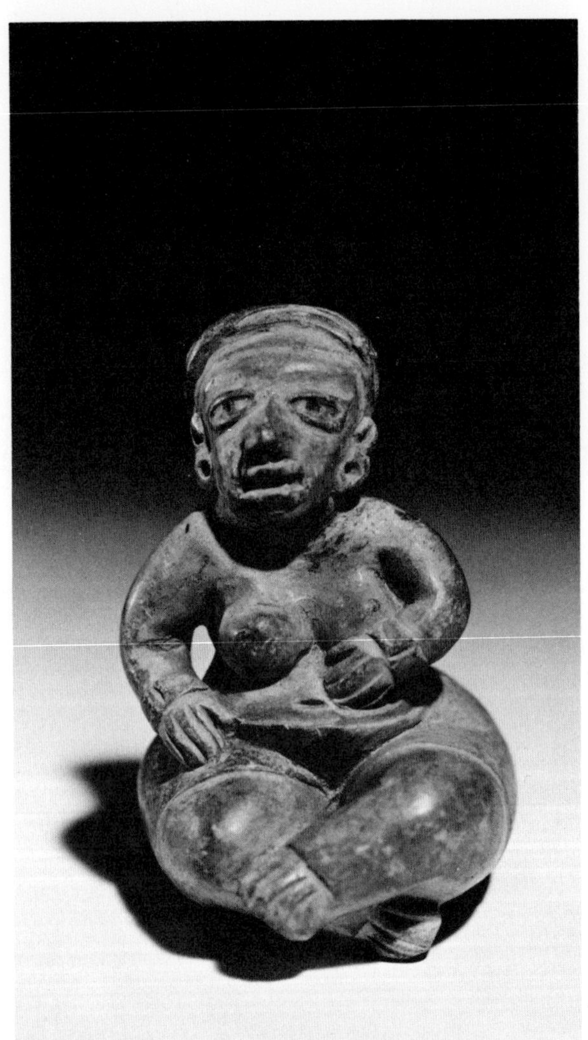

123. Seated Female Figurine
A beautifully modeled seated clay female figurine, this plump lady is wearing a textile bandeau in her hair, and a skirt around her waist. She is typical of the ceramics from the Playa de los Muertos region. Collected before 1875 by Joseph Jones. MAYA. Chaloma, Honduras. 800-500 B.C. 2" x 3½". 7594.

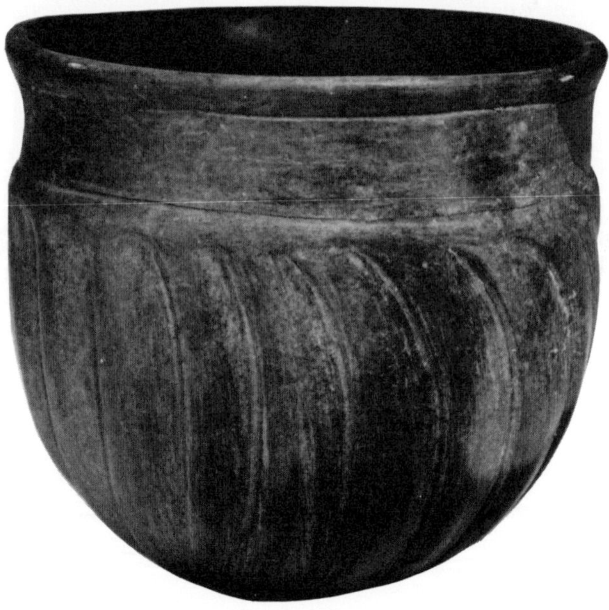

124. Fluted Bowl
With a rounded bottom, and sides gracefully embellished by a swirling fluted design, this grayware bowl is a fine representation of some of the utilitarian wares of the Maya. Collected by Dorothy Poponoe. MAYA. Playa de los Muertos, Ulua River, Honduras. 800-500 B.C. 6¾" x 7¾". 17/8468.

125. Tripod Polychrome Vase
A combination of painting, modeling and carving emphasize the beauty in this cylindrical vase with tripod supports. Much of the original paint is intact. MAYA. Ulua Valley, Honduras. 550-950. 8¼″ x 8½″. 24/3270.

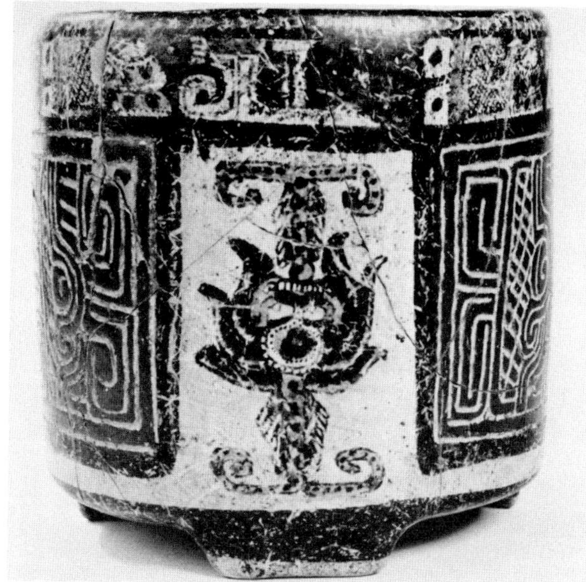

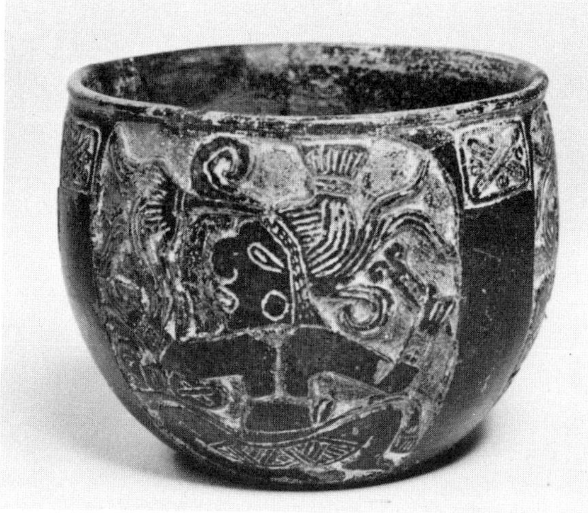

126. Carved Blackware Bowl
This small bowl has a shallow carved design of the usual priest or deity in panels on the sides, holding a wand in his hand. Presented by John S. Williams. MAYA. Ulua Valley, Honduras. 550-950. 4″ x 5¼″. 22/7138.

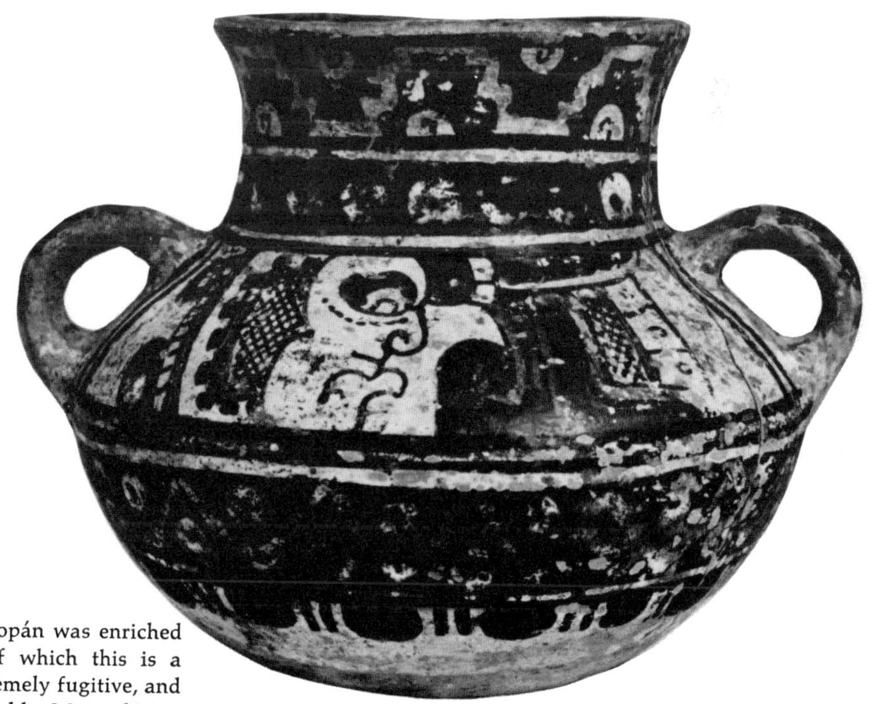

127. Polychrome Loop-handled Vessel
The great ceremonial center at Copán was enriched by brilliantly painted pottery, of which this is a typical example. This paint is extremely fugitive, and complete designs are rare. Presented by Mr. and Mrs. Donald C. Webster. MAYA. Copán, Honduras. 5¾″ x 6″. 550-950. 24/4303.

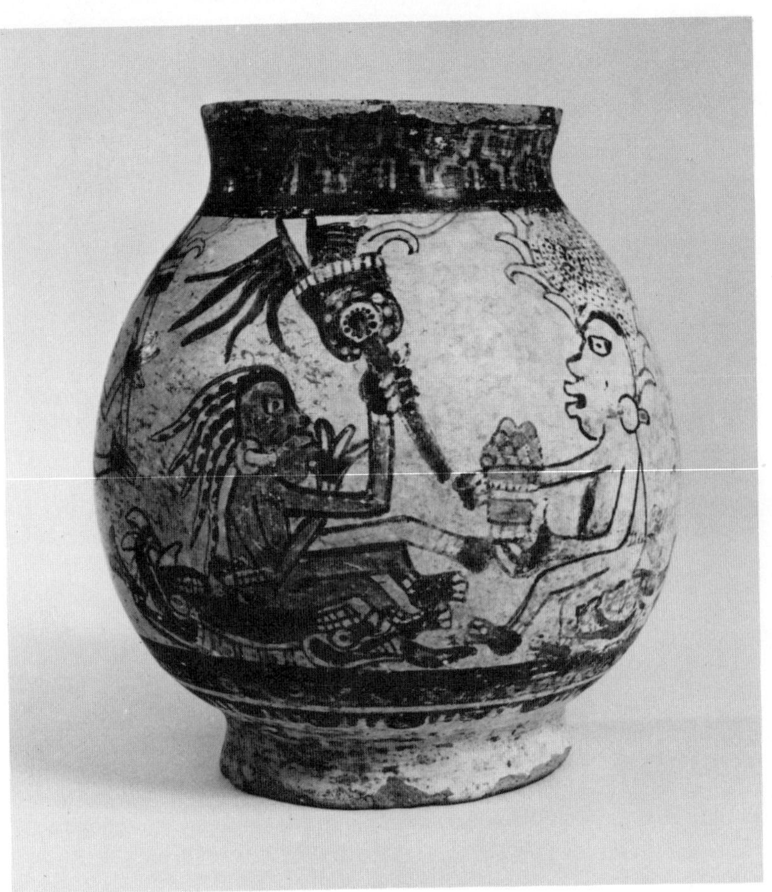

128. Polychrome Vase
An elaborately painted scene of two noblemen, one holding a huge feathered fan, and the other wearing an oversize textile turban. Presented by Alice K. Bache. MAYA. Copán, Honduras. 550-950. 5¾″ x 7½″. 24/4272.

129. Ceramic Shoe Pot
These derive their name from the shape; the off-center form is apparently for insertion into the *comal*, a type of oven used by Native Americans throughout the New World. The ingenious shape allows one to keep the contents of the vessel warm, while still dipping into it for food. Collected by C. Bransford in 1875. NICARAO. Ometepe Island, Nicaragua. 800-1200. 6½″ x 10″ x 6″. 3/2342.

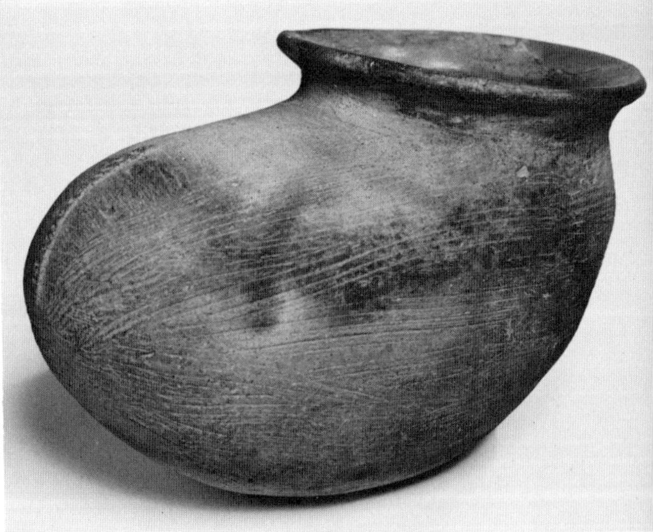

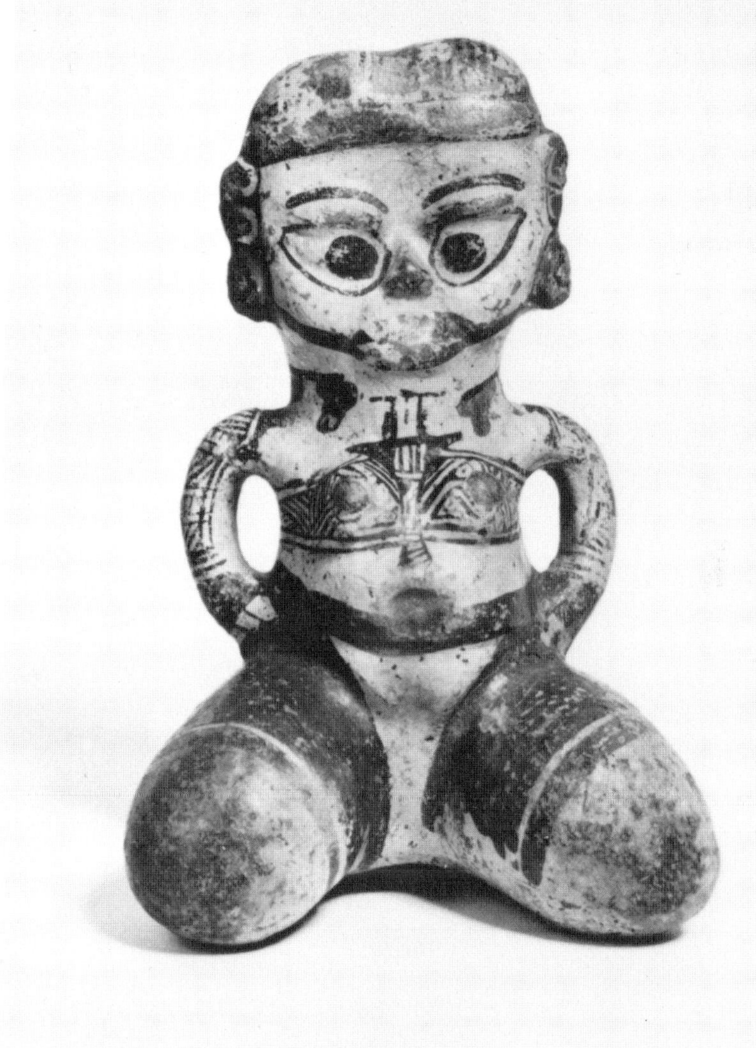

130. Seated Polychrome Figurine
Brilliantly painted effigies are found throughout Nicaragua and Costa Rica. The designs seem to represent body painting, tattooing, or perhaps textiles. This lady, apparently wearing a brassière, is typical of the more northerly area. NICARAO. Lake Nicaragua, Grenada, Nicaragua. 800-1200. 5¾″ x 7¾″. 13/6834.

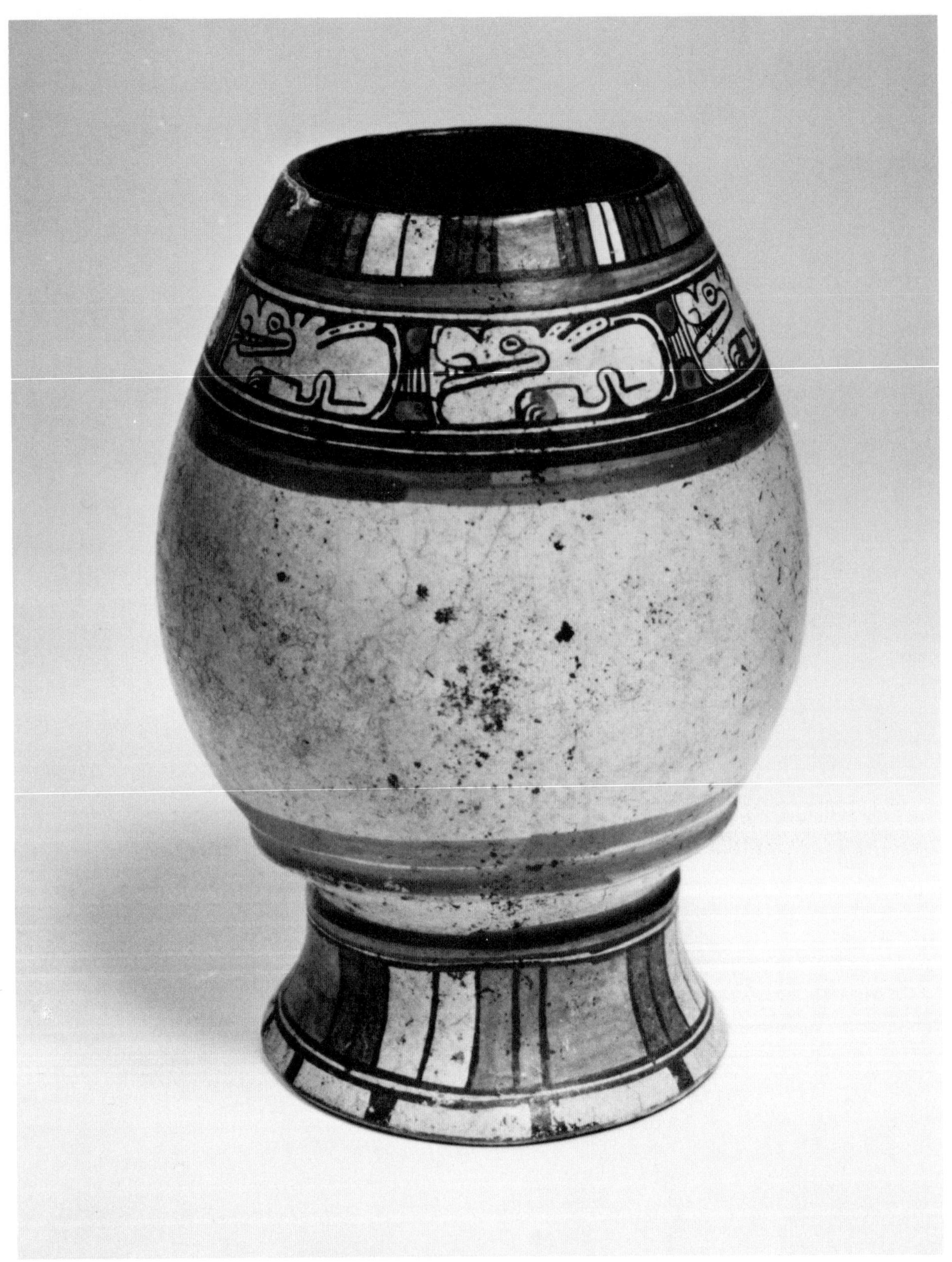

131. Globular Ring-base Vase
The cream slip on this graceful vessel gives a strong contrast to the brilliantly painted designs on the base and the rim. NICARAO. Moyogalpa, Ometepe Island, Nicaragua. 800-1200. 5½″ x 9″. 24/3695.

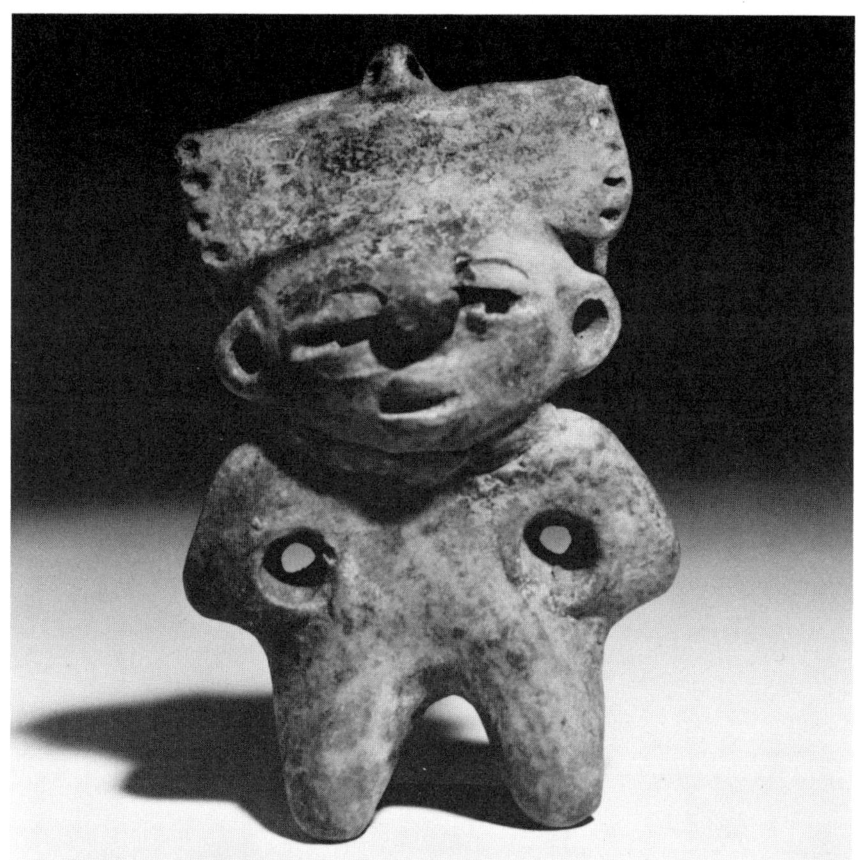

132. Buffware Figurine
The solid clay figurines with spread legs and arms akimbo are characteristic of this region of Central America. The peculiar headdress may represent a textile bandeau with a forehead bow. Presented by Theodore T. Foley. PIPIL. El Trunjo, El Salvador. 200 B.C.-550 A.D. 3½" x 5¼". 24/6306.

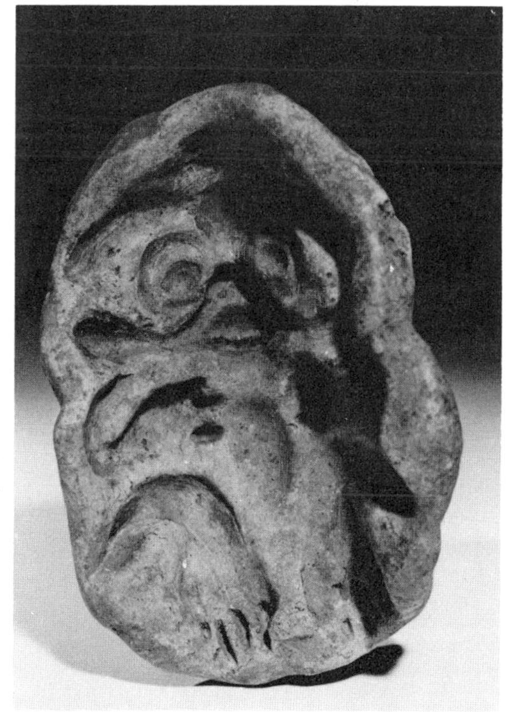

133. Clay Figurine Mold
The use of molds to produce large quantities of clay objects was common in prehistoric America. The original object was pressed into wet clay which is then fired, providing a mold from which many duplicates can be made. These are rare, since they usually become broken and discarded after years of use. Presented by Theodore T. Foley. PIPIL. Chalchuapa, El Salvador. 550-950. 3" x 4½". 24/6188.

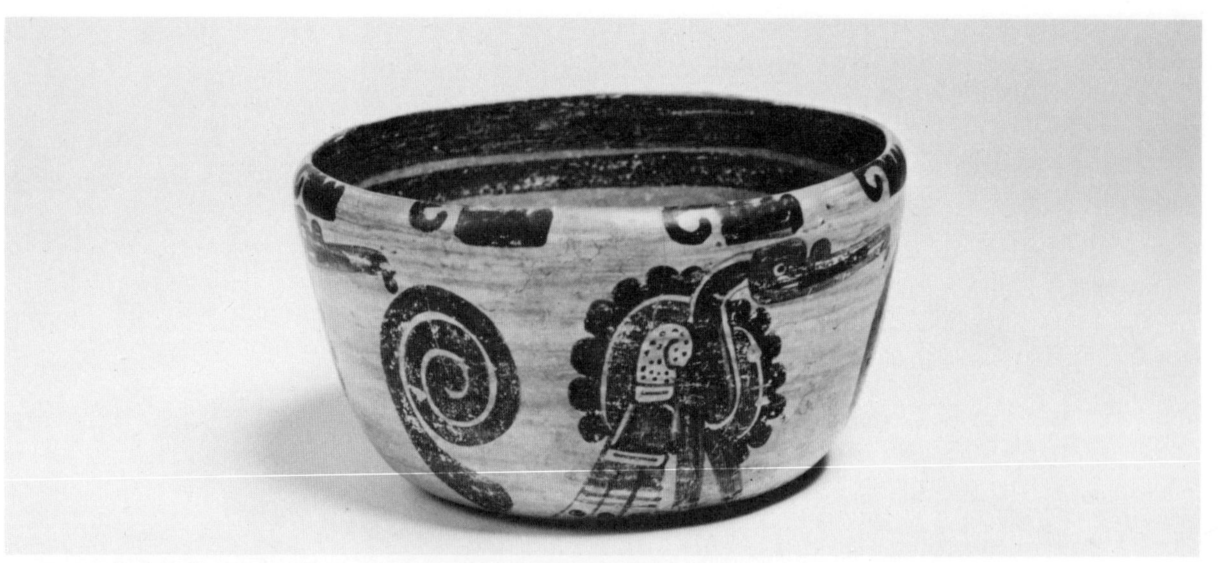

134. Small Polychrome Bowl
One of the brilliantly-painted Mayan ceramic vessels from this area is represented by this painting of a turkey with a spread tail. Collected by Marshall H. Saville. MAYA. San Salvador, El Salvador. 550-950. 4" x 7½". 9/9556.

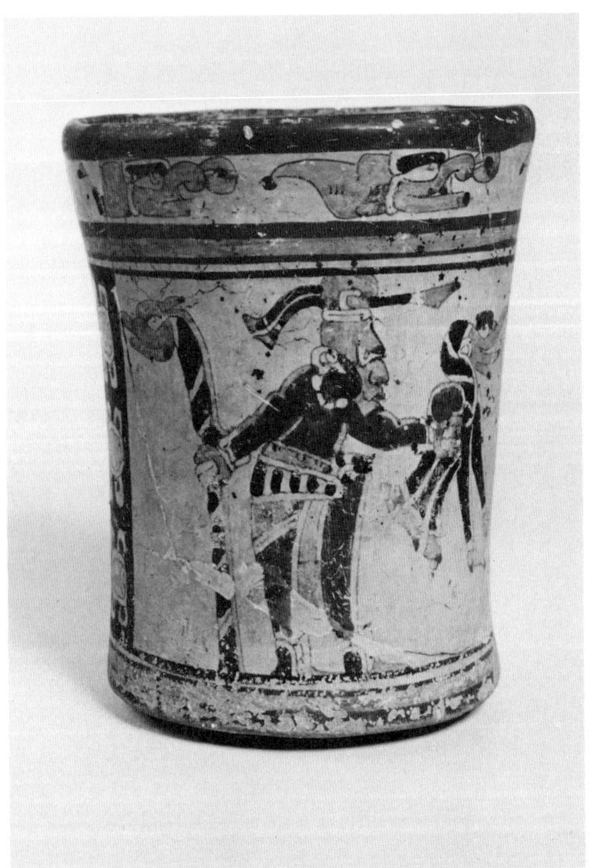

135. Painted Cylindrical Vase
This is the classic form of pottery from the Maya region; the design portrays a man in profile, holding an animal-headed staff in one hand, and a bird in the other. Presented by James B. Ford. MAYA. San Salvador, El Salvador. 550-950. 5¾" x 7¾". 9/9571.

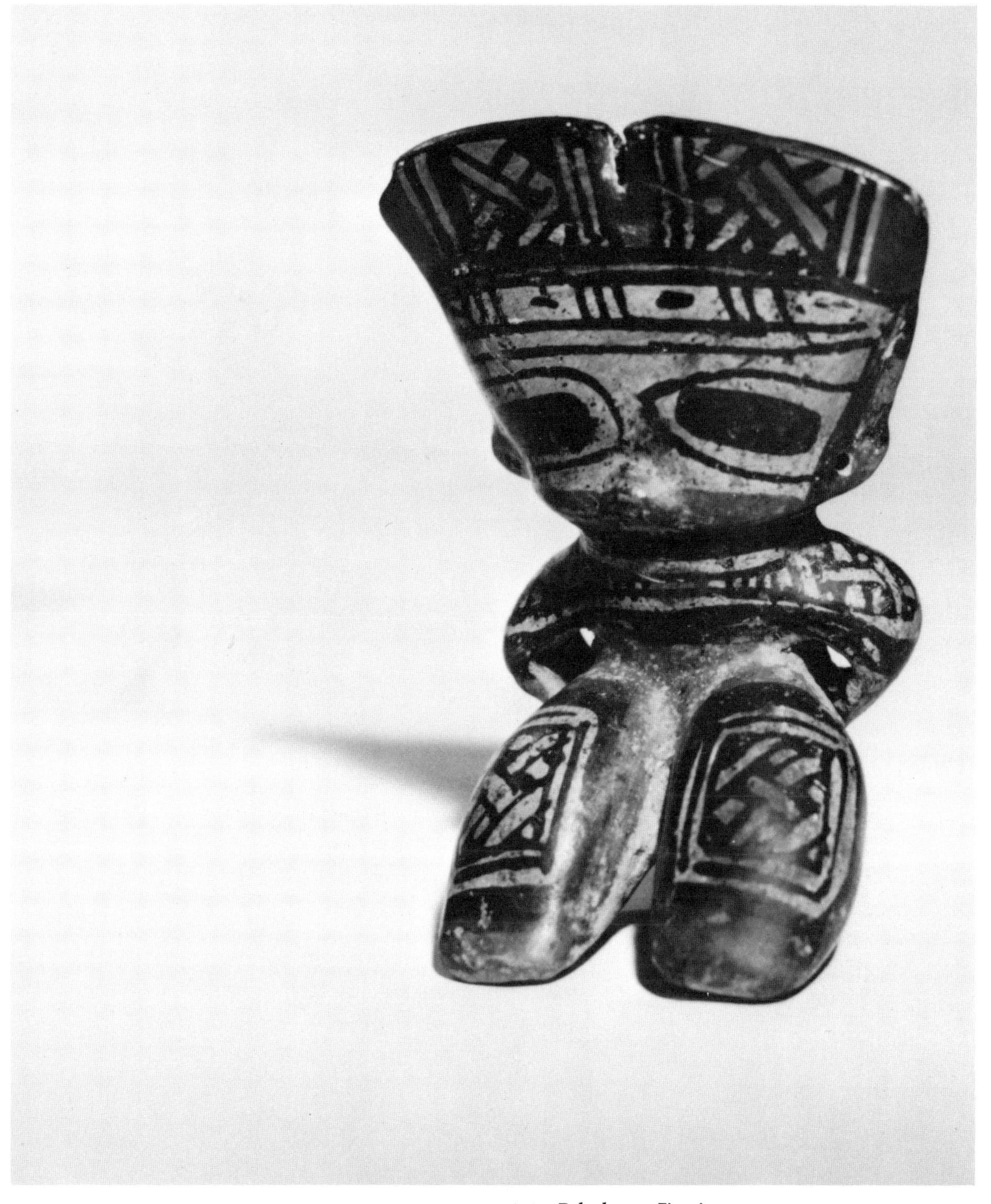

136. Polychrome Figurine

These seated clay effigies are found in many sizes; the decorations may represent tattooing, or textile motifs. The headdress probably represents a basketry "crown" or band; these are known to have been worn in the area, usually decorated with feathers thrust into the sides. CHOROTEGA? Florida, Línea Vieja, Costa Rica. 500-800. 3½" x 5½". 23/4167.

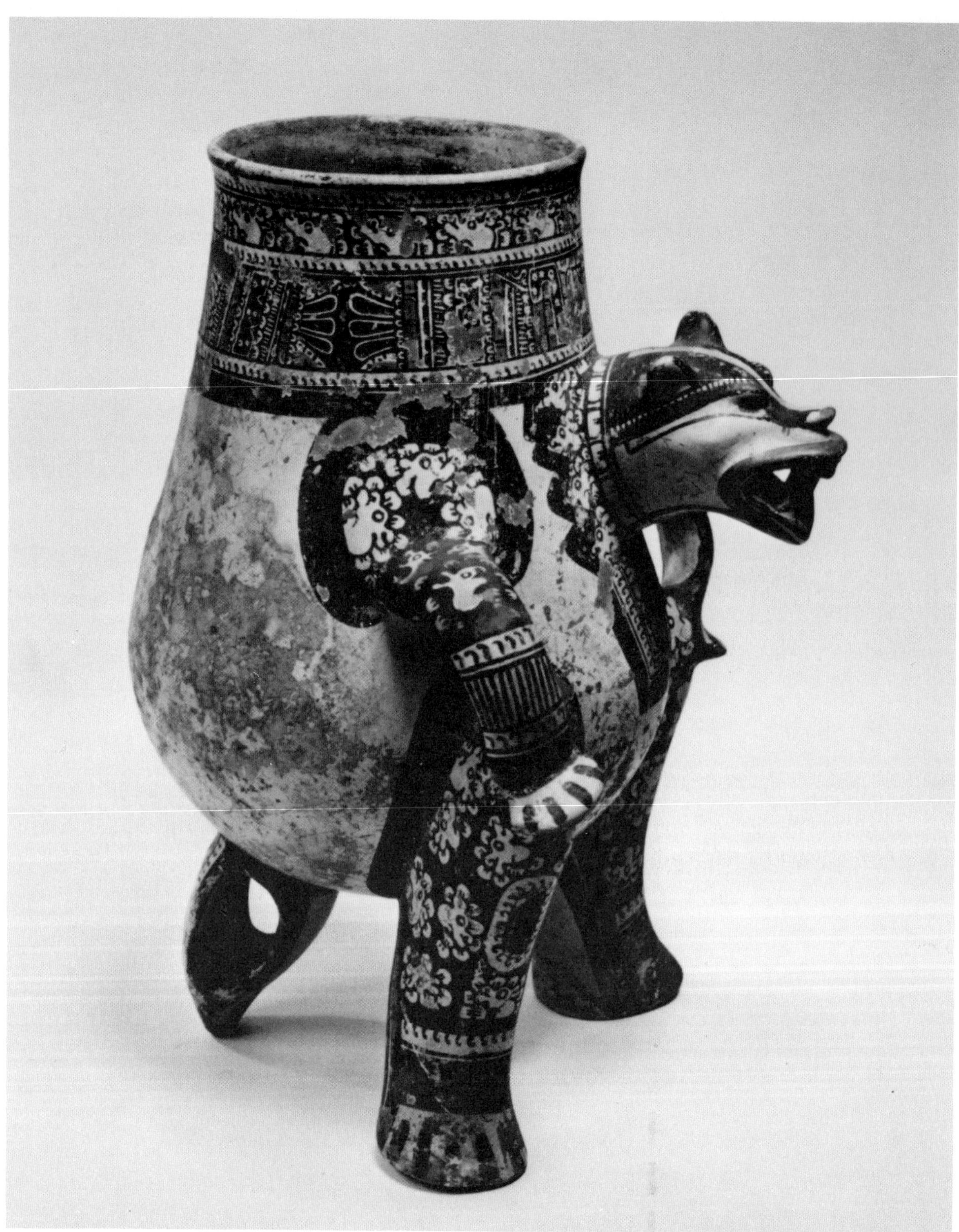

137. Polychrome Jaguar Vase
One of the most characteristic ceramic objects from this area are these jaguar vases with large globular bodies, brightly painted in psuedo-glyph designs. CHOROTEGA? Filadelfia, Guanacaste, Costa Rica. 800-1200. 11″ x 15¼″. 19/7240.

138. Large Polychrome Urn

(See color insert facing page 160)

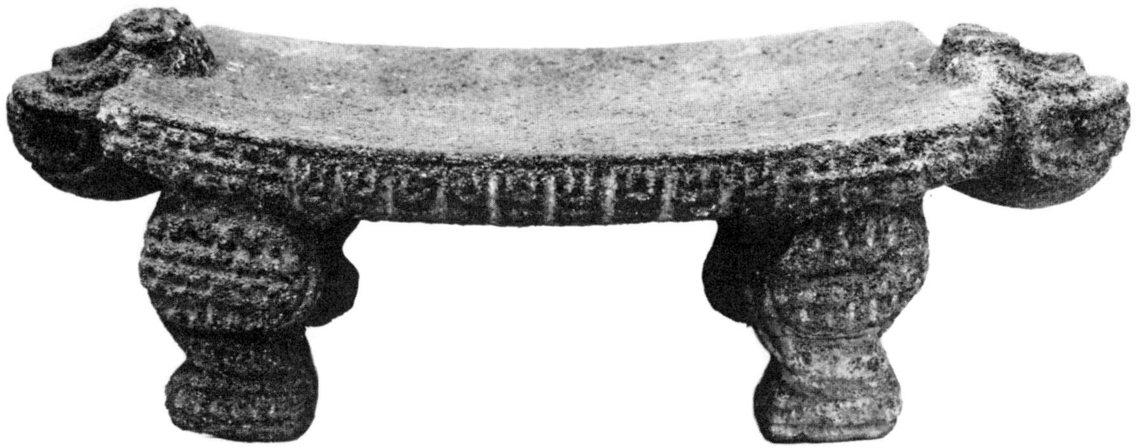

139. Ceremonial Metate

Carefully carved slabs, called *metates,* are common throughout lower Middle America. They were used for grinding up corn and other materials. This design, representing a two-headed jaguar, has intricately carved designs on the sides and legs. Presented by Minor C. Keith. CHOROTEGA? Las Mercedes, Costa Rica. 500-1200. 5″ x 15½″. 7/8152.

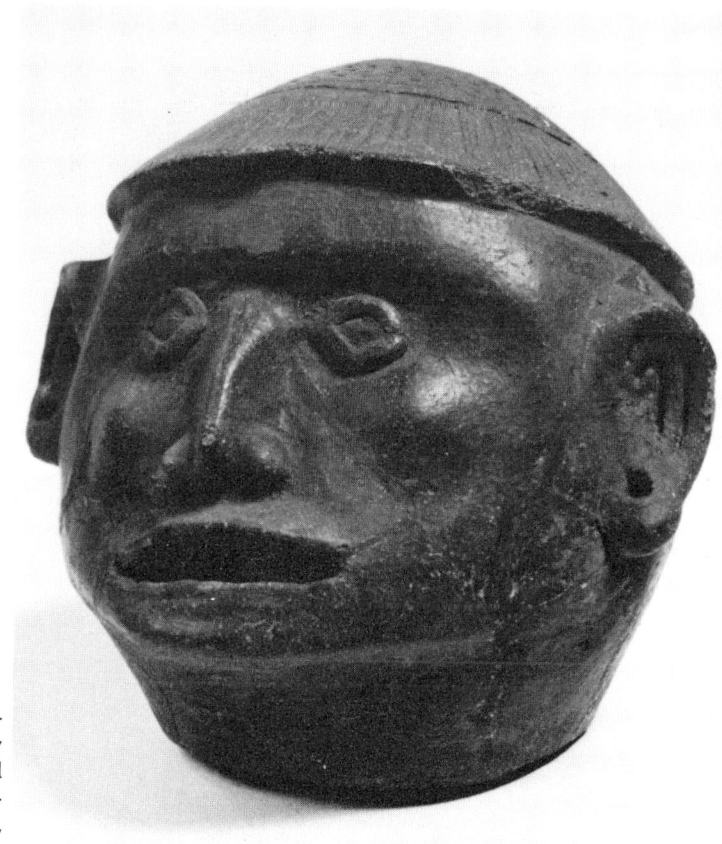

140. Redware Trophy Head Effigy

The taking of heads as trophies was a common practice in Middle America, and this modeled head effigy would seem to represent the custom. The perforated ear lobes may have held ornaments at one time. Presented by Minor C. Keith. CHOROTEGA? Las Mercedes, Costa Rica. 500-1500. 6″ x 6¾″. 7/5127.

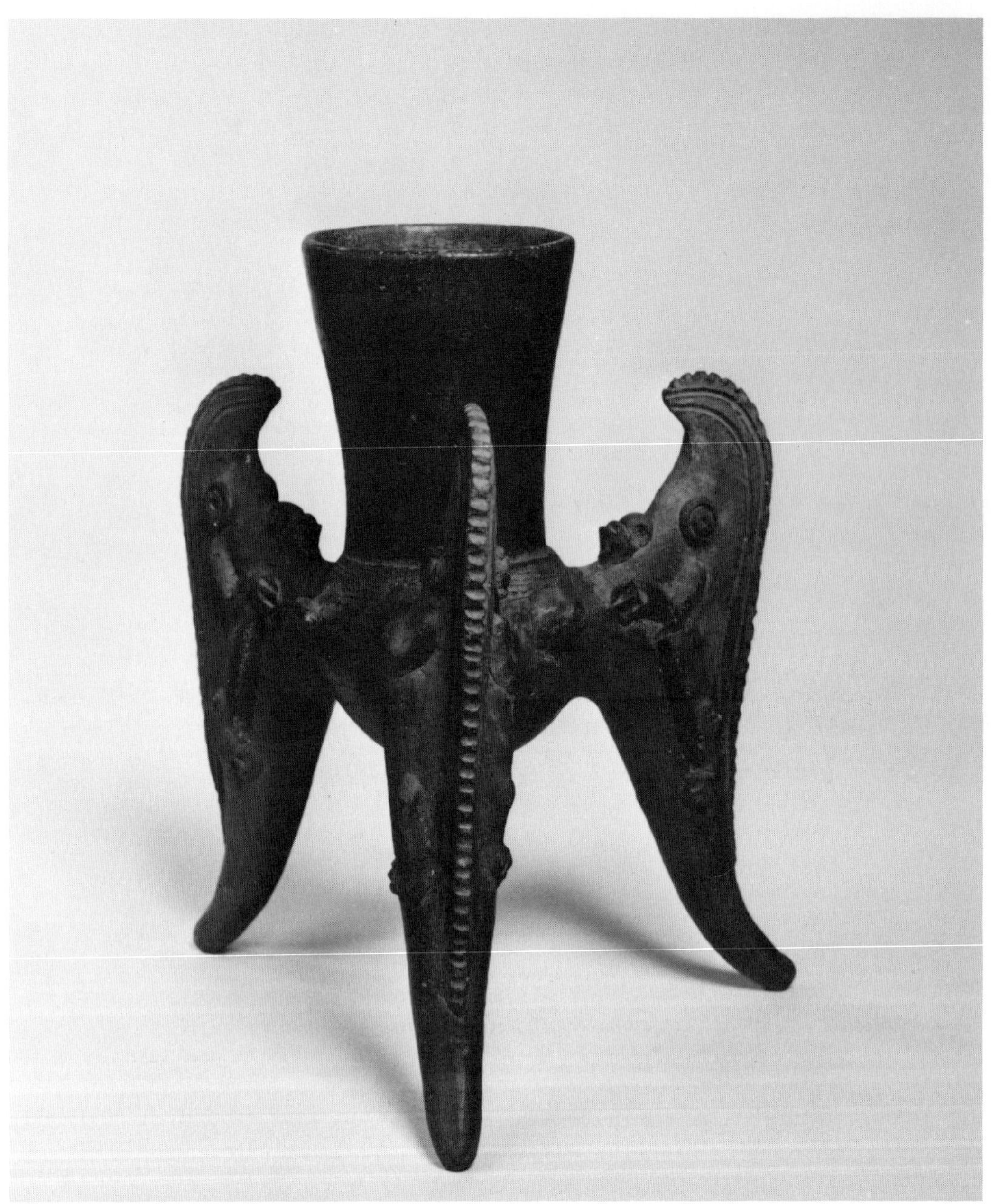

141. Brownware Tripodal Vase
One of the unusual forms familiar to this region are these vessels with elaborately modeled, molded, or carved supports. This example has legs apparently representing the crested iguana. There are pebbles in the bodies, providing a rattle. CHOROTEGA? Las Mercedes, Costa Rica. 500-800. 8½" x 11". 23/5572.

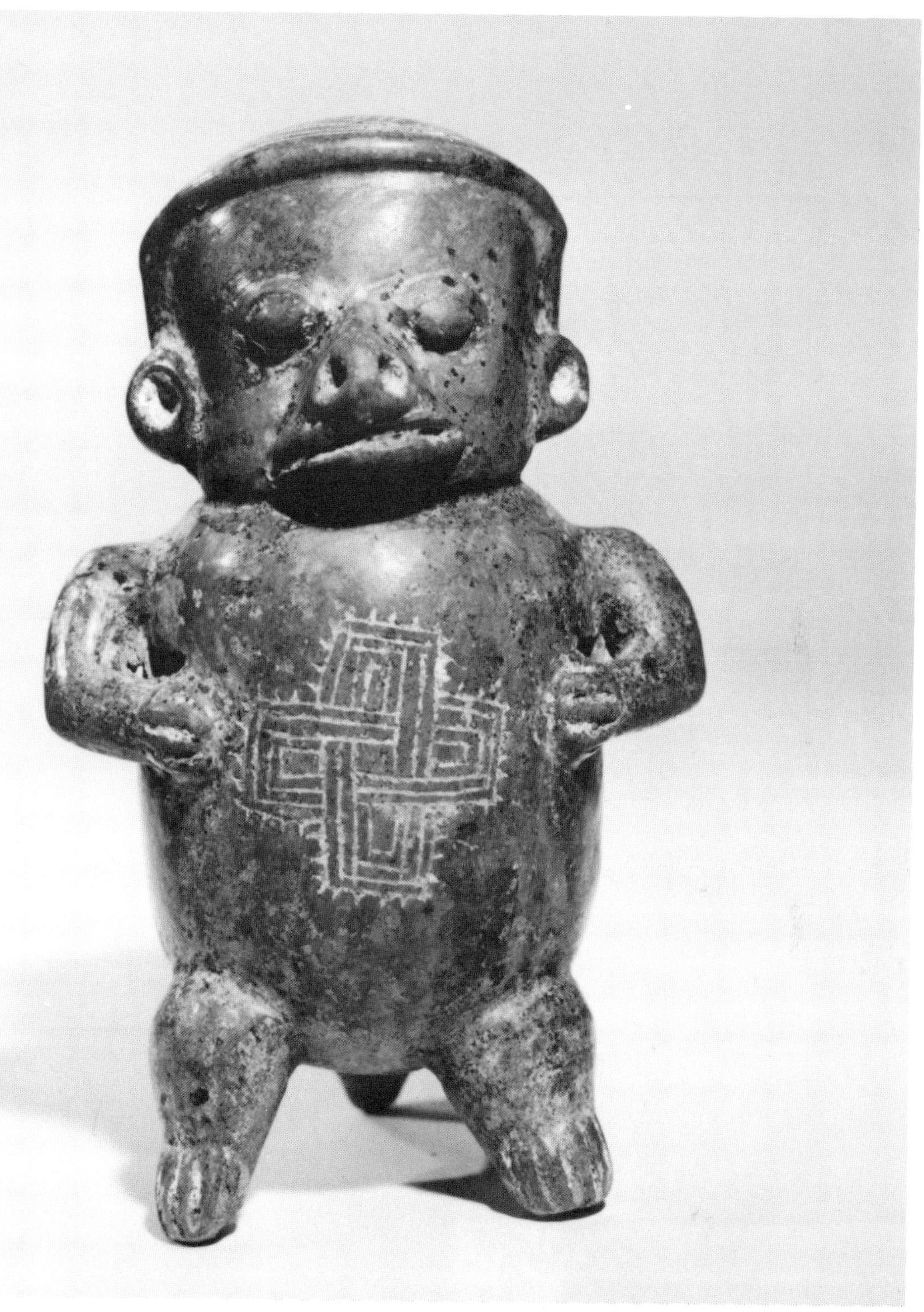

142. Hollow Redware Whistle
This figurine, in the form of an anthropomorphic effigy, has a fine incised decoration on the breast, which has been filled with white paint for contrast. NICOYA. Guanacaste, Costa Rica. 100-500. 4½" x 6¼". 23/5562.

143. Zoömorphic Incensario Cover

An abstracted modelling representing an iguana, sometimes confused with the old Crocodile God. These objects are the upper part of a two-piece *incensario*; the smoke was allowed to flow through the holes cut through the vessel. They are known in a variety of grotesque forms and sizes. Presented by Dr. and Mrs. Arthur M. Sackler. Nicoya. Guanacaste, Costa Rica. 800-1200. 8″ x 9¼″. 23/6310.

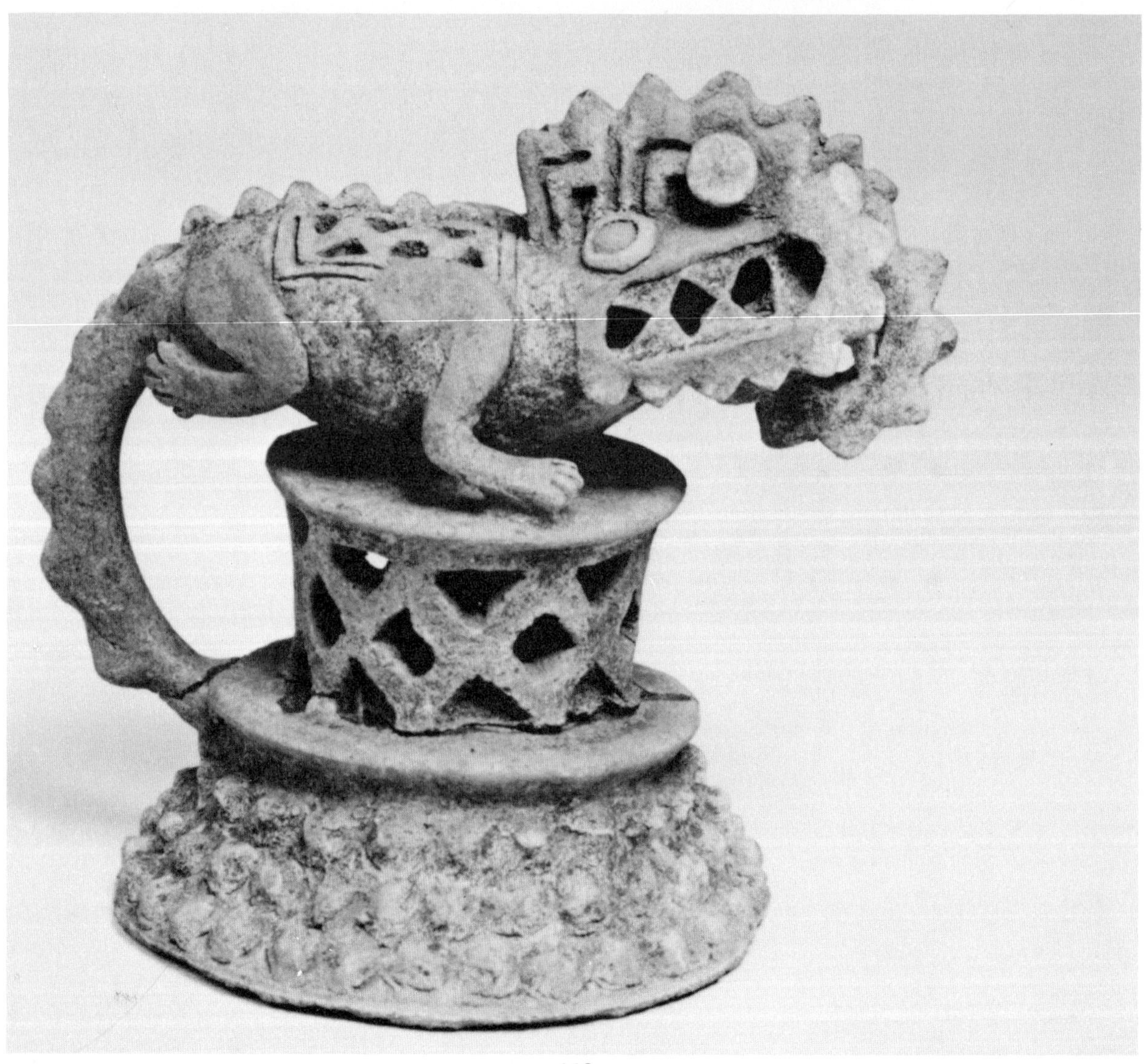

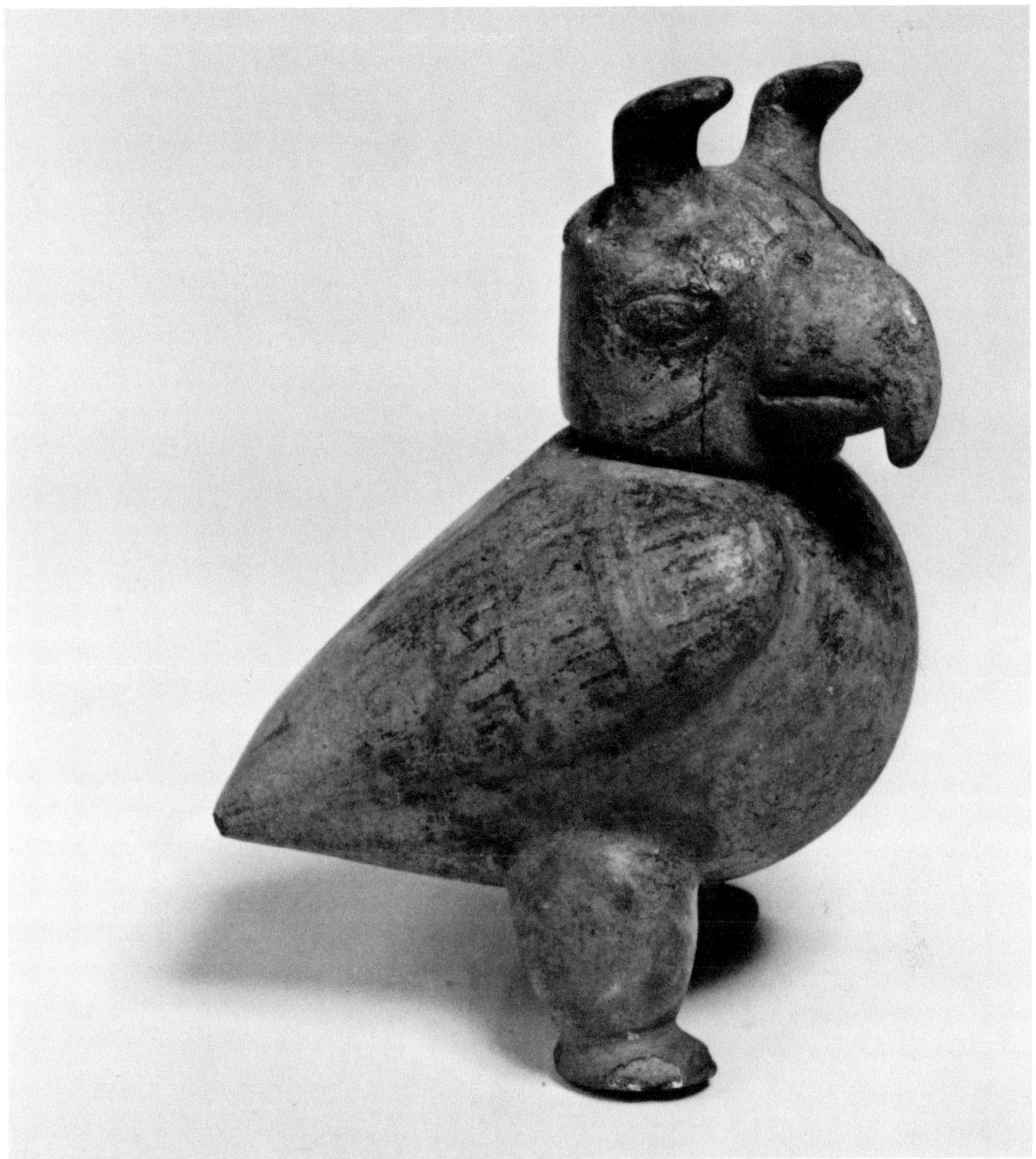

144. Two-piece Container
This effigy of a harpy eagle with a smooth, rotund body, is a fine example of a container in which the head and the body are made separately. By removing the head, objects can be placed within the body. Holes allow both parts to be fastened together for security. CHOROTEGA. Guanacaste, Costa Rica. 800-1500. 8″ x 8½″. 22/9216.

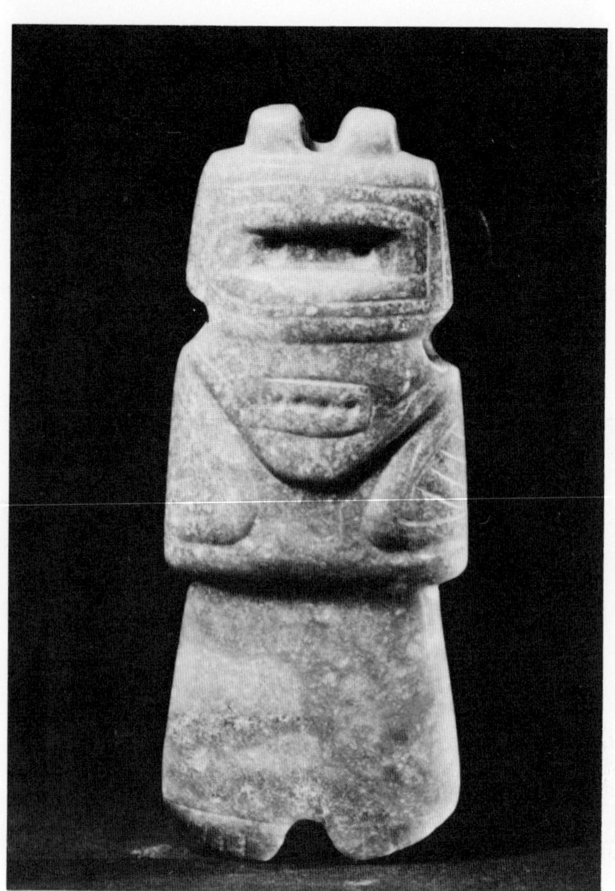

145. Jadeite Axe God

A particular form of jadeite found in the Costa Rican region was a popular material for ornaments throughout this southern area. These small pendants, commonly termed 'axe gods', were one of the most frequently worked forms. Nicoya. Guanacaste, Costa Rica. 300 B.C.-500 A.D. 4¼″ x 1¾″. 23/5748.

146. Carved Mace Head

The use of carved and polished stone club heads was widespread, and some of these were veritable esthetic masterpieces. This serpentine *maza* represents a jaguar head; a wooden staff was inserted into the vertical opening for use. Nicoya. Guanacaste, Costa Rica. 800-1500. 2¼″ x 3½″. 24/1043.

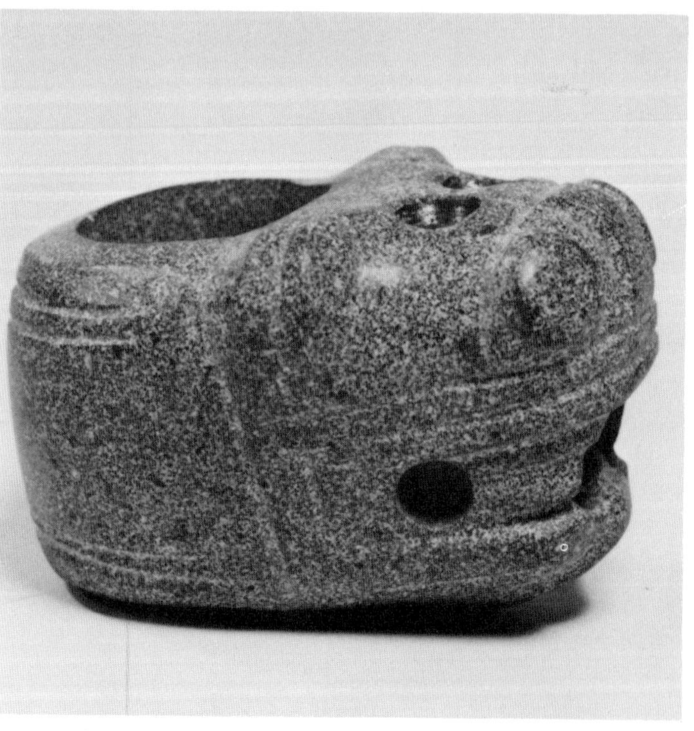

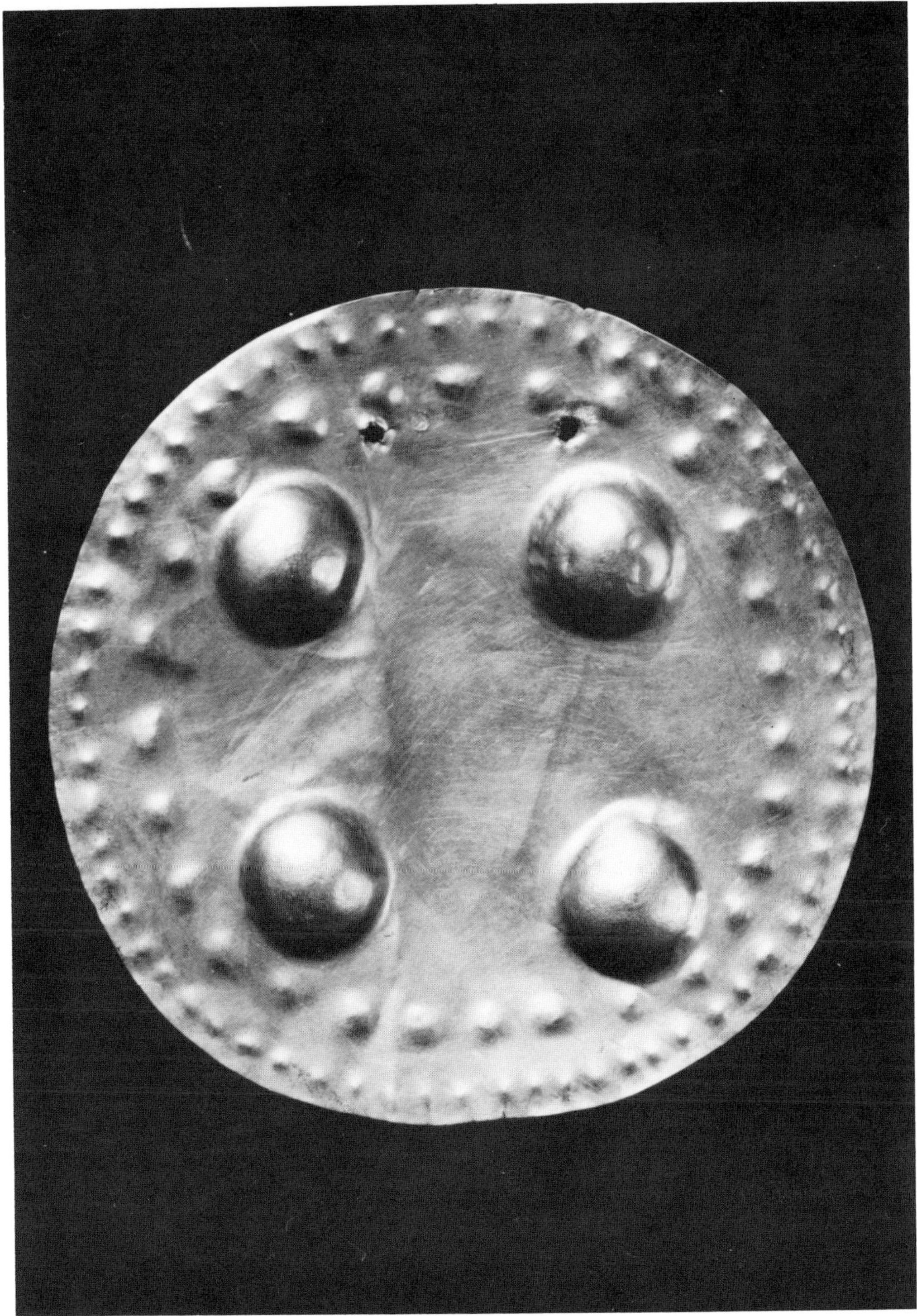

147. Embossed Gold Plaque
Hammered from a thin sheet of gold, this was worn on the breast as an ornament. These are found in many sizes, from 2 to 16 inches in diameter. CHOROTEGA? Las Indianas, Siquieres, Costa Rica. 1100-1525. Weight, 45.5 grams. D: 4¾″. 23/5013.

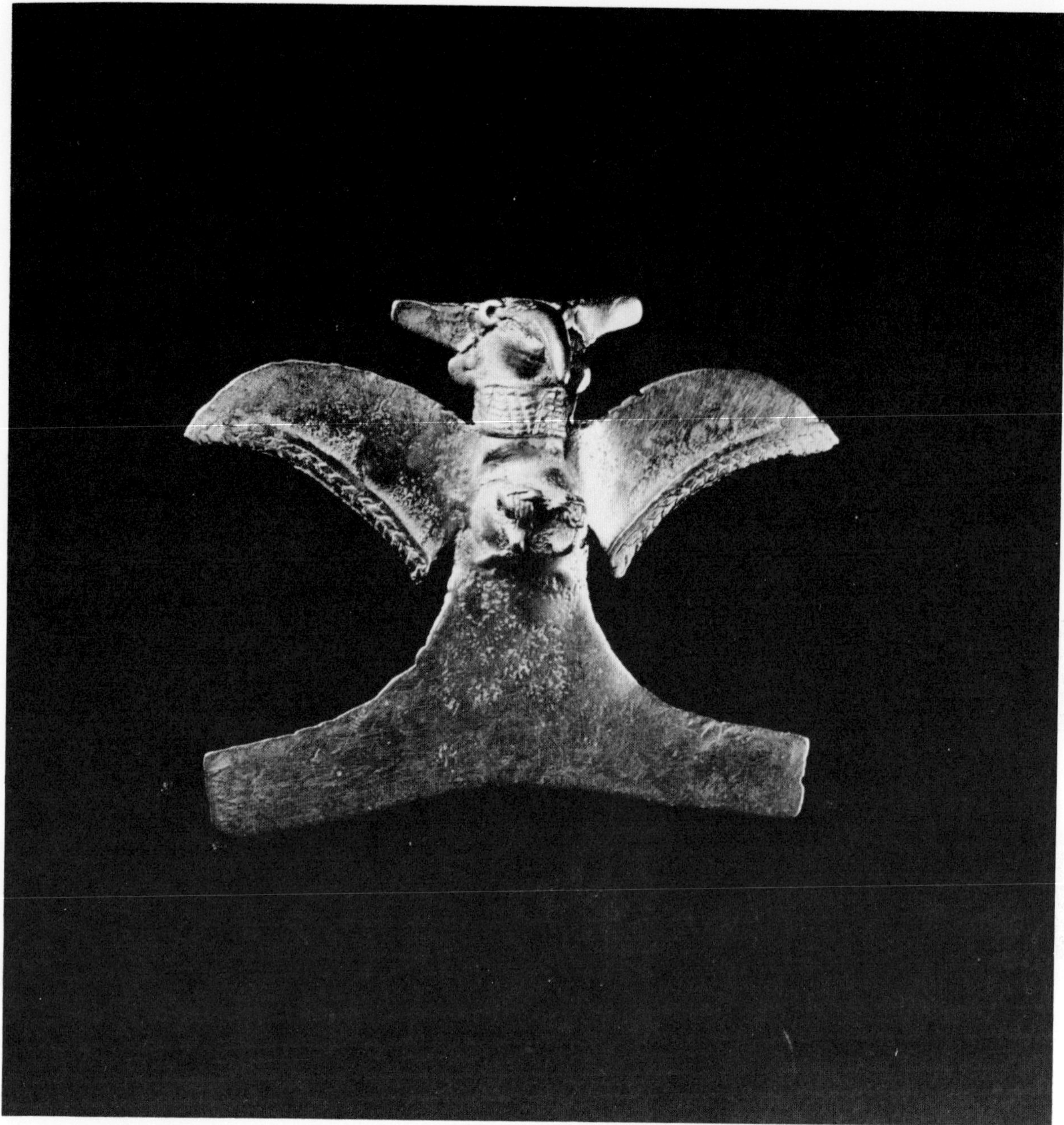

148. Cast Gold Pendant
Commonly called a *huaco,* these ornaments representing a bird are the most frequently seen cast gold objects from this region. Presented by Morton D. May. NICOYA. Guanacaste, Costa Rica. 1100-1525. Weight, 72 grams. 3″ x 4″. 24/4220.

149. Globular Bisque-ware Olla

For sheer beauty of form, the biscuit ware pottery from Costa Rica and Panama is one of the most remarkable ceramic productions of the Americas. The walls of these vessels are almost paper thin, and the tiny *adornos* which often decorate the shoulders of the vessels add a touch of piquant humor. Collected by Eva M. Harte. CHIRIQUÍ. Chiriquí, Panama. 1200-1525. 9" x 10¼". 23/6748.

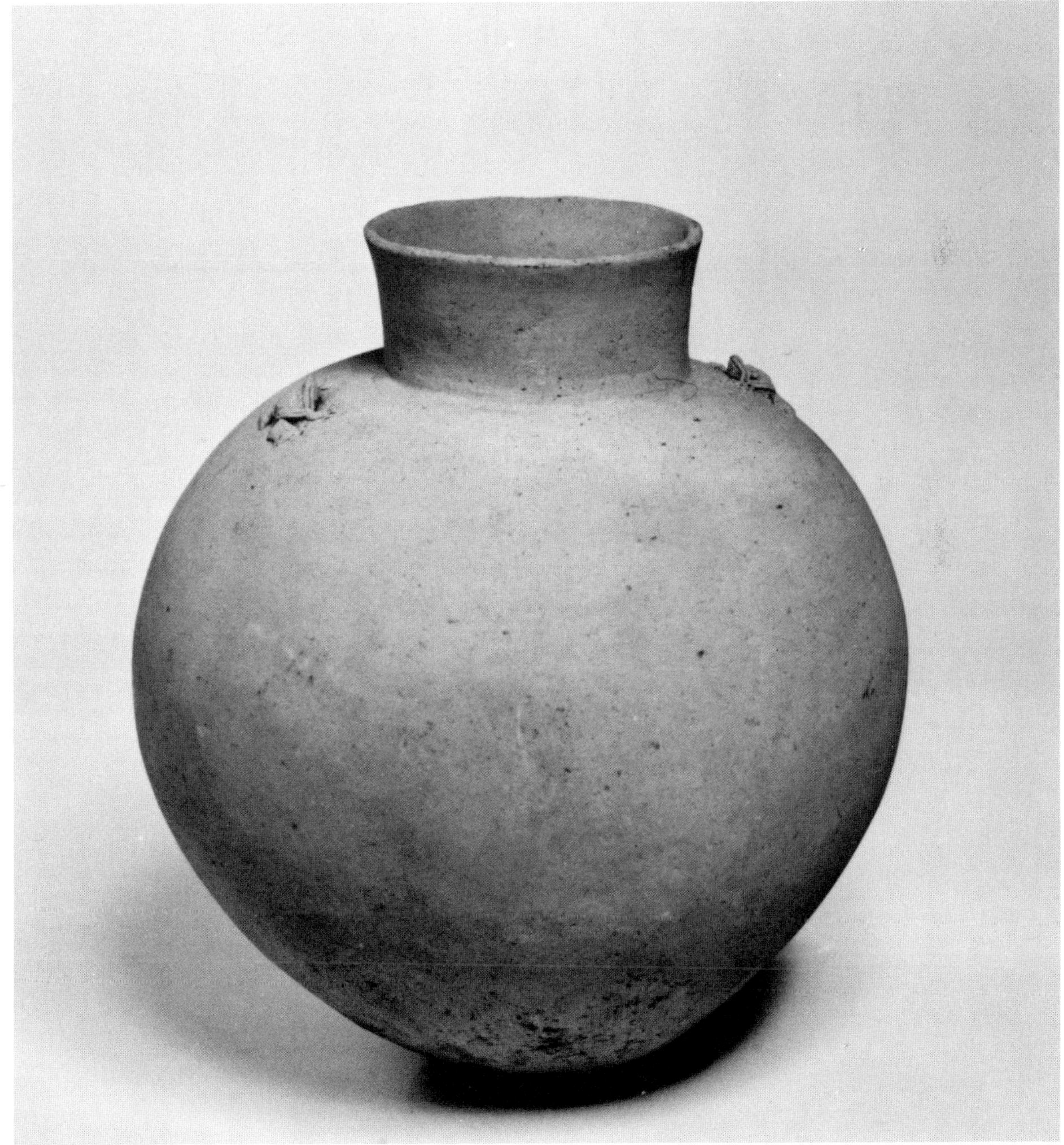

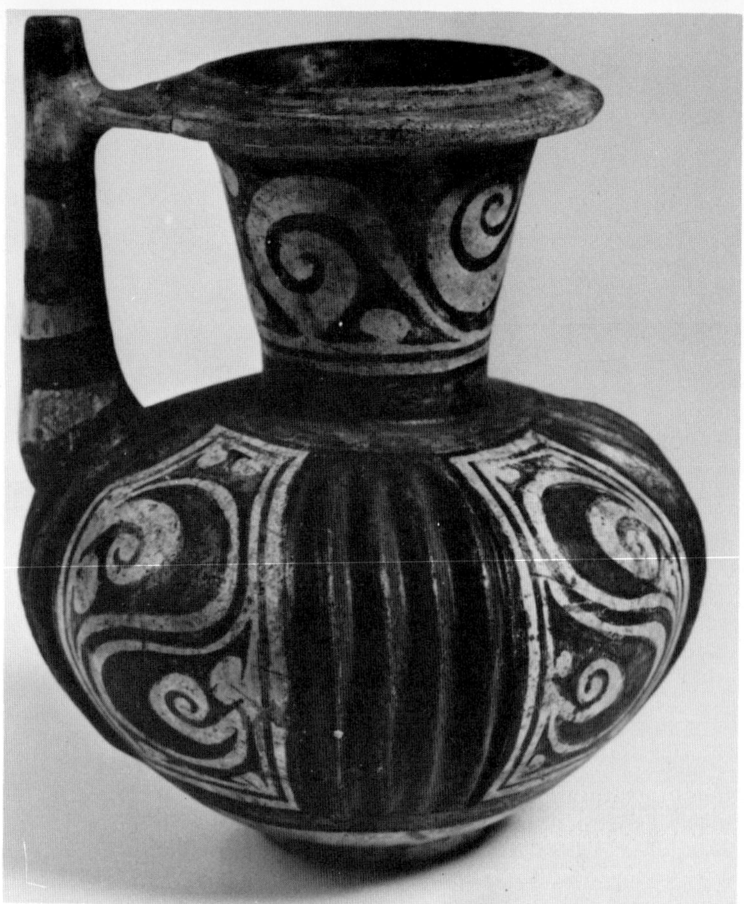

150. Polychrome Spouted Vessel
The swirling lines on these ceramic objects give them a freedom of design which makes them recognizable in any ceramic collection. This is a fine example of the classic style. Excavated by Neville A. Harte. COCLÉ. Río Grande, Coclé, Panama. 500-800. 6″ x 8¾″. 23/6753.

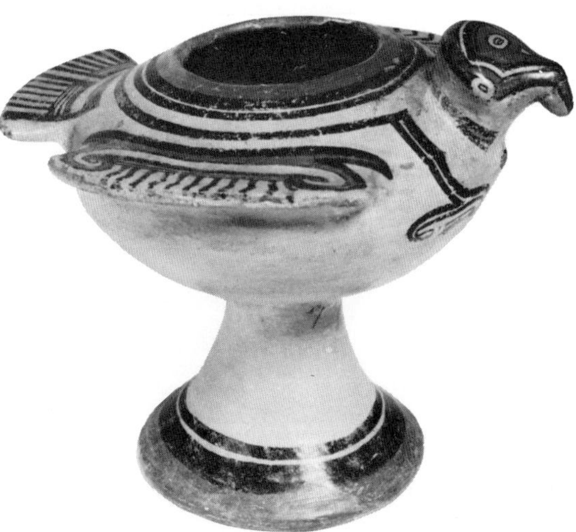

151. Painted Pedestal Bowl
One of the globular bird bowls with polychrome decoration, this saucy creature is representative of a wide variety of these vessels. Collected by Philip L. Dade. AZUERO. Santiago, Veraguas, Panama. 1200-1525. 9″ x 10″. 22/8351.

152. Polychrome Frutera
One of the more complex and intricately painted designs, this represents the Crocodile God, painted in the inside of a pedestal dish. Excavated by Eva M. Harte. AZUERO. Río de Jesús, Veraguas, Panama. 1200-1525. 5″ x 9¾″. 23/6784.

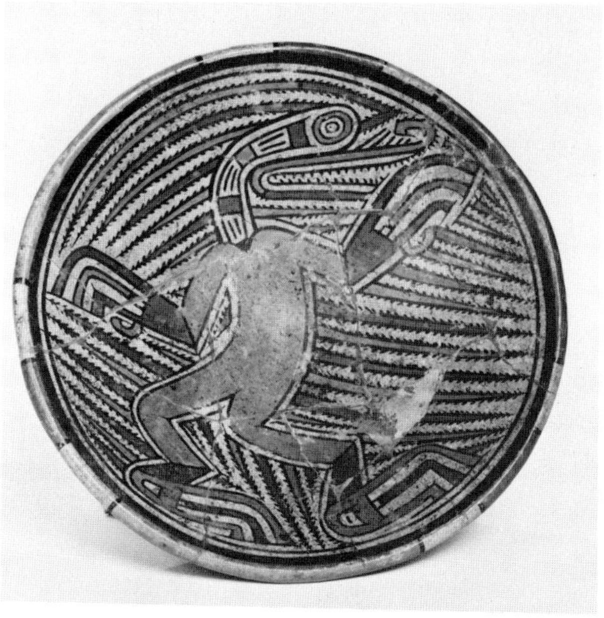

153. Large Painted Plate
(See color insert facing page 240)

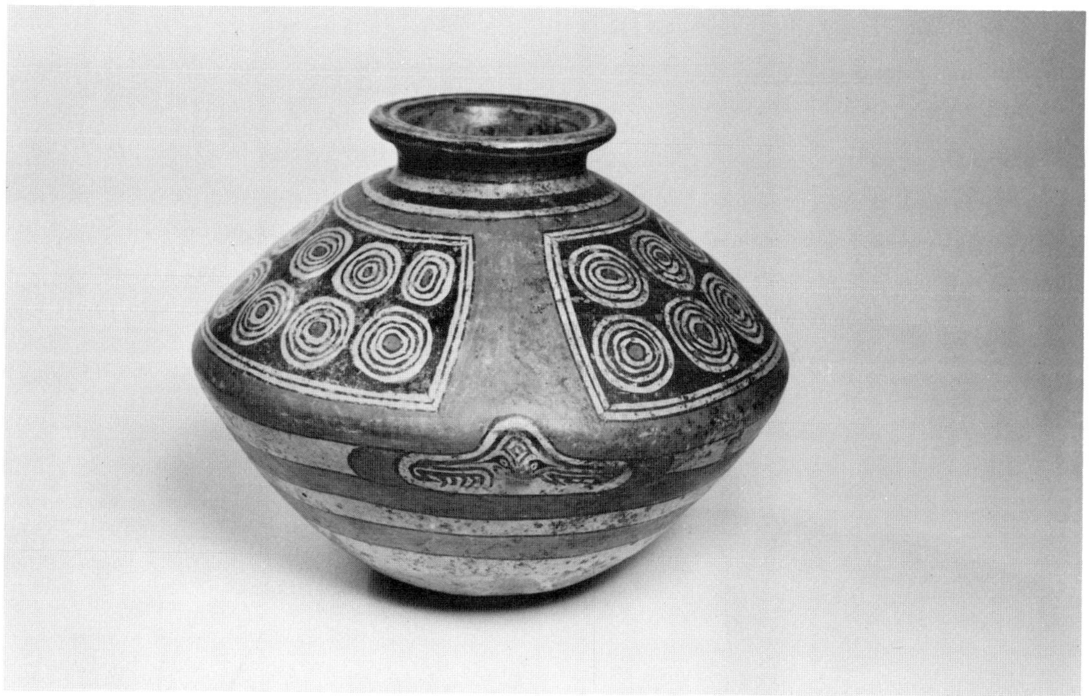

154. Large Globular Bowl
A simply-designed, powerful rotund form, this is a superb example of the work of the ancient Coclesanos. Collected by Philip L. Dade. AZUERO. Río Coclé, Coclé, Panama. 1200-1525. 9¾″ x 10¾″. 23/4799.

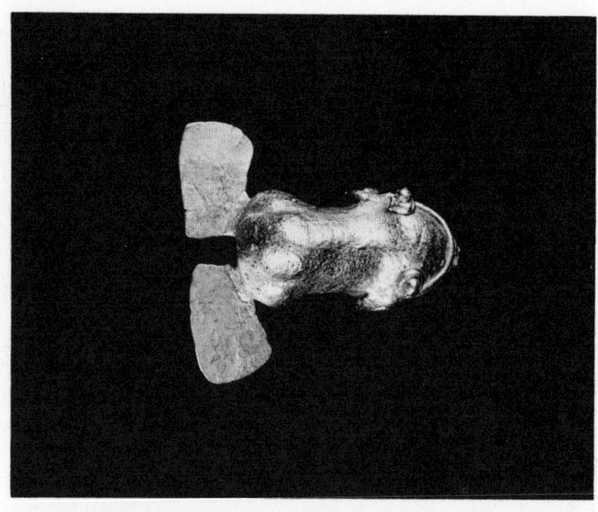

155. Cast Gold Frog
A small yellow tree frog was apparently an important animal in prehistoric Central America; many pendants were cast in gold in the form of this creature. This was collected before 1875 by George C. Dissette. CHIRIQUÍ. Bocas del Toro, Chiriquí, Panama. 800-1200. Weight, 12.5 grams. 1¼" x 1½". 8225.

156. Cast Gold Bead Necklace
The art of casting small gold beads was no mystery to the Coclesanos. This necklace is the type of bead common to the people of the Isthmus; such objects are found literally by the hundreds. COCLÉ. Río Grande, Coclé, Panama. 800-1200. Weight 9.5 grams. Length, 11 inches. 16/3866.

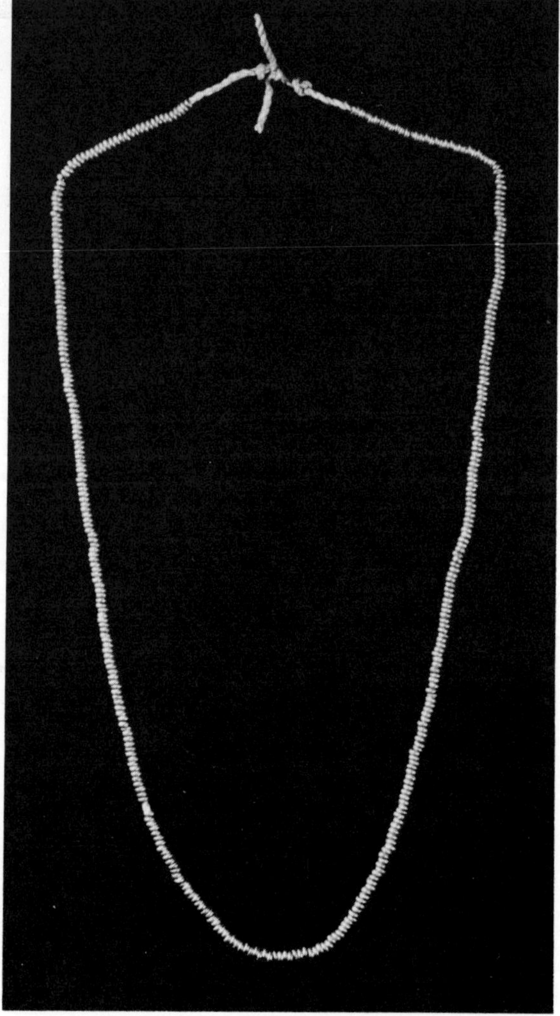

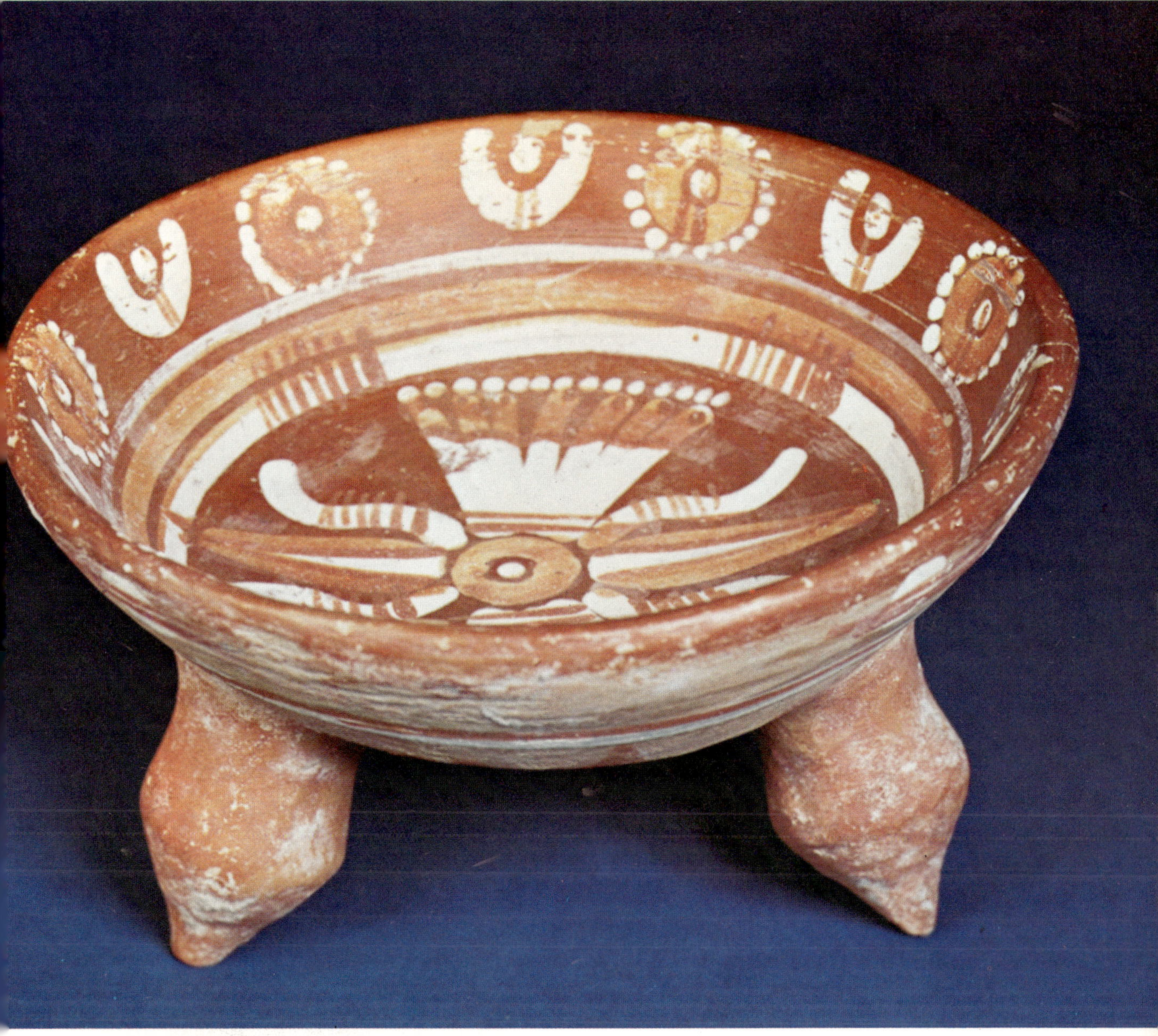

77. Painted Tripodal Bowl
This is remarkable for the amount of original paint which has survived; usually such vessels lose their color after burial in the earth over many centuries. Presented by William M. Lannik. GUERRERO, Mexico. 100 B.C.-250 A.D. (?) 4½" x 8½". 24/8.

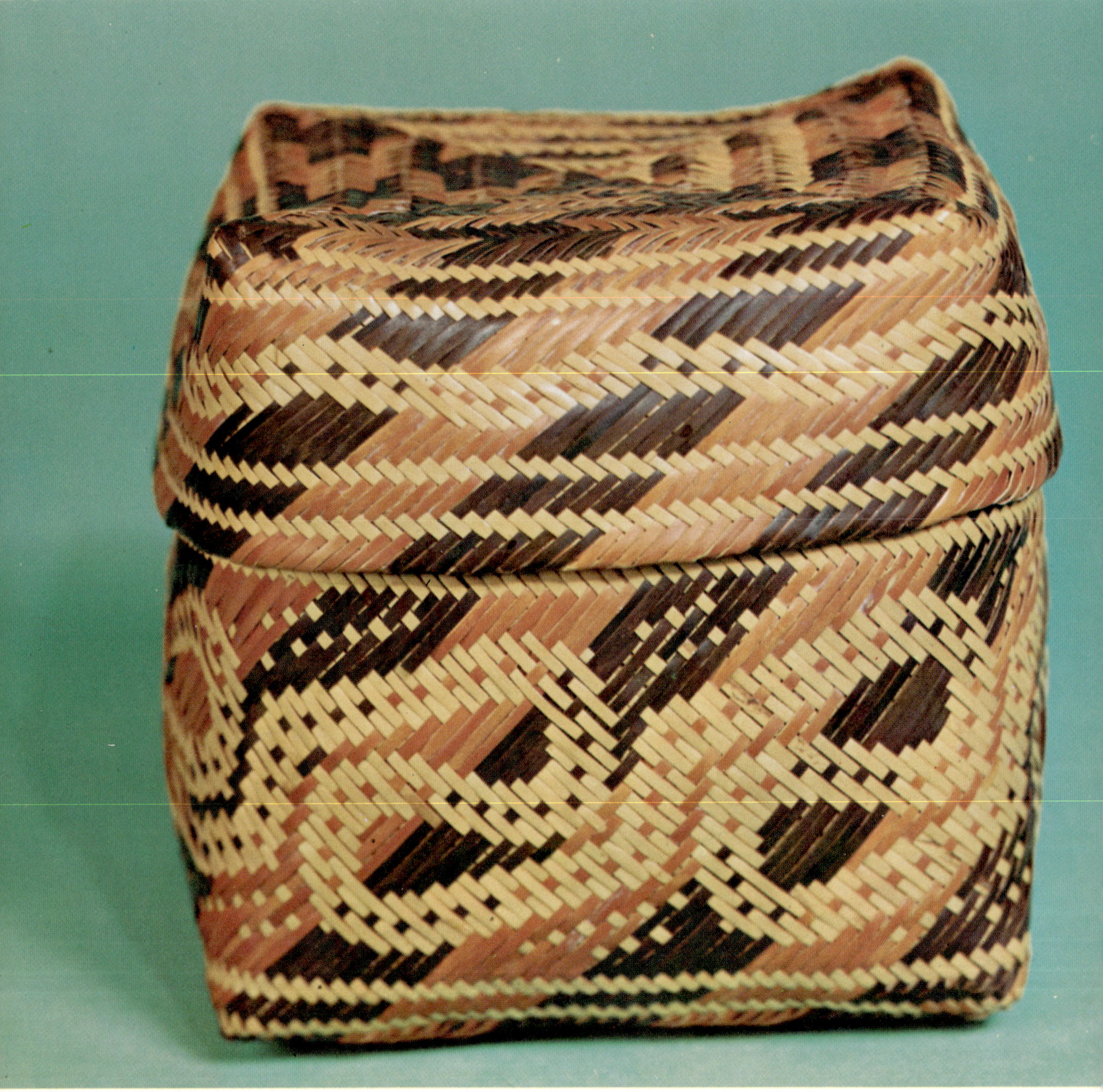

449. Double-weave Cane Basket
The brilliant black-and-orange coloring of these baskets makes them stand out in any collection. This design, called a worm track, is one of the few circular motifs found in basketry. Presented by Mr. and Mrs. William H. Schloss. CHITIMACHA. Grand Lake, Louisiana. 1900-1910. 6½″ x 7″ x 7″. 23/7276.

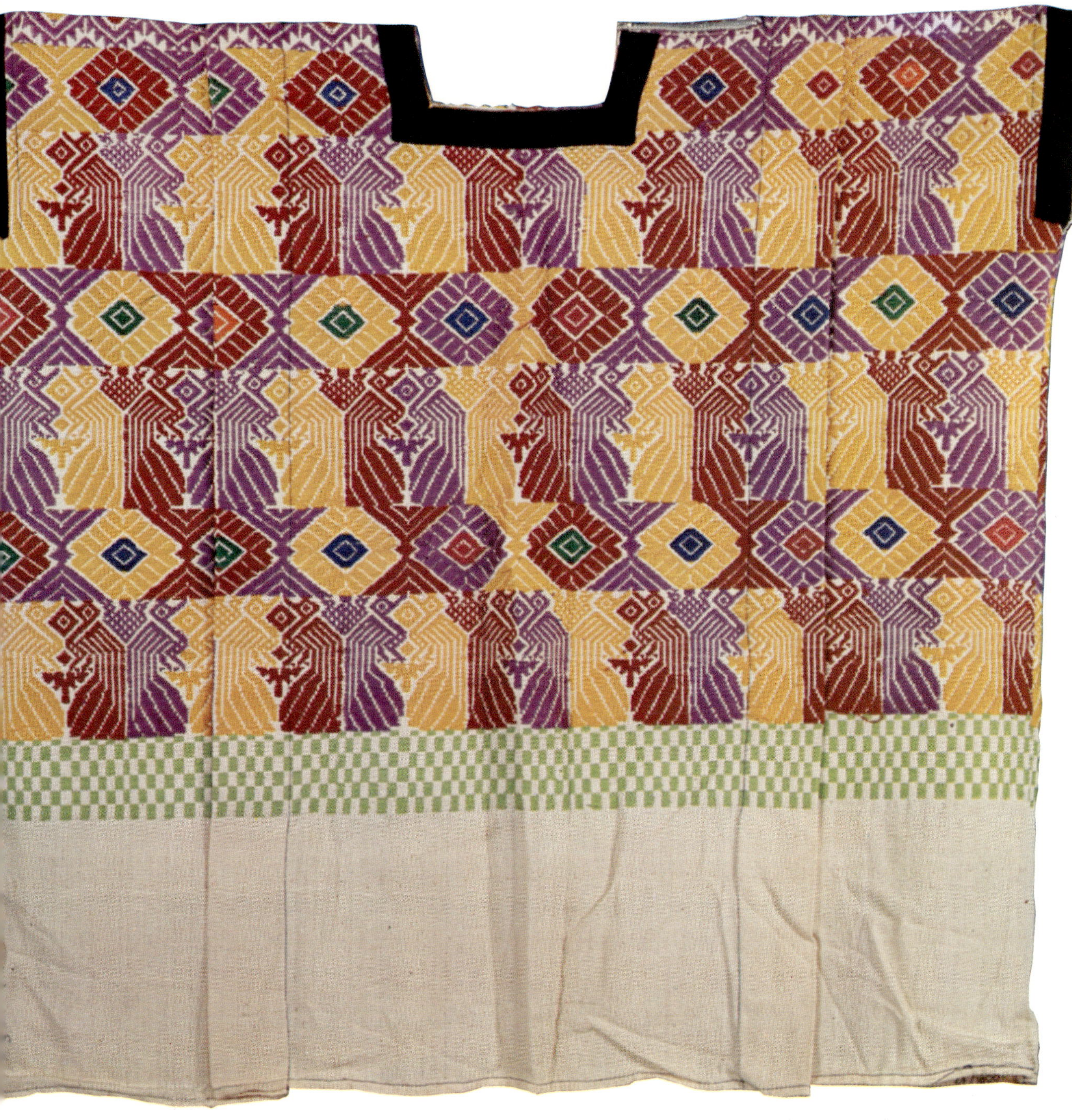

471. Modern Blouse

This is an example of the changes which have taken place in Maya weaving. The colors are commercial yarn, and the *huípil* is provided with a zipper for easier wearing. Yet the over-all effect is traditional, and it retains all of its splendor. Collected by Mrs. Mary W. Williams. QUICHÉ MAYA. Santo Tomás Chichicastenango, Guatemala. 1971-1972. 27″ x 28″. 24/1800.

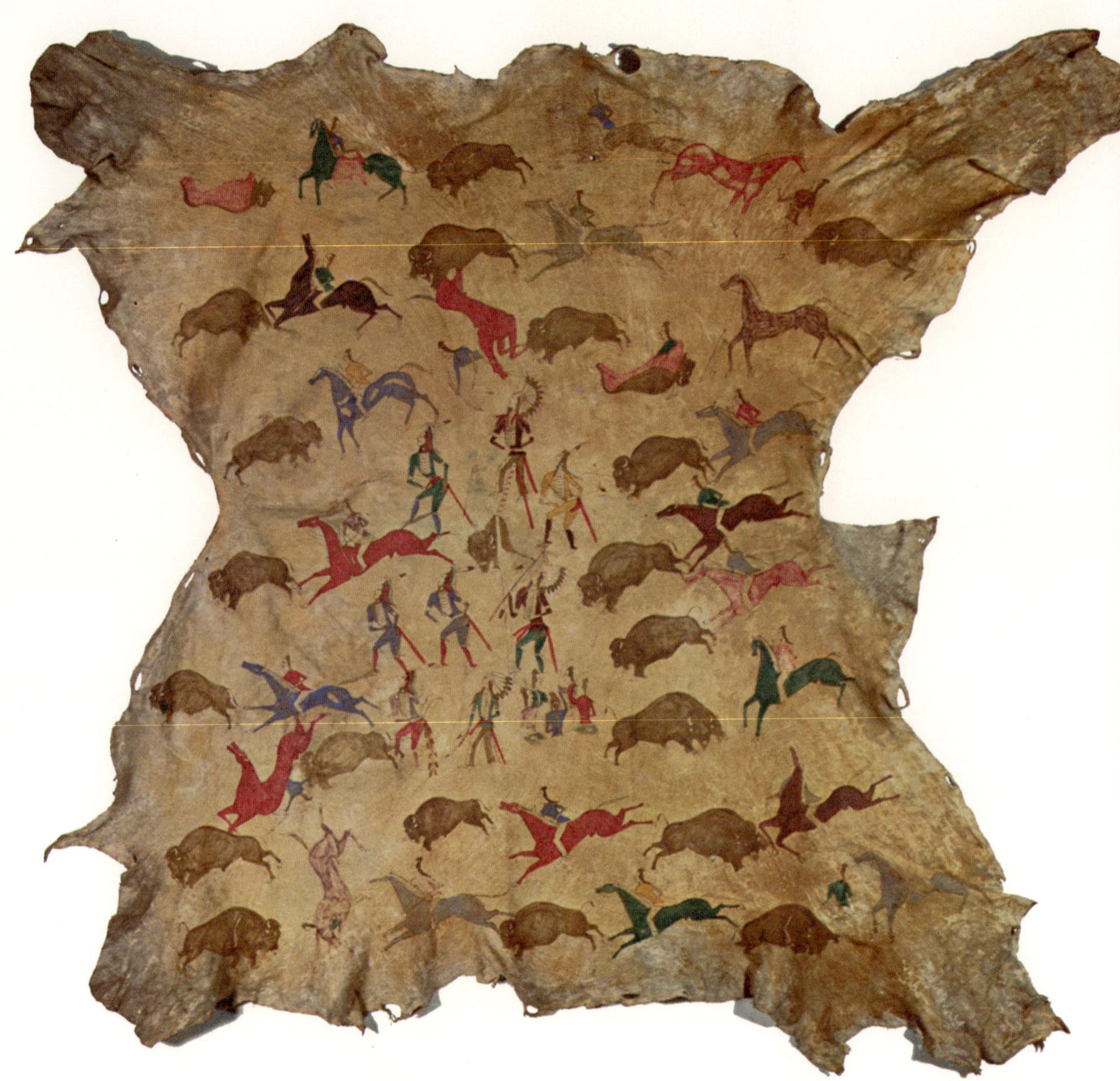

410. Painted Buffalo Hide

Buffalo hides were commonly painted in a variety of designs, providing the same surface that canvas does for the White artist. This example depicts the annual Sun Dance, given to bring back the buffalo. It was painted about 1900 by George Washakie, and obtained from him by Howard C. Means. SHOSHONI. Idaho. 1900. 69″ x 69″. 23/6400.

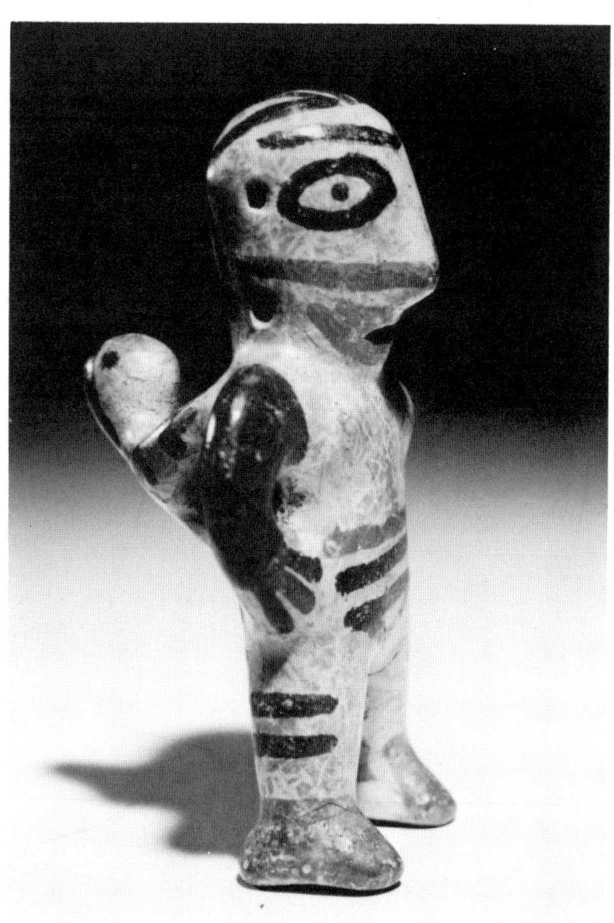

157. Polychrome Female Effigy
Painted in a linear pattern, with a baby on her back, this is an extremely abstracted form. Many of these are rattles or whistles. Excavated by Eva M. Harte. CHIRIQUÍ. Chiriquí, Panama. 1200-1525. 3″ x 4¼″. 24/518.

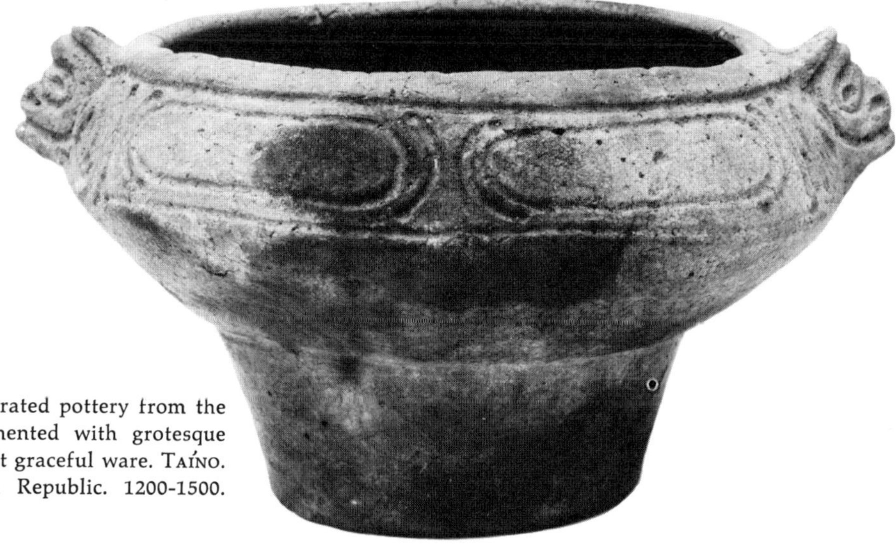

158. Buffware Vessel
The well-formed, linear decorated pottery from the West Indies is often ornamented with grotesque *adornos*, making a bizarre but graceful ware. TAÍNO. Santo Domingo, Dominican Republic. 1200-1500. 5½″ x 9¼″. 19/7662.

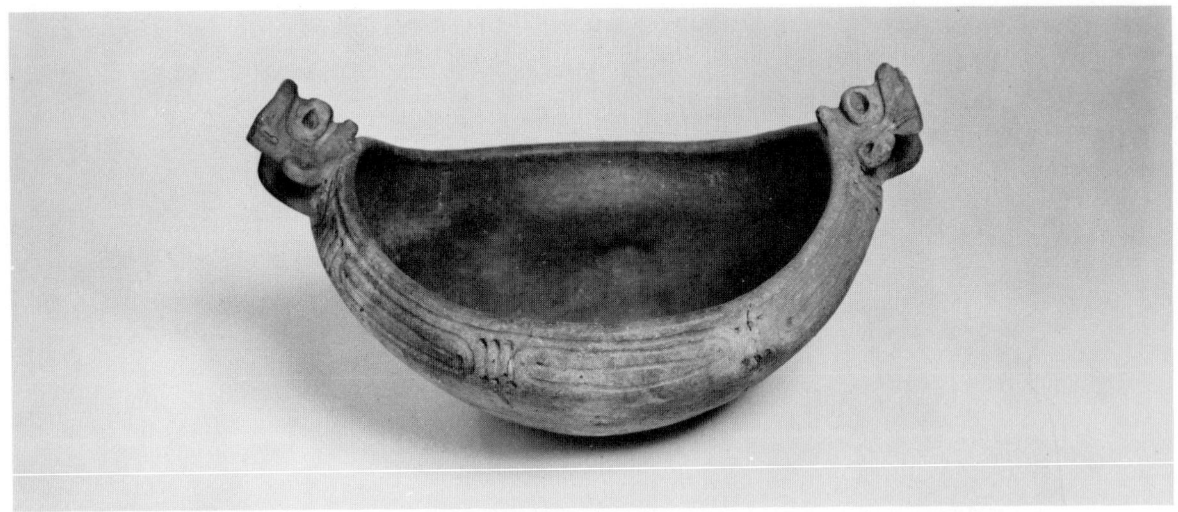

159. Double-headed Bowl
Although limited by a poor quality clay, the Taíno people produced a rich variety of ceramic vessels, many of them with a graceful, swelling form. The grotesque *adornos*, modeled in the forms of zoömorphic beings, were often attached to the rims of the bowls. TAÍNO. Santo Domingo, Dominican Republic. 1200-1500. 6″ x 11½″. 19/7696.

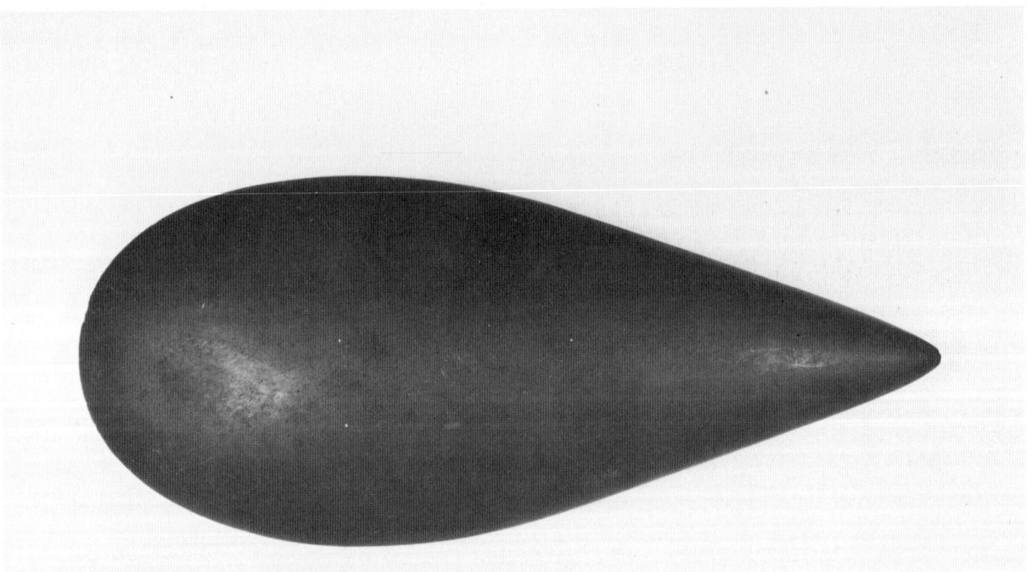

160. Petaloid Celt
One of the most remarkable sculptural triumphs of the West Indies are these beautifully-worked blades. They were used as cutting implements, embedded in a wooden haft. Their perfect form justifies their inclusion in any collection of artistic masterpieces. TAÍNO. Arecibo, Puerto Rico. 1200-1500. 4″ x 9½″. 10/9715.

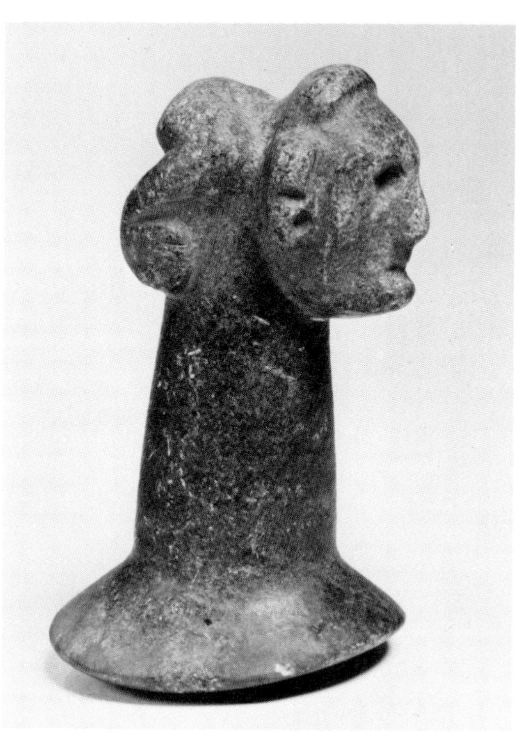

161. Carved Stone Pestle

Small stone pestles with sculptured human or animal forms on one end were common throughout the West Indies. This example has a squatting anthropomorphic figure carved on the top. Collected by H. E. Hurst. TAÍNO. Santiago, Dominican Republic. 1200-1500. 4¼″ x 7″. 12/7423.

162. Tri-point Stone

(See page 27)

163. Stone "Collar"

Such circular sculptures, believed to have a similar function to the stone *yugo* in Mexico, are also thought to be related to the ball game known to have been played in the West Indies. Collected by Frank D. Utley. TAÍNO. Arecibo, Puerto Rico. 1200-1500. 2¾″ x 16¼″. 3688.

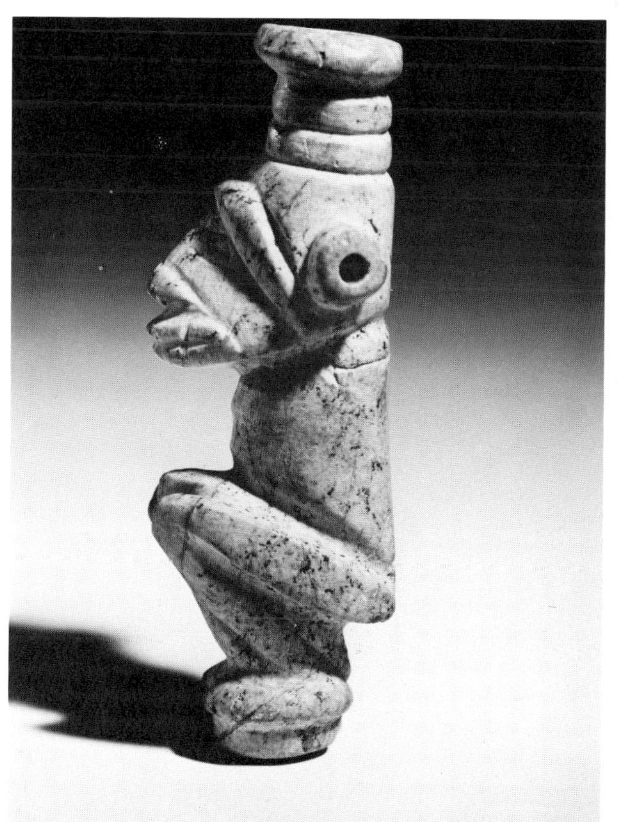

164. Sculptured Death's Head

(See page 26)

165. Zoömorphic Pendant

A wide variety of small carvings in stone or shell, and occasionally bone, are found throughout the eastern part of the Caribbean. They were probably used as charms. Collected by Lady Edith Blake. LUCAYAN. Caicos Island. 1200-1500. 1¼″ x 3¾″. 5/9238.

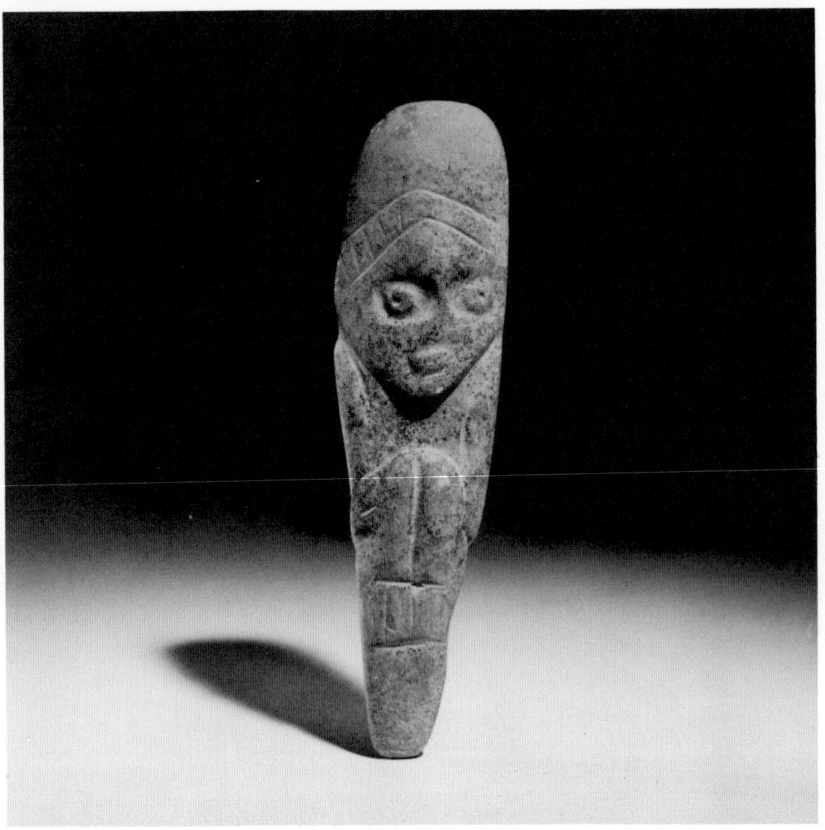

166. Anthropomorphic Celt
Carved from a celt, with human features and limbs, these probably were not used as axe blades, despite their origin. However, they may well have been lashed into a wooden haft, used for ceremonial purposes. CIBONEY. Haiti. 1200-1500. 2½" x 8¾". 22/7518.

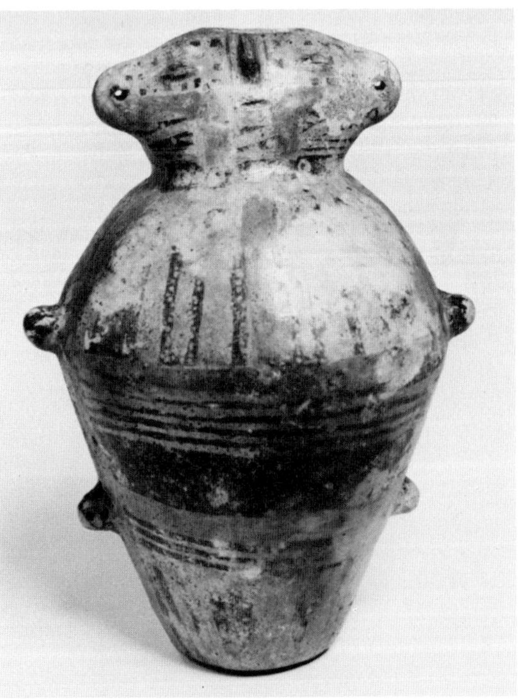

167. Effigy Vessel
The resist-ware technique on this anthropomorphic vessel is typical of the ceramics from the Quimbaya region. The design is achieved by overpainting on a design which burns off when the vessel is fired, leaving the decoration outlined in relief. Presented by James B. Ford. QUIMBAYA. Pereira, Cauca Valley, Colombia. 500-1500. 6½" x 9½". 9/9783.

168. Small Effigy Vessel
Commonly called a *brujo*, this modeled male figurine is found throughout the Cauca area in varying sizes. Presented by Dr. and Mrs. Arthur M. Sackler. CALIMA. Restrepo, Cauca Valley, Colombia. 500-1500. 3″ x 4″. 23/8978.

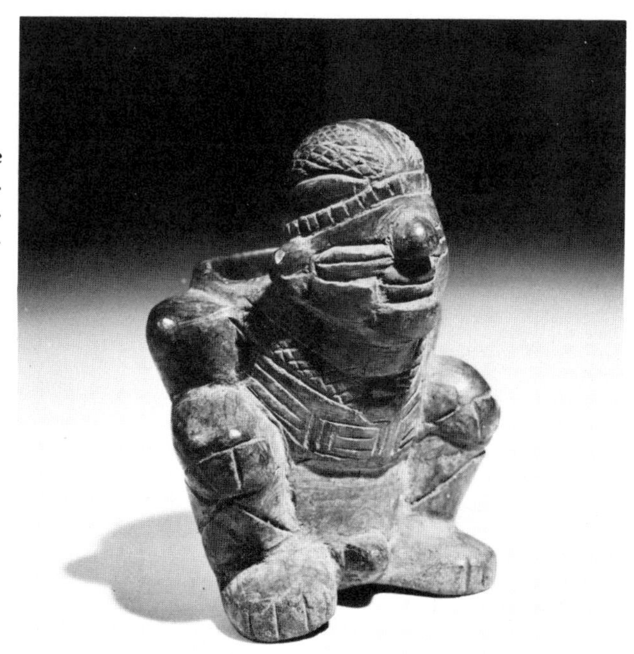

169. Geometrically-carved Bowl
This unique design is restricted to the Quimbaya region; two zoömorphic *adornos* are mounted on the rim of the deeply-carved redware vessel. Collected by Luther S. Livingston. QUIMBAYA. Quindió, Caldas, Colombia. 500-1500. 4½″ x 8¼″. 3/3875.

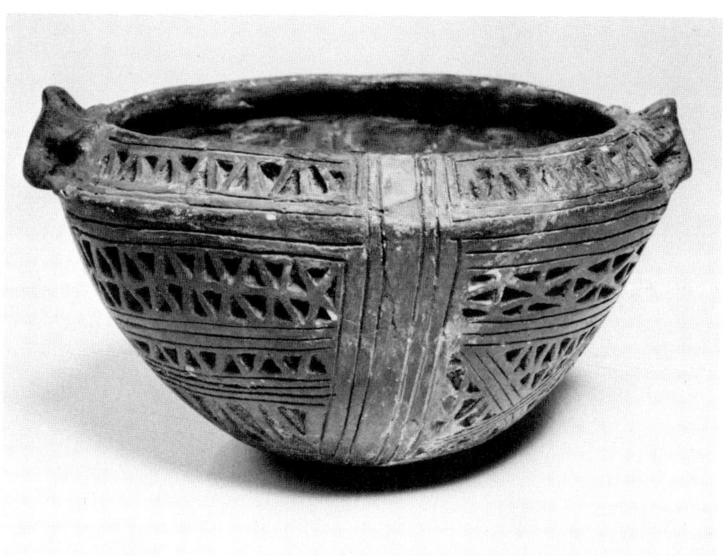

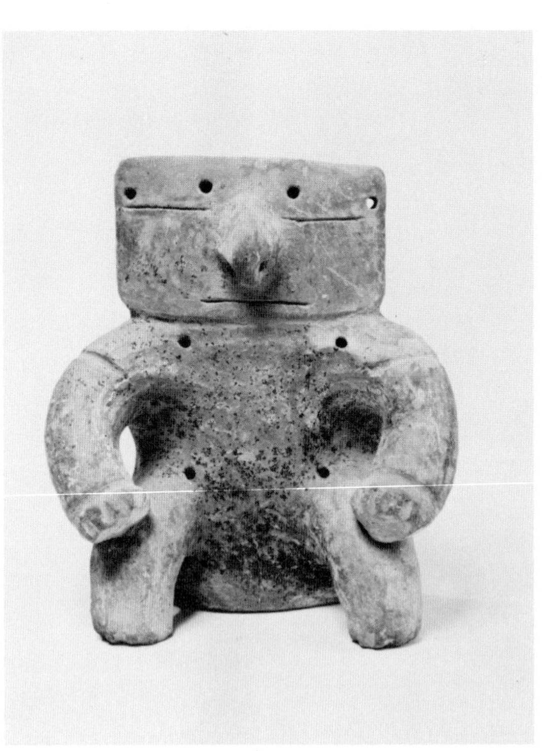

170. Solid Redware Effigy
Seated human figurines of this form were probably intended for use as funerary offerings. Occasionally they are found with gold nose rings or other jewelry inserted into the holes in the head. QUIMBAYA. Cali, Colombia. 500-1500. 6¼″ x 7″. 20/140.

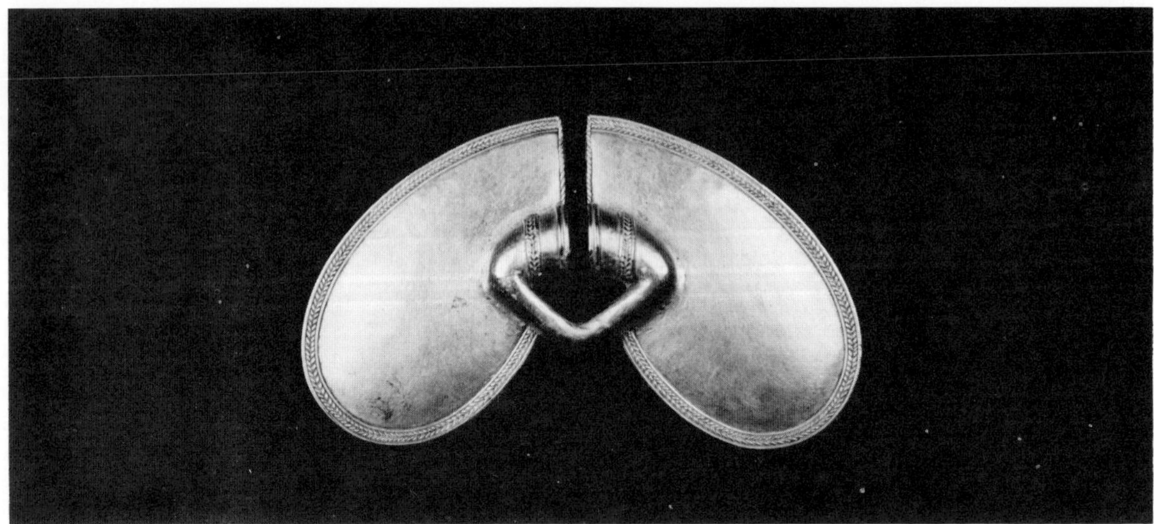

171. Gold Nose Ornament
These beautifully-worked flaring ornaments have a grace and delicacy reflecting a high level of civilization. They vary in size and elaboration. Weight, 26.5 grams. TAIRONA. Santa Marta, Colombia. 1200-1500. 2¼″ x 3⅛″. 24/7995.

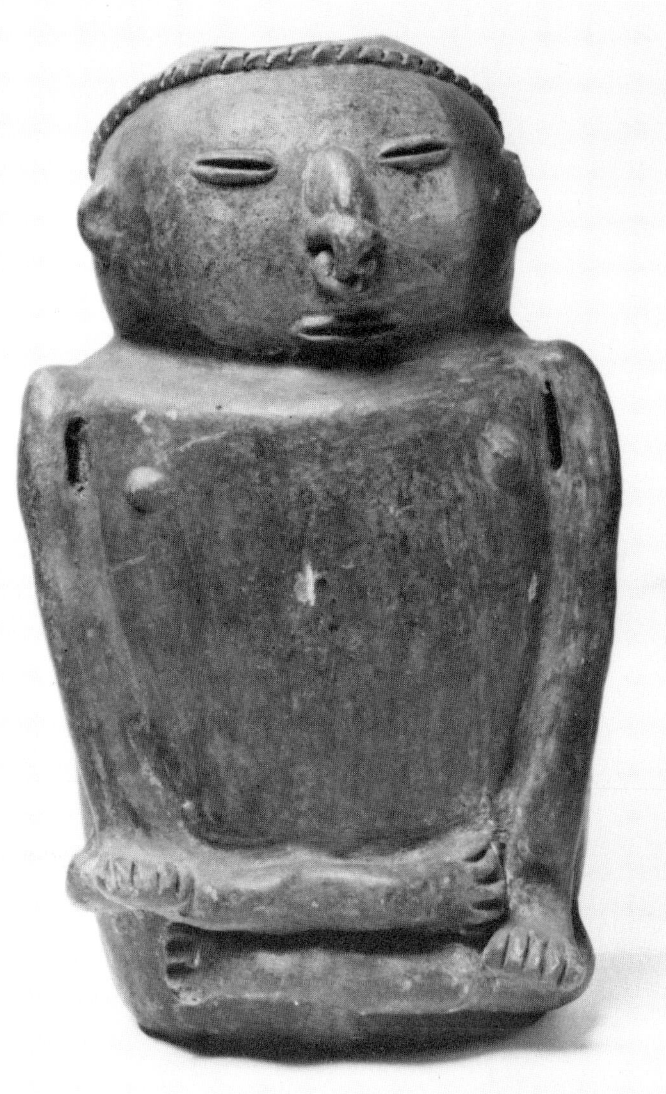

172. Human Effigy Vessel
Another form of the seated effigy figurine, this redware example features the well-modeled head but abstracted body and limbs so often found in South American ceramics. Presented by James B. Ford. QUIMBAYA. Pereira, Cauca Valley, Colombia. 500-1500. 6″ x 10½″. 9/9787.

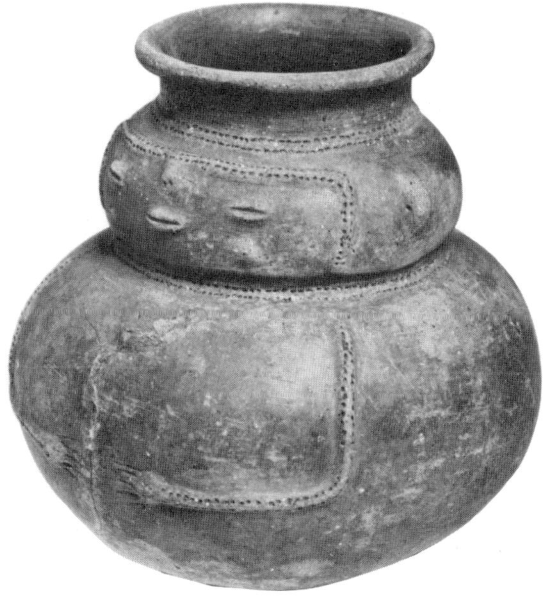

173. Effigy Vessel
The rotund body of this small brownware vessel has been ceremonially "killed" prior to interment. Presented by Mr. and Mrs. Donald C. Webster. TAIRONA. Santa Marta, Colombia. 1200-1500. 7½″ x 8″. 24/6756.

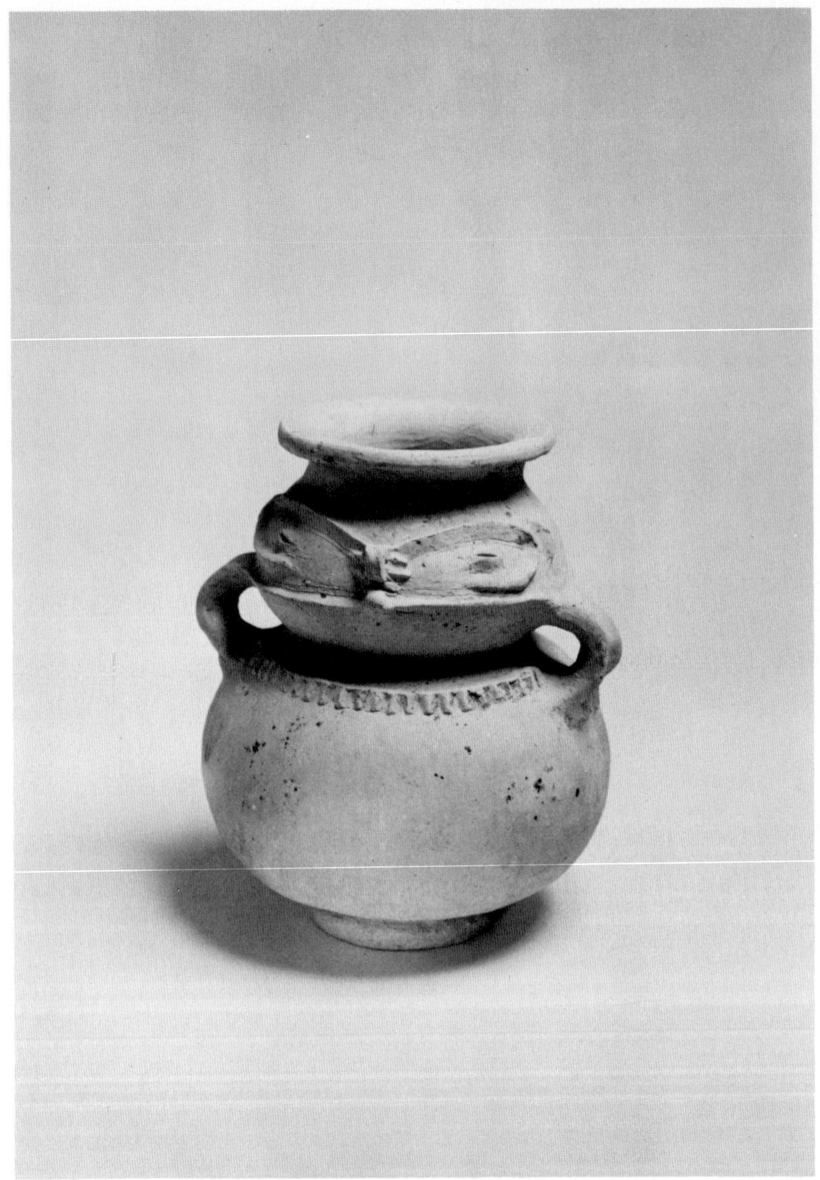

174. Orangeware Effigy Bowl
Formed by a raised linear decoration on the upper portion, this anthropomorphic vessel has the design features so familiar to one of the major cultures of Colombia. Presented by Mr. and Mrs. Donald C. Webster. TAIRONA. Santa Marta, Colombia. 1200-1500. 6″ x 8″. 24/6758.

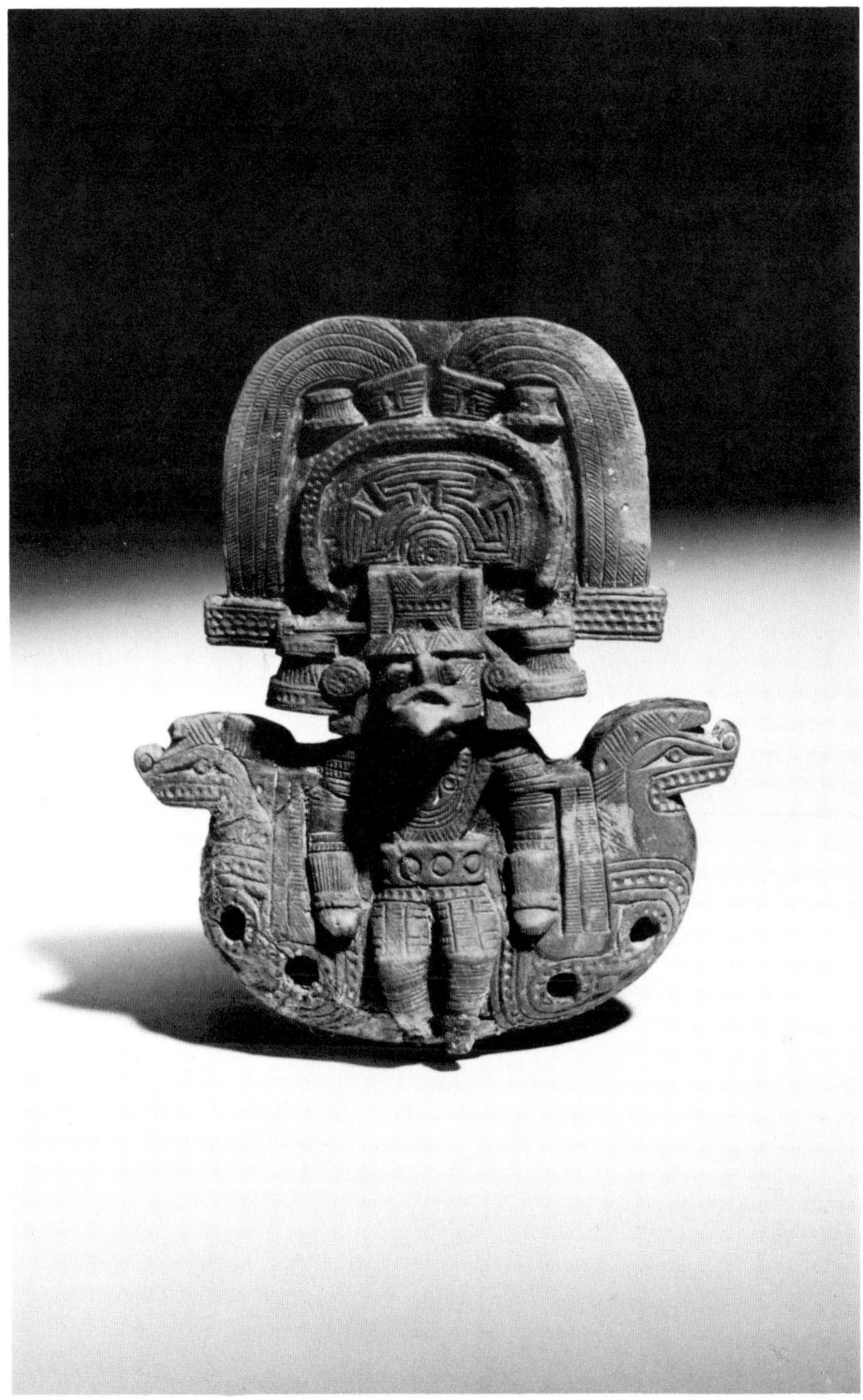

175. Carved Clay Ocarina
Some of the most ornately decorated ceramics in South America is this incised ware from Santa Marta. This 4-tone musical instrument has the design of a chieftain seated on a serpent throne; his headdress is composed of basketry and tropical bird feathers. Presented by Mr. and Mrs. Donald C. Webster. TAIRONA. Santa Marta, Colombia. 1200-1500. 4" x 4¾". 24/6783.

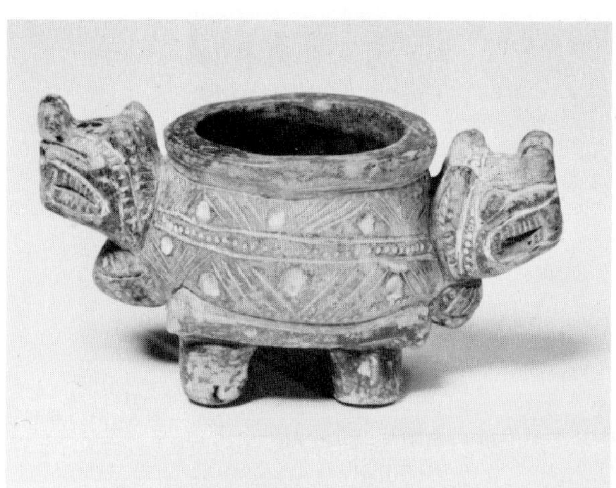

176. Grayware Urn

Another example of the finely-carved and modeled clay work of the Tairona is this small four-legged vessel. The design represents two serpent heads attached to a circular bowl. Collected by Borys Malkin. TAIRONA. Santa Marta, Colombia. 1200-1500. 2″ x 2¼″ x 3¾″. 24/6786.

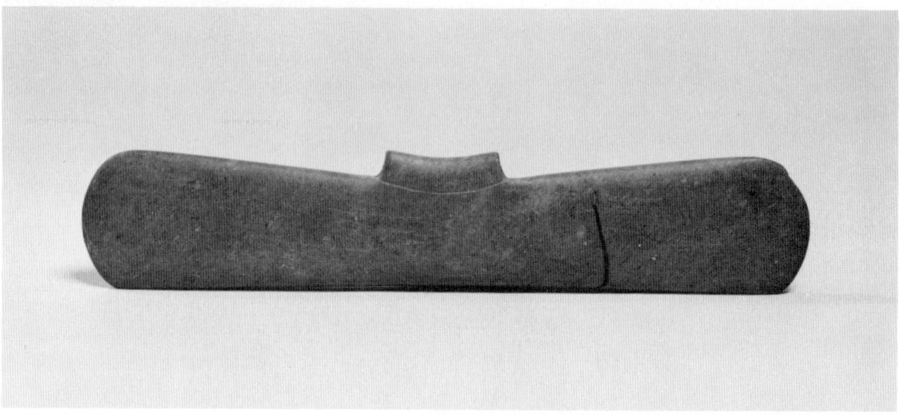

177. Smooth-ground Ornament

Carefully worked and polished, these are found in many sizes; some are known made from shell. They were drilled for suspension, presumably for use as pendants. Collected by Borys Malkin. TAIRONA. Santa Marta, Colombia. 1250-1500. 2″ x 15″. 24/6814.

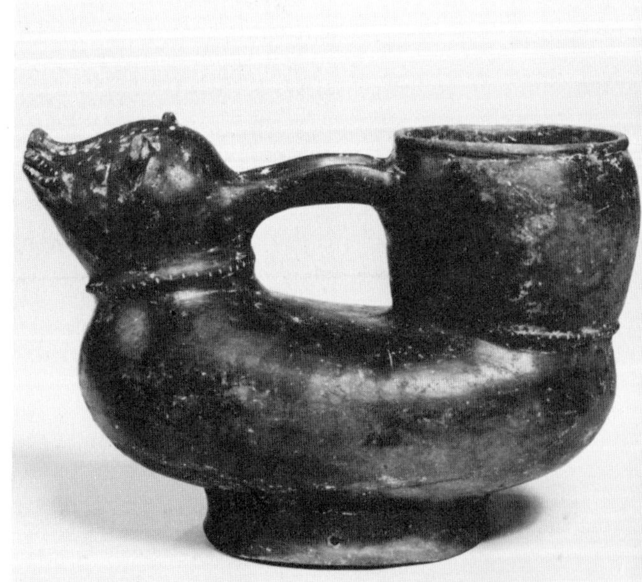

178. Blackware Effigy Vessel

The polished, graceful pottery of the Tairona is demonstrated by this globular body, spout, and zoömorphic head connected with a strap-handle. Presented by Mr. and Mrs. Donald C. Webster. TAIRONA. Santa Marta, Colombia. 1250-1500. 6½″ x 9¾″. 24/7057.

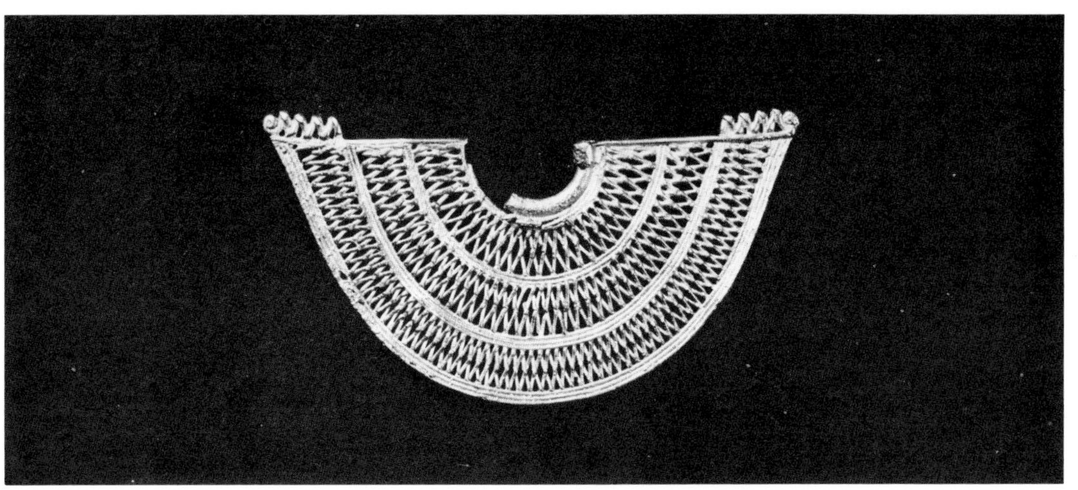

179. Cast Gold Ornament
Made in one piece, this filigree jewelry was probably worn as an ear ornament. The design and craftsmanship reflects a high degree of technological skill. Collected by Russell H. Millward before 1900. Weight, 8.5 grams. SINÚ. Santander, Colombia. 1250-1500. 1¼″ x 2¾″. 7/7102.

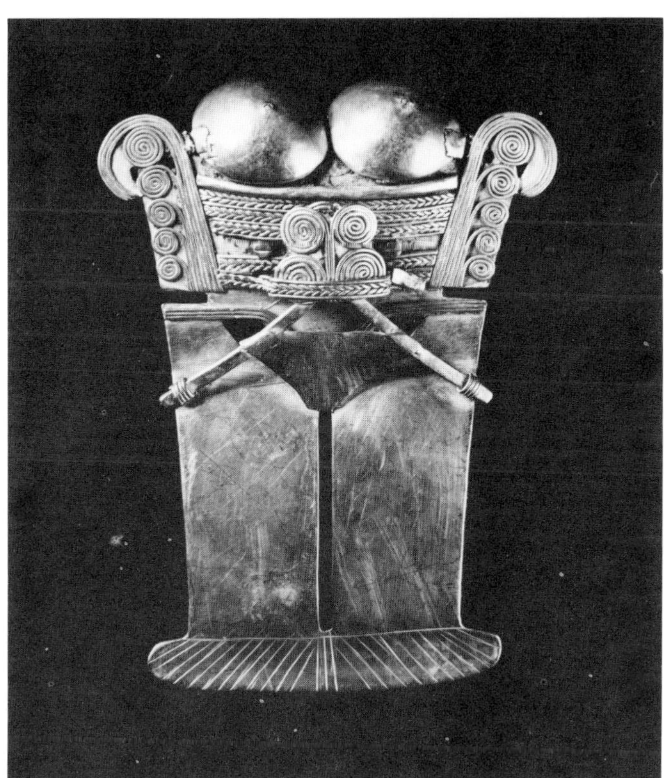

180. Gold Pendant
The design of this elaborate decoration is an abstracted human figure with a snout-like mask, holding two batons. These have been traded over a wide area, and are found in many sizes and styles. This was collected along the banks of the Sinú River before 1890. Weight, 98.5 grams. DARIÉN. Montería, Bolívar, Colombia. 1250-1500. 3¾″ x 5″. 5/851.

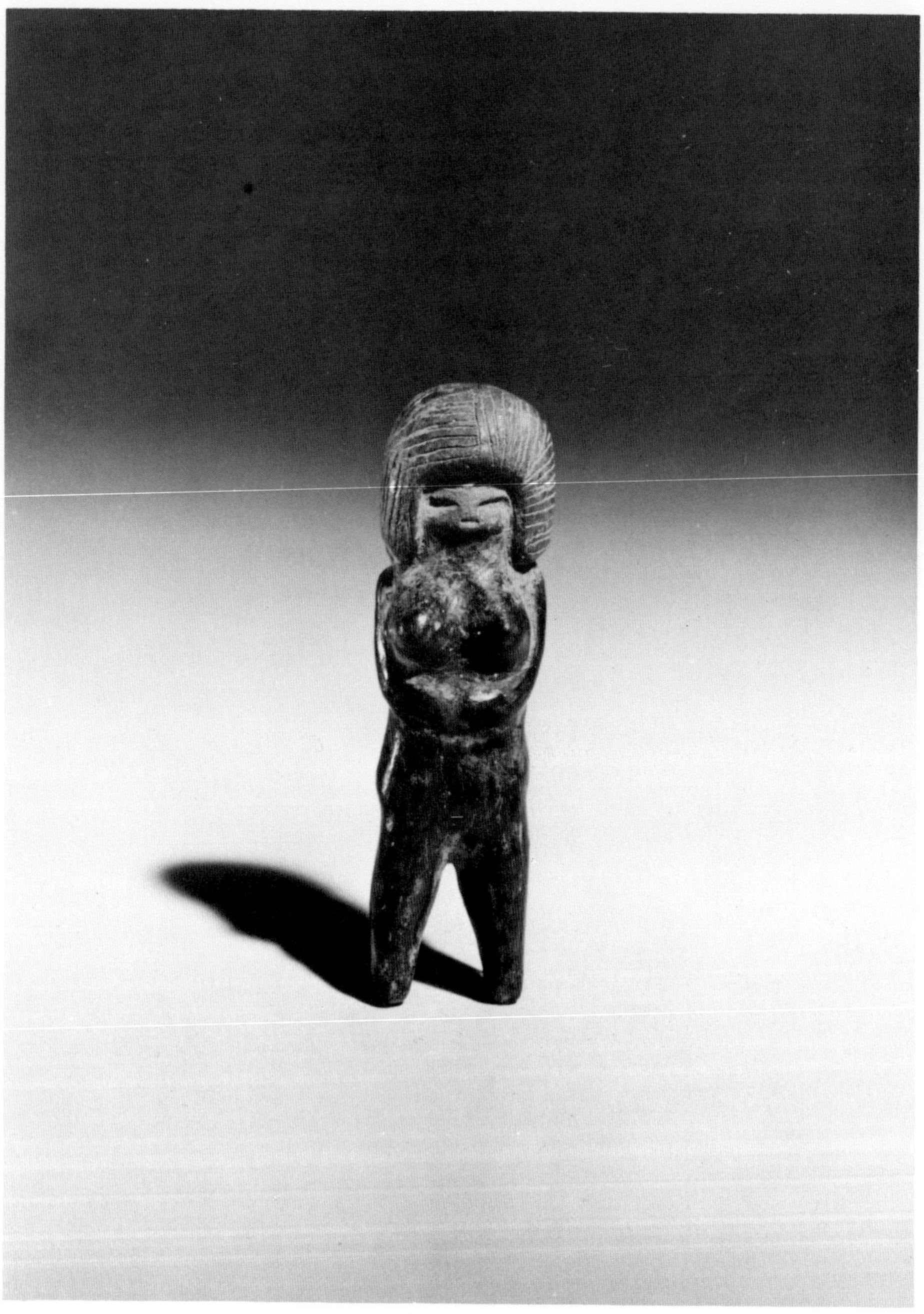

181. Solid Clay Figurine
The small modeled effigy of a nude female, found near the mouth of the Guayas River, represents the earliest New World culture from which pottery has thus far been found. The plainness of the body contrasts with the careful modelling of the hair and face. Presented by Alice K. Bache. VALDIVIA. Guayas, Ecuador. *Circa* 3000 B.C. Height: 3⅜". 24/8401.

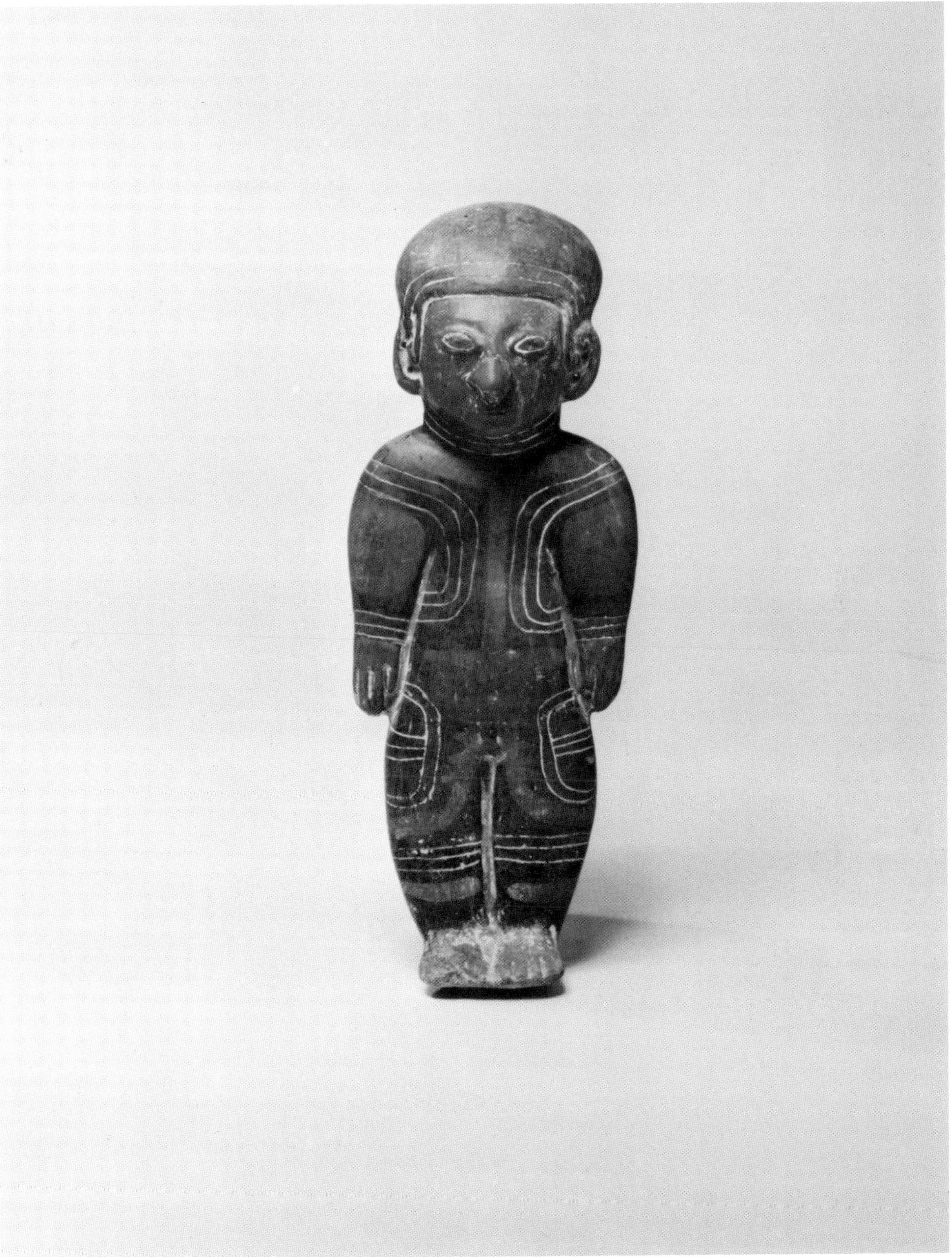

182. Orangeware Effigy
Modeled in the form of a human, this whistle has a hole in the top of the head which serves as the mouthpiece. The linear designs on the body possibly represent tattooing. GUANGALA. Manabí, Ecuador. 1000-500 B.C. 3¾″ x 10″. 24/6606.

183. Polychrome Figurine

This two-tone clay effigy is remarkable for the amount of original coloring which has survived. The design shows the style and arrangement of costumes worn by the ancient people. Presented by Dr. and Mrs. Anton Notey. BAHÍA. Los Esteros, Bahía de Manta, Ecuador. 500 B.C.-500 A.D. 5″ x 11″. 24/463.

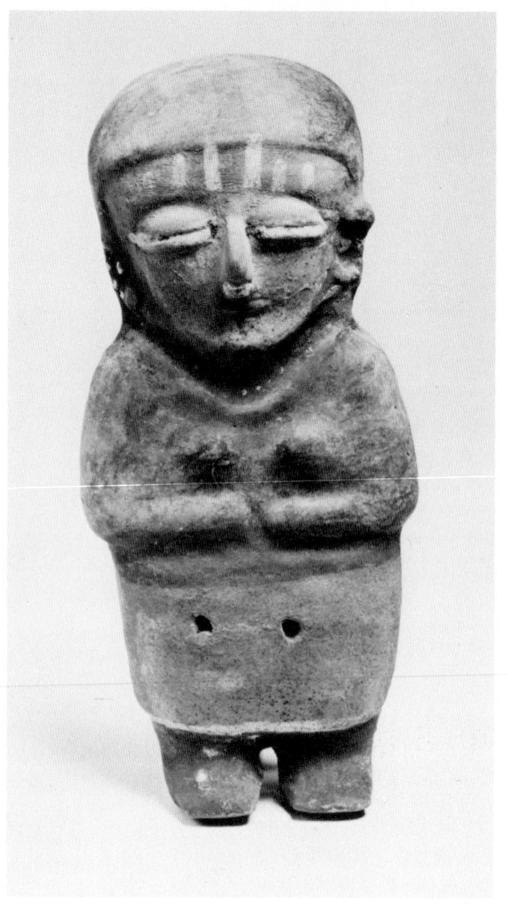

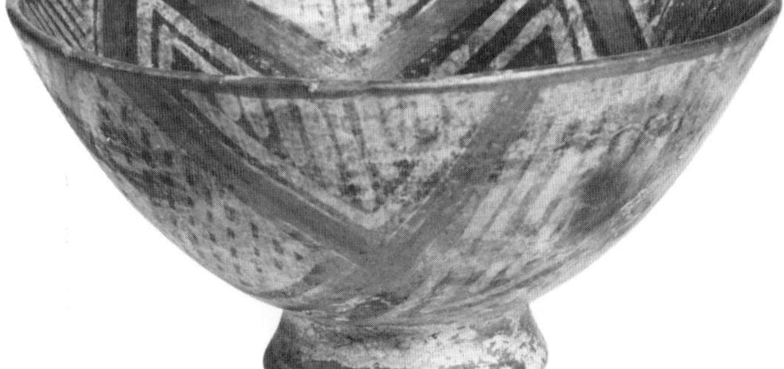

184. Resist Ware Bowl

Perhaps the most common form of pottery from this region is achieved by means of the application of a basic design, over which a second pattern is applied. When fired, the first decoration burns away, leaving a "negative" ornamentation. Collected by Marshall H. Saville, CARCHI. Angel, Ecuador. 500-1500. 4″ x 7¾″. 3/306.

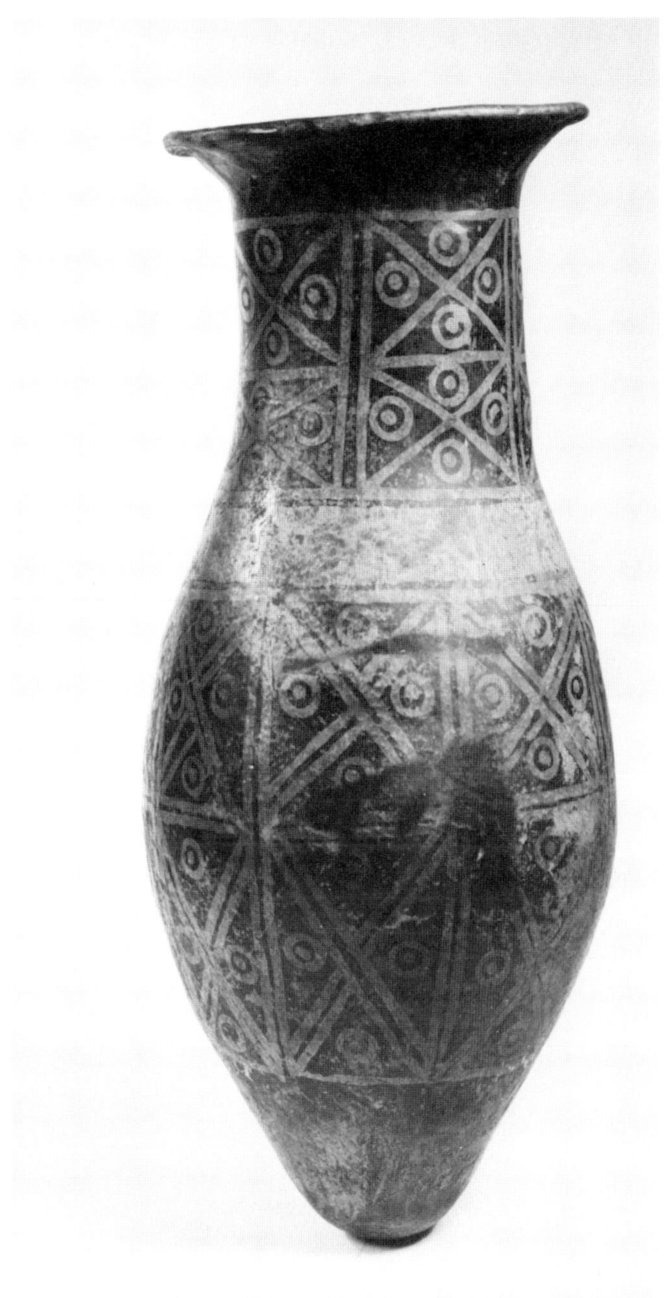

185. Burial Urn
Another form of the resist-ware ceramics, these graceful vessels were typical of the Carchi area. Collected by Marshall H. Saville. Carchi. Angel, Ecuador. 500-1500. 10½″ x 24½″. 3/1734.

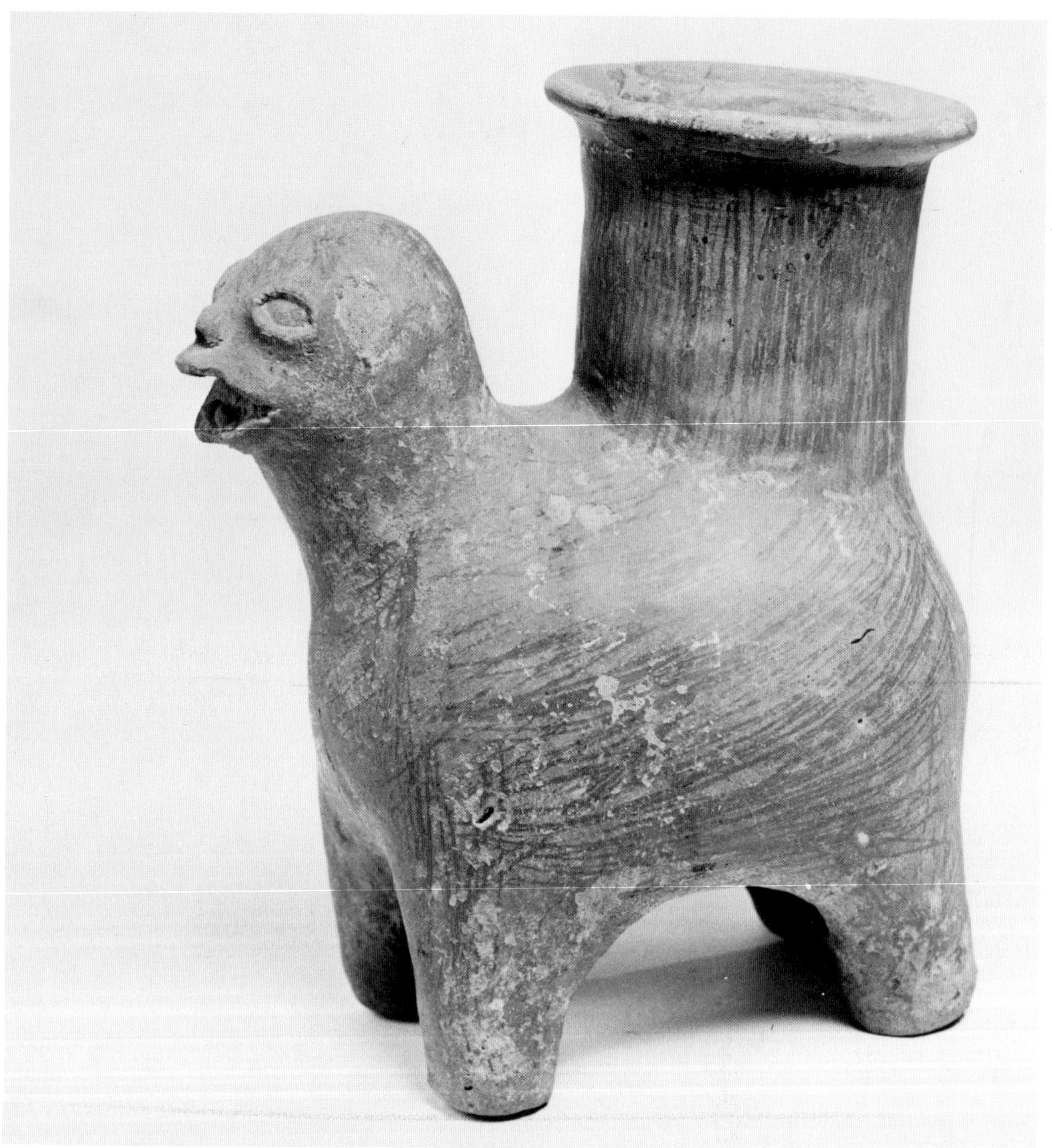

186. Jaguar Effigy Vessel
A modeled redware vessel from a little-known region of the Andes, this is another of the frequently-found burial urns from the Northern Highlands. Collected by Pedro Chiriboga. PICHINCHA. Ecuador. 500-1500? 5½" x 8¼". 3/6691.

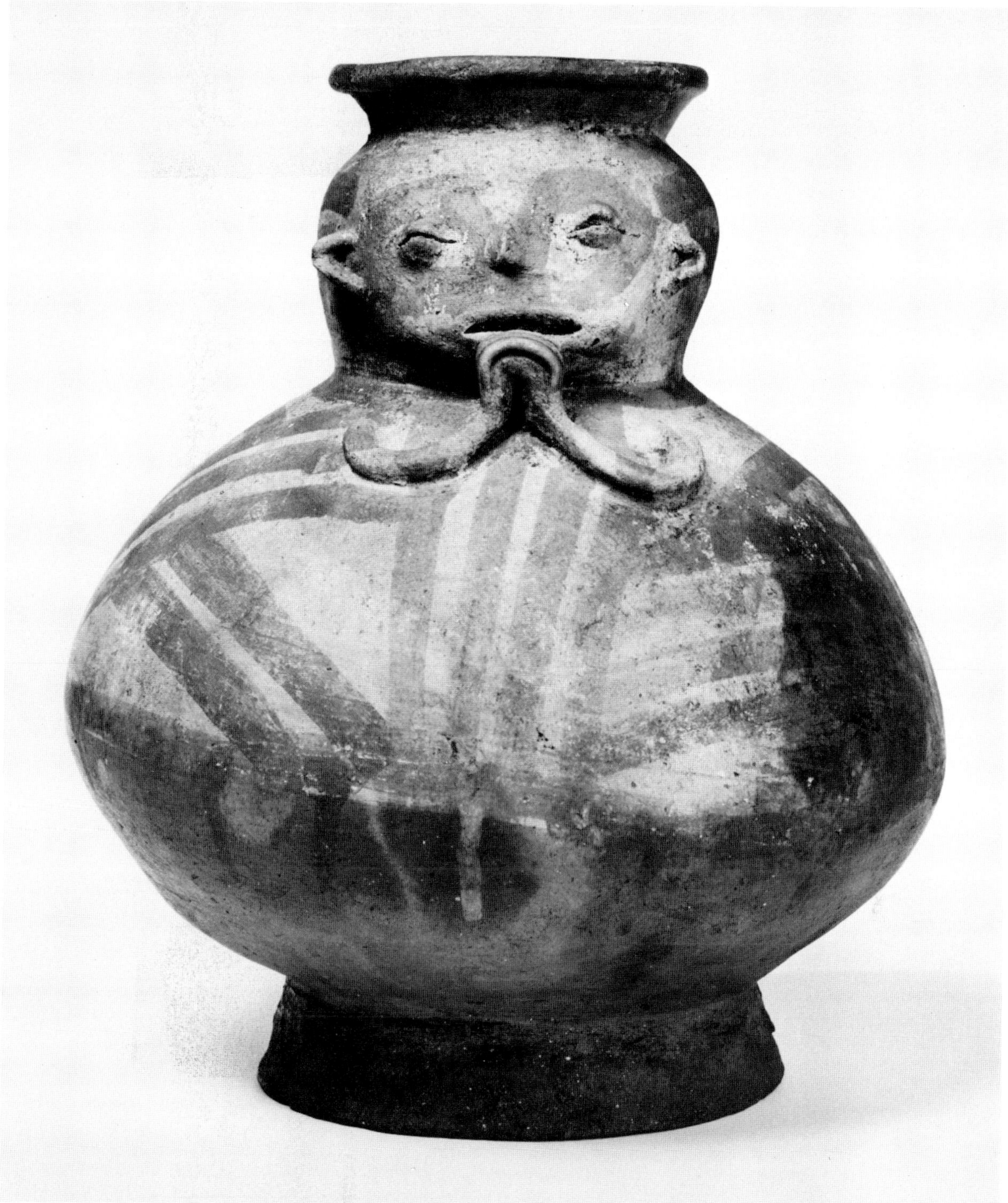

187. Effigy Urn
This redware vessel with rounded body and modeled head has appliqué clay arms clasped in front of the mouth. Collected by Marshall H. Saville. PURUJÁ. Pillaro, Tunguragua, Ecuador. 500-1500. 11″ x 12¾″. 1/3551.

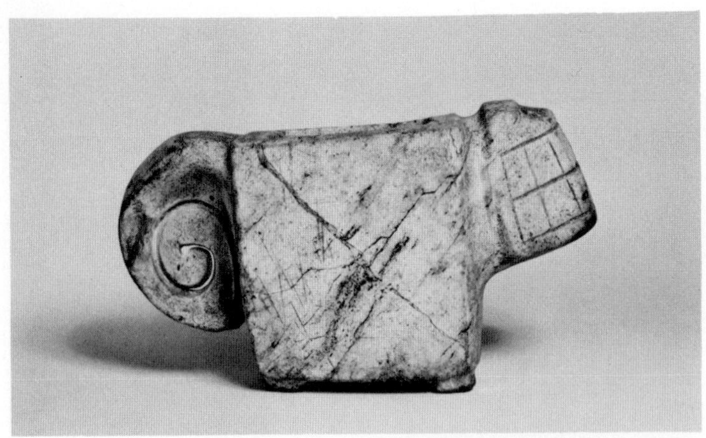

188. Rectangular Stone Mortar
Carved from white stone, this mortar in the form of a jaguar is unique to the Ecuadorean region. Presented by The Viking Fund. Inc. MANABÍ. Sesme, Manta, Ecuador. 500-1500. 6¼″ x 10½″. 21/1455.

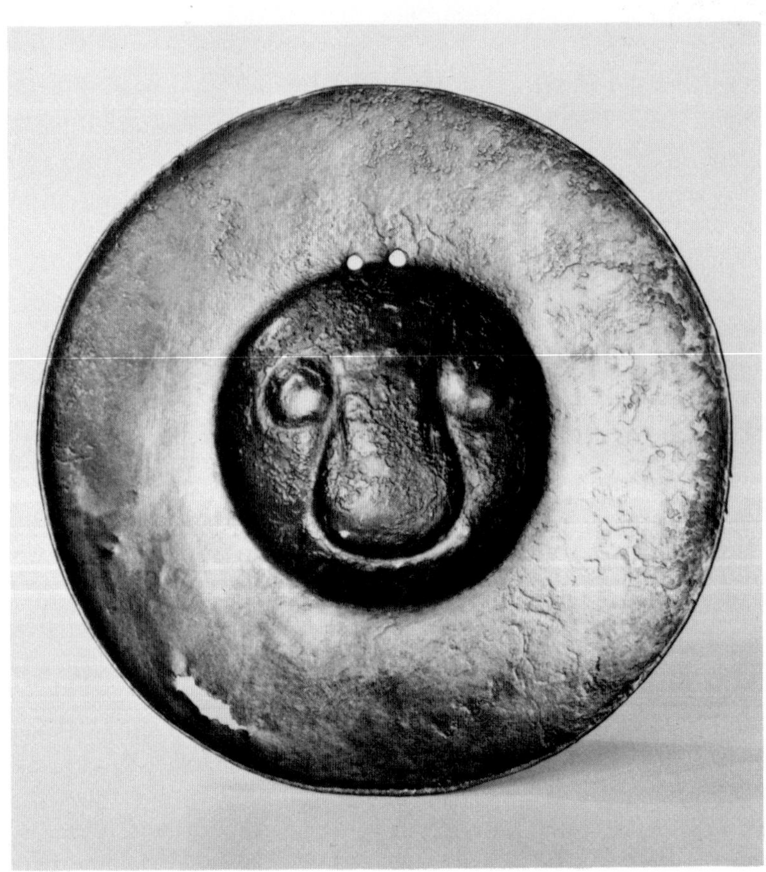

189. Hammered Copper Disc
Metalsmithing was an important art in the prehistoric Ecuadorean region. This repoussé disc has the head of a puma in the center. Two holes drilled through the center suggest that it was used for suspension, and it is more likely this was used for a gong, rather than worn on the person. Collected by Marshall H. Saville. TIAONE. Tiaone Valley, Esmeraldas, Ecuador. 500 B.C.-500 A.D. D: 9″. 1/5693.

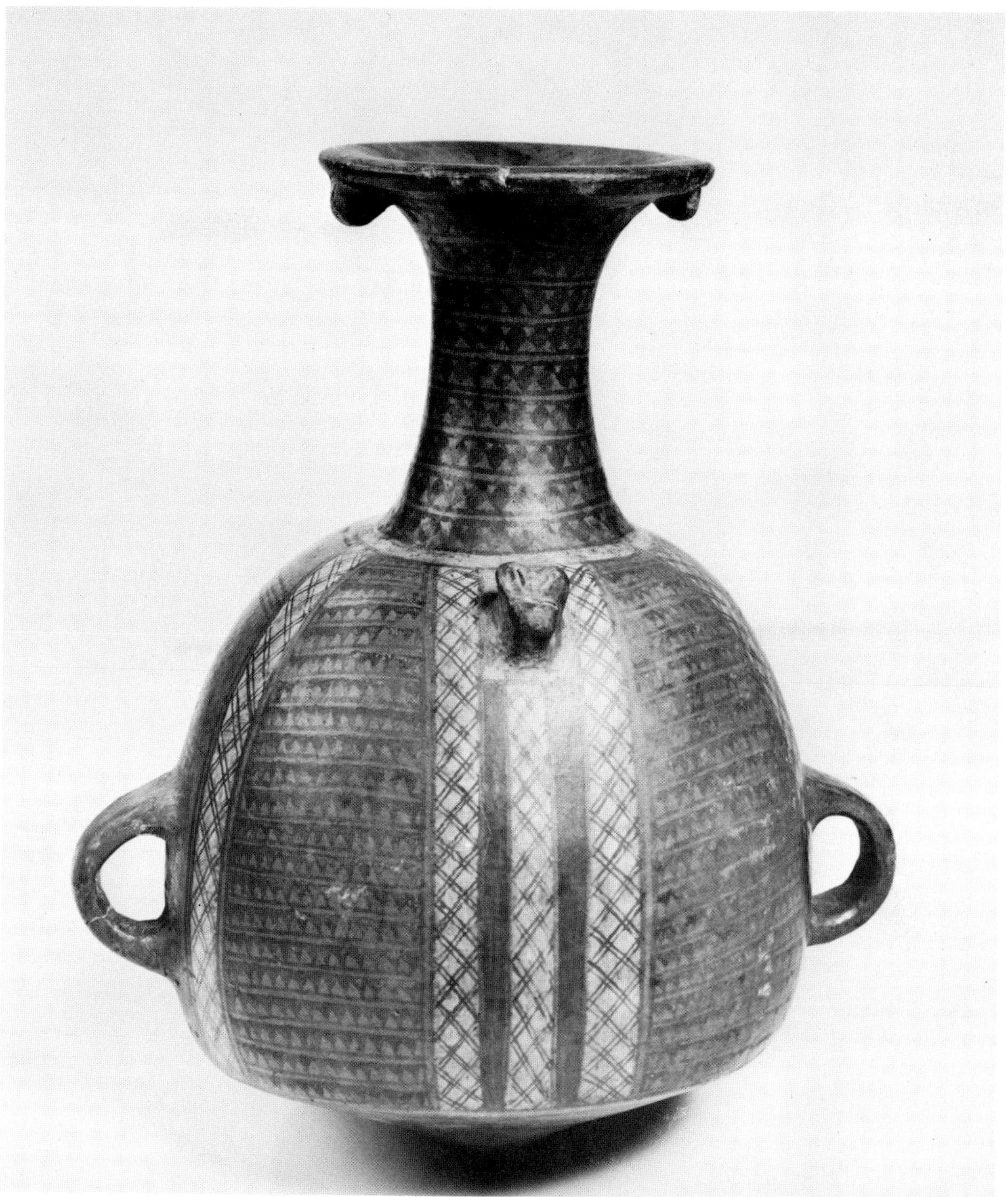

190. Polychrome Ceramic Urn
One of the most typical pottery forms designed by the Inca was the *aryballos*. This example, made in Ecuador, is an important indication of the range of the Inca Empire in the north. INCA. Chillanes, Bolívar, Ecuador. 1450-1520. 8¾" x 10½". 3/1069.

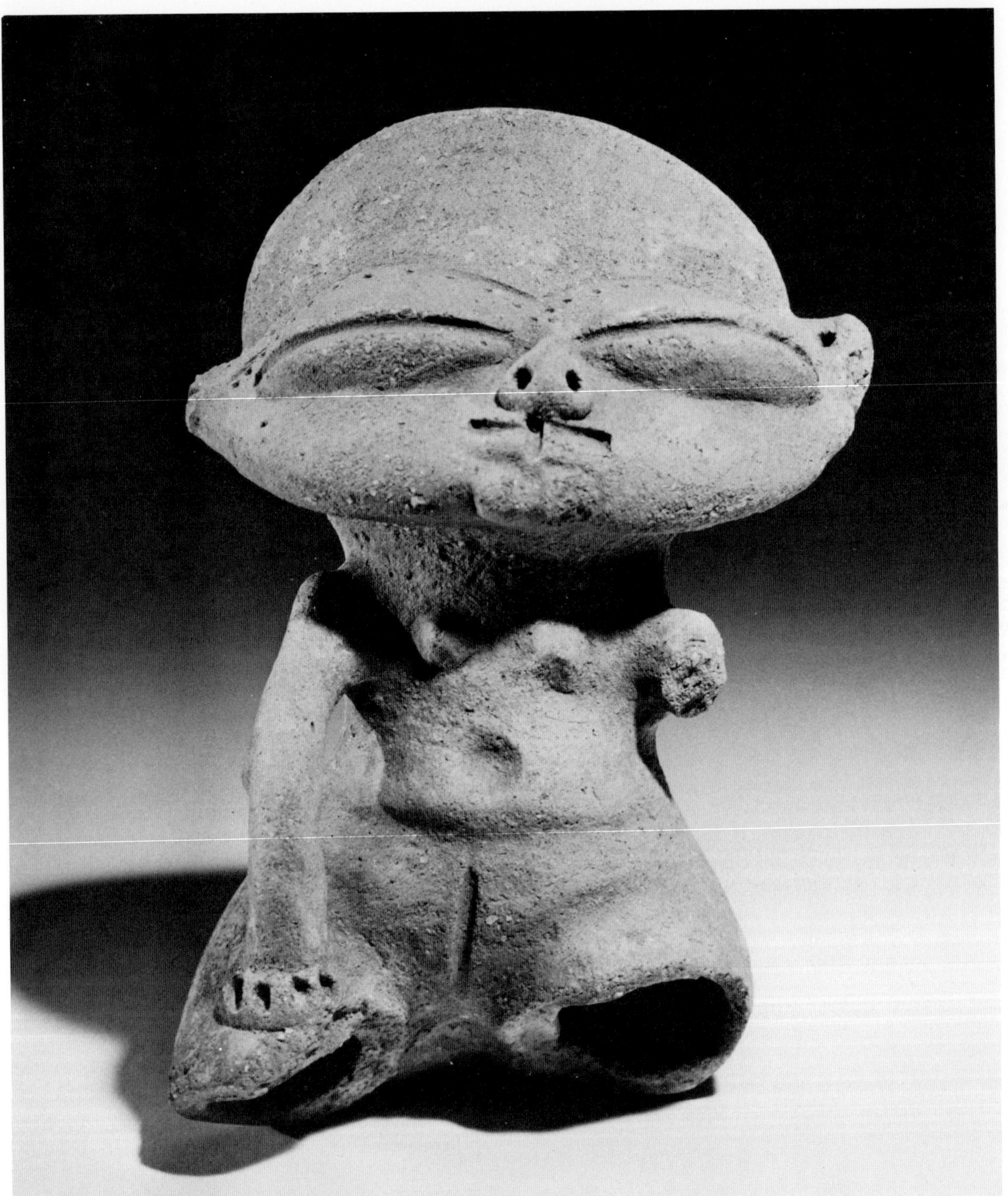

191. Buffware Effigy

The unusual facial features of these amusing figurines were restricted to an area in northern South America around Lake Valencia. This fragment reflects the globular quality of these wares. Collected by Luís H. Martínez. VALENCIA. Lake Valencia, Aragua, Venezuela. 1000-1500. 4½" x 6½". 4/9075.

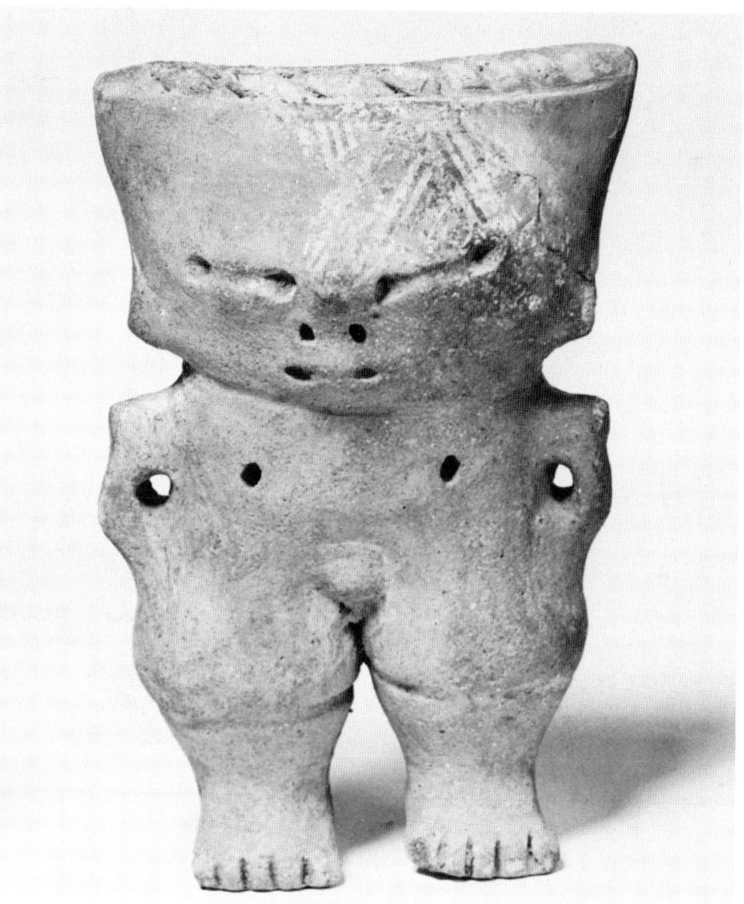

192. Painted Figurine
Another form of the bizarre effigy formations from the northern South America area is this grayware male figure with traces of red and white paint. Collected by C. F. Witzke. TIERRA DE LOS INDIOS. Niquitoy, Trujillo, Venezuela. 1000-1500. 4½" x 6¾". 4/8629.

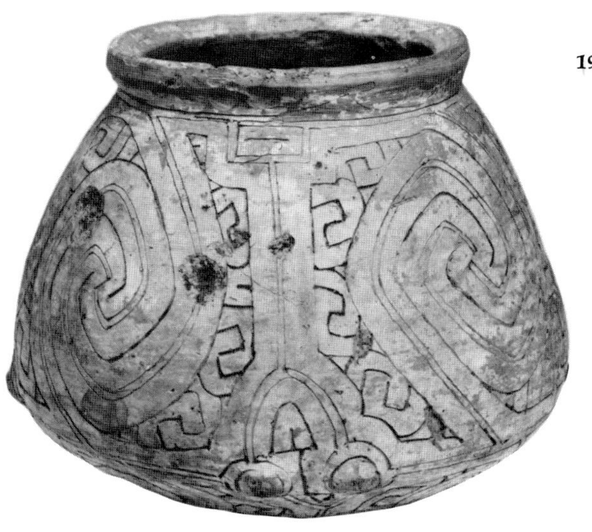

193. Carved Redware Bowl
This swelling, globular bowl is an example of a geometrically decorated pottery whose carved and incised decorations are distinctive, and found only at the mouth of the Amazon River. Presented by the Mattatuck Historical Society. MARAJOARA. Marajó Island, Pará, Brazil. 1000-1500. 6¼" x 7¼". 24/1938.

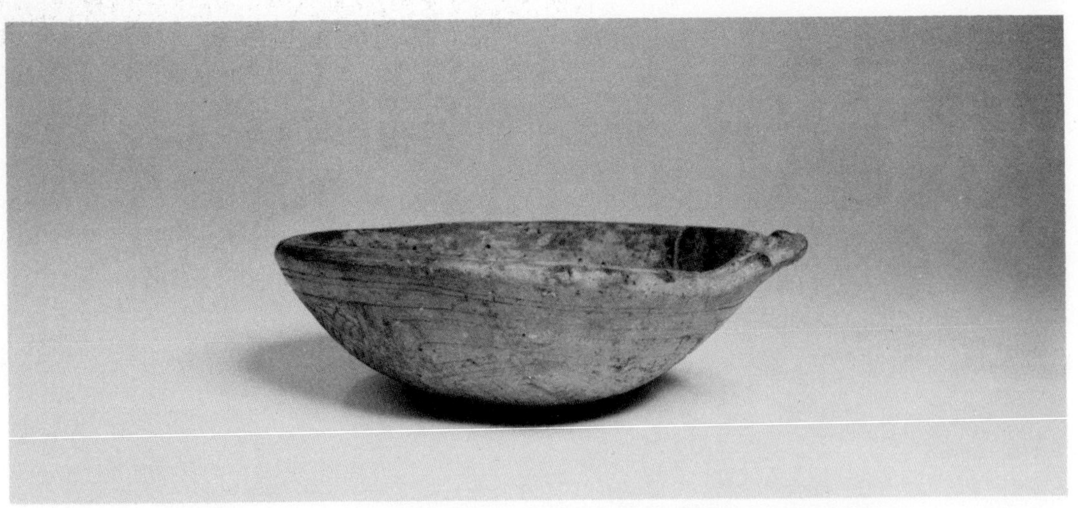

194. Shallow Redware Bowl
Bearing the excised and incised designs characteristic of the region, this retains all of the grace of early Amazon wares of northeastern Brazil. Collected by Hermann Immendorf. MARAJOARA. Marajó Island, Pará, Brazil. 1000-1500. 2½" x 7½". 18/778.

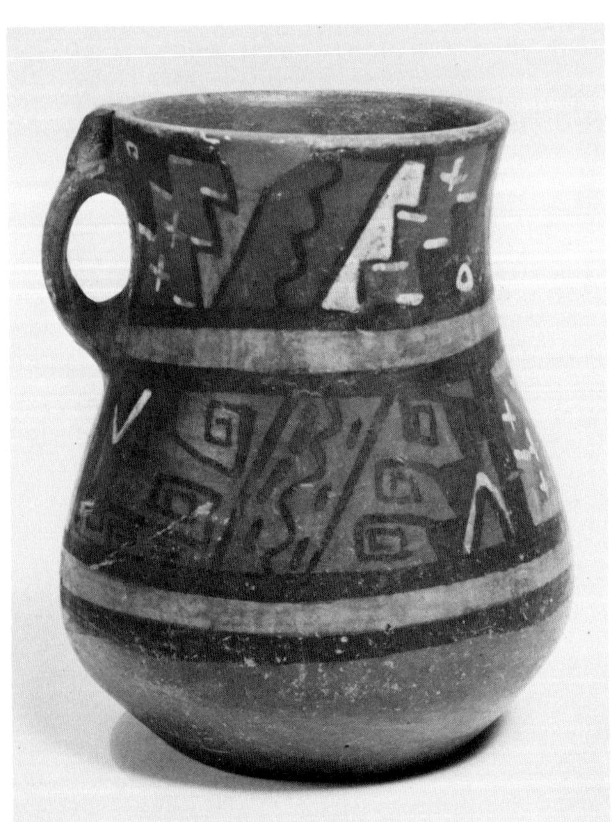

195. Polychrome Pitcher
In the angular style typical of the region, this black-and-white on redware vessel is a graceful example of ceramics from the middle years of Altiplano development. Collected by Adolph Bandelier. TIAHUANACO. Lake Titicaca, Bolivia. 750-1000. 4½" x 5¾". 6/3034.

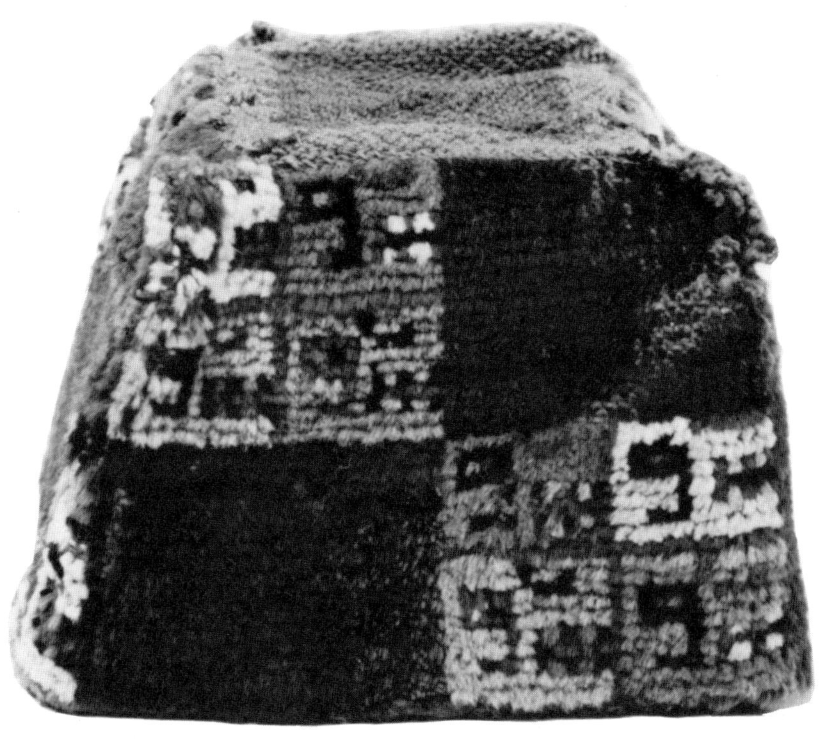

196. Man's Woven Cap
This lovely polychrome cap is woven in a knotted pile technique limited to the Tiahuanaco culture. The repeat-pattern design is the ubiquitous puma head so common during this period. TIAHUANACO. Bolivia or Peru. 750-1000. 3¼″ x 4½″ x 4½″. 24/3585.

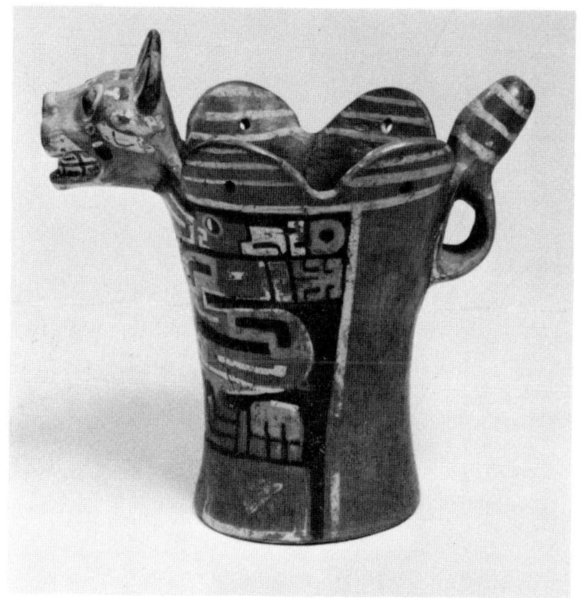

197. Flaring-rim Kero
Modelled with deep scallops around the rim, this *kero* has a powerfully worked jaguar head on one side. The design is completed in brilliant colors on the orangeware surface in a condor motif. TIAHUANACO. Bolivia. 500-700. 8¼″ x 8½″. 20/6314.

198. Polychrome Ring-base Jar
(See Title Page)

199. Double Shell Effigy

Two sea shells connected by a long stirrup spout are modeled in brown clay. Chavín pottery often reflects such natural features, making it particularly helpful in tracing prehistoric lifeways. CUPISNIQUE. Tembladera, Cajamarca, Peru. 500-200 B.C. 9¼" x 10¾". 24/3534.

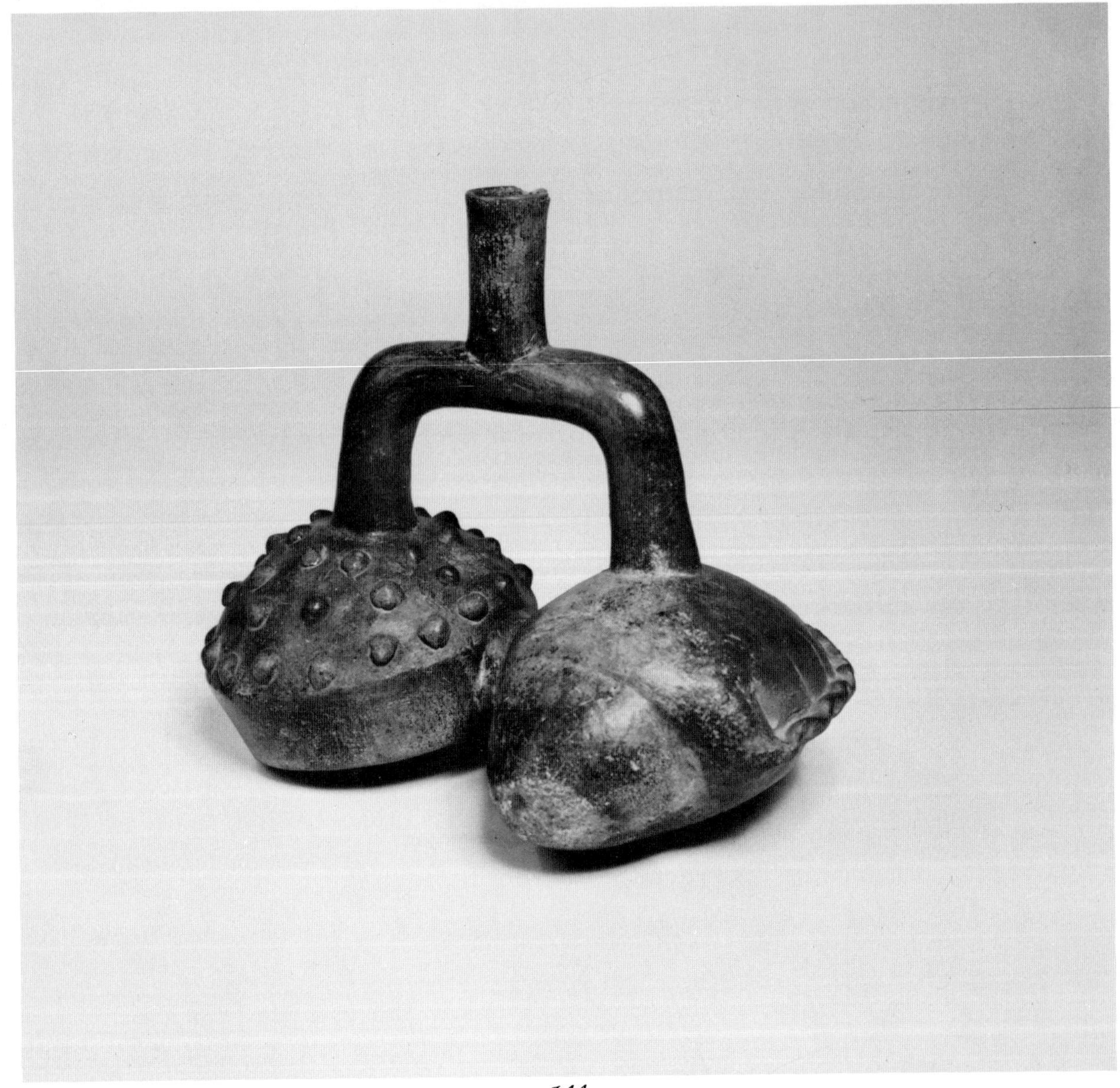

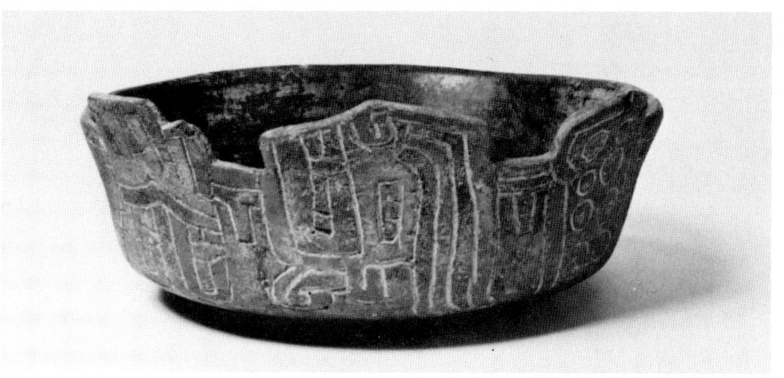

200. Shallow Incised Bowl
Far to the south in Peru, along the Paracas Peninsula, are the desert sites which yield pottery decorated by incising and colorfully pigmented designs. This linear pattern represents the Feline God, so frequently seen in this region. PARACAS. Paracas, Peru. 600-400 B.C. 4″ x 10″. 24/7528.

201. Globular Bridge-spouted Vessel
A characteristic form in the south are the thin-walled globular bowls with incised decorations, often with a whistle inserted in the neck. The design represents a falcon, native to the area. Presented by Dr. and Mrs. Arthur M. Sackler. PARACAS. Ocucaje, Ica Valley, Peru. 5¼″ x 6½″. 500-250 B.C. 23/8946.

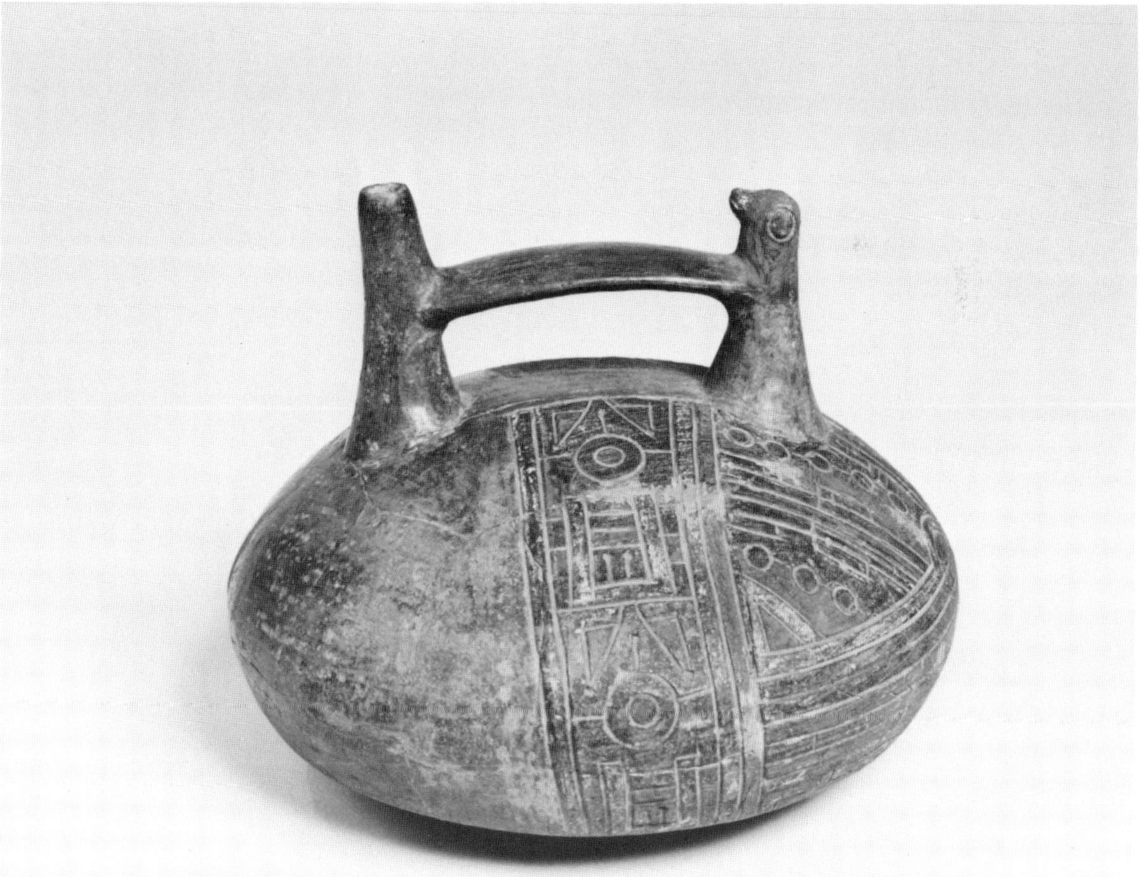

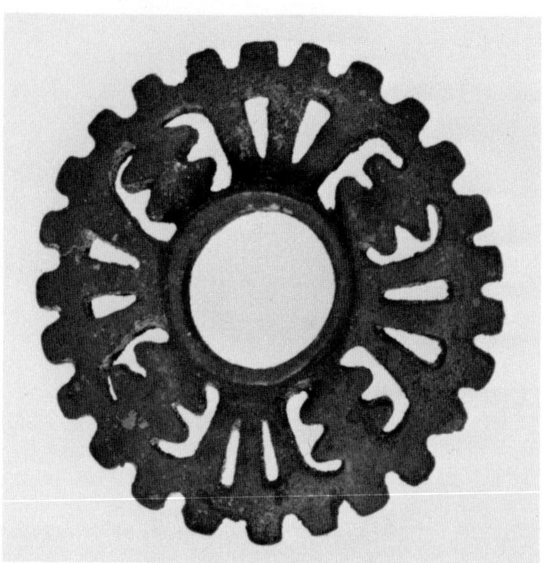

202. Bronze Mace Head
This circular bronze casting with a notched edge was intended for use with a wooden shaft, providing a mace or war club. Vicús. Ayabaca, Piura, Peru. 250-750. D: 3″. 23/8557.

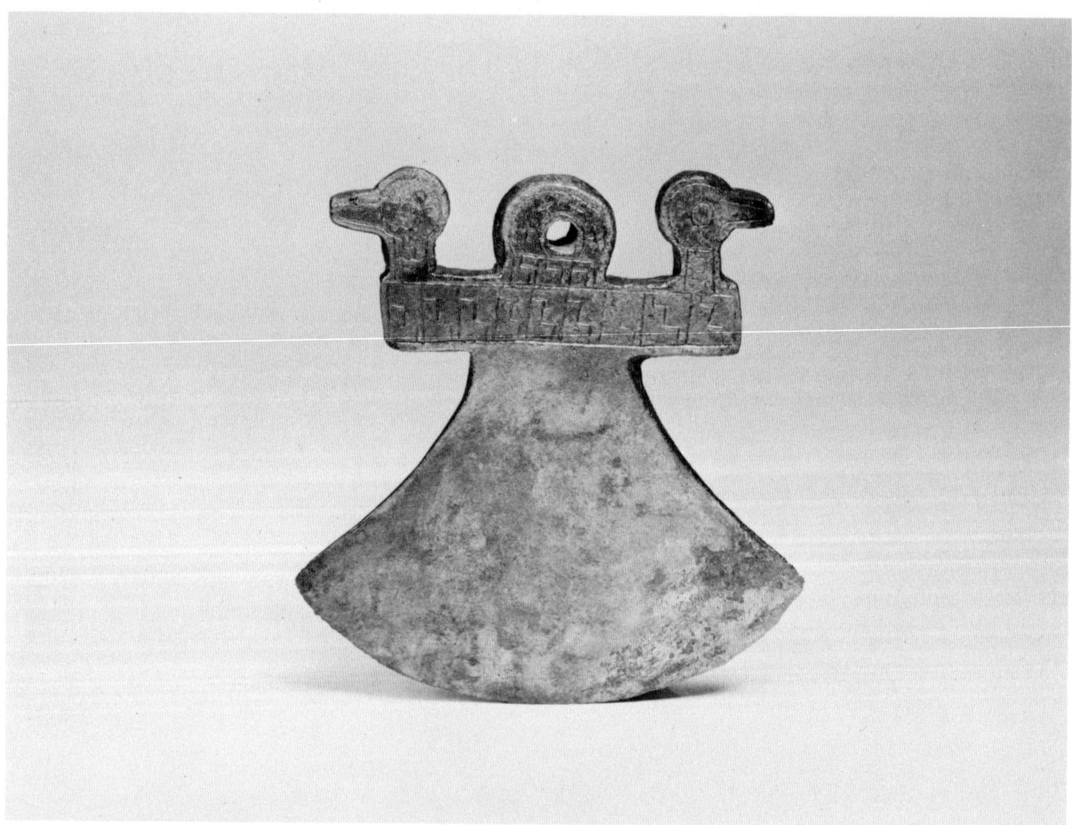

203. Cast Copper Blade
Intended for lashing to a wooden handle, this well-proportioned axe blade is decorated by incised geometric designs and two bird heads. Presented by Dr. and Mrs. Arthur M. Sackler. Vicus. Ayabaca, Piura, Peru. 250-750. 4¼″ x 4¼″. 23/9202.

204. Kneeling Prisoner

Another early ware, in the north of Peru, is found in the region of Ayabaca, where finely-modeled vessels decorated by resist technique, occur. This may represent a captive with his arms bound. Presented by Dr. and Mrs. Arthur M. Sackler. Vicús. Ayabaca, Piura, Peru. 200-500. 4″ x 8¼″. 23/8936

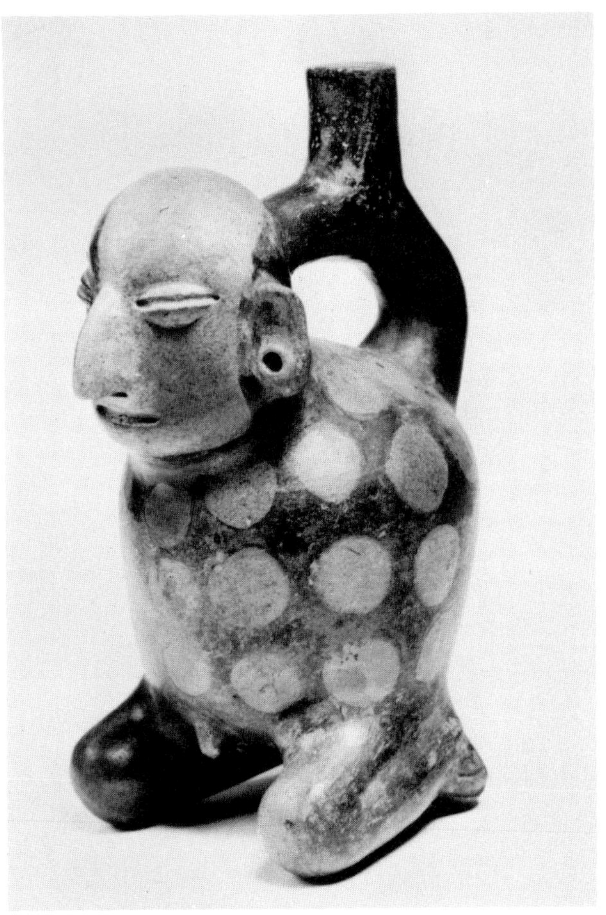

205. Double-bodied Vessel

With a design of a woman, joined to a large water vessel by two bridges, this is typical of the early horizon period in Peru. Presented by Dr. and Mrs. Arthur M. Sackler. Vicús. Ayabaca, Piura, Peru. 200-500. 7″ x 10″. 23/8940.

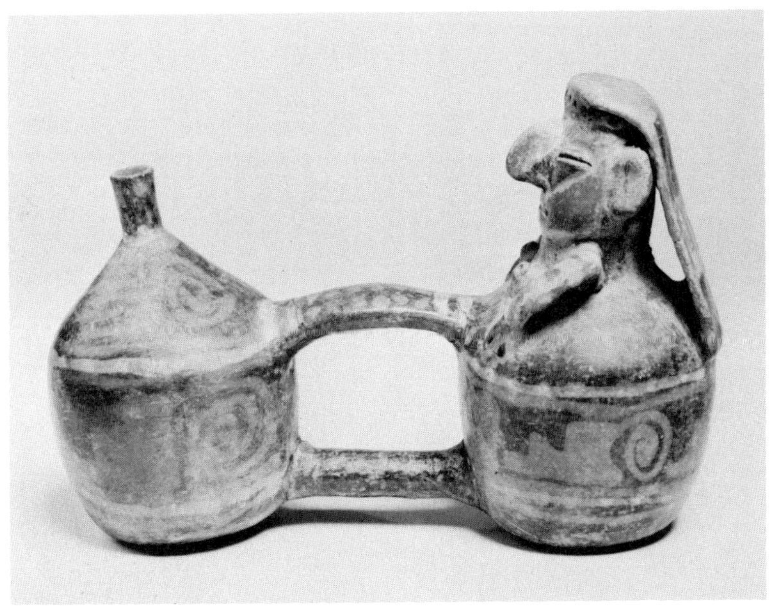

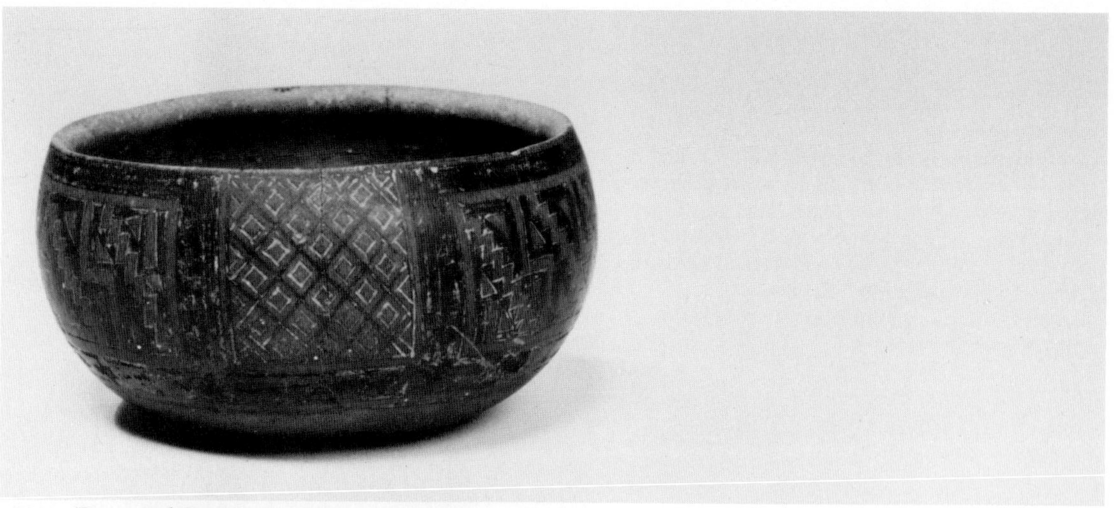

206. Decorated Gourd
These delicate linear designs are accomplished by burning the surface, presumably with a hot metal wire or rod. Often they are also painted. Collected by Hobart S. Geary. Lima, Peru. 1100-1476. 2½" x 5". 7/2763.

207. Human Effigy
A modeled vessel with the design of a seated, or squatting, man with a stirrup-spout on his back, this is typical of some of the sculptural wares of Peru. Presented by Dr. and Mrs. Arthur M. Sackler. Mochica. Chicama Valley, Libertad, Peru. 100-0 B.C. 3¾" x 6¼". 23/8960.

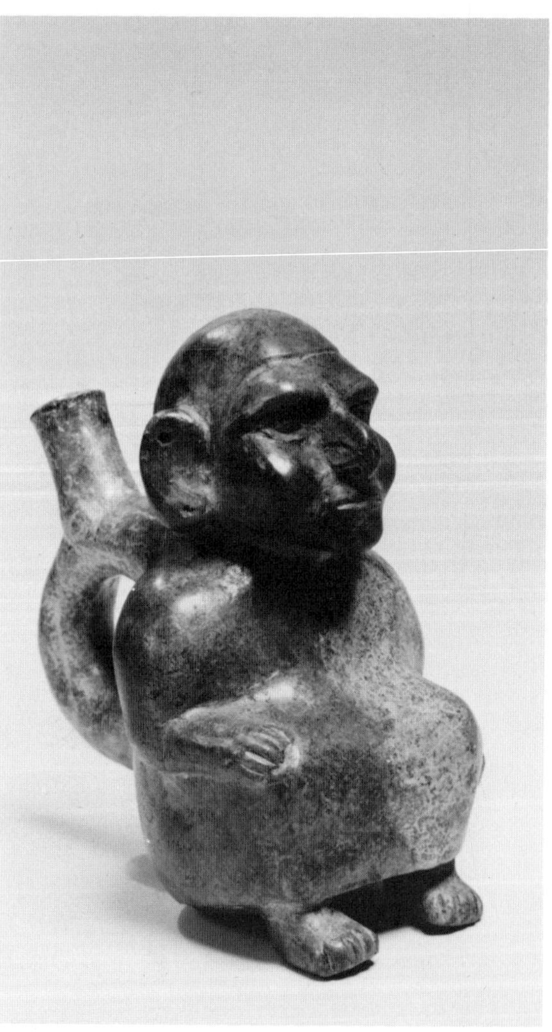

208. Painted Water Bottle

This cream-slipped redware vessel is decorated with brilliantly painted designs of a monster around the sides in red-brown. Collected by Harry Vanden Berg. MOCHICA. Chicama Valley, Libertad, Peru. 200-500. 6″ x 11½″. 15/7571.

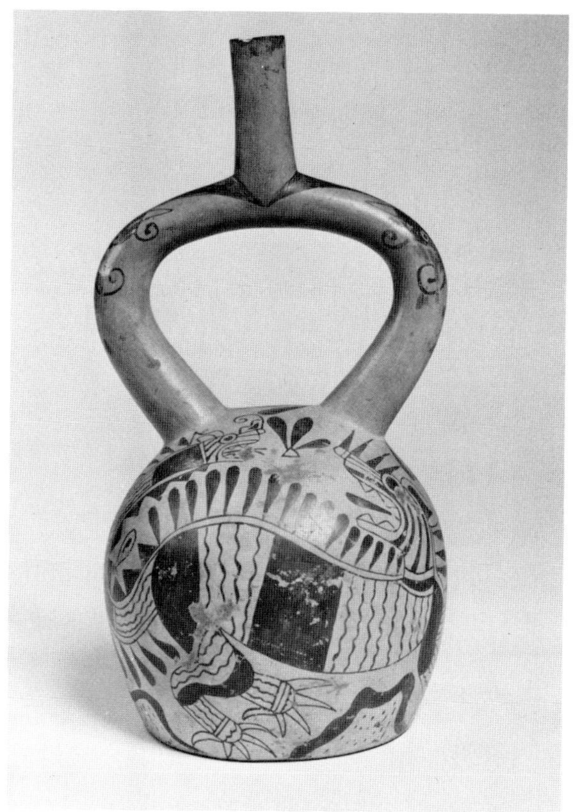

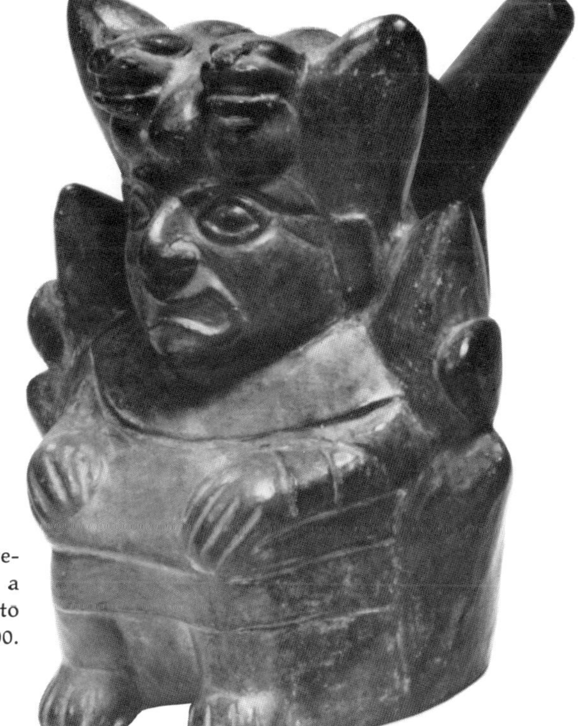

209. Grayware "Mountain Vessel"

So called because of the modelled peaks, this represents the anthropomorphic deity Ai-Apec with a serpent headdress. This iconography goes back to Chavín times. MOCHICA. Trujillo, Peru. 200-500. 5¾″ x 6½″. 24/7250.

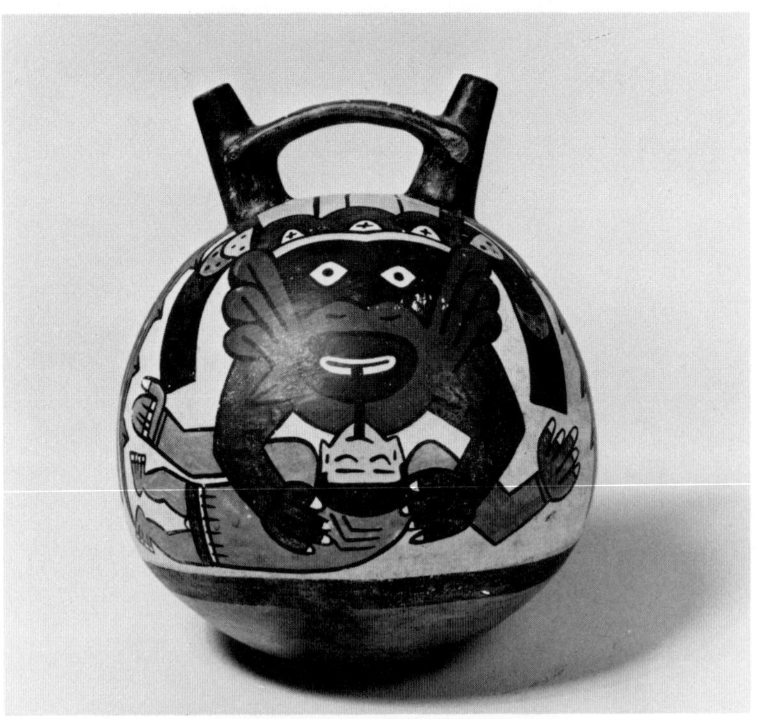

210. Double Spouted Vessel
This beautifully rounded vessel is painted with a polychrome design of a feline monster holding a person, presumably a dead victim, in his claws. NAZCA. Nazca Valley, Peru. 100 B.C.-200 A.D. 6″ x 7¼″. 22/5604.

211. Open-mouthed Bowl
The smoothly polished sides of this thin-walled bowl are decorated by painted designs of flying birds. Presented by John S. Williams. NAZCA. Nazca Valley, Peru. 100 B.C.-200 A.D. 3¾″ x 5″. 23/2260.

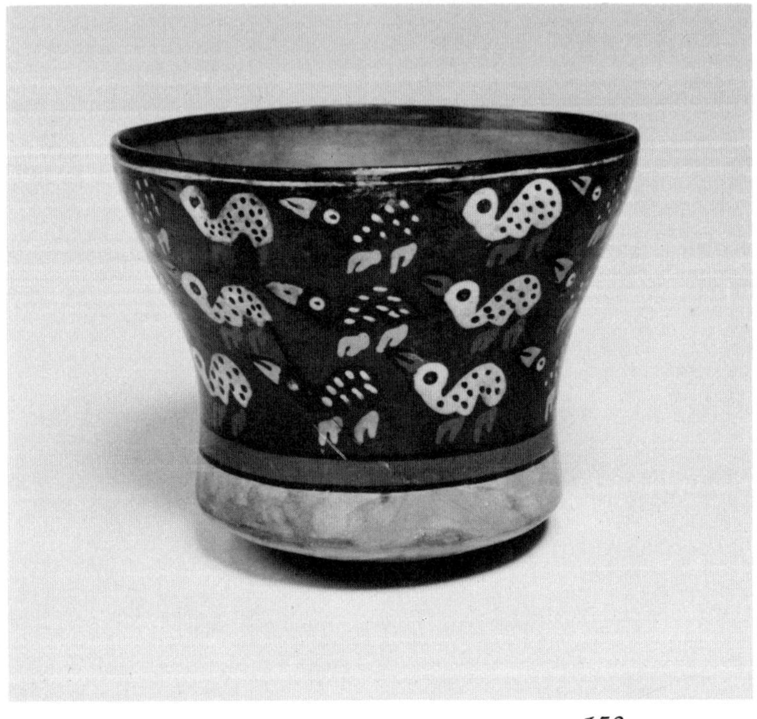

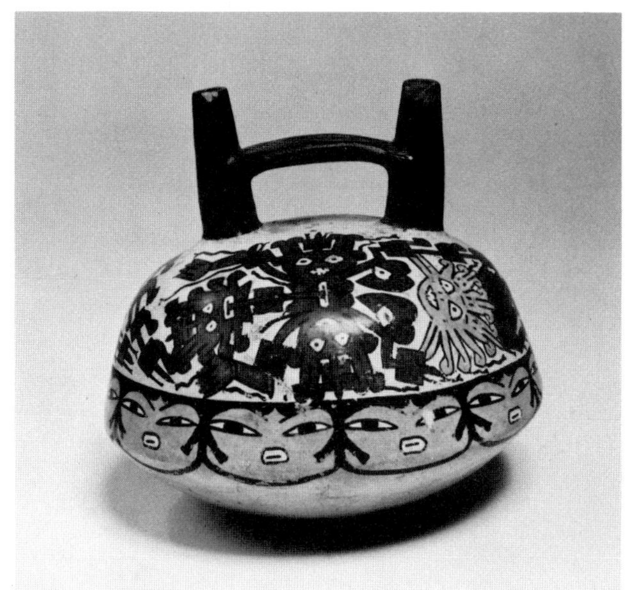

212. Polychrome Vessel

The graceful lines and perfect proportions of some of the best of the Peruvian pottery work is seen in this example. The designs are mythological creatures above a repeat band of human faces. Collected by Michel V. M. Schroder. NAZCA. Ica, Peru. 300-600. 5″ x 5″. 11/2669.

213. Polychrome Vase

(See color insert facing page 40)

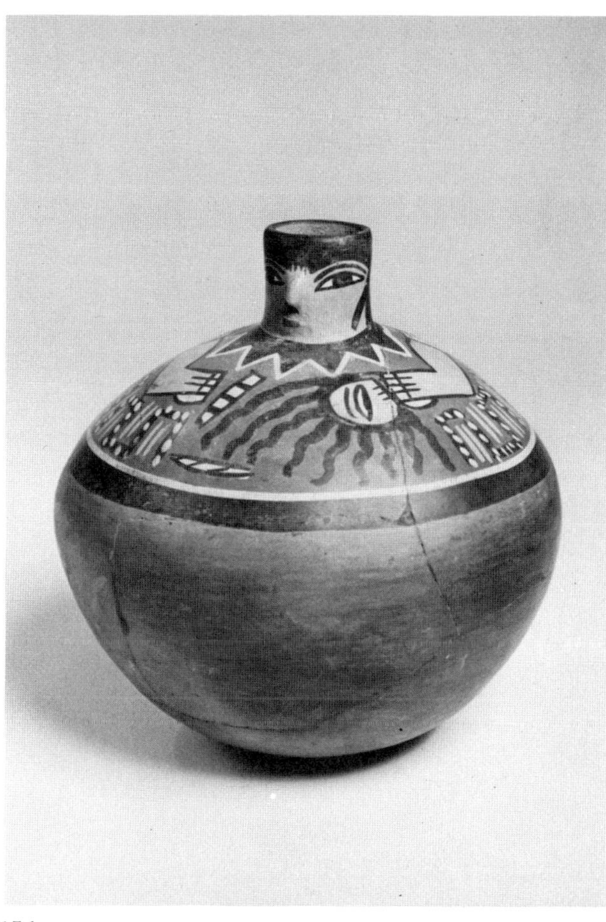

214. Polychrome Jar

A large globular-bodied vessel, painted to represent a human, this is a fine representation of the rotund form of many Peruvian ceramics. Collected by Michel V. M. Schroder. NAZCA-HUARI. Nazca Valley, Ica, Peru. 500-700. 7½″ x 7½″. 11/2798.

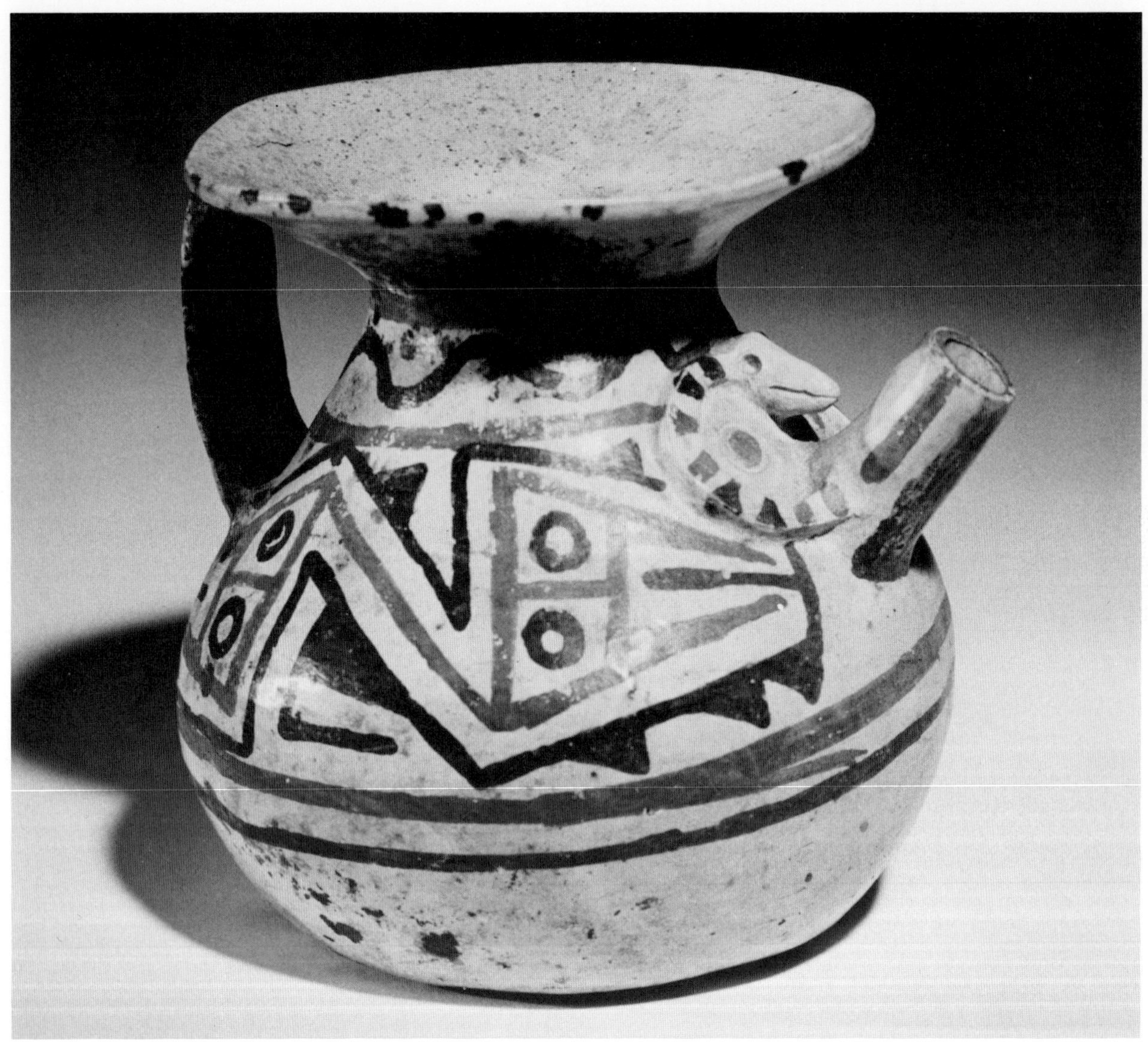

215. Painted Pitcher
A cream-slipped bowl with a protruding spout, this has a bird mask design on the side. Presented by Dr. and Mrs. Arthur M. Sackler. RECUAY. Ancash, Peru. 300-800. 4¼" x 4¾". 23/8973.

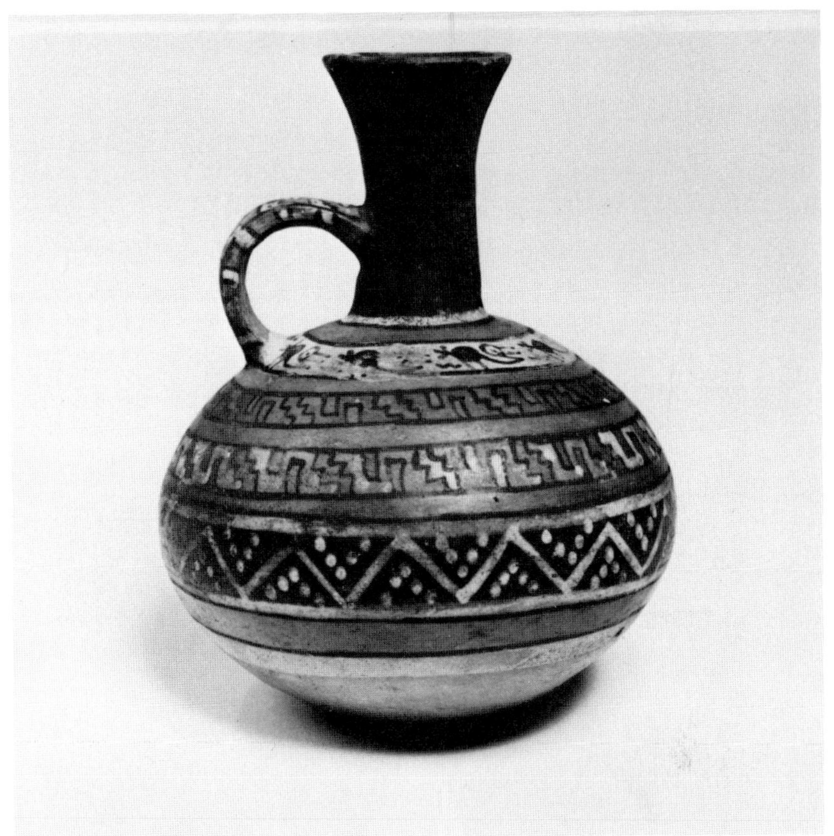

216. Polychrome Goblet
The artists of the Ica Valley often painted their ceramics with designs derived from textiles. This example was collected about 1830 and taken to England. The William L. Morkill Collection. ICA. Ica Valley, Peru. 1200-1476. 5¼″ x 7½″. 19/9237.

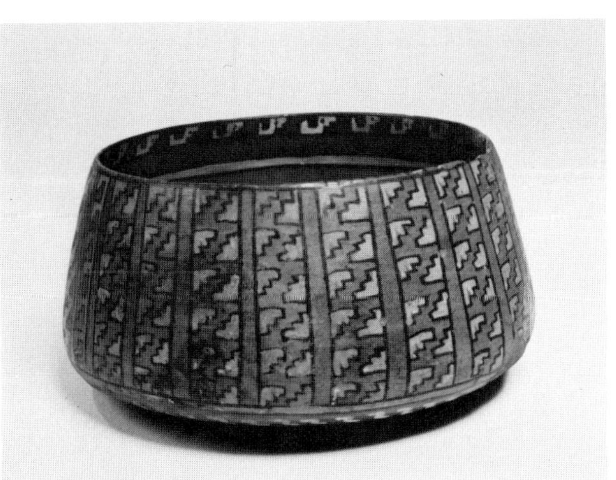

217. Ceramic Bowl
Another example decorated in the geometric style so favored by the South Coast artists. The Cranmore Collection. ICA. Ica Valley, Peru. 1200-1476. 3¾″ x 6½″. 19/6608.

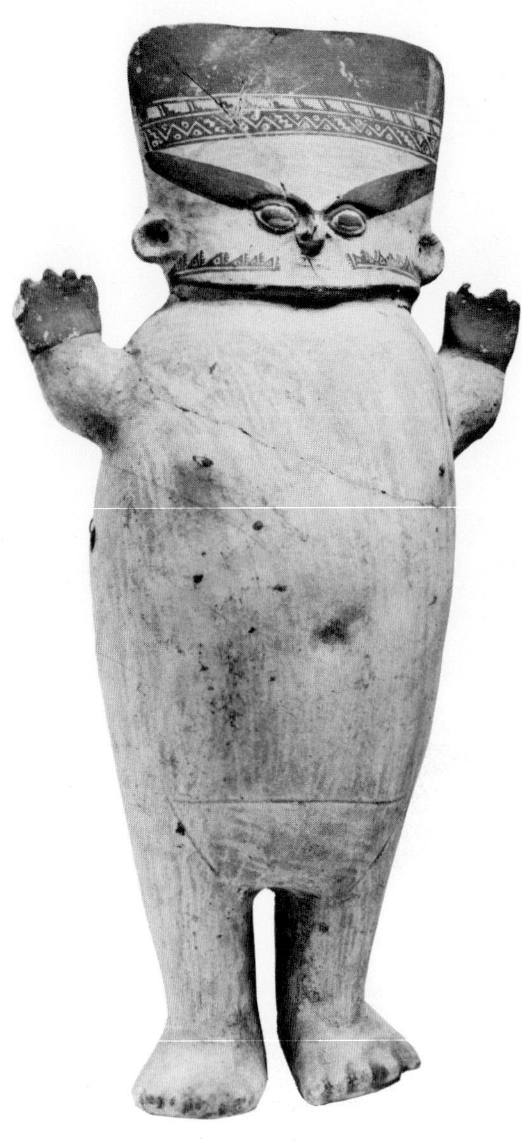

218. Large Female Effigy
These ovoid figurines are characteristic of the Chancay culture. Made from poor quality clay, and often painted in a sloppy fashion, they can readily be identified by their form and abstracted appearance. CHANCAY Lima, Peru. 1100-1476. 12½" x 24¾". 22/1790.

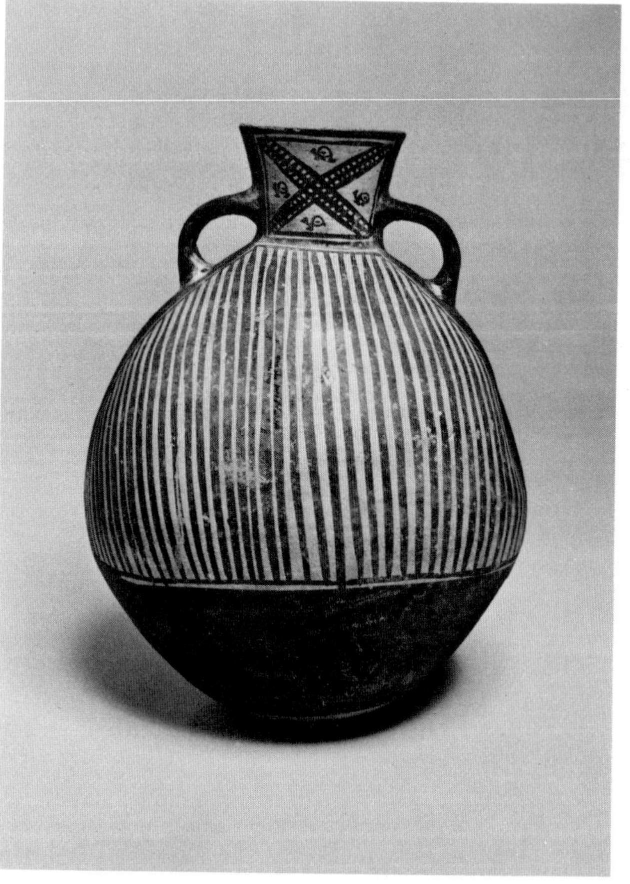

219. Globular Olla
Another example of the characteristic egg-shaped vessels from this region, this features a geometric design in brown on a cream-colored slip. Presented by William F. Stiles. CHANCAY. Chancay Valley, Peru. 1100-1476. 5¾" x 9". 23/8574.

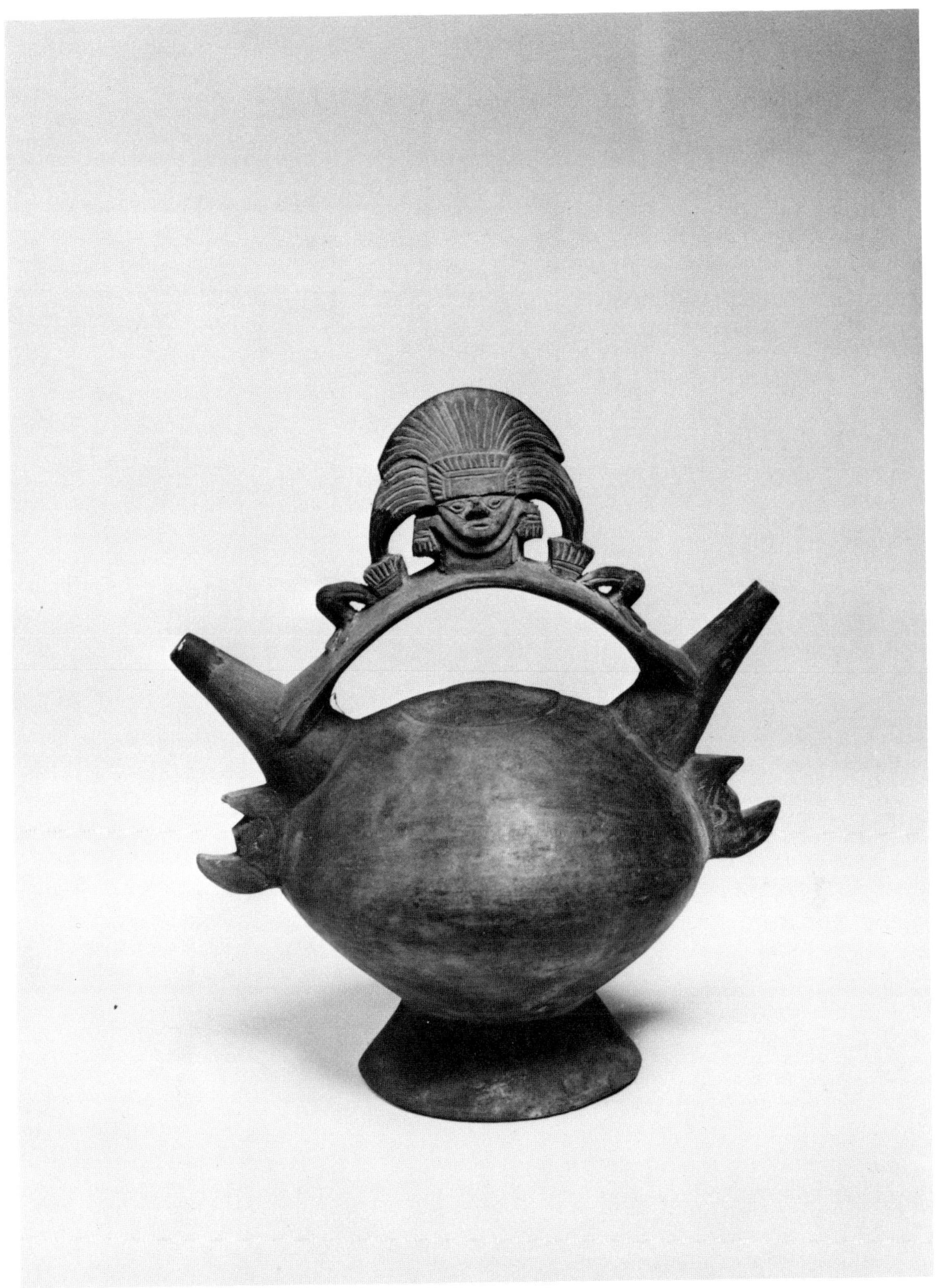

220. Elaborate Double-spout Vessel
The origin of the *tumi*, a characteristic headdress of Peruvian nobility, is well demonstrated by this modeled effigy wearing a splayed feather headgear. Two small birds are at his sides. The William L. Morkill Collection. LAMBAYEQUE. Lambayeque Valley, Peru. 1100-1476. 9" x 10¾". 19/9172.

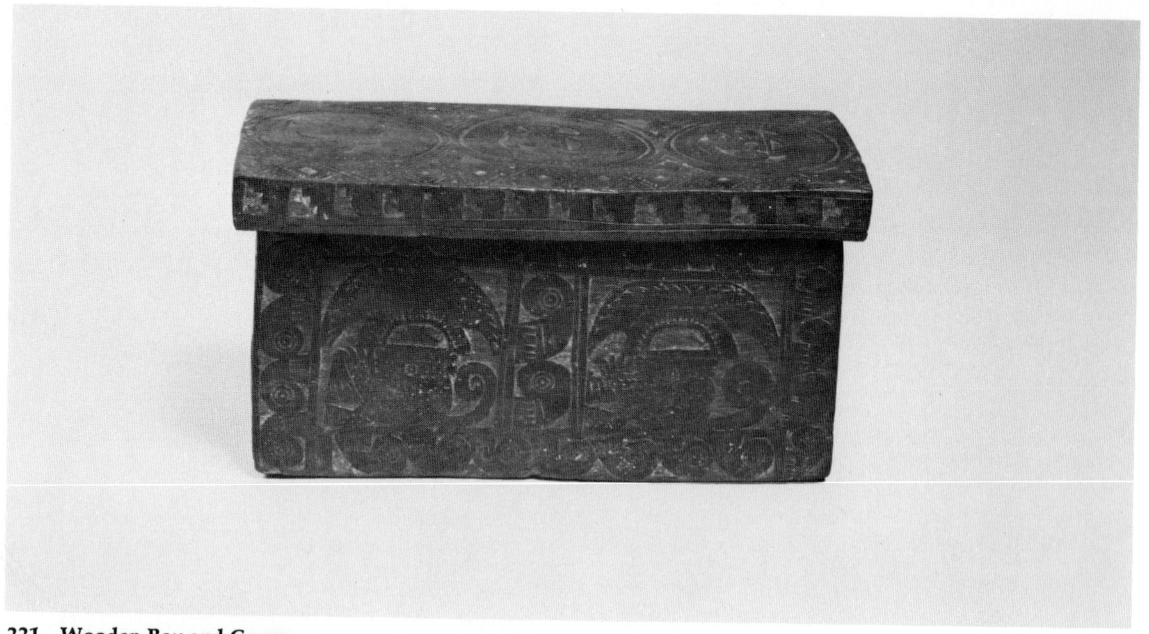

221. Wooden Box and Cover
Probably intended for storage of personal possessions, this is decorated by incised designs of the spotted ocelot or a similar leopard-like creature. CHIMÚ? Trujillo, Peru. 900-1200. 5″ x 9¼″. 19/7587.

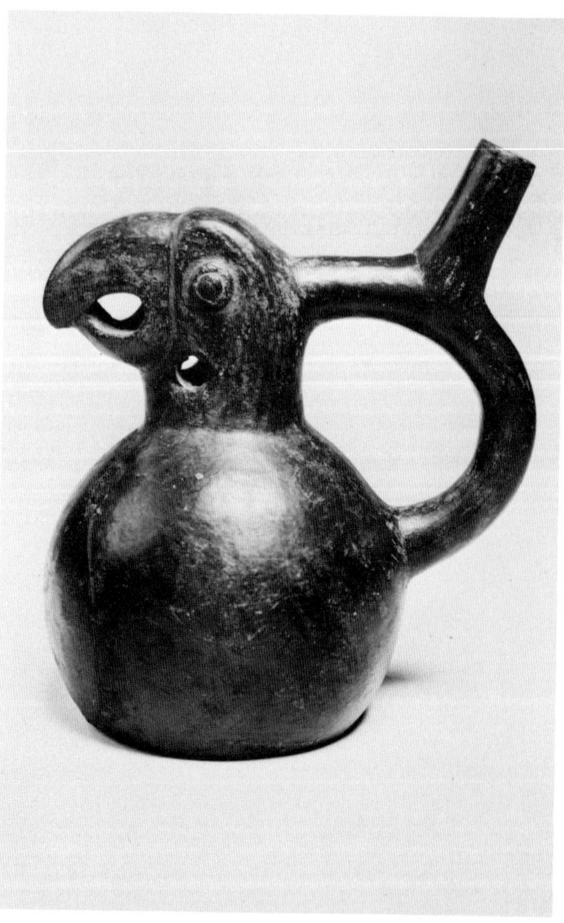

222. Parrot Effigy Vessel
The many examples of flora and fauna found in ancient Peru are often depicted in their ceramics. This fine blackware representation of a parrot is an example of the realistic quality in this ware. Collected by Harry Vanden Berg. CHIMÚ. Chicama Valley, Peru. 1200-1476. 7″ x 8¼″. 15/7649.

223. Maize God Deity

The stack of maize ears, topped by a figure with a headdress composed of maize, leaves little question as to the identification of this deity modeled in blackware. Collected by George G. Heye. CHIMÚ. Chicama Valley, Peru. 1476-1534. 7¼″ x 9″. 11/1359.

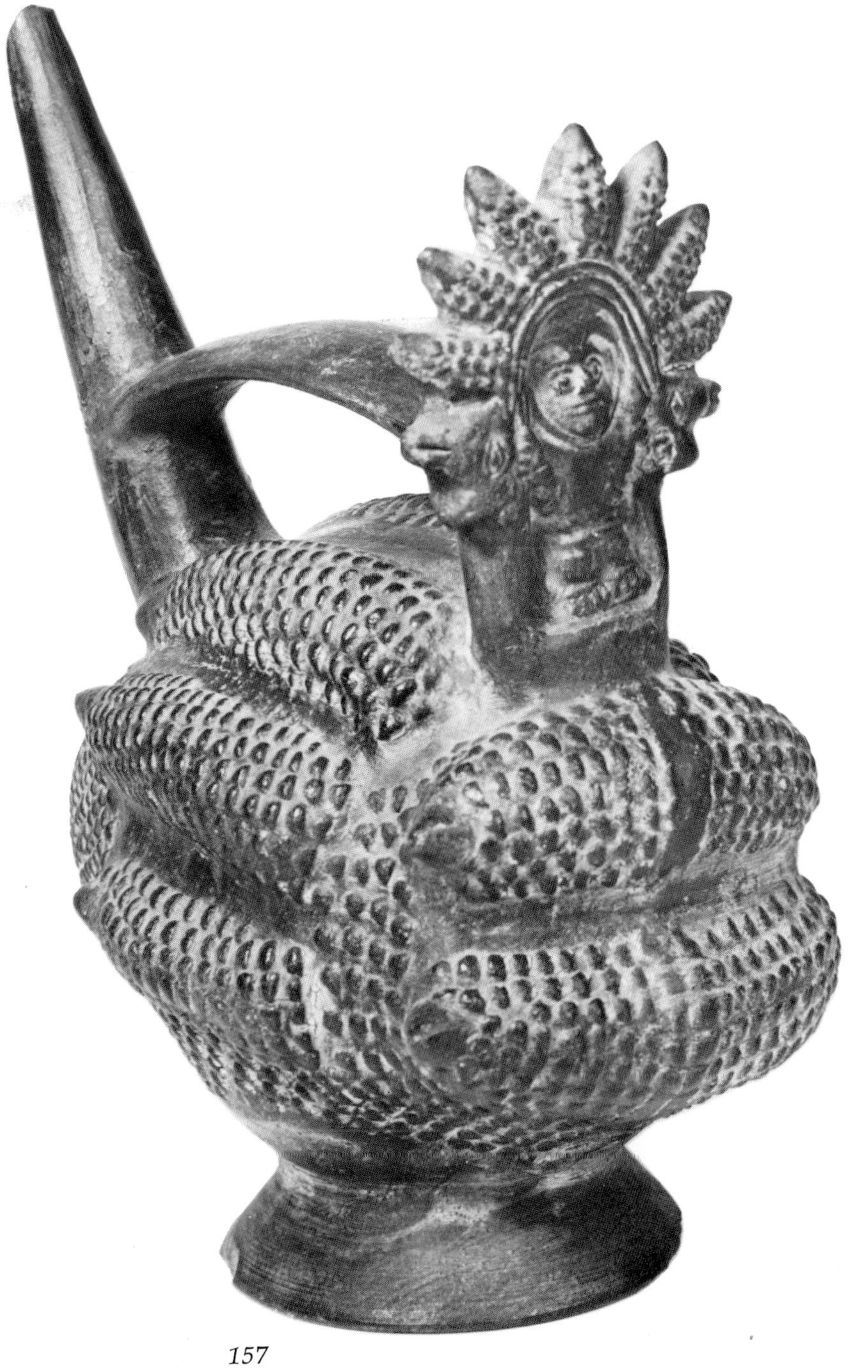

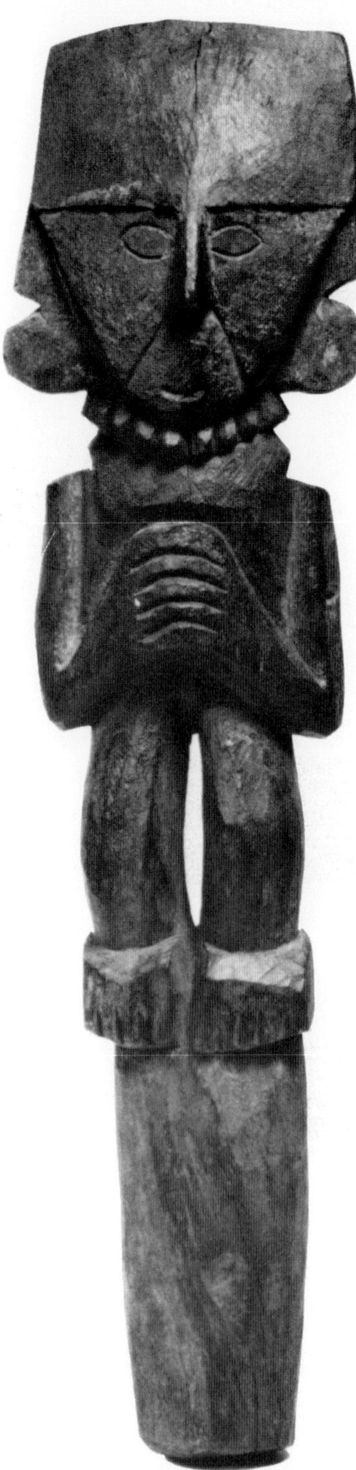

224. Sculptured Wooden Figure
Furnished with a base for insertion into the ground, these are believed to have served much the same purpose as our headstones for graves today; they may have been idols or ceremonial effigies. The Cranmore Collection. CHIMÚ. Trujillo, Peru. 1300-1476. 5¾" x 22". 19/6641.

225. Silver-plated Beaker
Hammered out of a sheet copper base, and "drawn" by processes still followed by contemporary silversmiths, this elongated goblet is decorated with the repoussé design of a human head. The metal was subsequently plated with silver. CHIMÚ. Lambayeque, Peru. 1300-1476. 2½" x 8¼". 19/7965.

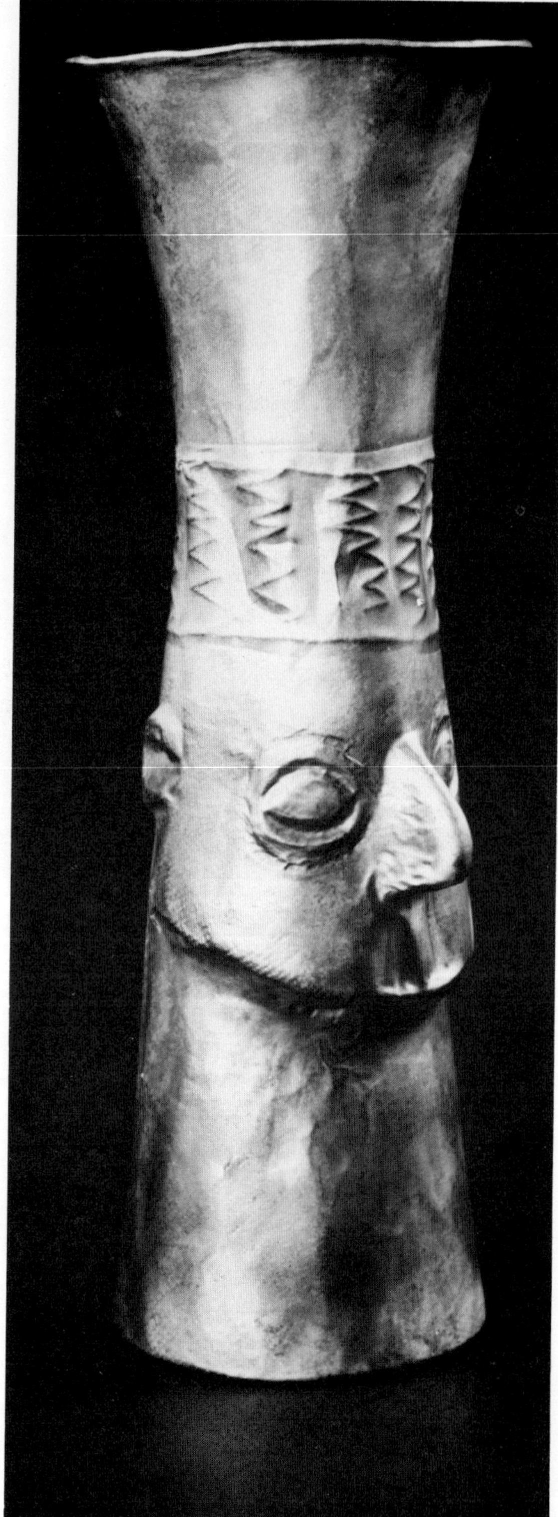

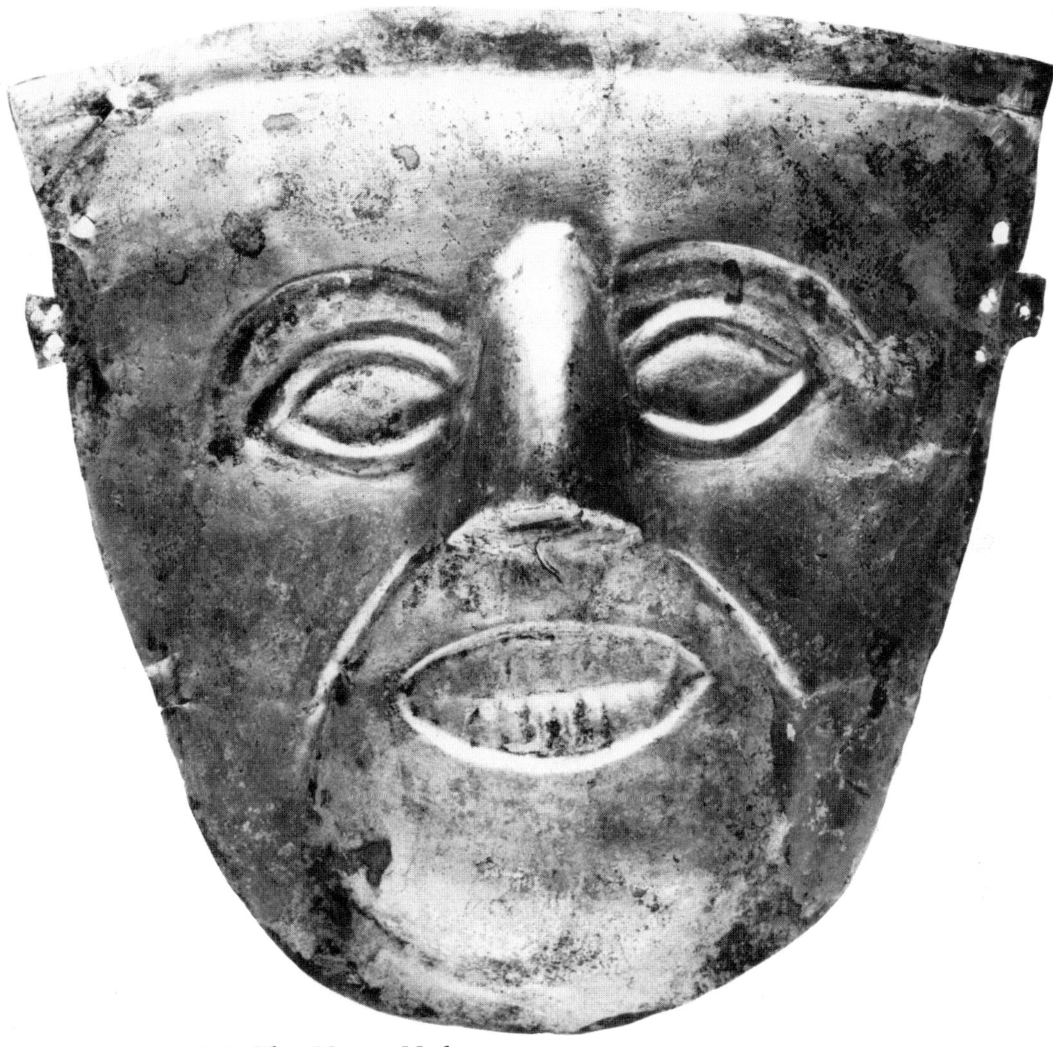

226. Silver Mummy Mask

Made from a flat sheet of silver, with holes for attachment to the mummy bundle, this bears a repoussé design of a face, perhaps that of the deceased. Collected by A. H. Verrill. CHIMU? Supe, Peru. 1000-1532. 6¾" x 7". 15/8574.

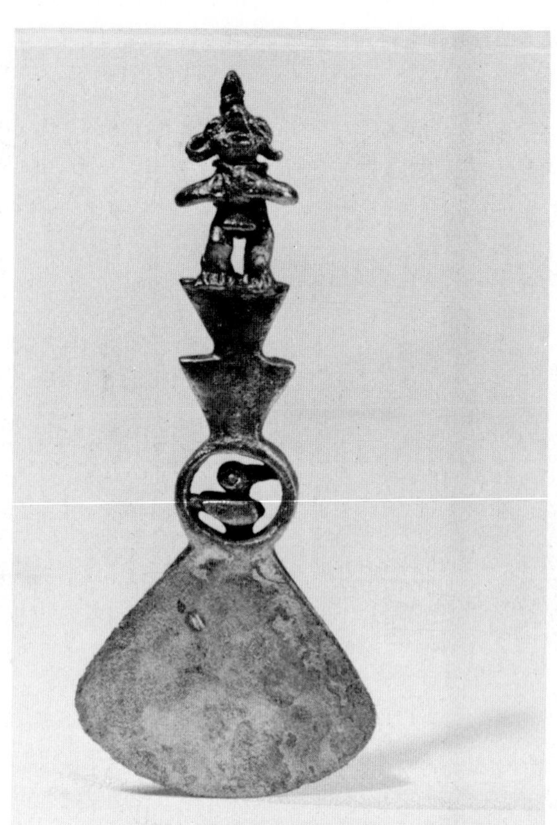

227. Cast Copper Blade

Elaborately designed with an openwork human, topping a bird in a circle, this blade is a fine example of the delicate casting of the Peruvian metalsmith. Collected by Maj. Otto Holstein. CHIMÚ. Chan Chan, Peru. 1300-1476. 1¾" x 3¾". 15/7166.

228. Cast Bronze Staff Head

Careful examination of this ornate object reveals the remarkable technical skill of the bronze caster. The design of four monkeys seated atop the central shaft, in various poses—together with eight bells attached by solid rings, each with its own clapper—were all cast in one piece. This apparently served as the head of a wooden staff, and provided a musical sound as the owner walked. Collected by A. H. Verrill. CHIMÚ. Chan Chan, Peru, 1300-1476. 2¼" x 3¾". 15/8589.

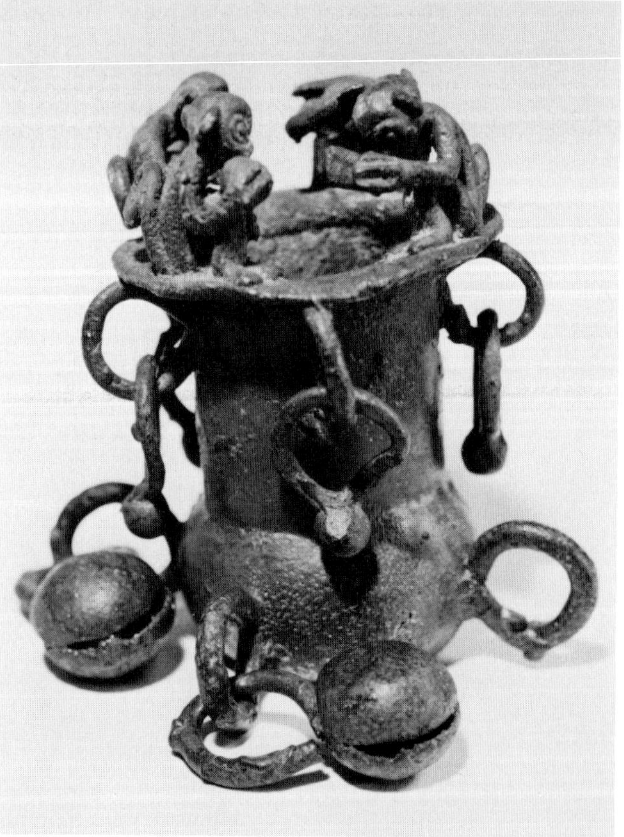

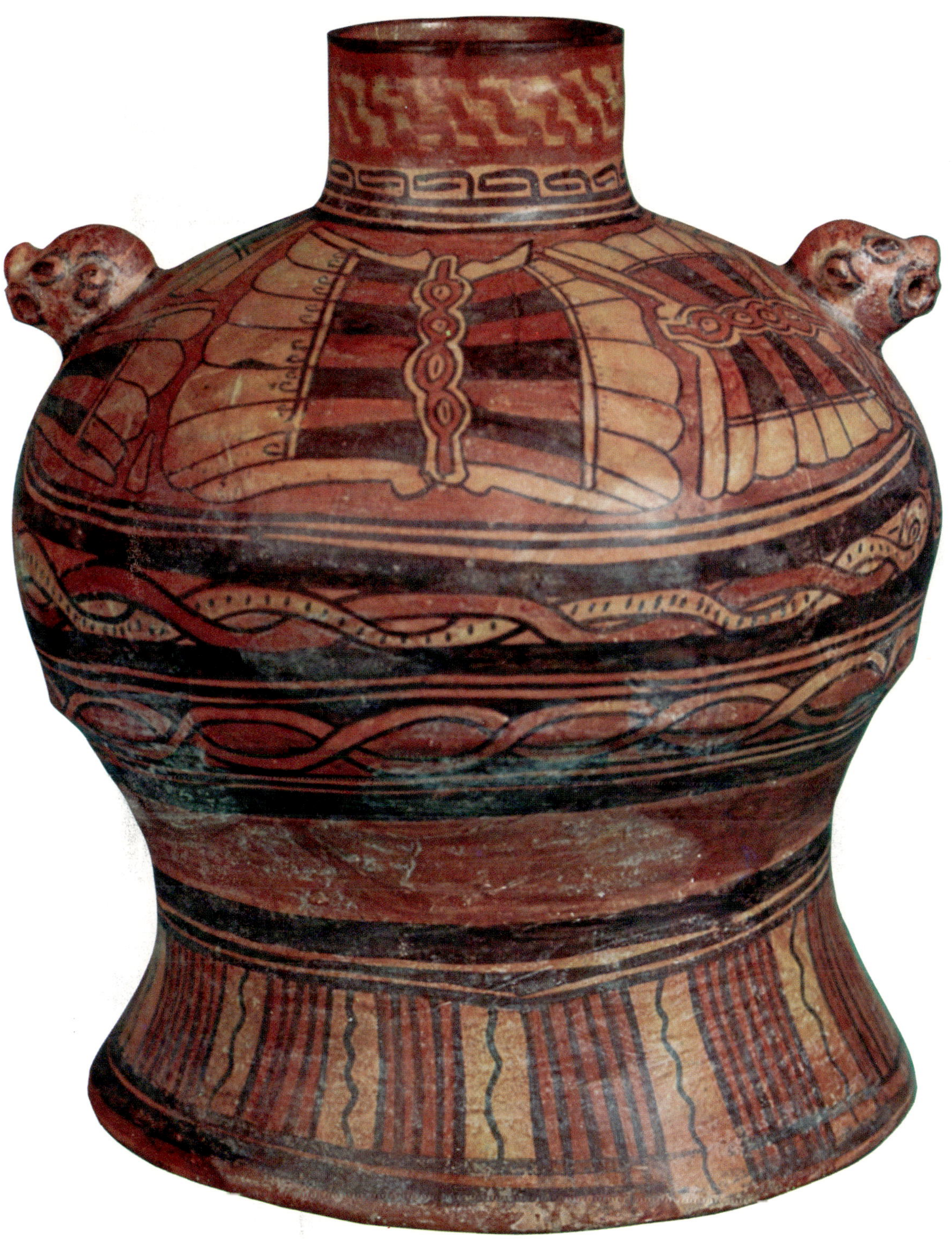

138. Large Polychrome Urn
A brilliantly painted polychrome vessel, probably a drum. Decorated with two jaguar heads on the sides. CHOROTEGA? Filadelfia, Guanacaste, Costa Rica. 800-1200. 13″ x 15½″. 23/5597.

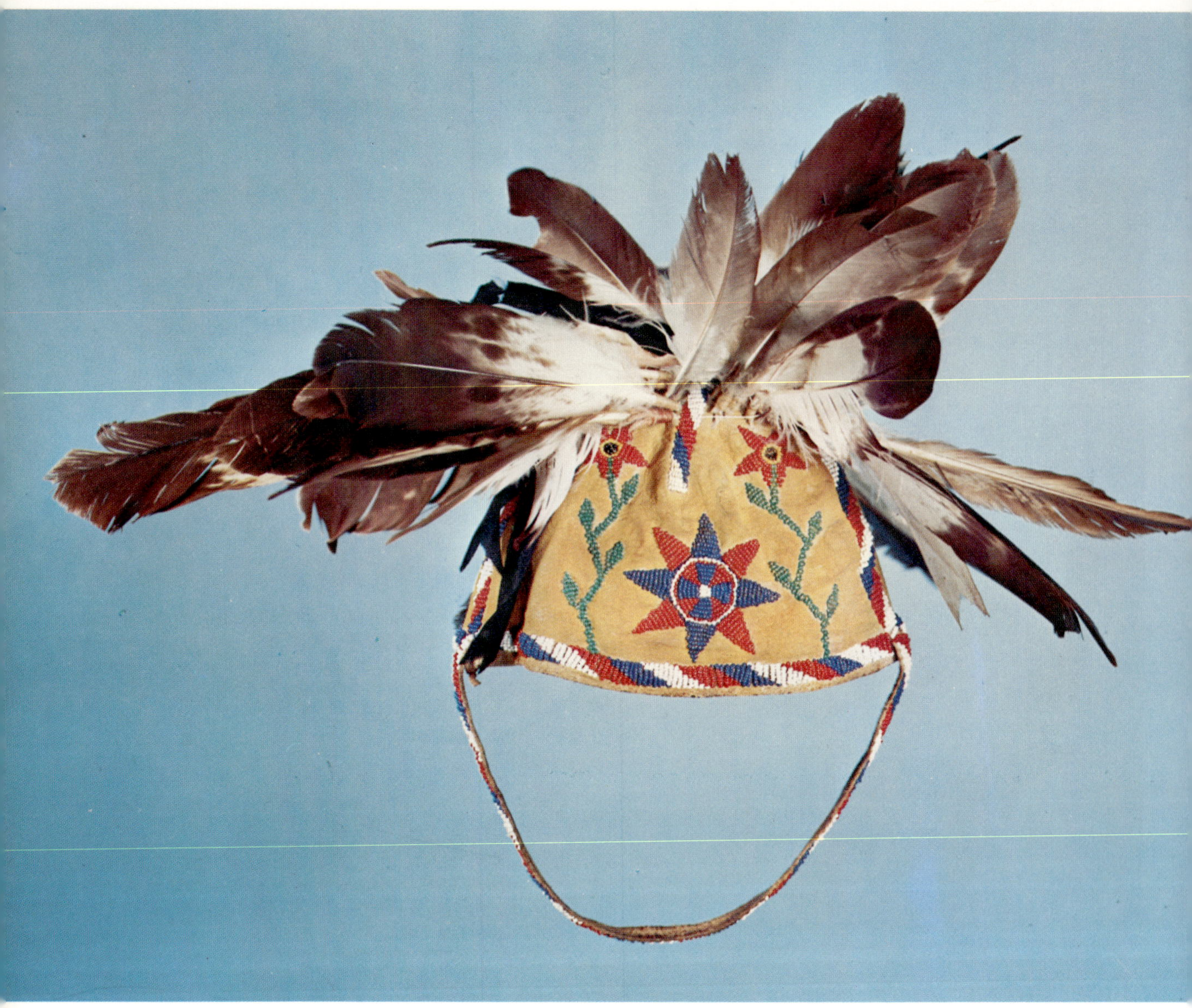

339. Feathered War Cap
Warriors wore such caps not only for protection from harm, but also in the realization that it made them more fearsome to their enemies. This yellow-painted deerhide cap is ornamented with eagle and hawk feathers, and beadwork designs. Collected by Irving S. Cobb. White Mountain Apache. Arizona. 1875-1880. 10″ x 23″. 20/8055.

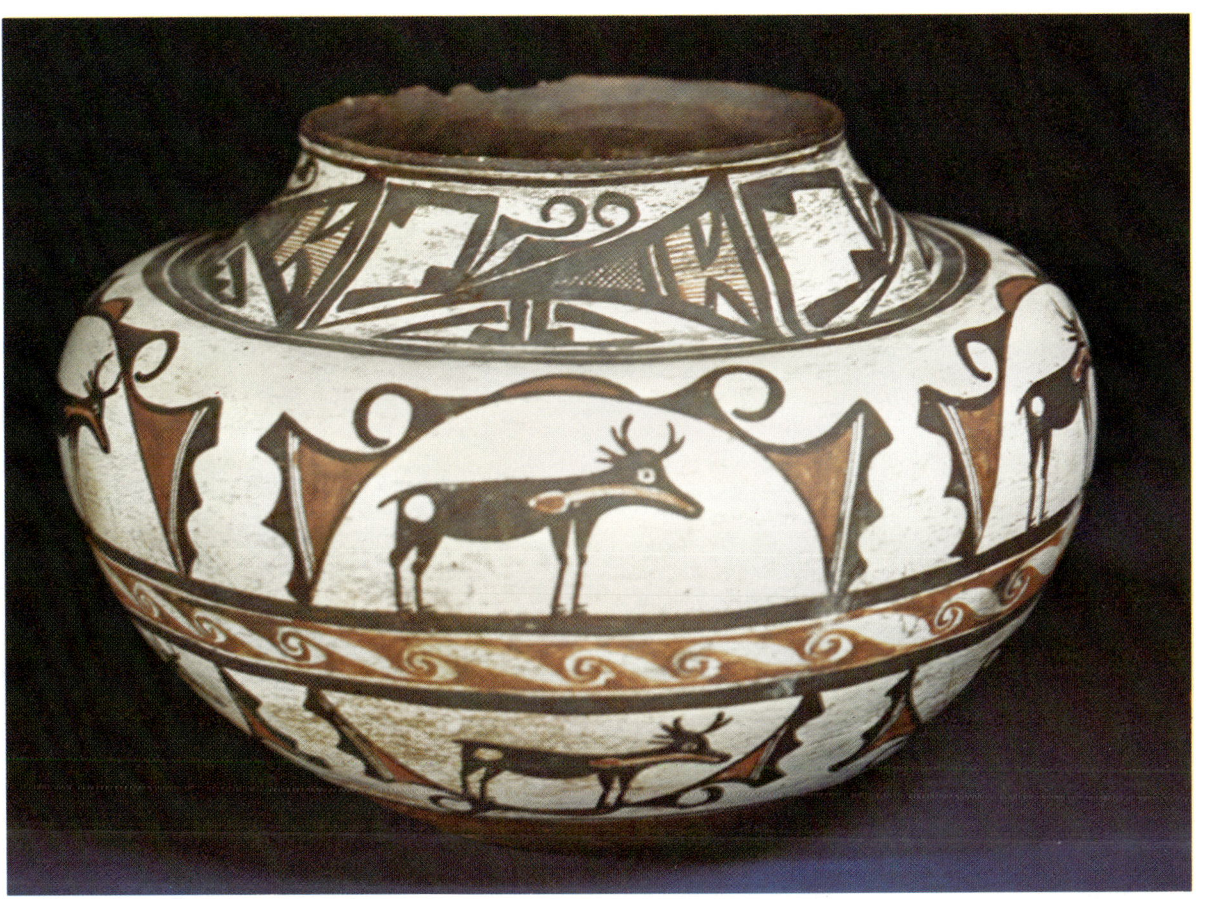

365. Polychrome Olla

The large thin-walled water vessels of this Pueblo are perhaps the most familiar ceramics from the Southwest. This was collected by Douglas D. Graham in 1880, and presented by Mmes. E. B. Lent, G. B. Oman, A. B. Young, and F. B. VanHouten. ZUNI. New Mexico. 1875-1880. 9″ x 11¾″. 22/7881.

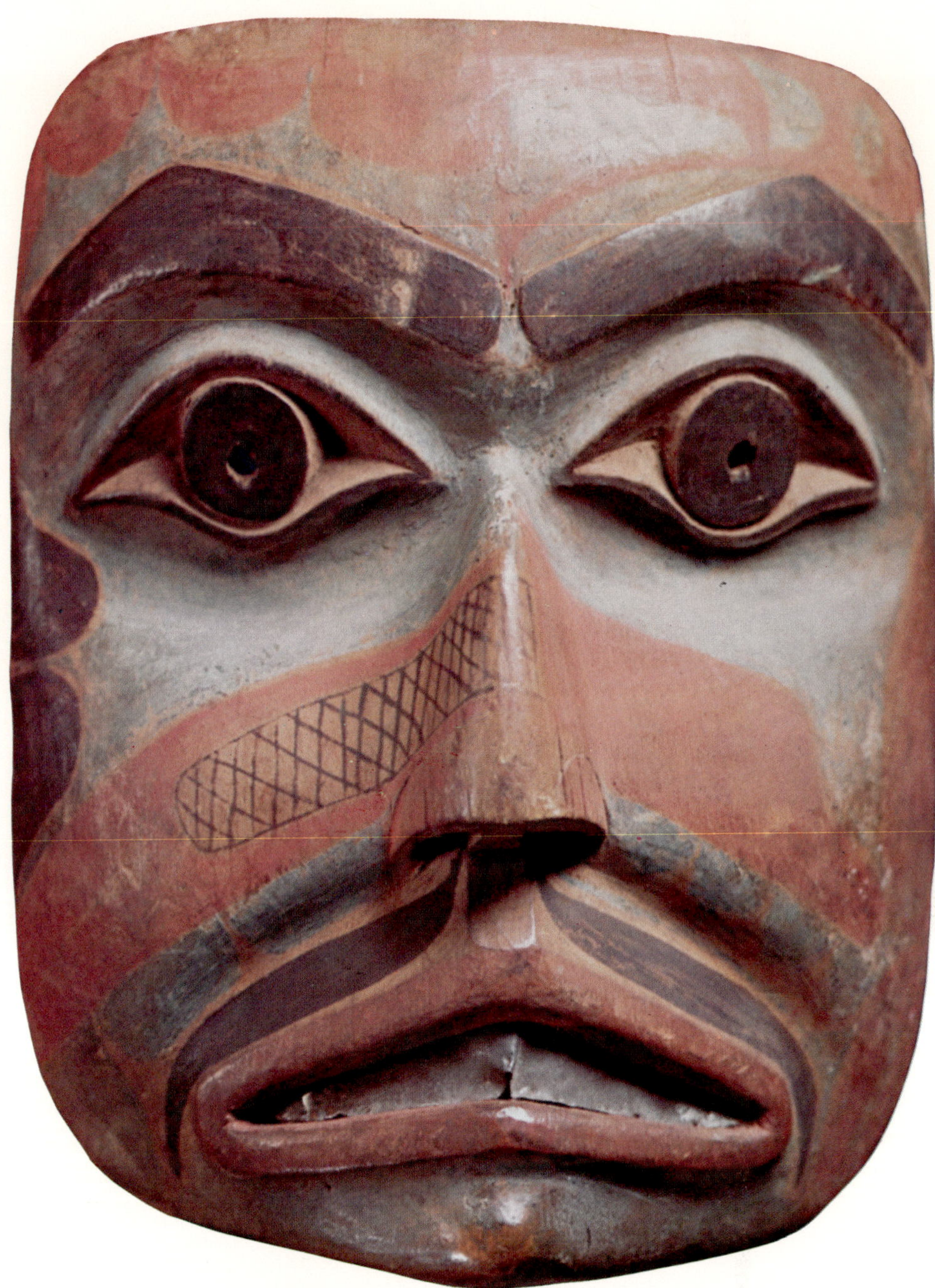

292. Face Mask

A large mask, decorated with tattooing or facial paint. As with so many carvings of this nature, it is almost impossible to identify the character without knowing what the original carver had in mind. KWAKIUTL. Vancouver Island, British Columbia. 1880-1900. 7¼" x 9¼". 1/9325.

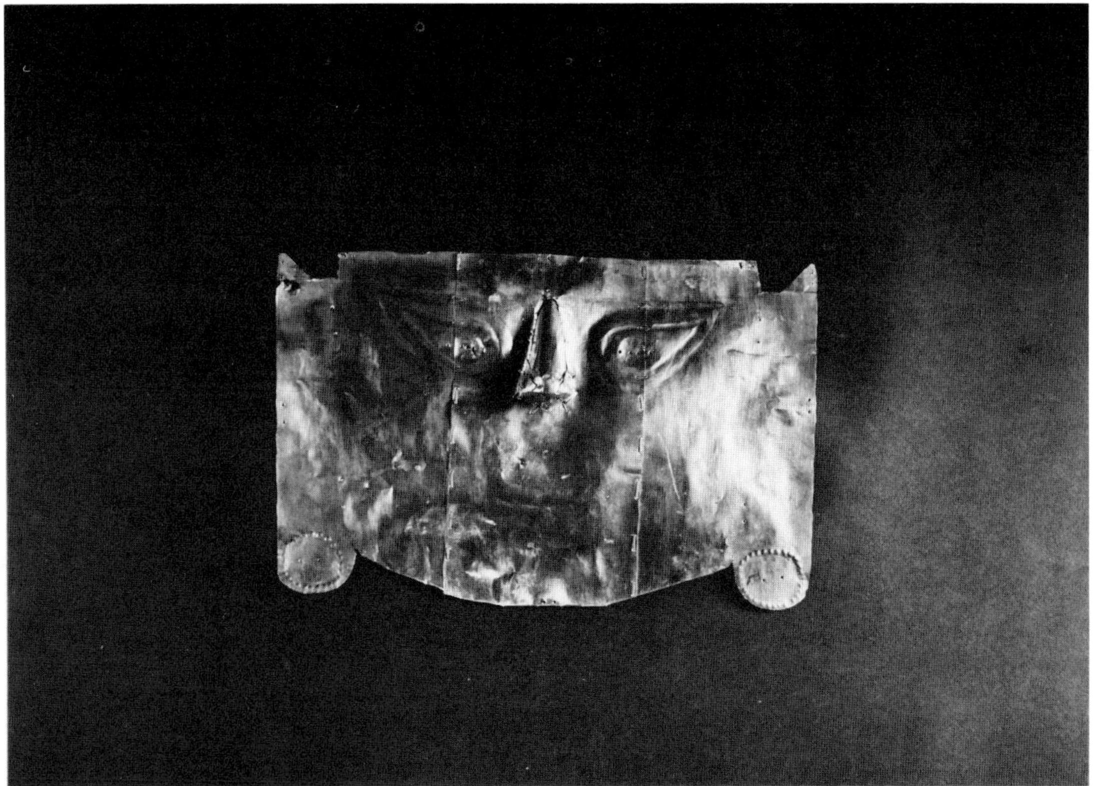

229. Hammered Gold Mask
For use on a mummy bundle of very wealthy rulers, these were made by the repoussé process in three pieces. Since the goldsmiths of this period had not yet mastered the art of soldering, the sheets were sewn together with gold wire. Eyes made of turquoise or greenstone beads were frequently attached to the sockets by wire. CHIMÚ. Lambayeque, Peru. 1100-1476. 8″ x 12″. 18/6590.

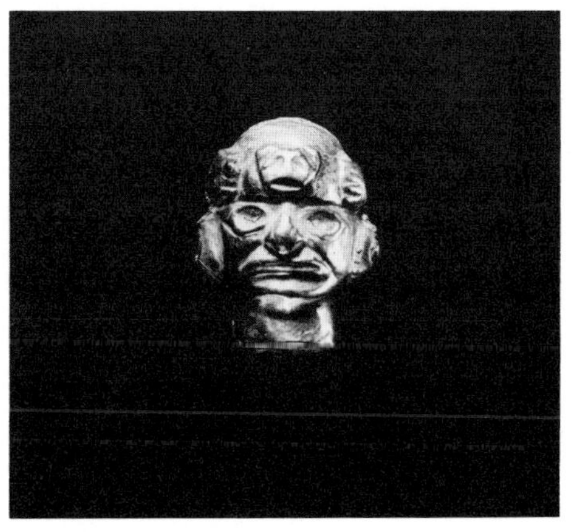

230. Miniature Gold Head
Formed by the repoussé process, this lovely miniature head has delicately formed features, surmounted by a headband with a puma head in the center. It is a fine example of Peruvian goldsmithing. Weight, 2 grams. CHIMÚ. Trujillo, Peru. 1300-1476. ¾″ x 1″. 23/4861.

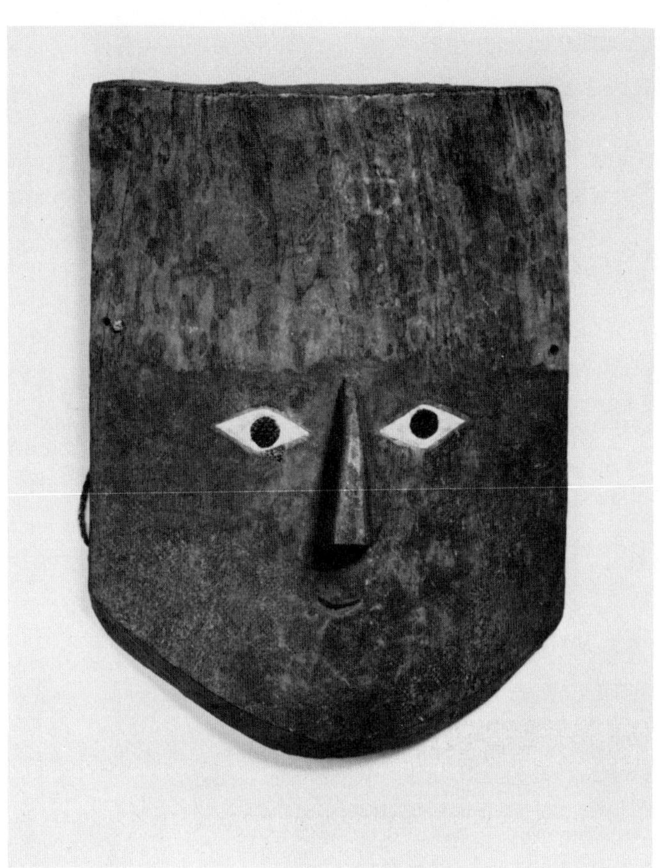

231. Wooden Mummy Mask
Intended for use with a mummy bundle, this flat board has been carved and painted to represent a face. It originally had a textile bandeau, and may also have had hair attached to the forehead. CHIMU? Trujillo, Peru. 1100-1476. 8½″ x 11½″. 11/50.

232. Blackware Paccha
One of the vessels unique to Peru was the *paccha,* a drinking vessel used with *chicha,* the primary beverage of the people. This example is decorated with a miniature aryballos, identifying it as of Inca chronology. INCA. Trujillo, Peru. 1476-1534. 6¾″ x 13¼″. 22/2431.

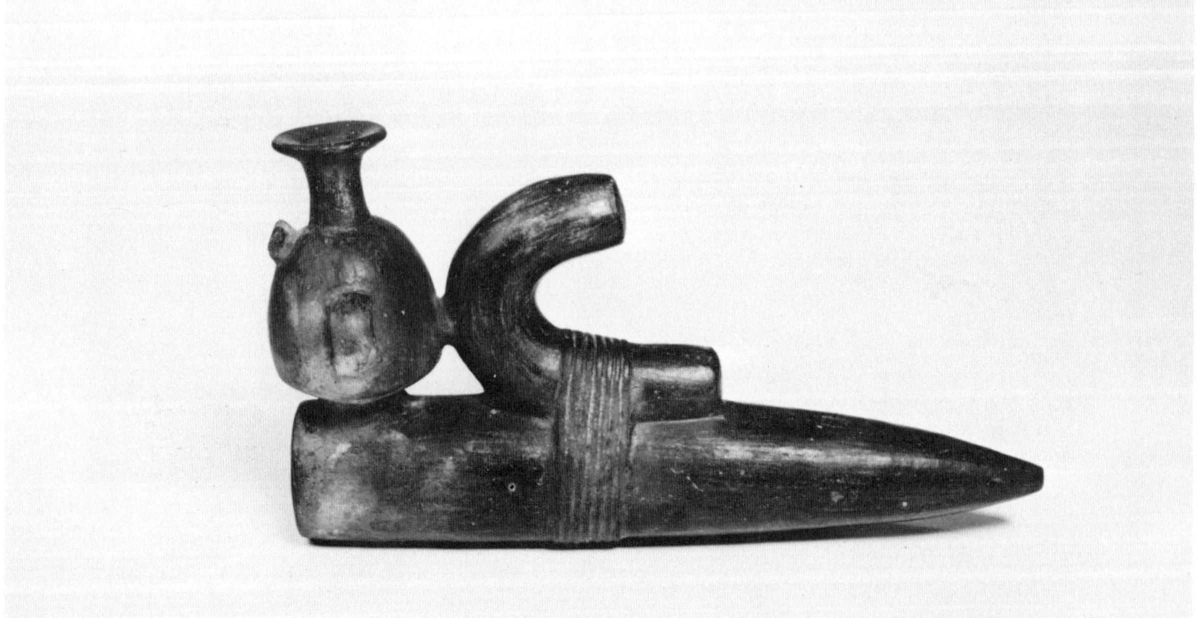

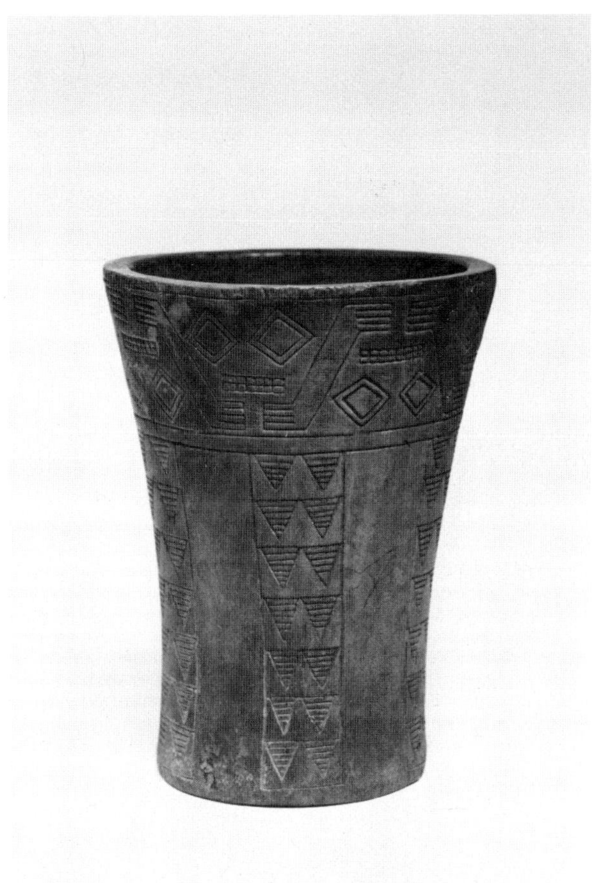

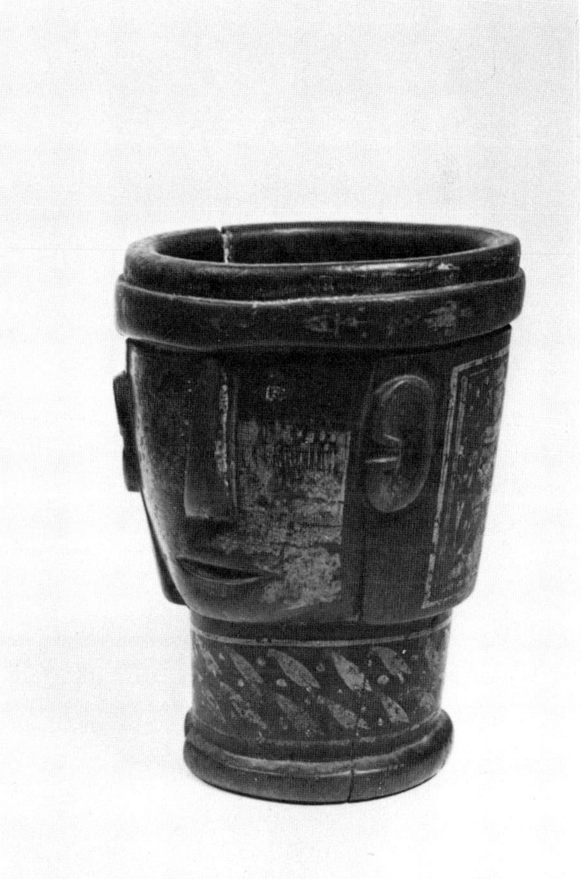

233. Carved Wooden Goblet
The *kero,* a drinking vessel of unique form, was common throughout ancient Peru; they were usually used in pairs during drinking ceremonies. This example has an incised geometrical decoration. INCA. Coastal Peru. 1476-1532. 5″ x 7″. 17/7382.

234. Anthropomorphic Goblet
The use of the *kero* was adopted by the Spaniards who saw it as a drinking vessel similar to the European forms with which they were familiar. They influenced the Inca artist to make the cup far more elaborately decorated, even to the extent of sculptural motifs, and polychrome lacquered designs. This is such an example, with a polychrome hunting scene in the rear of the vessel. INCA. Cuzco, Peru. 1550-1650. 6¼″ x 8″. 21/7455.

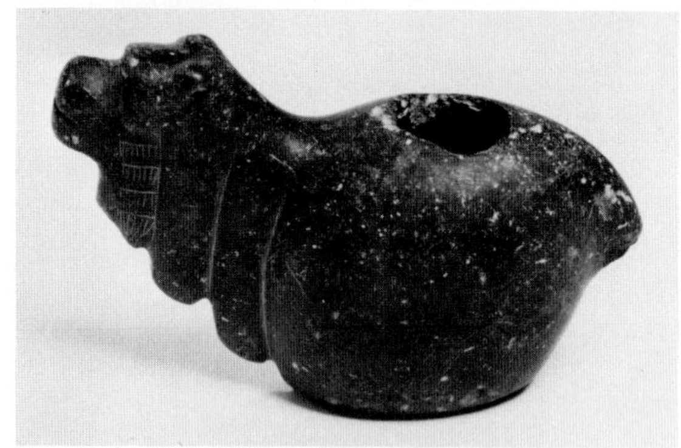

236. Carved Stone Cup
Sculptured in the form of a miniature llama, these were used as containers for paint, and are most commonly found in Inca sites. Presented by Harmon W. Hendricks. INCA. Arequipa, Peru. 1476-1532. 2½" x 4". 14/5500.

237. Featherwork Poncho
Applied onto a woven cotton base, with a geometric decoration in black, turquoise and orange feathers; these were obtained by trade from the Amazon region of the Andes. This was apparently worn by a person of considerable distinction; the designs may have served much the same purpose as the heraldic devices of Mediaeval Europe. Presented by Dr. and Mrs. Arthur M. Sackler. INCA? Peru. 1000-1500. 24½" x 27½". 23/9137.

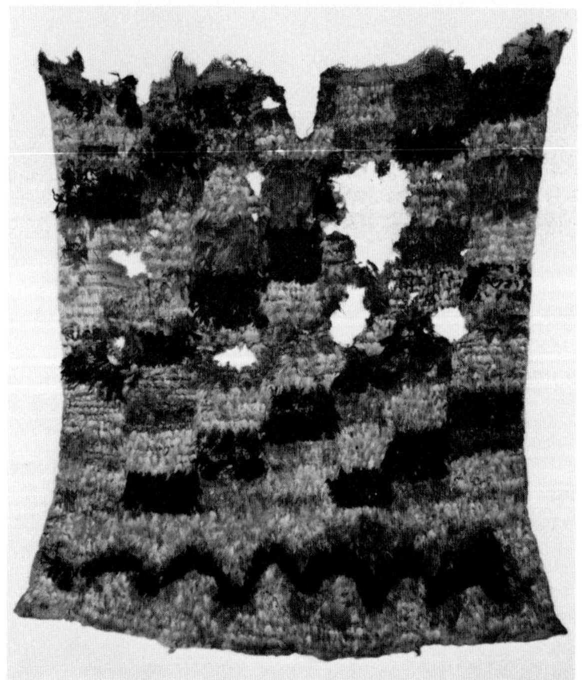

235. Carved Wooden Paddle
At one time, these were though to have some relationship to agricultural ceremonies. Today, they are variously regarded as steering paddles or leeboards, for use on watercraft. They are frequently elaborately carved or painted. Collected by George G. Heye. INCA? Ica, Peru. 1476-1532. L: 60". 16/3780.

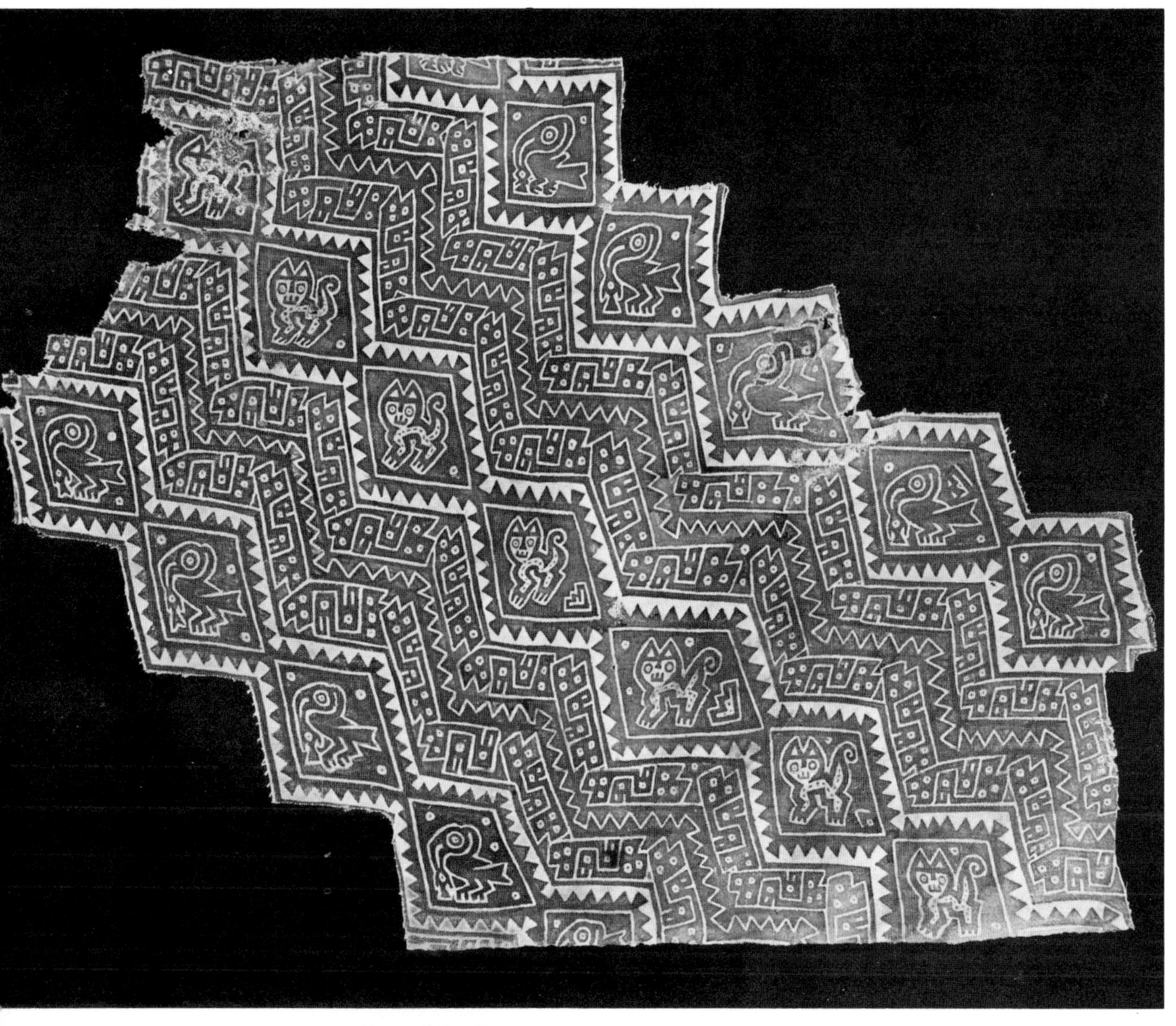

238. Painted Textile

A fragment of a once much larger textile, this is an example of the rich design and color familiar to the ancient Peruvian. The diagonal lines of birds and felines alternate with geometrical bands of zoömorphic heads. Coastal Peru. 1000-1300. 27½″ x 37″. 24/8379.

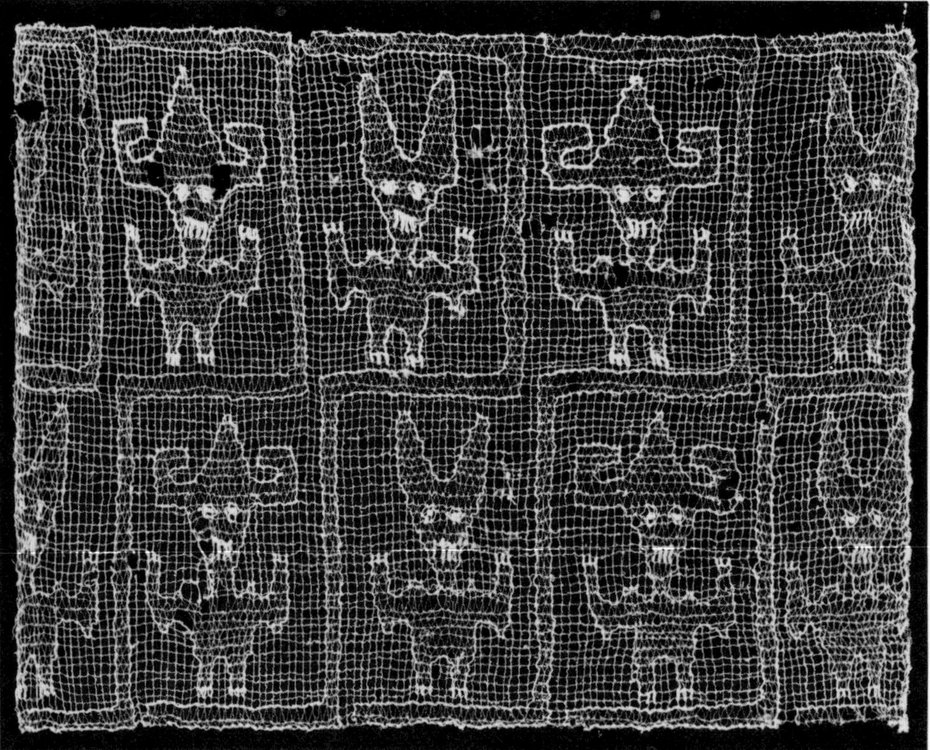

239. Cotton Openwork Textile
Commonly called "gauze," this is a complete textile worked in knotted-weft technique. The design represents six anthropomorphic creatures standing with hands upraised. The delicacy of these is equalled only by some of the finest Paracas embroideries. NAZCA? Peru. 13" x 17". 600-1000. 23/9080.

240. Tapestry Weave Fragment
(See color insert facing page 40)

241. Geometric Weave Textile
The intricately designed zoömorphic motifs in t fragment of a much larger textile presents an i triguing pattern. Such materials provided the ba fabric for many of the garments familiar to t ancient Peruvian. CHIMÚ. Trujillo, Peru. 1250-15 14" x 18". 21/2139.

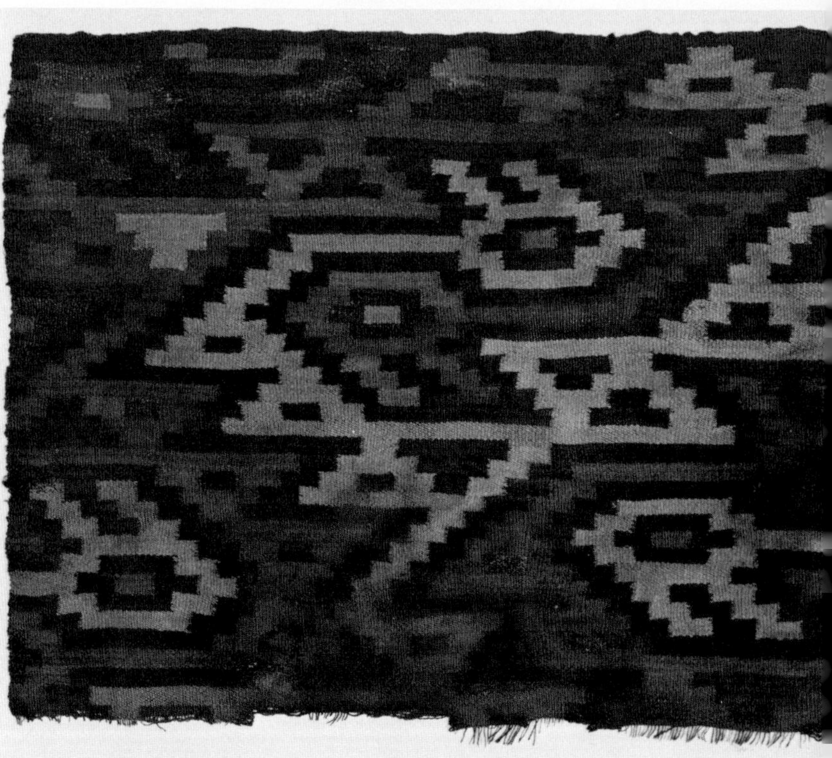

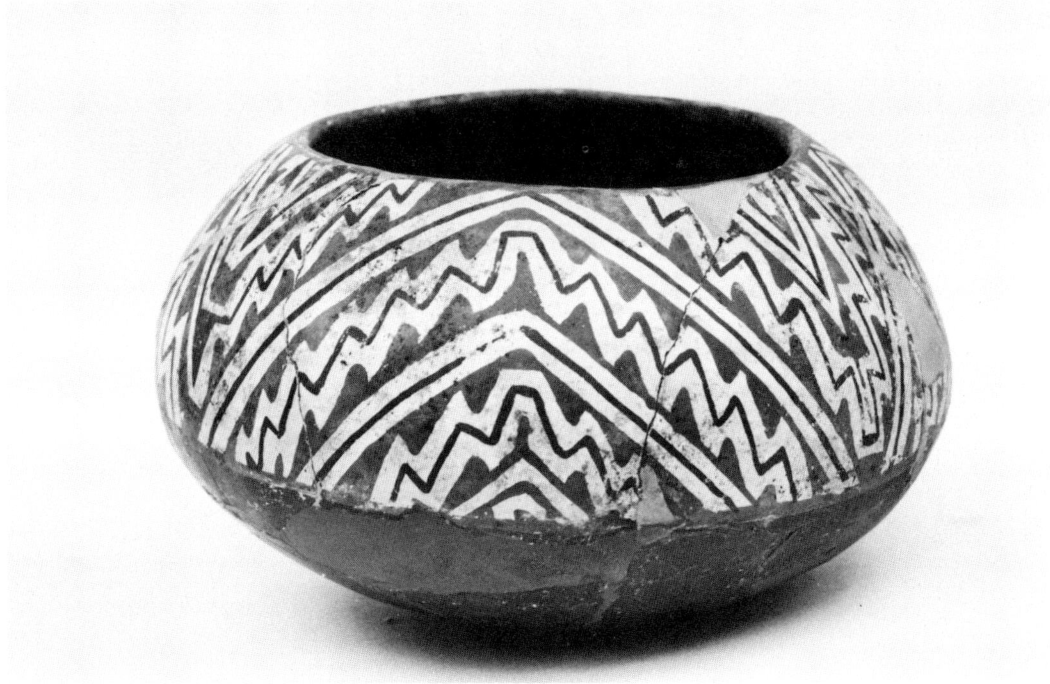

242. Polychrome Bowl
These brightly-painted, shallow bowls in red-brown, white and tan colors are typical of the Diaguita area. Collected by Samuel K. Lothrop. DIAGUITA. Compañía Baja, Coquimbo, Chile. 1000-1450. 3″ x 6¼″. 17/5153.

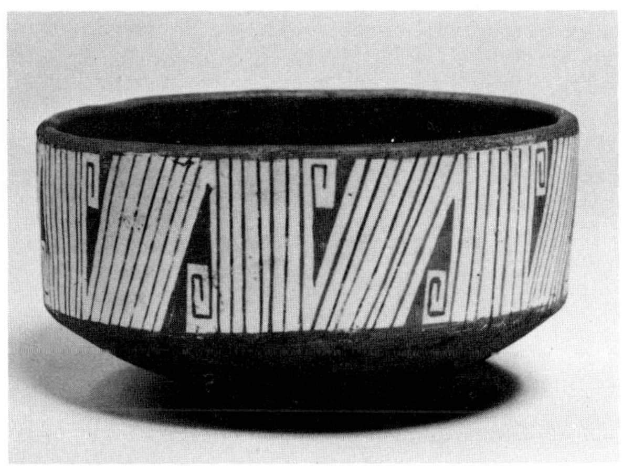

243. Ceramic Bowl
Decorated in polychrome colors, this carinated vessel is from the same prehistoric area as the preceding. Collected by Samuel K. Lothrop. DIAGUITA. Compañía Baja, Coquimbo, Chile. 1000-1450. 3″ x 6¼″. 17/5136.

244. Zoömorphic Container

A simple form, this cup is modeled in the shape of an animal similar to a rabbit; the red stripes on a cream base are found on many vessels from this southern area. Collected by R. E. Steinberg. CIÉNEGA. Cafayate, Salta, Argentina. 100-500. 4¼″ x 5″. 15/7423.

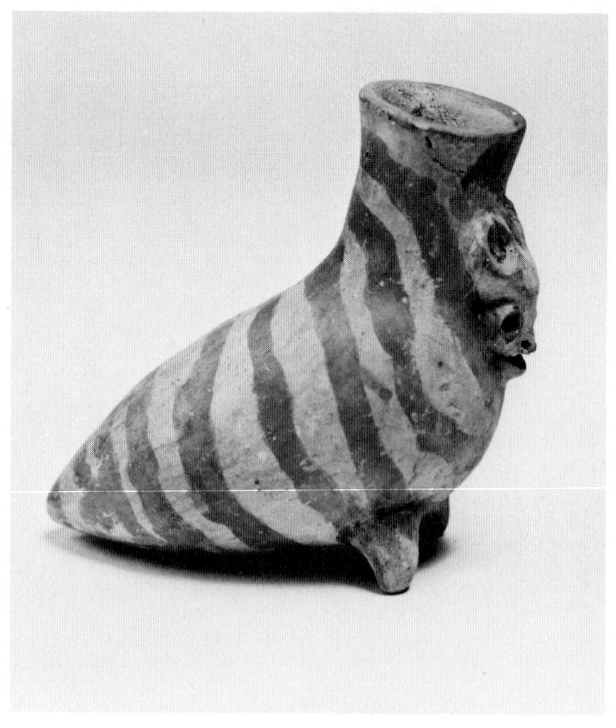

245. Polychrome Ring-base Jar

The rich red surface of this vessel has been painted with a black and white design in geometric patterns, and a strong fret treatment around the waist. CALCHAQUÍ. Tafí, Tucumán, Argentina. 500-1000? 5¼″ x 5½″. 8/9049.

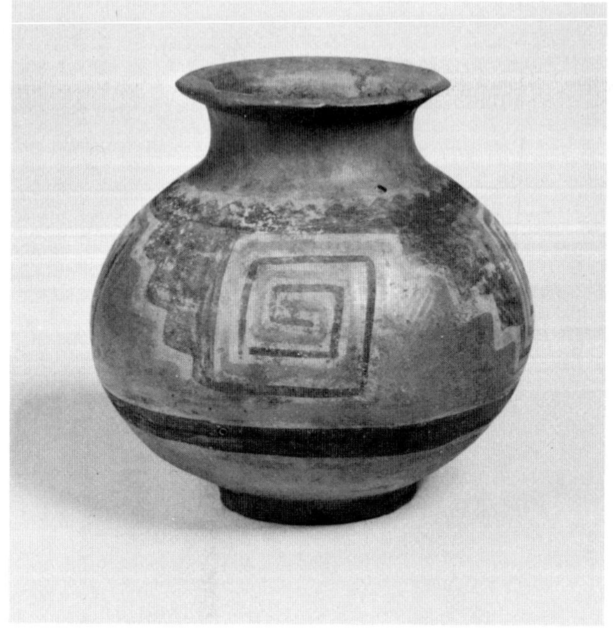

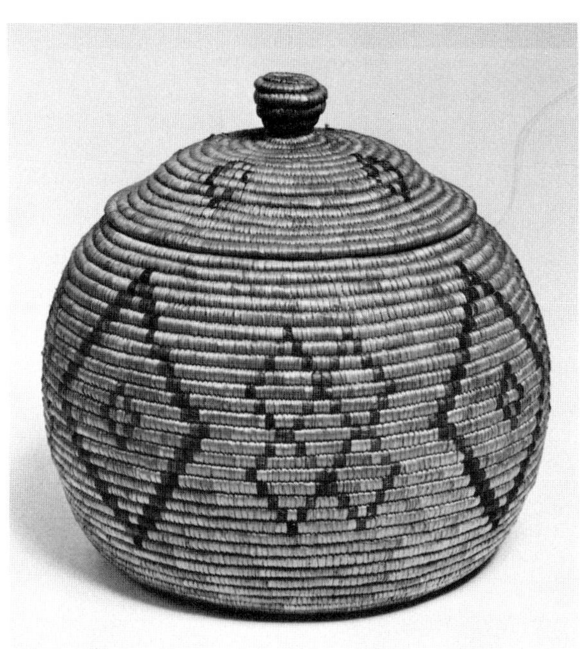

246. Woven Basket and Cover

Various local grasses were woven into containers for foods and other materials. They were often decorated with colored fibers; after the coming of the European, colored yarns were used. Collected by Clark M. Garber. Kuskwogmiut Eskimo. Kuskokwim, Alaska. 1920-1925. 6½" x 7½". 22/6534.

247. Carved Ivory Charm

Tiny ivory carvings were commonly used by the shamans in religious and social ceremonies. This standing nude male with arms akimbo is an excellent example of the type. Nuwukmiut Eskimo. Point Barrow, Alaska. 1875-1880. 1" x 3". 24/8705.

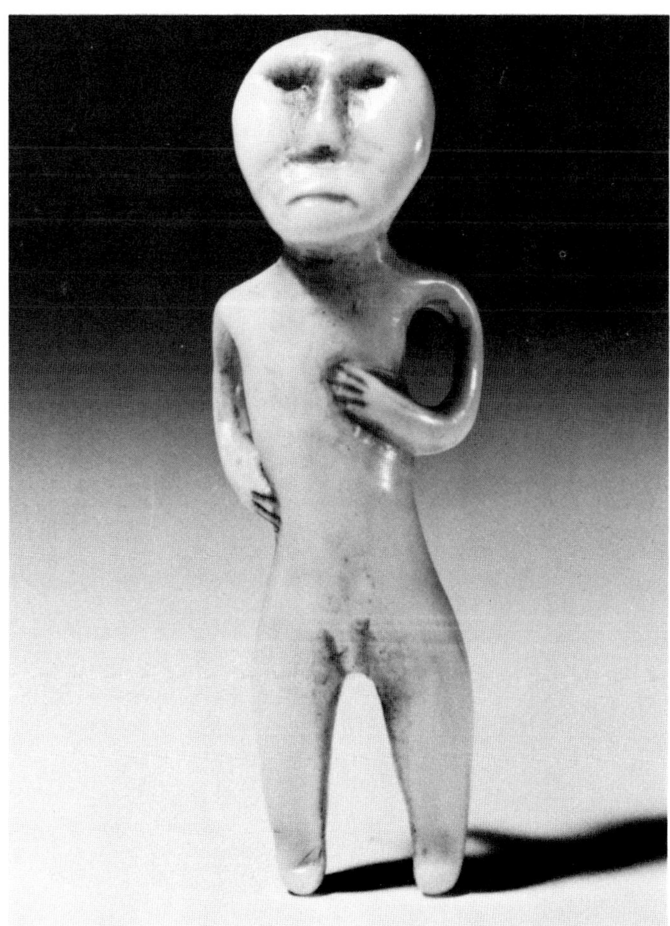

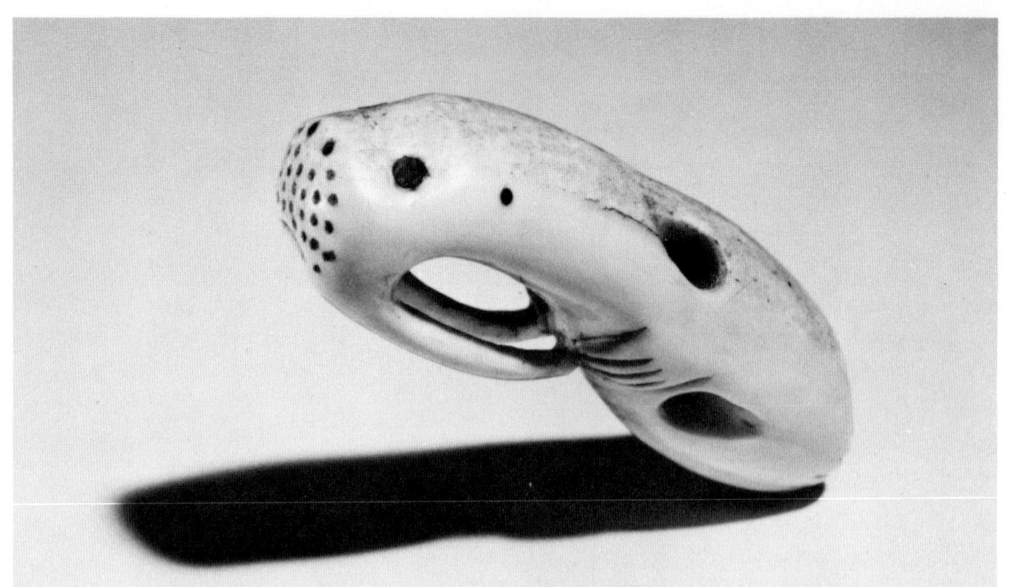

248. Carved Ivory Toggle
Sculptured from a walrus tusk, this has inlaid eyes, and was intended for use as a toggle lashing. NUWUKMIUT ESKIMO. Point Barrow, Alaska. 1875-1880. L: 3½". 24/8706.

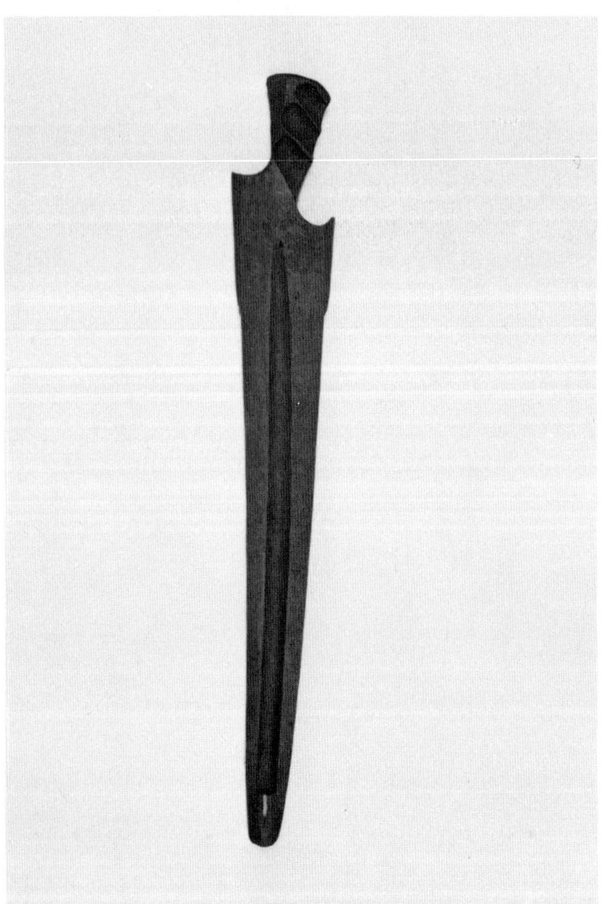

249. Wooden Atlatl
The *atlatl*, a prehistoric implement in use until the invention of the bow, continued in Eskimo culture to the present time. This example has been carved to precisely fit the hand and to give a graceful form to the wooden shaft. It was collected sometime before 1850 and taken to England, where it was acquired by Mrs. Thea Heye. KAVIAGMIUT ESKIMO. Sledge Island, Cape Nome, Alaska. 2¾" x 19¼". 17/6335.

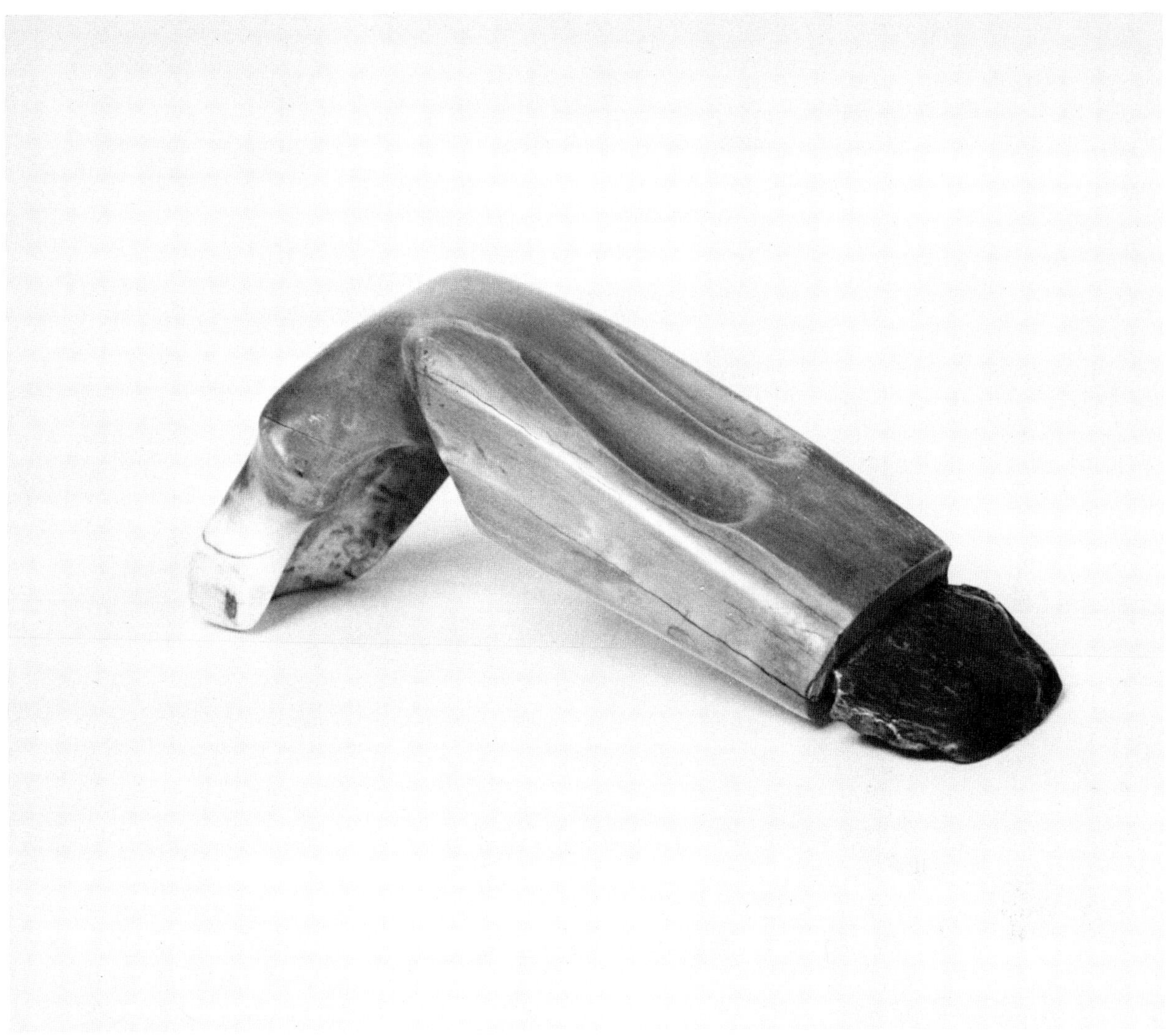

250. Bone Hide Scraper
Another example of the extraordinary care taken to fit an object to its specific use is this hide scraper, made to fit only the hand of the user. With an inlaid polished jade blade, it is a work of art as well as effectively functional. Collected by Judge Nathan Bijur. SIDARUMIUT ESKIMO. Point Hope, Alaska. 1860-1875. 1½" x 5". 20/8883.

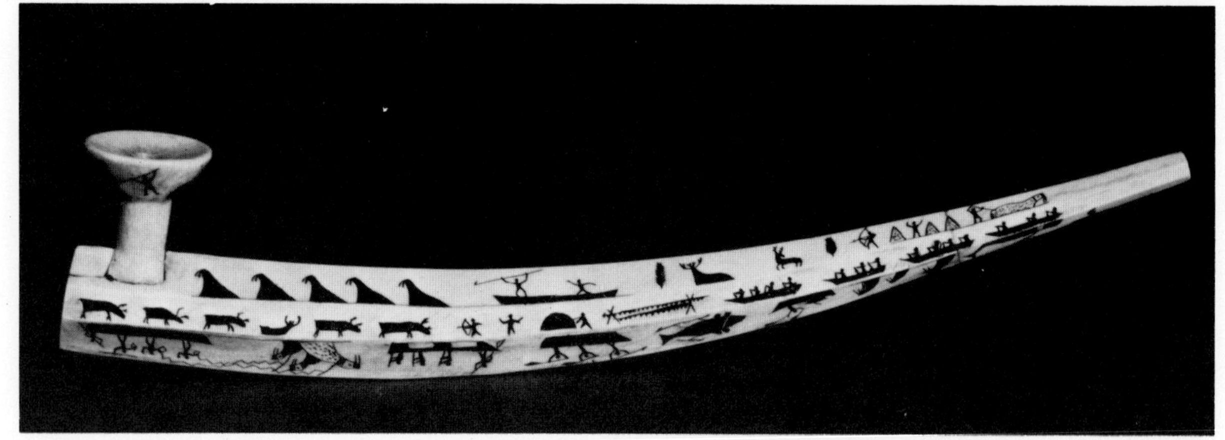

251. Carved Ivory Pipe
Tobacco traveled completely around the world, leaving the New World, going to Europe, and finally returning to the Eskimo *via* Russia, as indicated by this pipe design. The stem is a walrus tusk, into which the bowl has been fitted. MALEMIUT ESKIMO. Kotzebue Sound, Alaska. 1890-1900. 2¼″ x 12″. 6/2445.

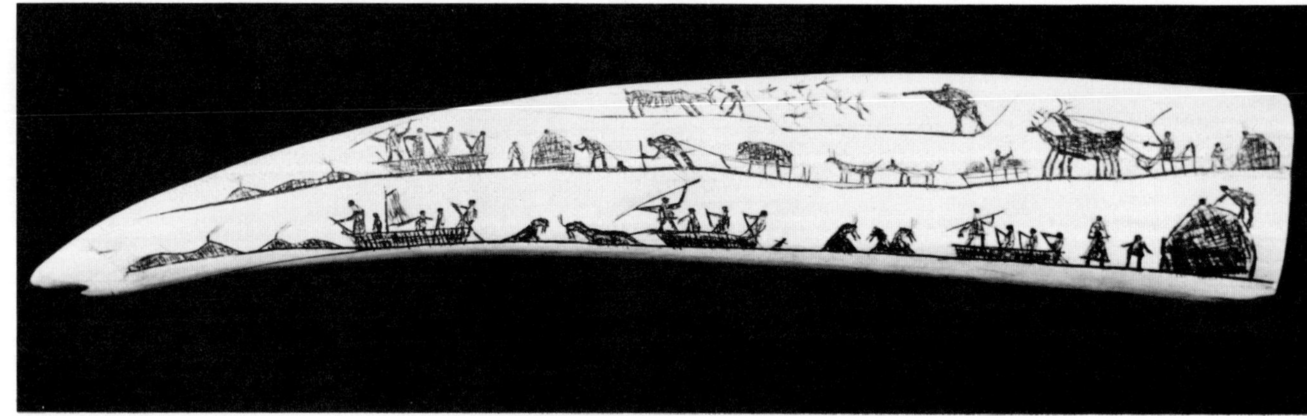

252. Incised Walrus Tusk
Tusks were frequently used as a surface for decoration. This example depicts a group of hunters pursuing whales and caribou. The designs were incised with a sharp point—jade or stone in earlier days, and steel knives after the coming of the European—after which, charcoal mixed with grease was rubbed into the lines for contrast. Collected by J. E. Standley. NUWUKMIUT ESKIMO. Point Barrow, Alaska. 1875-1890. 1½″ x 10″. 5/3507.

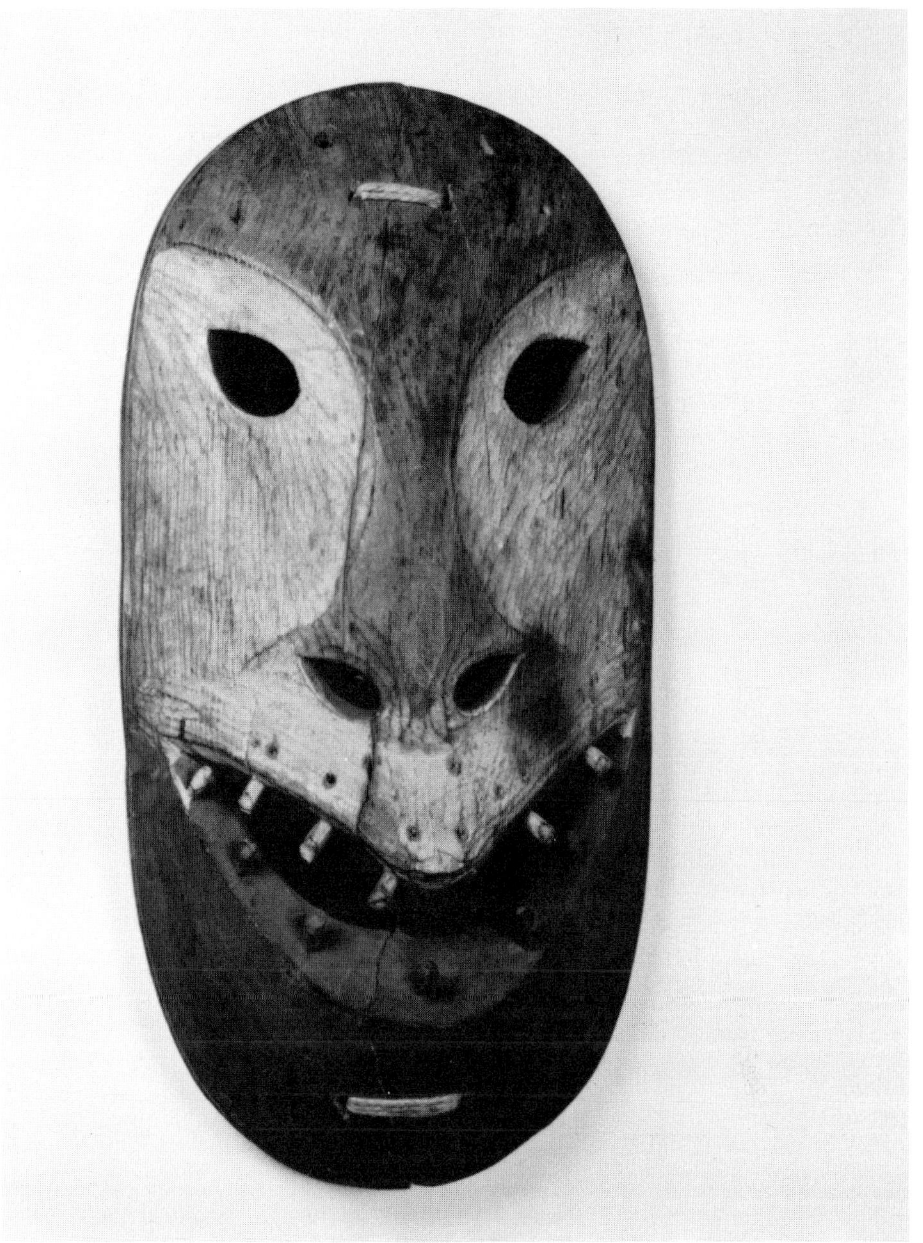

253. Carved Dance Mask

The use of elaborate or grotesque dance masks was a well-known art among the Eskimo people. They depicted humorous, sacred or secular personations of the many human and animal forms of the region. This mask was originally decorated with snow goose feathers which have since been lost. Collected by G. B. Gordon. Kuskwogmiut Eskimo. Mamtrek, Alaska. 1875-1890. 3¾" x 8½". 1/6818.

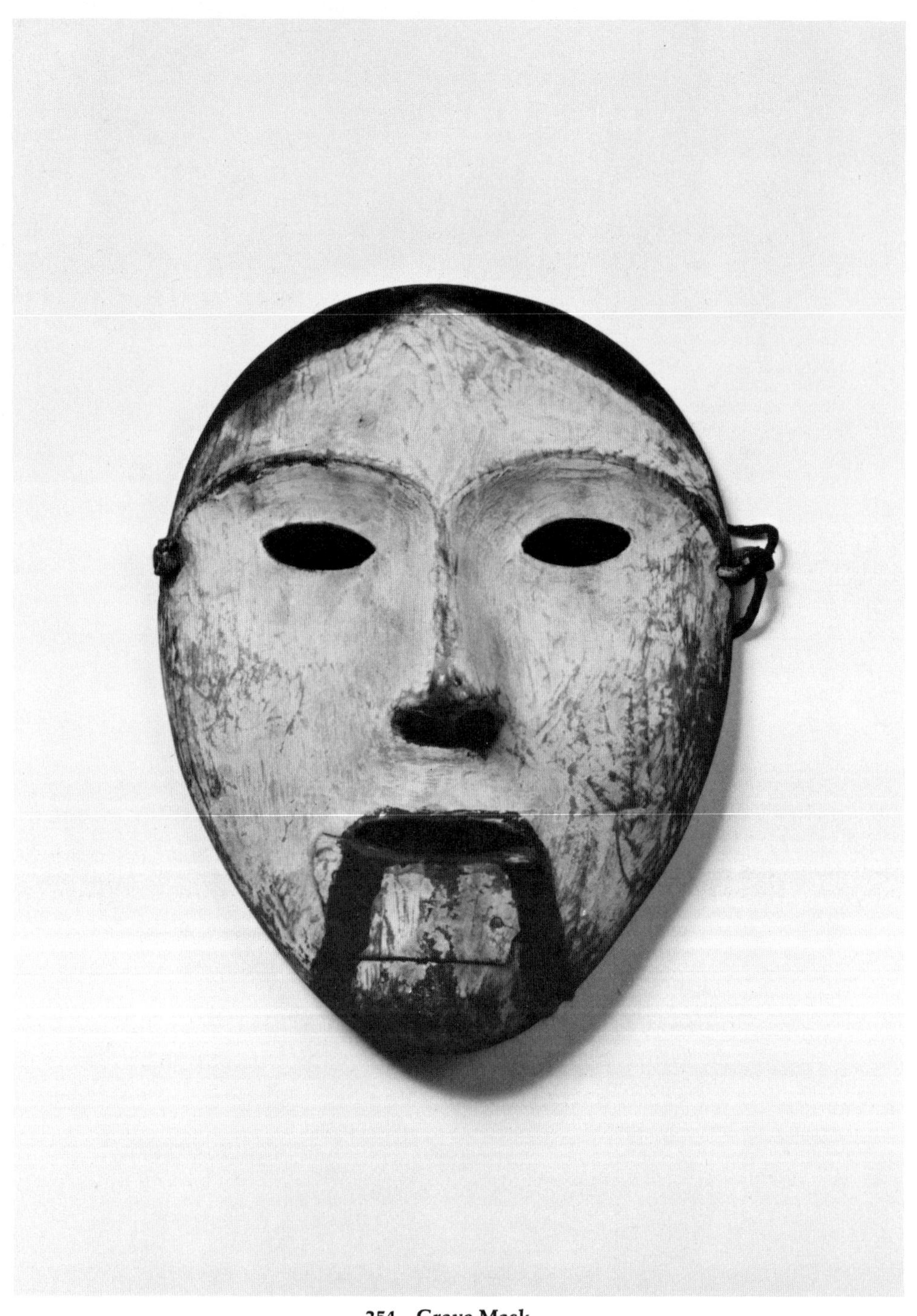

254. Grave Mask
So called because they are often found in burials, these were used equally for ceremonies, and were not just restricted to funerary usage. Presented by the Academy of Natural Sciences of Philadelphia. KAVIAGMIUT ESKIMO. King Island, Alaska. 1875-1890. 11½" x 7½". 16/7603.

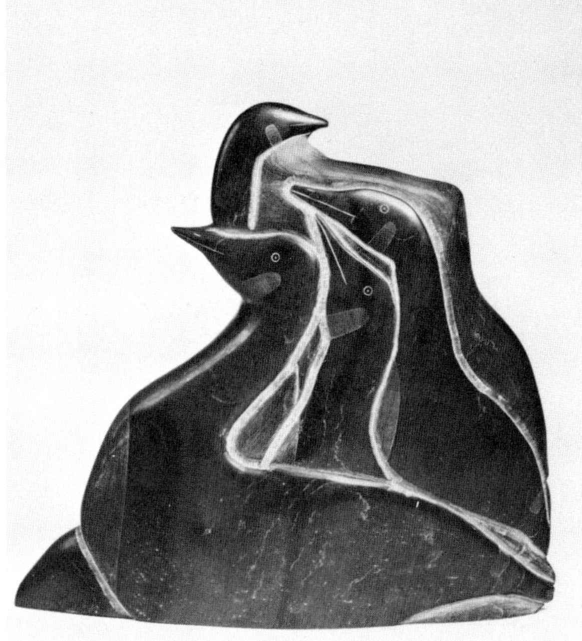

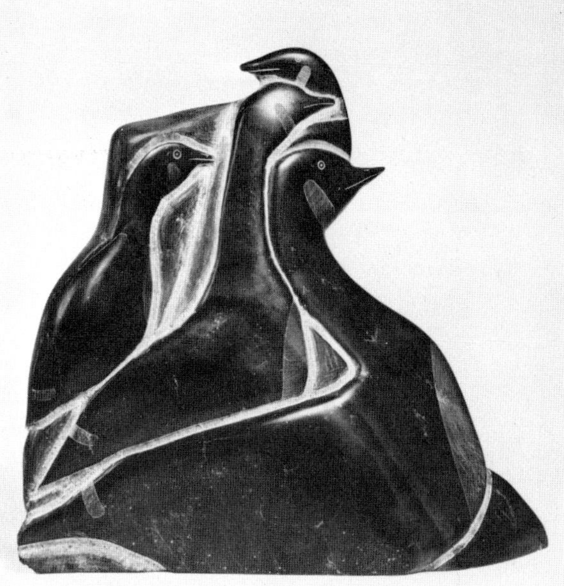

255. Steatite Sculpture
One of the recent arts of the Canadian Eskimo people is the carving of steatite into a variety of esthetically pleasing forms. Although introduced by Whites, this takes advantage of the inherent talents of the native artist, and has been developed into a major art form. This sculpture combines four birds in a well-balanced composition. ESKIMO. Hudson Bay, Québec, Canada. 1972. 11½" x 12½". 24/8704.

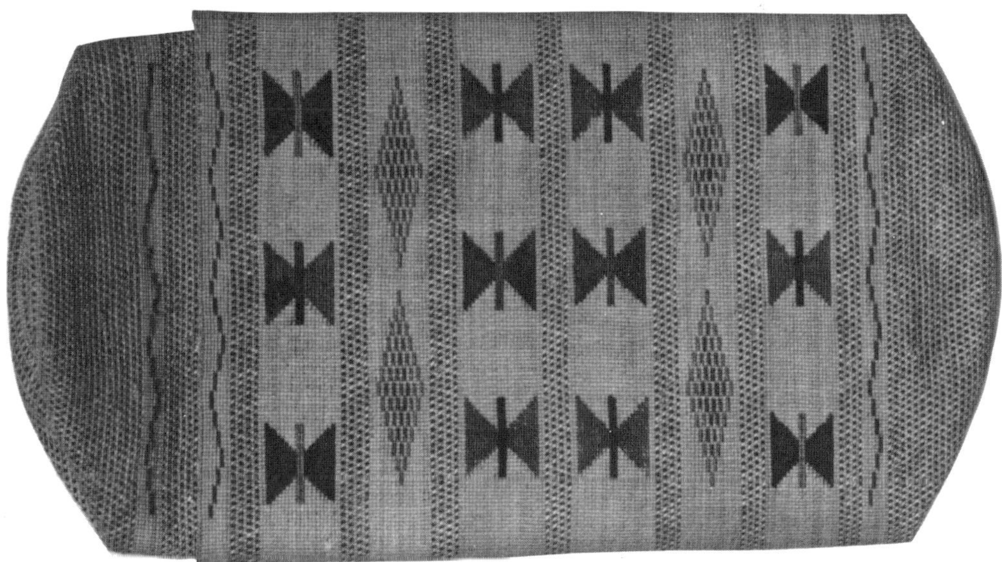

256. Woven Wallet
Sea grasses were woven into incredibly fine-textured containers. This cigar case, although woven for the White tourist trade, is among the most remarkable basketry products of the New World. Collected by S. Prescott Fay. ALEUT. Aleutian Islands, Alaska. 1890. 3¼" x 6". 21/9000.

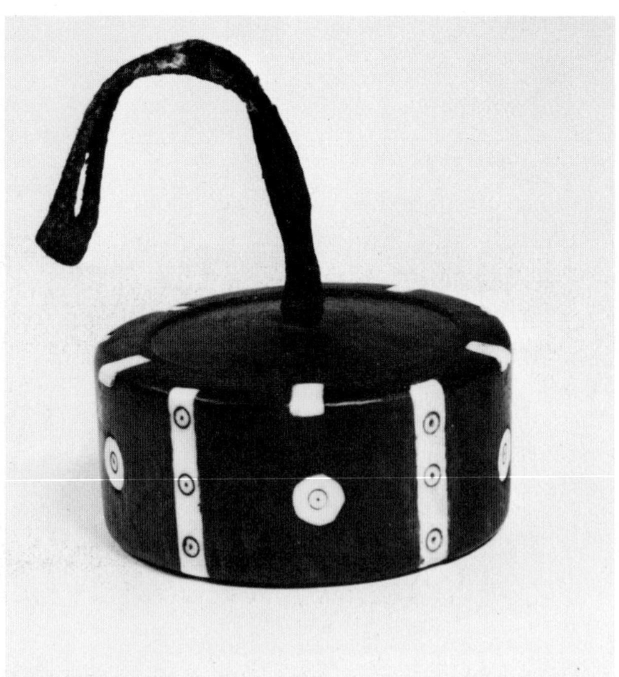

257. Wooden Snuff Box
Driftwood was commonly made into implements, containers and various other objects. The use of snuff, introduced by Europeans, was a common practice in Alaska, and small boxes were made for the purpose. This one has been decorated with carved ivory inlays. Presented by James B. Ford. ALEUT. Port Heiden, Aleutian Is. 1878-1890. 1″ x 2¾″. 6/2381.

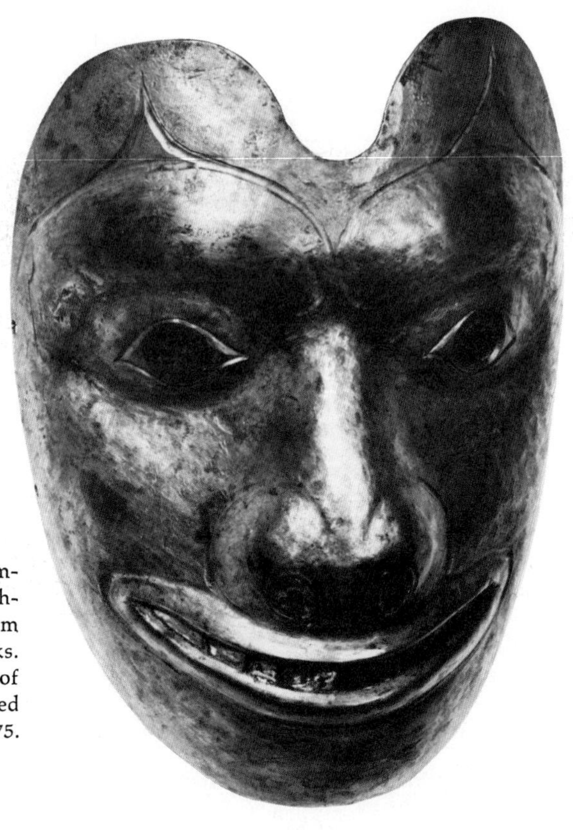

258. Hammered Copper Mask
Copper, originally obtained in native lodes and hammered to form, was an important metal in the Northwest. Later, sheet copper became available from traders, or was peeled off the hulls of shipwrecks. This mask, representing a bear, is a fine example of the art. The teeth are inlaid abalone shell. Collected by Joseph Keppler. TLINGIT. Alaska. 1850-1875. 6¼″ x 8½″. 20/6954.

259. Forehead Ornament
(See page 14)

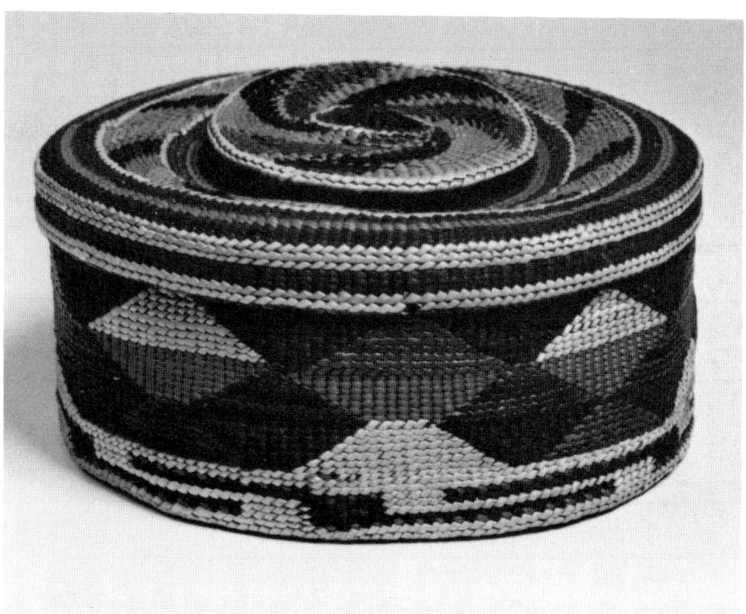

260. Polychrome Basket and Cover
Brilliantly-dyed spruce root was woven into various forms of basketry containers. The hollow handle of the cover of this basket has some seeds inserted, to provide a pleasing sound. Bequest of Mrs. Mary H. Davis. TLINGIT. Sitka, Alaska. 1880-1900. 2¾" x 6¾". 22/1932.

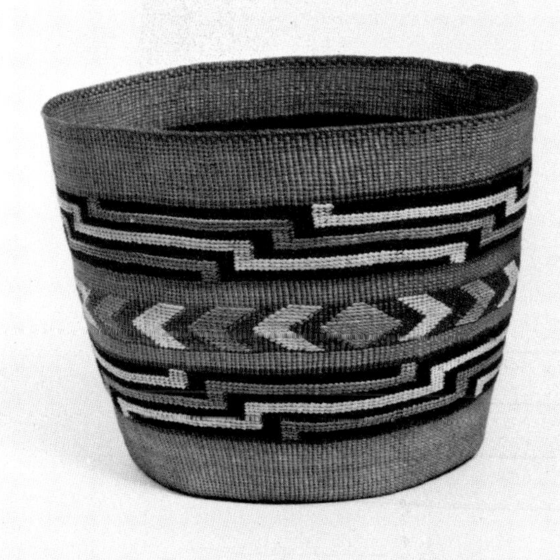

261. Woven Basket
Another form of design in spruce root, this is one of the familiar flat-bottom containers from Alaska. TLINGIT. Yakutat, Alaska. 1880-1900. 6¼" x 8". 20/1693.

262. Painted Hat

The designs on this carefully woven basketry hat depict a killer whale painted in red, black and green. Such a hat was not necessarily indicative of a chief; it could have been worn by any person with sufficient wealth or social position to own one. Collected by D. F. Tozier. HAIDA. Queen Charlotte Islands, British Columbia. 1890-1900. 6½" x 14". 6/9226.

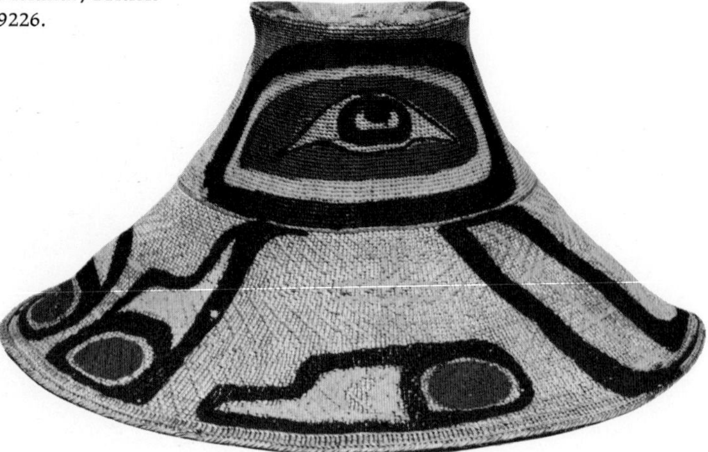

263. Movable Bird Mask

Carved to represent the head of a seagull, this mask has rotating eyes, and a beak which opens and closes with the pulling of strings by the wearer. Collected by G. T. Emmons. HAIDA. Queen Charlotte Islands, British Columbia. 1875-1890. 7" x 19". 1/2177.

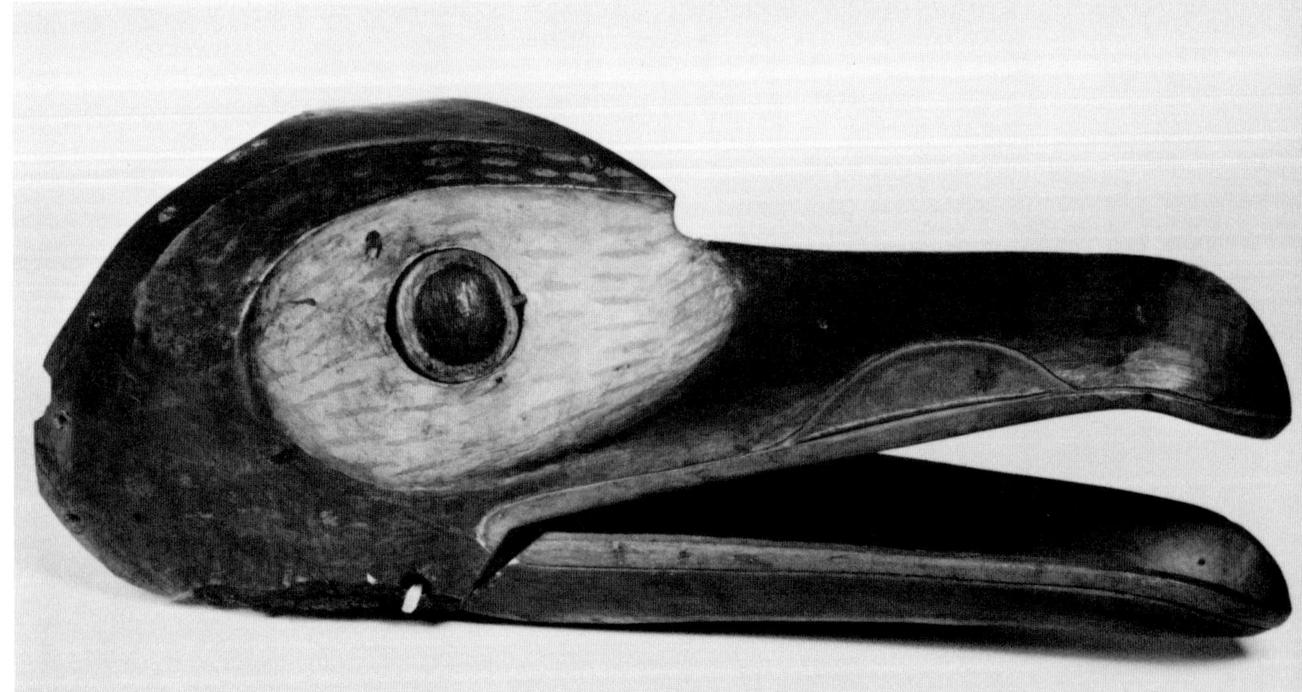

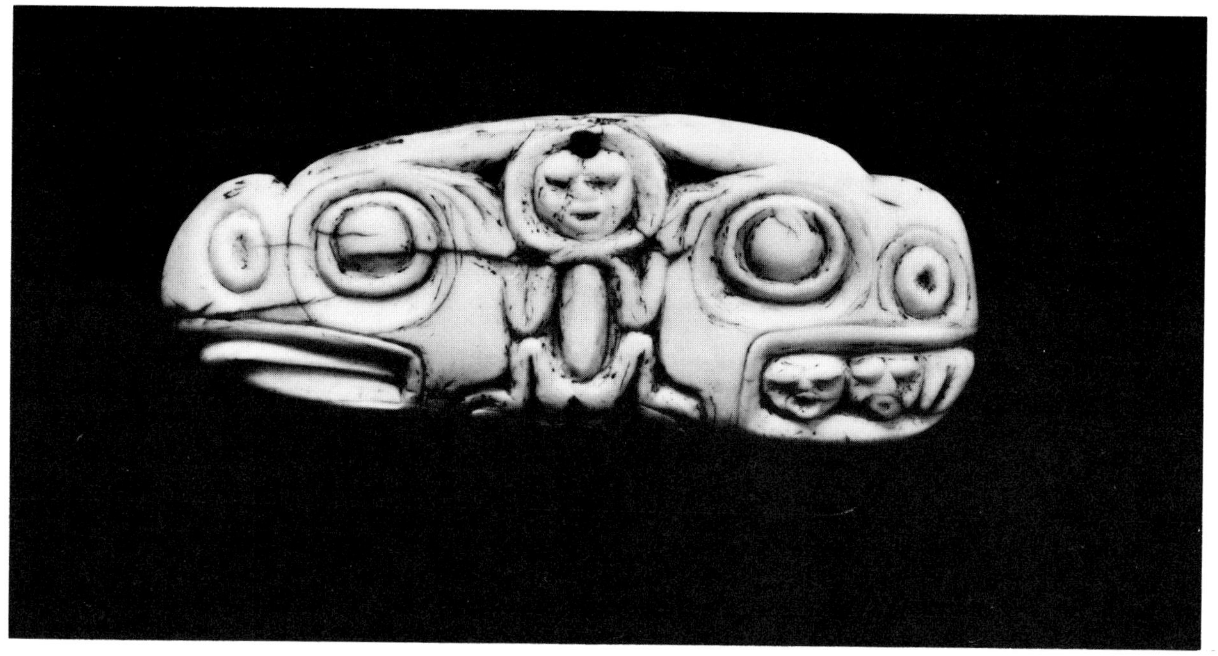

264. Ivory Charm
Killer whale teeth were used for their ivory. This example demonstrates the technique of the carver in following the outlines of the tooth in his design. The representation is that of a spirit figure, providing a guardian for the shaman who used it in his ceremonies. Collected by G. T. Emmons. Tlingit. Yakutat, Alaska. 1875-1890. 1¾" x 4½". 4/1671.

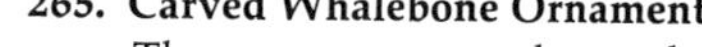

265. Carved Whalebone Ornament
These are worn as charms by shamans. The designs vary, depending entirely upon the purposes involved. Many are so abstract that they can only be identified by the carver or the individual wearing them. Presented by Mrs. Eugene F. Barnes. Haida. Kasaan, Alaska. 1880-1900. 3" x 5½". 21/6815.

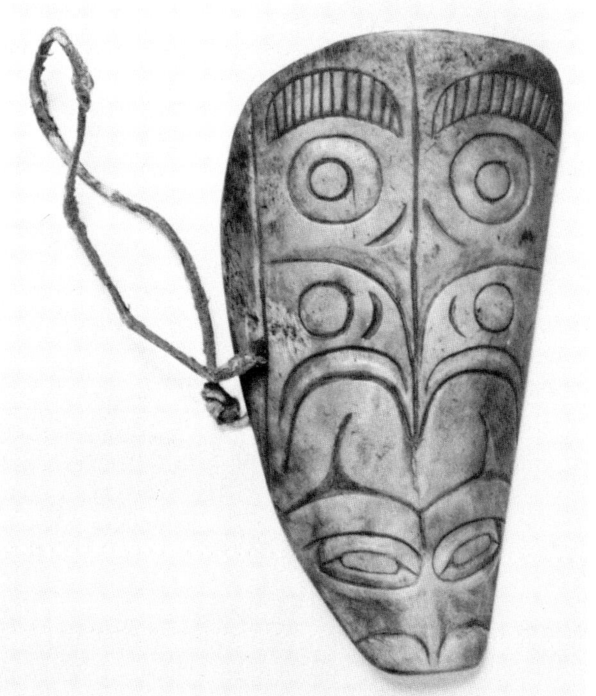

266. Raven Rattle
(See color insert facing page 240)

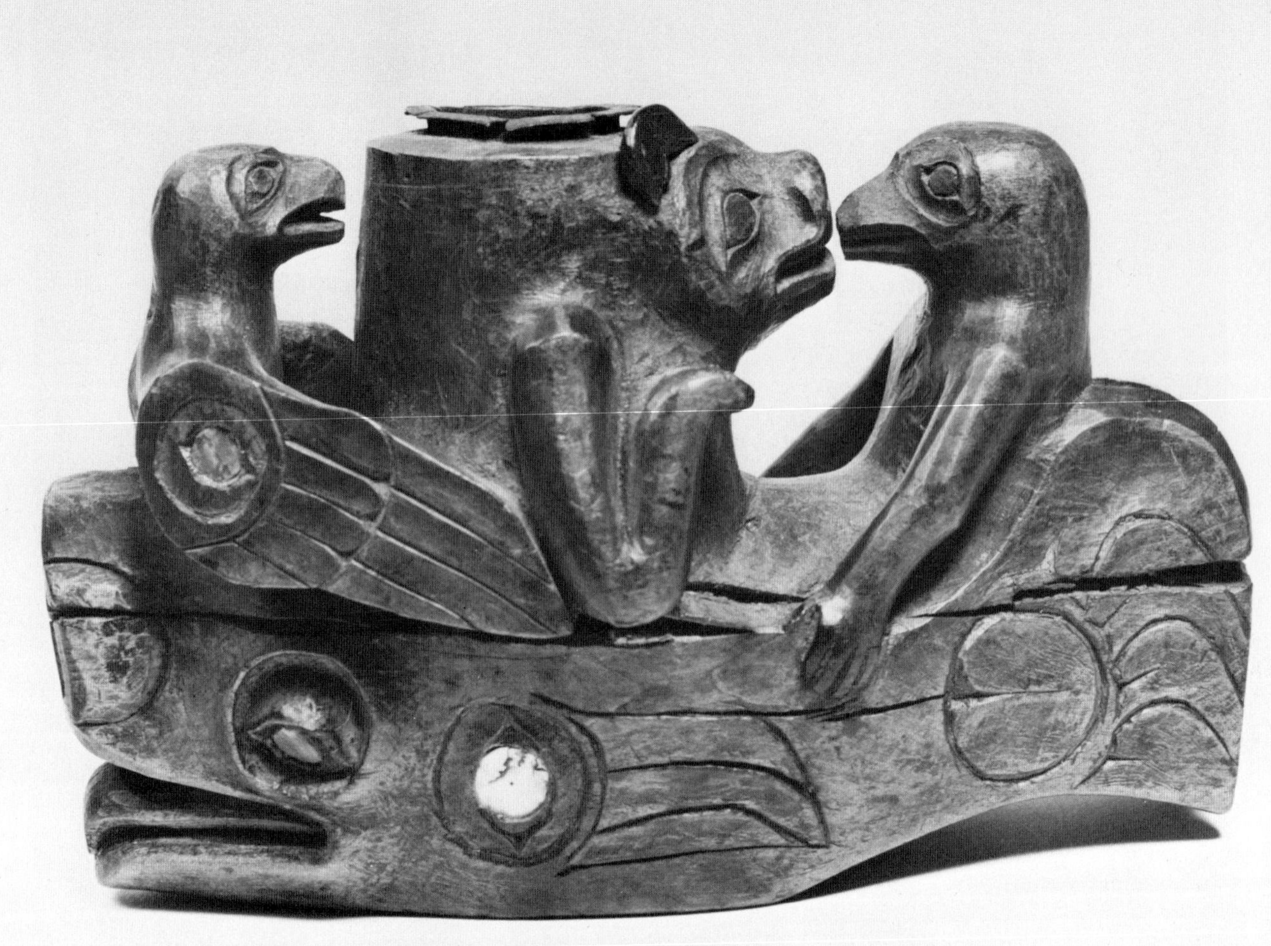

267. Cedarwood Pipe
The elaborately-worked pipe bowls are found throughout the Alaskan Coast. This design represents a mythical spirit canoe in which a bear, an eagle, and a "bird man" are sailing. Collected by G. T. Emmons. TLINGIT. Taku, Alaska. 1870-1890. 5½" x 9". 2/9169.

268. War Helmet
(See color insert facing page 240)

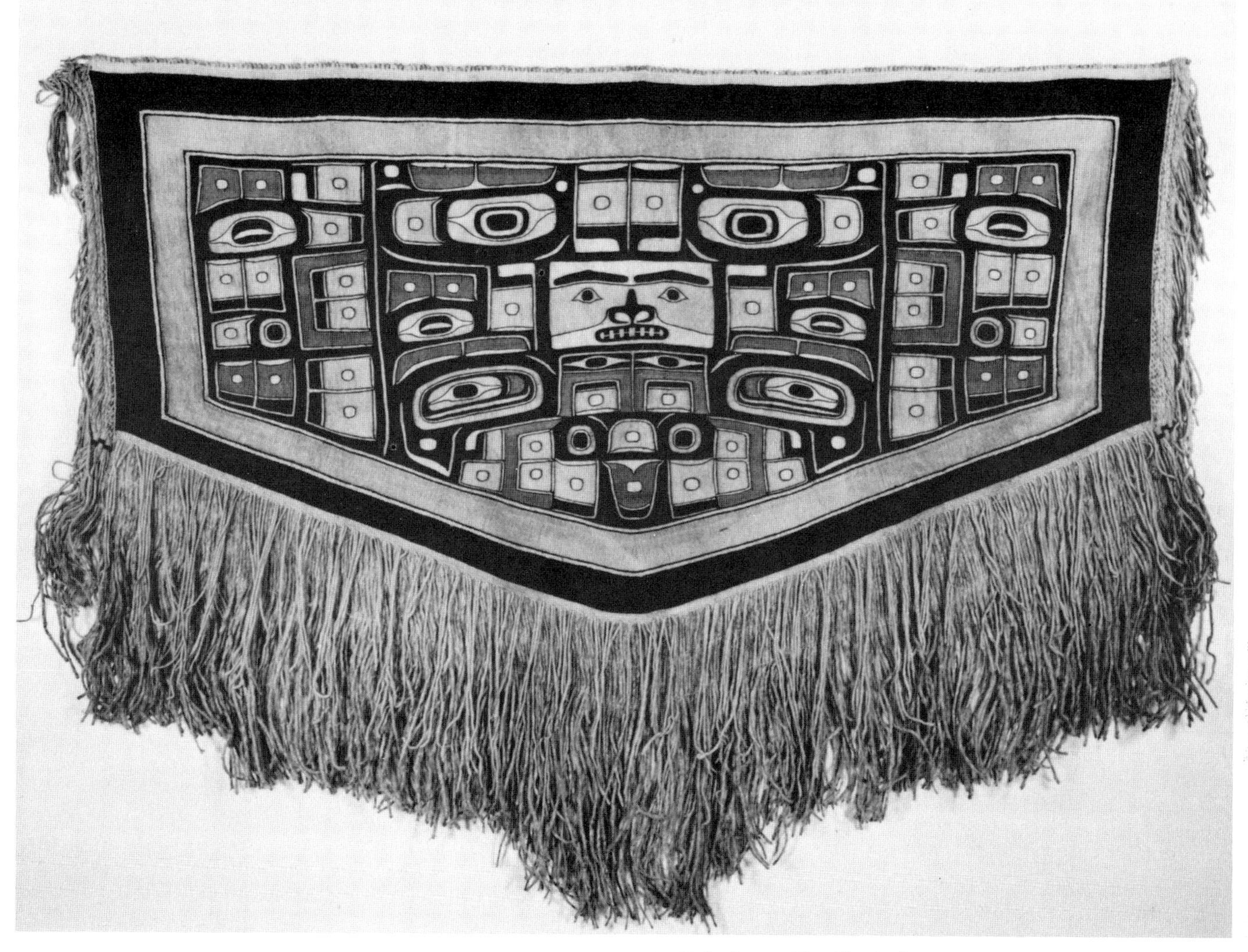

269. Polychrome Shoulder Robe
Commonly termed the "Chilkat Blanket" after the Tlingit group who specialized in its manufacture, this is one of the most familiar products of the Northwest Coast tribes. It is typified by a technique of weaving cedar bark and mountain goat wool in a variety of zoömorphic designs. This represents the killer whale in an abstract pattern. Collected by M. W. Pope. TLINGIT. Yakutat, Alaska. 1860-1875. 52½" x 70". 16/1693.

270. Halibut Hook

Even the everyday implements were often finely carved. This form, peculiar to the Northwest Coast, was intended for halibut fishing. The design represents a man—presumably the owner, holding his hoped-for catch. A bone barb is lashed to the fork; the balance of the hook allows it to lay flat on the ocean floor. TLINGIT. Sitka, Alaska. 1880-1890. 6¼″ x 9″. 23/6175.

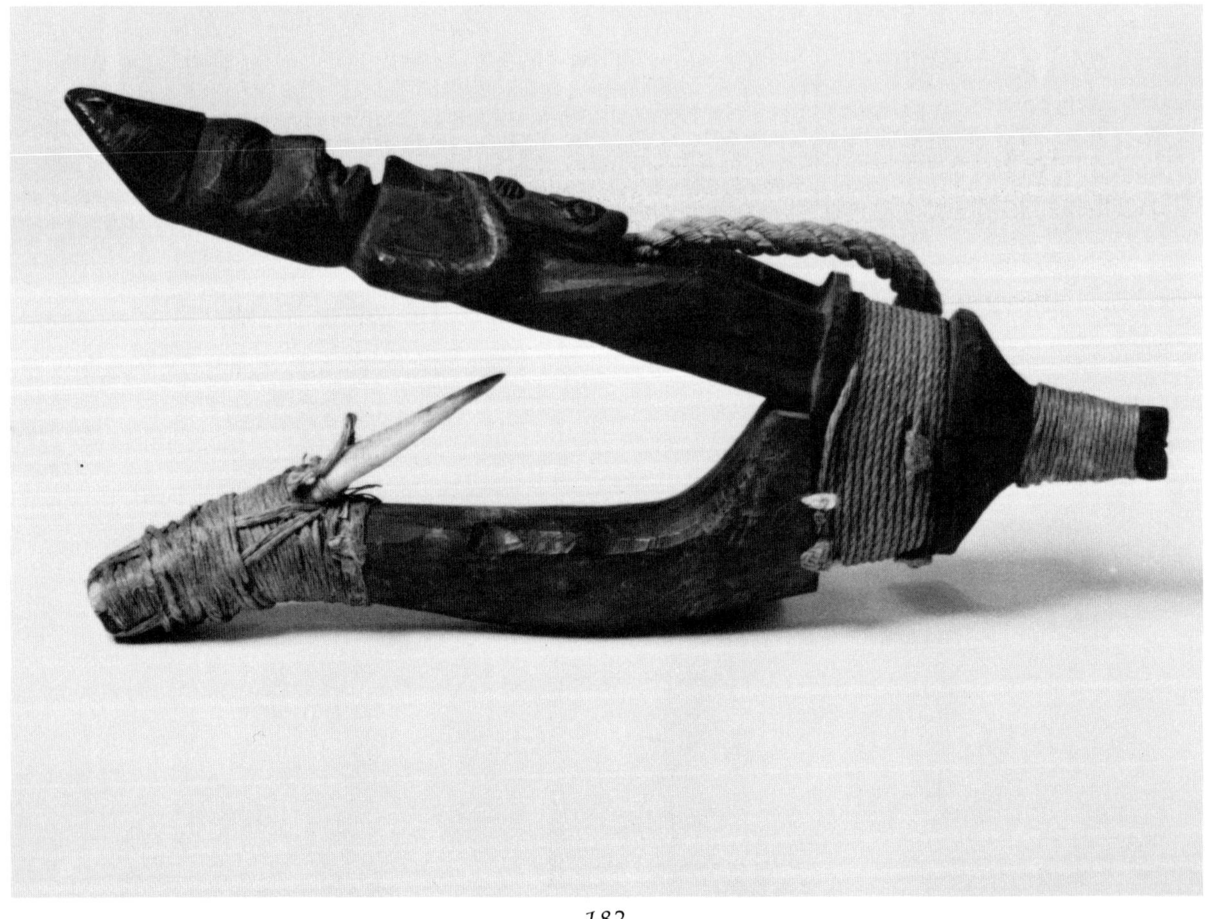

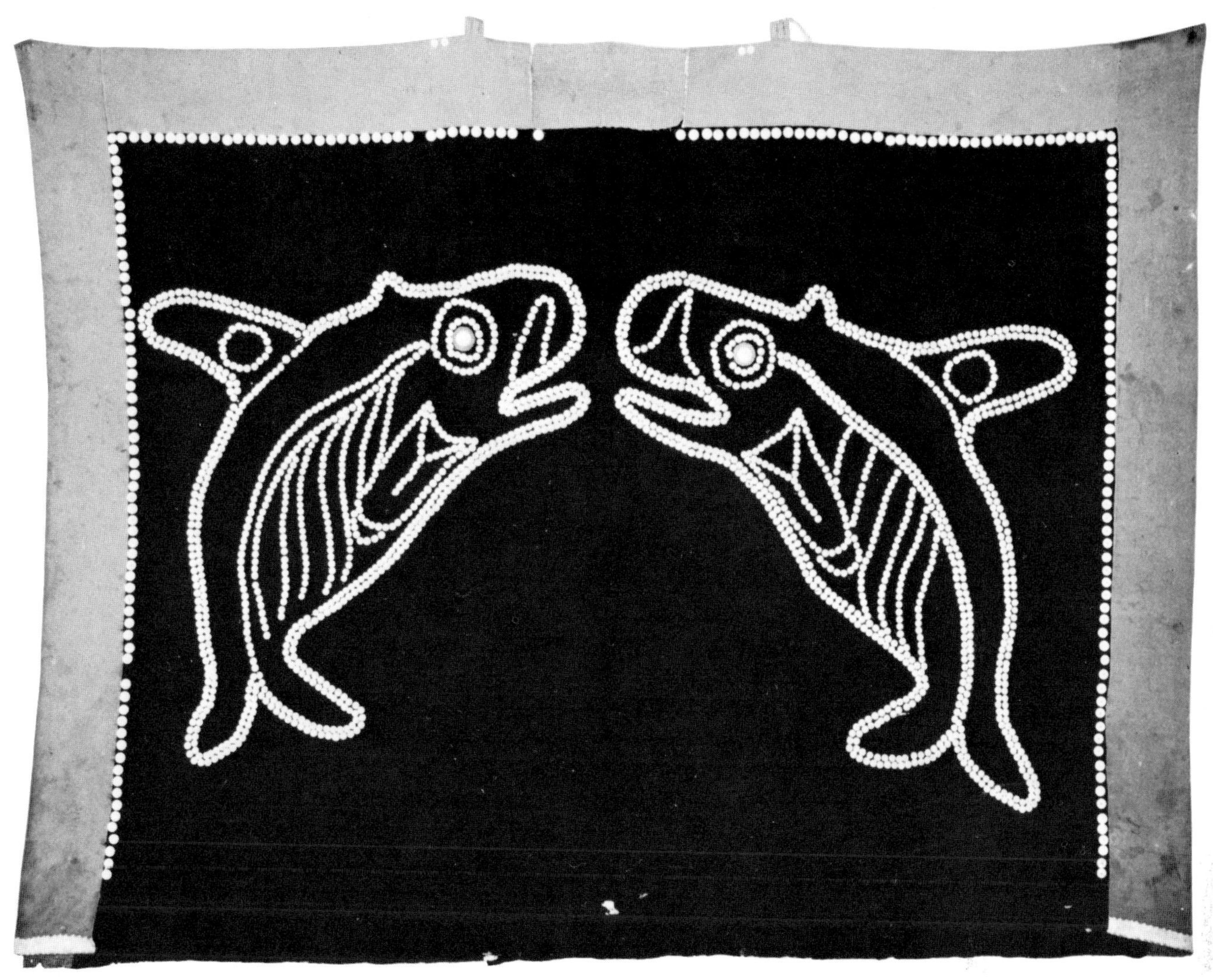

271. Button Blanket
Various shoulder coverings were commonly worn in the coastal area; many of these were beautifully ornamented. This trade cloth blanket is made of trade cloth decorated with two killer whales executed in pearl buttons and abalone shell; it would have been worn only on ceremonial occasions. Collected from Chief Kyan. TLINGIT. Ketchikan, Alaska. 1920-1930. 58″ x 62″. 23/6180.

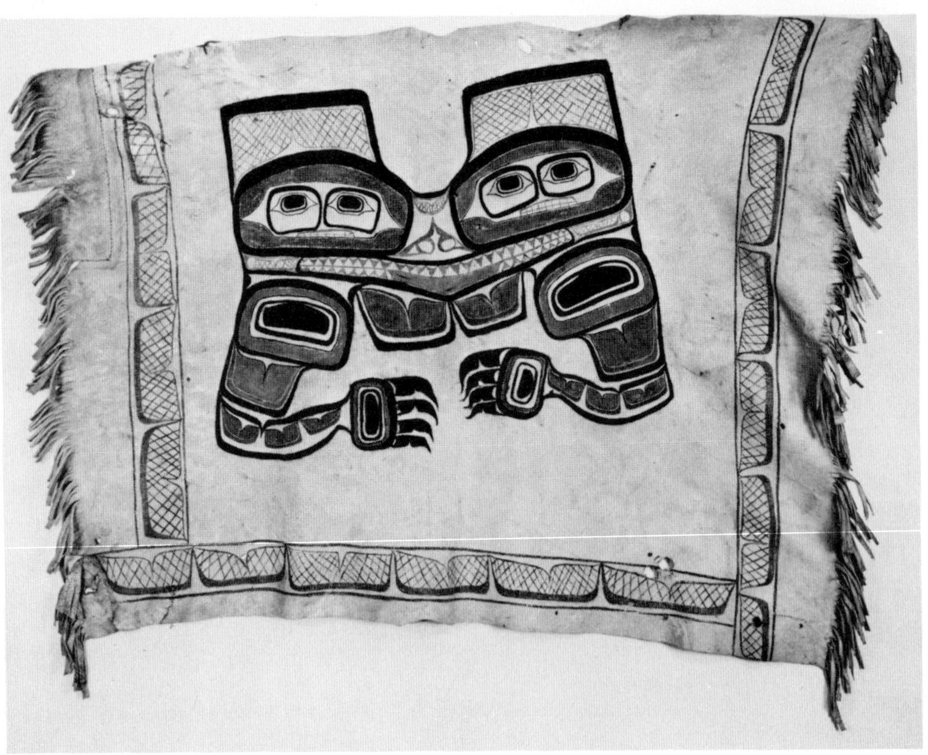

272. Painted Dance Robe
Sketched in red, blue and black on hide, the design on this garment represents the brown bear. Collected by G. T. Emmons. TLINGIT. Klukwan, Alaska. 1880-1900. 40" x 59". 5/6905.

273. Caribou Hide Robe
Another example of the decorated garments from the Northwest is this cape painted with an anthropomorphic design in red and black. TLINGIT. Sitka, Alaska. 1875-1890. 51" x 70". 8/1796.

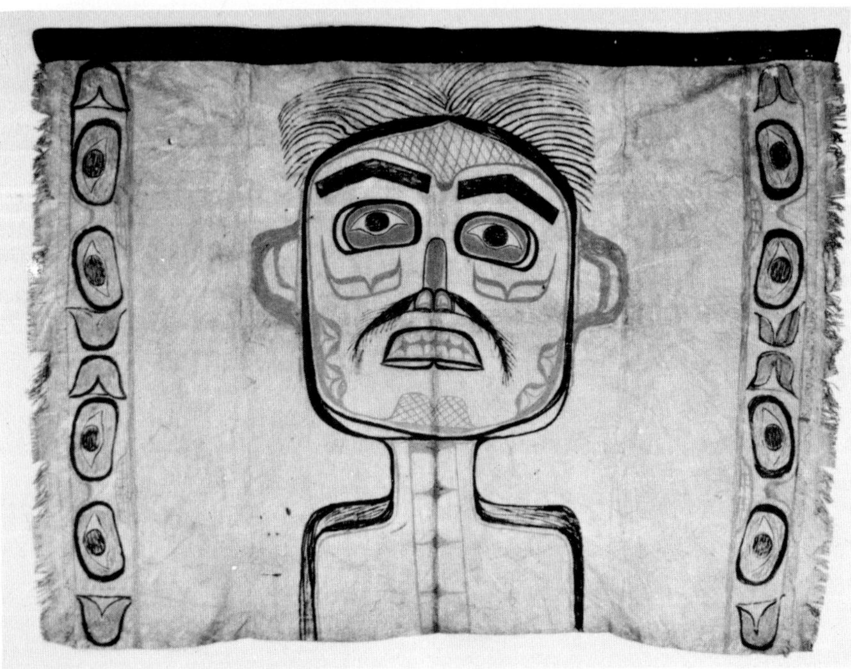

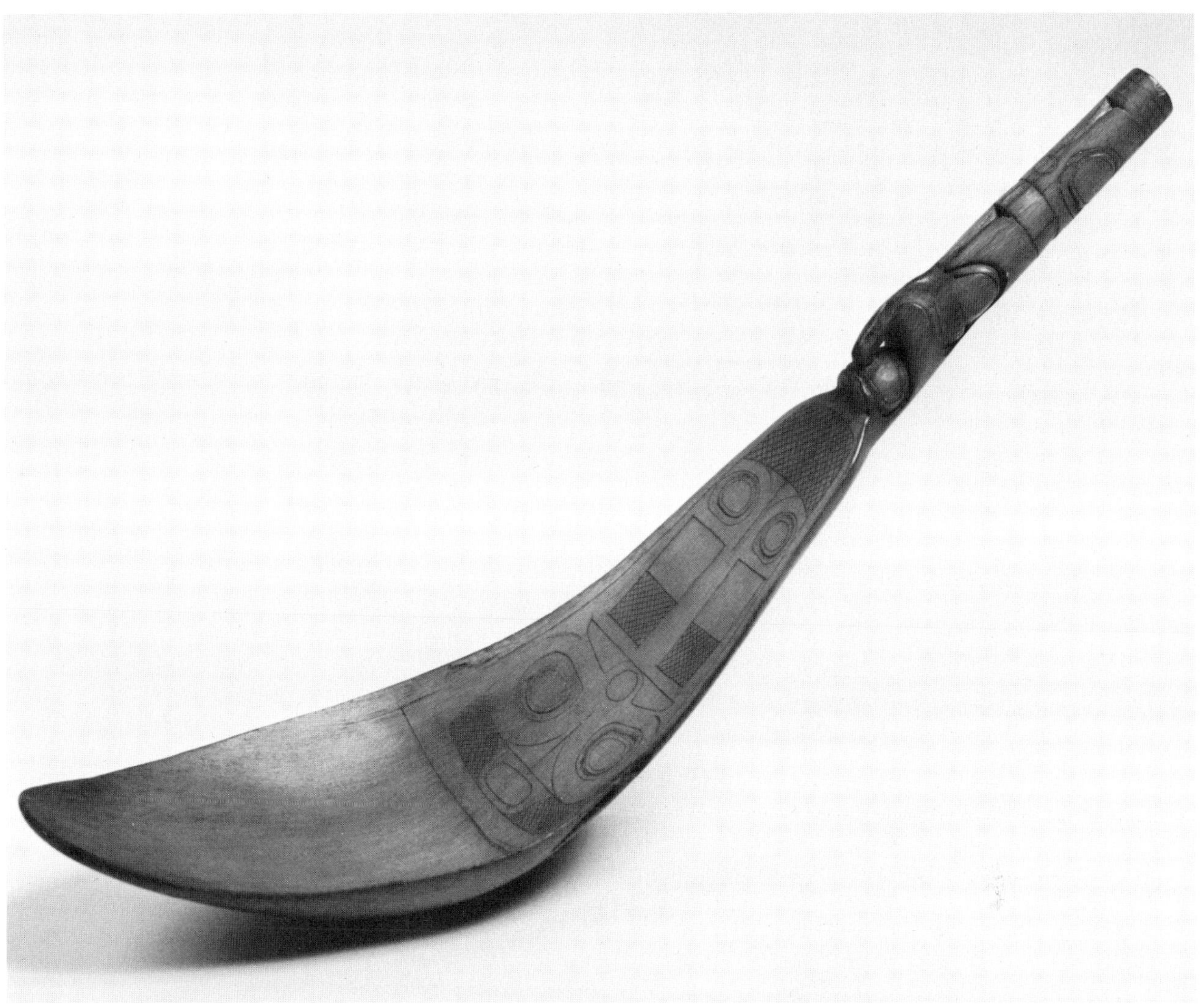

274. Horn Ladle

This carved and incised spoon was made from the horn of the mountain sheep. These were softened by boiling, and then worked into the desired shape, after which they were decorated. Collected by J. E. Standley. HAIDA. British Columbia. 1880-1900. 3″ x 12″. 5/3279.

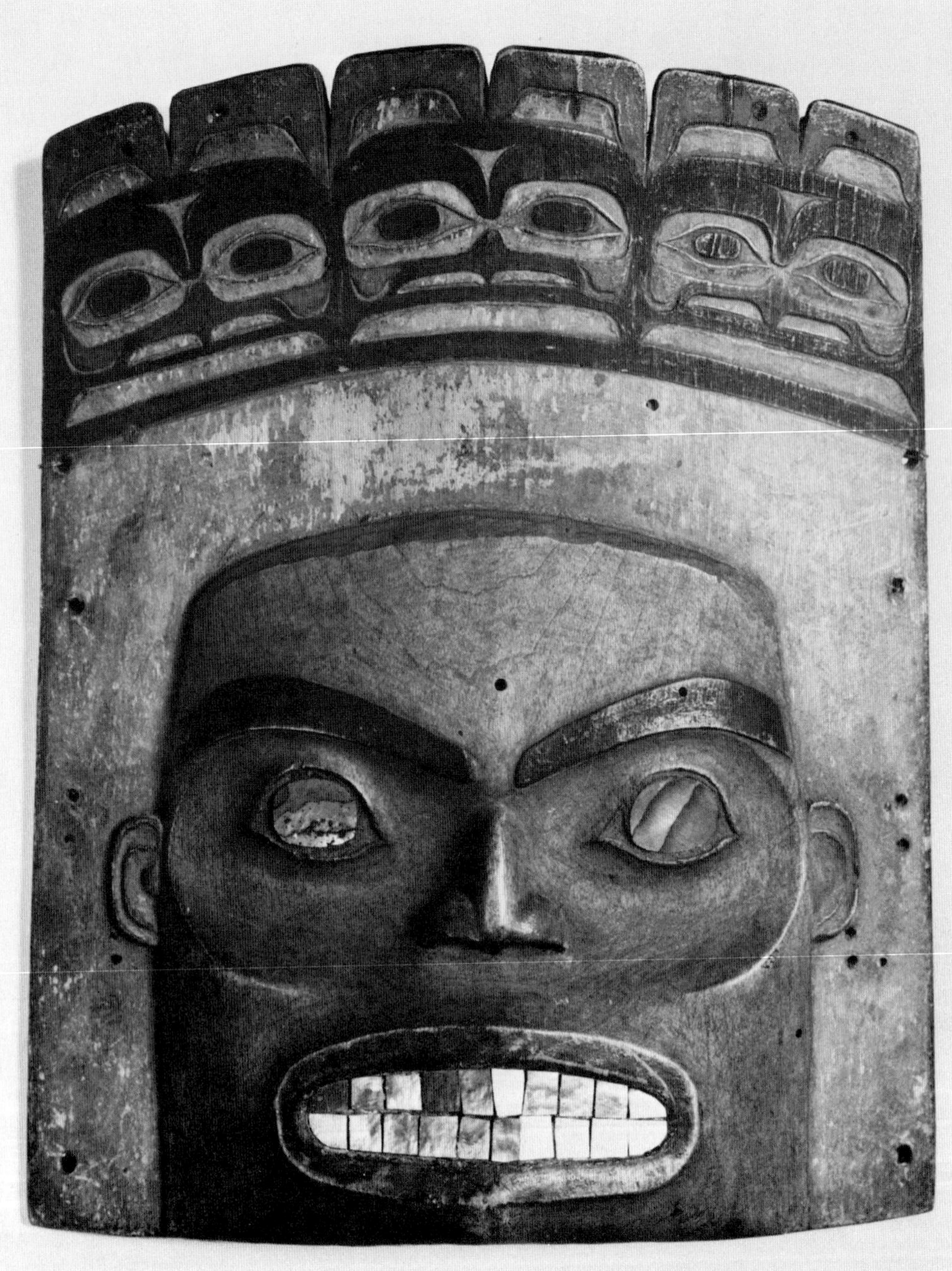

275. Carved Frontlet

Carefully carved and painted in the form of a human, with inlaid abalone shell teeth, this placque was worn on the forehead by wealthy individuals. Three hawk spirits are above the single figure, apparently representing his guardian spirits. Collected by Thomas Crosby. HAIDA. Skidegate, Queen Charlotte Islands, British Columbia. 1860-1875. 5¾" x 7¾". 1/8947.

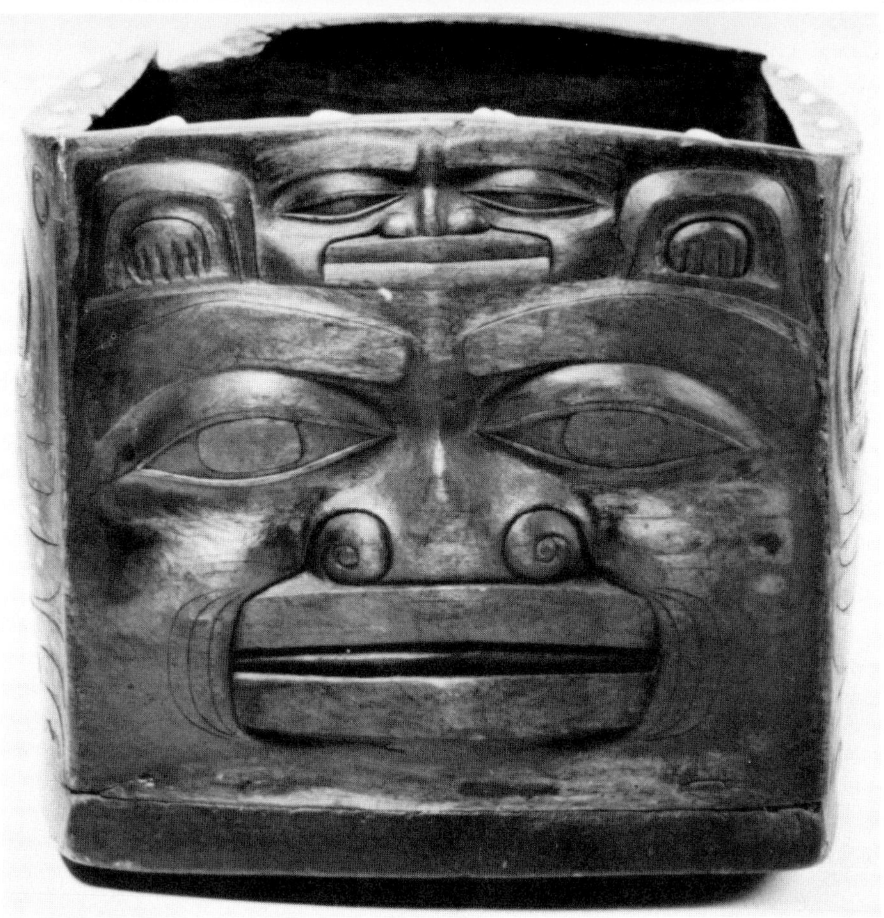

276. Storage Box
Many types of boxes were used in the area—plain ones for everyday use, and more elaborately carved styles intended for personal possessions, such as this example. These were crafted with a one-piece wrap-around side lashed together at one corner. HAIDA. Queen Charlotte Islands, British Columbia. 1850-1875. 10″ x 11″ x 13″. 15/4534.

277. Shaman's Rattle
Globular rattles were primarily used by shamans in religious ceremonies. The carving on this example is the killer whale. Collected by Rev. Thomas Crosby. HAIDA. Kloo, Tanoo Island, Queen Charlotte Islands, British Columbia. 1850-1870. 4¾″ x 12″. 1/8026.

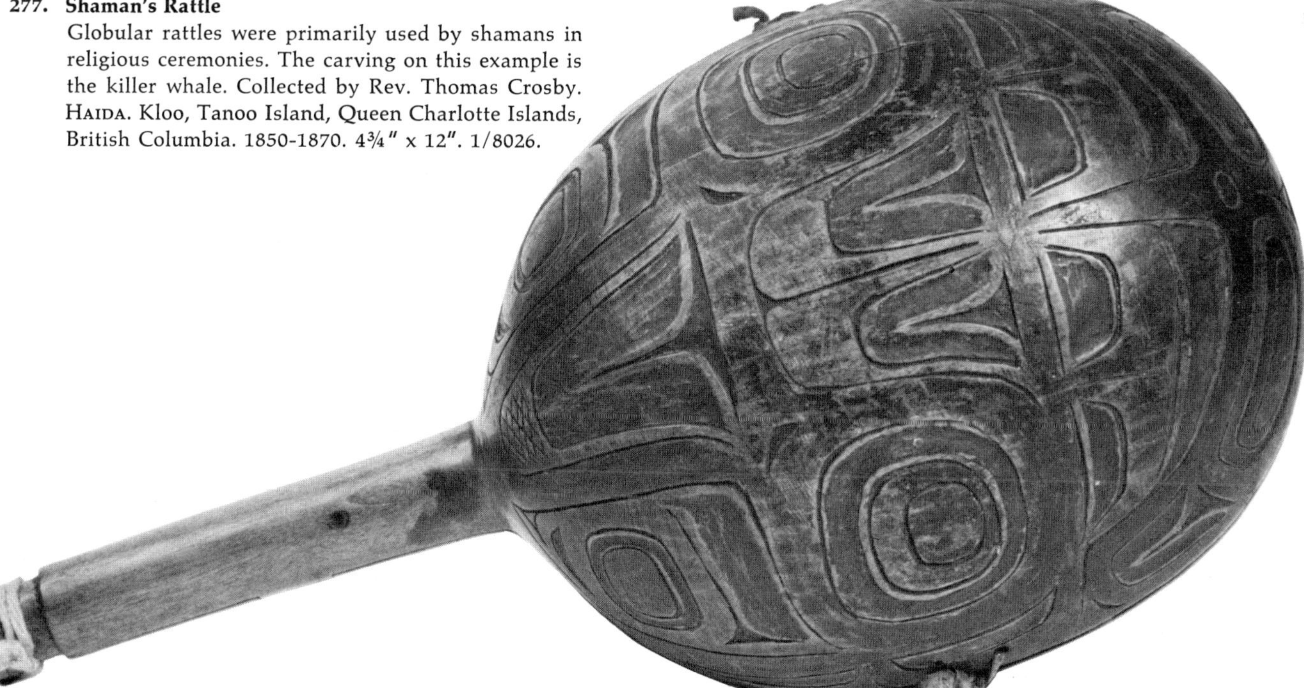

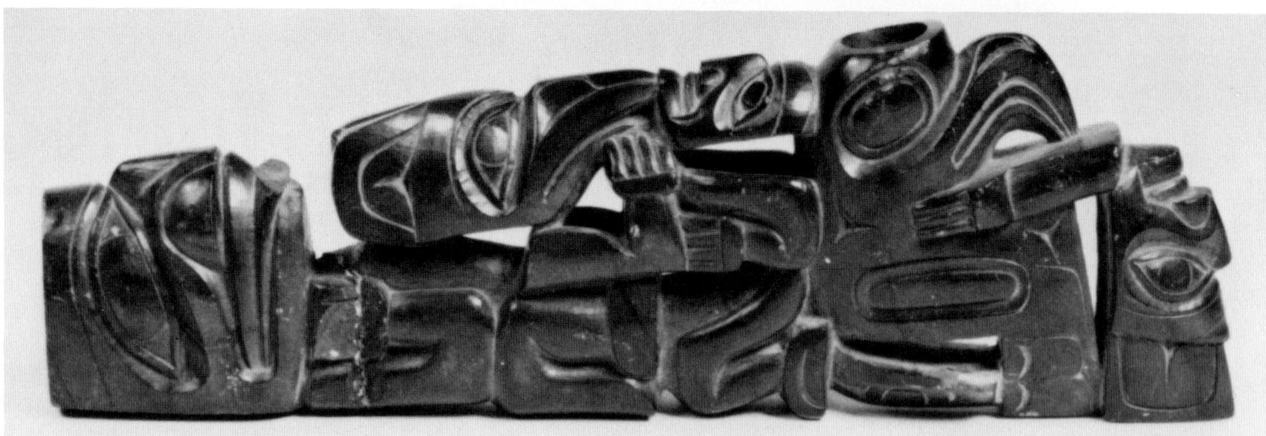

278. Argillite Pipe

Carved from a clay-like stone commonly called "black slate," although the rock has no cleavage, these pipes were intended for decoration only. The source of the raw material was controlled by the Haida people, who worked it into many objects for the tourist trade. Many of these sculptures are art treasures today. HAIDA. Skidegate, Queen Charlotte Islands, British Columbia. 1880-1900. 2½" x 7¼". 22/9183.

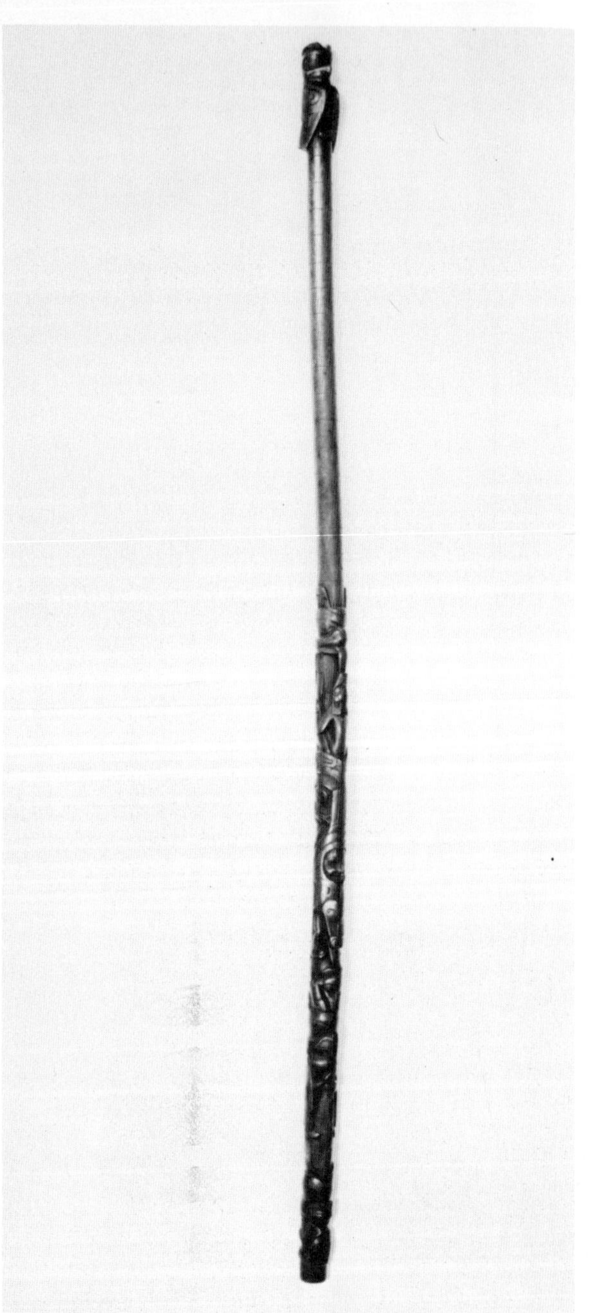

279. Speaker's Staff

Ceremonial staffs were important, since they represented the authority of the owner. Frequently they were pounded on the floor for emphasis, or to gain attention. This chief's staff has an owl on top, with other animal and human figures on the base. Collected by G. T. Emmons. TSIMSHIAN. Nass River, British Columbia. 1860-1870. L: 70". 6/4582.

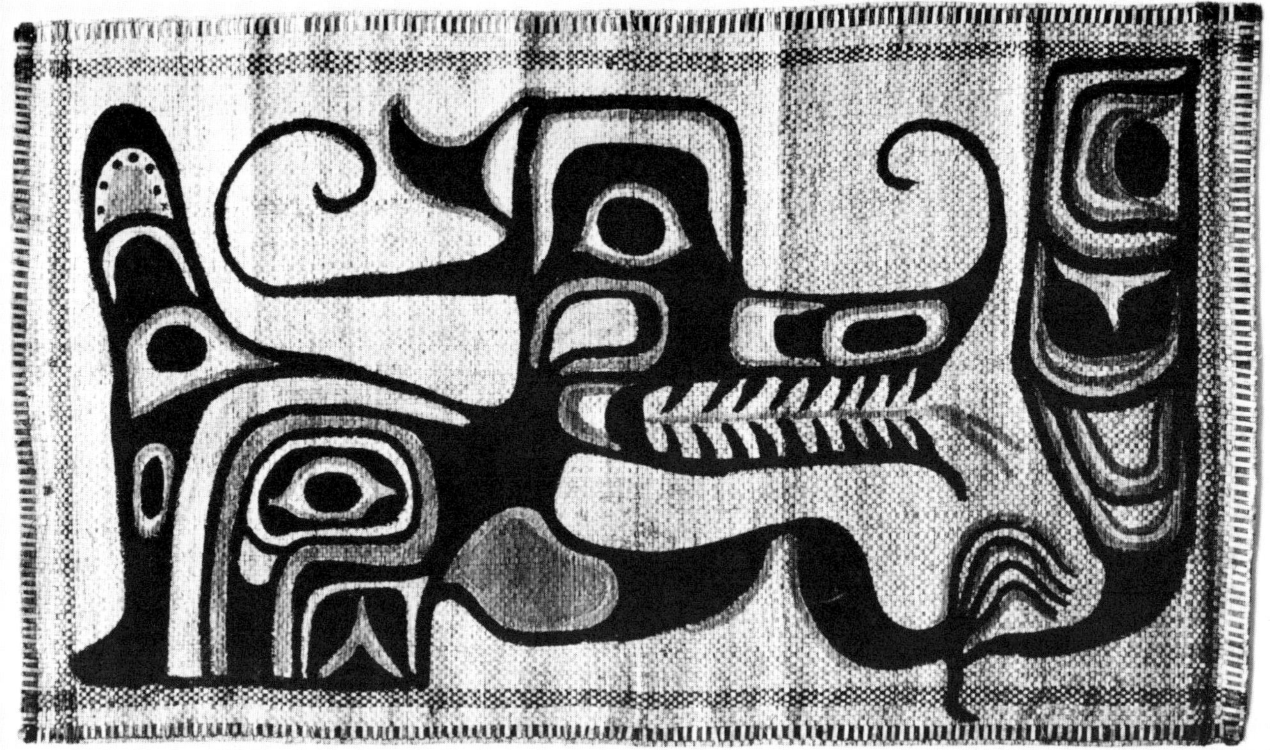

280. Cedar Bark Mat

Strips of cedar bark, pounded and flattened for working, were woven into garments, matting and many other objects. This example has been painted with a strong red, black, blue and green design representing a mythical serpent. KWAKIUTL. Kitimat, British Columbia. 1900-1910. 39″ x 68½″. 19/5016.

281. Carved Rattle

Representing a human head, this has been further decorated by the addition of blue, white and red paint. It was collected by a member of the U.S. Fish Commission shortly after the purchase of Alaska. HAIDA. Kasaan, Prince of Wales Island, Alaska. 1875-1880. 5″ x 11″. 2/431.

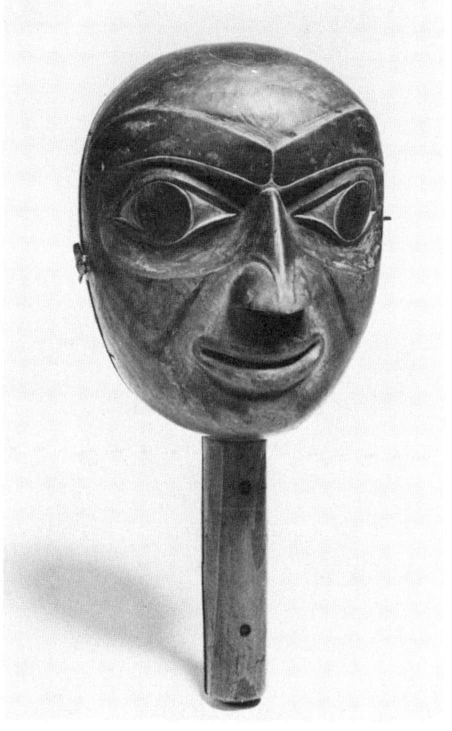

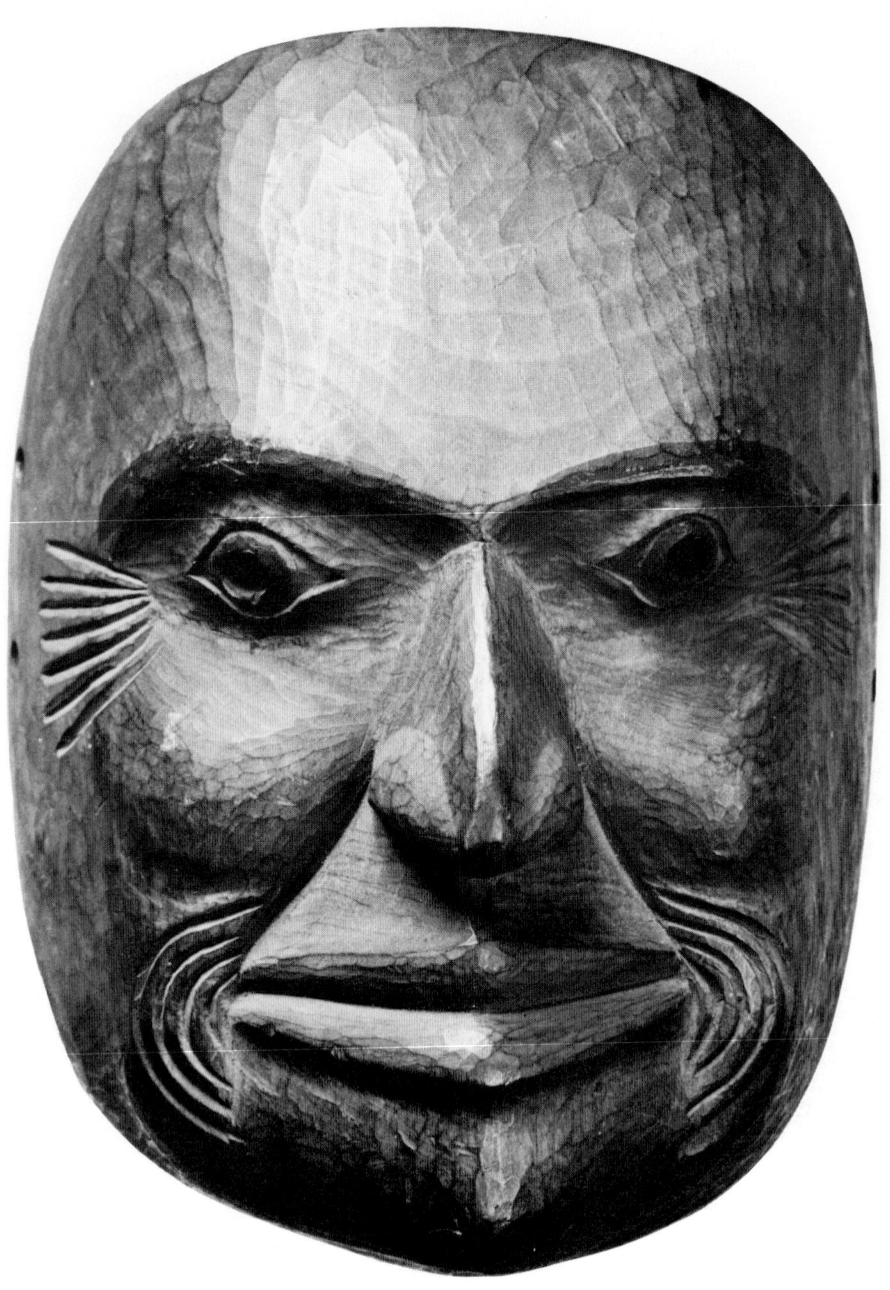

282. Human Face Mask
An example of a mask which in all probability represents the portrait of an actual individual, this has a vitality and sculptural quality far above most carvings of this type. Collected by G. T. Emmons. NISKA. Nass River, British Columbia. 1850-1860. 7″ x 9½″. 1/4233.

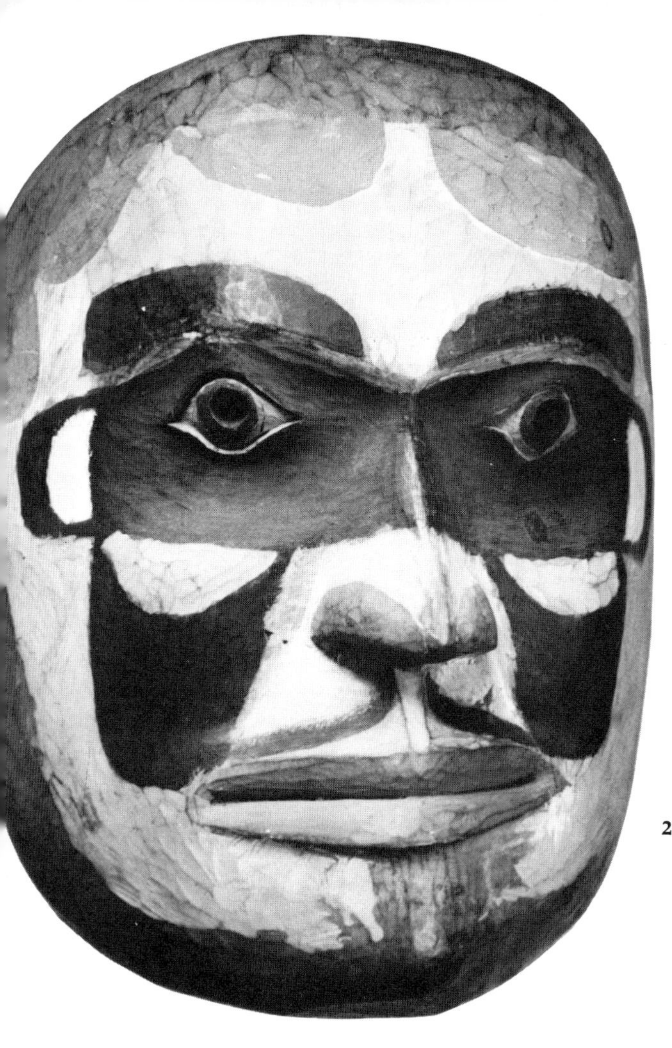

283. Painted Mask
Faces were often painted or tattooed; this mask depicts a man whose face has been decorated for a ceremony. Collected by G. T. Emmons. NISKA. Kitlakdamik, Nass River, British Columbia. 1850-1875. 7¼″ x 9¼″. 1/4225.

284. Horn Ladle
A two-piece ladle, made from the horns of a mountain goat and a mountain sheep, with the design of a squirrel in the mouth of a wolf, and a man holding a spear—perhaps a hunter. Collected by G. T. Emmons. NISKA. Nass River, British Columbia. 1865-1880. 3″ x 10″. 9/8080.

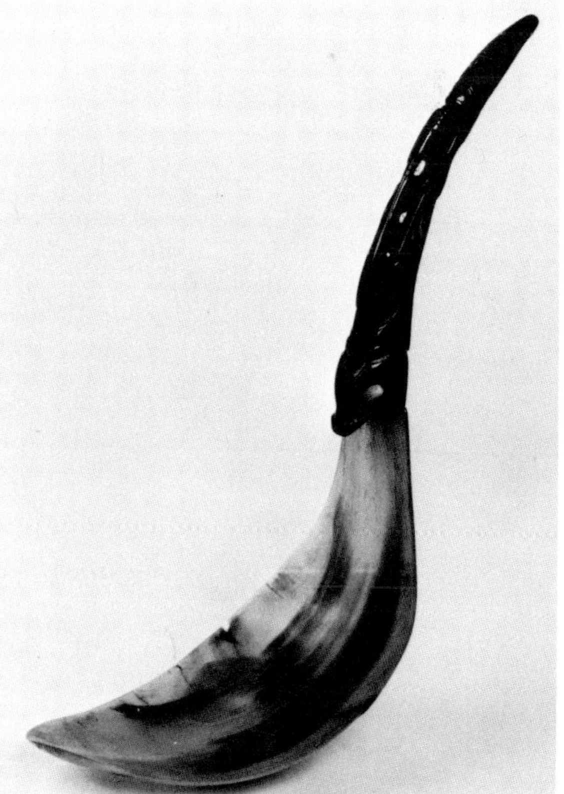

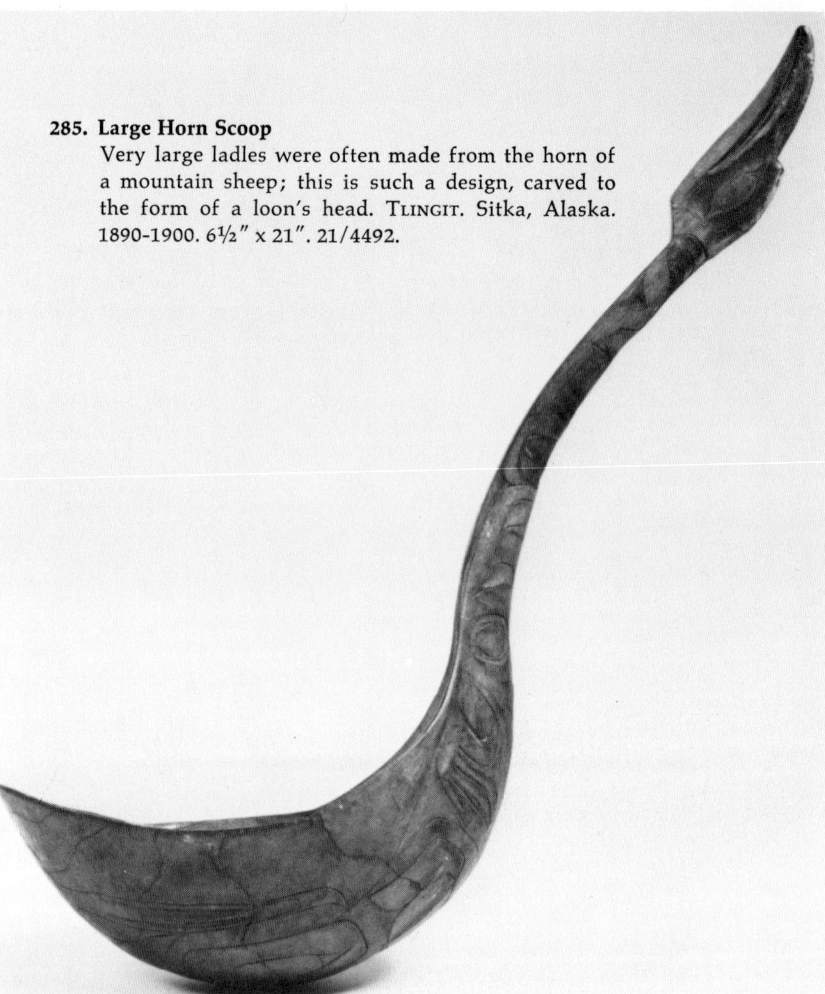

285. Large Horn Scoop
Very large ladles were often made from the horn of a mountain sheep; this is such a design, carved to the form of a loon's head. TLINGIT. Sitka, Alaska. 1890-1900. 6½" x 21". 21/4492.

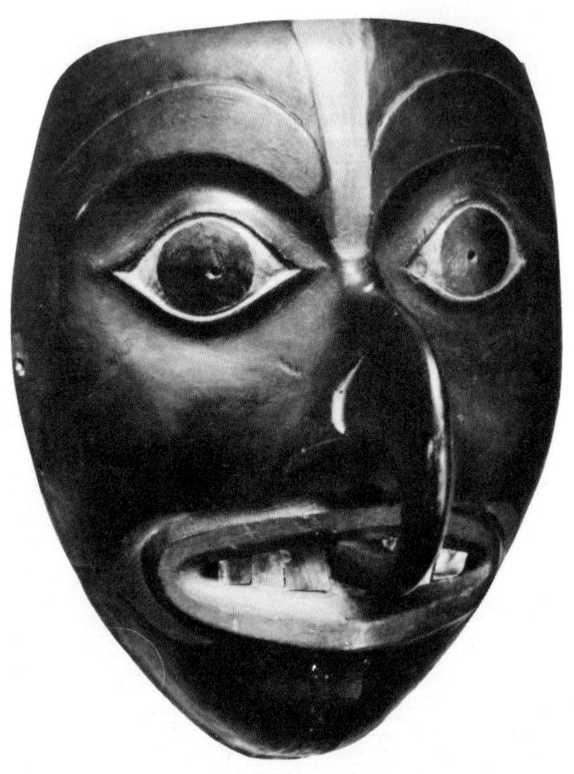

286. Wooden Hawk Mask
A finely carved and polished mask with the original paint still in excellent condition. The mouth is set with abalone shell inlaid into the wood. Collected by G. T. Emmons. TLINGIT. Prince of Wales Island, Alaska. 1890-1900. 6½" x 8¼". 15/1325.

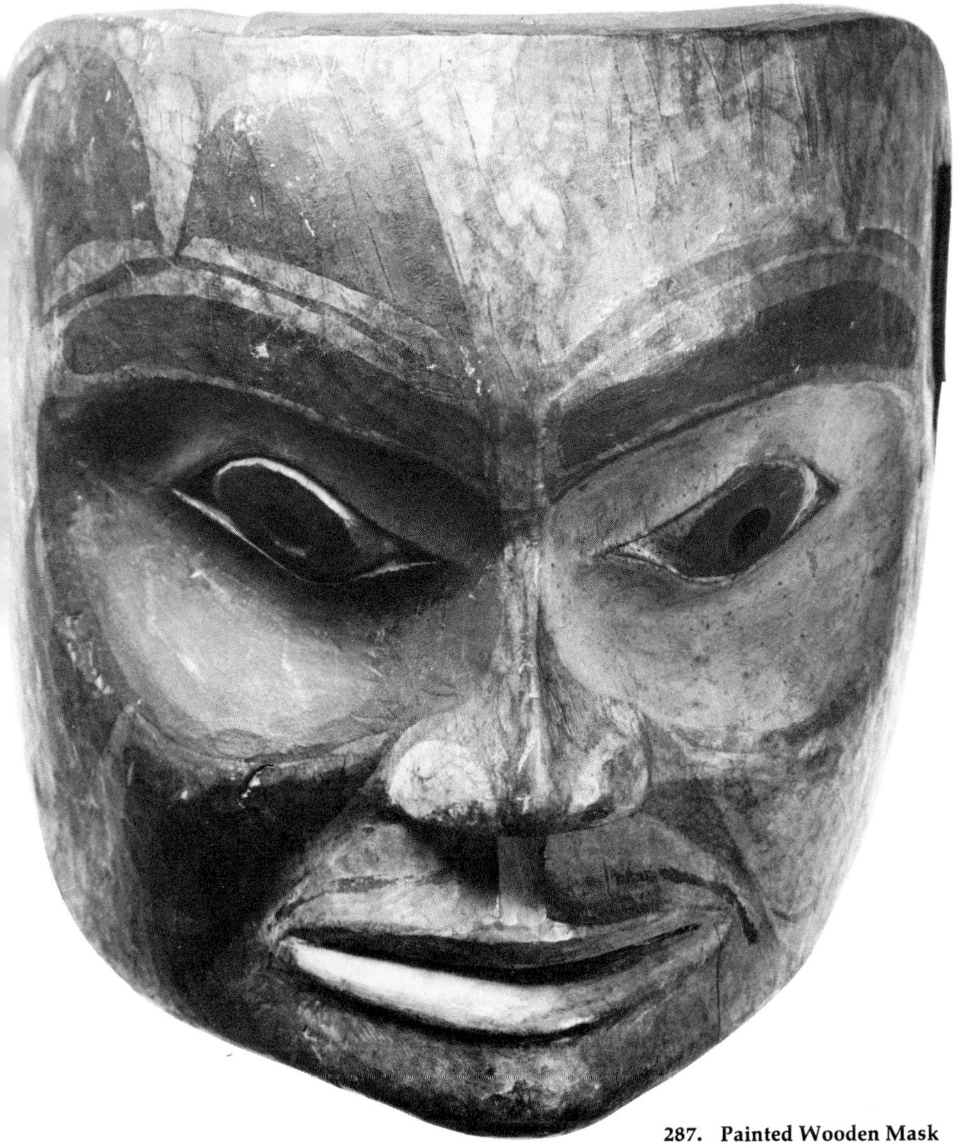

287. Painted Wooden Mask

The design on the face represents the dorsal fin of the killer whale. This may indicate the family of the man wearing it, or the creature he was portraying in a ceremony. Collected by G. T. Emmons. NISKA. Kitlakdamik, Nass River, British Columbia. 1860-1875. 8½" x 7¾". 1/4243.

288. Wooden Dance Staff

A very long wand is frequently part of the ceremonial equipment used during performances in the homes of the Northwest Coast people. This might be used for emphasis, or as a dramatic part of the costume. This represents the Raven, with human hair decoration. HAIDA. Queen Charlotte Islands, British Columbia. 1890-1910. 6¾" x 81". 15/4341.

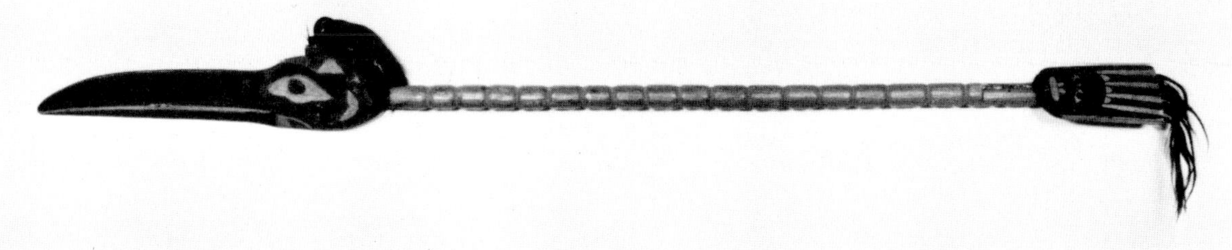

289. Beaded Neck Ornament
(See color insert facing page 280)

290. Fighting Knife
Wealthy individuals had richly worked war knives made of wood, copper, steel or whalebone. This example, with a carved wooden handle representing the Raven, has inlaid abalone shell eyes and teeth. The blade is of steel. TLINGIT. Wrangell, Alaska. 1850-1875. L: 17". 19/7446.

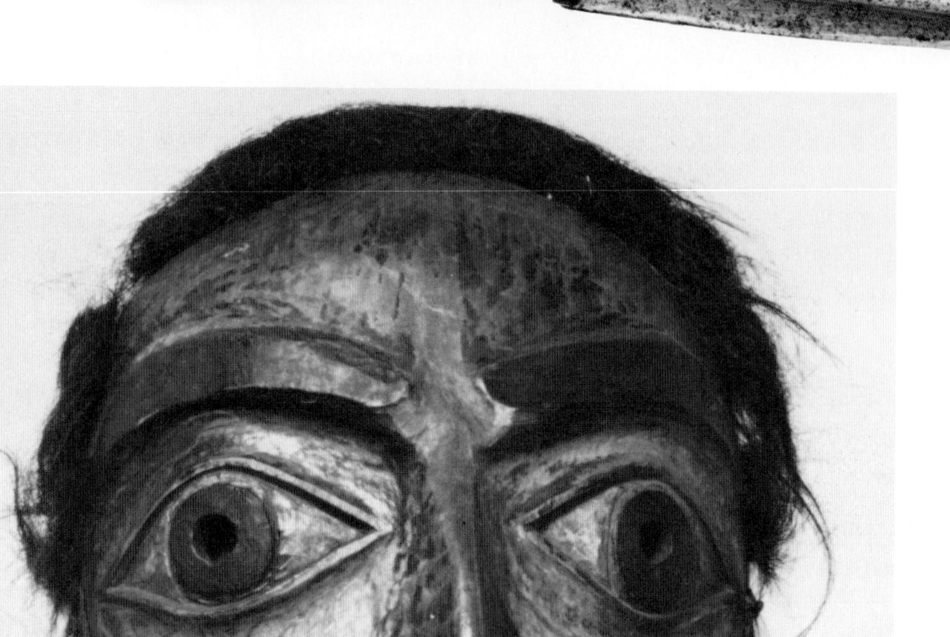

291. Large Dance Mask
Some of the very elaborate performances employed masks decorated with human hair and other materials. This probably represents Tsonoqua, a mythological cannibal giant who lived in the woods. She brought wealth to the people. KWAKIUTL. Vancouver Island, British Columbia. 1850-1875. 9" x 14". 8/1573.

292. Face Mask
(See color insert facing page 160)

293. Painted Mask
(See color insert facing page 280)

294. Movable Mask
Fitted with ear flaps which open when in use, this mask represents the wolf. It is one of the many zoömorphic masks used during the course of the annual ceremonial calendar. Collected by G. T. Emmons. KWAKIUTL. British Columbia. 1880-1900. 9″ x 16″. 5/4246.

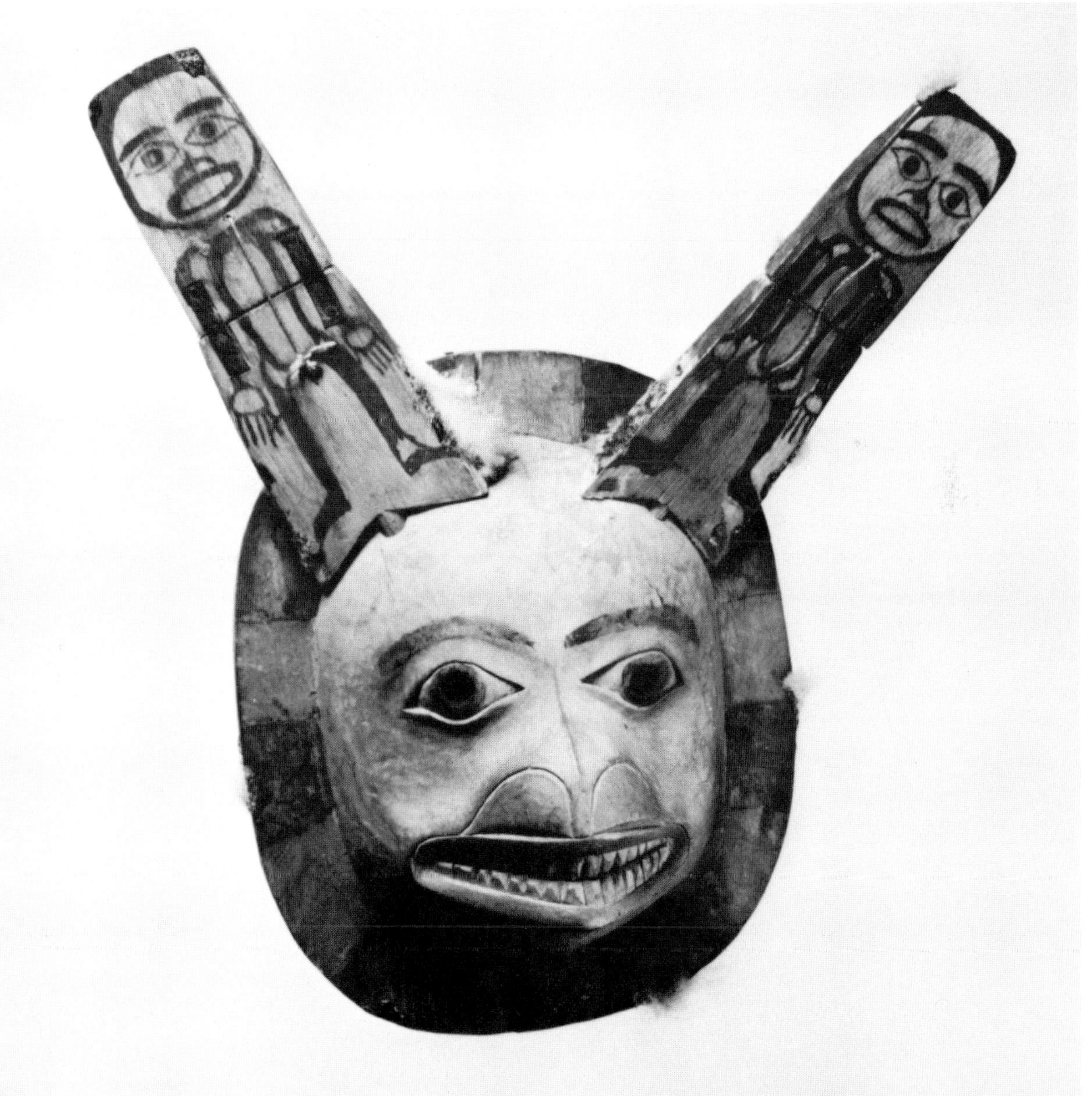

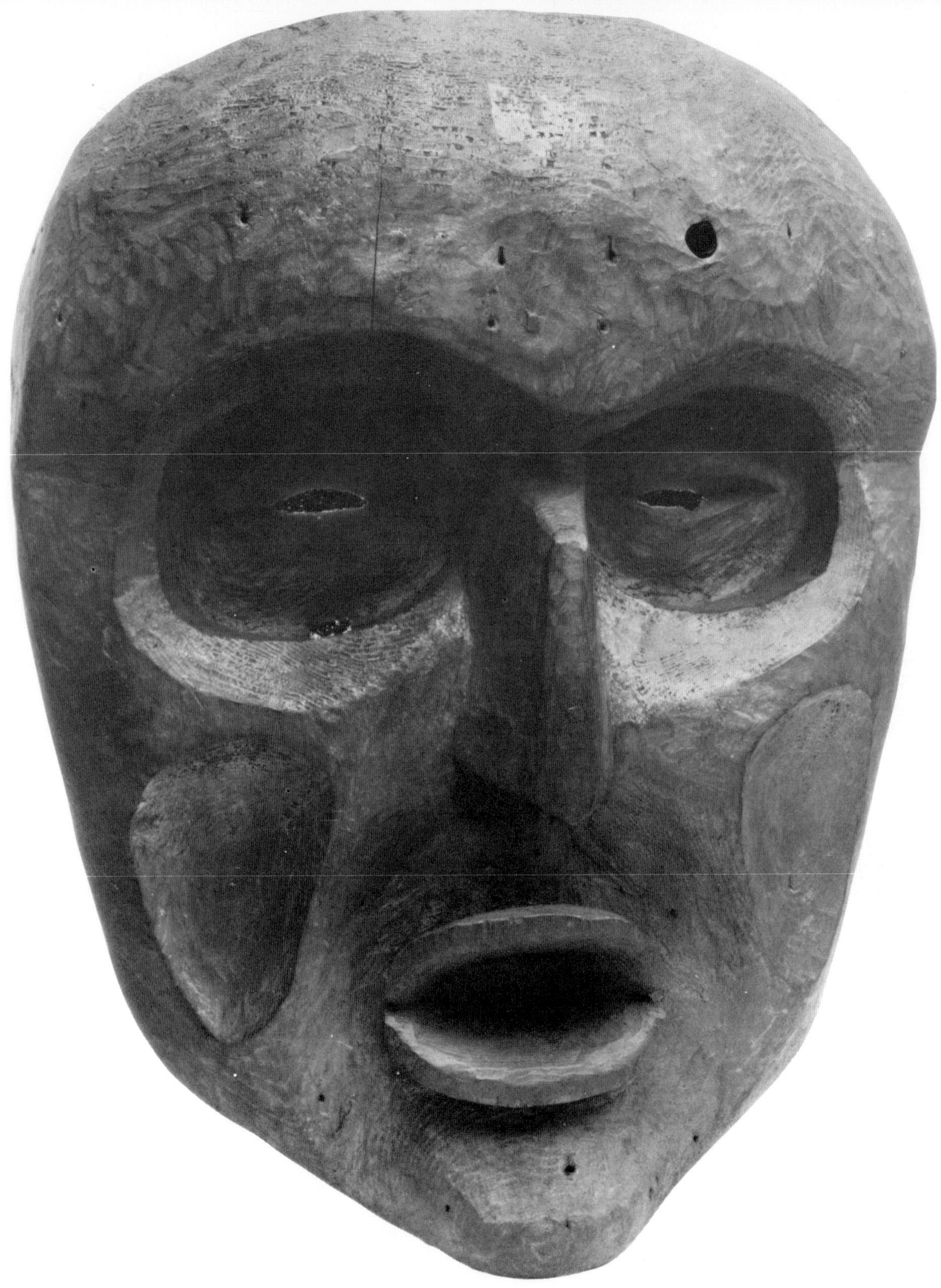

295. Very Large Mask
A representation of Tsonoqua, the giant who lives in the woods and eats naughty children. She brings good fortune and treasure to those who deserve it. Collected by G. T. Emmons. KWAKIUTL. Quatsino, Vancouver Island, British Columbia. 1860-1870. 17″ x 22″. 1/2176.

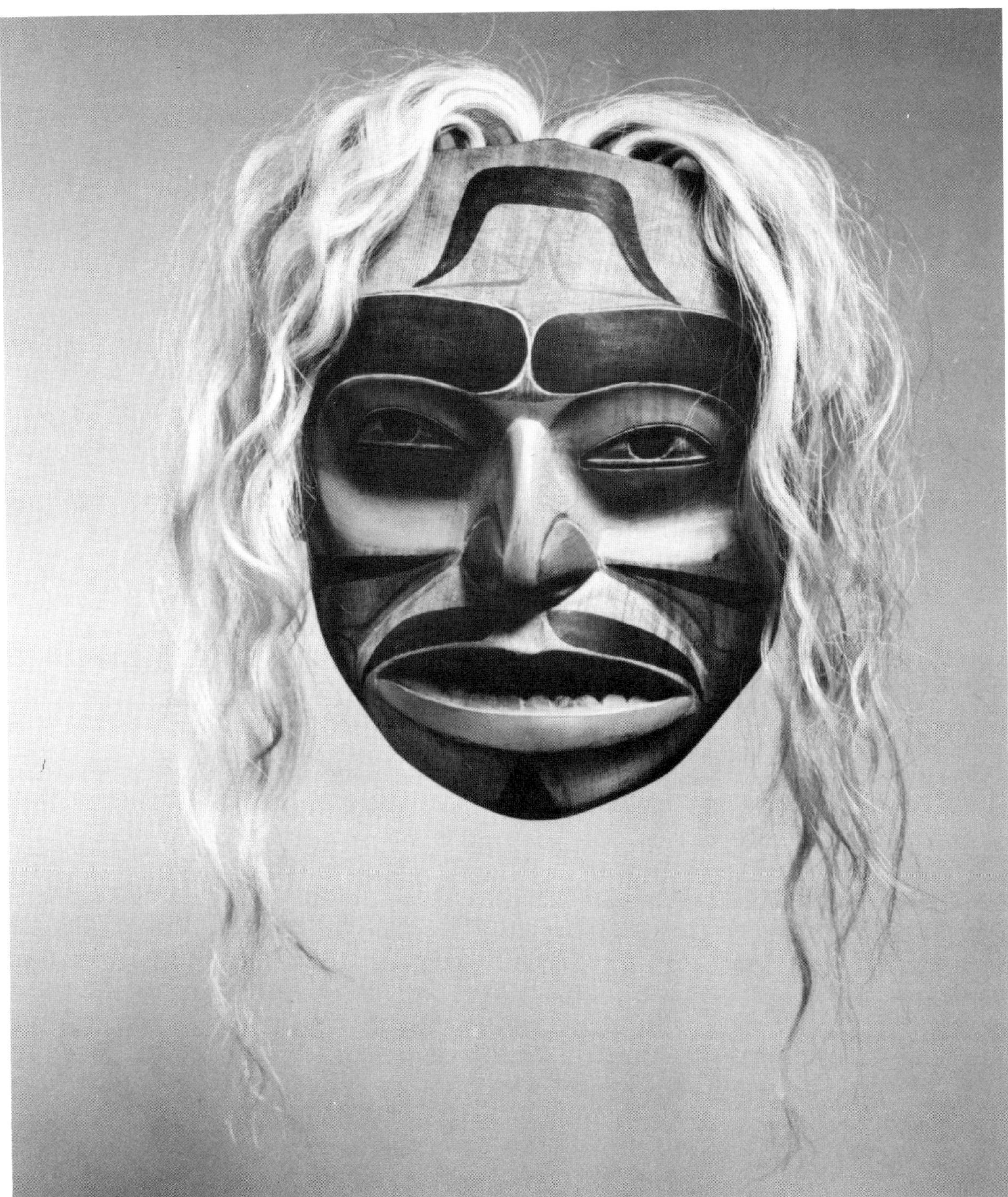

296. Modern Carved Mask

The art of the Northwest Coast people is still a vibrant force. This mask, carved in 1971 by Tsungani, is a fine example of the work being produced today. In design, balance and execution, it has all of the qualities of the 19th Century sculpture. Indeed, it is quite likely that many of the older carvings looked just as this does when they too, had aged only a year or two. TLINGIT. Alaska. 8½" x 9½". 24/6487.

297. Painted Hide Drum

(See color insert facing page 200)

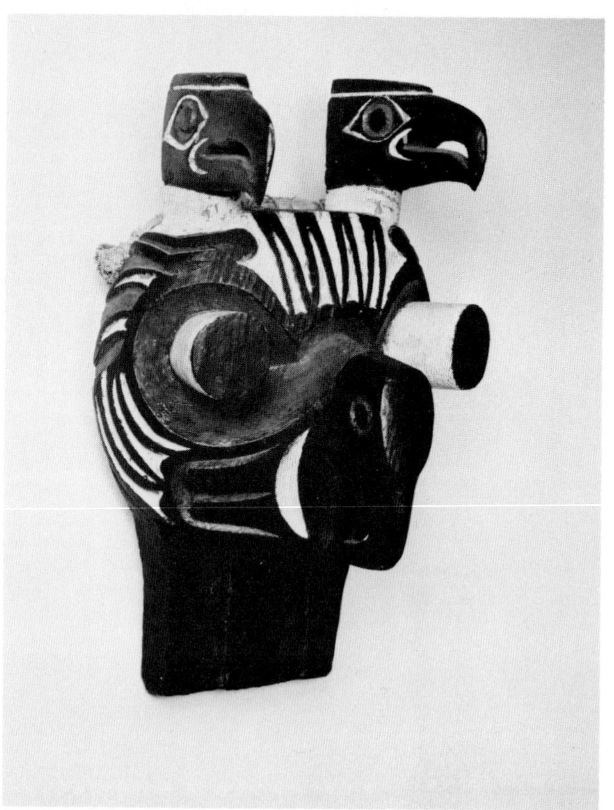

298. Sky Being Mask
A powerful design representing Swaixwe, the mythical Sky Bird who came down to earth and lives in lakes. This is unique to the Salish people, although it was later adapted by others in the area. A collar of swan feathers is wrapped around the base when in use. Collected by G. T. Emmons. COWICHAN. Nanaimo, Vancouver Island, British Columbia. 1890-1900. 11″ x 18″. 18/1063.

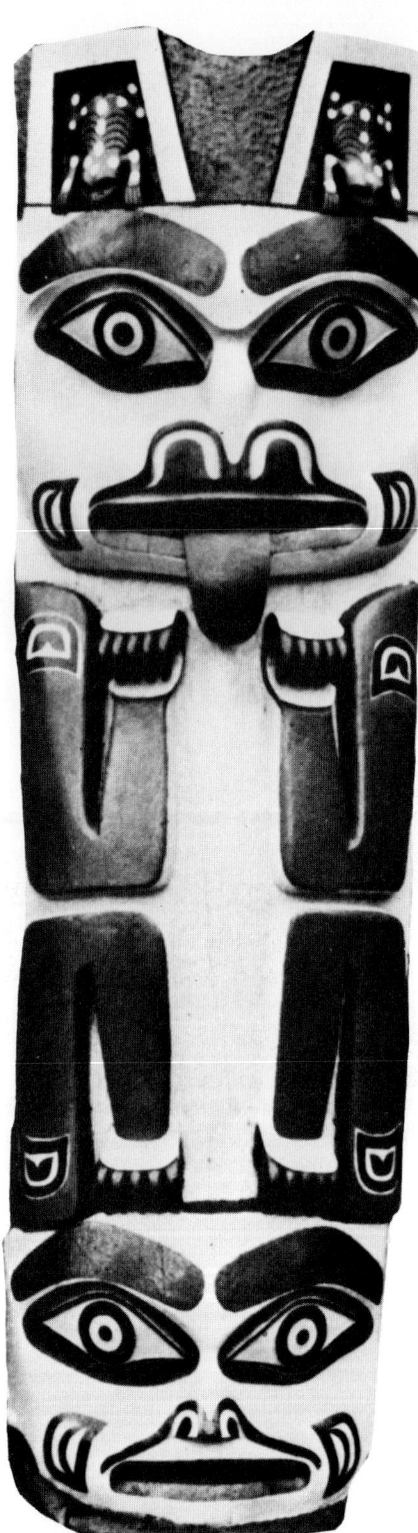

299. Carved House Post
These were used inside the large wooden dwellings to support the roof, or often to provide further decoration to the interior. This represents the Sea Bear, and has a frog carved in each ear. It was presented as a token of respect to Chief Frog Ears of Sukkwan by the people of a neighboring village. HAIDA. Cordova Bay, Alaska. 1850-1875. 4′ x 11½′. 15/9199.

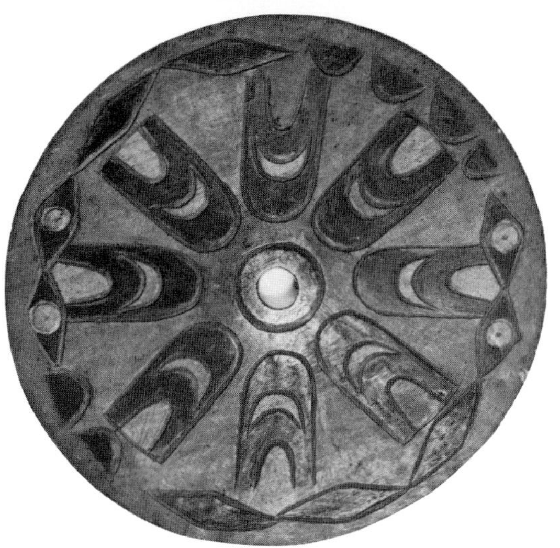

300. Wooden Spindle Whorl
Salish weaving involved a variety of very large looms and spinning sticks, to produce the extremely coarse yarns required. Large cedar wood spindle whorls were used to balance these long sticks; they were decorated with a variety of incised designs. COWICHAN. Duncan, Vancouver Island, British Columbia. 1880-1890. D: 9″. 16/2781.

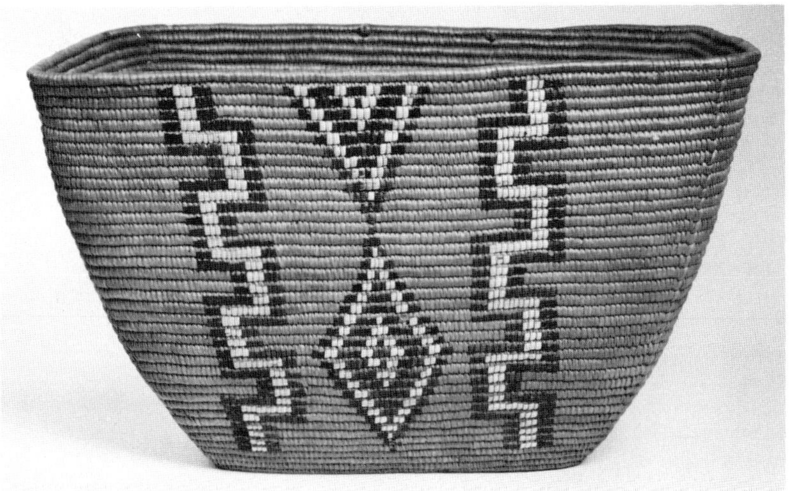

301. Storage Basket
Along the Fraser River, a great variety of sturdy, well-woven baskets are made, often with strong, brilliant designs. The geometric fret-and-lozenge patterns on this example are typical. LILLOOET. Fraser River, British Columbia. 1880-1900. 8″ x 13¾″. 18/8911.

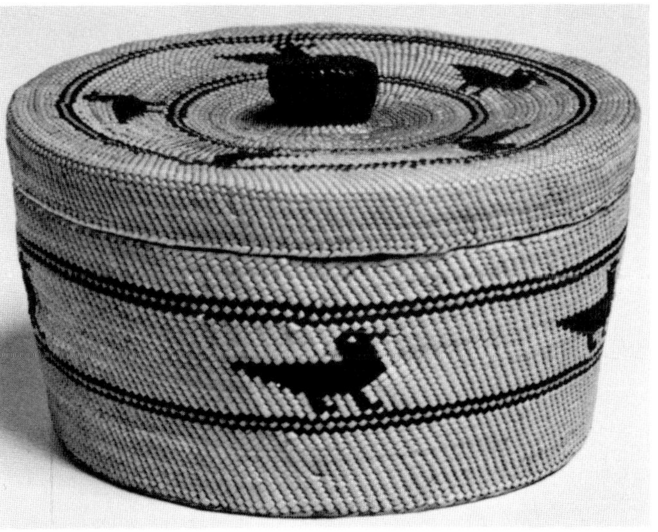

302. Basket and Cover
The people around the Pacific Northwest region weave a very fine variety of basketry into many forms. This tightly woven example has a row of sea birds around the sides. NOOTKA. Nitinat, Vancouver Island, British Columbia. 1880-1890. 1¾″ x 3¼″. 11/8269.

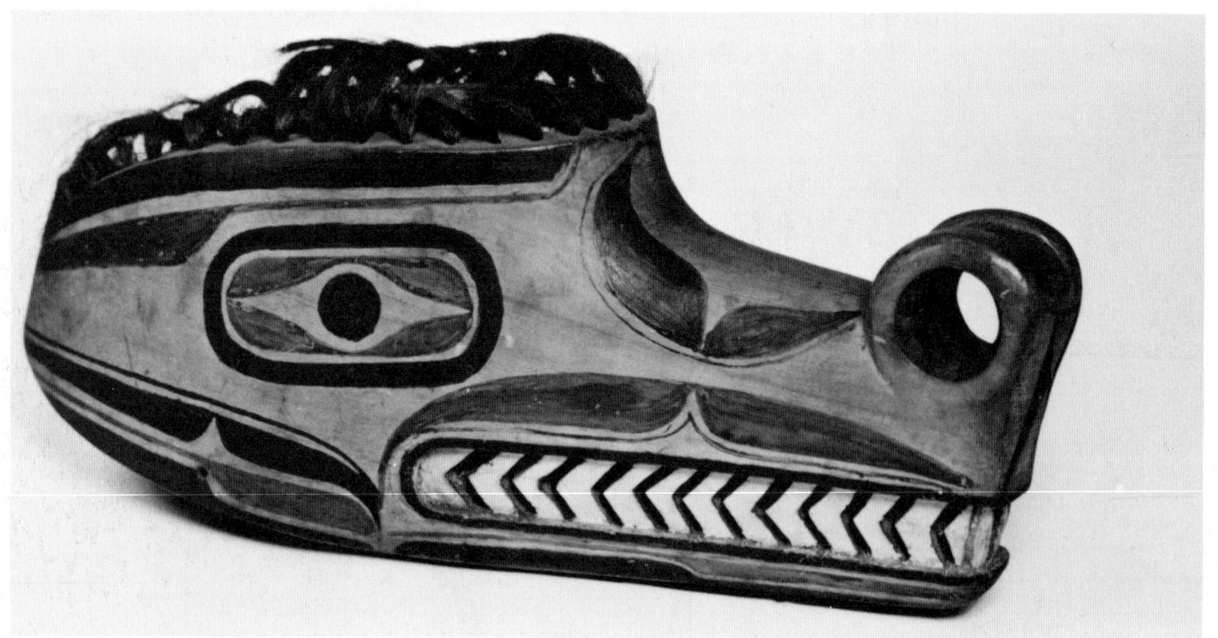

303. Carved Dance Mask

The Nootka style of mask differs from other carvings in the Northwest Coast. Often, box-like forms are employed; this is a smoother, more fluid style, painted in the usual orange and black colors and decorated with horsehair. The design represents the wolf, one of the most frequently impersonated beings. Collected by D. F. Tozier. NOOTKA. Ahousat, Vancouver Island, British Columbia. 1875-1890. 7″ x 17½″. 6/9489.

304. Woven Basket

Made with a series of wolf heads in black and blue around the sides, this is a coarser style of weave than **302** . Collected by Leo J. Frachtenberg. MAKAH. Neah Bay, Washington. 1910-1915. 5½″ x 10¼″. 6/413.

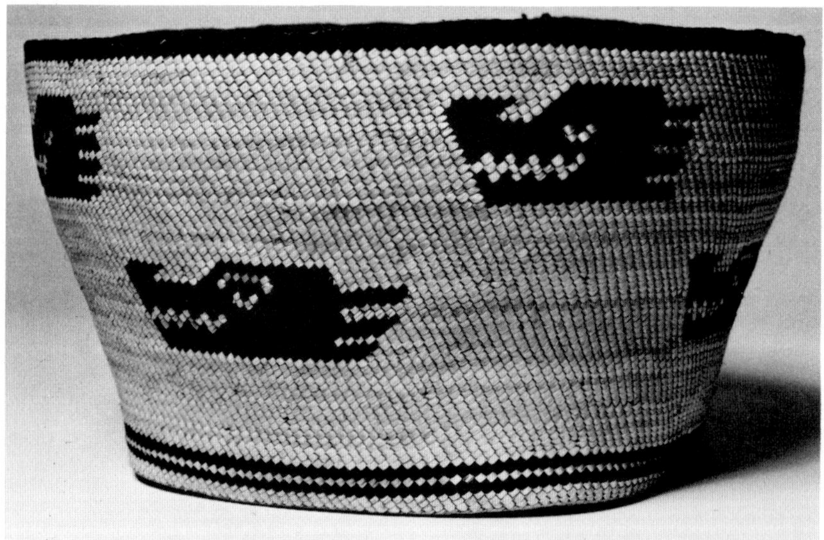

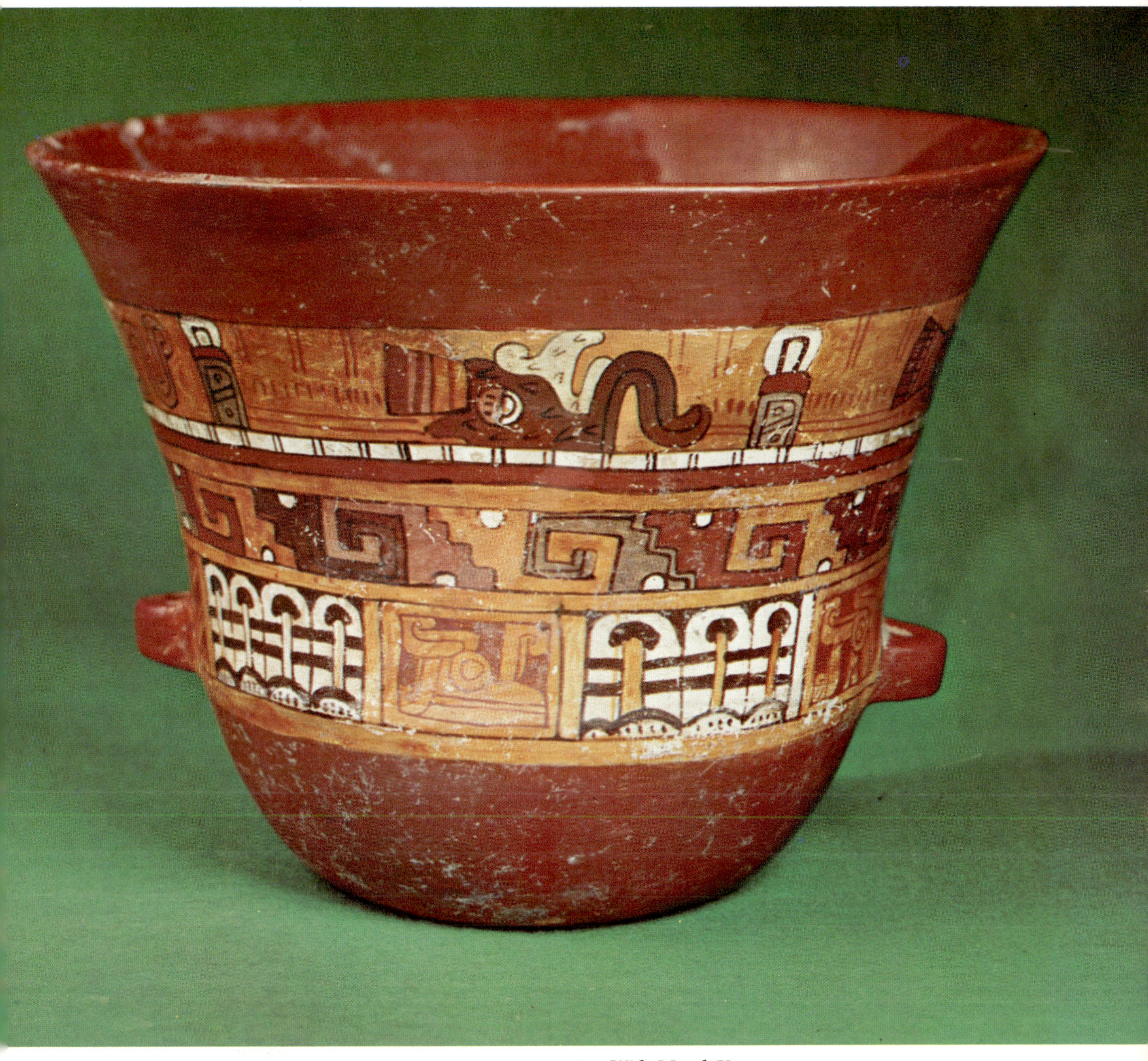

87. Wide Mouth Urn

The pottery from Cholula is famous for its brilliance in design and color. This example demonstrates those qualities very effectively. CHOLULA. Puebla, Mexico. 1350-1520. 10″ x 14″. 24/1147.

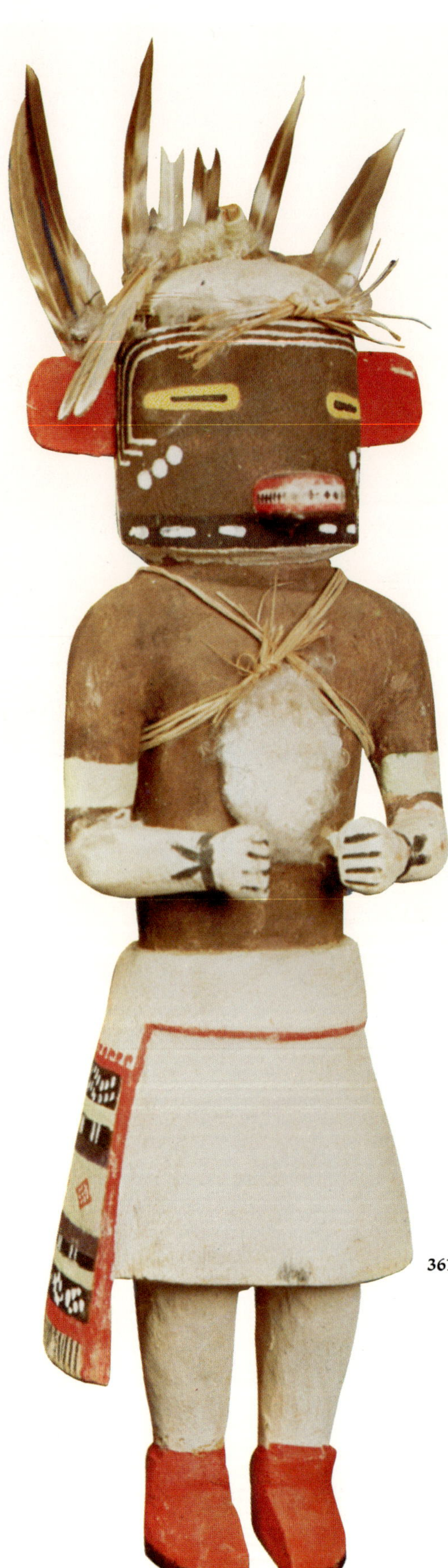

361. Kachina Figurine

Another example of the *tihü*, which are intended for educational purposes, rather than as objects to be worshipped. This is an example of the more modern form, offering ample evidence of the continuation of the art. Today these become wholly sculptural, emphasizing all of the body detail which was so conventionalized in the earlier example. This design represents Laqán, the Squirrel Kachina. Collected by John L. Nelson. Hopi. Shungopovi, Arizona. 1930-1940. H: 12″. 18/7555.

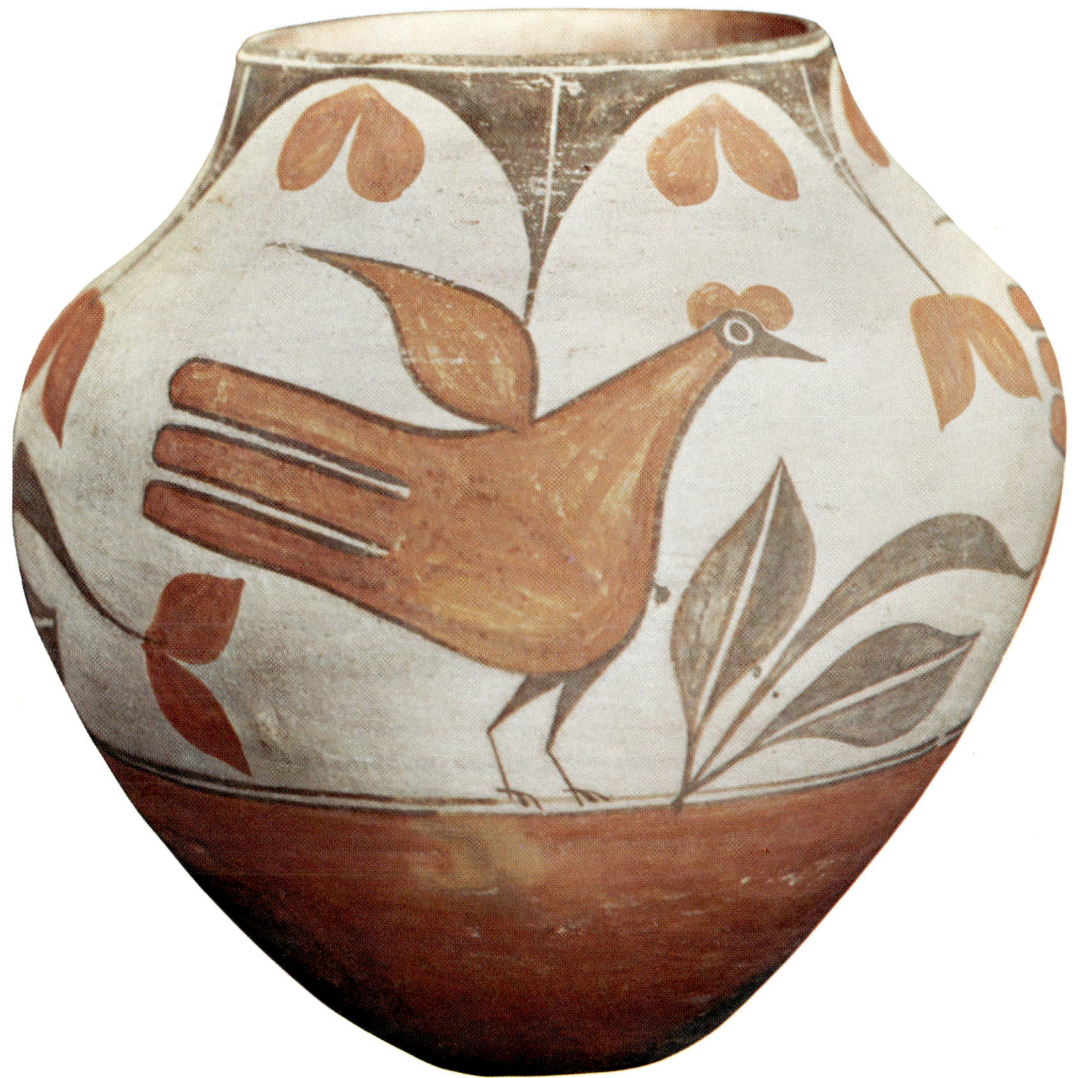

370. Painted Olla
The bird design on this vessel is characteristic of one of the smaller villages, but one which produces some of the finer wares of the Rio Grande Valley. Collected by John L. Nelson. ZIA. New Mexico. 1900-1910. 10½" x 10¾". 16/5746.

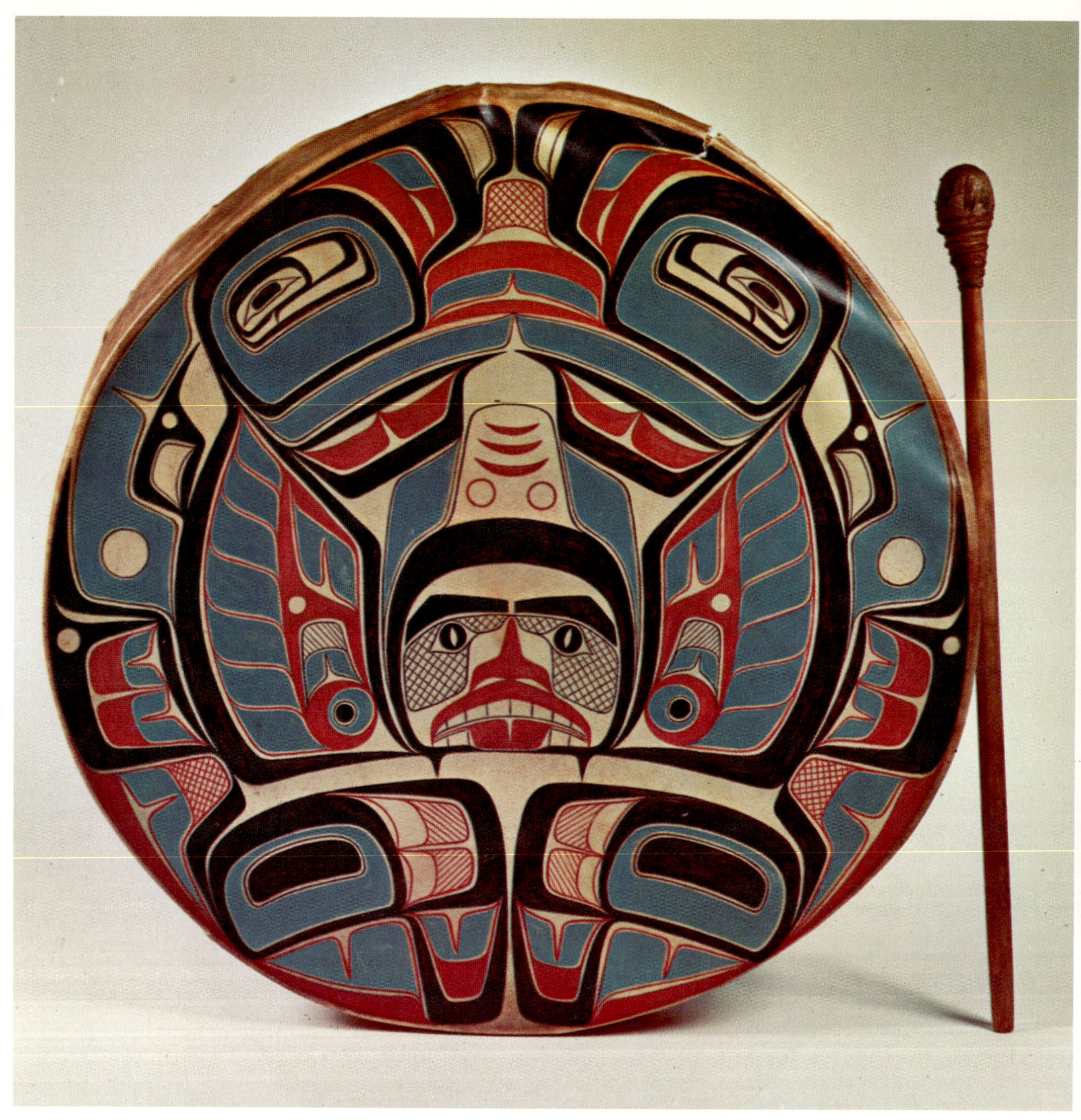

297. Painted Hide Drum

Also a modern example of Northwest Coast art, this drum was made by Duane Pasco in 1971. It has a fluid sense of design and rhythmic balance which allows it to fit very smoothly into the scope of this exhibition. TLINGIT. Alaska. D: 20″. 24/6858.

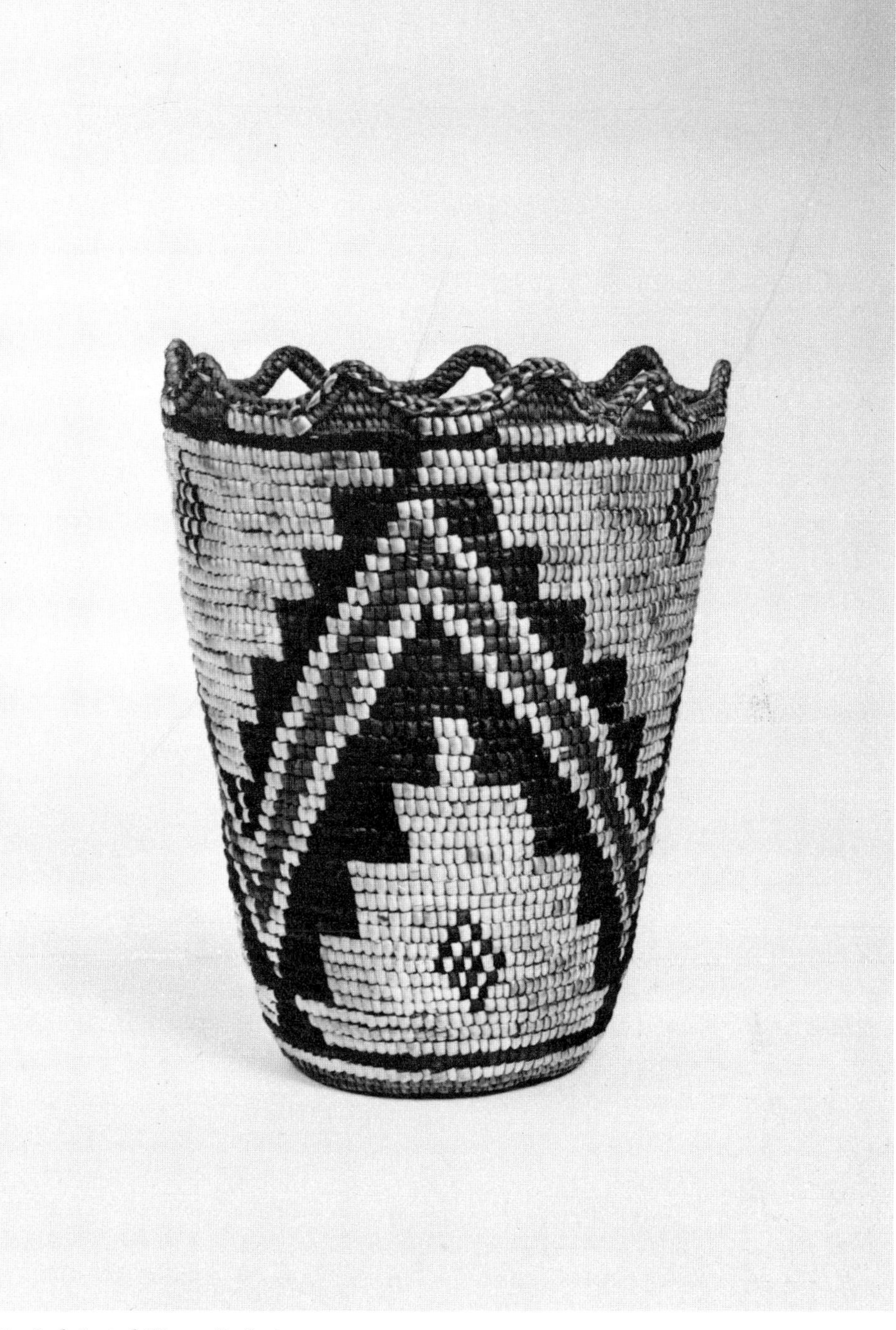

305. Imbricated Weave Basket

A style limited to this region is employed by the Pacific Northwest people in the creation of these sturdy gathering and storage baskets. The looped rim was a later concession to tourist demand. Collected by Frederick W. Skiff. KLIKITAT. Washington. 1900-1910. 9½″ x 12″. 15/6453.

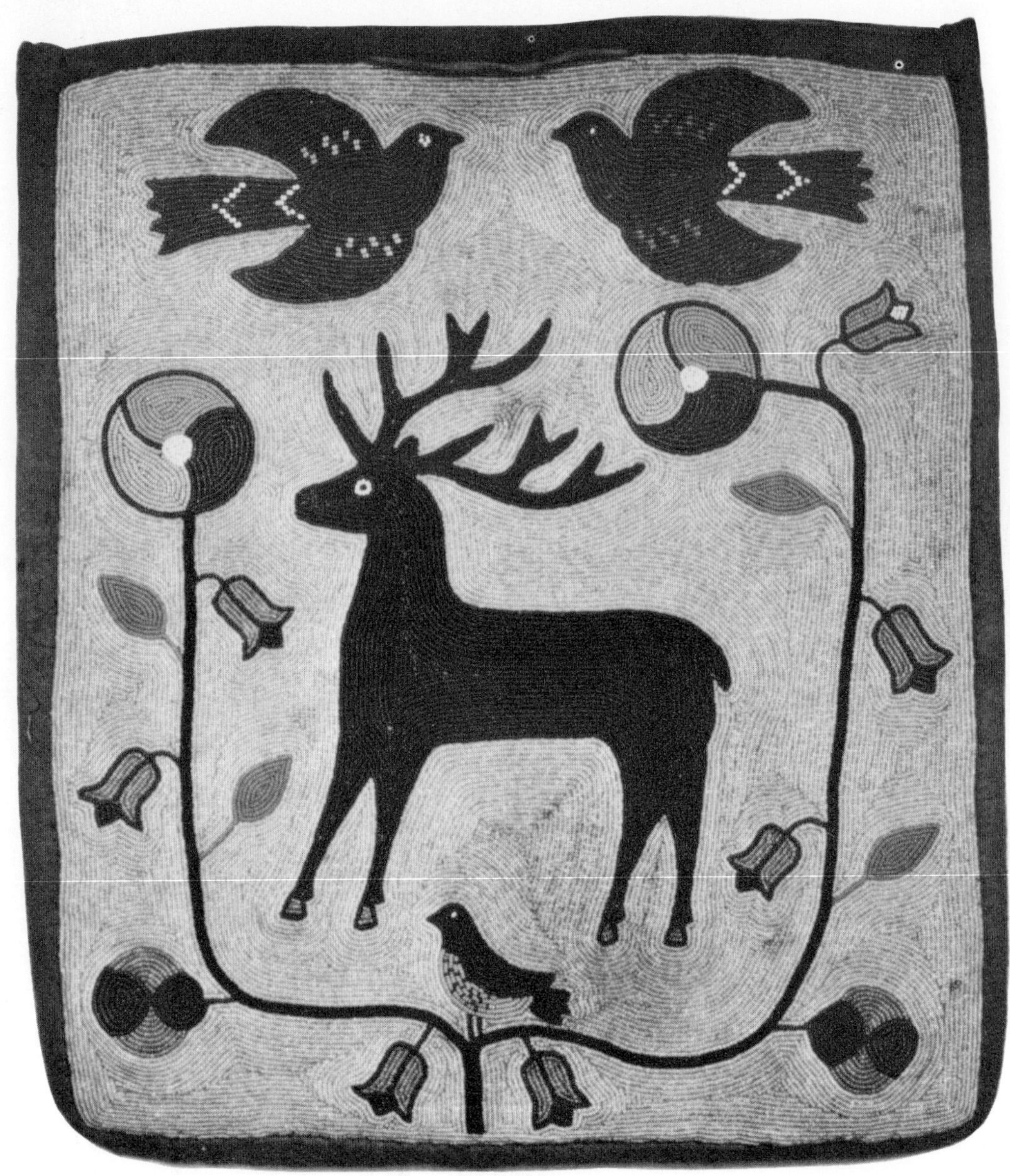

306. Beaded Wallet
This style of beadwork is done in a continuous apliqué form, with various zoömorphic forms in a wide range of colors. The strong designs make these attractive costume accessories. Collected by Frederick W. Skiff. YAKIMA. Washington. 1900-1910. 14¼″ x 16¾″. 13/8466.

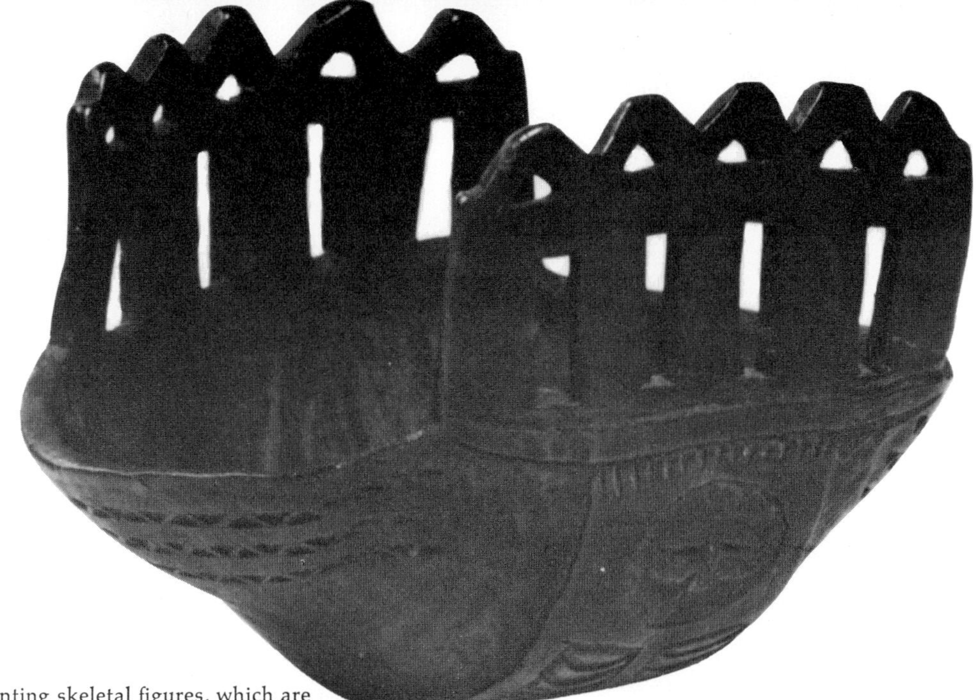

307. Carved Horn Bowl
With designs representing skeletal figures, which are typical of the area, this bowl is a classic form. It is fashioned from the horn of the mountain sheep. Collected and presented by Charles F. Nesler. WASCO. Oregon. 1875-1880. 4½" x 5½". 10/5467.

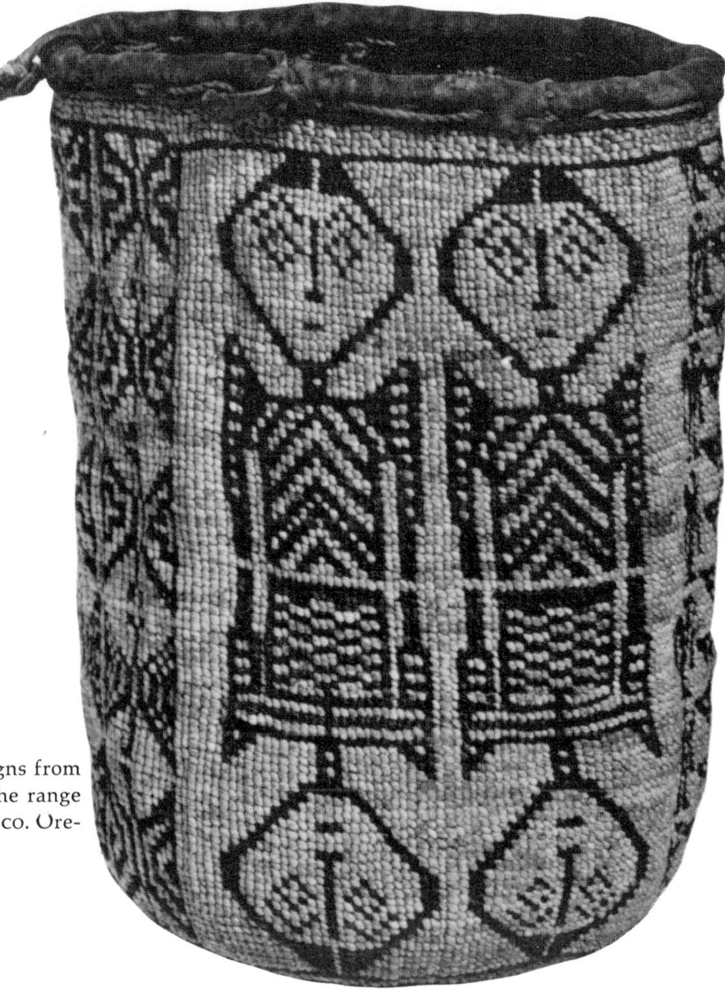

308. Soft-Weave Basket
Also bearing the characteristic skeletal designs from this tribe, the soft weave is diagnostic of the range of basketry from the Pacific Northwest. WASCO. Oregon. 1870-1880. 6" x 9¼". 15/4624.

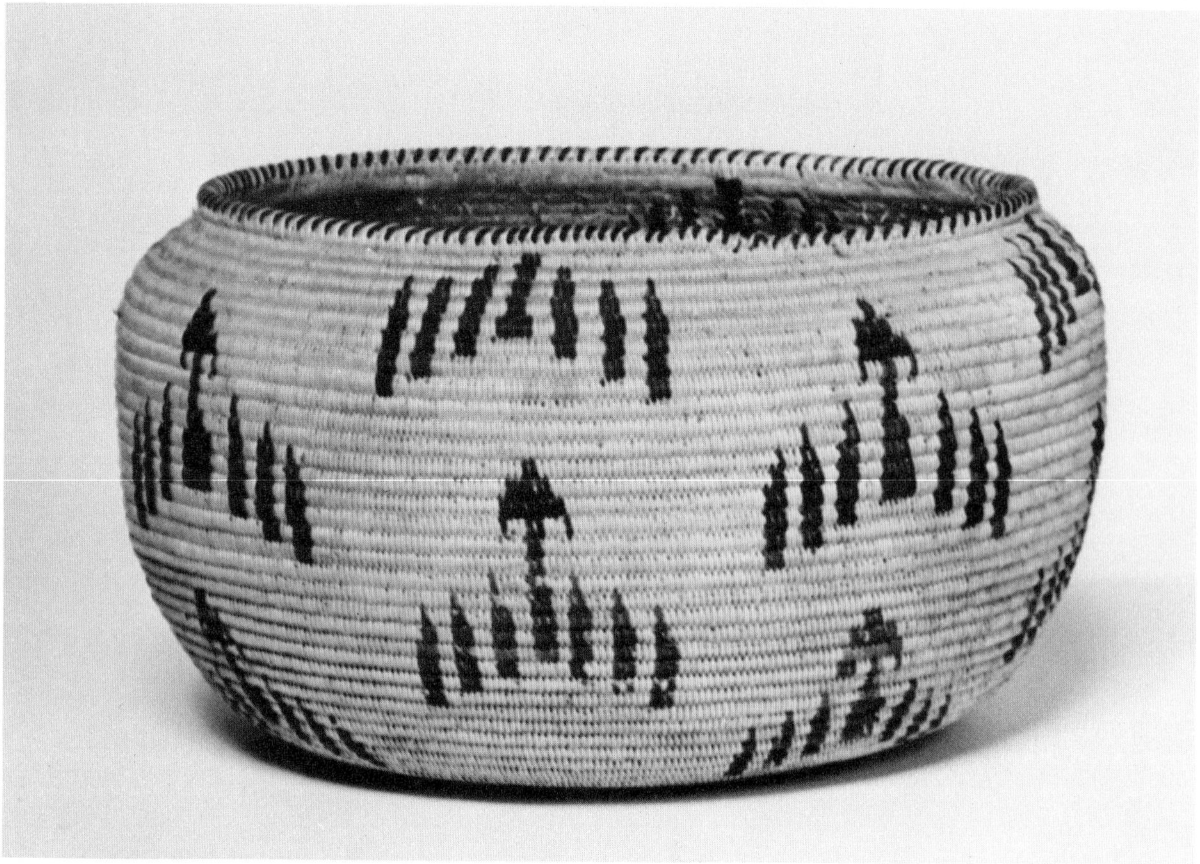

309. Bowl Basket
Some of the finest basketry in North America comes from the least likely areas. This beautifully woven basket, with repeat designs around the sides, is an example of the work of one of the most famous weaving groups. Collected by Mrs. Helen J. Stewart. Washo. Nevada. 1915-1925. 4¼″ x 7¾″. 16/3956.

310. Ring-necked Basket
Another fine example of tightly-woven basketry from the Great Basin region is this coil-weave container with a zigzag pattern in black around the sides. Collected by Mrs. Helen J. Stewart. Paiute. Moapa, Nevada. 1915-1925. 4″ x 5¾″. 16/4015.

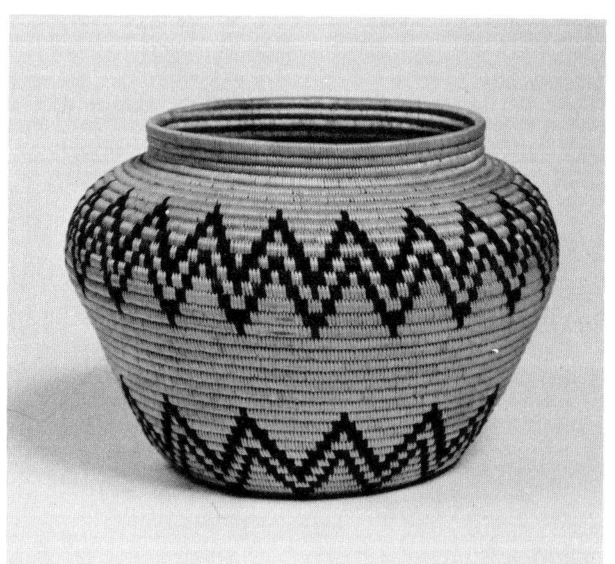

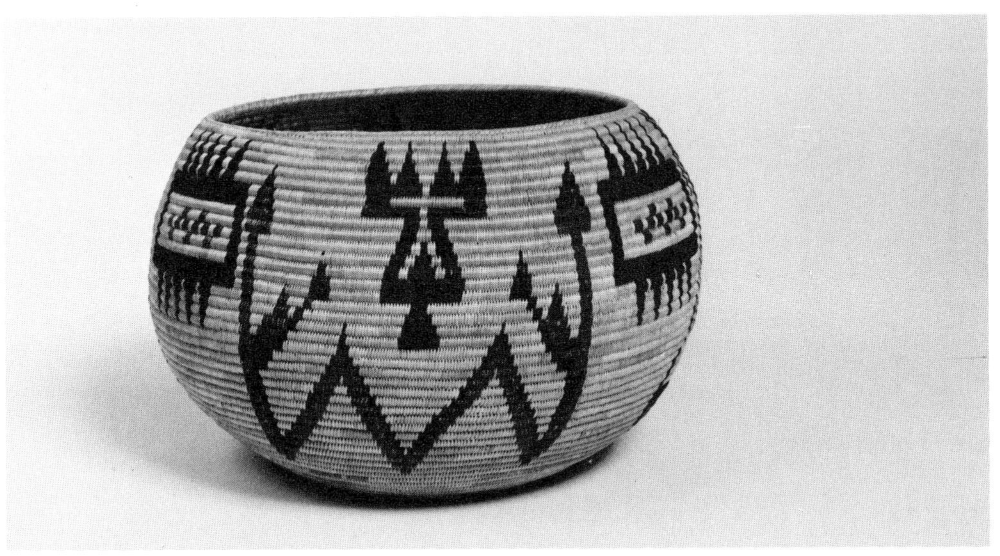

311. Polychrome Weave Basket
The multiple designs in black and red-brown maintain the high technical proficiency of the Basin weavers. Collected by M. R. Harrington. PAIUTE. Mono Lake, California. 1905-1910. 5½" x 7¾". 14/2136.

312. Beaded Basket
The strong basketry surface of this bowl container has been completely covered by trade beads, sewn on in geometric designs. These were intended primarily for tourist sale. PAIUTE. Nevada. 1945-1965. 3½" x 6". 21/3693.

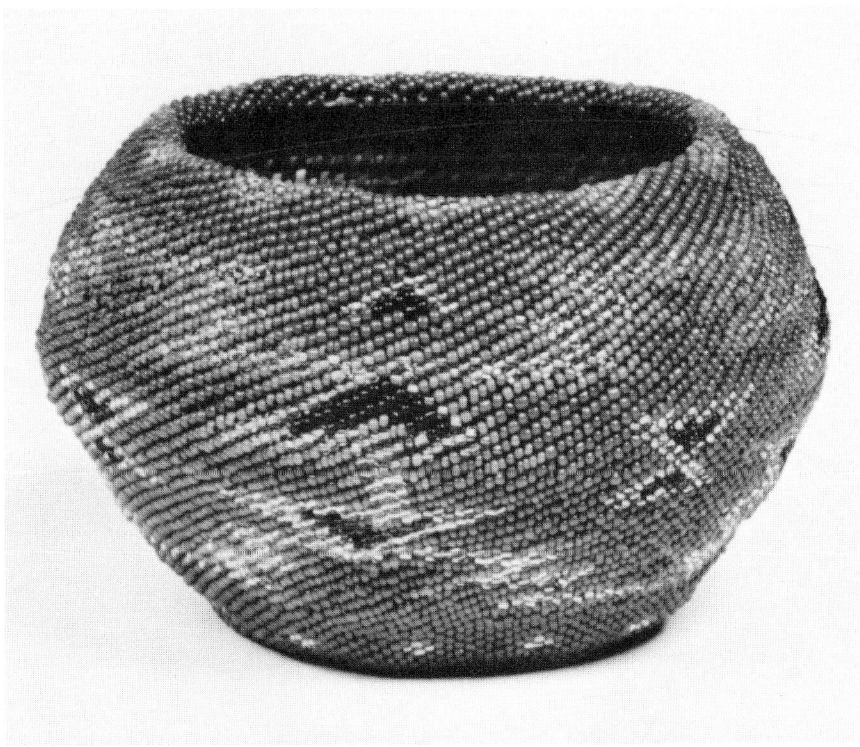

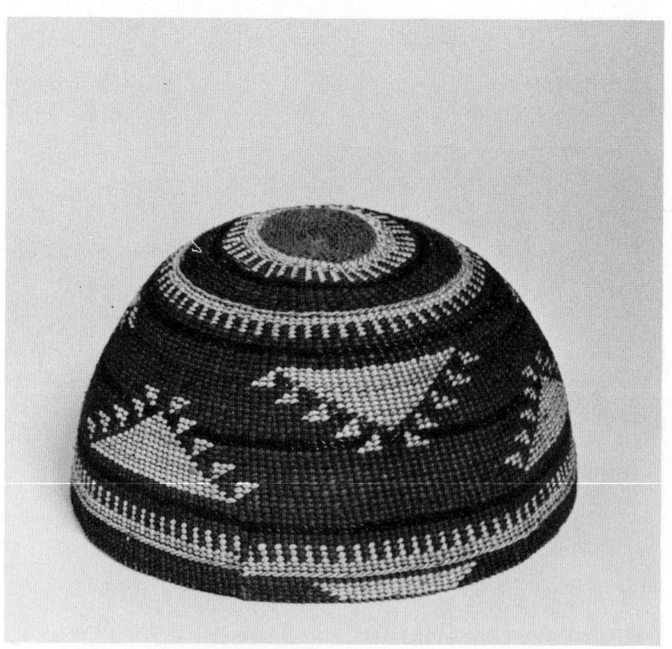

313. Woman's Basketry Hat
Carefully woven basketry hats were commonly worn by the women of Oregon and northern California, both for decoration and to protect the head from the tumpline used to carry heavy burdens. Presented by Mrs. Martha G. Hervey. KAROK. Klamath River, California. 1880-1890. 3½" x 6½". 8/5686.

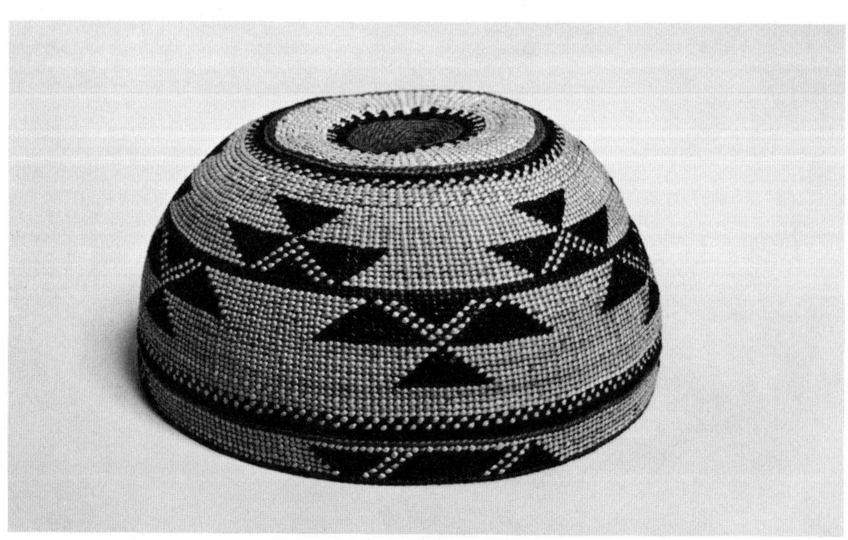

314. Woman's Basketry Hat
Another example of the woven hats worn by women, this offers a contrasting design to #313. Presented by Mrs. Russell Sage. KAROK. Klamath River, California. 1880-1890. 3" x 6½". 4/8788.

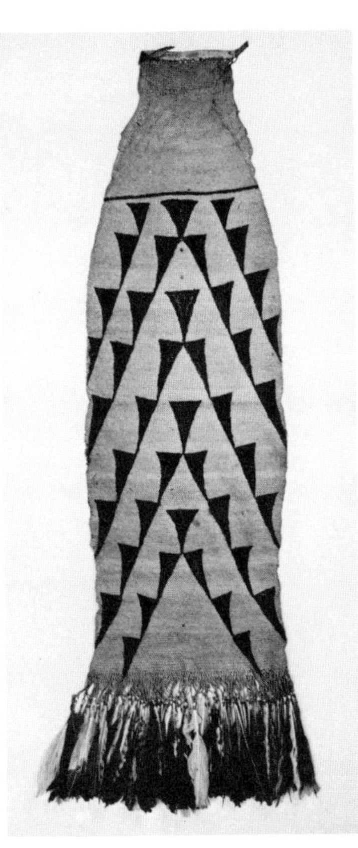

315. Woven Textile Headdress
Made of milkweed fiber in a net-weaving technique, these are worn by shamans performing in the Jumping Dance. Painted geometrical designs are applied in red, blue or black. Collected by Grace Nicholson. KAROK. California. 1890-1910. 10″ x 36″. 20/2927.

316. Carrying Basket
Made for the purpose of carrying ceremonial equipment, this particular design is limited to the northern California region. Collected by Grace Nicholson. KAROK. California. 1890-1910. 7¾″ x 24¾″. 15/1864.

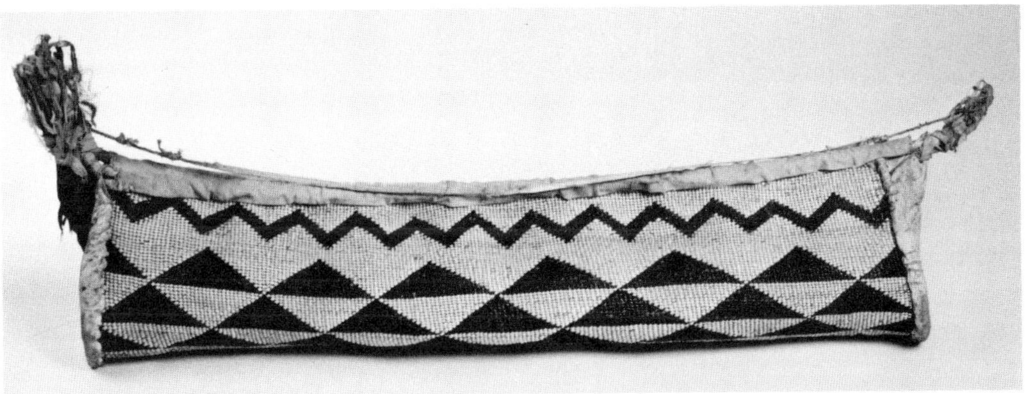

317. Small Covered Basket
Woven in a combination of maidenhair fern and bear grass dyed with lichen, this is an unusual form found only among the Karok. This example was made by Mrs. Hitchcock, a famous weaver. Presented by Mrs. Thea Heye. KAROK. California. 1900-1920. 3½″ x 3¾″. 18/8227.

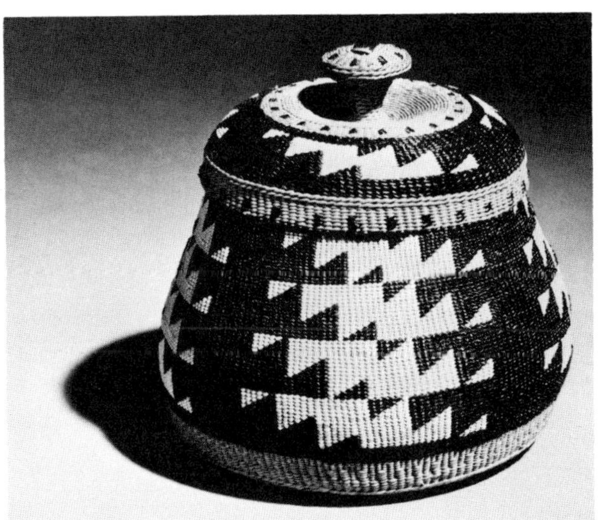

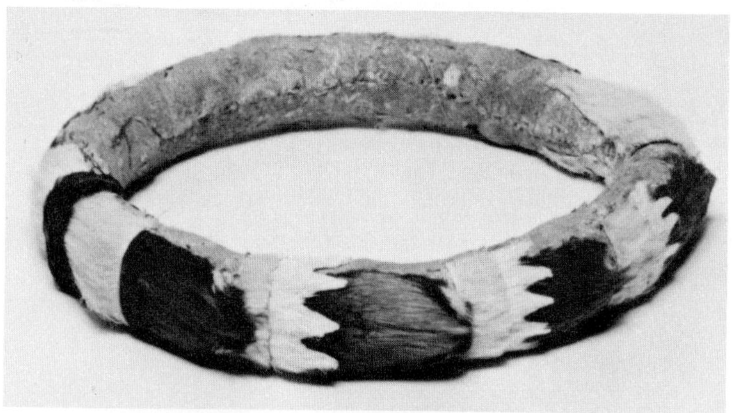

318. Feather Head Ring
Worn by performers in the Jumping Dance and the White Deer Dance, these buckskin-wound circlets are decorated with woodpecker feathers. The base is bundles of grass. Collected by Grace Nicholson. YUROK. California. 1900-1910. 1½″ x 8½″. 15/7029.

319. Painted Bow
Decorated in geometric designs in black, orange, red and other colors, these are not only functional weapons, but attractive objects as well. Many of the older bows were sinew-backed for greater strength. Collected by Mrs. Augusta Rankin. MODOC. California. 1880-1900. 2½″ x 35¼″. 11/8717.

320. Feather Headband
These beautiful costume decorations are ornamented with fifty woodpecker scalps applied to a buckskin base in rows. Other feathers are often included for contrasting effect. These are worn on the forehead during the White Deerskin Dance. Collected by A. Brizard. HUPA. California. 1880-1890. 9″ x 36″. 1210.

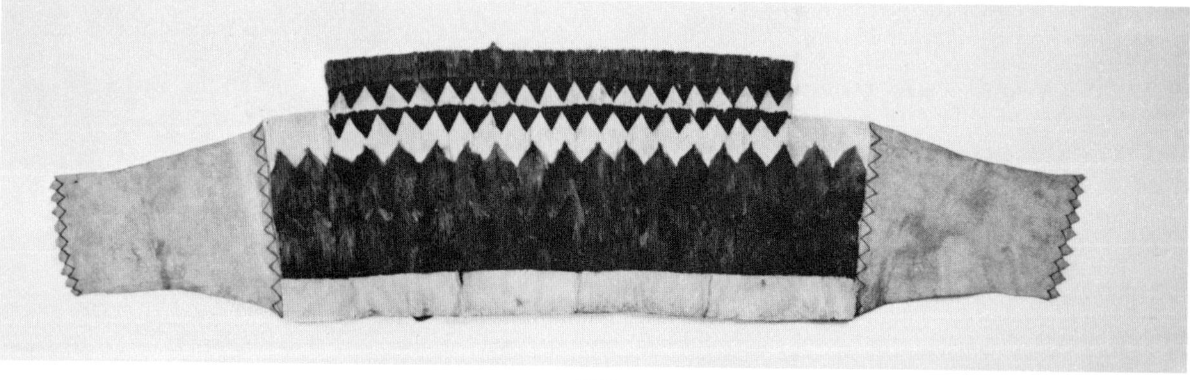

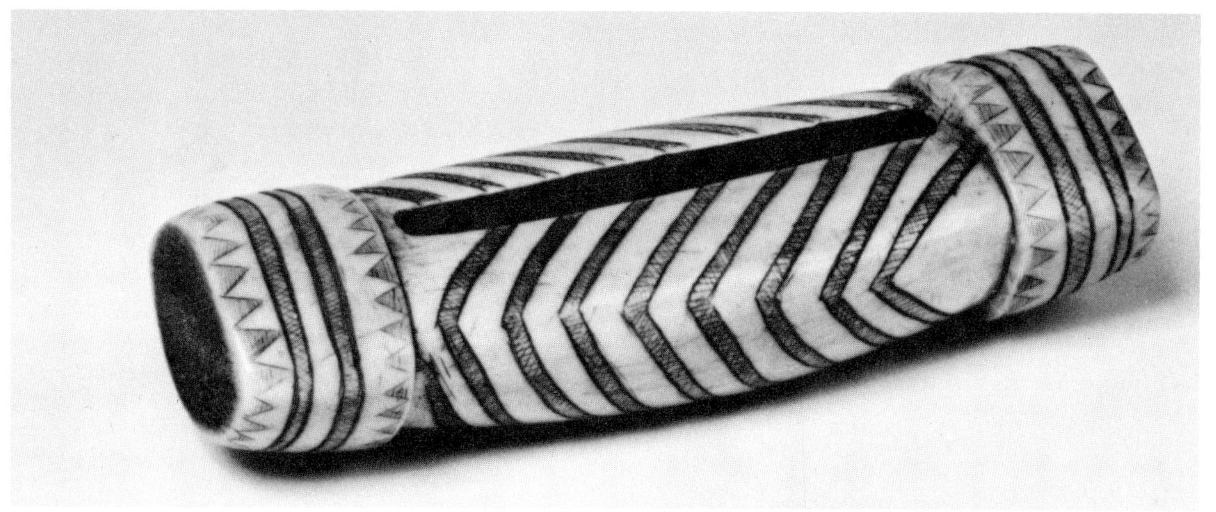

321. Elk Antler Purse
These small purses, intended for the storing of the dentalium shell currency used in the California area, are unique to a half-dozen tribes. Incised in various geometric designs into which black or red pigment has been rubbed, they acquire a soft patina with use. Presented by Mrs. Thea Heye. HUPA. California. 1880-1900. 1¼″ x 2″ x 5¼″. 10/8163.

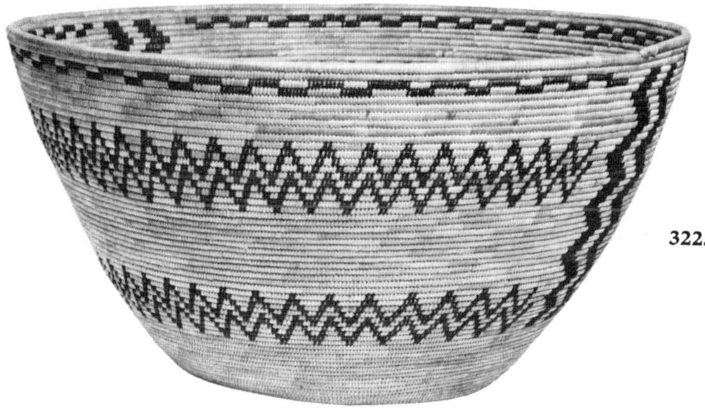

322. Storage Basket
The basic foods of the California people are stored in wide-mouthed containers of this type. Although the decorations are simple, they form a pleasing effect when woven in contrasting colors to the buff base. Collected by Mrs. Thea Heye. YOKUTS. Tulare Lake, California. 1890-1900. 8½″ x 16½″. 11/4863.

323. Bowl Basket
Woven in the "rattlesnake design" characteristic of the basketry from this tribe, the red-brown and black decorations combine to produce a pleasing pattern. YOKUTS. Tulare Lake, California. 1880-1900. 7¼″ x 12¼″. 6/990.

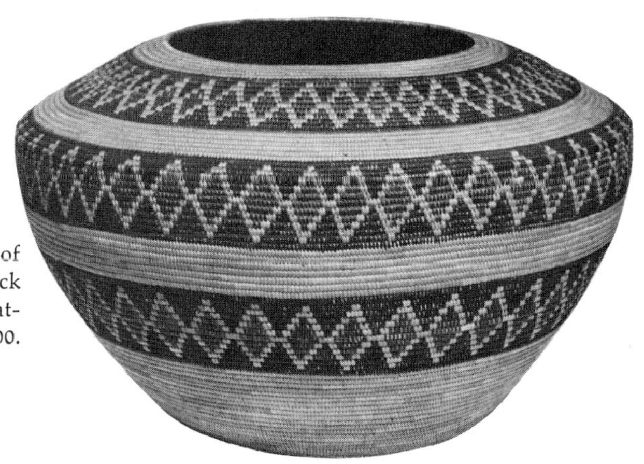

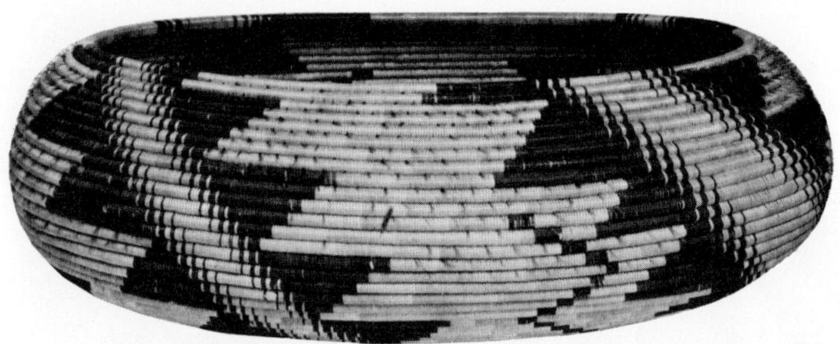

324. Canoe Basket

The basketry of this tribe is universally conceded as representing the finest work in the New World. This oval basket combines delicate design with tiny feathers interwoven into the basic coils. Collected by Judge Nathan Bijur; presented by Mr. and Mrs. Harry Bijur. POMO. California. 1880-1900. 5¼″ x 15½″. 23/5701.

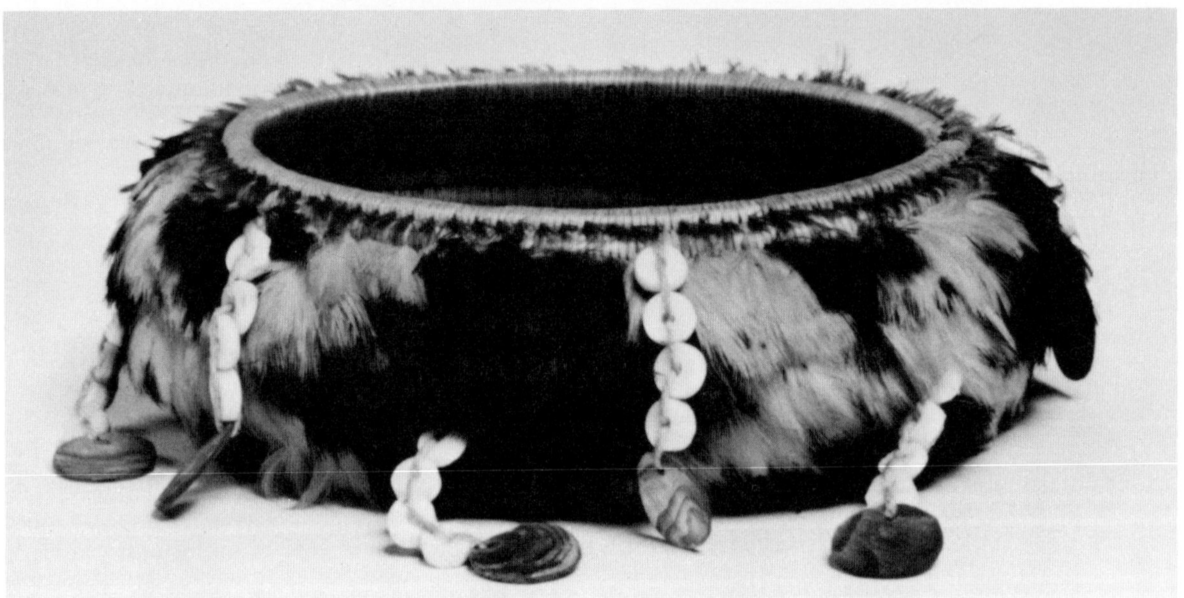

325. Feather Decorated Basket

The ability to work delicate bird feathers into the coils of the weaving was an art at which these people excelled. This is a good example of the "gift baskets" which were given away, or often burned in a funeral pyre. The ornaments are shell beads attached in strings to the rim. Collected by Frank M. Covert. POMO. California. 1875-1890. 1¼″ x 5¾″. 1185.

326. Miniature Feather Basket

(See page 16)

327. Miniature Baskets

As a simple *tour de force* of the basket-weaver's skill, these incredibly small baskets are complete in every respect—weaving, black-on-buff design, and overall form. They were made primarily for tourist sale, or occasionally as an example of pride in craft work. Presented by Mrs. Thyra Maxwell. POMO. California. 1900-1920. (A) ⅛″; (B) ⅛″ x ¼″; (C) ⅜″ x ½″. 24/8371.

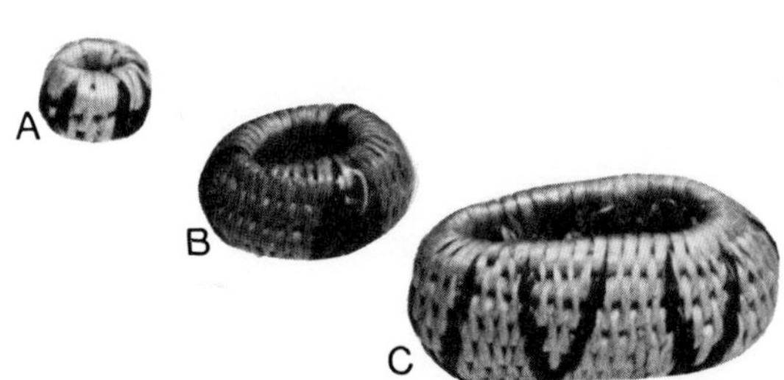

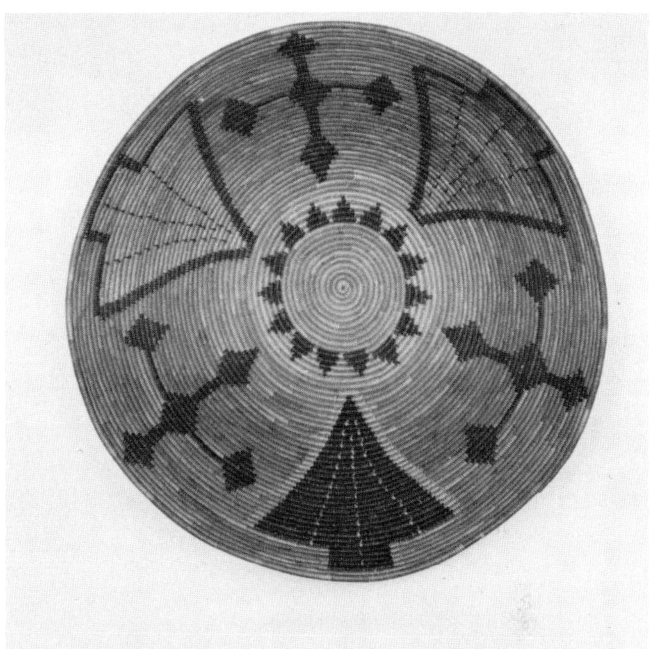

328. Large Bowl Basket
Fine basketry is not confined to the northern California area. The southern peoples provided a high level of skill in their containers, as this example demonstrates. The work from this tribe is commonly termed "Mission" basketry, although the term applies equally to all peoples living in and around the early missions of the Pacific Coast. DIEGUEÑO. California. 1875-1900. D: 15½". 24/3083.

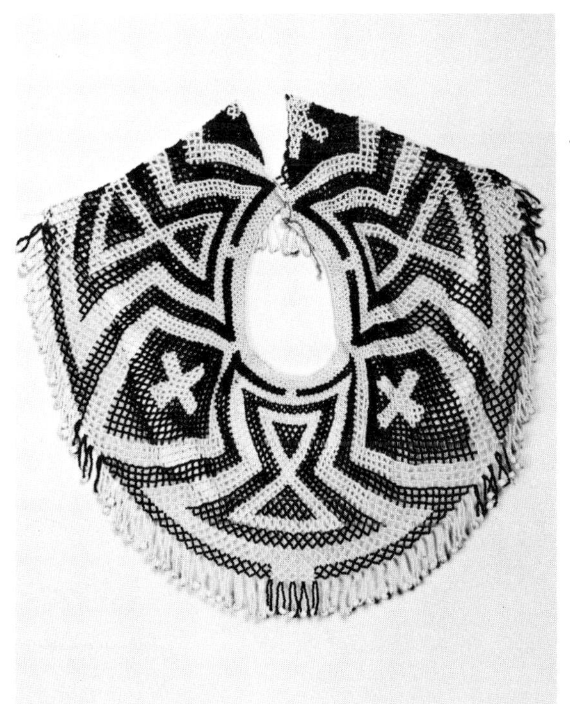

329. Beadwork Collar
Woven in a netting technique, these open-work collars in blue and white were worn by women shortly after the introduction of Venetian beads. Note the similarity in design and technique to **473** . Collected by William M. Fitzhugh. MOHAVE. Arizona. 1890-1900. 15" x 16". 19/3804.

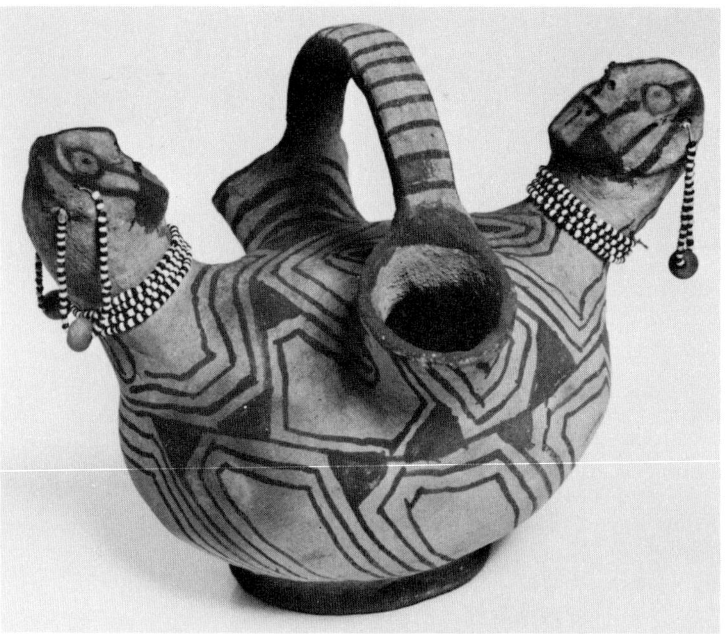

330. Clay Effigy Bowl
Made in the buffware clay, and decorated in geometric patterns typical of the region, this is adorned with two anthropomorphic heads and blue-and-white beadwork. These were produced for the tourist trade. Collected by William M. Fitzhugh. MOHAVE. Yuma, Arizona. 1880-1900. 6¼″ x 8″. 19/4434.

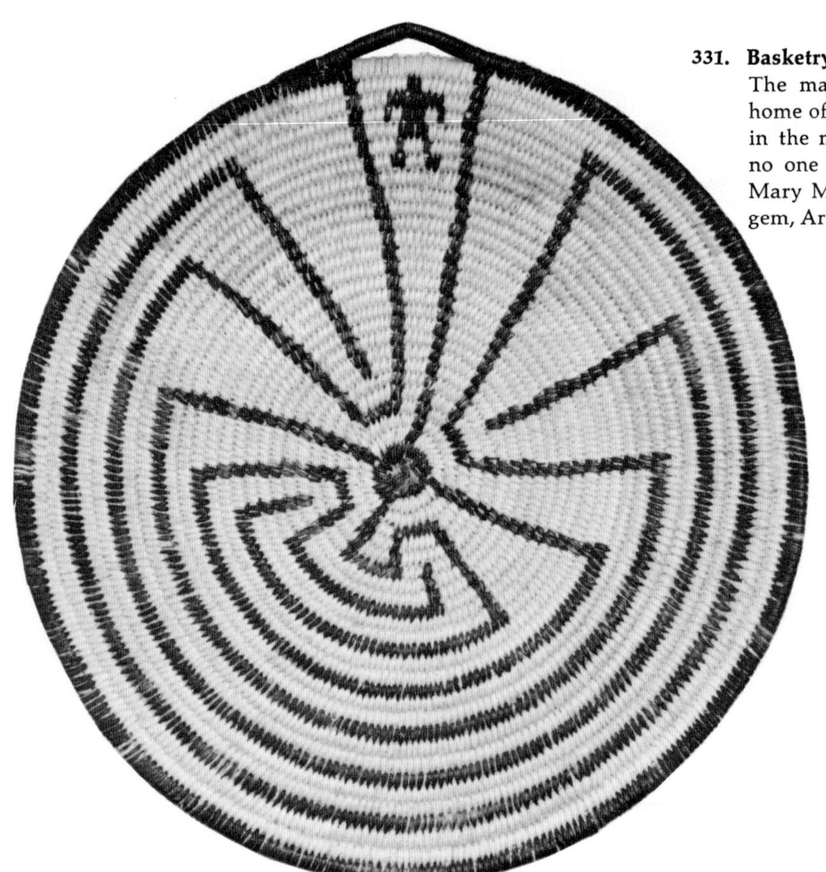

331. Basketry Placque
The maze design, called Siuhü Ki, represents the home of a legendary Pima supernatural who lives far in the mountains, where trails become so confused no one can follow him. This was made in 1964 by Mary Miguel. Presented by Tom Bahti. PIMA. Anagem, Arizona. D: 10″. 23/6218.

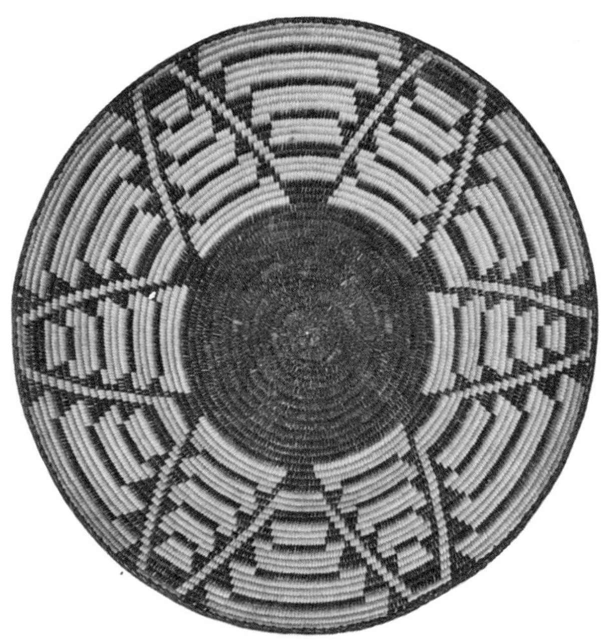

332. Large Bowl Basket
In the flower pattern seen frequently in the work of this tribe. Collected by John Lawrence. PIMA. Arizona. 1920-1921. 3¾″ x 16″. 23/765.

333. Basketry Tray
Another typical pattern seen in Pima basketry is this design which has many variants. Collected by Frederick W. Skiff. PIMA. Arizona. 1880-1900. 4″ x 18″. 15/6484.

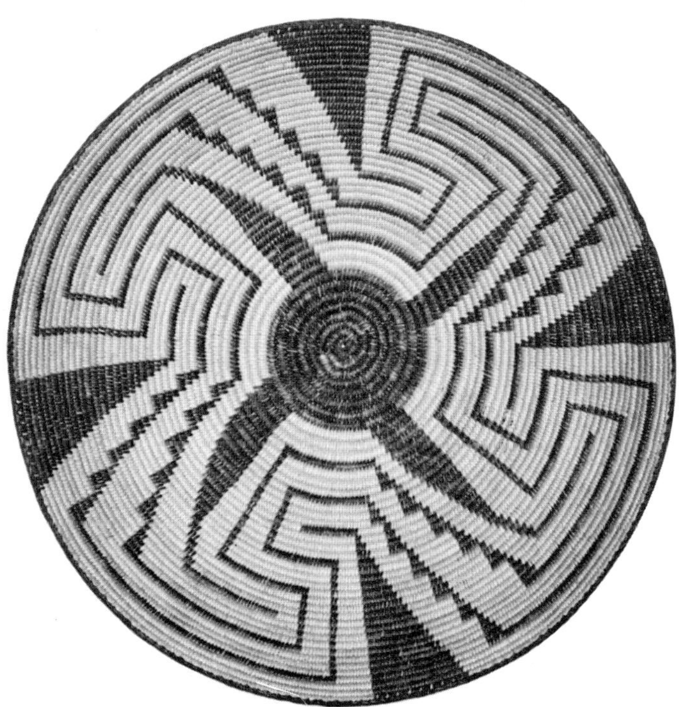

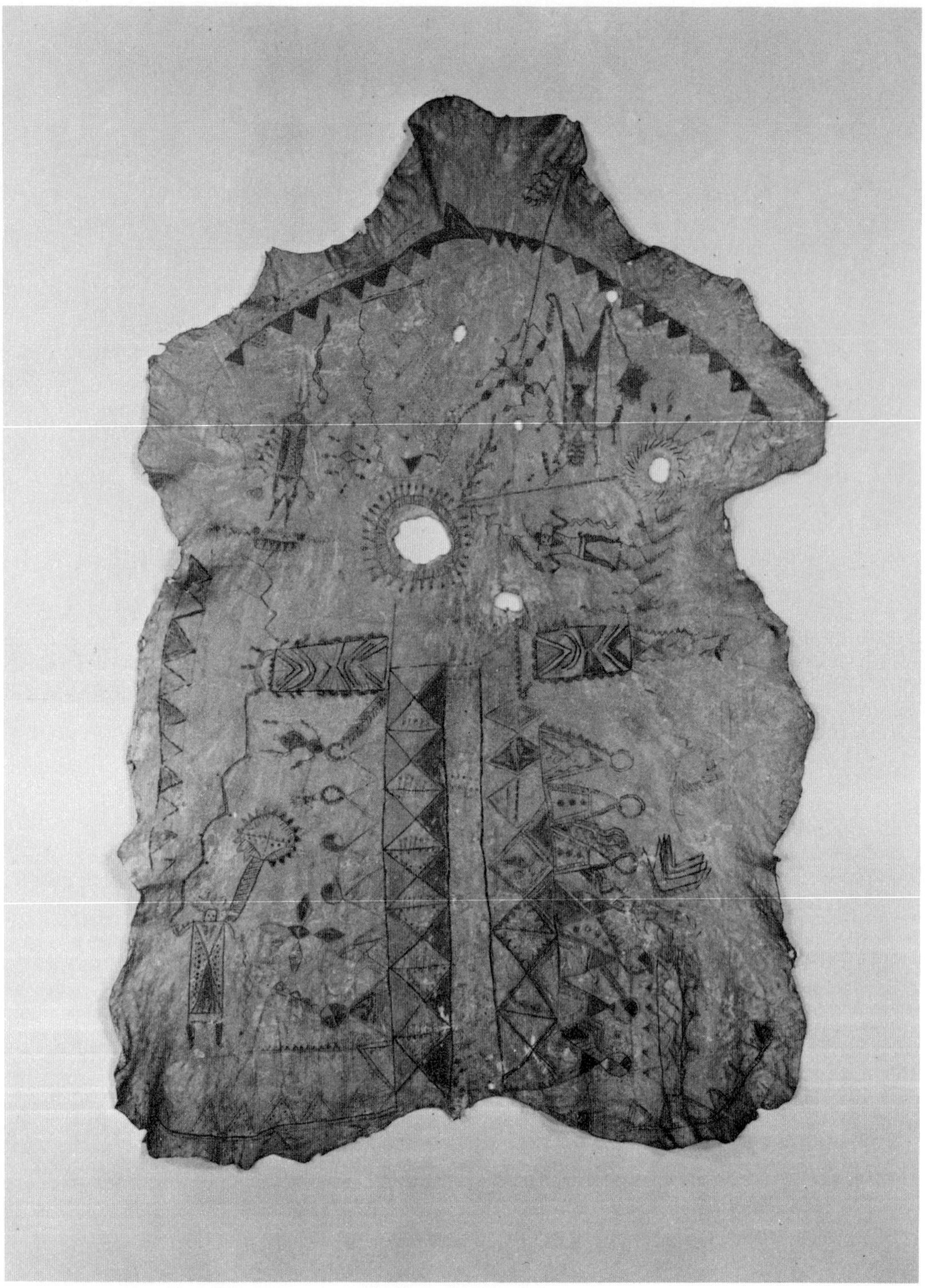

334. Painted Medicine Hide

Singers or religious shaman commonly used deer hides with painted decorations symbolic of religious beings. This "poncho" is such a garment. It was collected during the Army pursuit of Geronimo in 1880. CHIRICAHUA APACHE. Arizona. 1875-1880. 32" x 50". 20/3519.

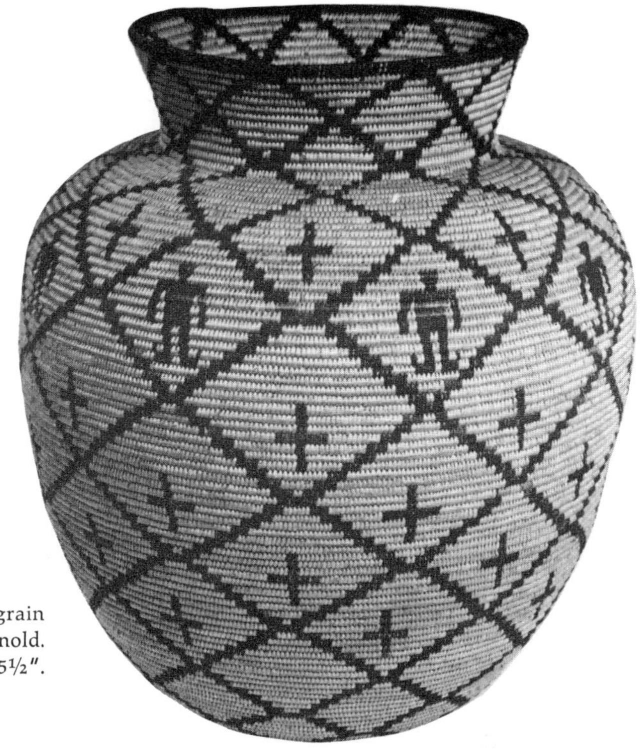

335. Storage Basket
This style is commonly used for the storage of grain and other foodstuffs. Presented by Mrs. Hicks Arnold. WESTERN APACHE. Arizona. 1890-1900. 12¾" x 15½". 13/1864.

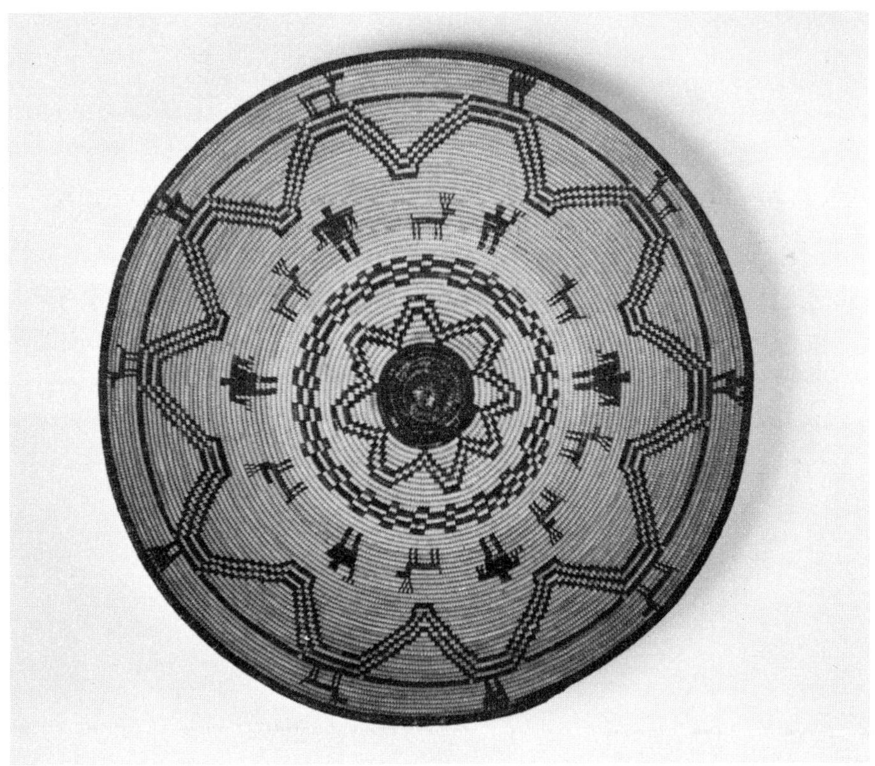

336. Bowl Basket
A large black-and-cream bowl basket with animal and human designs distinctive of the work of this tribe. The designs represent the hunters and quarry. Presented by John S. Williams. WHITE MOUNTAIN APACHE. Arizona. 1880-1900. D: 16½". 23/7869.

337. Basketry Tray

A complex weave, with the star, zoömorphic and geometric designs so popular with these weavers, this features the interesting "offbeat" example of two tiny human figures around the rim. WHITE MOUNTAIN APACHE. Arizona. 1880-1900. 4" x 17¾". 5/9388.

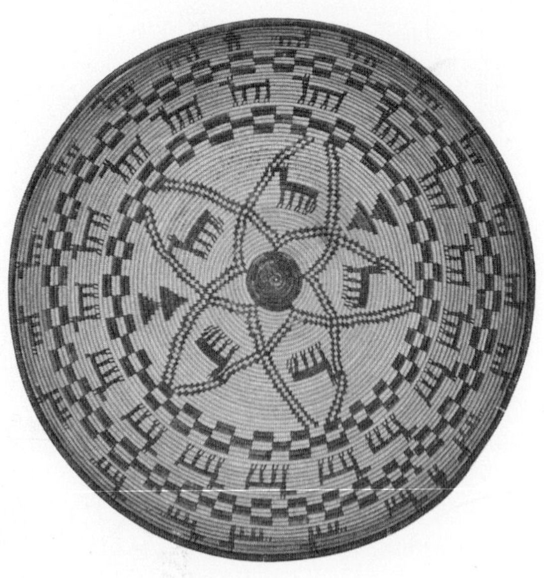

338. Polychrome Basket

Another variety of Apache basketry is that exemplified by this star design, executed in black and light tan on the natural cream base. Collected by Charles F. Nesler. MESCALERO APACHE. New Mexico. 1880-1890. D: 18¼". 10/5351.

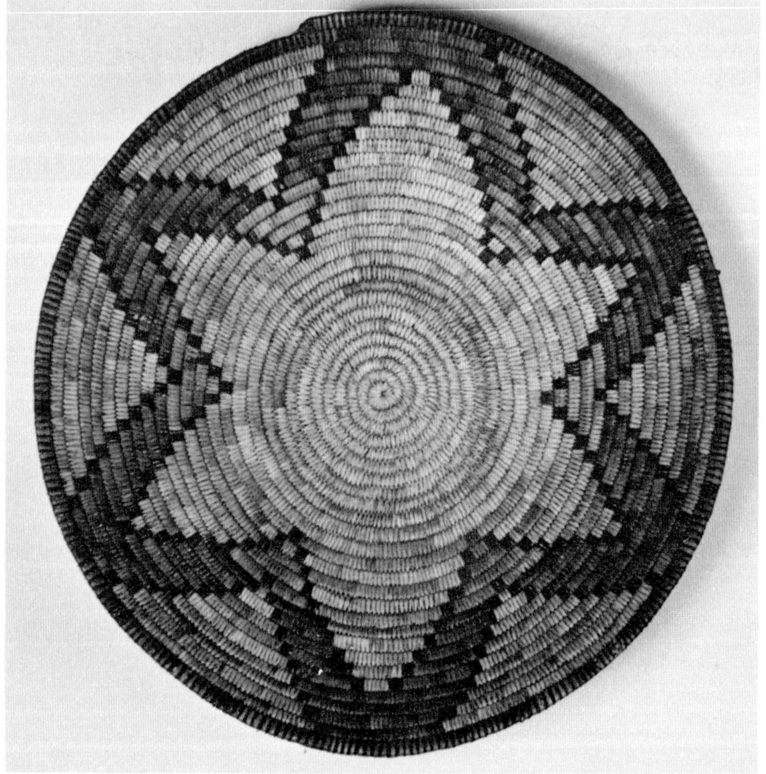

339. Feathered War Cap

(See color insert facing page 160)

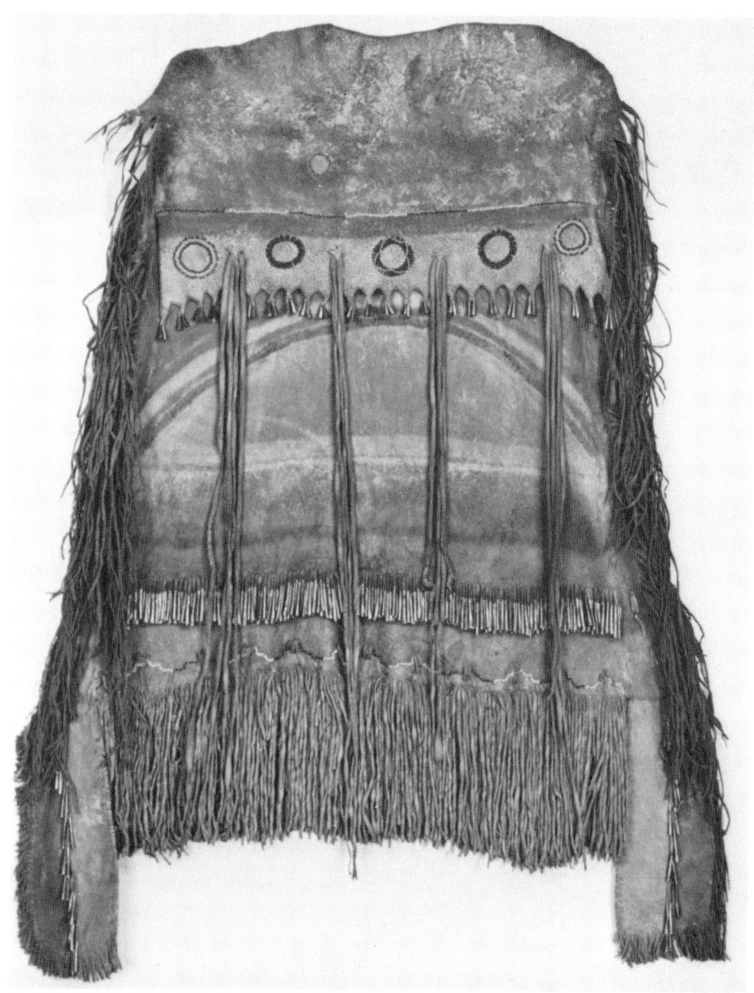

340. Buckskin Skirt
Made of buckskin, painted and beaded, this is also equipped with a long fringe to give additional grace, and tin cones to provide pleasing sounds. These were worn by the *Gahn*, or Mountain Spirits who appeared during the girl's puberty ceremony. Collected by Irving S. Cobb. WHITE MOUNTAIN APACHE. Arizona. 1880-1900. 26″ x 35″. 20/8054.

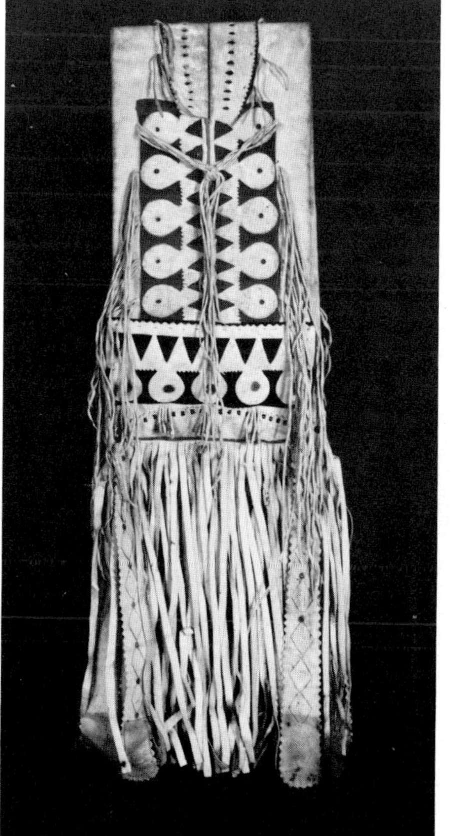

341. Cutwork Saddle Pouch
The technique of cutting away portions of rawhide and sewing it to a red trade-cloth base provides a colorful design to this "envelope pouch" used by the women. Collected by M. R. Harrington. CHIRICAHUA APACHE. Fort Lawton, Oklahoma. 1880-1890. 10″ x 75″. 2/1201.

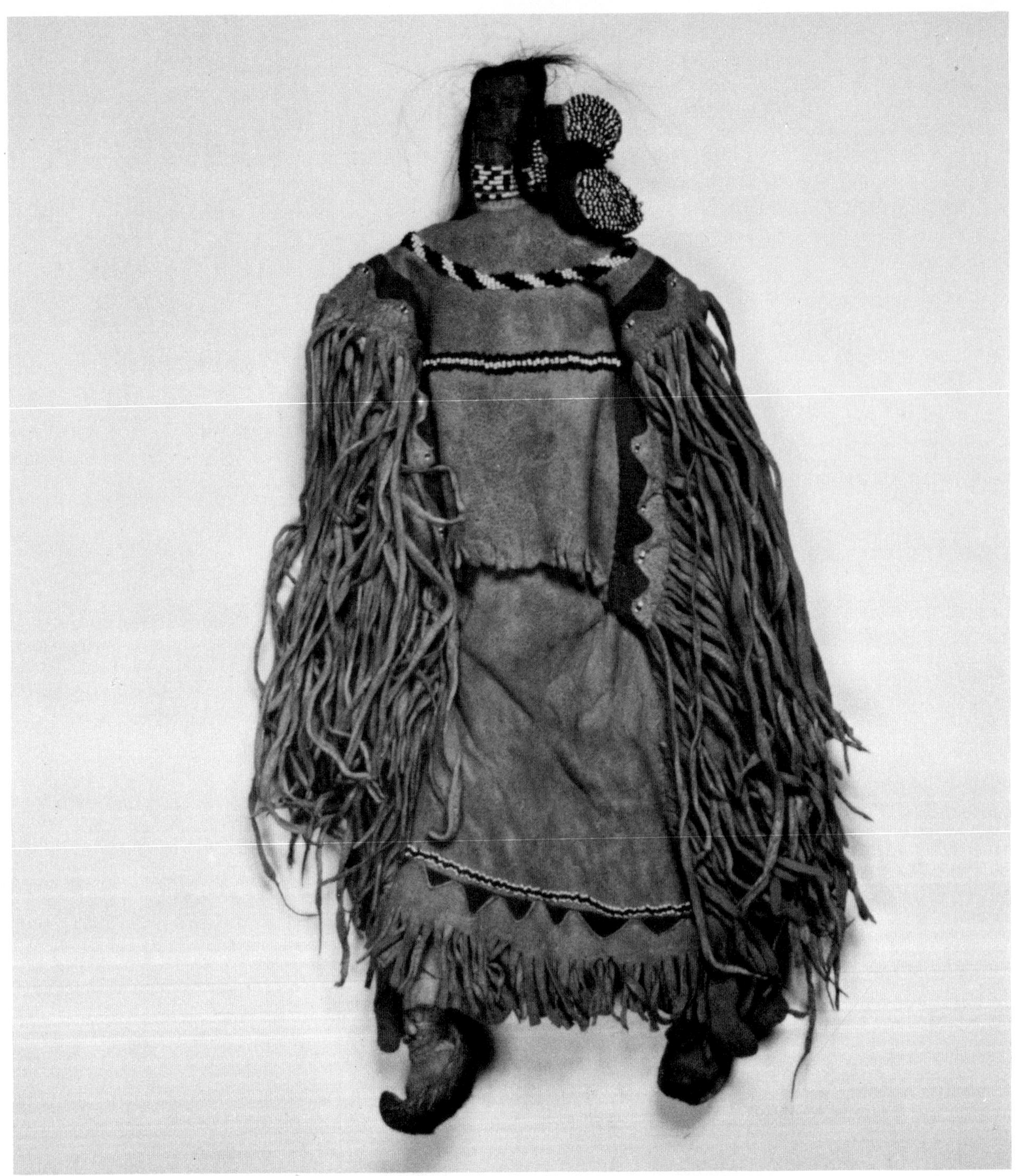

342. Costumed Doll
The attire of the adult is often well rendered by many of these Indian-made figurines. This doll, although made for the tourist trade, is a faithful replica of the costume and hair-dress of an Apache woman. Collected by Emil W. Lenders. CHIRICAHUA APACHE. Arizona. 1890-1900. 7" x 20". 2/3234.

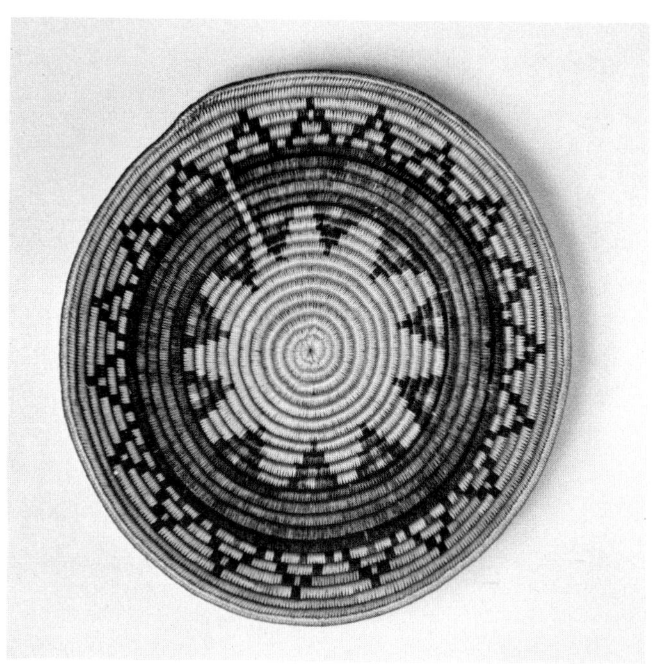

343. Ceremonial Basket
The so-called "wedding basket" of the Navajo is in reality often made by the neighboring Paiute, who faithfully execute the traditional designs, and then trade them for food or craftwork. Presented by Mrs. Thea Heye. NAVAJO. Arizona. 1900-1920. D: 14½". 11/5314.

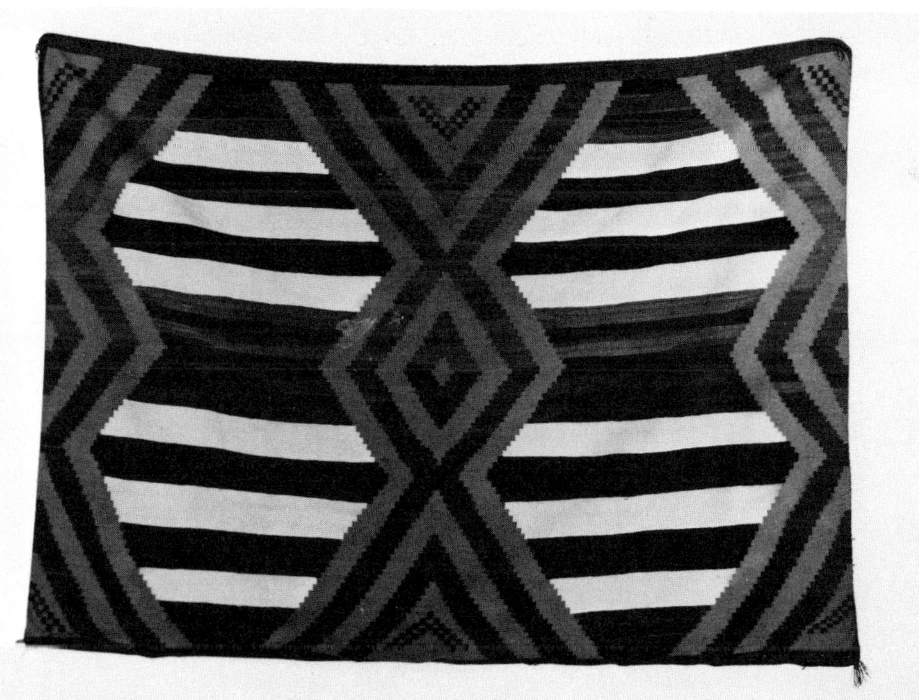

344. Woven Wool Blanket
Although familiarly known as a "Chief's Blanket," this design was not restricted to such individuals. Any person wealthy enough to purchase one could wear it. Collected by Dr. Joseph J. Asch; presented by Mrs. Asch. NAVAJO. Arizona. 1880-1900. 53¾" x 74½". 19/7318.

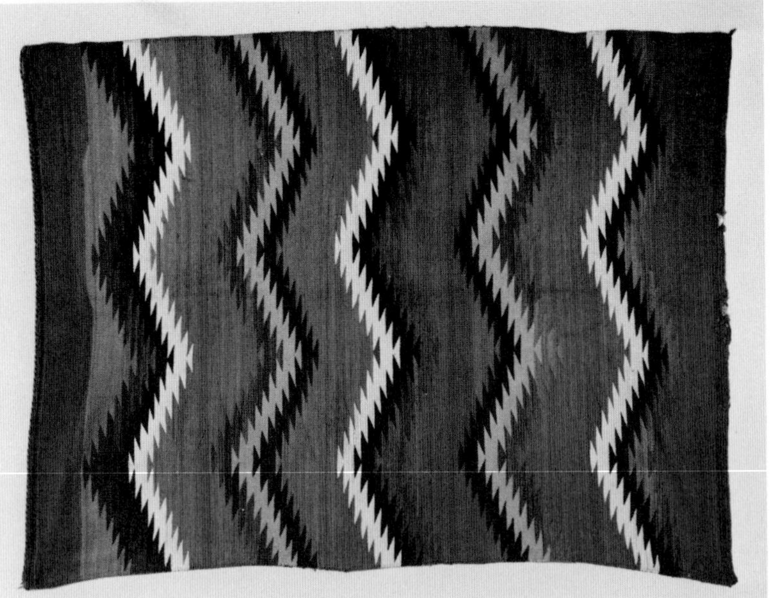

345. Zigzag Blanket
These brilliant textiles enjoyed a wide popularity throughout the Southwest, and were the forerunners of what has become a basic Navajo economic staple. Collected by George G. Heye. Navajo. New Mexico. 1890-1900. 56" x 76". 18/8590. *(See detail on back cover.)*

346. Bordered Blanket
A fine example of a later period, this wool textile was created for the then-burgeoning tourist trade, and shows the skill of the weaver in the first quarter of the 20th Century. Presented by Henry Siefke. Navajo. Arizona. 1915-1920. 45" x 65". 24/7136.

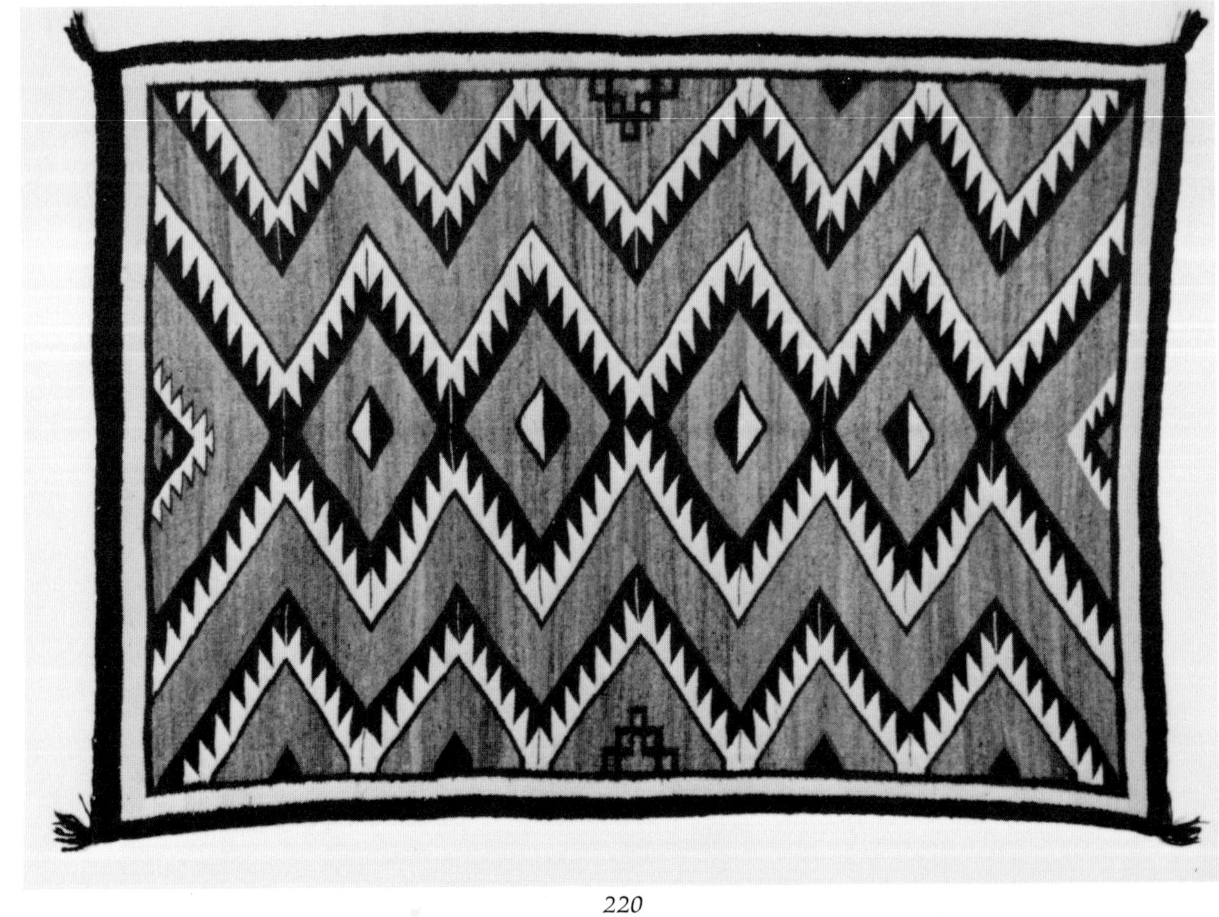

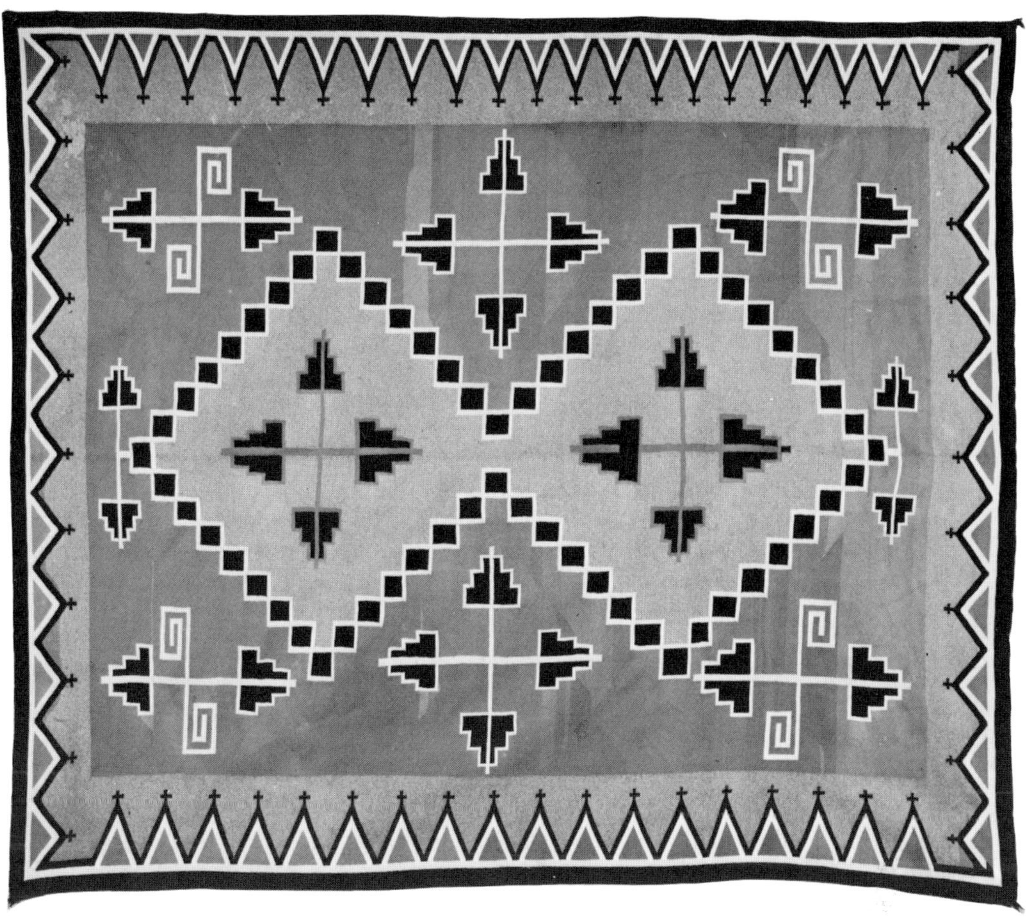

347. Oversize Woolen Textile

The tremendous size of this rug is equalled only by the intricate design carefully woven from commercial yarns. These usually served as wall hangings more than as floor coverings. Collected by J. Charles Andrews. Presented by Mrs. Andrews. NAVAJO. Arizona. 1895-1900. 96″ x 115″. 23/2058.

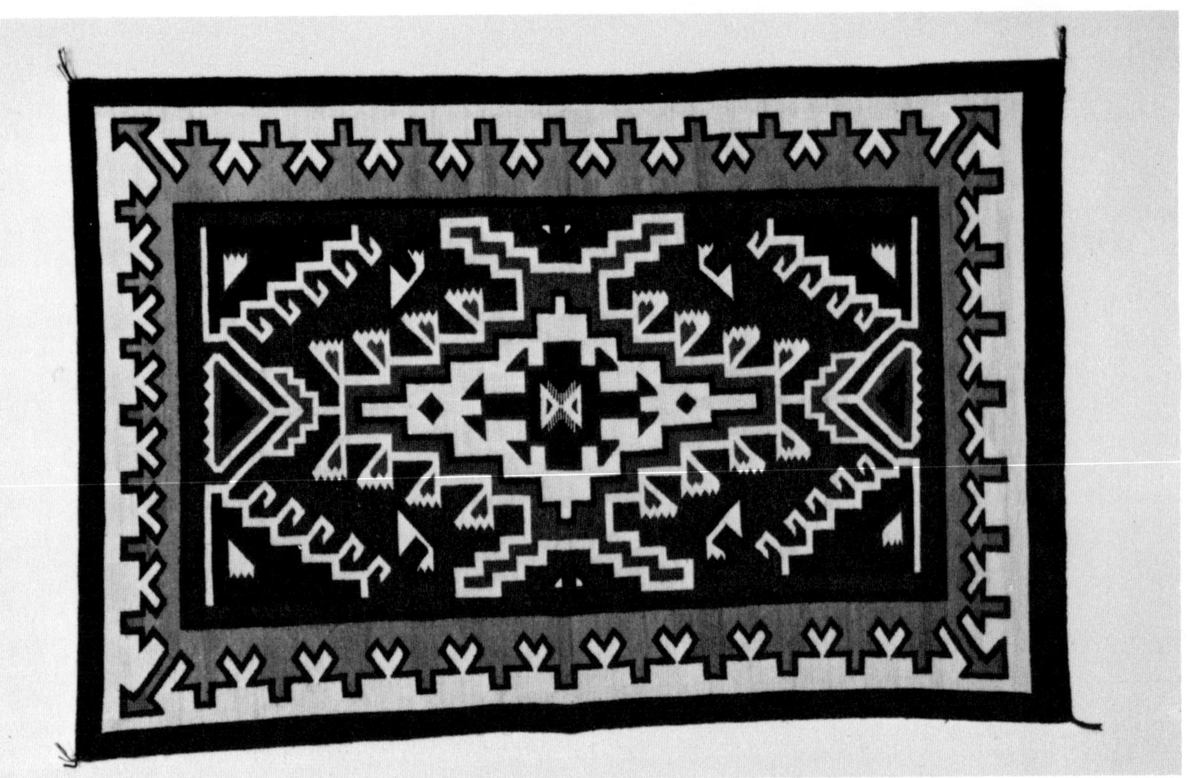

348. Classic Rug
A fine example of the "Two Gray Hills" style of weaving, this combines the tight weave and intricate design popular in that area with the pleasing color combination which has made these textiles so popular with non-Indians. Presented by IBM Gallery of Arts and Sciences. NAVAJO. New Mexico. 1950-1955. 46" x 69". 24/1070.

349. Germantown Textile
Woven of yarns brought into the trade from Germantown, Pennsylvania, this is a fine example of the weaving produced toward the end of the 19th Century. Note the weaving combs, bow and arrow. Collected by Genl. Nelson A. Miles. Presented by Mrs. Samuel K. Reber and Maj. Sherman Miles. NAVAJO. Arizona. 1875-1885. 49¼" x 73¾". 14/2209.

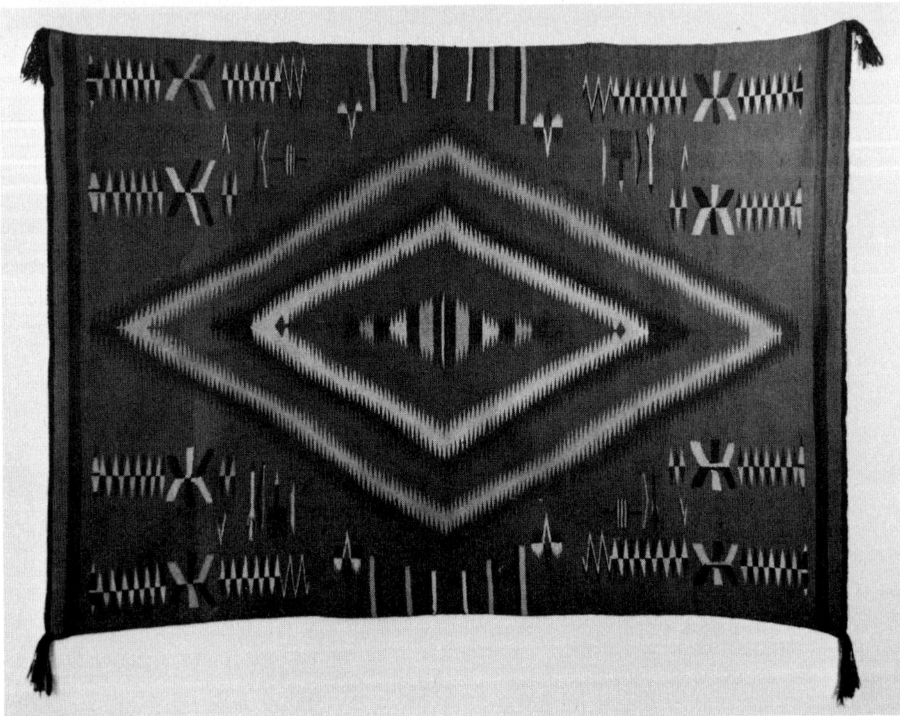

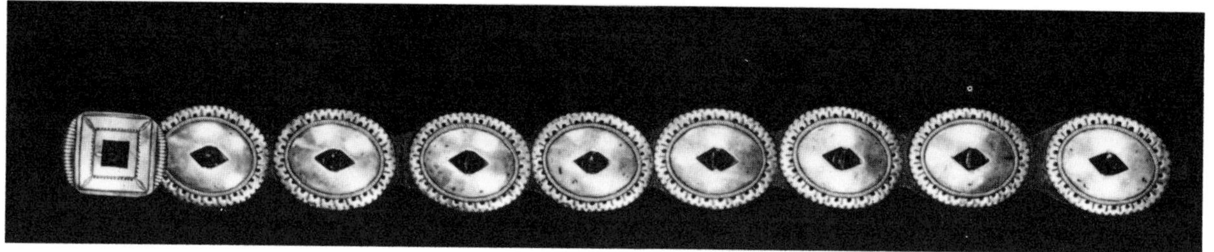

350. Silver Belt
Made up of eight hammered *conchas* and a buckle, this is typical of the early work of the Navajo silversmith. It was obtained from John Wetherill about 1910. Bequest of Katherine Harvey. NAVAJO. Arizona. 3″ x 38″. 23/2450.

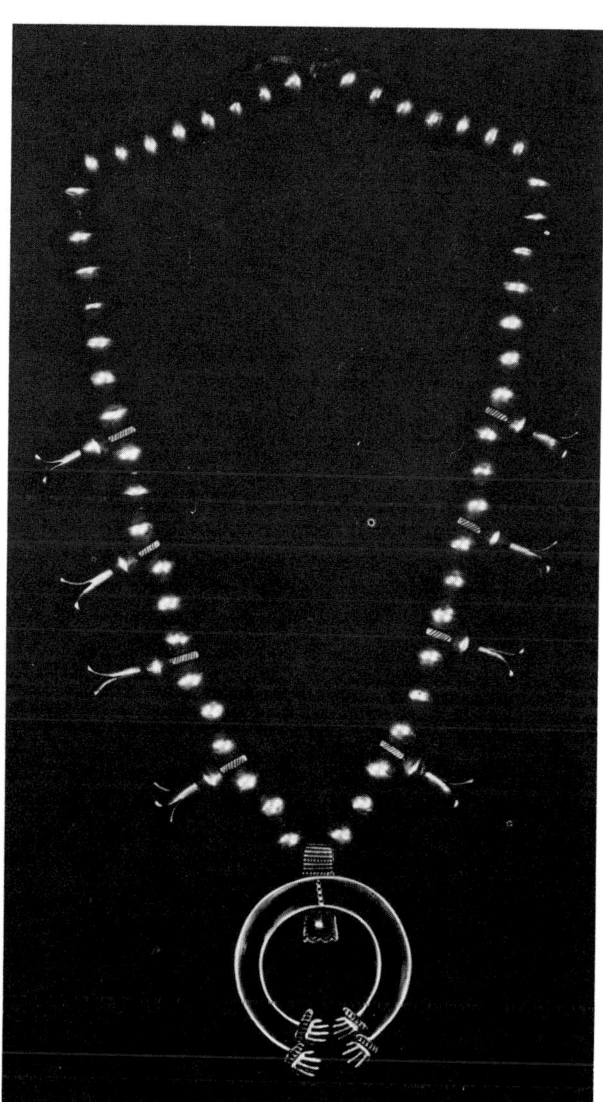

351. Silver Necklace
The "squash blossom necklace" is one of the most familiar items of native American jewelry today. This example was collected by Dr. Byron Cummings in 1910. NAVAJO. Ganado, Arizona. L: 16″. 24/745.

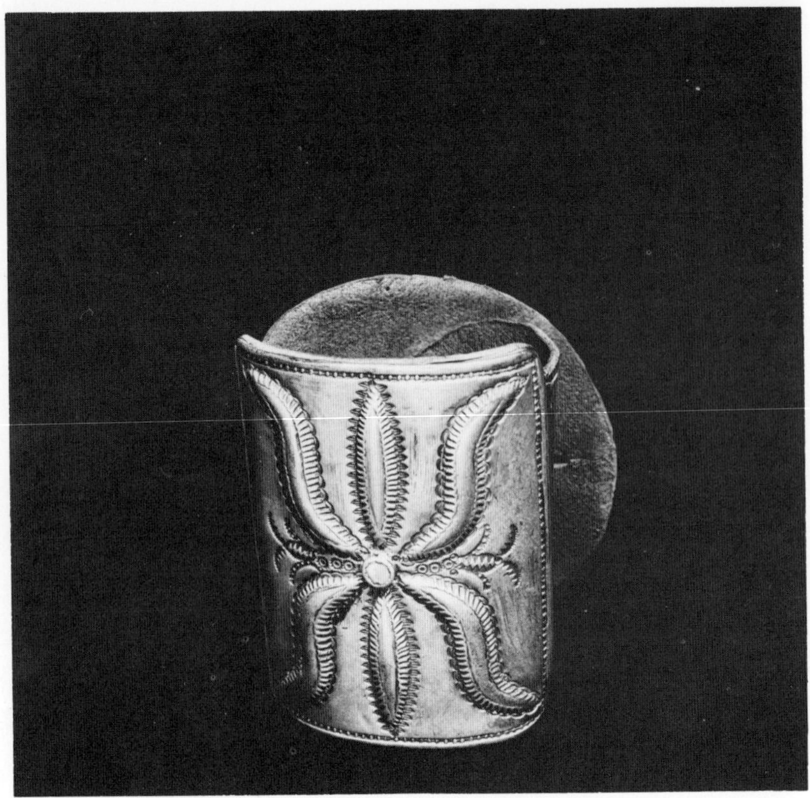

352. Silver Bowguard
The hammered silver *ketoh* was used to protect the wrist from the impact of the bowstring. Later, these became jewelry decorations. The design represents the Spider Woman, a mythological being. NAVAJO. New Mexico. 1920-1925. 2¼" x 3½". 20/3537.

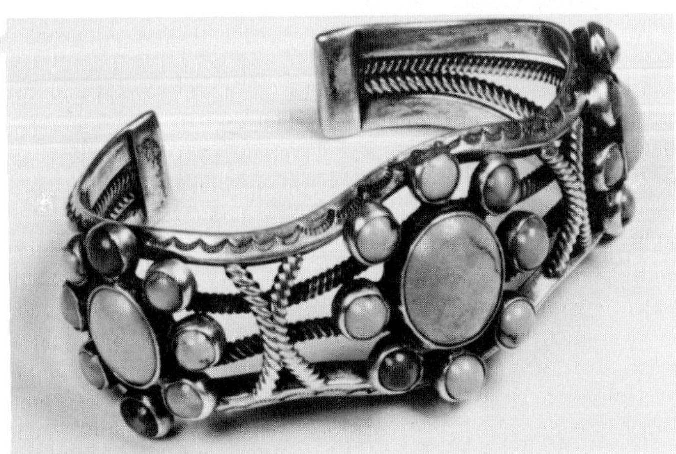

353. Cast Silver Bracelet
Made of cast silver set with 24 turquoise arranged in the clusters typical of such jewelry, this is an excellent example of Southwestern silverwork at its best. Bequest of Hope Violet Lea. ZUNI. New Mexico. 1920-1930. 1¼" x 3". 24/3622.

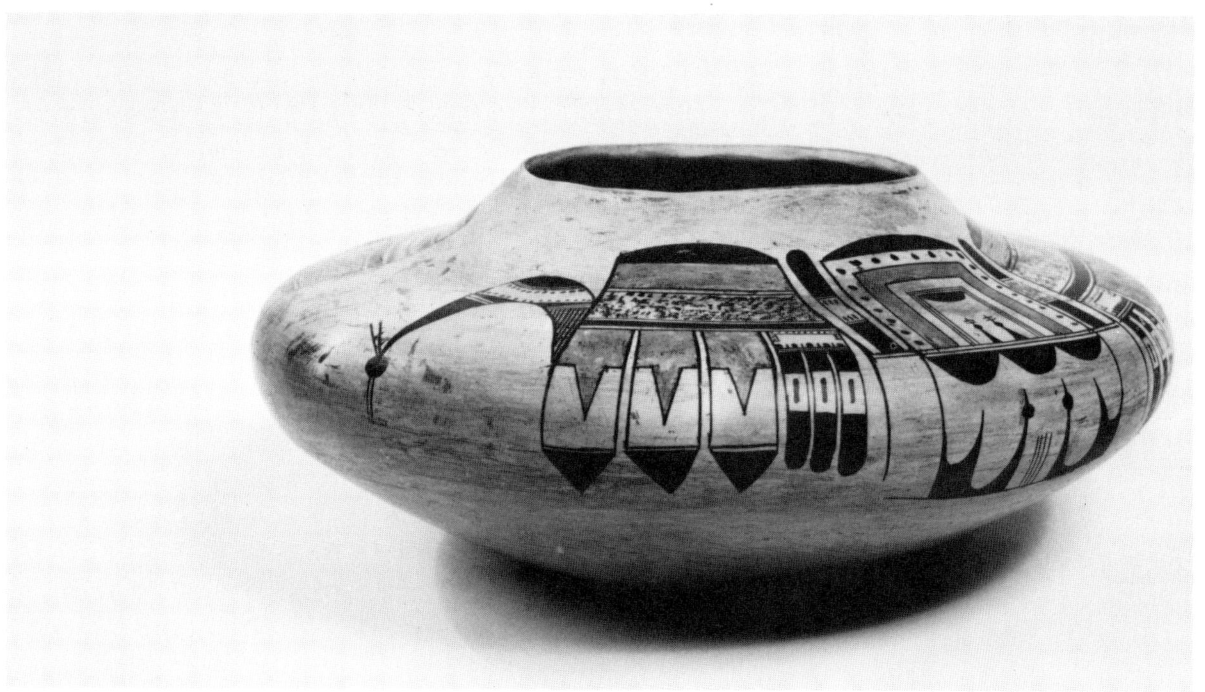

354. Pottery Bowl
At the turn of the century a young Hopi woman named Nampeyó became intrigued by the designs on prehistoric pottery sherds then being excavated by J. W. Fewkes. She adapted many of these to her own pottery, and gained a reputation as a ceramic innovator which is still remembered with respect. Presented by Mrs. Clark G. Dailey. Hopi. Hano, Arizona. About 1900. 5½″ x 13″. 22/2846.

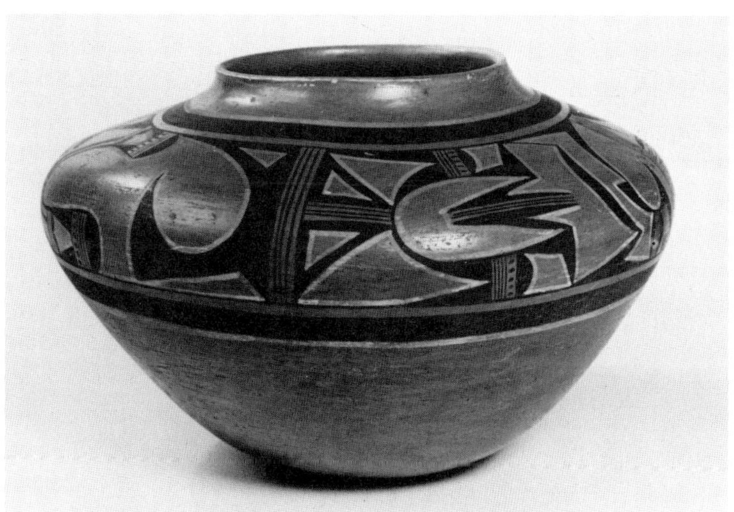

355. Redware Olla
The large, beautifully curving vessels for which Nampeyó was famous is exemplified by this olla. It was made by her daughter, Fannie, who continued the excellent work until very recently. Presented by Misses Alice and Florence M. Ewing. Hopi. Hano, Arizona. 1915-1920. 9½″ x 13″. 24/6860.

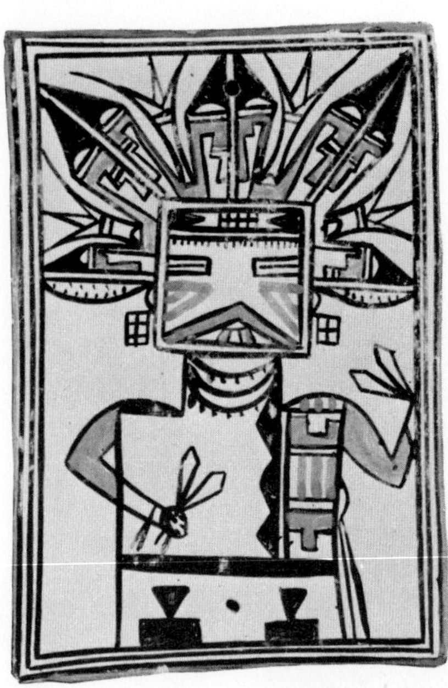

356. **Clay Tile**
For a brief period, small, flat clay tiles were made in the Hopi villages for sale to tourists. They were popular at the time for use in the homes in the Southwest. This is an example, portraying a Shálako Maiden wearing a mask and woven costume. Presented by Mrs. Elton Gannett. HOPI. Walpi, Arizona. 1895-1910. 4¾" x 7¾". 24/4432.

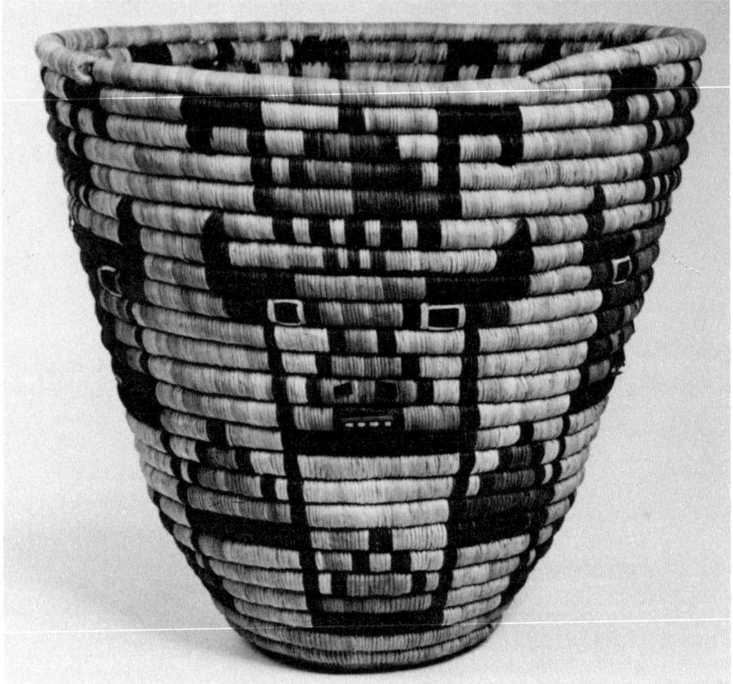

357. **Coiled-Weave Basket**
A particular style of very tightly-wound coil weaving is found only on Second Mesa. This storage basket has the design of Wakás, the Cow Kachina, on the sides. Collected by John L. Nelson. HOPI. Shungopovi, Arizona. 1930-1935. 11¾" x 13". 18/959.

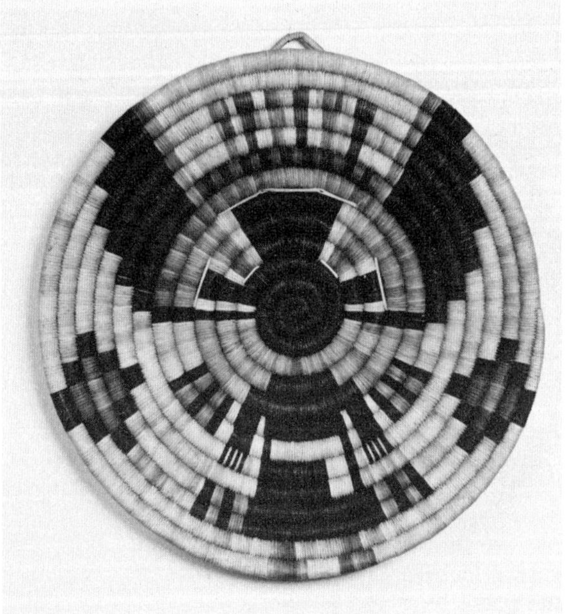

358. **Basketry Placque**
Another example of the coiled weave technique is this flat tray, used for corn meal and also as a wall hanging. It has the design of Angswüsnasómtaka, the Crow Winged Being, in her feathered costume. Collected by John L. Nelson. HOPI. Shungopovi, Arizona. 1930-1935. D: 13". 18/966.

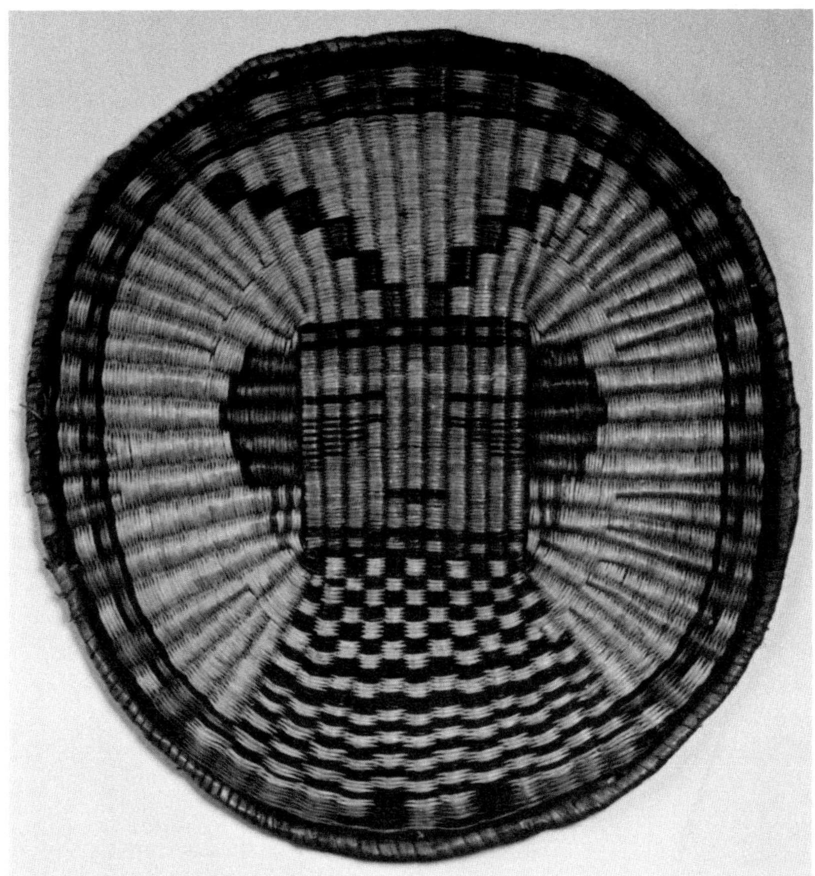

359. Wicker Weave Placque
A second type of Hopi basketry is the use of wicker, as in this example with the design of Poli Mana, the Butterfly Maiden. From the William Randolph Hearst Collection. Hopi. Oraibi, Arizona. 1930-1940. D: 14″. 23/2790.

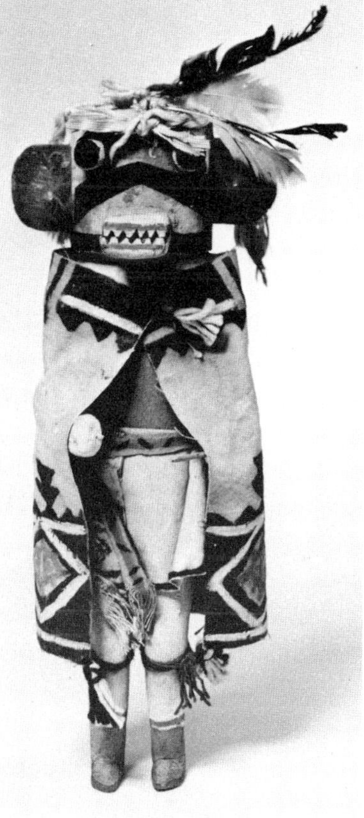

360. Kachina Figure
Commonly termed a "Kachina Doll", these are faithful replicas of the costume and regalia of a masked human personator. In this instance the design represents Torécama Kachina. Collected by H. R. Voth. Hopi. Oraibi, Arizona. 1895-1900. H: 14″. 18/6191.

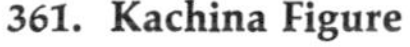

361. Kachina Figure
(See color insert facing page 200)

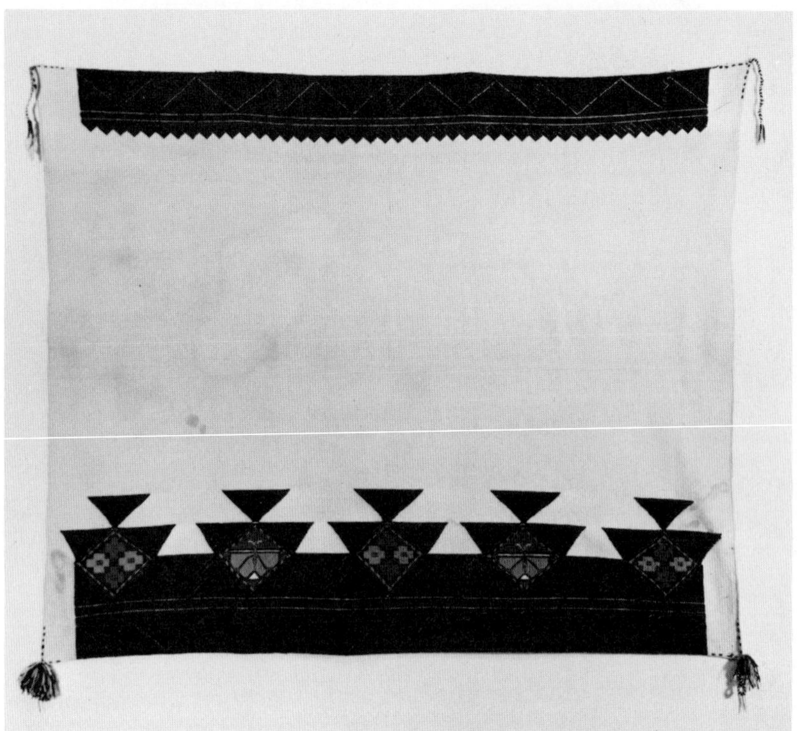

362. Ceremonial Shawl
These brilliantly brocaded garments are woven by men, and are worn by women, by dancers in various ceremonies, and by priests on occasion. Presented by Mrs. Harcourt Amory. HOPI. Arizona. 1935-1950. 56" x 70". 23/2870.

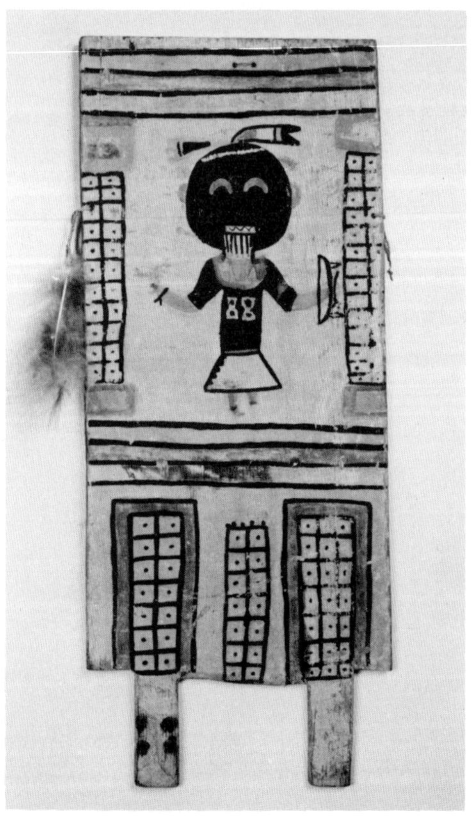

363. Woman's Dance Board
Carried in the hands by women performers in Women's Society dances, the *manayauwi* is painted in a variety of designs; this represents Chakwaina Kachina, and ears of corn. *See* #9. HOPI. Oraibi, Arizona. 1900-1905. 8¾" x 21". 9/578.

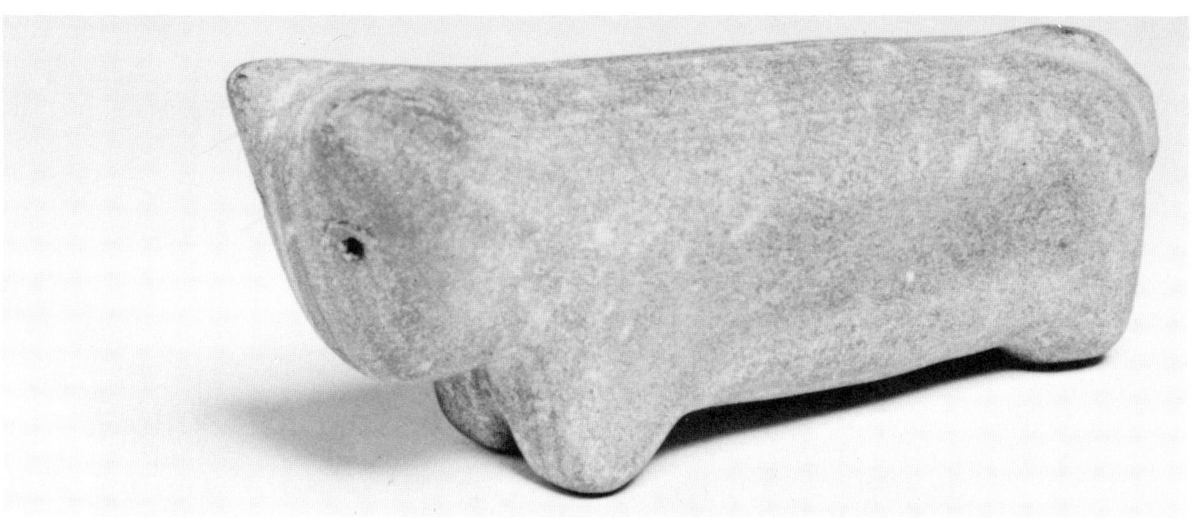

364. Stone Fetish

A tremendous variety of small stone carvings were made and used by the Pueblo people. Many were intended for success in hunting, others were for curing or witchcraft purposes, and some were for strictly personal needs. Later, these became favorite objects for tourist sale. This example represents a cougar, or mountain lion. Collected by Lancelot Ely. ZUNI. New Mexico. 1930-1940. 2½″ x 7″. 21/5038.

365. Polychrome Olla

(See color insert facing page 160)

366. Geometric Design Olla

Another type of Zuni design is this finely-painted design on a white slip base. It was also collected by Douglas D. Graham, and presented by Mmes. E. B. Lent, G. B. Oman, A. B. Young, and F. B. VanHouten. ZUNI. New Mexico. 1875-1880. 10¾″ x 13¼″. 22/7879.

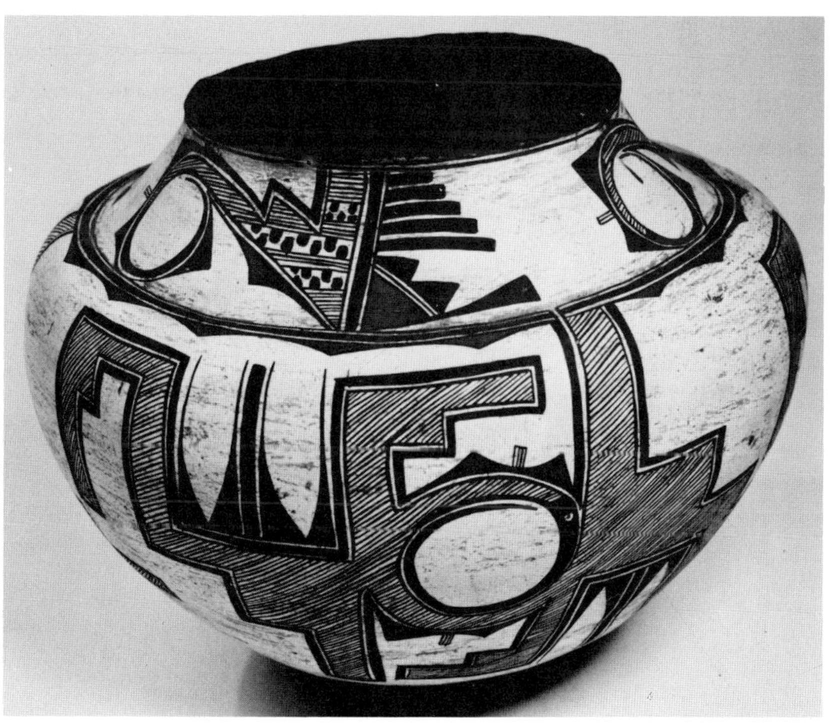

367. Embroidered Woolen Shawl

An entirely different type of shawl is the style from the Eastern Pueblos. This example, woven of wool dyed black, and commercial yarns, has a design adapted from early Spanish garments. Presented by Admiral and Mrs. Alexander S. Wotherspoon. ACOMA. New Mexico. 1900-1920. 41″ x 52″. 24/7827.

368. Modern Clay Bowl

(See page 18)

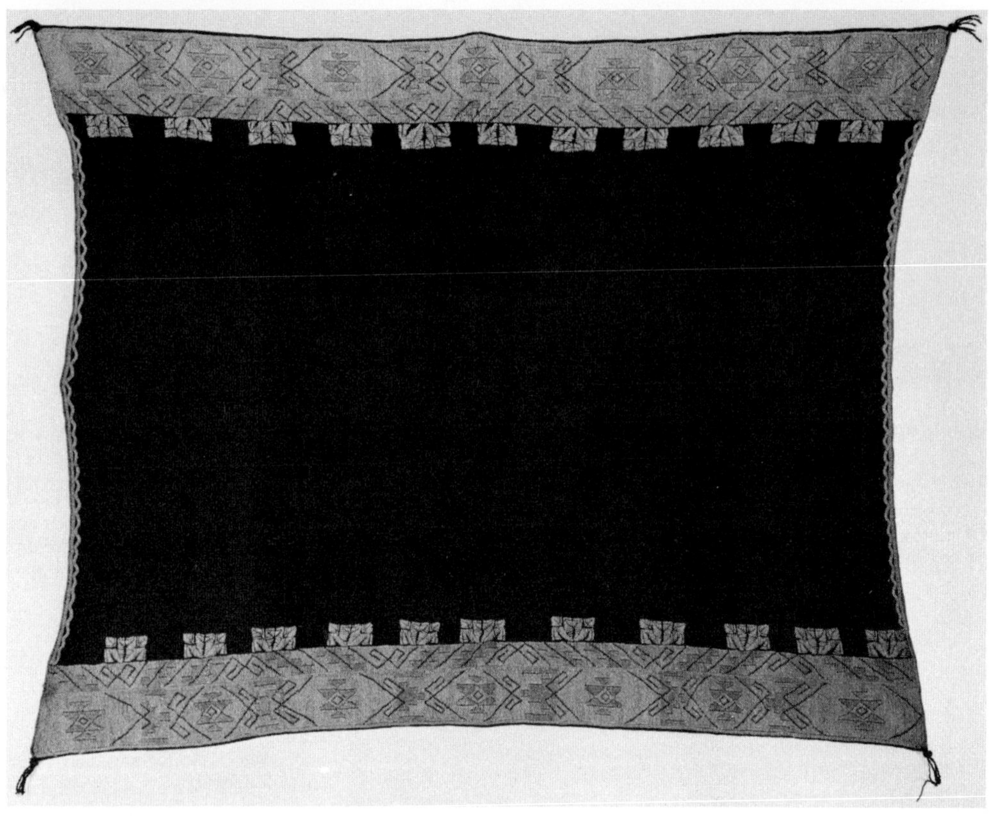

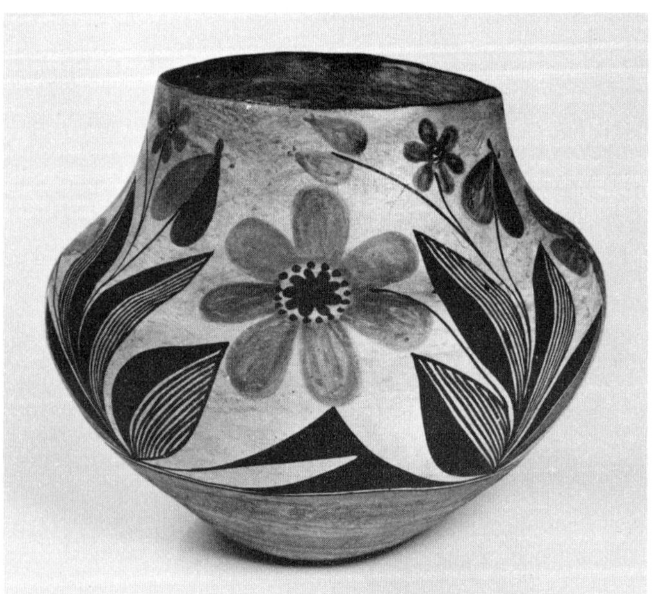

369. Polychrome Water Vessel

The ceramics from Santa Ana are far less common than from some of the other villages. This has the typical sunflower design on the sides. Collected and presented by Margaret J. Sharpe. SANTA ANA. New Mexico. 1910-1920. 9¼″ x 10½″. 22/5231.

370. Painted Olla
(See color insert facing page 200)

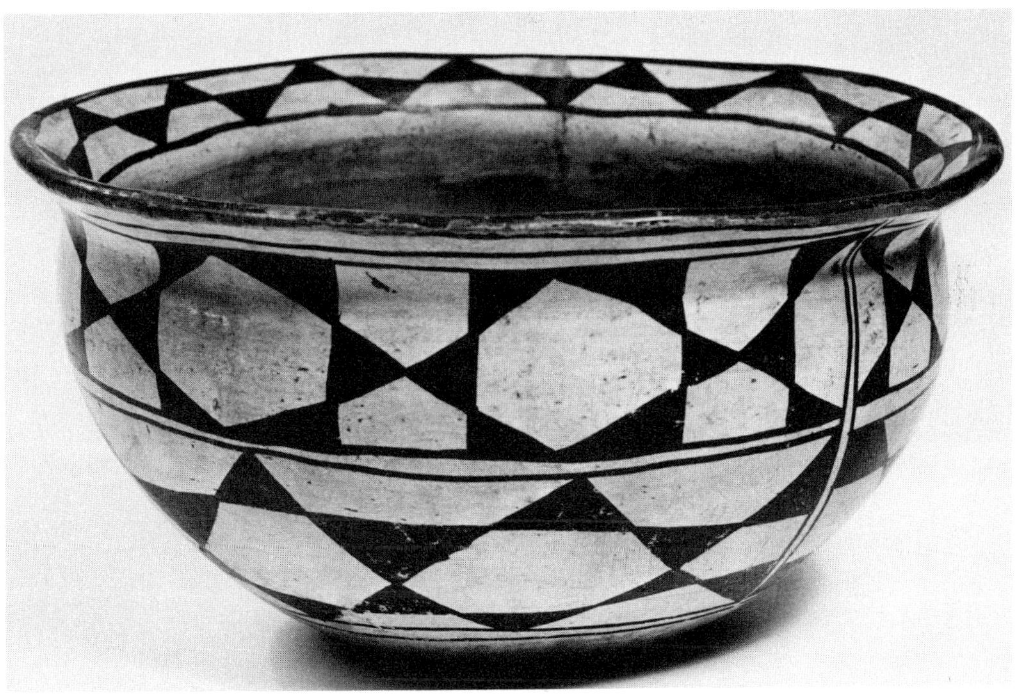

371. Black-on-Creamware Bowl
The strong triangular designs on the sides of this vessel identify it as coming from one of the major southern Rio Grande Pueblo areas. Collected by Jesse L. Nusbaum. SANTO DOMINGO. New Mexico. 1910-1920. 5" x 10¾". 5/673.

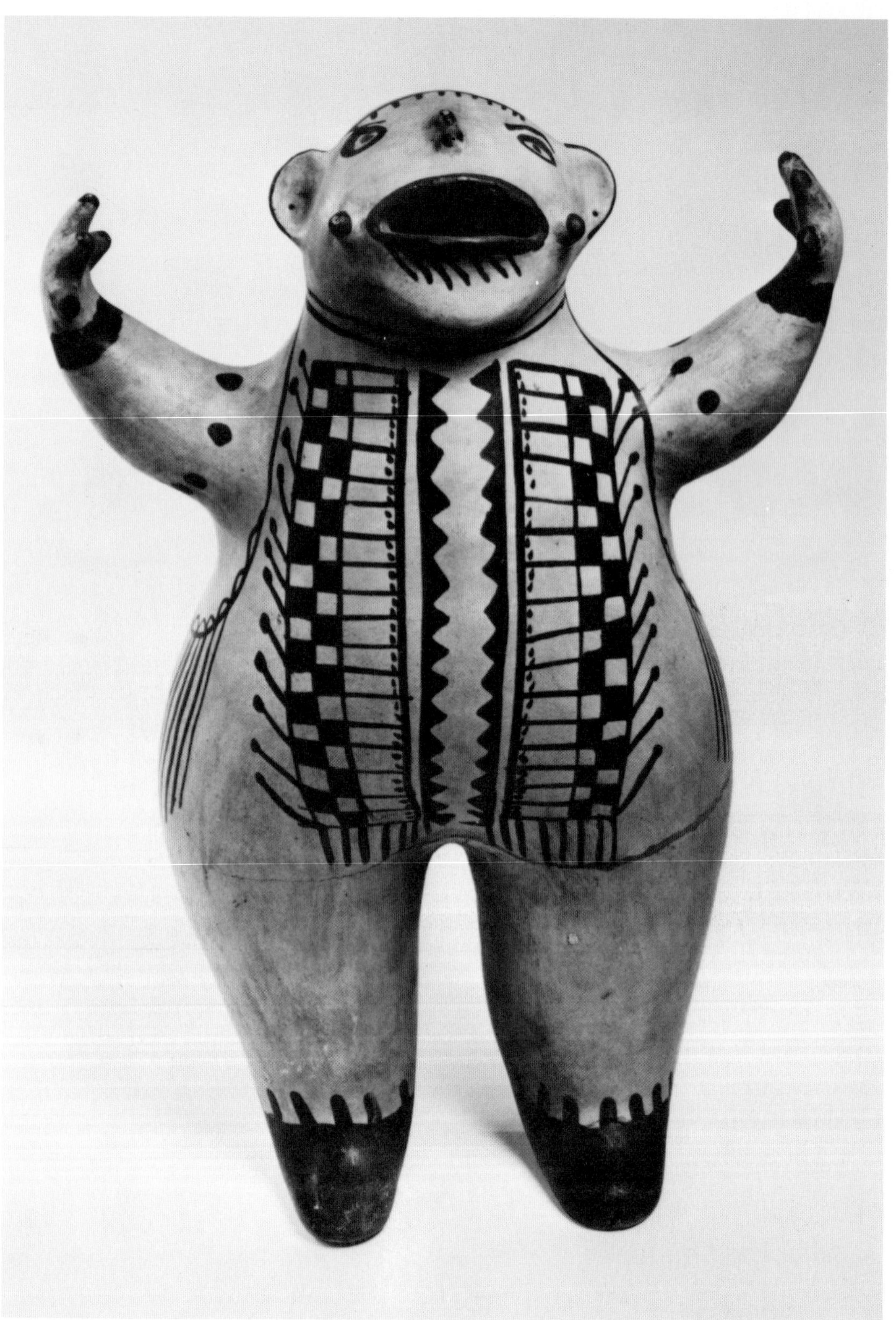

372. Standing Human Figure
These amusing effigies have been produced at Santo Domingo and Cochití for many years; the design represents clothing. They are intended primarily for sale to outsiders, and have no traditional function. SANTO DOMINGO. New Mexico. 1910-1930. 11″ x 18½″. 19/6726.

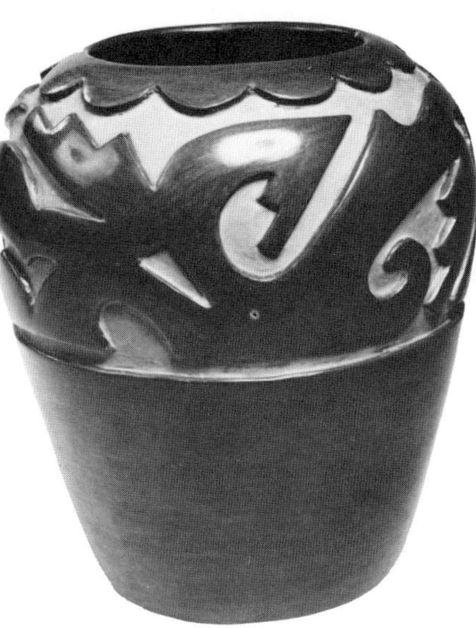

373. Carved Redware Vase
Another style of ceramics is the form shown here, in which the modeled clay is carved while moist, and then fired. The designs are found in a wide variety of motifs. This was made by Margaret Tafoya in 1962. SANTA CLARA. New Mexico. 8″ x 9¾″. 24/3736.

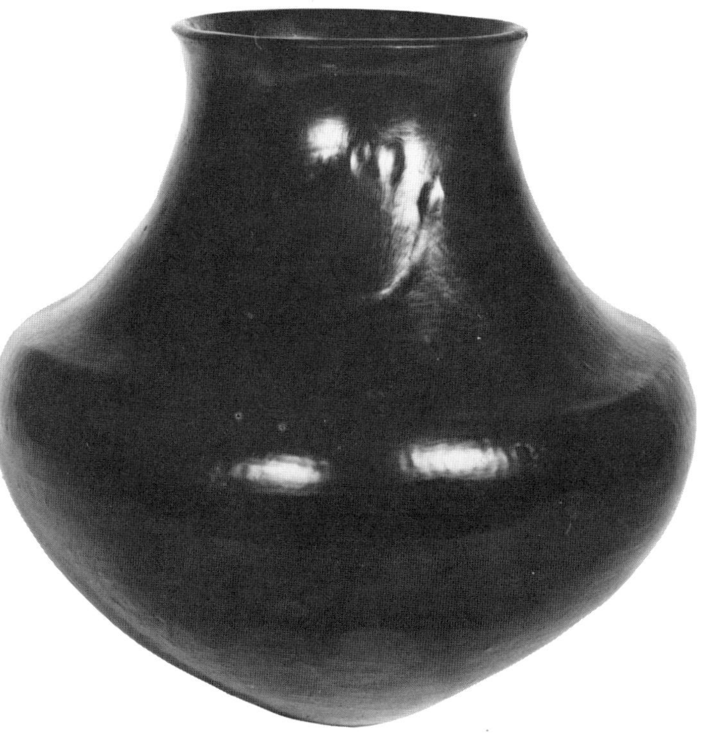

374. Blackware Tinaja
The large vessels of this style are magnificent examples of Pueblo ceramic artistry. The impressed bear-paw design is characteristic of pottery from Santa Clara. SANTA CLARA. New Mexico. 1920-1930. 10½″ x 12″. 21/7389.

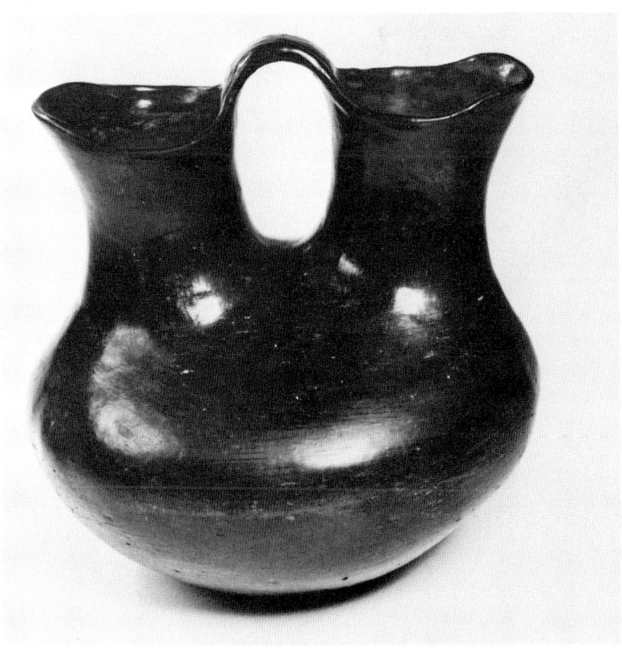

375. Double-spouted Vase
These beautifully formed vessels are commonly termed "Wedding Jars", from the mythology which has built up around their use. The graceful shape is enhanced by the firm burnishing of the surface with a polishing stone. SANTA CLARA. New Mexico. 1900-1920. 9½″ x 11″. 15/8260.

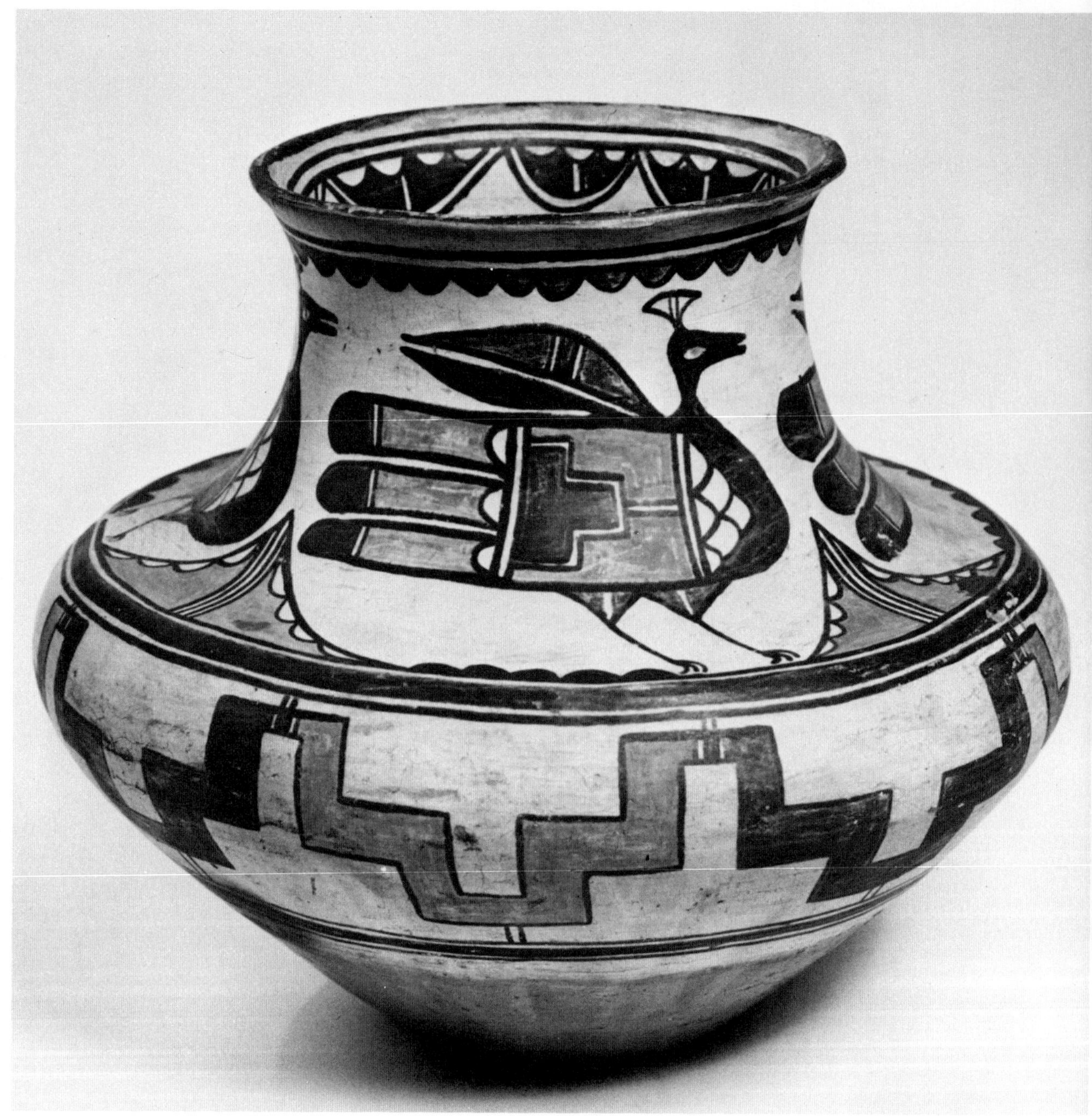

376. Polychrome Olla
The older type of pottery from the upper Rio Grande frequently includes bright colors and strong linear patterns. This shows the most characteristic form and design. Collected by Jesse L. Nusbaum. SAN ILDEFONSO. New Mexico. 1900-1920. 10″ x 10″. 5/3883.

377. Matte-finish Bowl

Undoubtedly the best known pottery from the New Mexico Pueblo area is the oxidized ware from San Ildefonso. Developed about 1919 by Julián and María Martínez, it was a revival of prehistoric pottery, but in a new and more sophisticated form. Presented by Harriet Roeder in memory of her mother, Harriet K. Roeder. SAN ILDEFONSO. New Mexico. 1930-1940. 5¼" x 8¾". 22/7597.

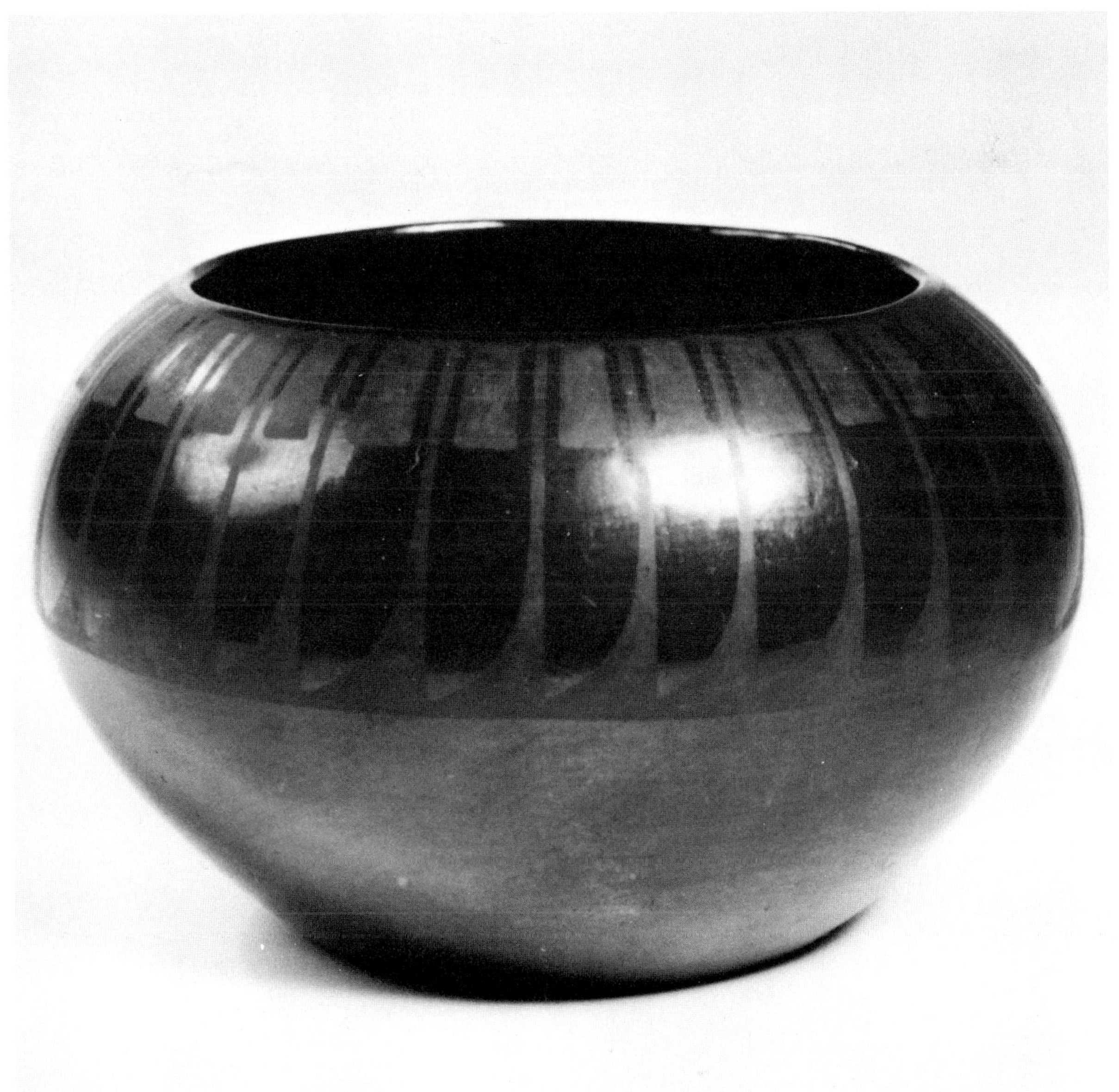

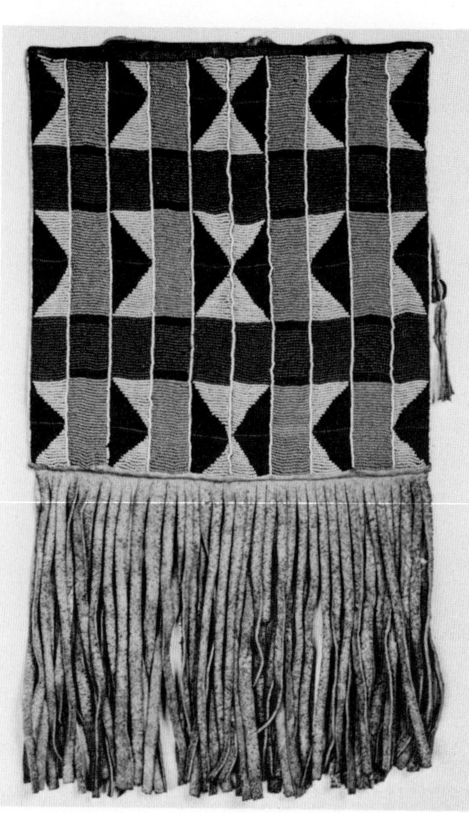

378. Beaded Pouch

Lacking pockets, the Indian people tended to make use of a variety of pouches and bags. This flat wallet style is typical of the Northern Plains and Plateau region; it has been decorated in a colorful geometric pattern. CROW. Montana. 1900-1910. 11″ x 21″. 24/1969.

379. Man's Buckskin Shirt

(See color insert facing page 280)

380. Elk Tooth Dress

The use of elk teeth to decorate costumes was a common practice, although their scarcity made such objects extremely valuable. This dress would have been very expensive, even though some of the elk teeth are imitations carved from bone. Collected by William Wildschut. CROW. Montana, 1890-1910. 38″ x 56″. 14/3597.

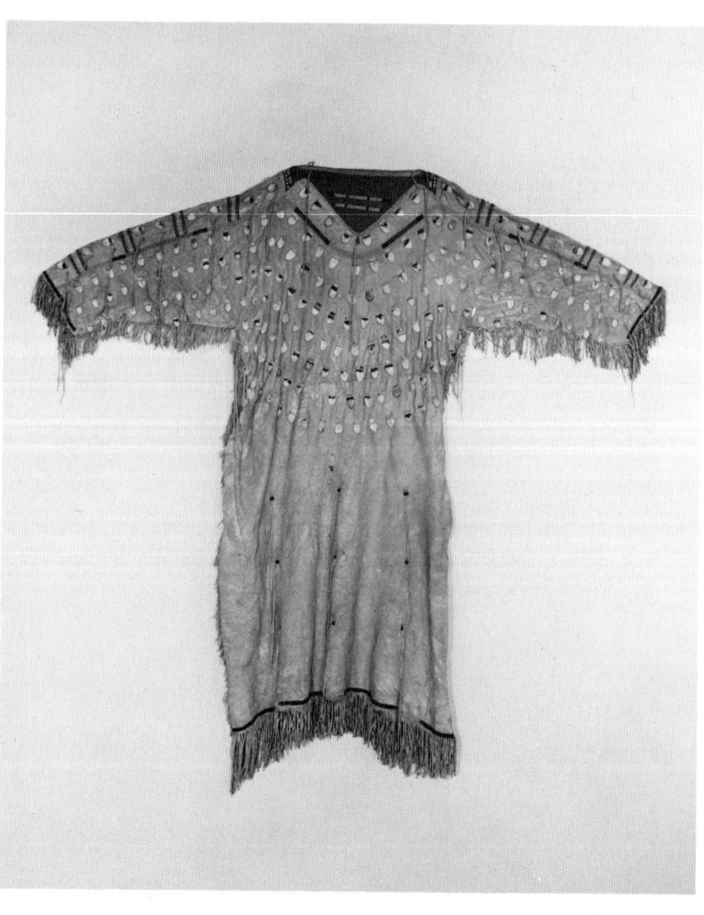

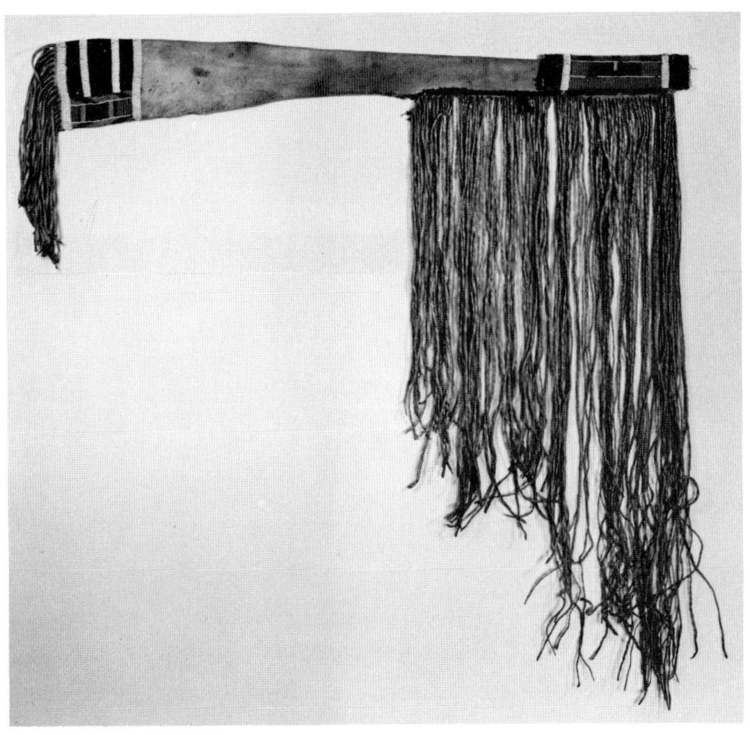

381. Gun Sheath
Carbines and rifles were kept in scabbards such as this—constructed on the pattern of the bow-case quiver. The beadwork and very long fringing are typical of the Northern Plains tribes. Presented by Mr. and Mrs. Percy H. Whiting. CROW. Montana. 1880-1900. 45″ x 45″. 23/1301.

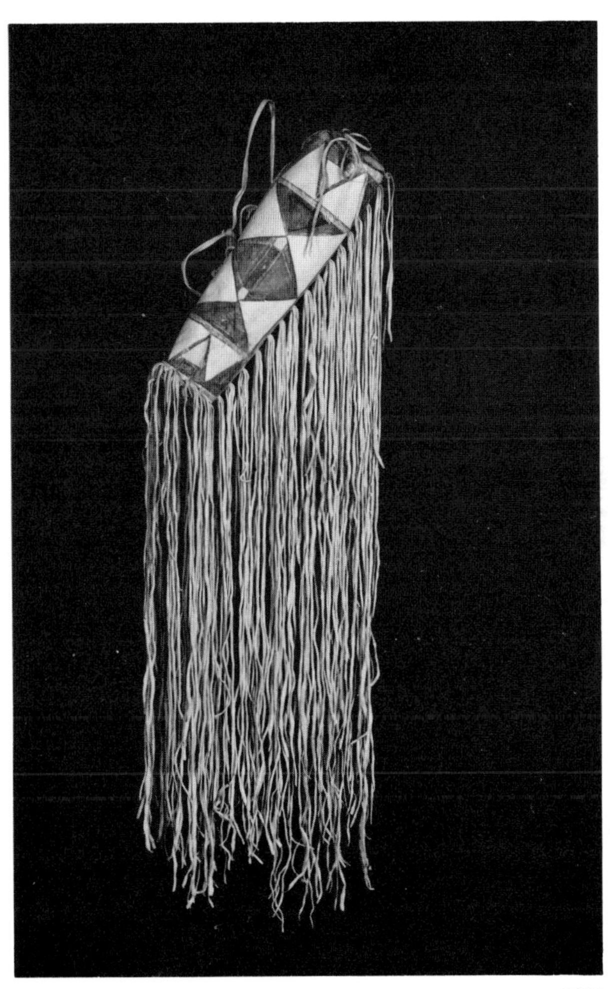

382. Bonnet Case
The protection of feathered bonnets was vital, and cylindrical rawhide cases were devised for the purpose. These were painted in geometric designs. Collected by William Wildschut. CROW. Montana. 1900-1910. 19″ x 48″. 11/7685.

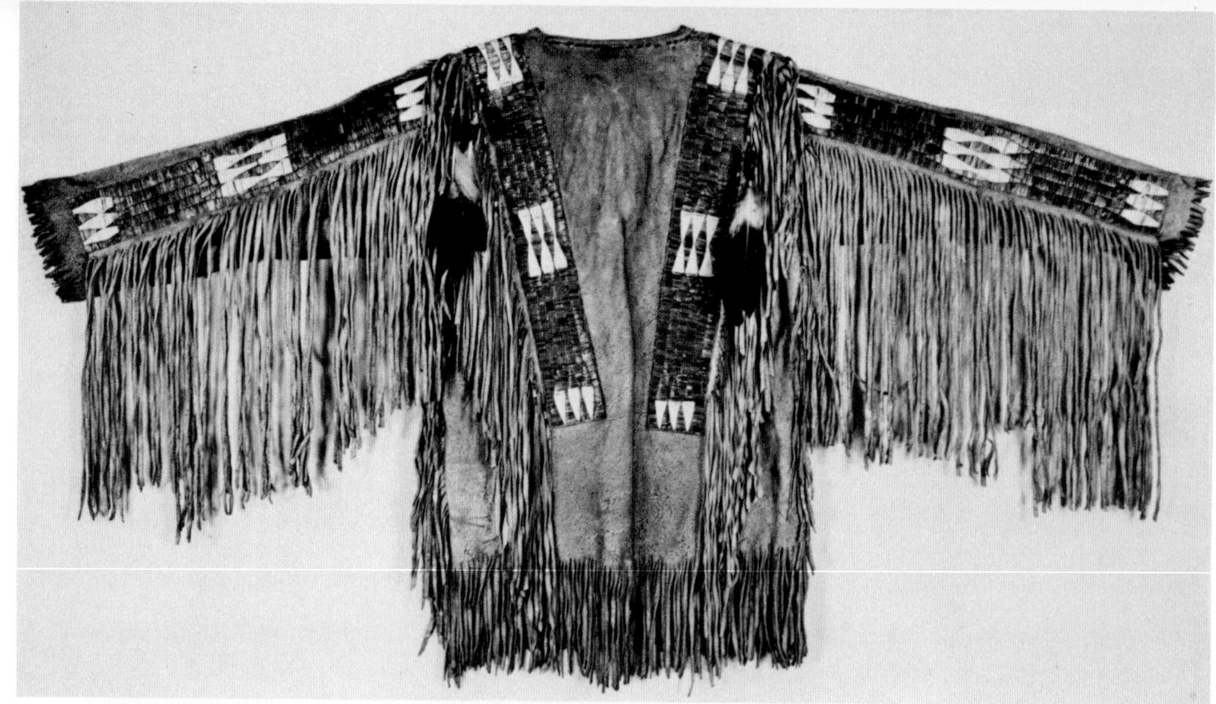

383. Buckskin War Shirt
Men's costumes were often quite brilliant in color, and elaborately decorated. This quilled shirt is a fine example of what the well-dressed man would wear during the days of the buffalo. Collected by Alanson B. Skinner. TETON SIOUX. 1880-1900. 60" x 63". 14/3485.

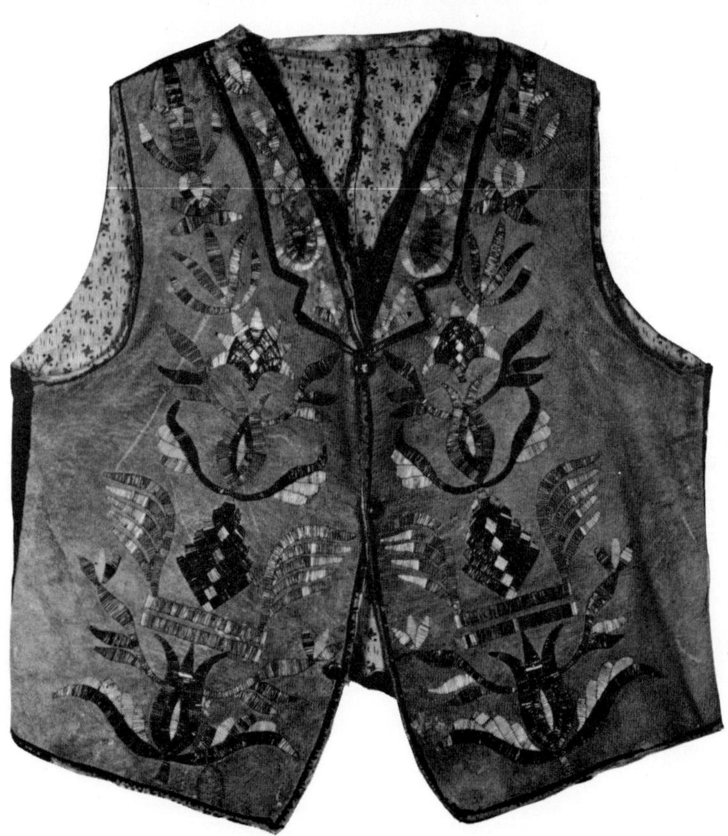

384. Quilled Vest
With the arrival of European immigrants, several types of garments new to the Indian became popular, among which was the vest. This example has polychrome porcupine quillwork in realistic designs on front and back. Presented by William L. Guthman. SANTEE SIOUX. Lake Traverse, Minnesota. 1880-1890. 16" x 22". 23/5010.

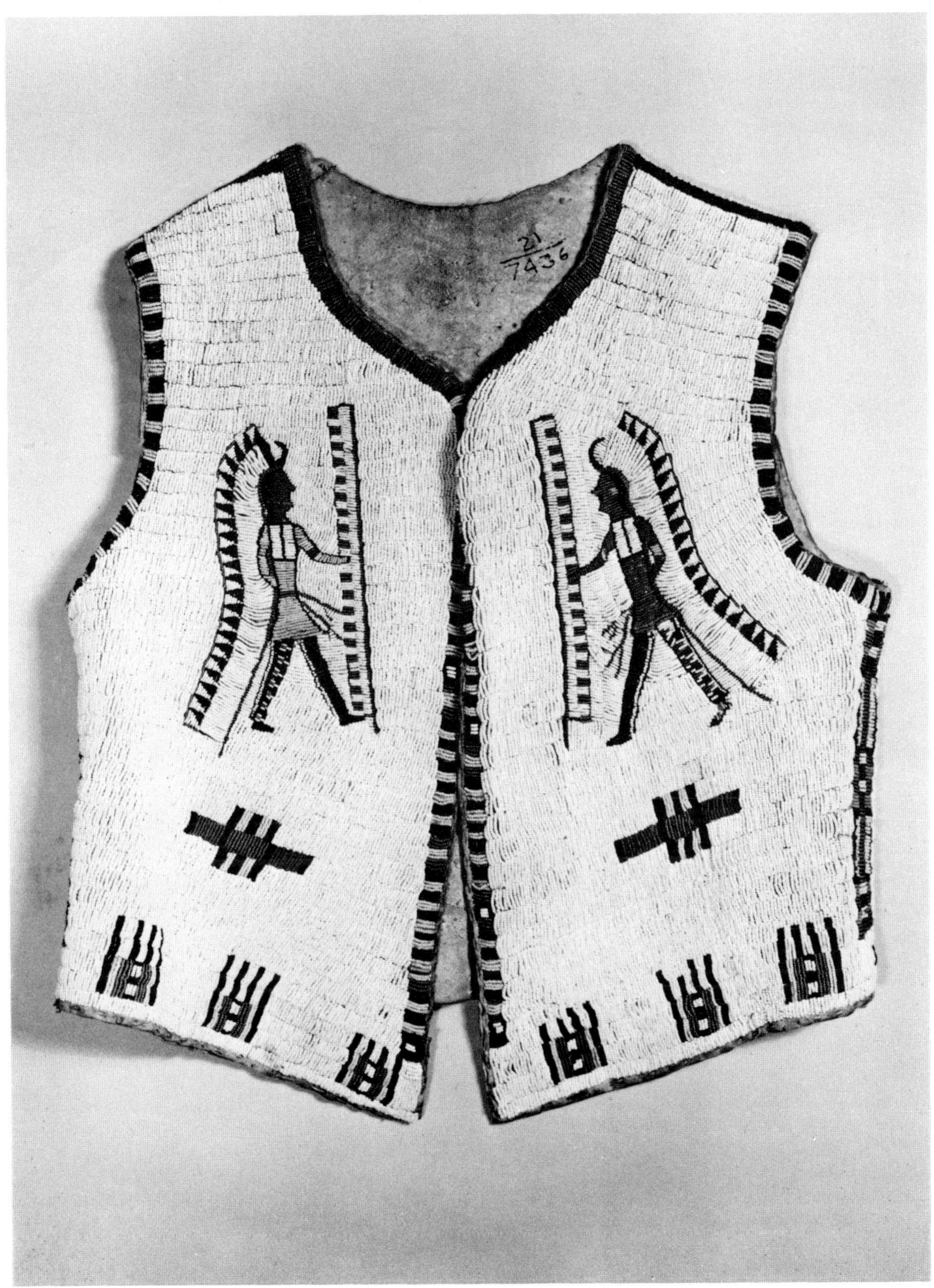

385. Man's Beaded Vest
Another style of vest is this buckskin garment, with pictorial designs beaded on the surface of the material. It is a striking example of the ability of the beadworker to create lifelike designs with trade beads. SIOUX. South Dakota. 1880-1890. 18″ x 20″. 21/7436.

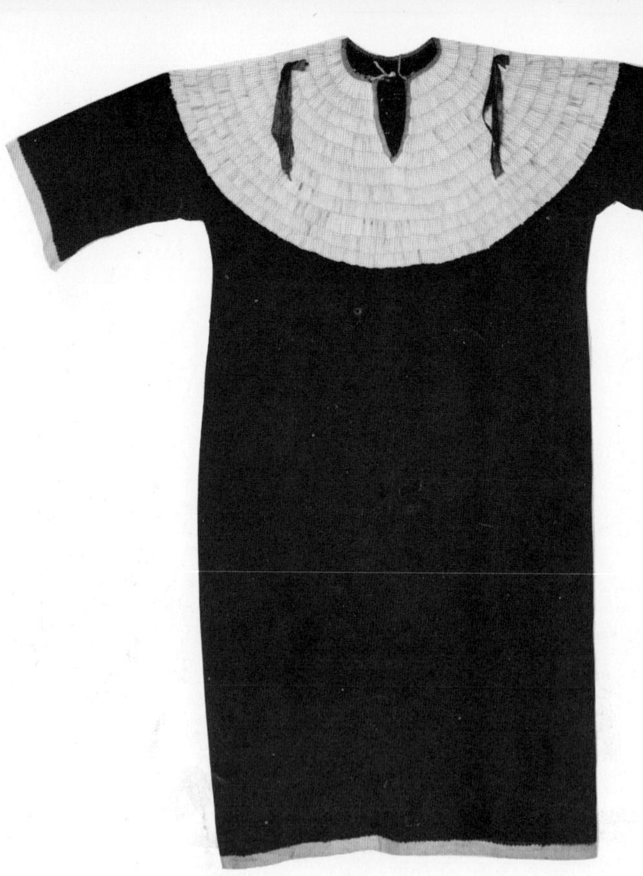

386. Trade Cloth Costume

Dentalium shells were highly esteemed, and objects which were decorated with them were very valuable. A dress of this type would have been available only to an extremely wealthy person. The shells came over a long trade route from the Pacific Northwest. Collected by Fred R. Meyer. BLACKFOOT. Wyoming. 1880-1900. L: 53″. 2/5996.

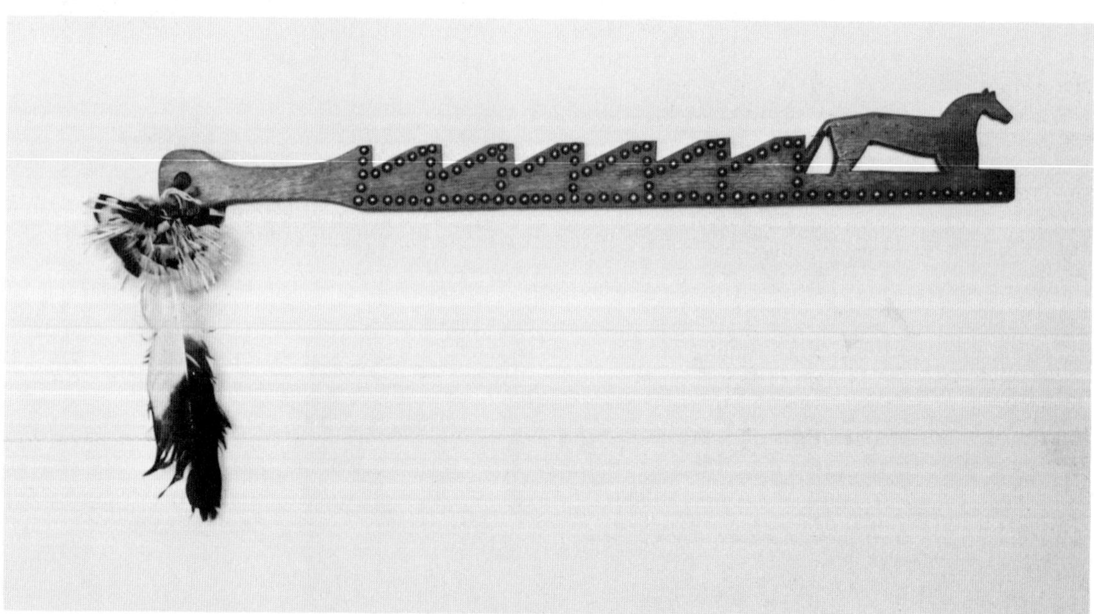

387. Wooden Dance Club

Carved into a horse at one end, and decorated with brass tacks obtained in trade, this has a small feather cluster decoration. These were used by the various Soldier Societies in public performances. Sometimes they were carried by Society guards in policing ceremonies, much as a baton to keep back the crowd. SIOUX. South Dakota. 1870-1890. L: 28″. 16/7185.

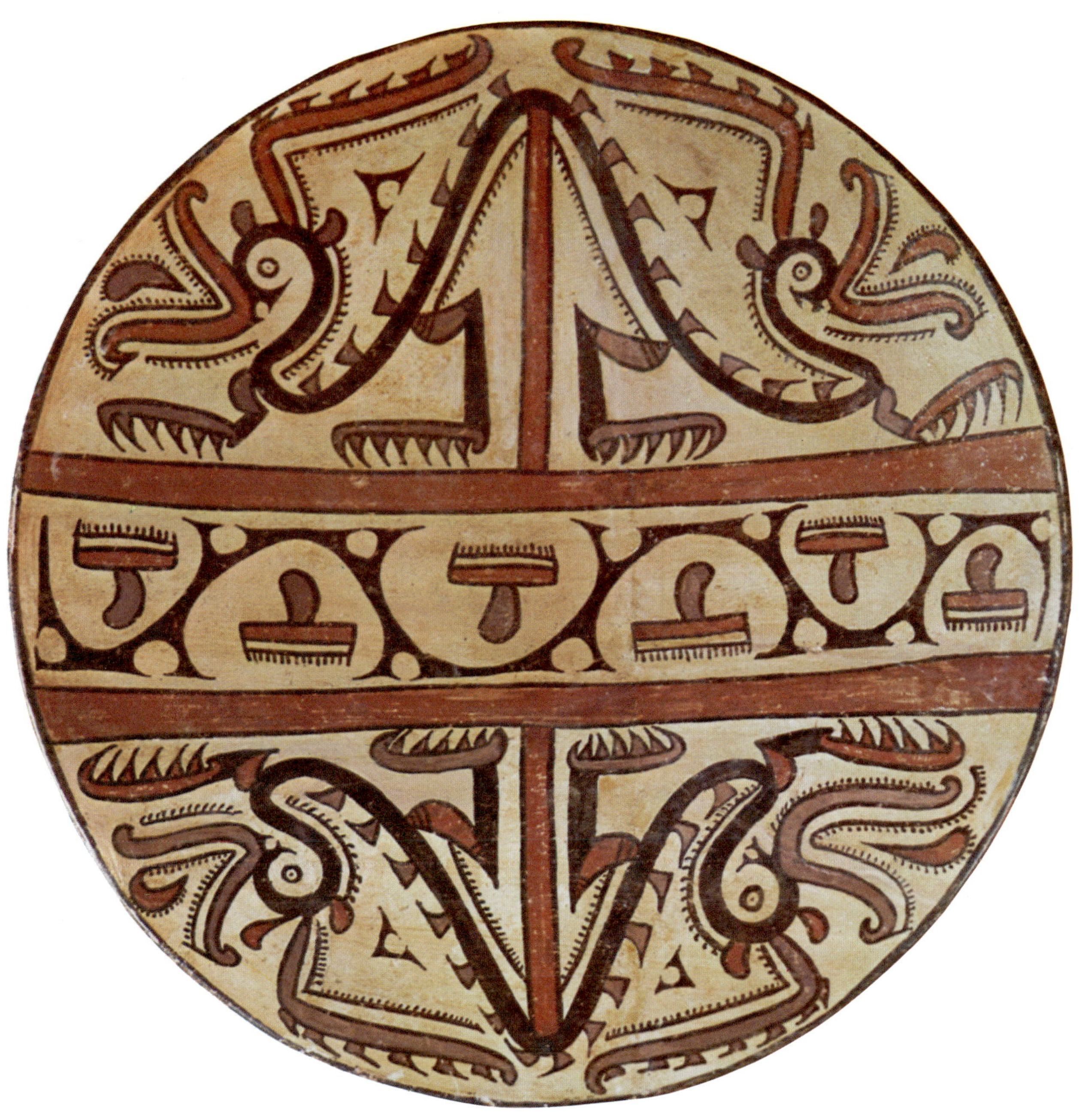

153. Large Painted Plate

This extremely complex design portrays several birds above and below the central band, in which are painted what are apparently six weaving combs. Collected by Philip L. Dade. Coclé. Río Coclé, Coclé, Panama. 1¾″ x 12″. 500-800. 22/9478.

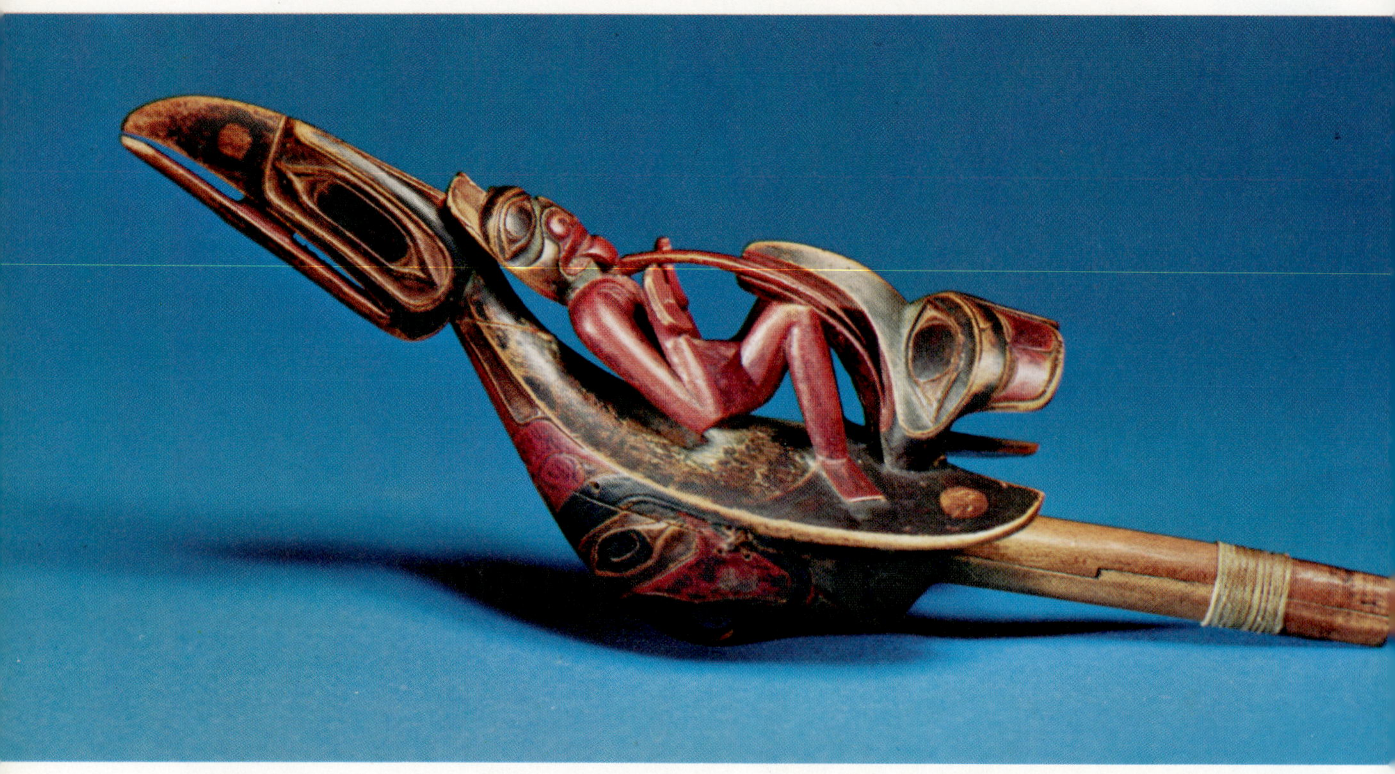

266. Raven Rattle

The most characteristic form of rattle among the people of the Northwest Coast is a design combining the raven, carrying a man, a frog, and a hawk on the under-belly in conventionalized form. Presented by Harmon W. Hendricks. Although collected from the Kwakiutl at Alert Bay, this is more likely made by Haida carvers. Alaska. 1875-1880. L: 12¾″. 11/5174.

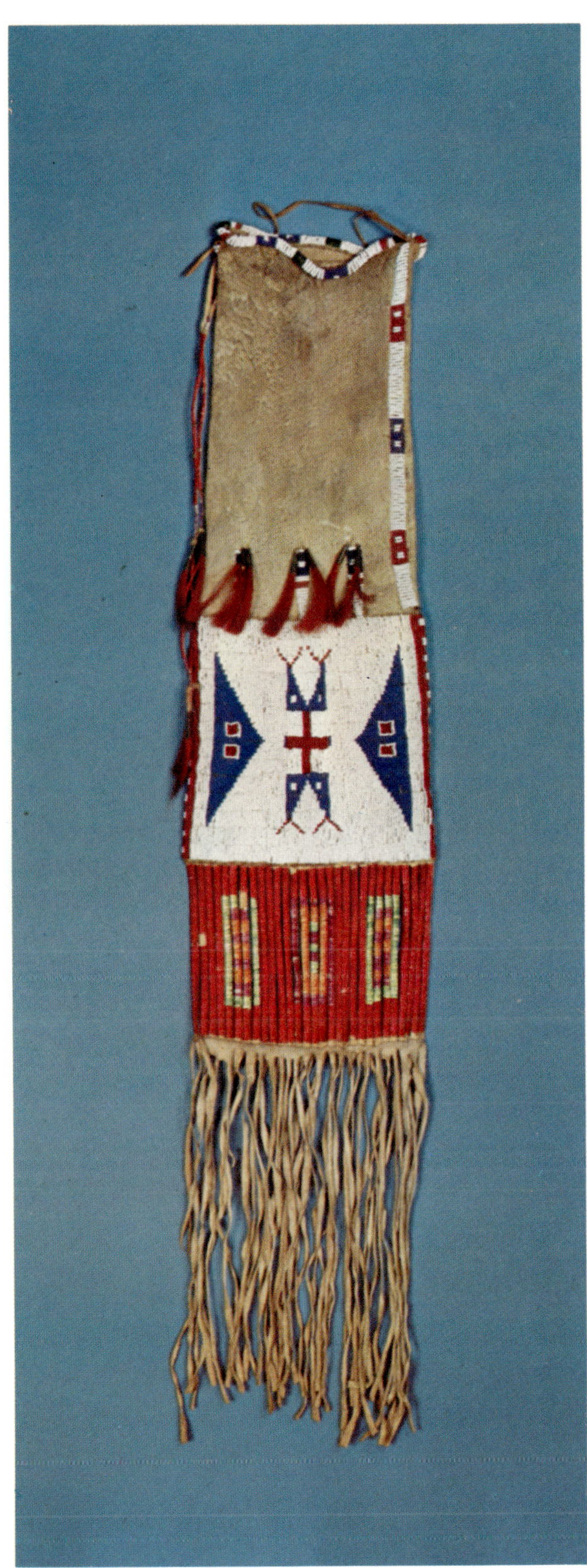

392. Buckskin Pipe Bag

A man's smoking materials, including his pipe bowl, stem, tobacco, strike-a-light and other equipment, were all carried in pouches of this design. They were usually decorated with beadwork or quilling. Collected by Maurice A. Gottlieb, and presented by David K. Spiegel. TETON SIOUX. Rapid City, South Dakota. 1880-1900. 7½" x 34". 19/8669.

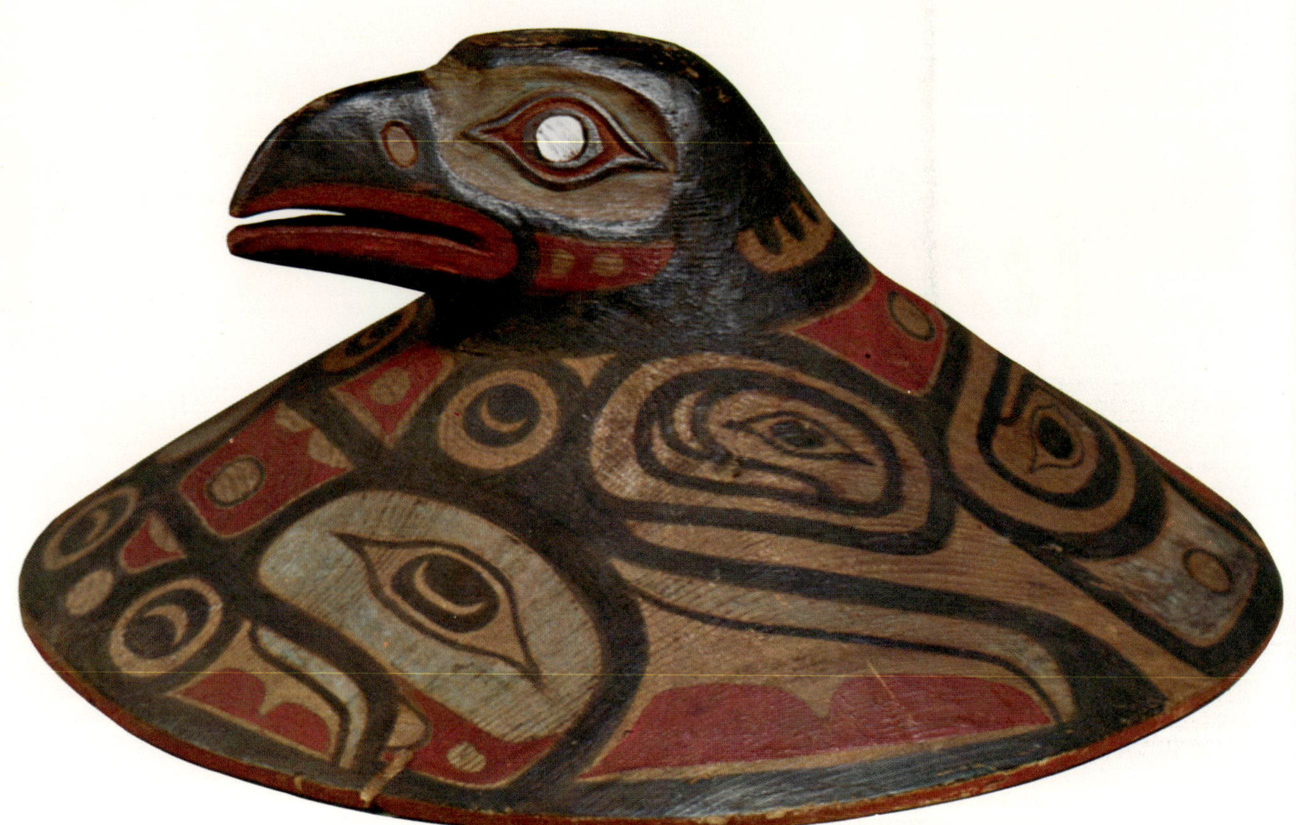

268. War Helmet

These sturdy carved wooden hats were used for protection as well as for identification. The painted design and carved form atop the helmet identifies the wearer as a member of the Raven Clan. The eye is inlaid with abalone. Presented by Mrs. Thea Heye. TLINGIT. Sitka, Alaska. 1880-1900. 7¼″ x 16″. 11/2947.

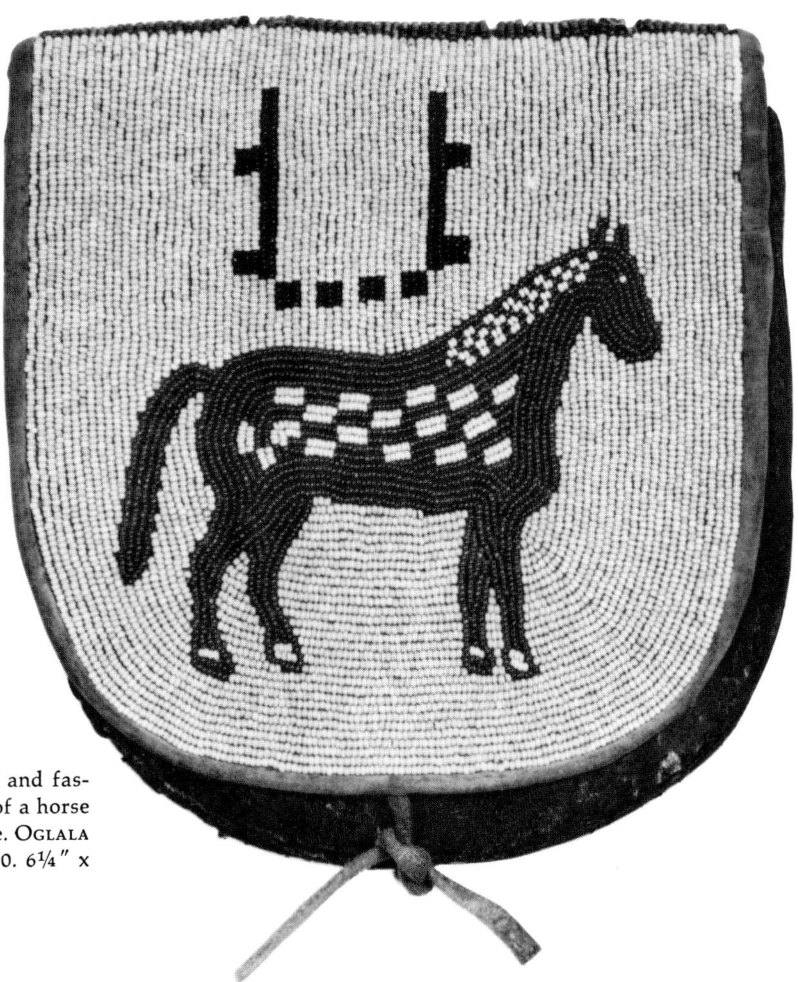

388. Belt Pouch
Small pouches of this type were decorated and fastened or looped to a belt. This has designs of a horse and two pipes. Presented by Mrs. Thea Heye. OGLALA SIOUX. Pine Ridge, South Dakota. 1880-1900. 6¼″ x 6¼″. 15/8451.

389. Beaded Moccasins
(See page 19)

390. Quill-decorated Moccasins
An earlier form of footwear decoration was the use of dyed porcupine quills, applied to the surface of buckskin moccasins. This pair was collected by Richard Joste. BRULÉ SIOUX. South Dakota. 1870-1880. L: 11″. 16/2512.

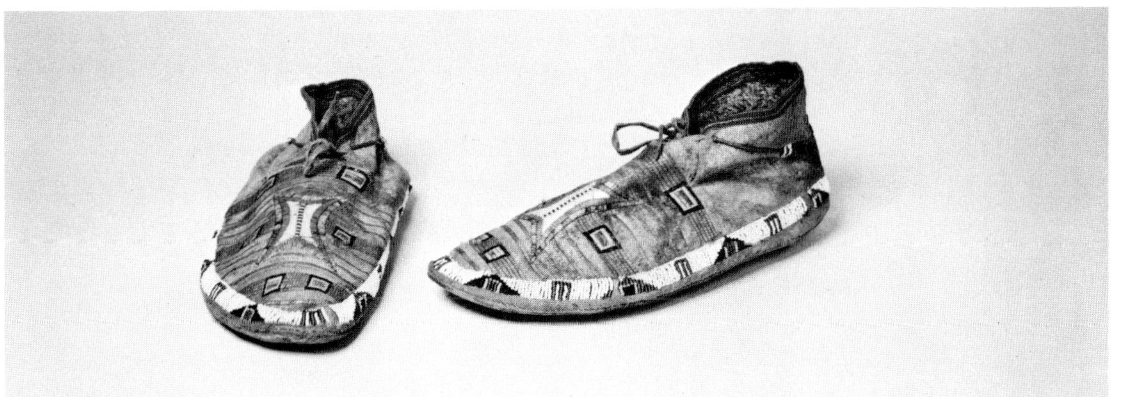

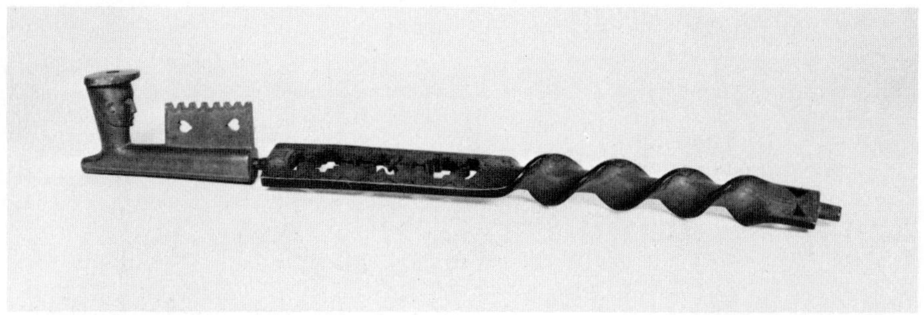

391. Pipe Stem and Bowl
Smoking was important to the Plains Indians, who used tobacco—or a mixture of vegetal materials commonly called *kinnikinnik*—primarily for ceremonial purposes. Social usage was known, of course, but this was secondary to the religious needs. This wooden stem and carved catlinite bowl were typical of the mid-Century style. TETON SIOUX. South Dakota. 1850-1860. 4¼" x 33½". 23/4100.

392. Buckskin Pipe Bag
(See color insert facing page 240)

393. Horn Ladle
Mountain sheep horn was used for many objects, most particularly spoons and ladles. This example was collected by Nate Salsbury. Presented by Mrs. Nate Salsbury. SIOUX. South Dakota. 1880-1900. 5½" x 17". 10/8342.

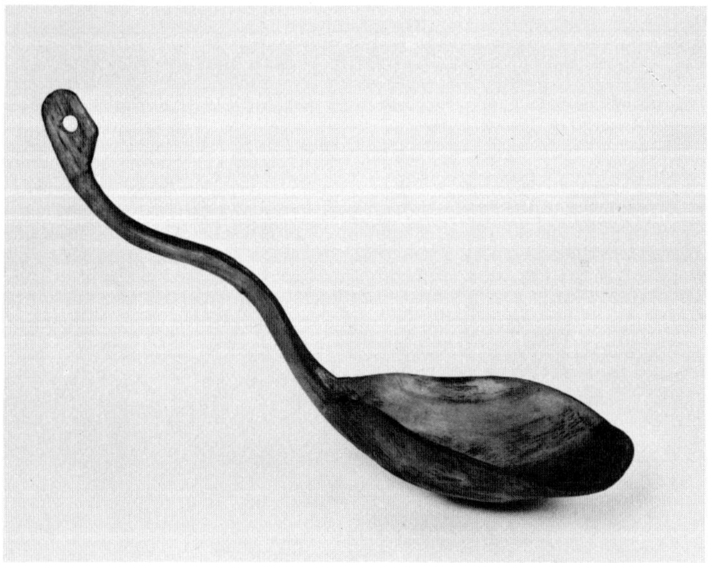

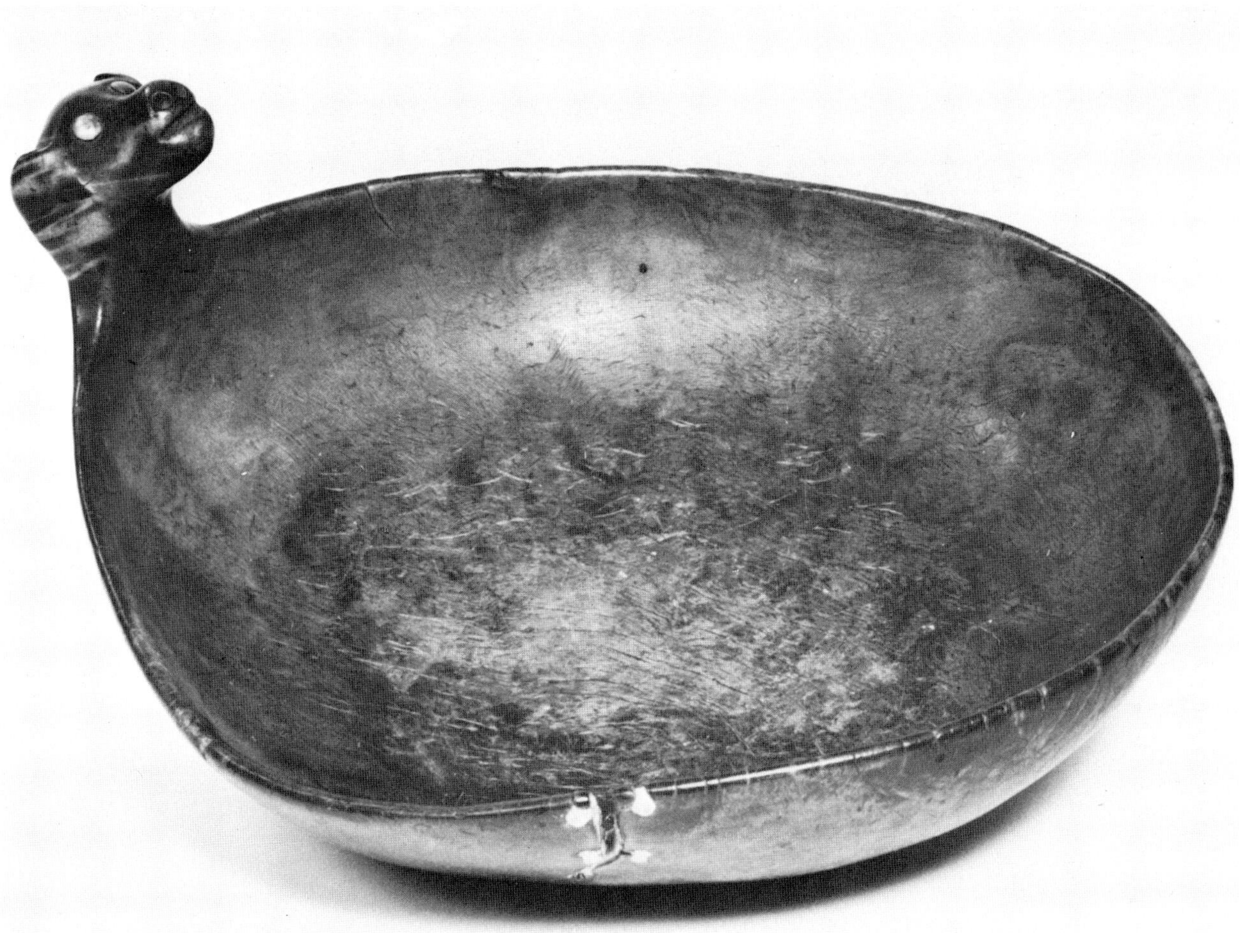

394. **Carved Medicine Bowl**

The Midéwewin Ceremony was known to the Eastern Plains people, who had their own paraphernalia, including such elaborate bowls as this. This example has a bear's head carved on the rim. Collected by L. Palm. Sisseton Sioux. Minnesota. 1850-1870. 7" x 13". 3/6828.

395. **Wooden War Club**

A weapon common to the Plains and Woodlands people is the gunstock club, named for its resemblance to the European arm. This had a trade spearpoint and brass tacks imbedded into the wood for decoration. Collected by H. W. Palm. Sisseton Sioux. Browns Valley, Minnesota. 1875-1890. 7" x 30¼". 9/7364.

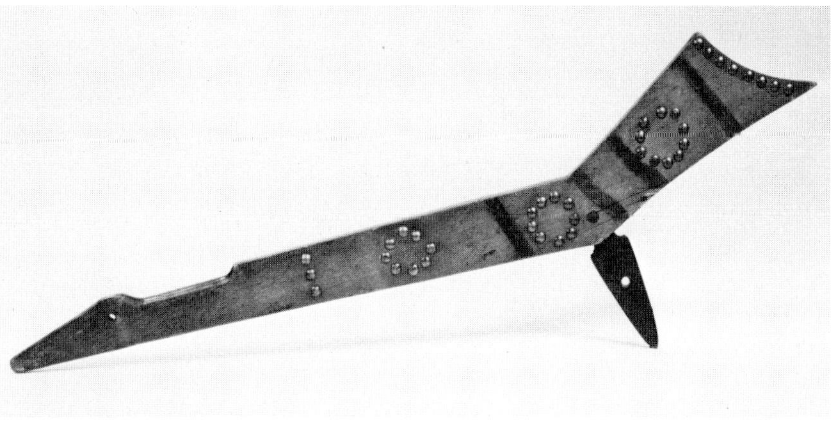

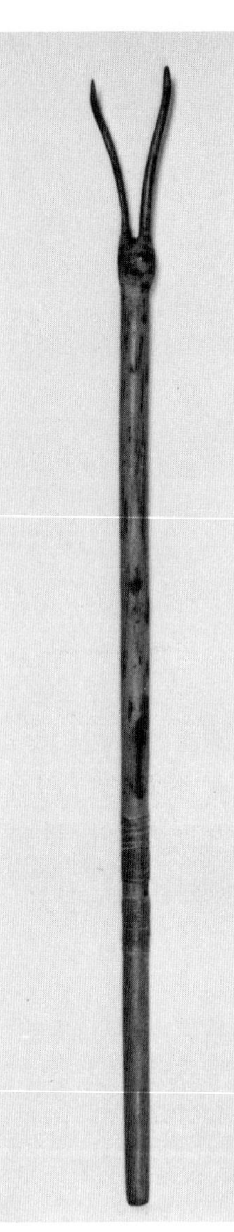

396. Courting Flute
An instrument of this type was used by a young man to woo his lady love. The decoration is a carved representation of a bird, painted yellow and red. Collected by Frances Densmore. TETON SIOUX. Standing Rock, South Dakota. 1900. L: 25". 6/7944.

397. Wooden Song Stick
The use of mnemonic devices was one way in which many Indian groups overcame the lack of writing. This song stick was used by the song leader to remind him of the phrase sequences as he led the group in a ceremony. The incised designs are not "readable" by everyone; it requires training to know how to employ such a device. They are therefore not true writing, but serve primarily as memory aids. Collected by L. Palm. SISSETON SIOUX. Minnesota. 1850-1875. 2" x 13". 4/418.

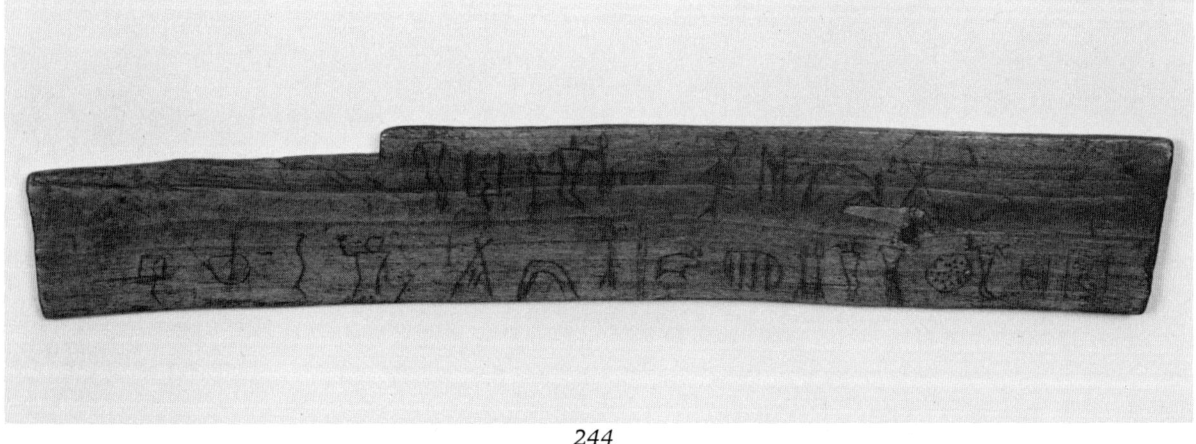

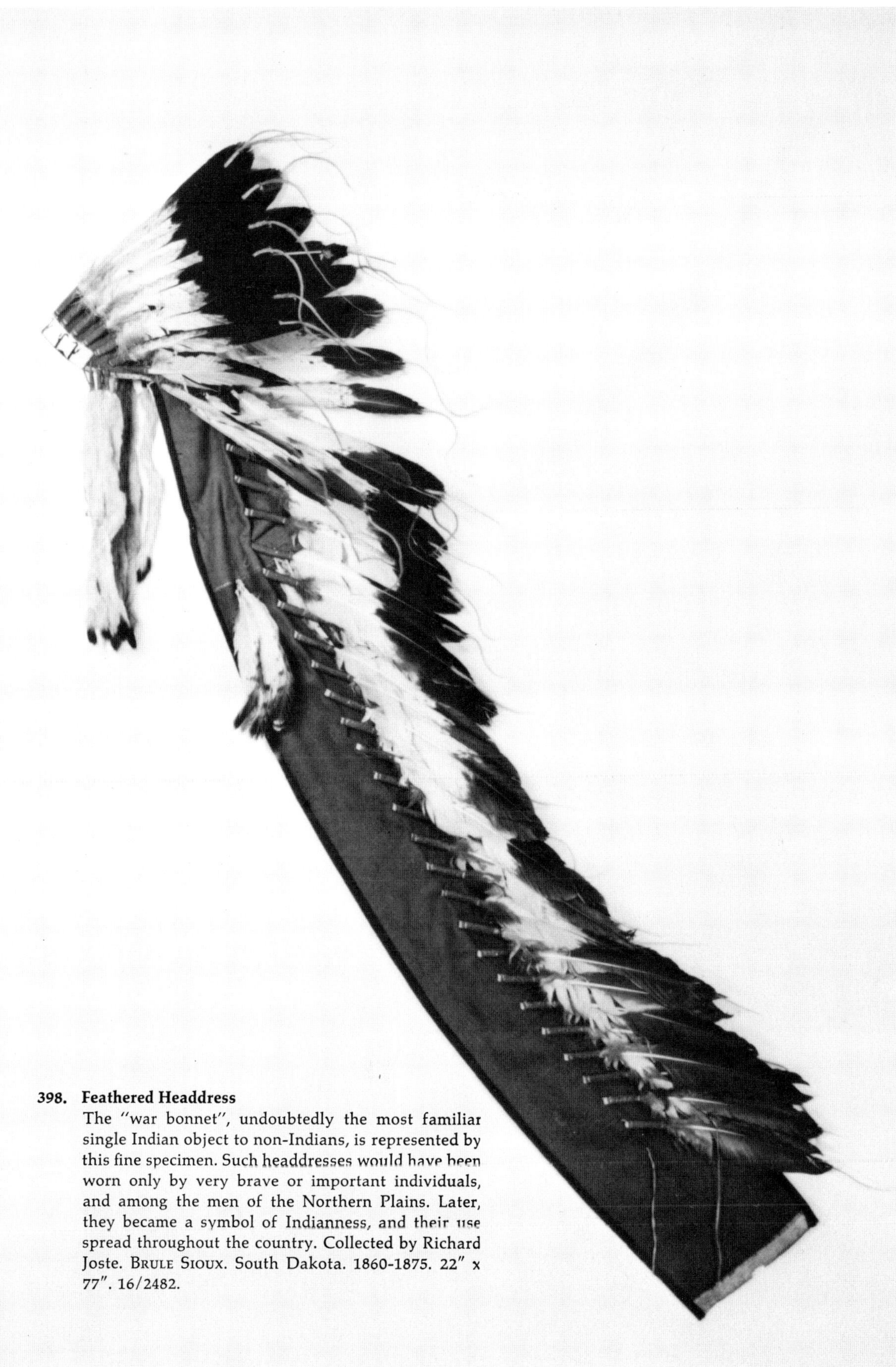

398. Feathered Headdress
The "war bonnet", undoubtedly the most familiar single Indian object to non-Indians, is represented by this fine specimen. Such headdresses would have been worn only by very brave or important individuals, and among the men of the Northern Plains. Later, they became a symbol of Indianness, and their use spread throughout the country. Collected by Richard Joste. BRULE SIOUX. South Dakota. 1860-1875. 22" x 77". 16/2482.

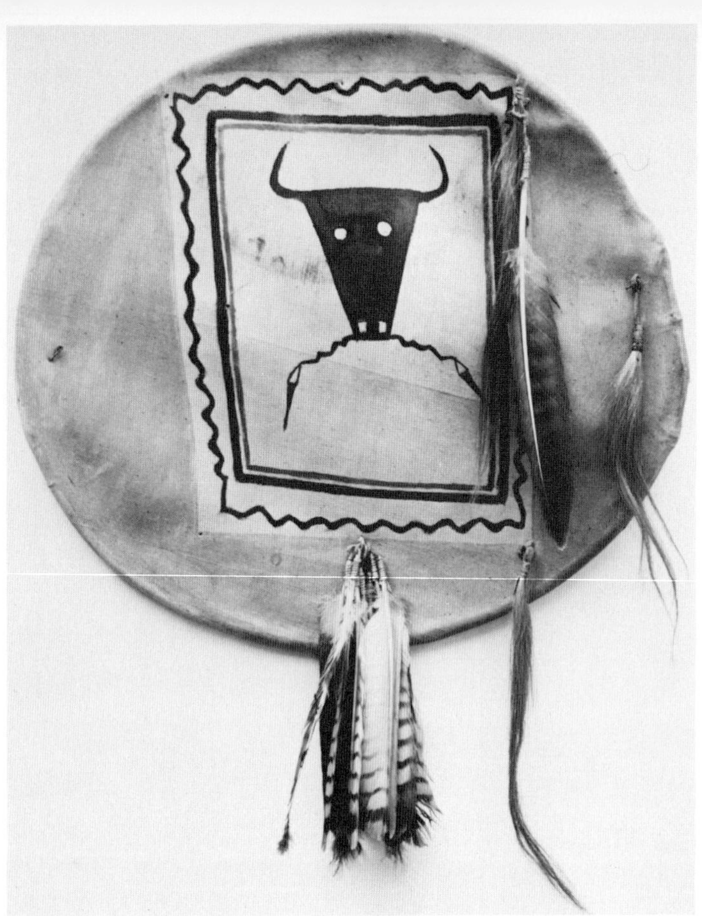

399. Ghost Dance Shield

During the height of the Ghost Dance, such objects were made of muslin, with symbolic designs painted upon them. These were believed to have the power to deflect bullets. This portrays a buffalo head, with medicine feathers suspended from the surface. Collected by Frances Densmore. TETON SIOUX. Standing Rock, South Dakota. 1890. D: 19". 6/7911.

400. "Sunburst" Hide

Geometrical designs were painted by the women, and used by them as robes, overcoverings, or blankets. This is a classic example of the decoration called "sunburst", or the "feathered circle". SIOUX. South Dakota. 1860-1880. 70" x 106". 15/2832.

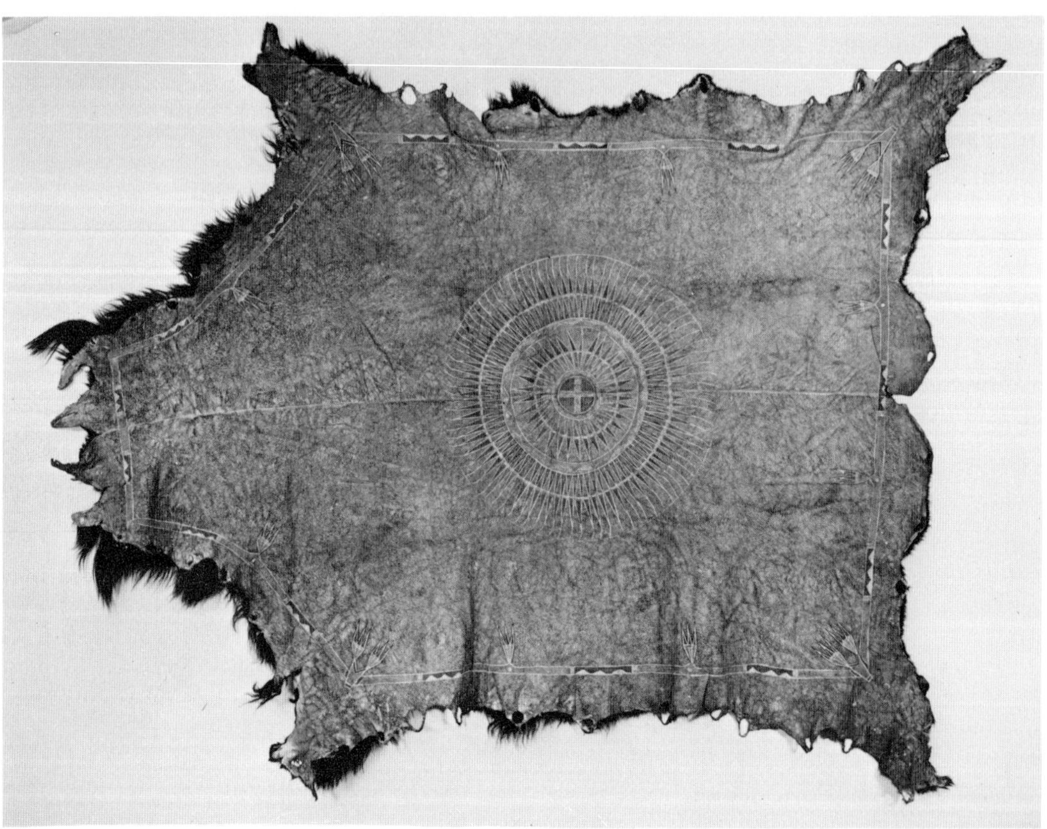

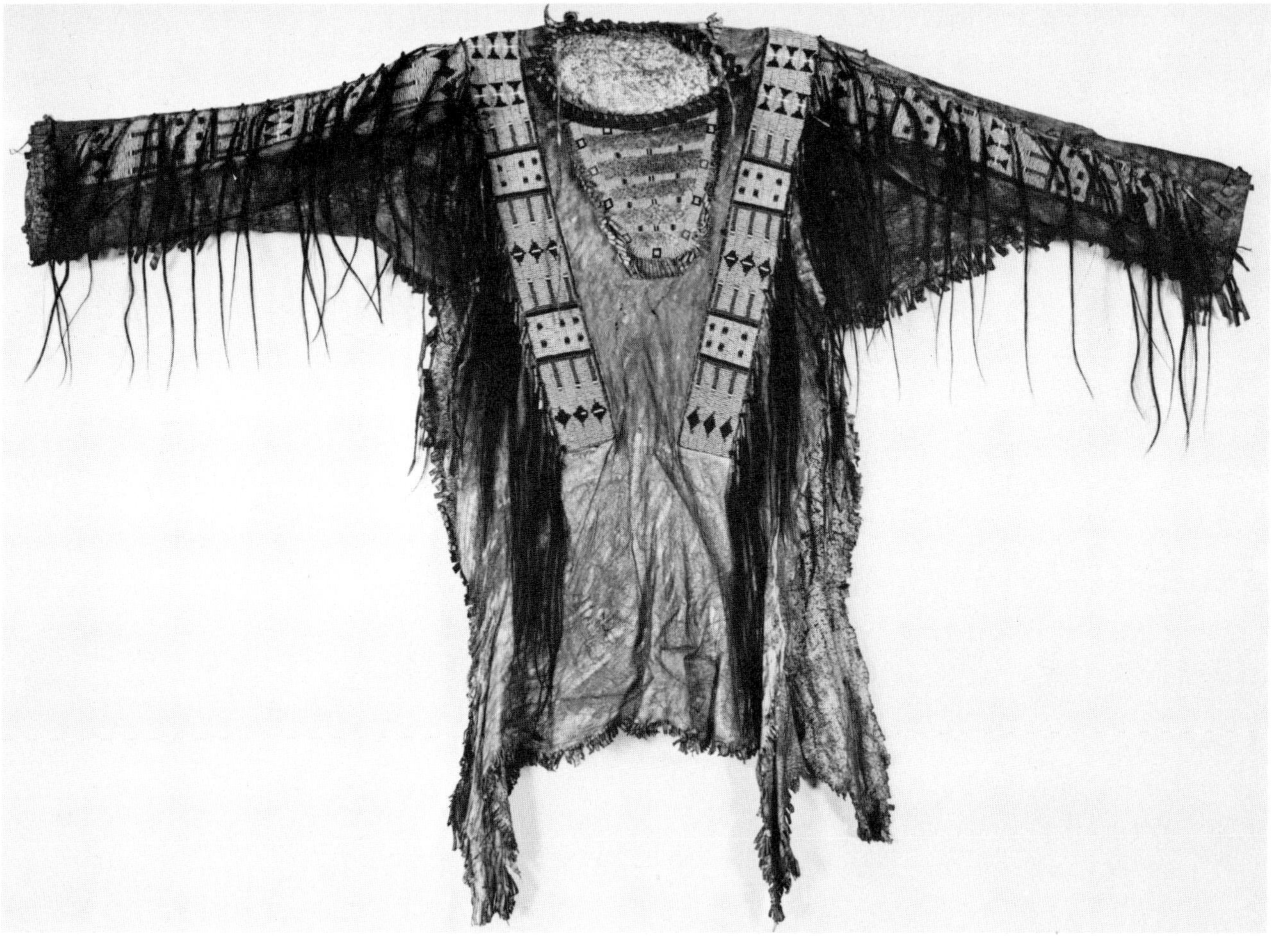

401. Painted War Shirt
A fine buckskin shirt, painted with blue pigment, and decorated with brilliant beadwork designs, this has the so-called "scalp lock" hair fringing common to Northern Plains garments worn by men. TETON SIOUX. South Dakota. 1860-1880. W: 57". 10/7455.

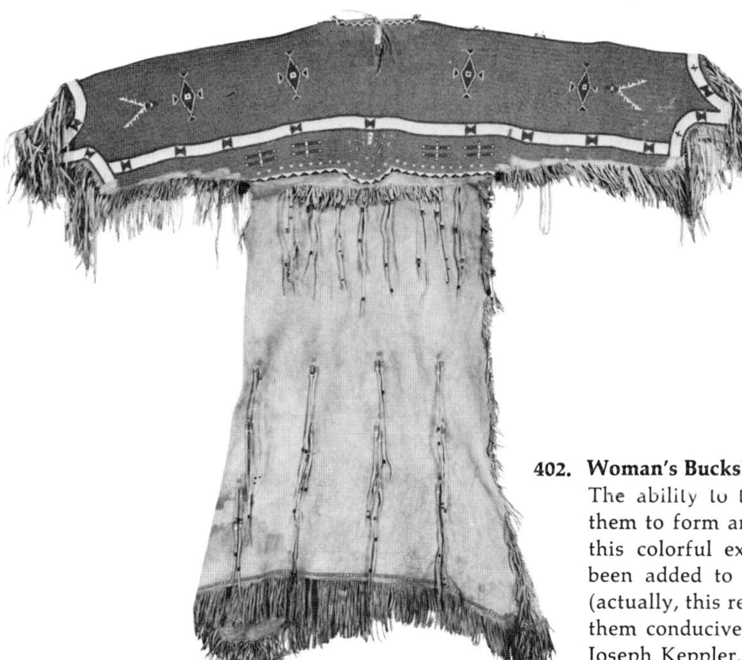

402. Woman's Buckskin Dress
The ability to take two large deer hides and tailor them to form an attractive dress is demonstrated by this colorful example. A heavily beaded yoke has been added to the skirt. The weight of the beads (actually, this represents just that much glass) makes them conducive to an upright posture. Collected by Joseph Keppler. MANDAN. North Dakota. 1875-1890. 40" x 60". 19/4964.

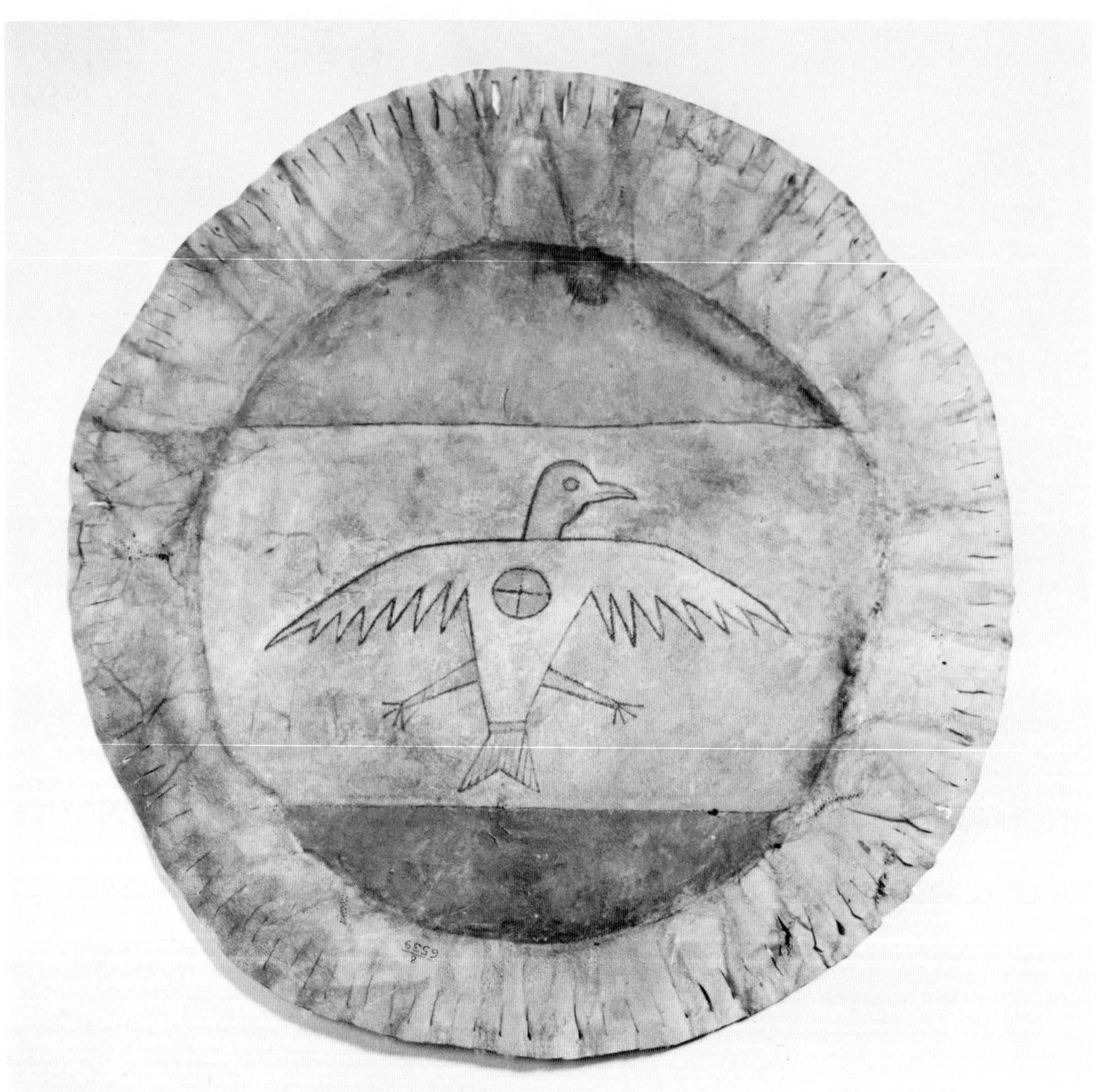

403. Buffalo Hide Shield

The hump of the buffalo was used to make the great circular shields which were effective protection during the early days of Plains warfare. It was only with the introduction of the Winchester that bullets could penetrate the tough hide. These were often decorated with colorful painted designs and sacred medicine objects. Collected by Henry G. Bayer. SIOUX. South Dakota. 1870-1880. D: 20″. 8/6539.

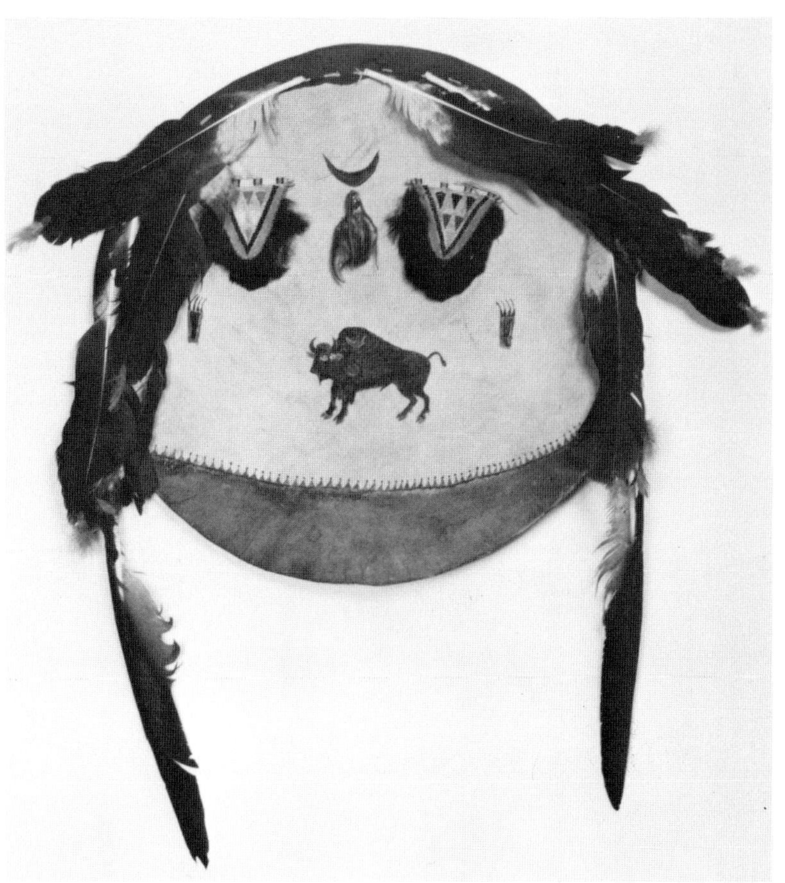

404. Dance Shield
Lighter weight shields were usually made for use in ceremonies. This example, made of deer hide, has medicine objects to make the shield as effective as the heavier buffalo hide disks. The bear claws and ears indicate the bravery of the owner. Collected by William Wildschut. CHEYENNE. Montana. 1880-1900. D: 20". 14/2108.

405. Painted Buffalo Hide
Another traditional design frequently painted on these hides is the "box and border", also painted by the women. This design is said to represent the internal viscera of the buffalo in an abstract pattern. Presented by John Jay White. CHEYENNE. Lamedeer, Montana. 1875-1880. 55" x 77". 10/4314.

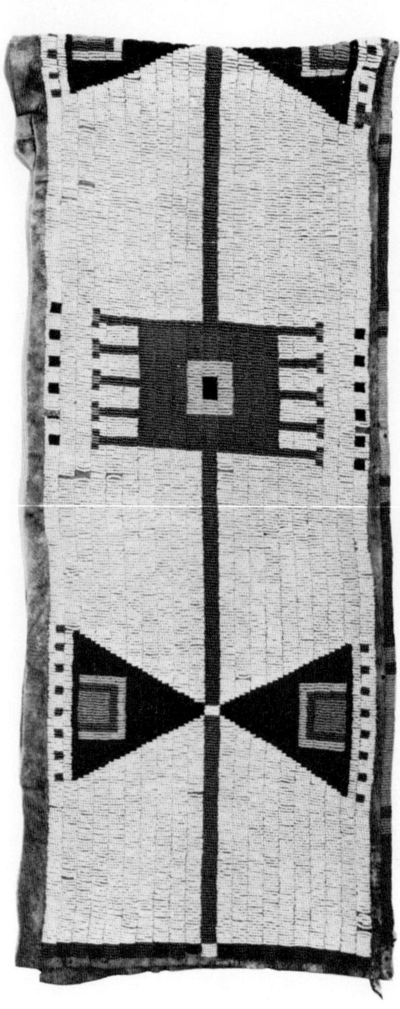

406. Beaded Panel
A wrapping for a baby carrier, prior to being attached to the frame, this was decorated with beaded designs similar to **408.** NORTHERN CHEYENNE. Montana. 1880-1900. 11″ x 27″. 10/5096.

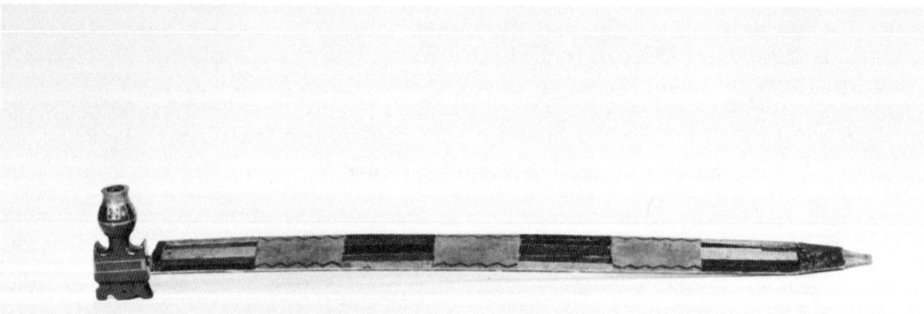

407. Pipe Stem and Inlaid Bowl
Another type of bowl is this variety, familiarly called the Micmac Bowl, although it occurs throughout the lower Canada region. This bowl of catlinite is inlaid with lead and black stone. BLACKFOOT. Alberta, Canada. 1875-1880. L: 30½″. 12/6111.

408. Beaded Baby Carrier
Babies were protected by devices of this nature, which provided comfort, as well as allowing the mother to carry the baby safely on horseback, or to leave the infant for a short time. The wooden slats kept the child's head from being injured. Presented by Foster Hannaford. SIOUX, South Dakota. 1880-1890. 13″ x 46″. 20/2029. →

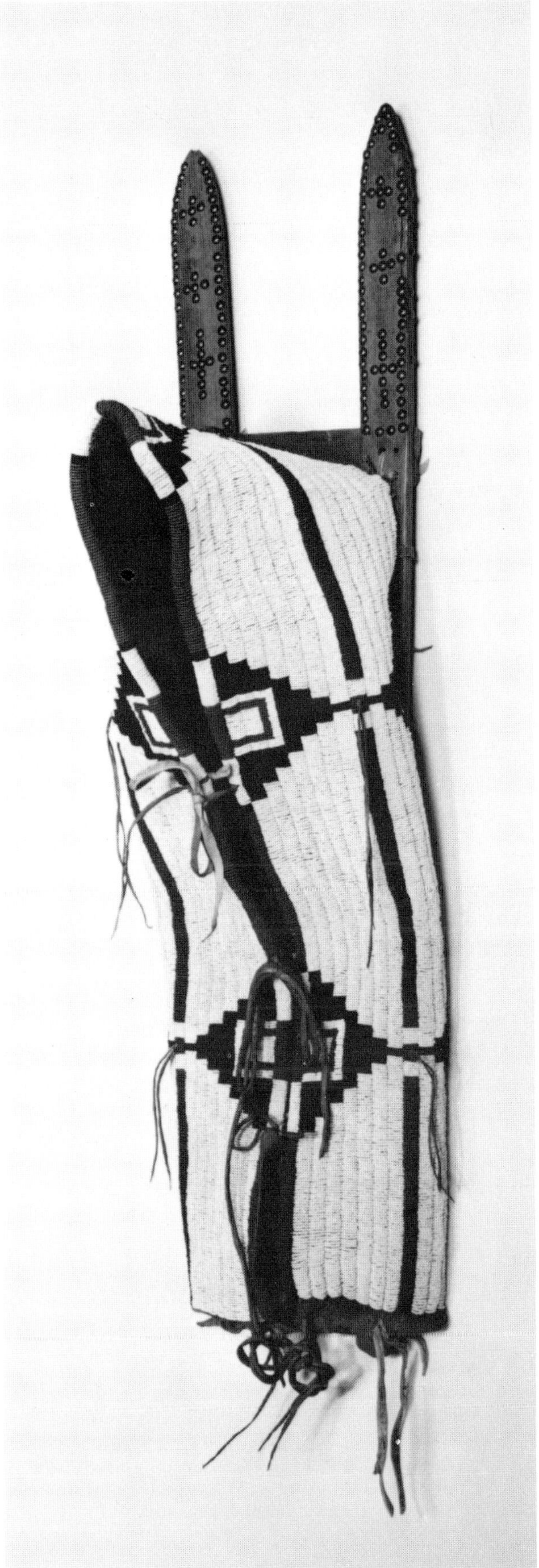

409. Beaded Pipe Bag

The scalloped top of this pouch identifies it as coming from a more northerly region, either the Plateau or lower Canada section. BANNOCK. Ft. Hall, Idaho. 1870-1880. 6½" x 21". 16/4518.

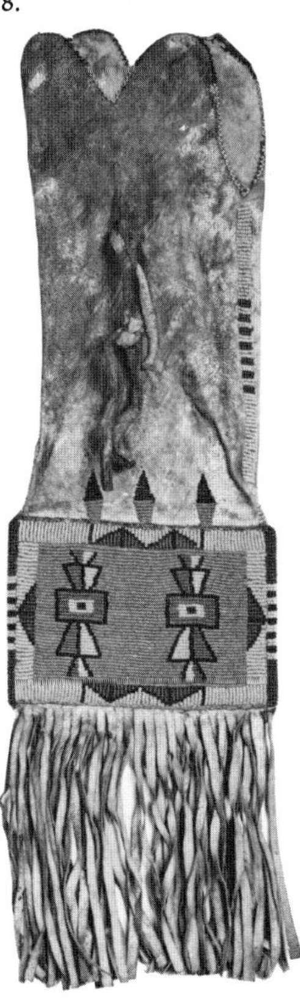

410. Painted Buffalo Hide
(See color insert facing page 120)

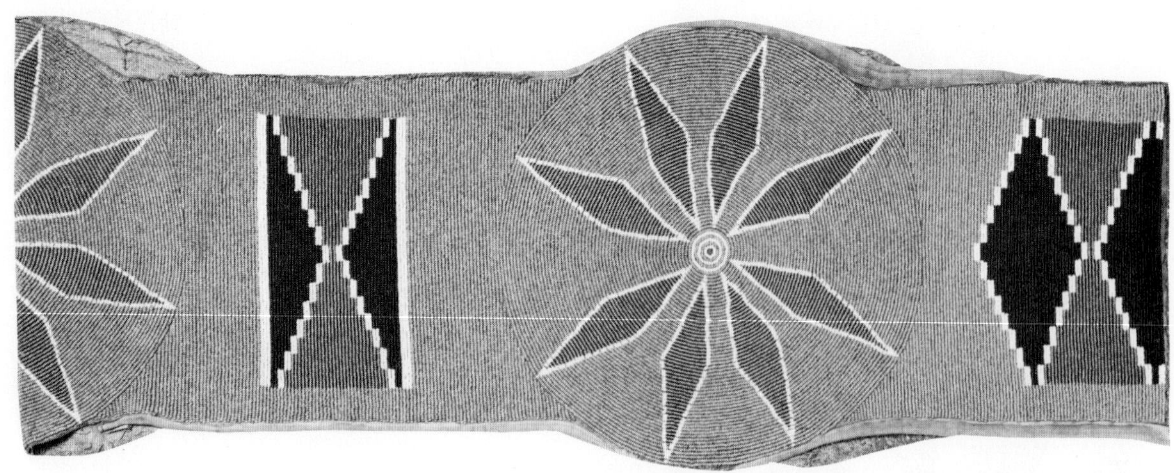

411. Blanket Strip
Trade cloth, and elk or buffalo hides were made into blankets for protection against the cold winters. They were often decorated with various ornaments. This wide beadwork strip was sewn to the blanket, acting as a "belt" as well as a decorative feature. Collected by Joseph Keppler. PAWNEE. Nebraska. 1875-1880. 10″ x 27″. 2/9644.

412. Parflèche
Although bearing the French name "for arrows", these are commonly used to carry foodstuffs. The envelope form allows the folded sheet of rawhide to expand as it is filled; there are regularly decorated with geometrically painted designs. Collected by M. R. Harrington. PONCA. Oklahoma. 1900-1910. 13″ x 28″. 3/6732.

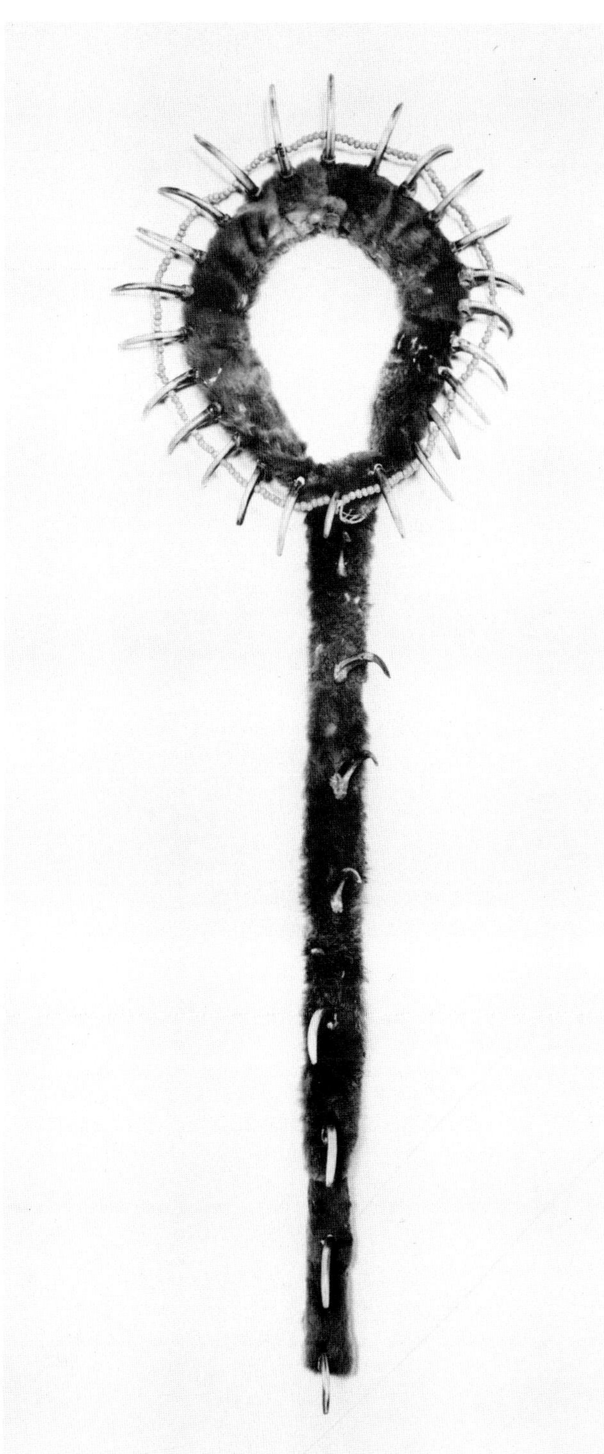

413. Bear Claw Necklace
A brave warrior often proved his stature by obtaining the claws of a grizzly bear, and making them into a status necklace. These not only had considerable social significance, but were powerful medicine objects as well. Such a necklace with otter fur streamer, would have been the pride of any man, and held an extraordinary value. Collected by T. R. Roddy. OSAGE. Oklahoma. 1875-1880. 17″ x 53″. 3/6324.

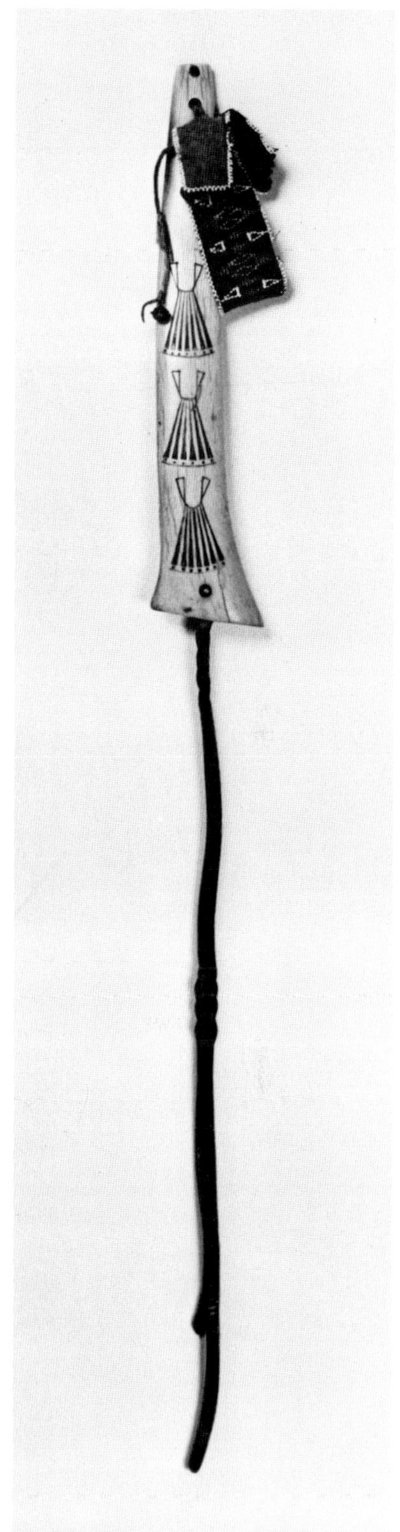

414. Elk Antler Quirt
Antler and bone was frequently used for quirts; this elaborately decorated masterpiece was incised, and had color rubbed into the lines. Collected by M. R. Harrington. SAUK-FOX. Oklahoma. 1910-1915. 2″ x 36″. 2/7442.

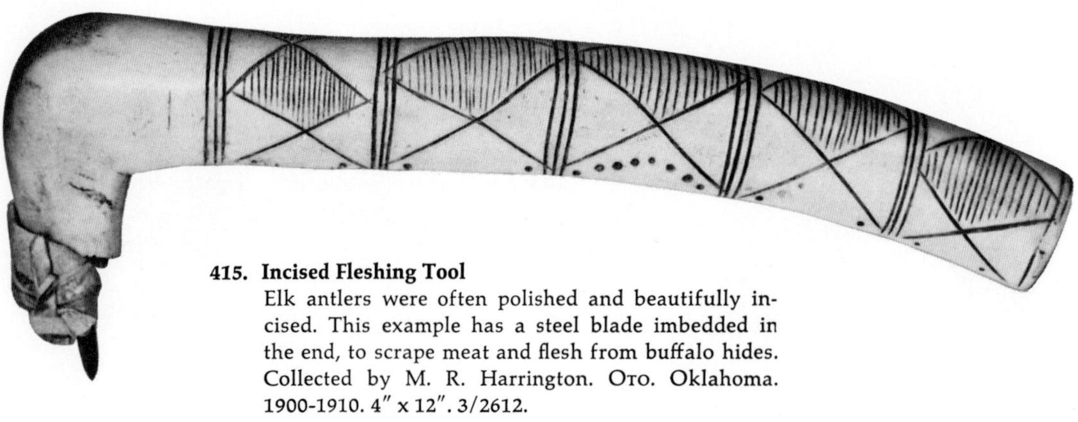

415. Incised Fleshing Tool
Elk antlers were often polished and beautifully incised. This example has a steel blade imbedded in the end, to scrape meat and flesh from buffalo hides. Collected by M. R. Harrington. Oto. Oklahoma. 1900-1910. 4″ x 12″. 3/2612.

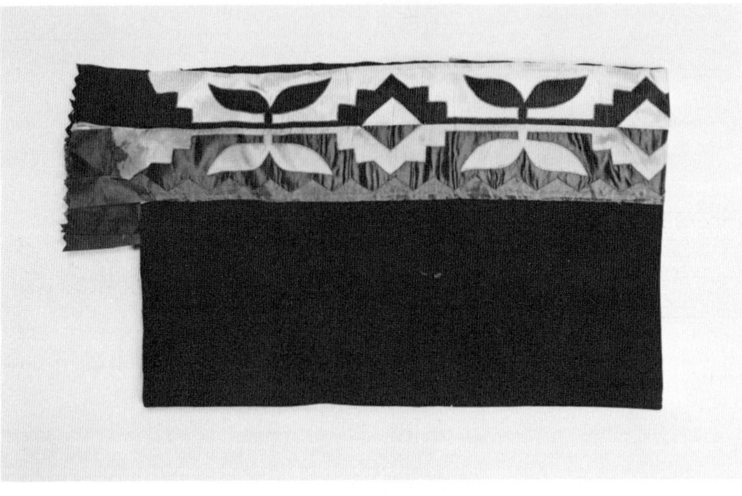

416. Trade Cloth Skirt
The use of scraps of silk became an art among the Midwestern tribes. This woman's skirt of blue trade cloth has been beautifully decorated with silk ribbon appliqué work. Collected by M. R. Harrington. Oto. Black Bear Creek, Oklahoma. 1900-1910. 18″ x 31″. 12/829.

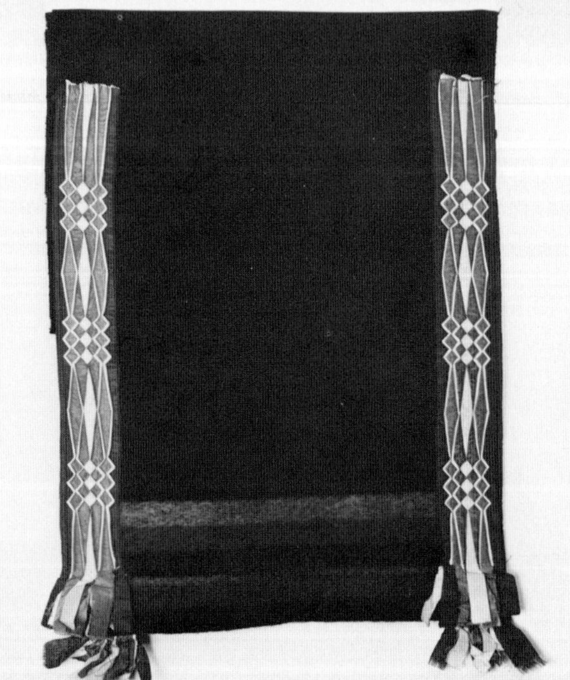

417. Breech Cloth
Another example of the breech cloth, this has been decorated with silk ribbon work in a geometric pattern. Osage. Oklahoma. 1890-1910. 14½″ x 21″. 21/2595.

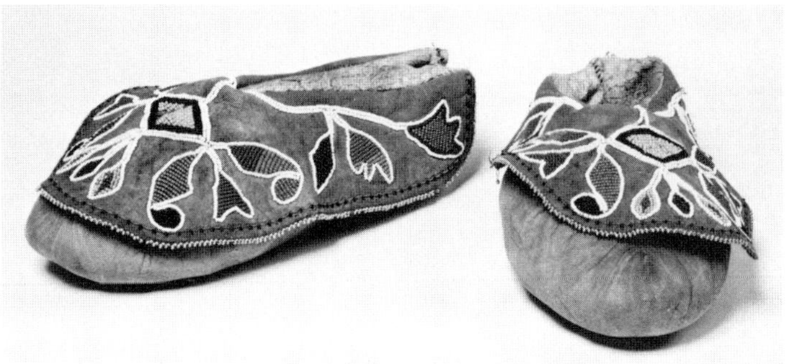

418. Bead Decorated Moccasins
The style of moccasins made by the Midwestern people is quite different from most of the Plains styles. This has the puckered toe, and wide flaps, which are typical of the area. The design is the familiar floral pattern. Collected by Milford G. Chandler. POTAWATOMI. Wisconsin. 1880-1900. 4½" x 10¾". 14/715.

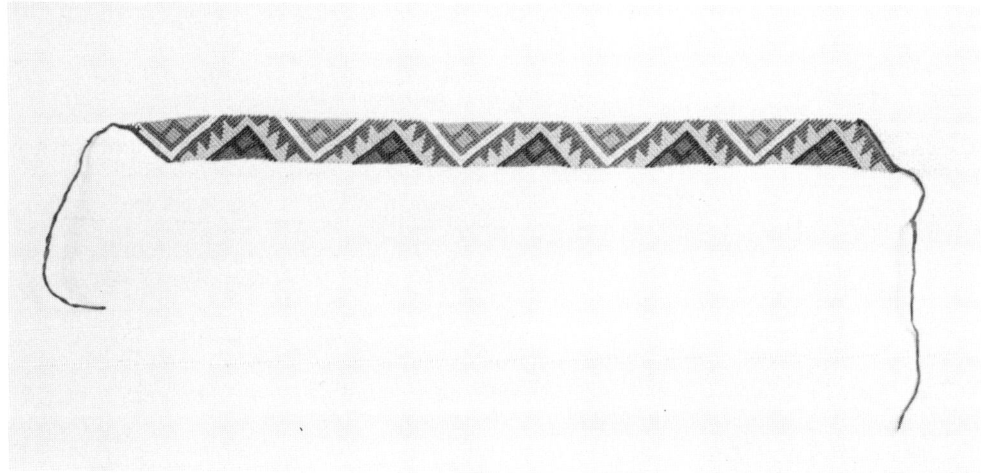

419. Woven Neck Band
Unique to the Midwest area are these neck bands, woven of beadwork on a bias, with a geometric design. Collected from Frank Michigan by David C. Vernon. POTAWATOMI. Wisconsin. 1910-1925. 1" x 18". 24/1771.

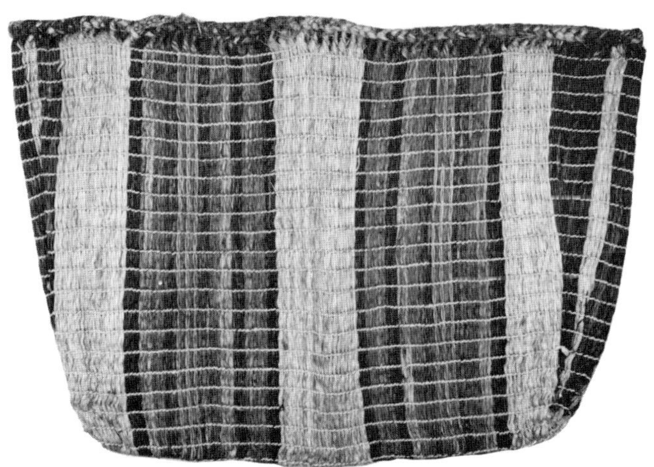

420. Food Container
The use of several fibers common in the area for weaving containers for storing foodstuffs was a necessary art. This woven bark fiber sack was used for shelled corn. Collected by M. R. Harrington. POTAWATOMI. Kansas. 1905-1910. 18½" x 27". 2/7534.

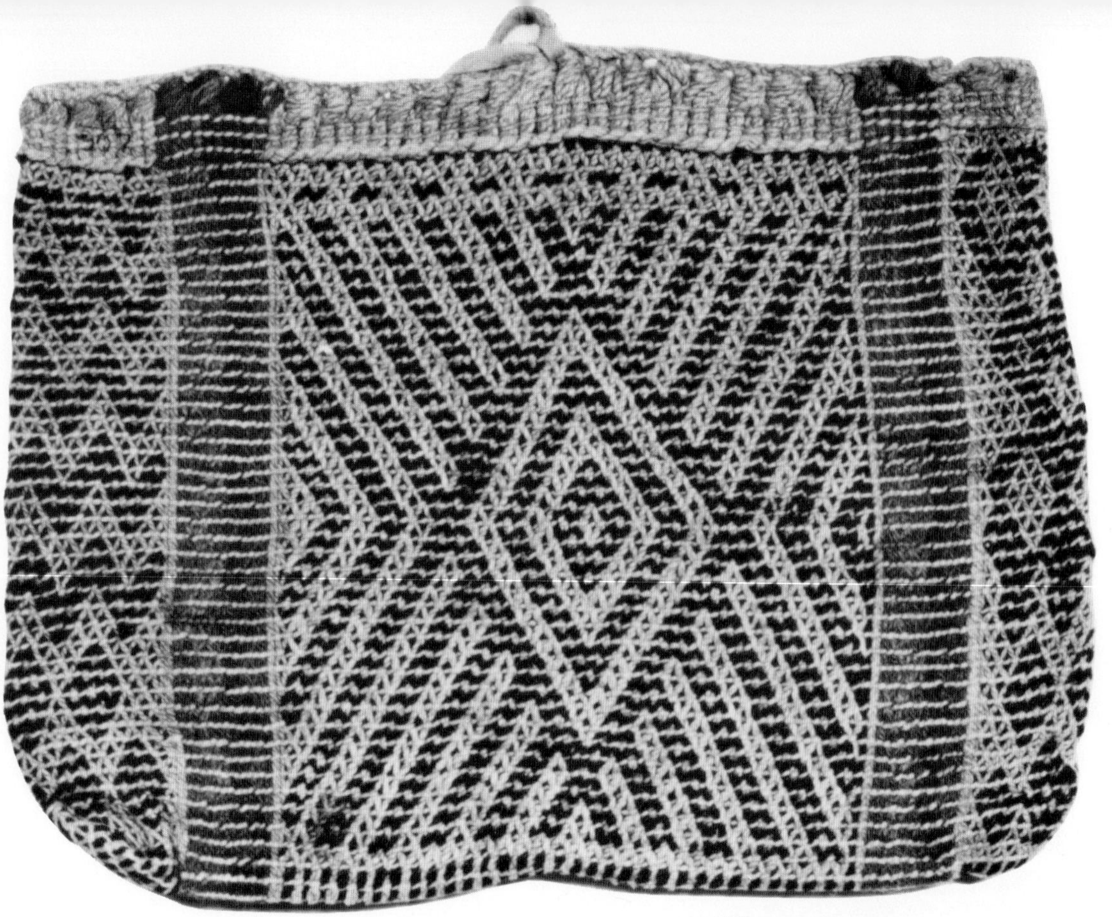

421. Woven Yarn Bag

These were woven on a suspension loom in many sizes and designs. The larger bags were used to store personal medicine bundles and possessions; the smaller ones were more commonly used for charms, fetishes and herbs. Collected by Milford G. Chandler. WINNEBAGO. Thurston, Nebraska. 6¼″ x 8¾″. 1890-1910. 14/907.

422. Otter Fur Turban

One of the more unusual forms of headwear of the American Indian was the turban or wrap-around hat. This is made of otter fur decorated with beadwork, and has an eagle claw fetish attached. Collected by David C. Vernon. WINNEBAGO. Thurston, Nebraska. 1890-1900. 5½″ x 9″. 24/2153.

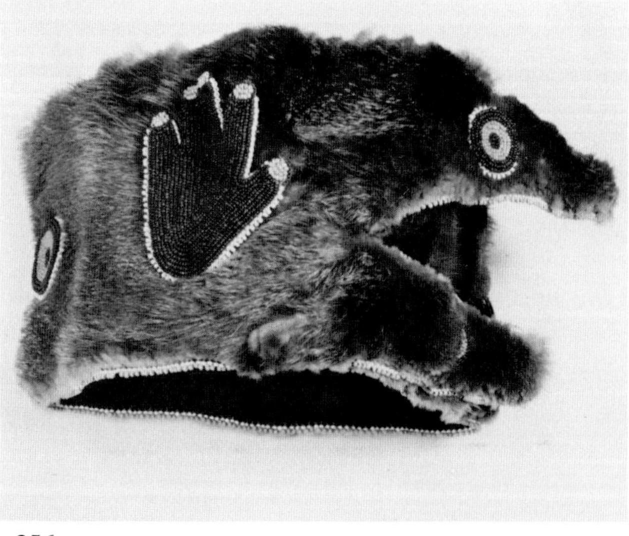

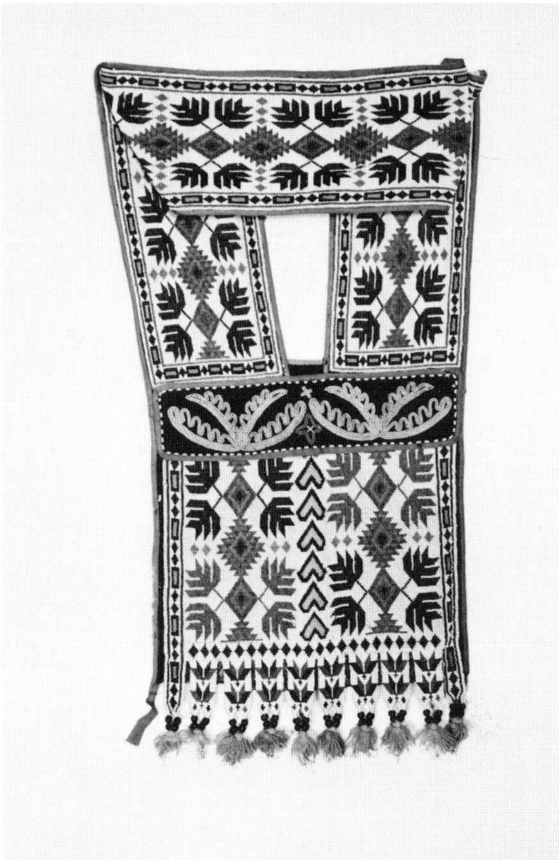

423. Bandolier Bag

The use of these extra large heavily beaded carrying pouches was restricted to the area around the Great Lakes. They became so ornate that in time they lost the function of a container, and simply became a decorative part of the man's costume. Presented by Harry E. Tebrock. MENOMINI. Wisconsin. 1880-1900. 15½" x 27½". 24/7259.

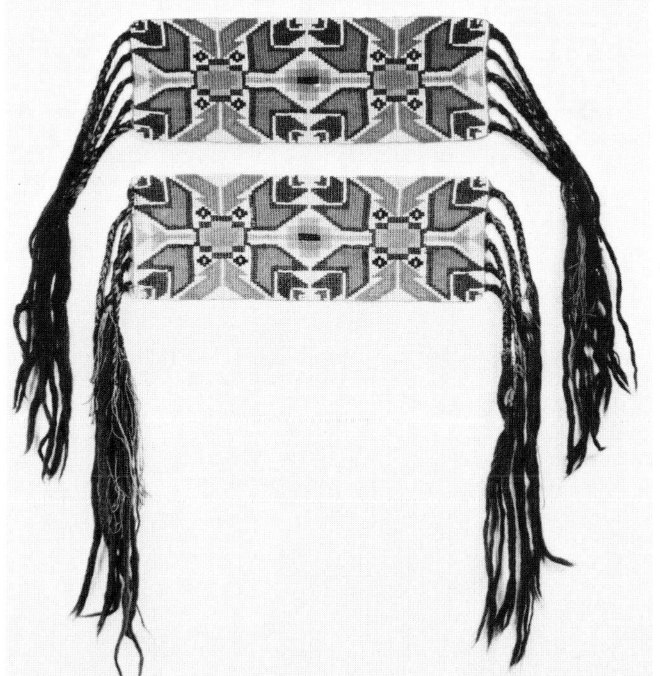

424. Beaded Garters

The well-dressed person had as one of the parts of his costume beaded garters of this type. The geometric design, woven in brilliant colors, is not always a sure method of identification; designs were often traded back and forth. MENOMINI. Wisconsin. 1900-1910. 3½" x 10". 21/3398.

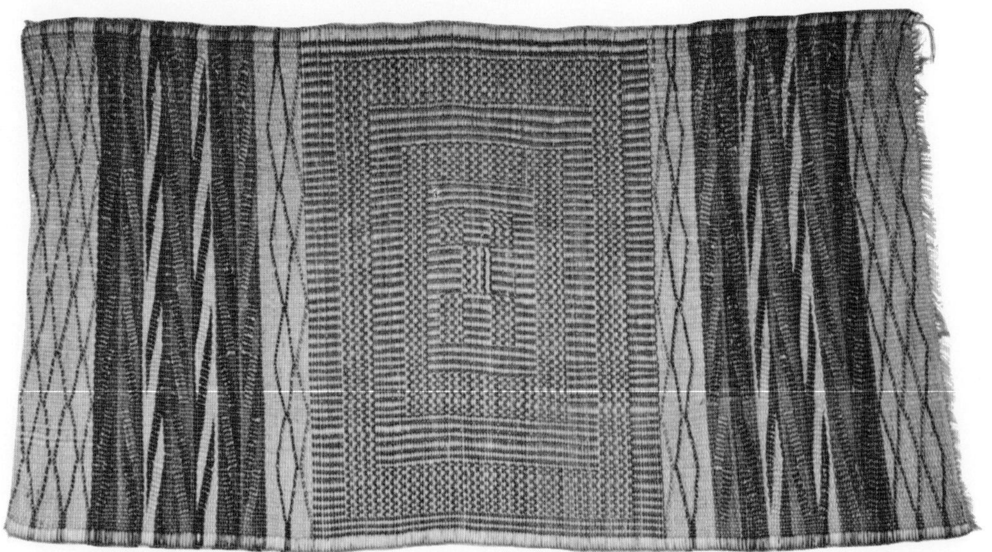

425. Sleeping Mat
Woven of rush, these were in almost every home. Some were plain, while others were dyed in various colors and woven to provide additional beauty. MENOMINI. Wisconsin. 1900-1910. 37″ x 66″. 14/9649.

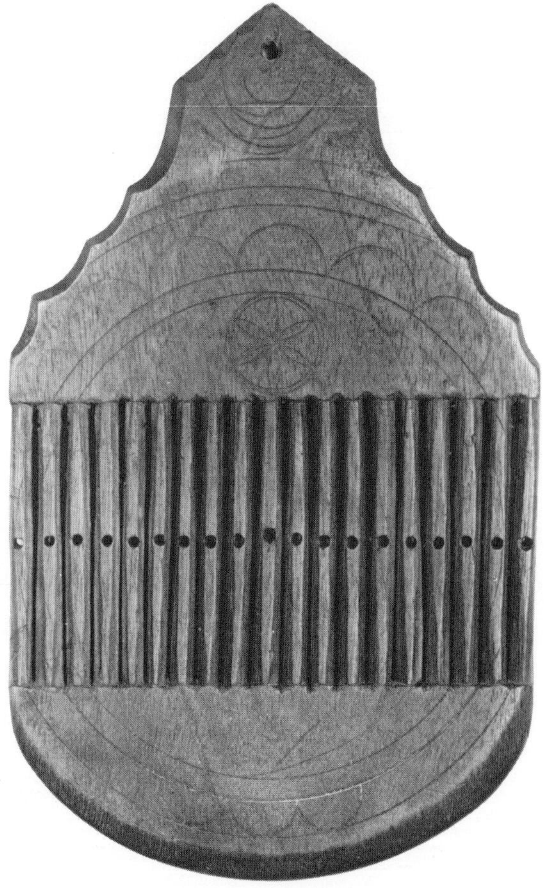

426. Beadwork Heddle
Beadwork strips, such as **419** and **424**, were woven on wooden heddles; these were often so carefully carved and decorated that they became artworks in themselves. Collected by M. R. Harrington. KICKAPOO. Oklahoma. 5″ x 8¼″. 1880-1890. 2/5031.

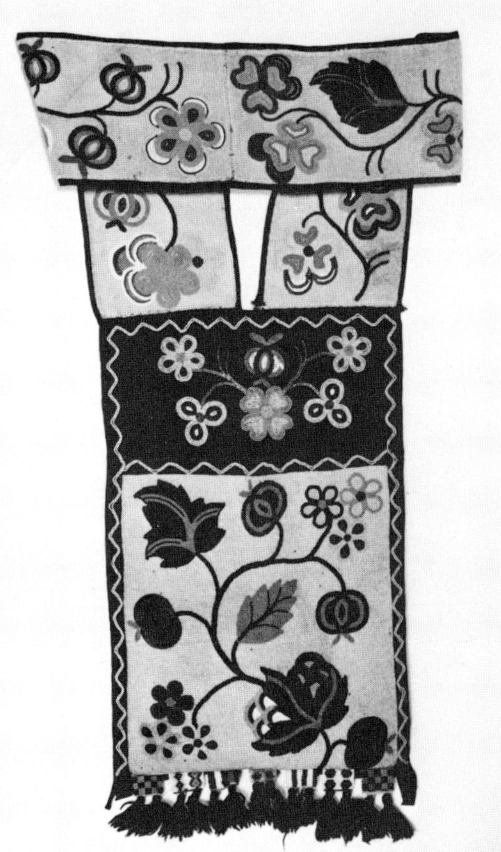

427. Beaded Bandolier Bag

This example no longer retains the pocket for carrying objects; it is simply a decorative panel, an adjunct to the man's dress-up costume. Collected by George H. Bingenheimer. CHIPPEWA. Saginaw, Michigan. 1890-1900. 19″ x 33½″. 12/2182.

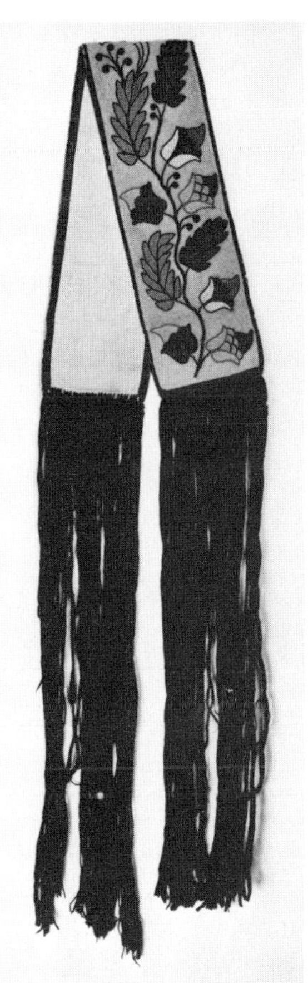

428. Beaded Sash

A beautifully worked sash with graceful fringed ends, this provided a colorful decoration to a person's costume. Presented by Elizabeth P. Hatecke. CHIPPEWA. Michigan. 1915-1925. 11″ x 44″. 24/4255.

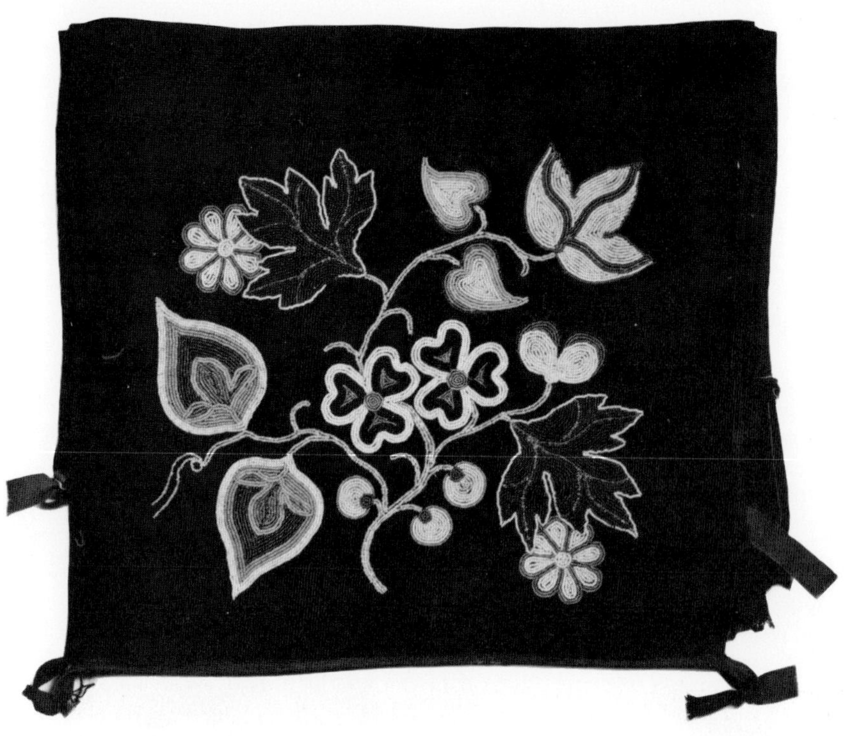

429. Breech Cloth
Part of the male costume was the breech cloth; this example is beaded in a polychrome floral pattern on velveteen. Presented by Frederick Schaefer in memory of his father, Rudolph J. Schaefer. CHIPPEWA. 1905-1910. 18″ x 21″. 23/2572.

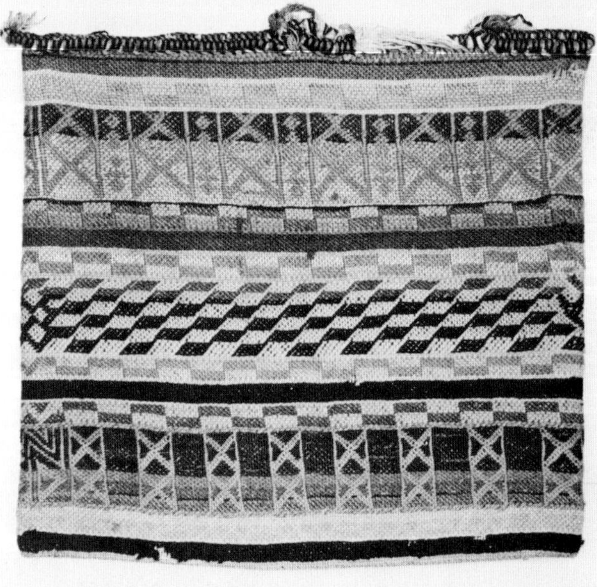

430. Yarn Bag
Large yarn bags were woven in geometric designs for storing or carrying personal possessions. CHIPPEWA. Rice Lake, Wisconsin. 1920-1930. 18¾″ x 20½″. 19/574.

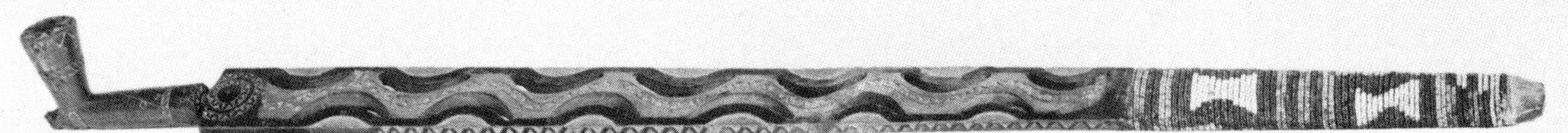

431. Quill Decorated Pipe
This magnificent pipe stem and carved catlinite bowl was collected and taken to England some time before 1845. OJIBWA. Ontario, Canada. 2¼″ x 33½″. 3/2850.

432. Bark-and-Quill Box
An oval birchbark box decorated with quill work and sweet grass, this is typical of the work of the northern Great Lakes people. Collected by Frederick Johnson. OJIBWA. Parry Island, Ontario, Canada. 1920-1930. 3″ x 6″ x 8″. 16/2568.

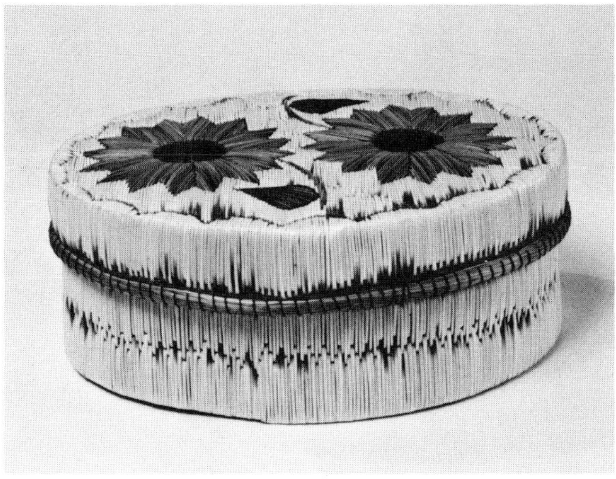

433. Wooden War Club
(See page 20)

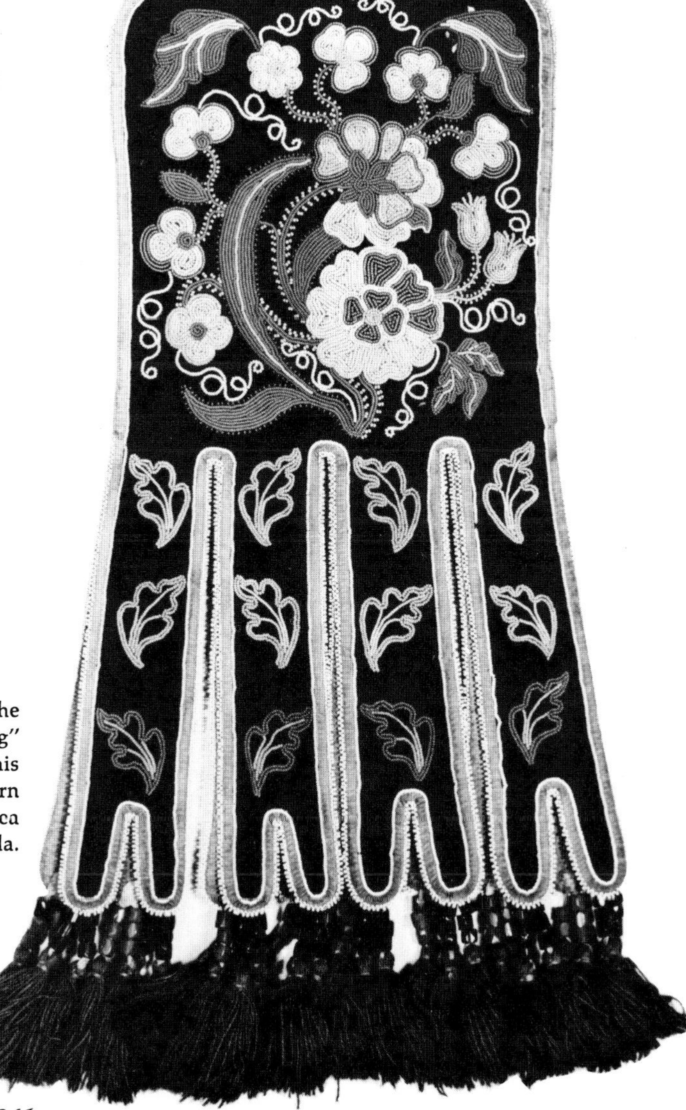

434. Beaded Firebag
Another of the great variety of pouches from the Midwest, this design, variously termed a "firebag" or an "octopus bag", because of the long tabs, this found over a wide area, as far west as southern Alaska. It apparently first developed in the Cree area of lower Ontario or Alberta. CREE. Alberta, Canada. 1880-1890. 9½″ x 20″. 19/6592..

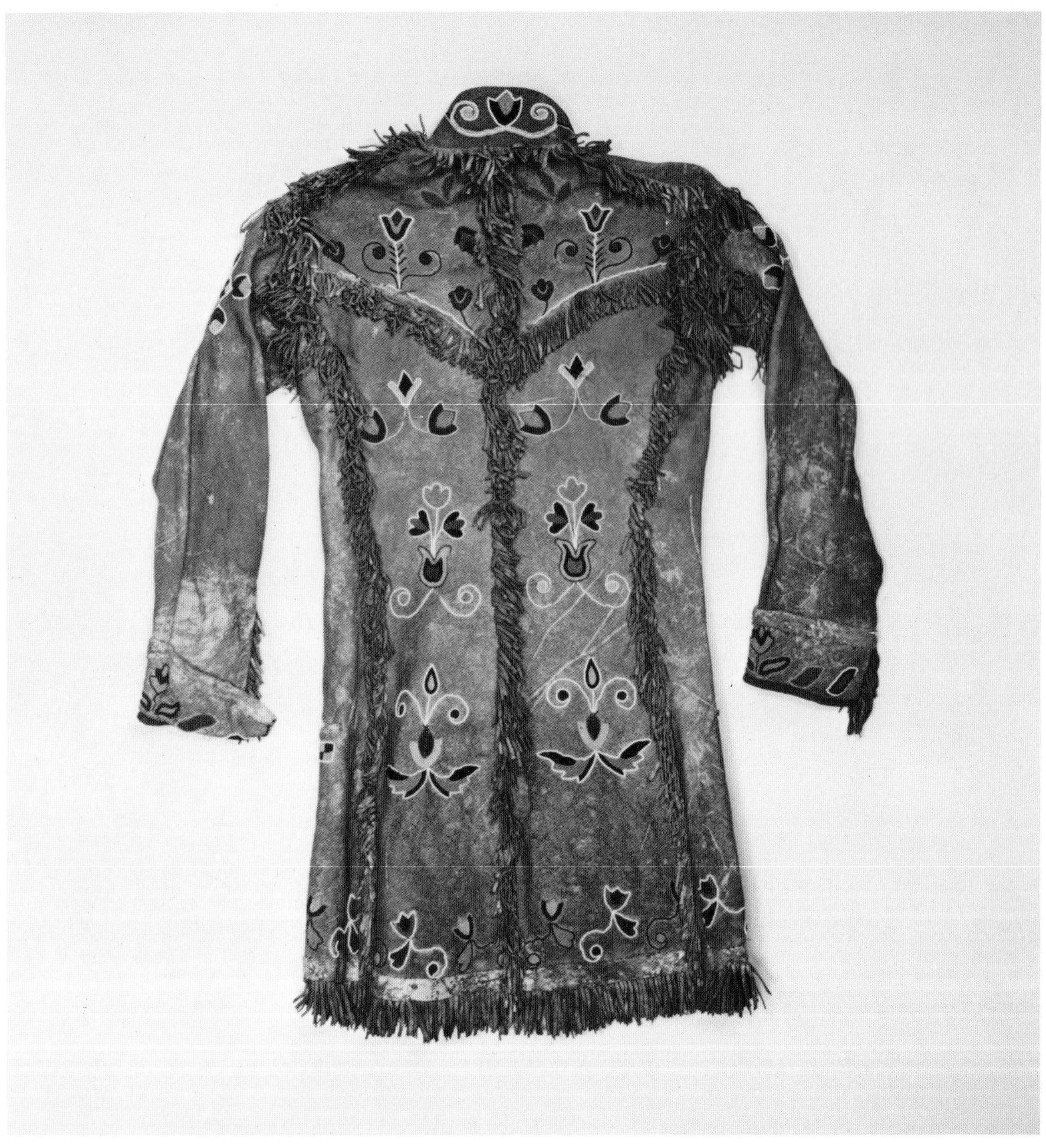

435. Tailored Buckskin Coat
Painted yellow with earth pigments, with a floral decoration, this garment reflects a considerable degree of White influence in the cut of the material, as well as the use of buttons as fasteners. Collected by William Randolph Hearst. Cree. Alberta, Canada. 1890-1910. 24" x 44". 20/2047.

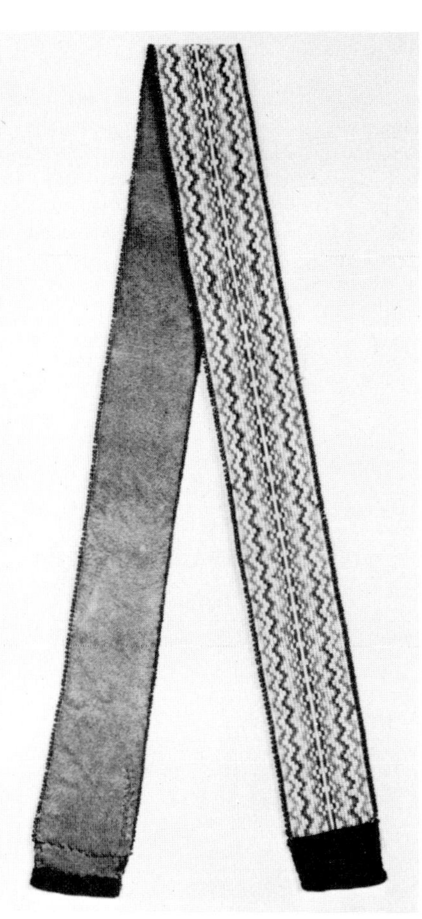

436. Woven Quill Belt
Very fine quills from bird feathers, were dyed and woven on a small loom to produce intricately-designed strips for costume ornamentation. This belt is an example of a craft found only in northwestern Canada. The technique is quite different from that of the Plains Indians, whose quill work was executed in an appliqué fashion. Collected by Donald Cadzow. CHIPEWYAN. Great Slave Lake, Canada. 1890-1900. 1½" x 14". 7/1075.

437. Birchbark Container
The *mokok* is a standard type of container found throughout the Woodlands area. These are made from elm or birch bark, and are often decorated by scraping away the surface, leaving the design in bold relief. Collected by Frederick Johnson. ALGONKIN. Golden Lake, Ontario, Canada. 1920-1930. 4½" x 6". 15/4438.

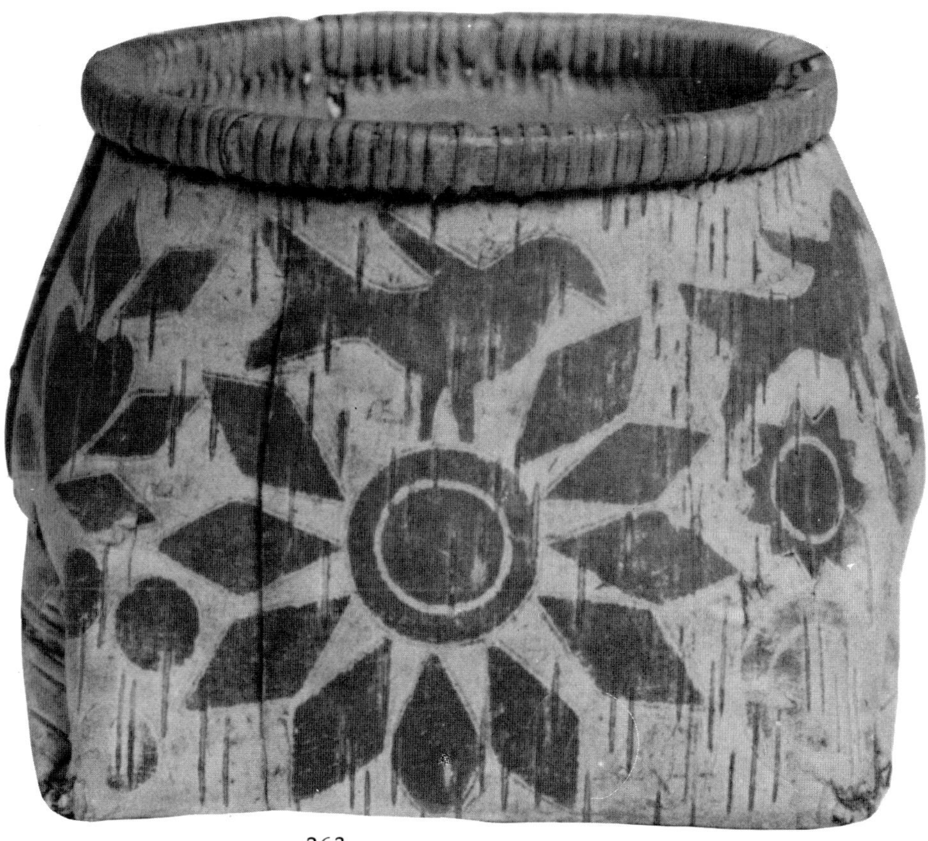

439. Finger-woven Sash

Variously termed an "Assumption Sash", or "Arrowhead Sash", depending upon the precise design, these were used as wrap-around belts into which small objects were thrust for carrying. Collected by M. R. Harrington. SHAWNEE. Oklahoma. 1850-1860. 6" x 51". 2/532.

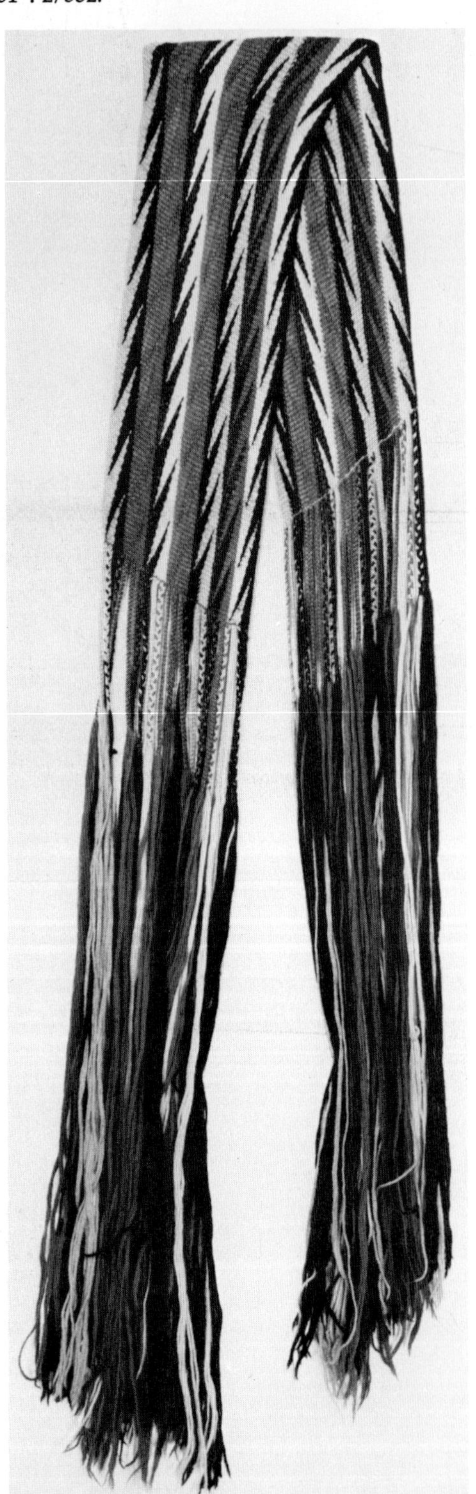

438. Cigar Container

Although made for the tourist trade, in the mundane form of a case for cigars, this still represents the fine moose-hair appliqué work so typical of these people. Presented by Thyra Maxwell. HURON. Québec, Canada. 1850-1875. 3" x 5¾". 23/2164.

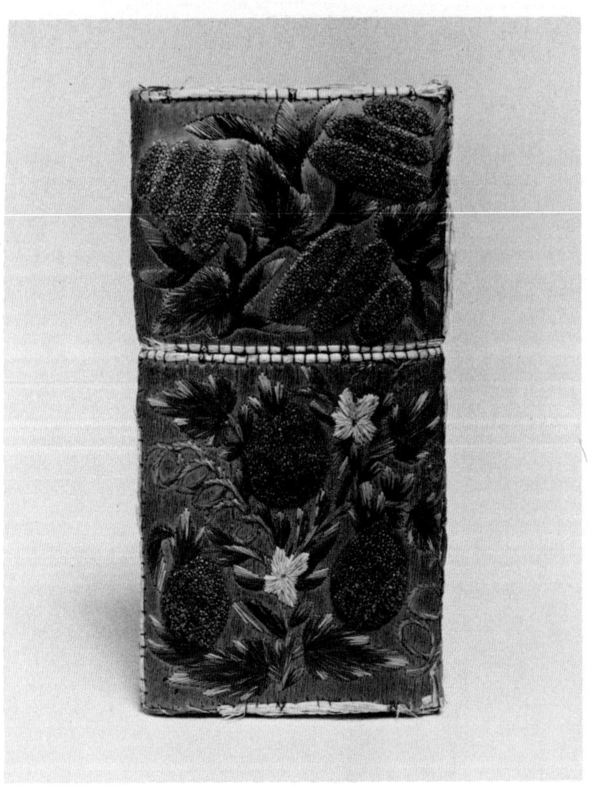

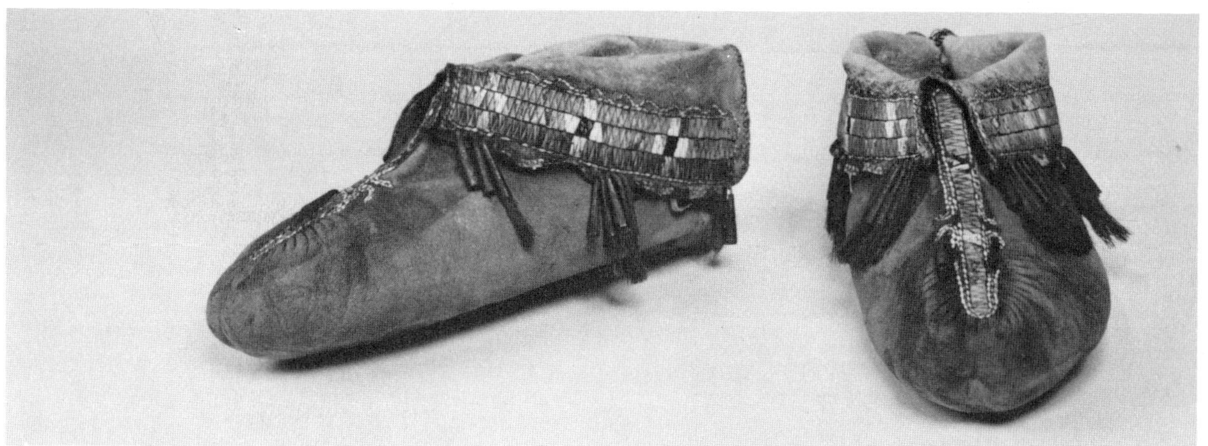

440. Quilled Moccasins
These moccasins are representative of the footwear which the Eastern Woodlands people wore during Colonial days. The colorful quillwork is further embellished by trade "jinglers" and dyed deer hair. LENNI LENAPE. Pennsylvania. 1775-1800. L: 10". 3/6411.

441. False Face Mask
(See page 22)

442. Cornhusk Mask
The use of twisted cornhusk to make a variety of objects was an art frequently executed by the Iroquois. One of the most frequently manufactured objects were the Huskface or Beggar Masks, worn by the beggars during Midwinter Feast ceremonies. This example, made in 1950, is an indication of the continuance of an old custom. Collected by William F. Stiles. SENECA. New York. 12¼" x 12¾". 24/2792.

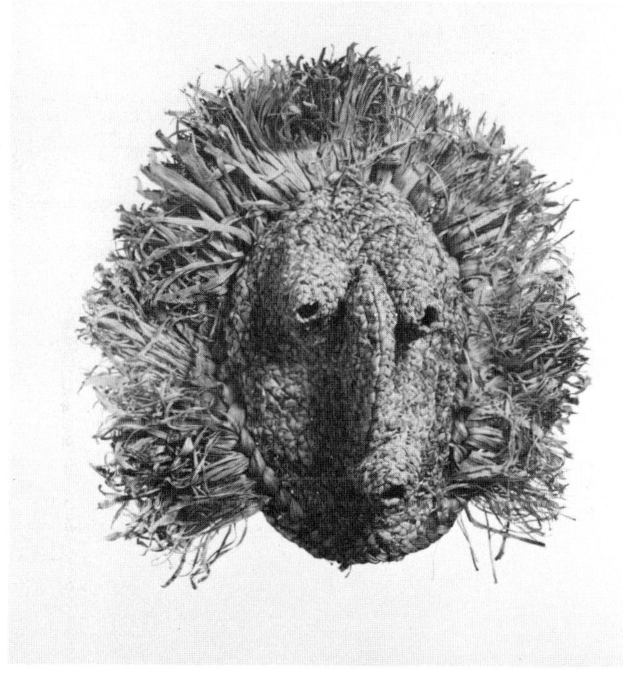

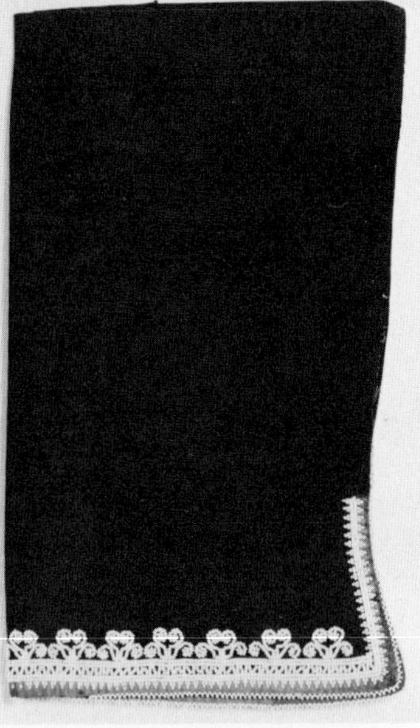

443. Beaded Leggings

Trade cloth in black, blue and red was popular among the Iroquois people for garments. This pair of leggings is typical of the form which extended from the knee to the ankle. The designs are executed in small beads applied to the surface in a floral design. Collected by Joseph Keppler. Seneca. Cattaraugus, New York. 1890-1900. 9" x 17½". 2/9662.

444. Wooden Ladle

These carved burl spoons and ladles are ornamented with effigies of birds and animals. The hook on the end prevents the ladle from slipping down into the bottom of the bowl. Collected by Joseph Keppler. Seneca. Tonawanda, New York. 1860-1870. 4¾" x 7½". 2/9611.

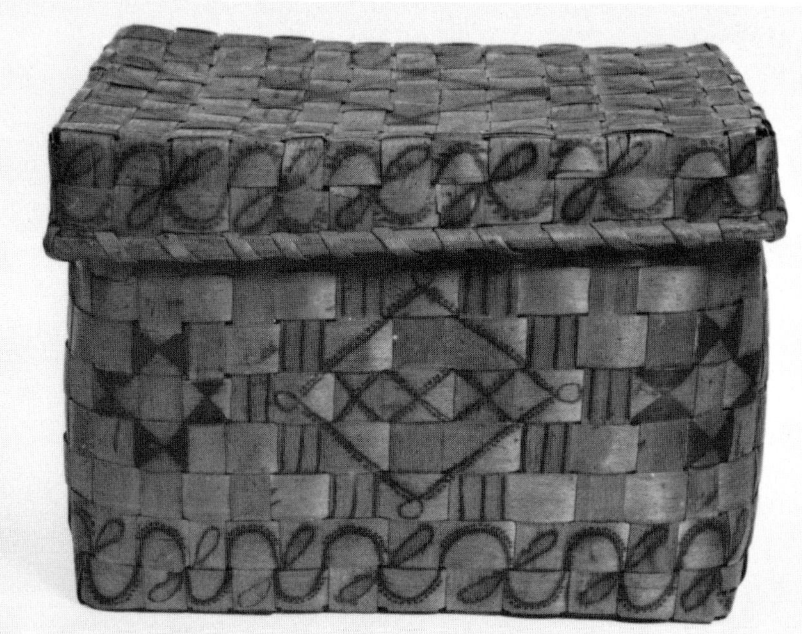

445. Splint Basket
These rectangular baskets were common throughout the eastern part of the country. They are often decorated by painting, or a stamped design provided by vegetal dye and hand-cut dies of wood. MOHEGAN. New Haven, Connecticut. 1860-1870. 7¼" x 10¾". 11/3516.

446. Bark Container
Another example of the common bark box and cover is this oval receptacle decorated with a forest scene. PASSAMAQUODDY. Calais, Maine. 1875-1890. 3¼" x 5" x 9¾". 22/4008.

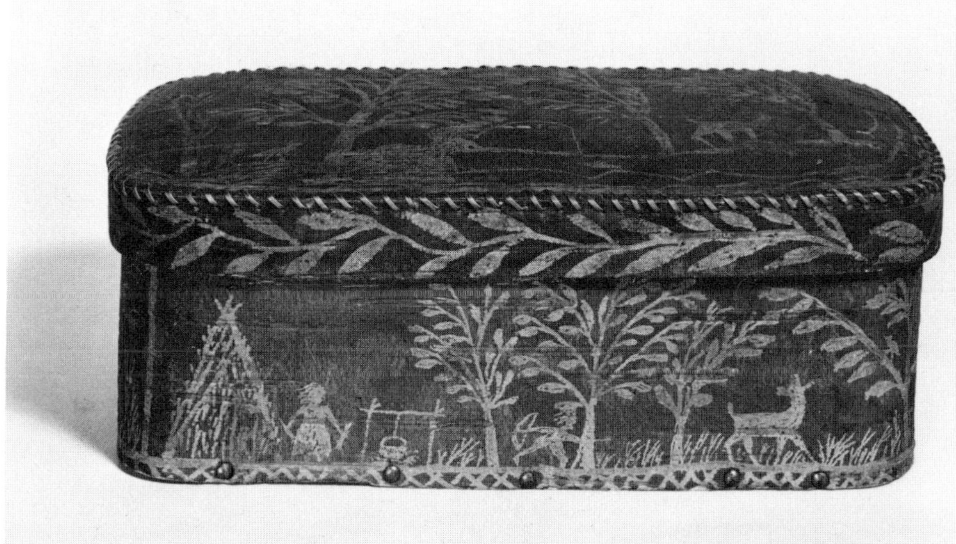

447. Quill-decorated Box
(See color insert facing page 40)

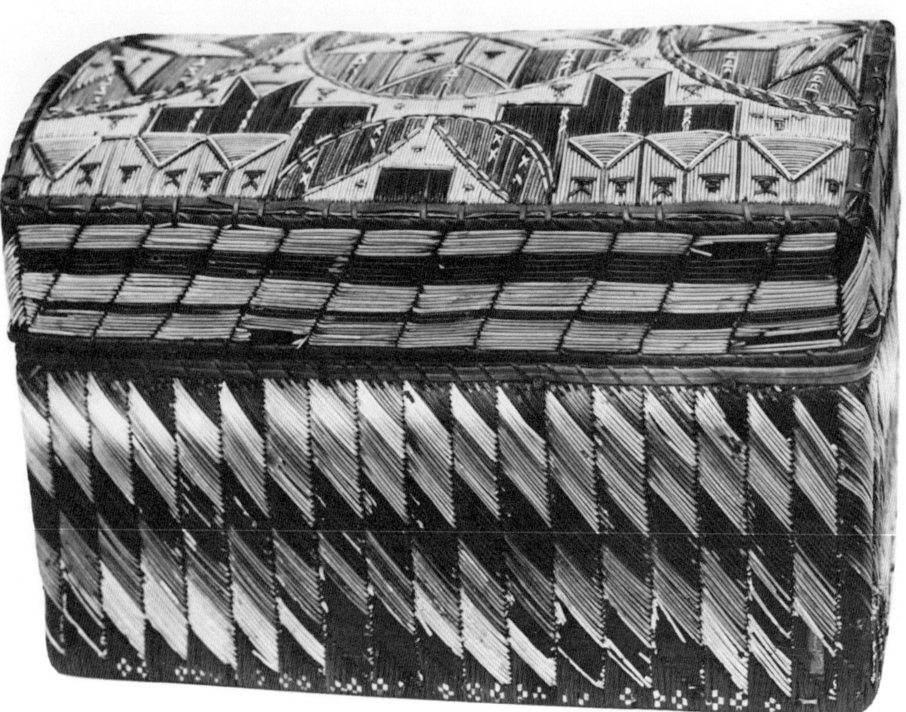

448. Quill-decorated Chest
An older type, this has been decorated with appliqué quilling, dyed with vegetal dyes, and some commercial color. MICMAC. Nova Scotia, Canada. 1850-1860. 7¾" x 8½" x 11". 21/8658.

449. Double-weave Cane Basket
(See color insert facing page 120)

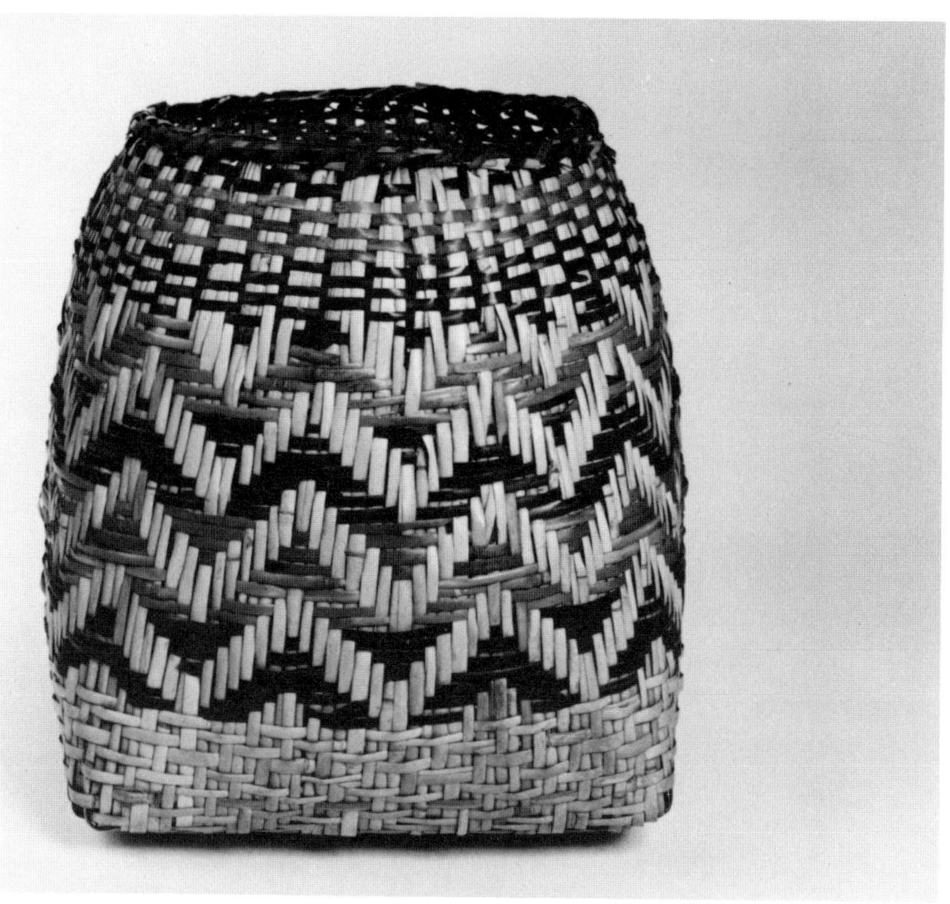

450. Cane Basket
A large, generously proportioned container of the type used for storage throughout the Southeast. These are woven of river cane, and occasionally are made in a double weave for strength. Collected by Frank G. Speck. CHEROKEE. Qualla, North Carolina. 1920-1930. 11½" x 12½". 15/8663.

451. Steatite Pipe Bowl
An art which has continued from prehistoric times to the present is the carving of small pipe bowls. Often they are decorated with the effigies of tiny animals; in this example, a squirrel is depicted. Presented by William deF. Haynes. CHEROKEE. Qualla, North Carolina. 1875-1900. 1½" x 2¼". 10/2445.

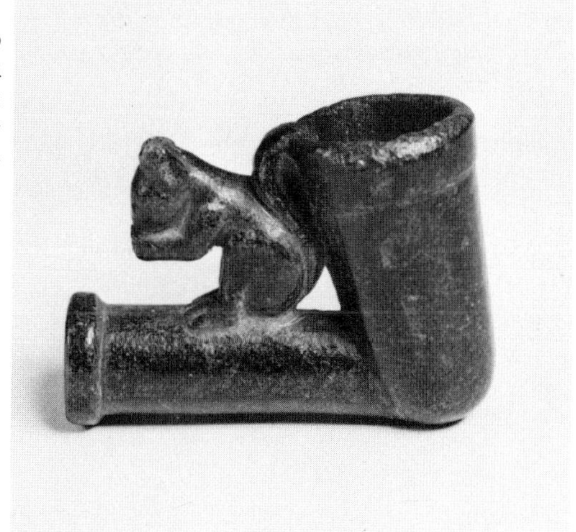

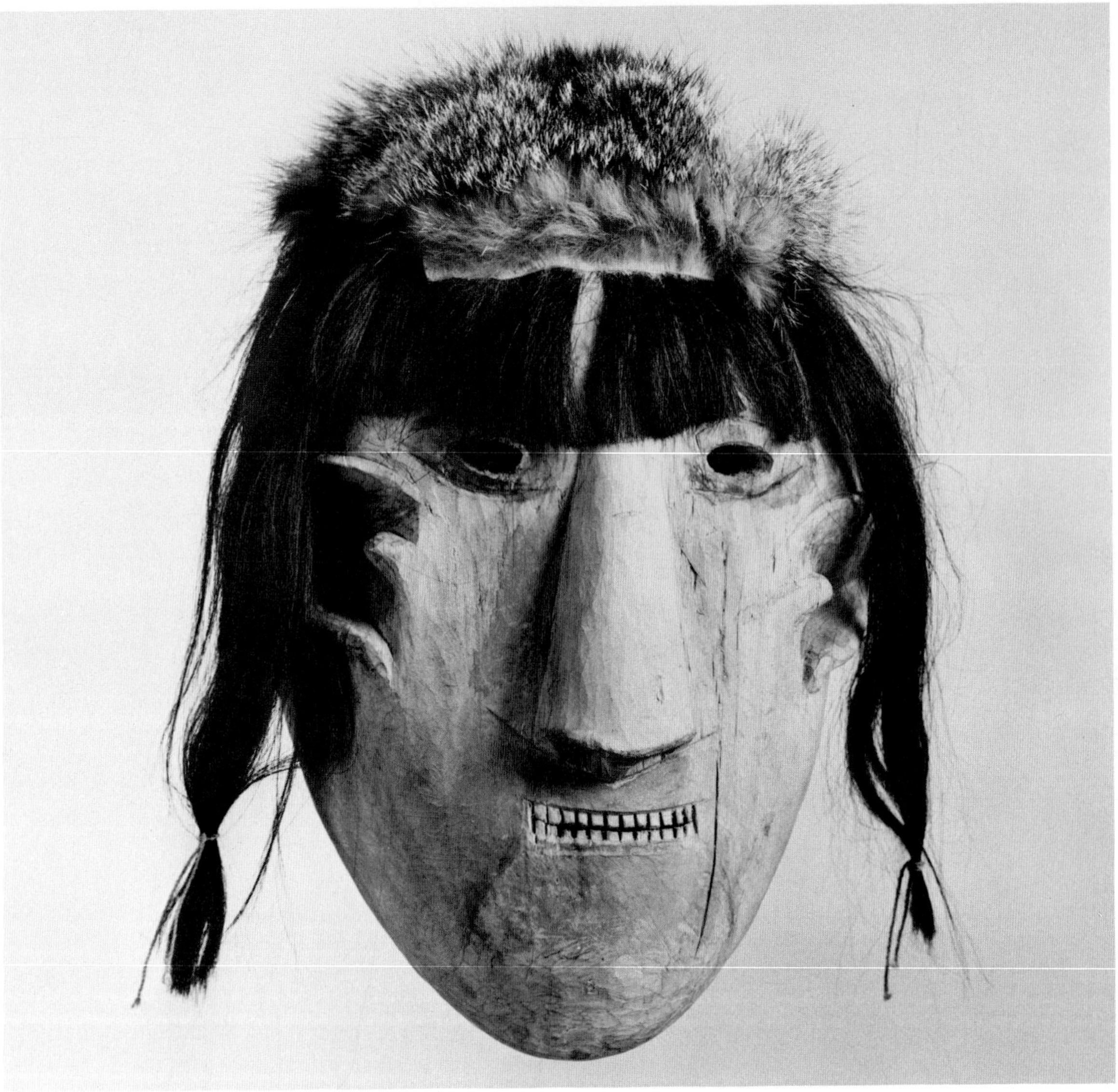

452. Wooden Mask

The so-called "Booger Masks" occur in a variety of sizes and shapes. They are used in the Midwinter Feast ceremonies, and represent a group of beings not unlike the False Face groups of the Iroquois. This depicts an Indian. Collected by Frank G. Speck. CHEROKEE. Qualla, North Carolina. 1920-1930. 8″ x 11½″. 18/5765.

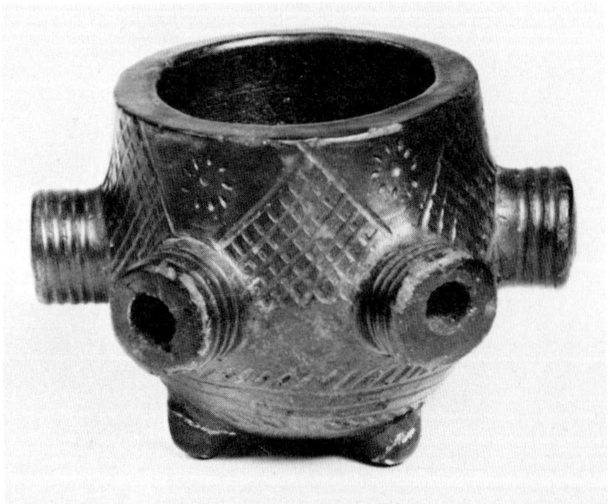

453. Community Pipe Bowl

These clay bowls, with four, six, or eight openings in the sides, are contemporary examples of an ancient vessel. Such "community pipes" were apparently used by several persons at one time, each inserting a long reed into the opening. Collected by George J. Niebuhr. CHEROKEE. Qualla, North Carolina. 1920-1925. 2¾″ x 4″. 16/3169.

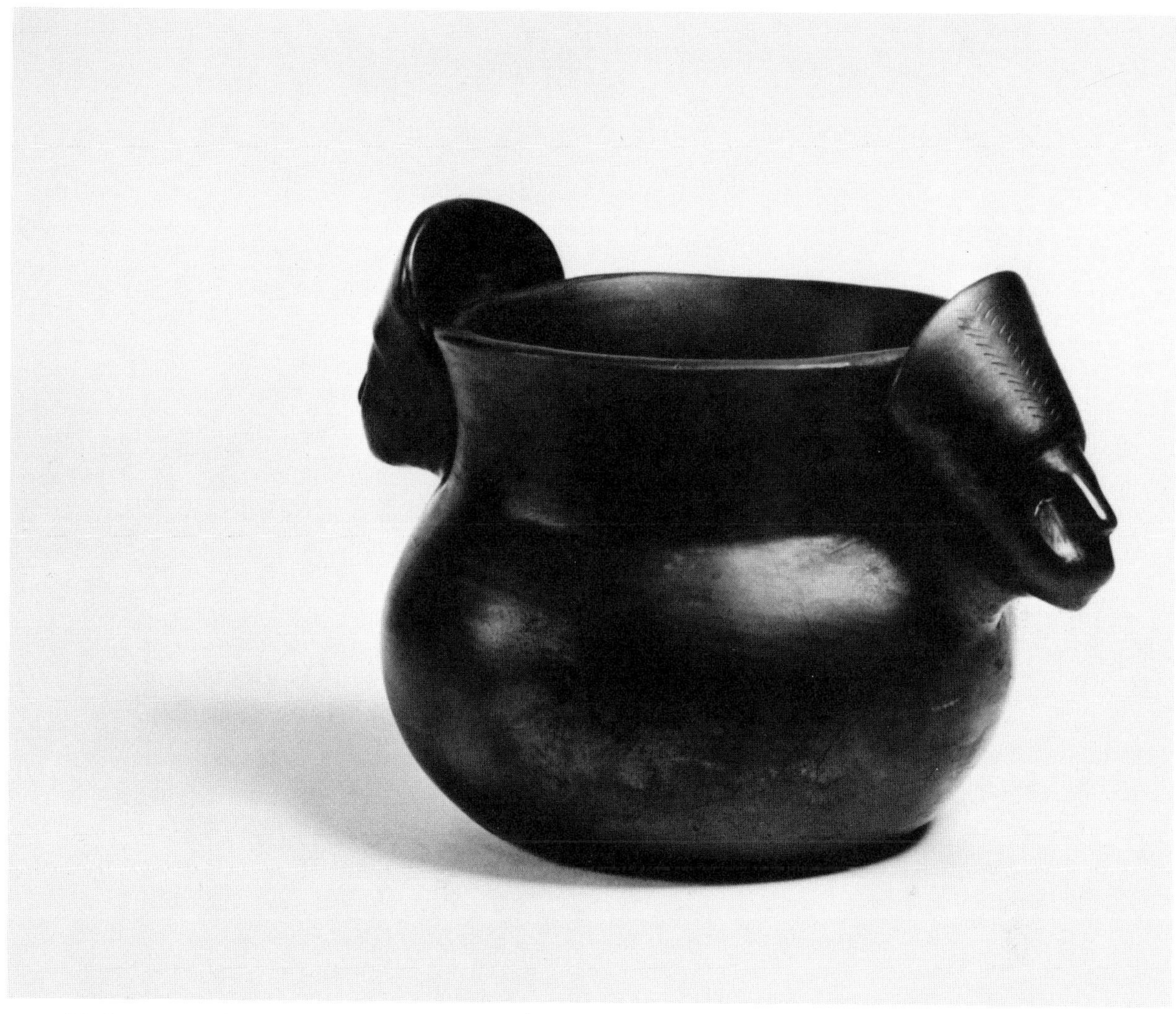

454. **Blackware Vessel**
Ornamented with two large modeled clay heads, this is a fine specimen of the oxidized pottery made today in the Southeast. This was made in 1973 by Mrs. Sara Ayers; excepting for the modeled feather-bonneted heads, it is very similar to ware produced in the same region five hundred years ago. CATAWBA. North Carolina. 6" x 11". 24/8724.

455. **Cloth Appliqué Costume**
(See page 21)

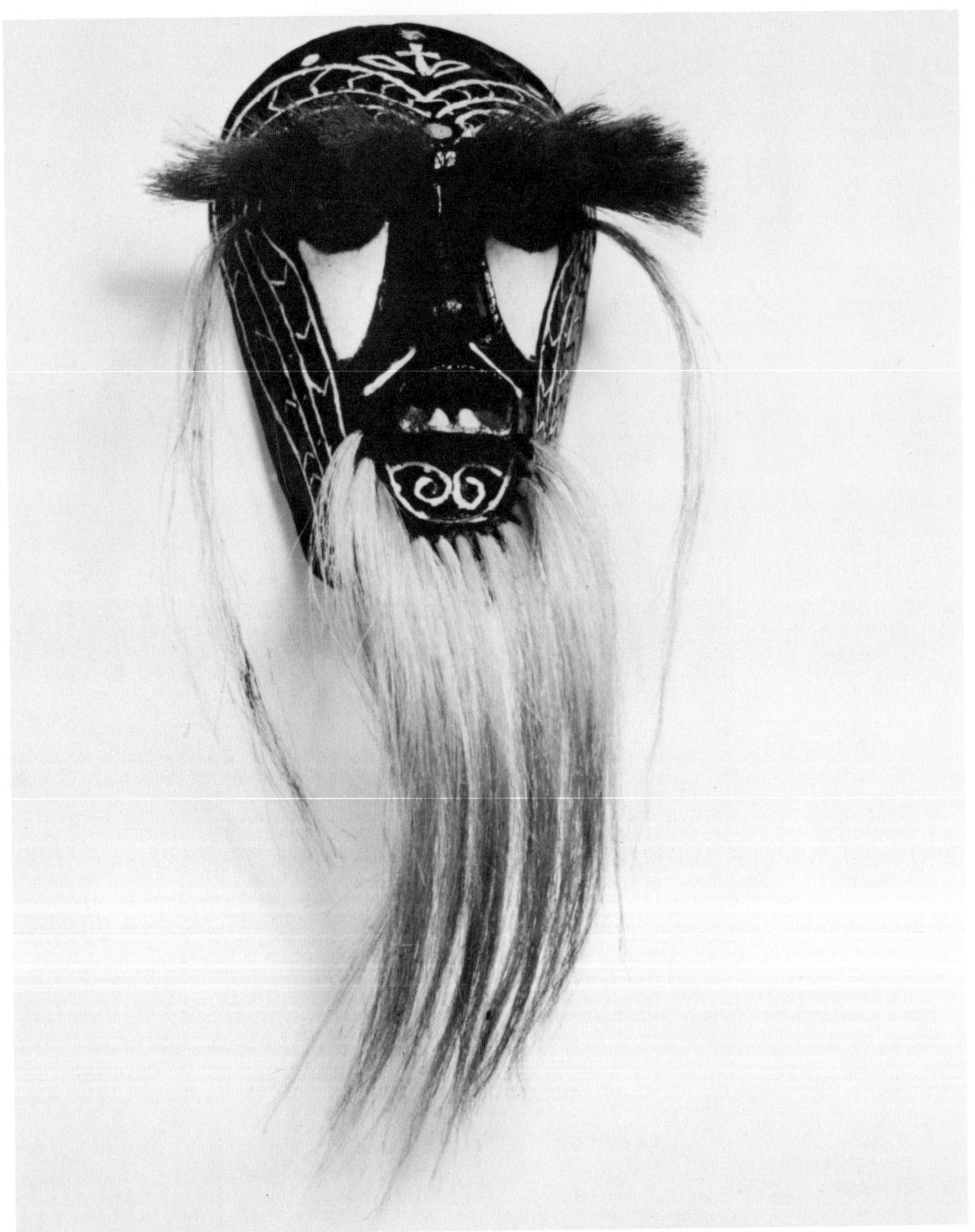

456. Carved Wooden Mask

Carved of soft wood, with elaborate horsehair trimming, these masks are decorated by sharply cut incising. This tribe lives on both sides of the Arizona-Mexican border; although the people are actually of Mexican origin. The masks are used in the Pascola (Easter) ceremonies by dancers representing animals. Collected by Edward H. Davis. YAQUI. Guadalupe, Arizona. 1910-1920. 5½" x 8". 10/4755.

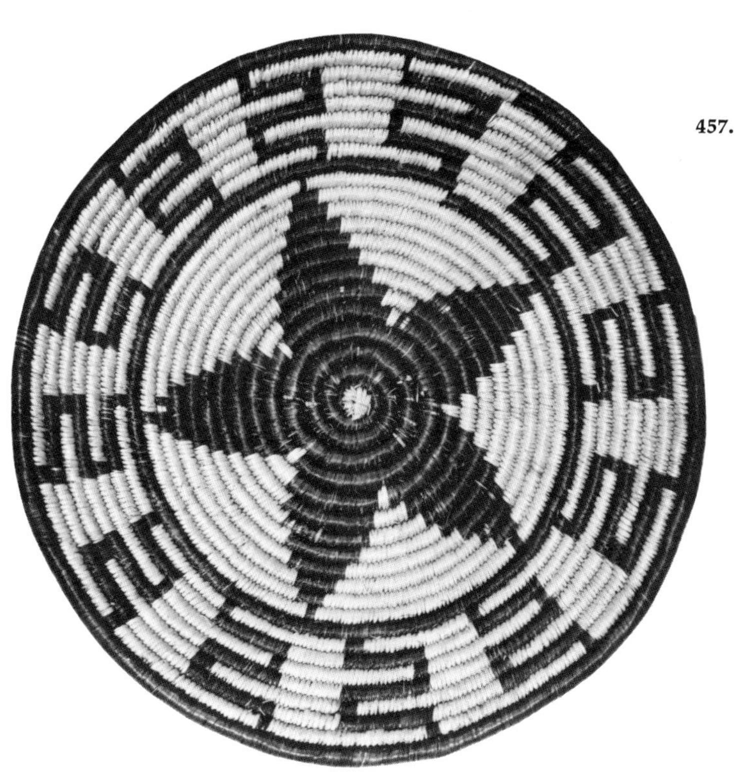

457. Basketry Tray

An old craft which has been continued and developed into an art, basketry objects have become an economically important part of Seri life. These are woven of *torote,* and dyed with plant roots. Collected by Richard Felger. SERI. El Desemboque, Sonora, Mexico. 1962-1963. D: 14″. 23/3489.

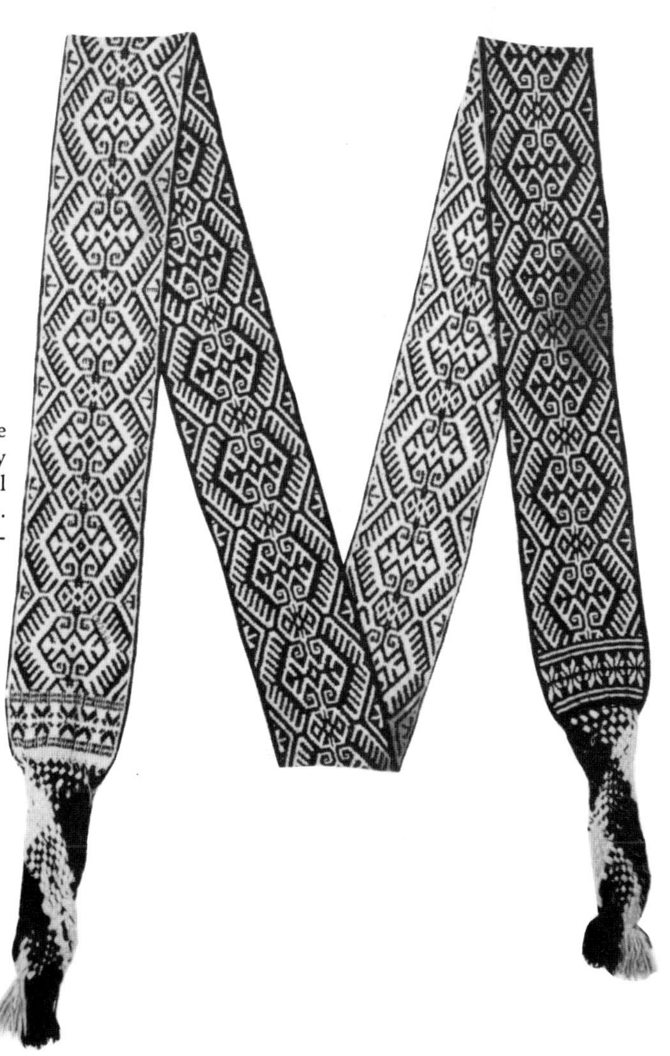

458. Woven Belt

Created on a waist loom, these are customarily made in brown, black and white in geometric designs. They often are worn wound around the waist, with small articles tucked into them. Collected by Donald B. Cordry. HUICHOL. La Mesa, Nayarit, Mexico. 1925-1930. 4″ x 42″. 19/5501.

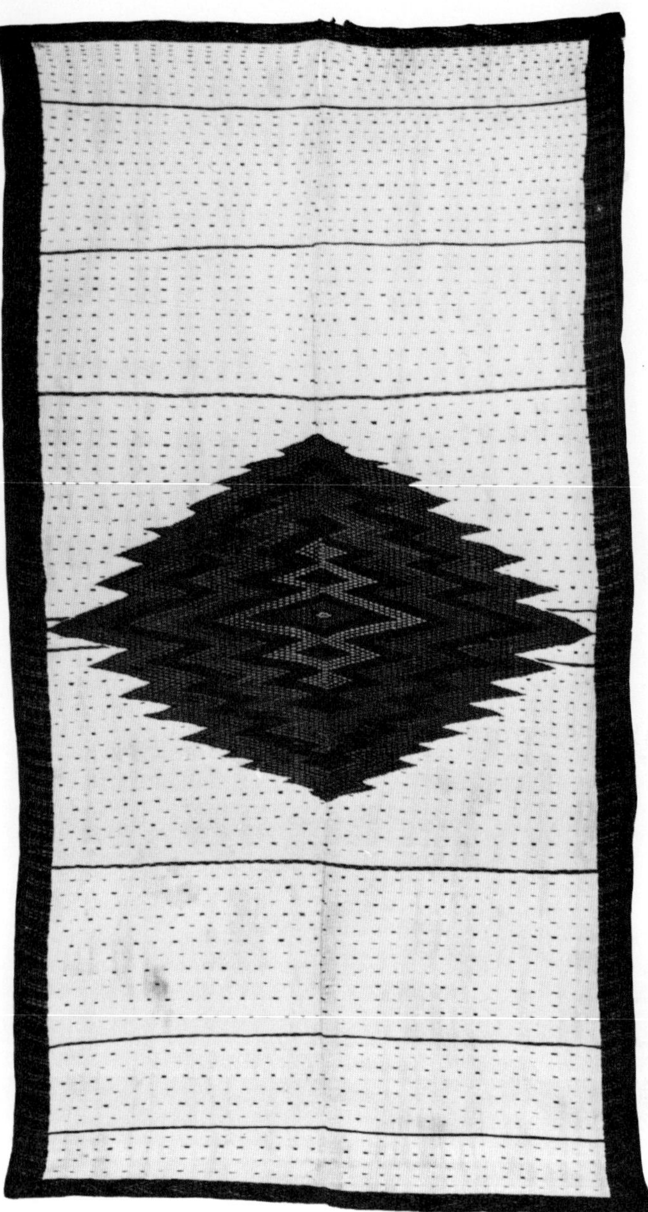

459. Woolen Serape
A white and pink-colored blanket, this is in the *serape* style, commonly found throughout northern Mexico. The diamond-shaped ornamental center is often pierced for the insertion of the head. SALTILLO. Coahuila, Mexico. 1870-1875. 52″ x 96″. 11/7026.

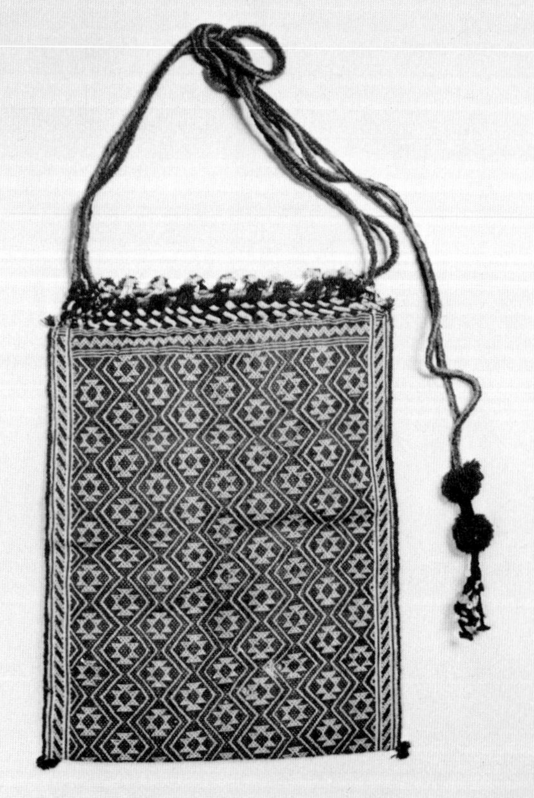

460. Textile Pouch
The design woven into the textile fabric, and the style of this pouch, are both modern examples of prehistoric work made by the early Mexican peoples. Collected by Edward H. Davis. AZTEC. San Bueno, Mexico. 1915-1920. 11½″ x 23¼″. 11/9485.

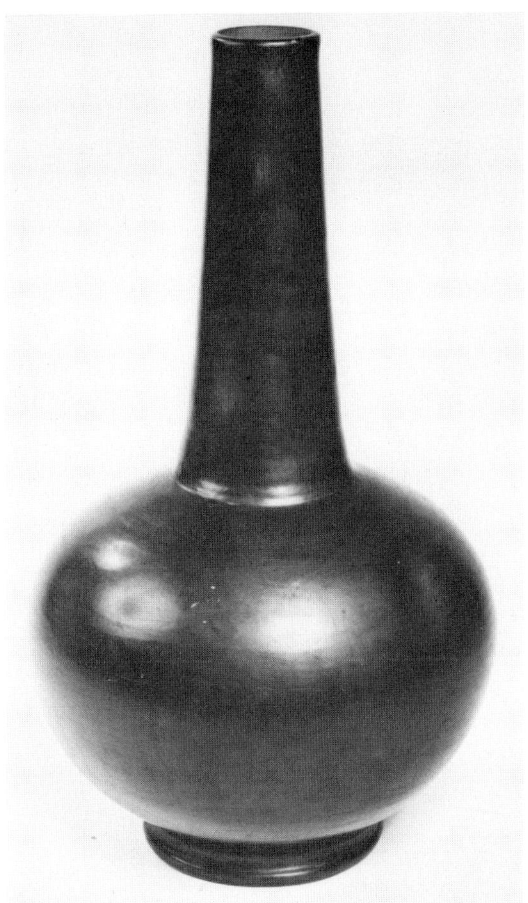

461. Blackware Vase
A beautifully-proportioned vessel, with a richly modeled globular base, this is typical of the fine work still being created in central Mexico. Collected by Elena Eritta. ZAPOTEC. San Bartolo Coyotepec, Oaxaca, Mexico. 1972. 7½" x 14¼". 24/7540.

462. Open-work Bowl
Finished off in a highly burnished surface, this bowl has a decoration achieved by cutting out triangular chunks of clay while the vessel is still damp. The color results from firing the pottery in a reducing atmosphere. Collected by Lewis Krevolin. ZAPOTEC. San Bartolo Coyotepec, Oaxaca, Mexico. 1973. 12" x 12". 24/8752.

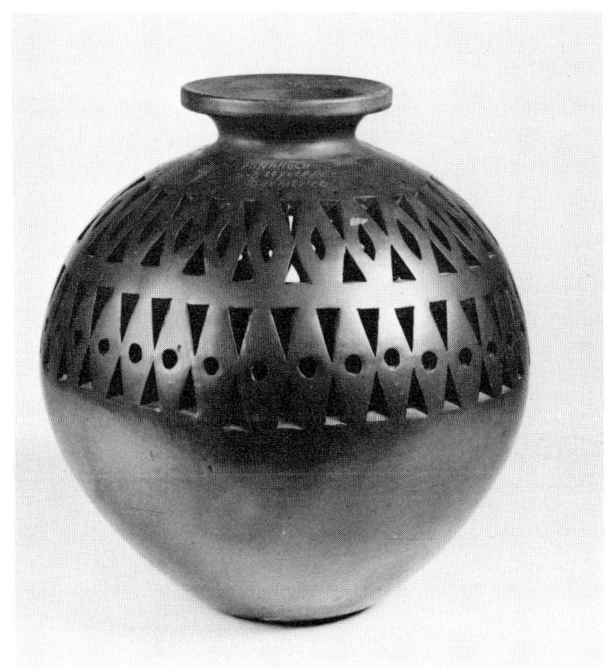

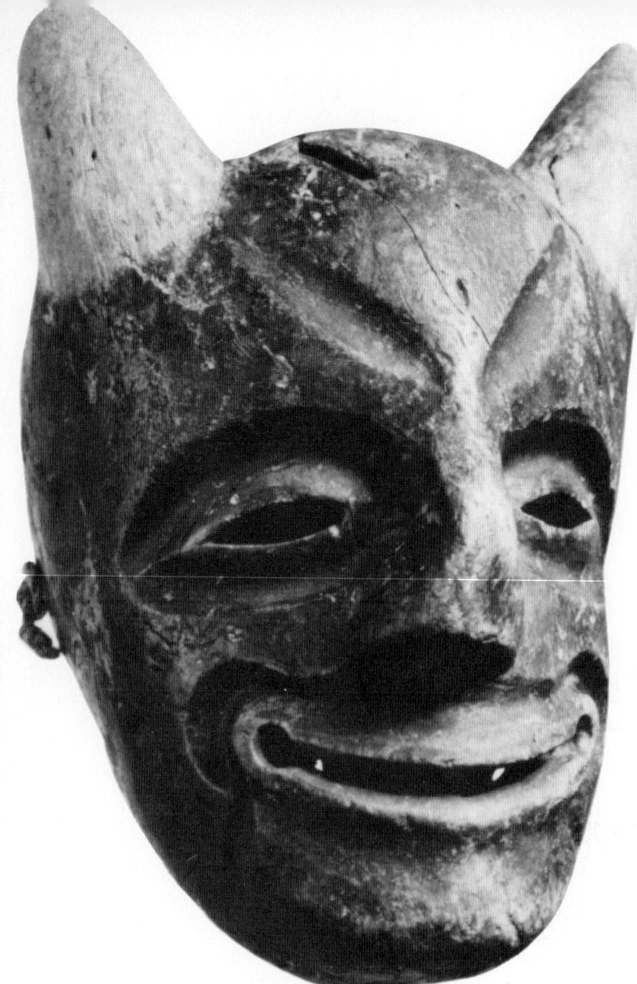

463. Devil Mask
Carved from a soft balsa wood, this represents the Devil, and is a fine example of classic Mexican mask sculpture. Collected by Bernard Bevan. ZAPOTEC. Yálalag, Oaxaca, Mexico. 1875. 8″ x 13″. 20/1610.

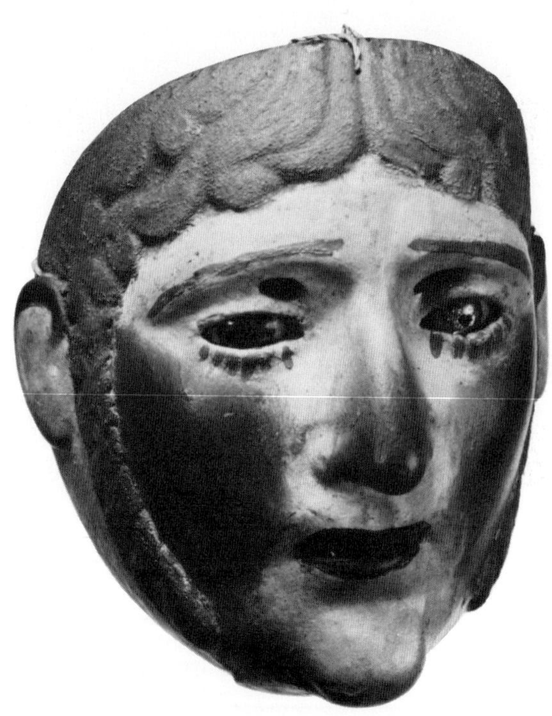

465. Painted Wooden Mask
Worn by performers in the Baile del Tun, this mask represents a European; the *tun* dancers wear elaborate tubular structures on their backs while performing. Collected by Samuel K. Lothrop. QUICHE' MAYA. San Juan Mixcoi, Guatemala. 1925-1926. 6½″ x 8″. 16/831.

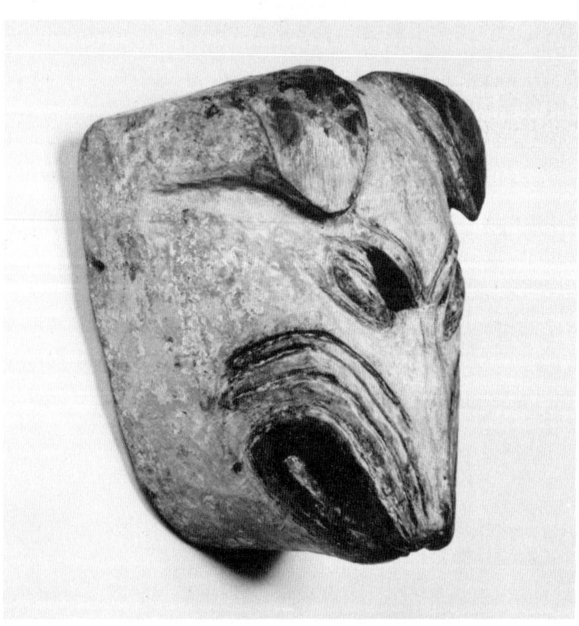

464. Zoömorphic Mask
A small painted representation of a dog, this is used in some of the animal dances. Traces of the original paint still survive. Presented by Aaron Furmann. TZOTZIL. Chiapas, Mexico. 1900-1910. 6¼″ x 7¼″. 22/8750.

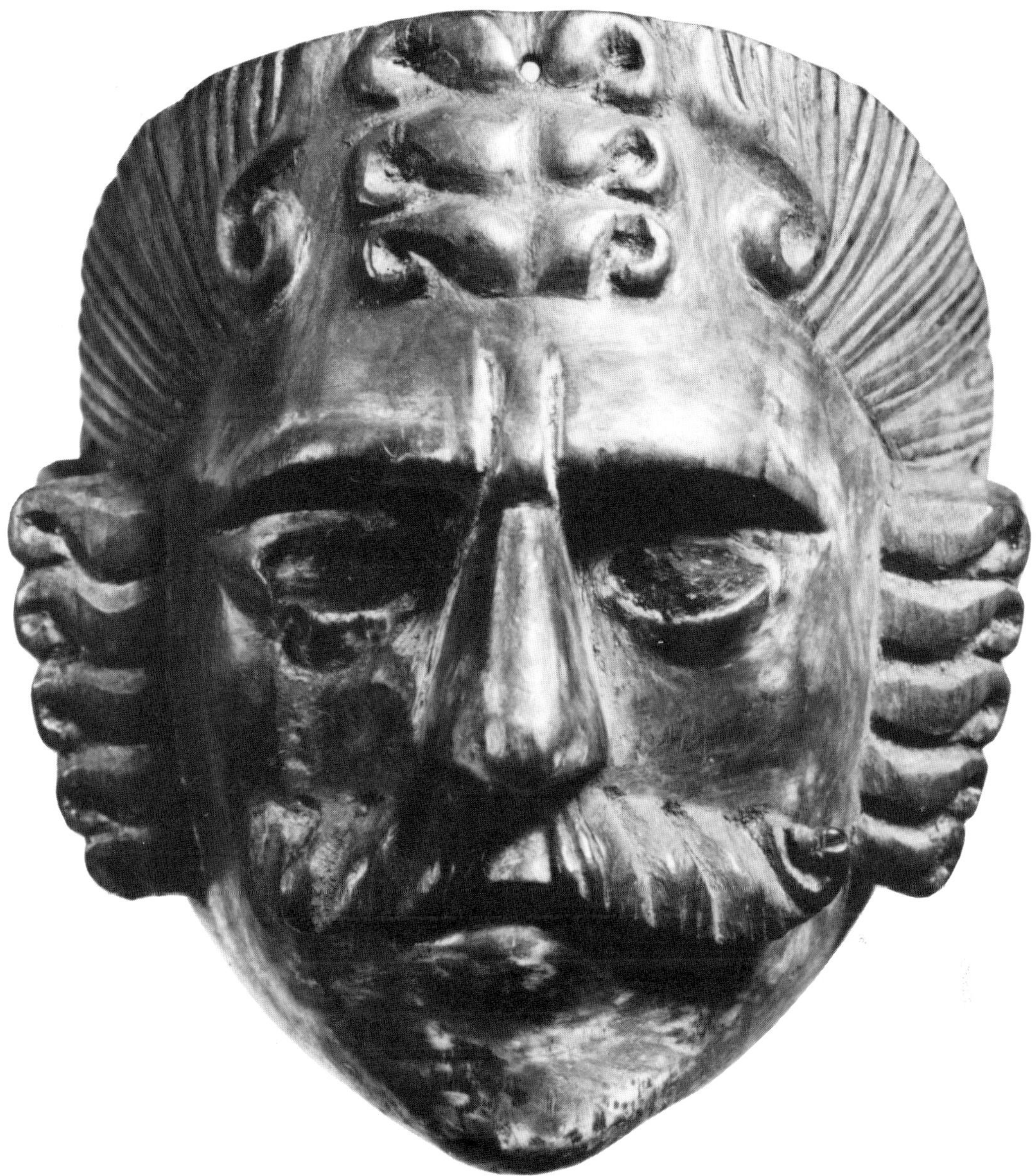

466. Carved Dance Mask

An older style of mask, this is the type used in the *Baile de la Conquista*, in which male performers reënact the invasion of the Spaniards. This is a classic example of Mayan mask carving. Presented by Aaron Furmann. QUICHÉ MAYA. Santo Tomás Chichicastenango, Guatemala. 1880-1900. 6¾" x 7½". 22/8758.

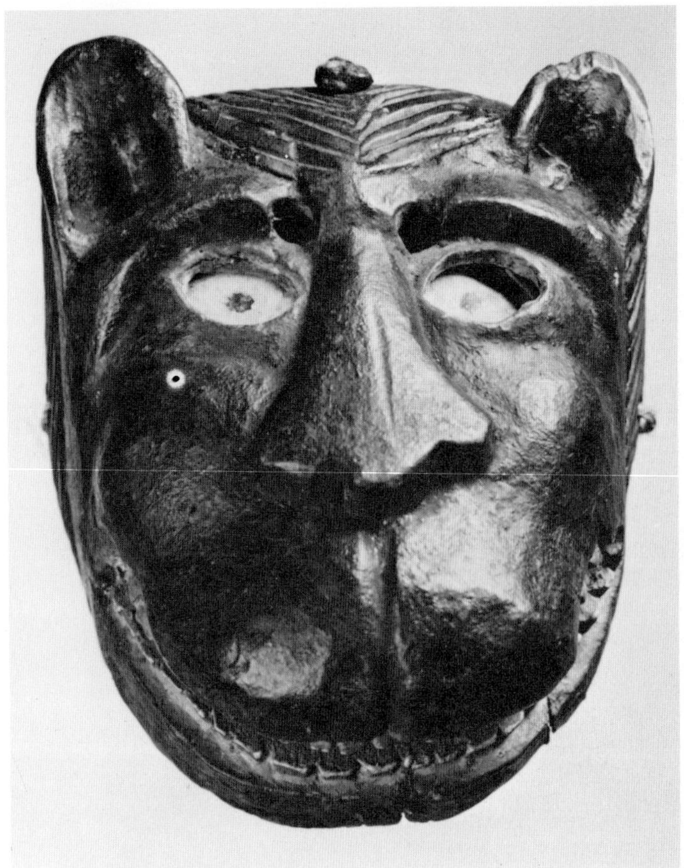

467. Animal Mask
An old example, representing the Puma, *Balam*, this is a continuation of prehistoric Mayan animal masking customs. Collected by Samuel K. Lothrop. QUICHÉ MAYA. Totonicapán, Guatemala. 1890-1900. 7″ x 8″. 14/5613A.

468. Woman's Blouse
Textiles have changed little since ancient times, although almost none of the prehistoric examples have survived: we must depend upon pottery figurines for prototype illustration. This *huípil* is unfinished, but gives a good idea of the garment in process. Collected by Samuel K. Lothrop. QUICHÉ MAYA. Totonicapán, Guatemala. 1910-1920. 35½″ x 44″. 16/720.

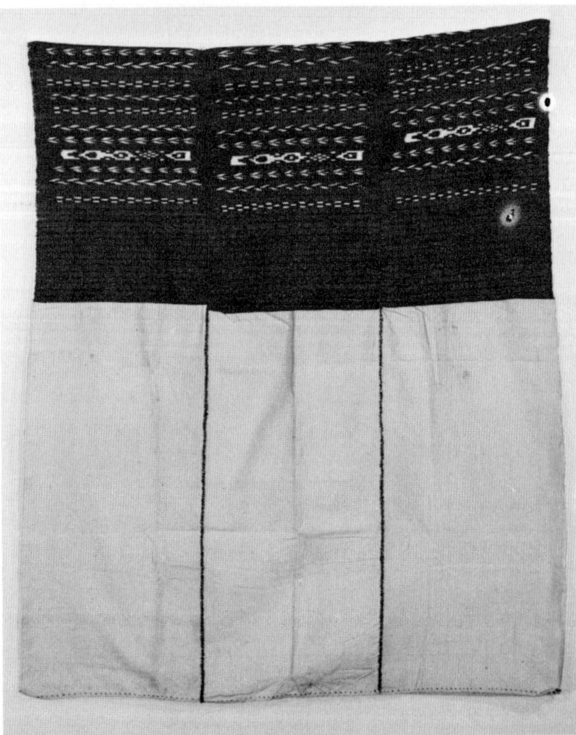

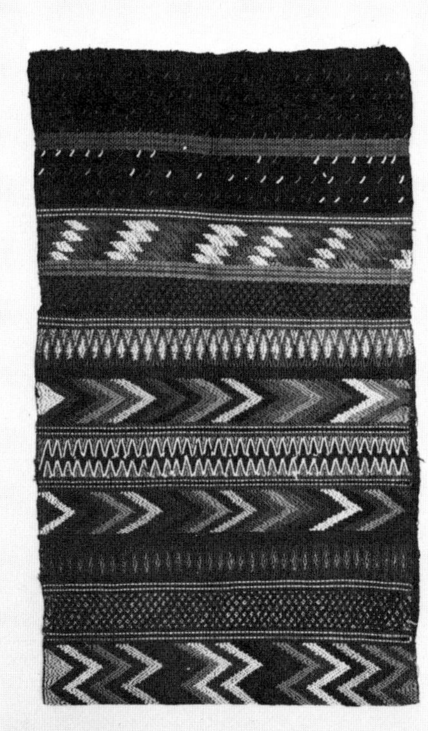

469. Panel for Blouse
These are woven separately, on waist looms, and then sewn together to form the finished women's *huípil*. This is a fine example of modern-day Maya weaving. Presented by Mrs. Harcourt Amory. QUICHÉ MAYA. Santiago Sacatepéquez, Guatemala. 1920-1930. 13½" x 23". 23/2497.

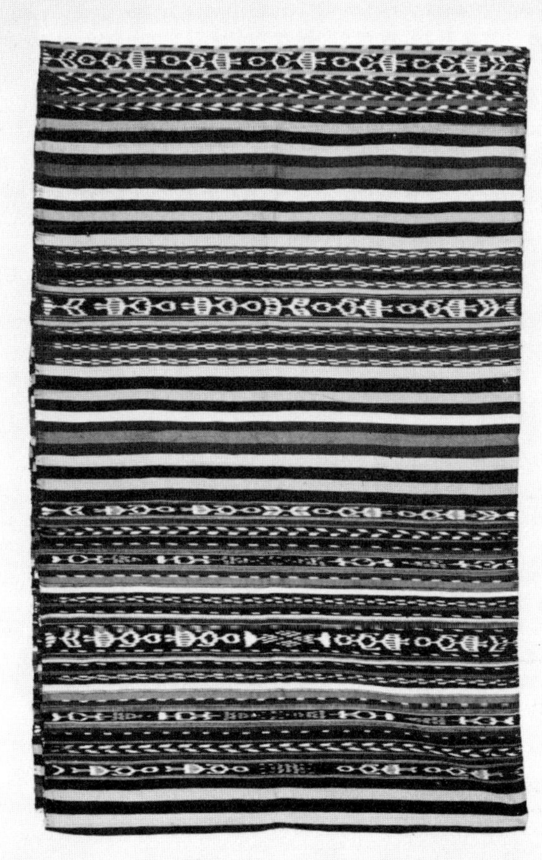

470. Woven Head Shawl
The *perraje* is worn over the shoulders, or the head, to provide warmth and protection. This brilliantly decorated textile has been worked by the tie-and-die, or *ikat*, technique. Collected by Samuel K. Lothrop. QUICHÉ MAYA. Totonicapán, Guatemala. 1910-1920. 24" x 39". 16/729.

471. Modern Blouse
(See color insert facing page 120)

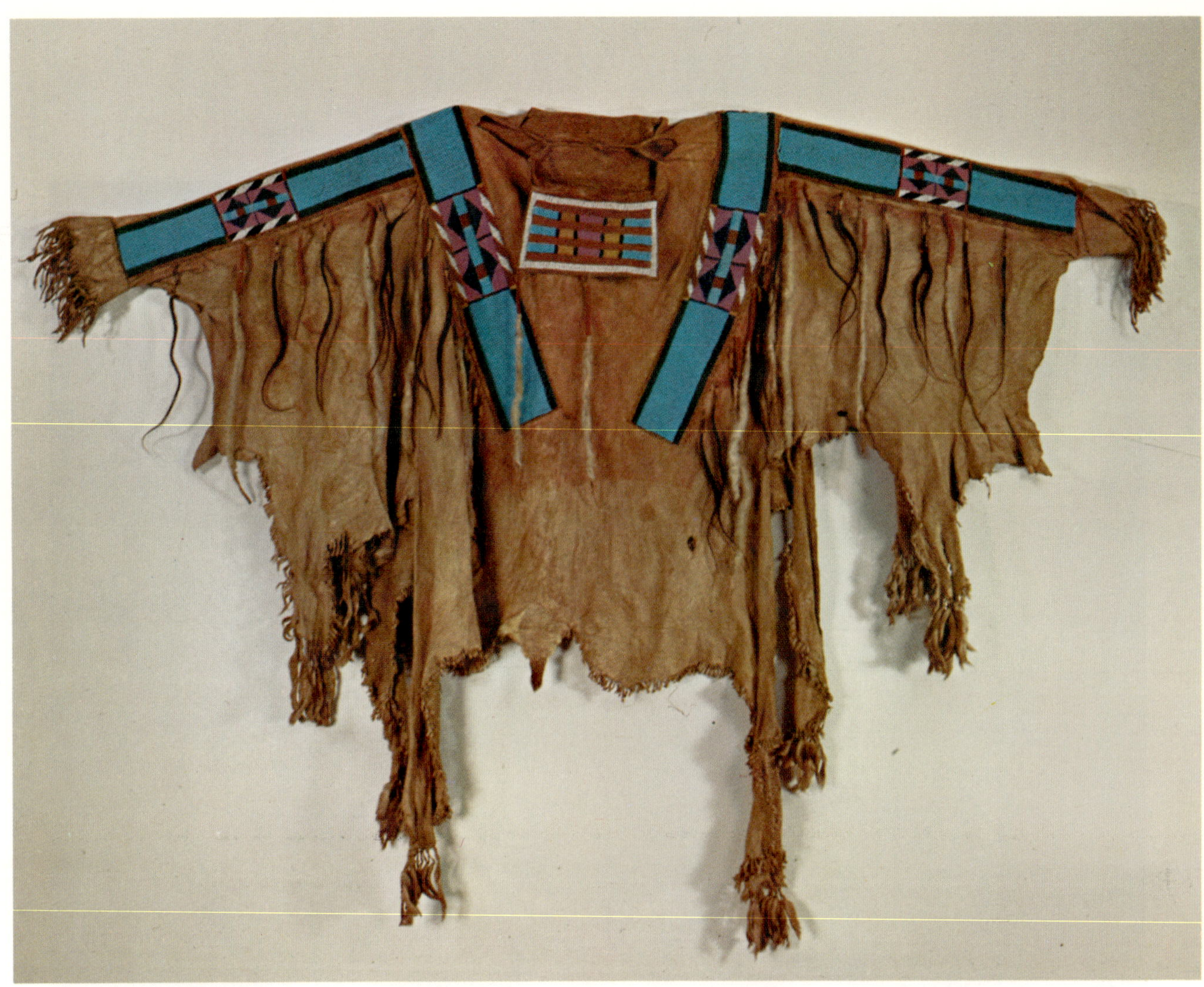

379. Man's Buckskin Shirt

These people were the dandies of the Northern Plains, dressing themselves in some of the finest garments Indian *couteriers* ever designed. This example has ermine fur, beadwork and trade cloth panelling to embellish the grace of the shirt. Collected by Nate Salsbury. Presented by Mrs. Nate Salsbury. CROW. Montana. 1875-1880. 44" x 53". 10/8320.

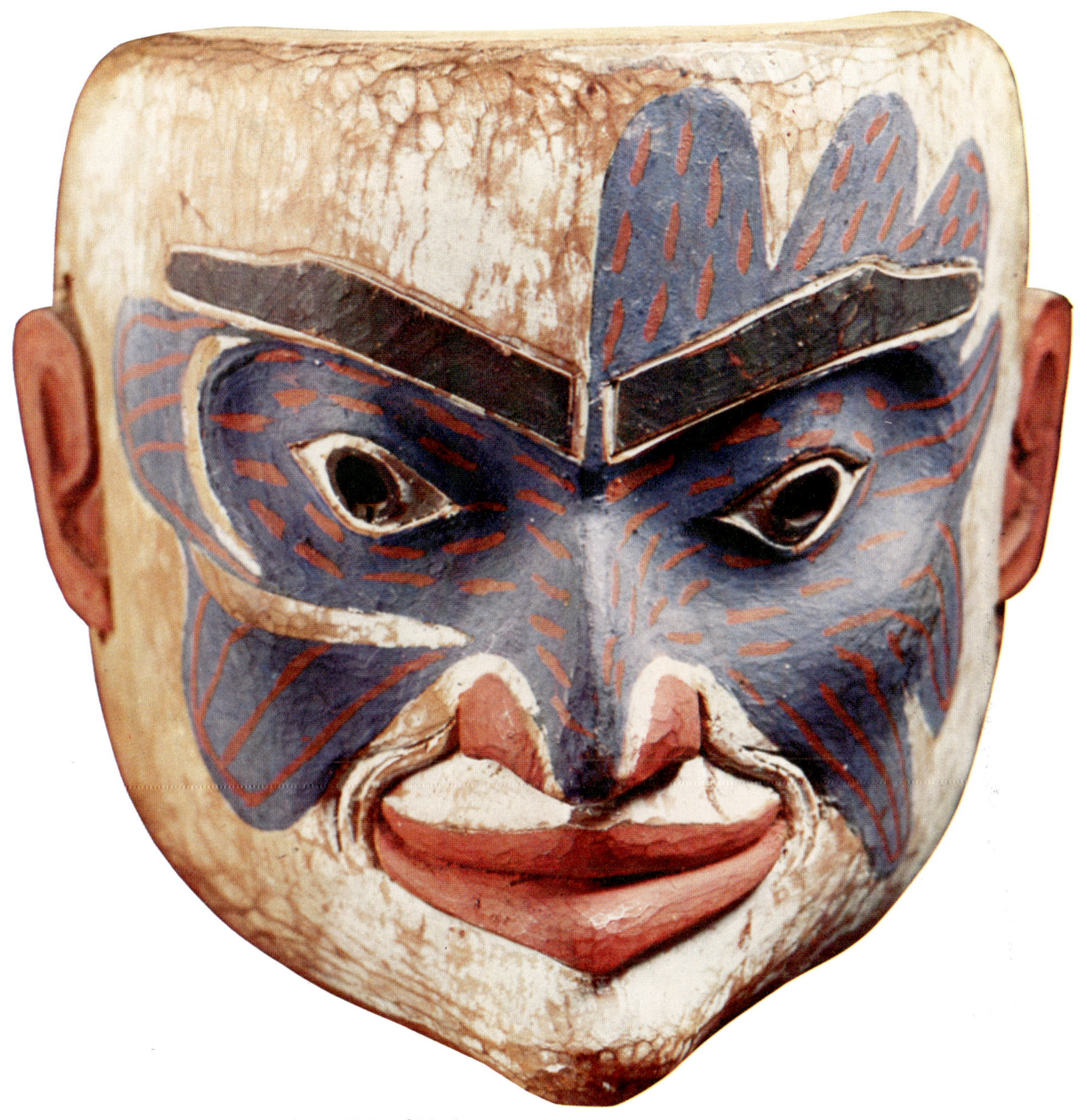

293. Painted Mask
With much of the original paint intact, this is an excellent example of the dramatic appearance of many of these objects when in use. BELLA BELLA. British Columbia. 1880-1890. 8″ x 9″. 8/1586.

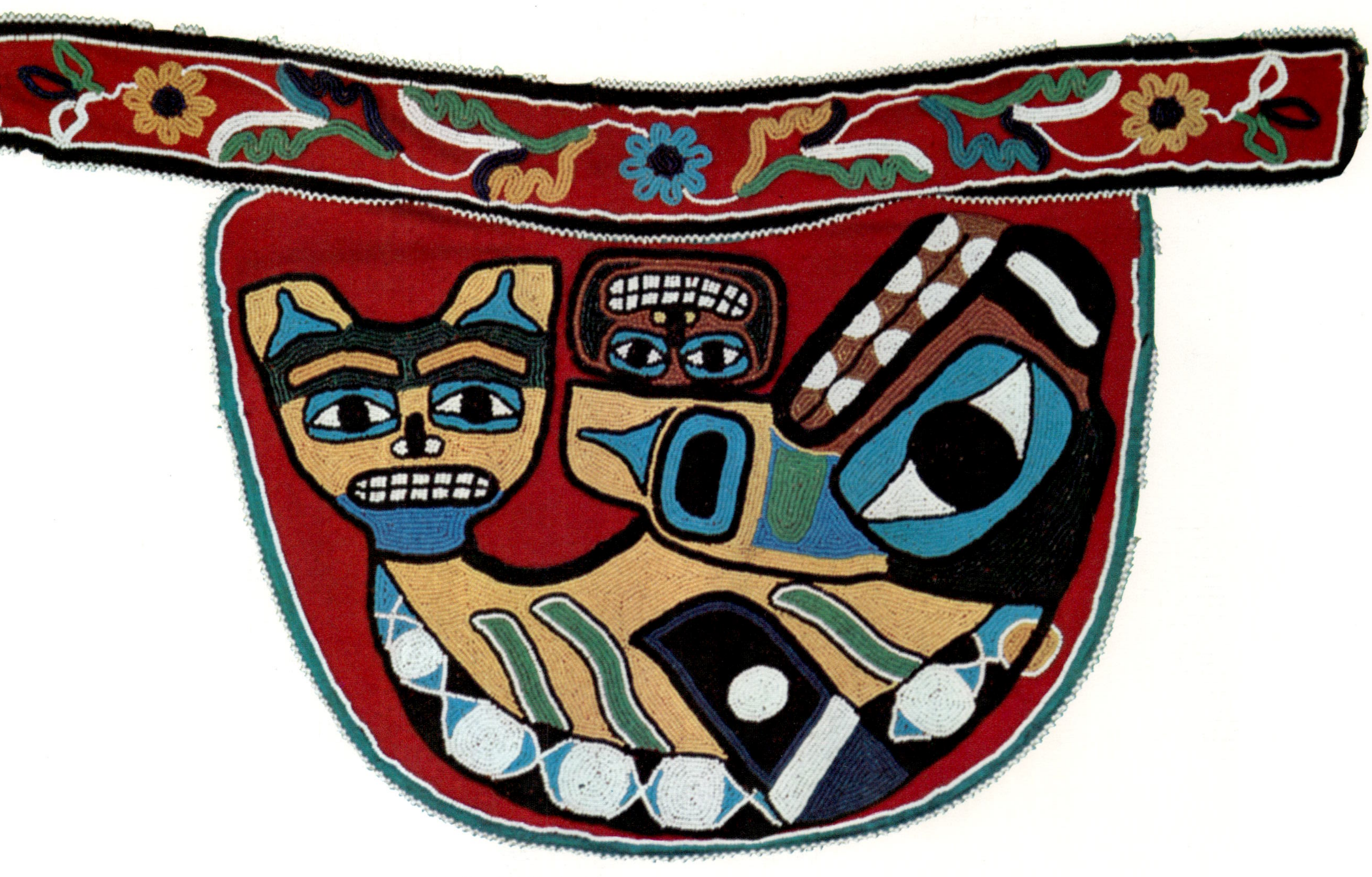

289. Beaded Neck Ornament

Elaborately decorated bibs were made to conceal the unsightly neck line following the adoption of European shirts. This heavily beaded design on trade cloth represents the killer whale. TLINGIT. Sitka, Alaska. 1890-1910. 8″ x 11″. 24/7455.

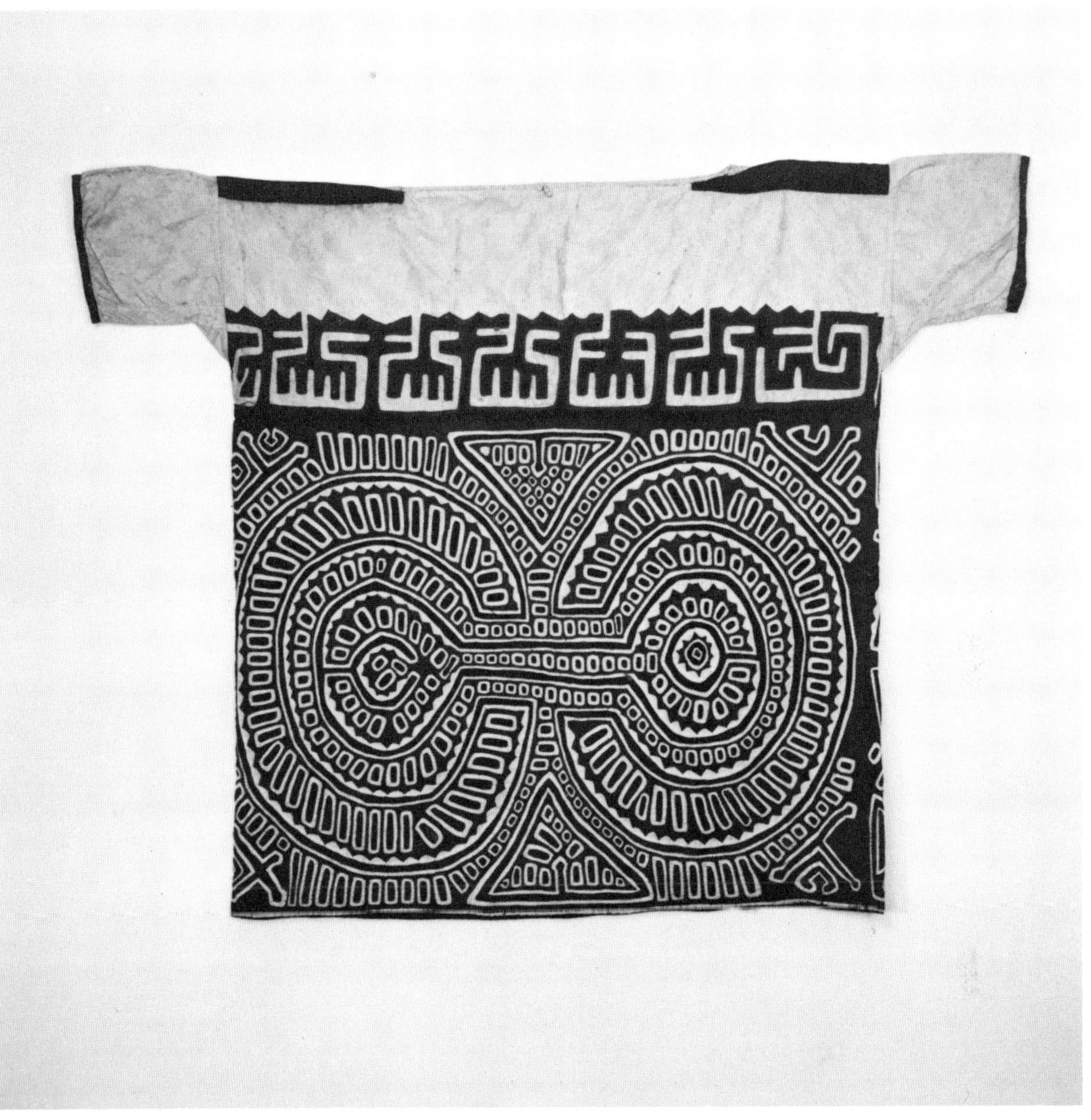

474. Woman's Appliqué Blouse

These fascinating garments have become familiar to many non-Indians today. The remarkable skill of the Cuna women in patiently cutting and sewing the hundreds of tiny cloth pieces into elaborate patterns is well illustrated in this *mola*. Many of the panels are used for pillow covers, wall decorations, and other home furnishings. Collected by A. Hyatt Verrill. CUNA. San Blas, Panama. 1910-1915. 27″ x 36″. 8/3627.

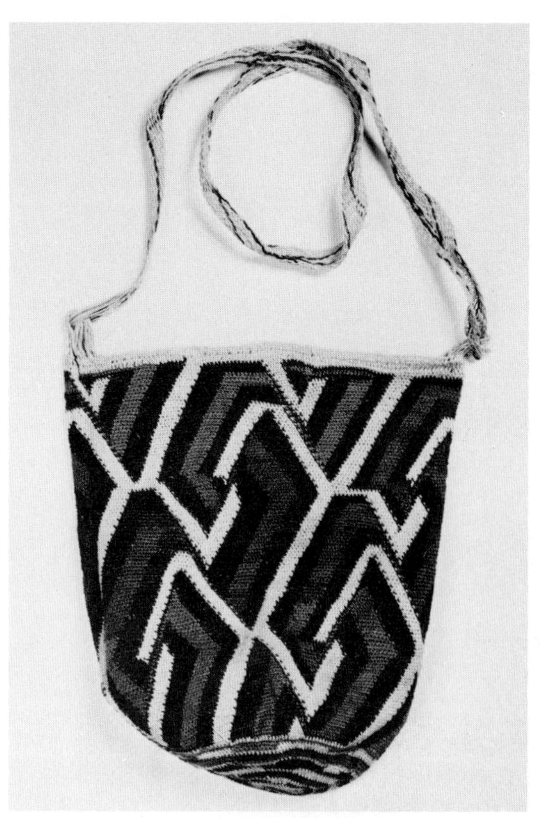

475. Net-woven Pouch
This has a well-balanced geometric design produced by an interlacing technique typical of these bags. This type of weaving is distributed throughout the Americas, but is most prolific in Central and South America. Collected by A. Hyatt Verrill. CUNA. San Blas, Panama. 1910-1915. 9″ x 16″. 8/3626.

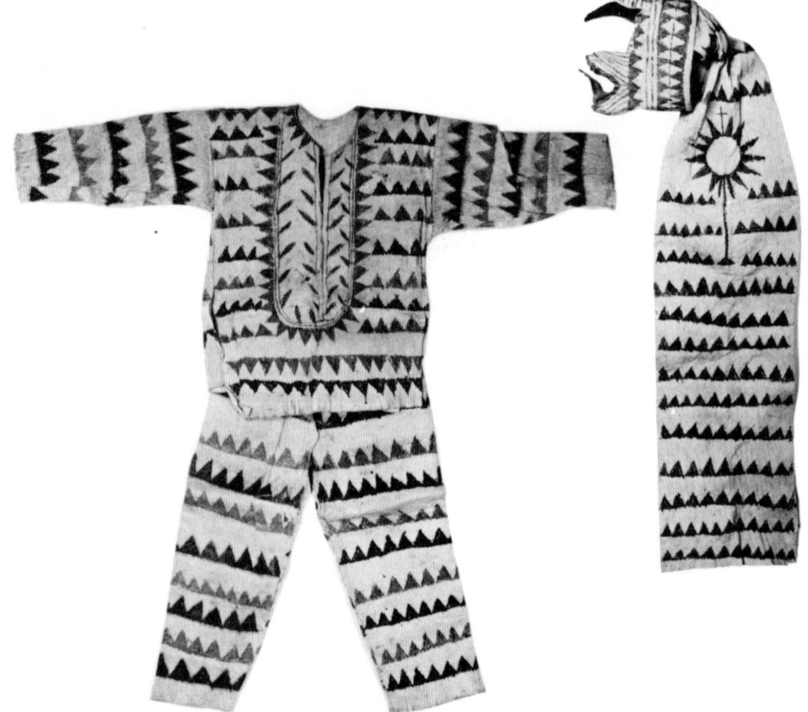

476. Bark Cloth Costume
Used in the Kuqua Dance, this costume has a real deer skull fastened to the bark blouse. The coat and trousers, surprisingly enough, are patterned after European tailoring. Collected by A. Hyatt Verrill. GUAYMÍ. Coclé, Panama. 1910-1915. 15″ x 58″. 13/1733. (*3 parts*).

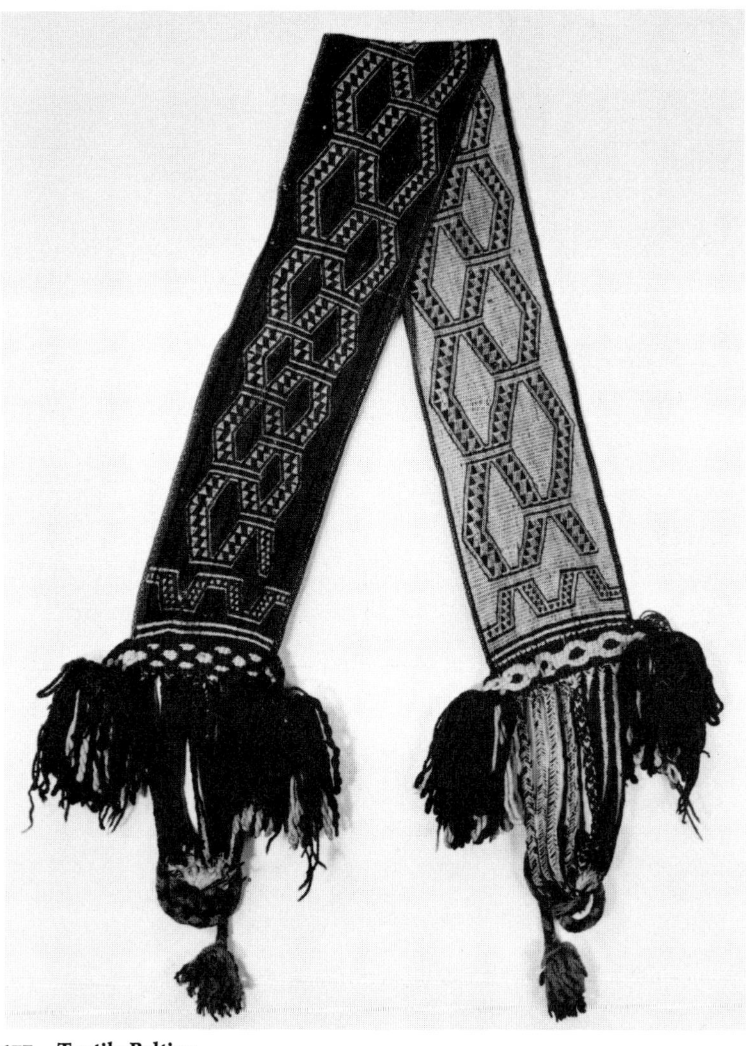

477. Textile Belting
Some of the most surprising weaving comes from little-known areas. This wide belt is worn for all dress-up occasions by men. Collected by Gregory Mason. GOAJIRA. Goajira Peninsula, Colombia. 1910-1930. 5″ x 32″. 18/9609.

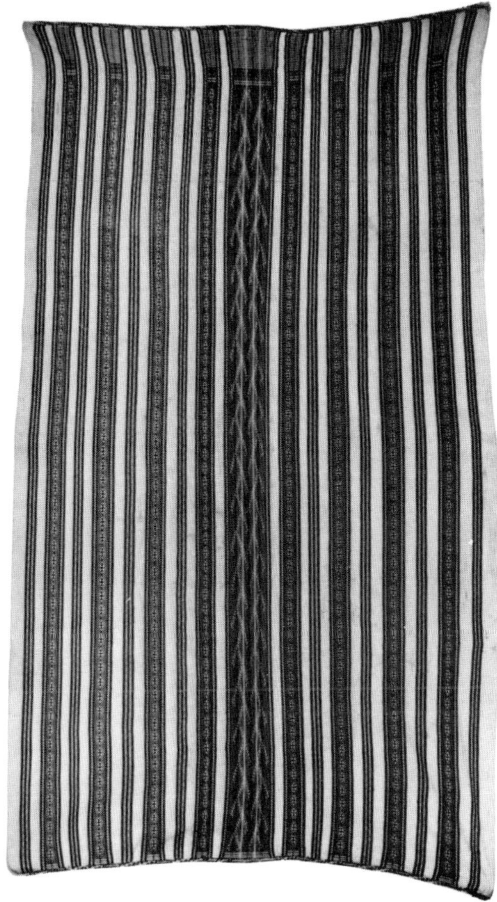

478. Textile Blanket
The common covering for general use is this type of panel, with colorful designs woven into it. Presented by Louis G. Huntley. GOAJIRA. Goajira Peninsula, Venezuela. 1915-1925. 44″ x 79″. 19/9597.

479. Woven Cane Basket

This rectangular double basket, while apparently a basket and cover, is also often separated to provide two containers when the need arises. Collected by A. Hyatt Verrill. Carib. Noseño River, British Guiana. 1910-1915. 7" x 11½". 7/5066.

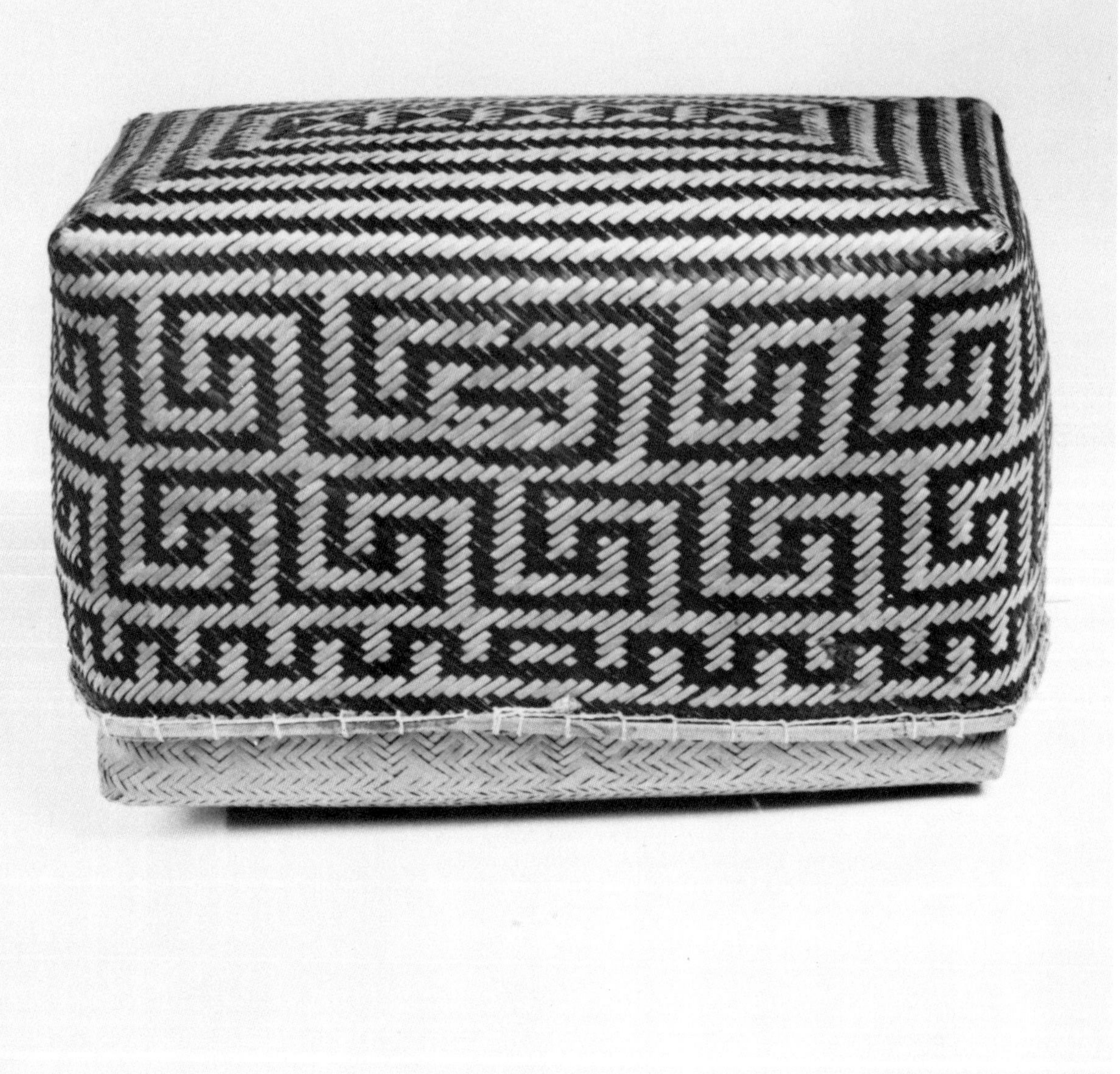

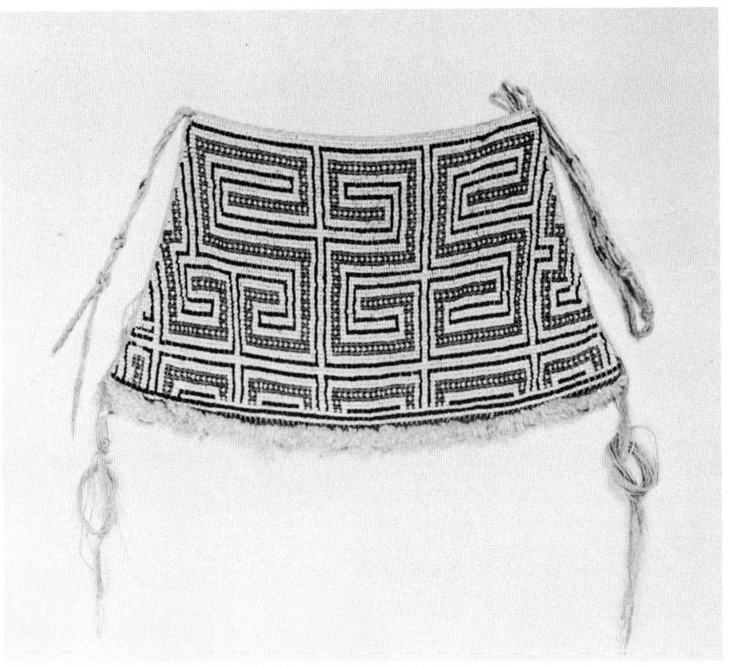

480. Woman's Apron
These beautifully designed and beaded aprons are worn by women throughout the Arawak region. Their contrast with the tan skin color provides a pleasing contrast. Collected by A. Hyatt Verrill. AKAWAI. British Guiana. 8″ x 14¼″. 4/9917.

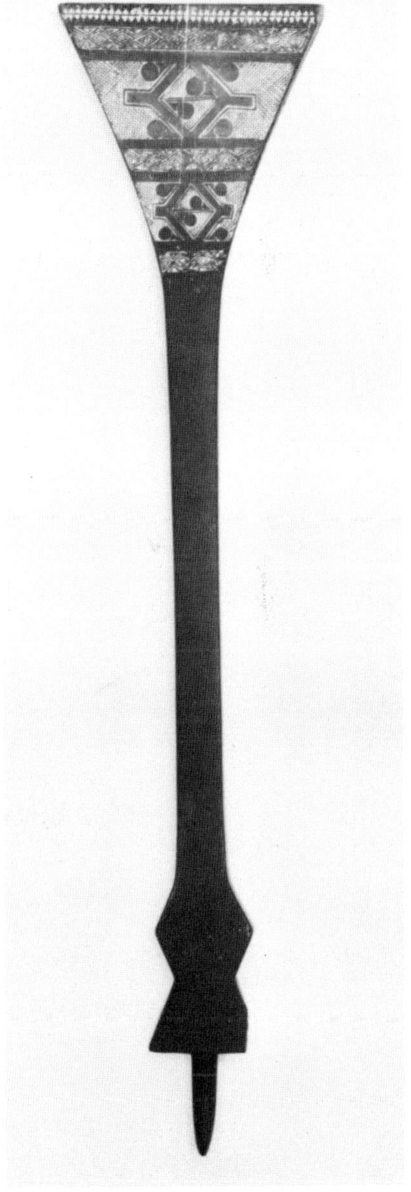

481. Incised Wooden Club
The extremely delicate designs incised on these weapons provides a startling contrast—the beauty of the pattern with the function of the club. This was collected in London, where it had been taken at the end of the 18th Century. ARAWAK. British Guiana. L: 34″. 19/6161.

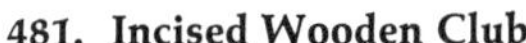

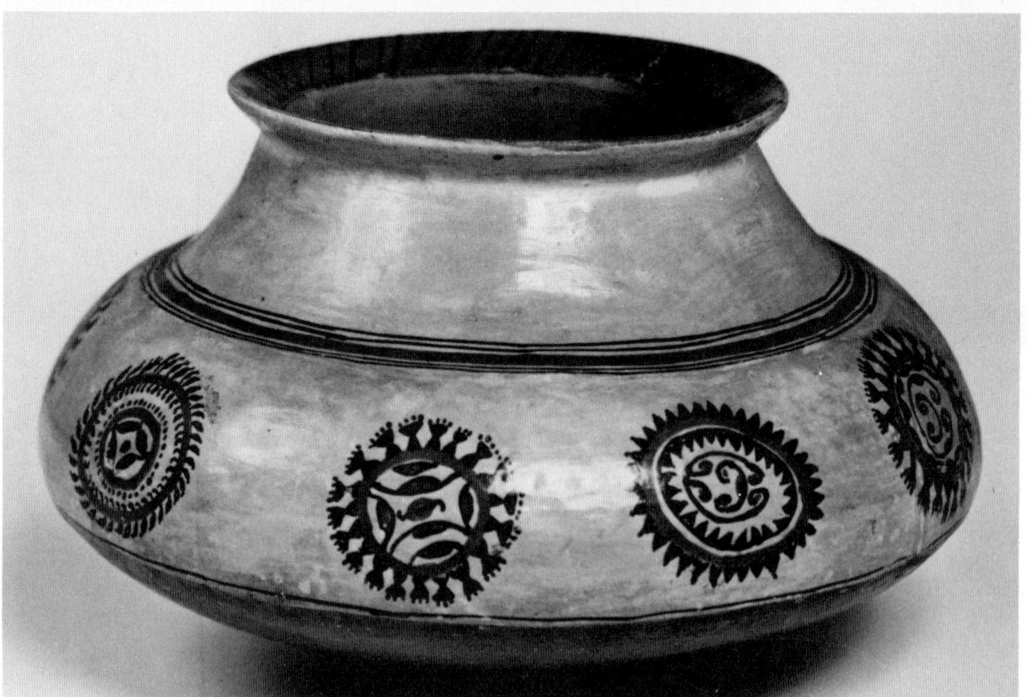

482. Polychrome Jar
The two-color design in black and red on a white slip, provides a strong contrast and pleasing effect. Copal is melted after firing, to give the surface a varnished appearance. Presented by E. Erskine Loch. CANELO. Sarayacu, Oriente, Ecuador. 1920-1925. 6½″ x 11″. 19/4787.

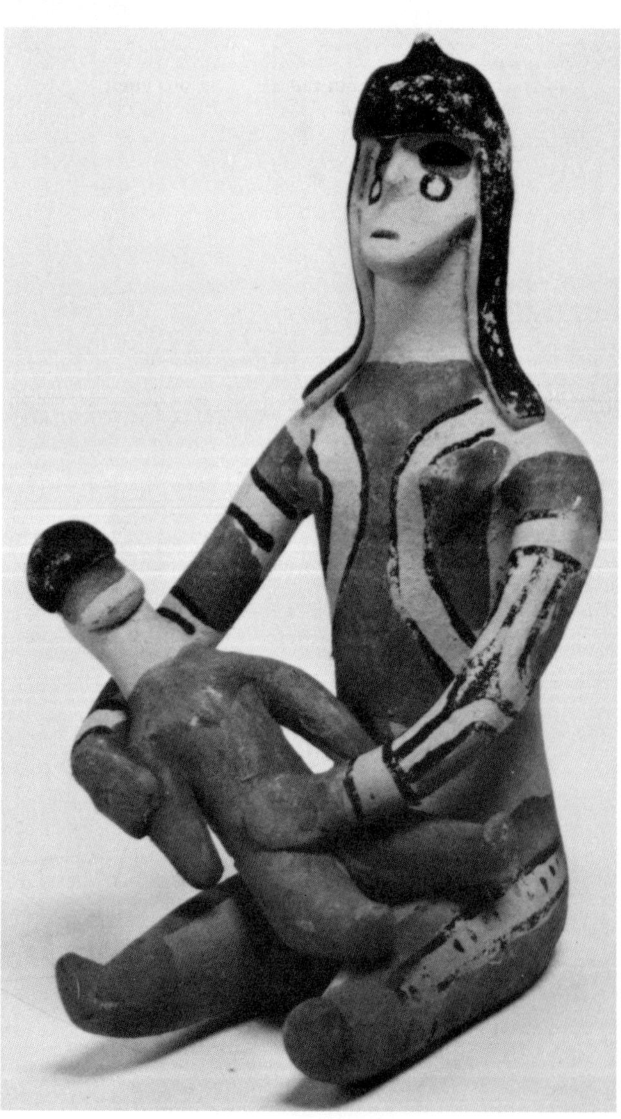

483. Mother and Child Figurine
These colorfully modeled and painted figurines, while made today for tourists, are similar to those which have traditionally been made by the Carajá women. Collected by Clovis P. Correa. CARAJÁ. Goyaz, Brazil. 1960. H: 5¼″. 23/9851.

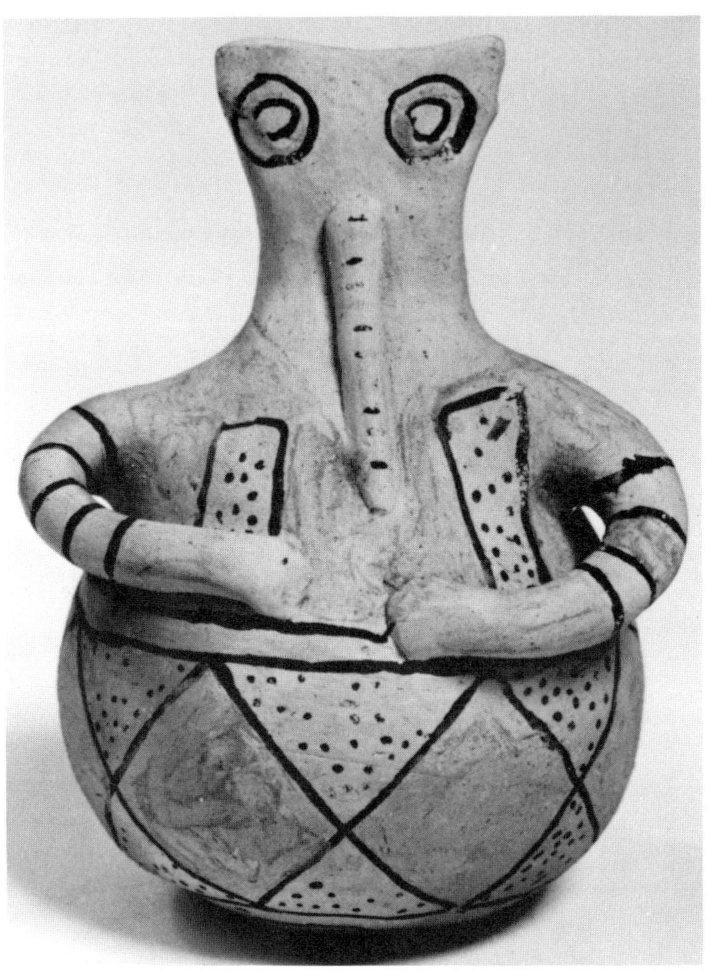

484. Pottery Figure
A new style, developed within the past decade, has given rise to some quite bizarre, but intriguing techniques in clay. This example is painted with yellow and black geometrical designs. Collected by Clovis P. Correa. CARAJÁ. Goyaz, Brazil. 1966. 3¾" x 5¼". 23/9841.

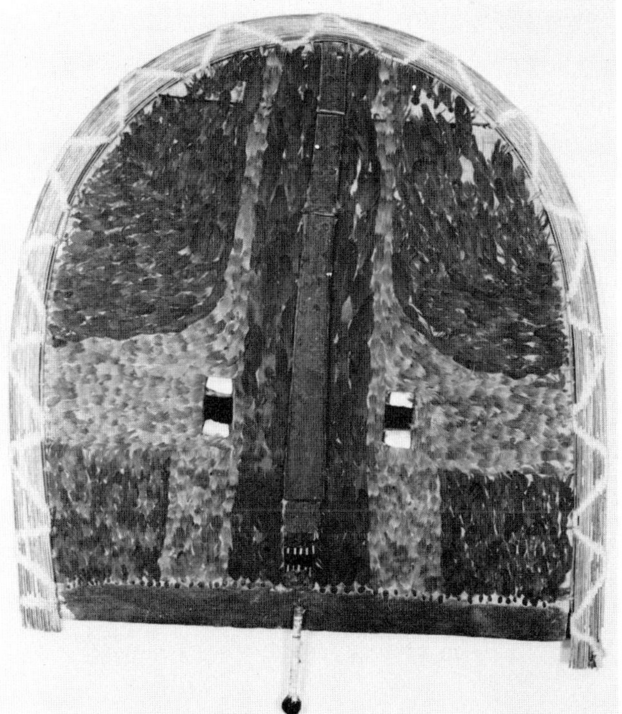

485. Feather-decorated Mask
These huge *Cara Grandes* are worn (actually carried) by men in the Banana Festival rites, when they appear in pairs, representing the souls of enemies killed in battle. Normally these have a large corona of macaw feathers; this has lost that fringe. Collected by Borys Malkin. TAPIRAPÉ. Goyaz, Brazil. 1960. 33" x 34". 23/8320.

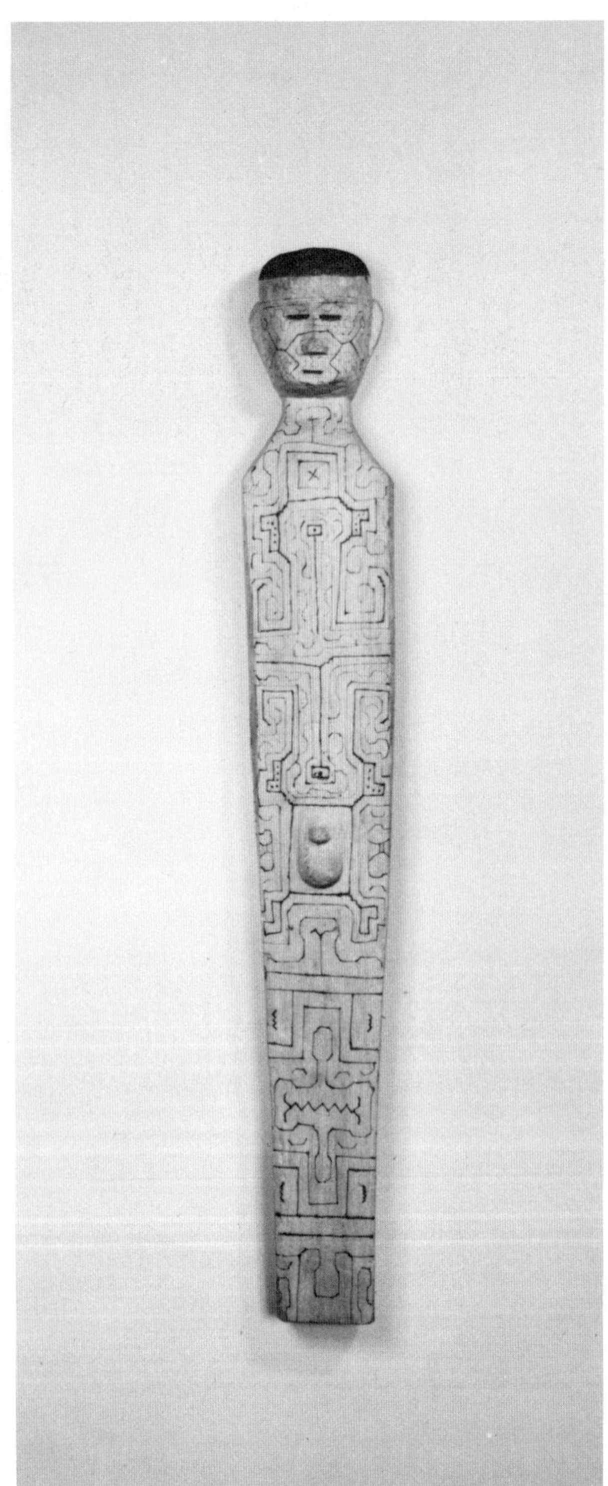

486. Painted Balsa Figure

The delicately-painted geometric lines on this figurine repeat the same designs styles as are found on textiles and pottery from this region. Presented by Malcolm Delacorte. SHIPIBO. Ucayali, Peru. 5¾″ x 36¼″. 23/1606.

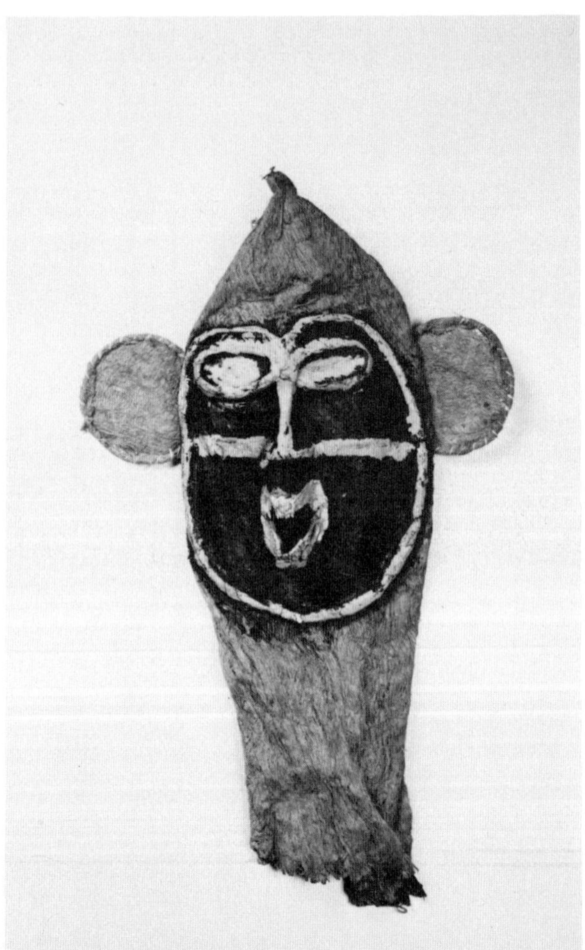

487. Bark Cloth Mask

Hammered bark cloth has been fastened to an animal skull, and subsequently coated with black gum and white paint to present a powerful form. These are used in religious ceremonies impersonating various zoömorphic beings. Collected by Arthur H. Fisher. COCAMA. Marañón, Peru. 1905-1915. 12¼″ x 21¼″. 14/9738.

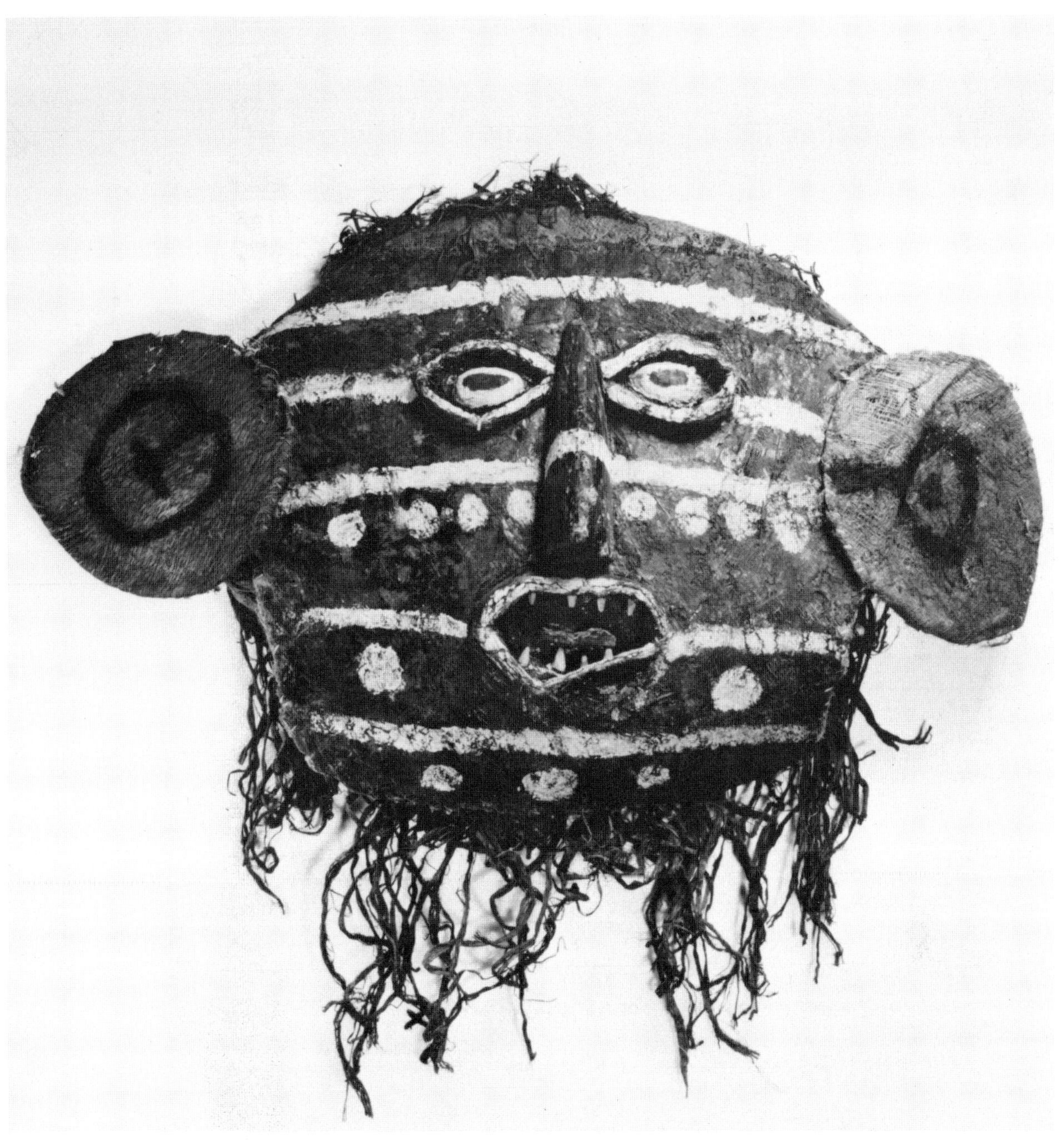

488. Bark Spirit Mask
These heavily overpainted masks are built on a bark cloth base, and decorated with bark fringing. They represent the various spirits who come to officiate at the Girls' Puberty Ceremony. Collected by Harald Schultz. TUKUNA. São Paulo de Olivença, Brazil. 1945-1955. 24" x 40". 24/7970.

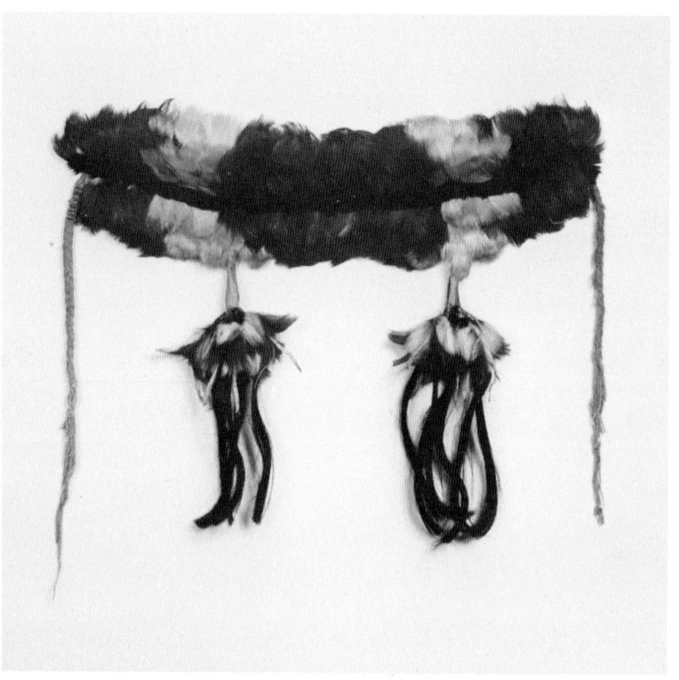

489. Feathered Headband
The brilliant feathers of various tropical birds are sewn to fiber cordage to provide headbands such as this example, worn by adult males. JÍVARO. Oriente, Ecuador. 1920-1930. 13″ x 20″. 18/9111.

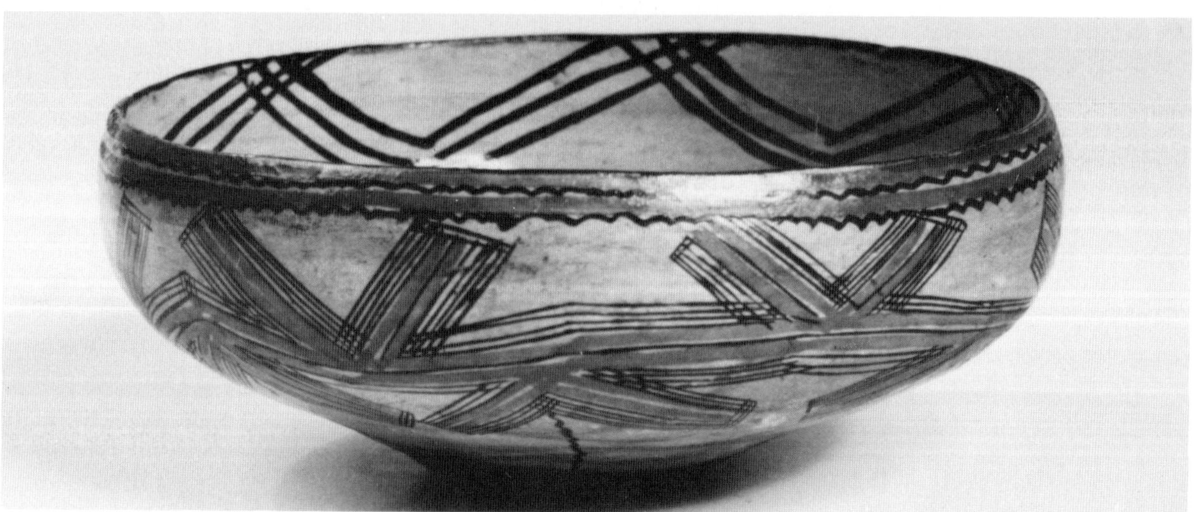

490. Buffware Bowl
The thin walls of these delicately-formed vessels are a triumph of the ceramist's art. The geometric design has been overpainted with resin, resulting in a shiny varnished appearance. Presented by E. Erskine Loch. ZÁPARO. Oriente, Ecuador. 1920-1925. 3″ x 8″. 19/4759.

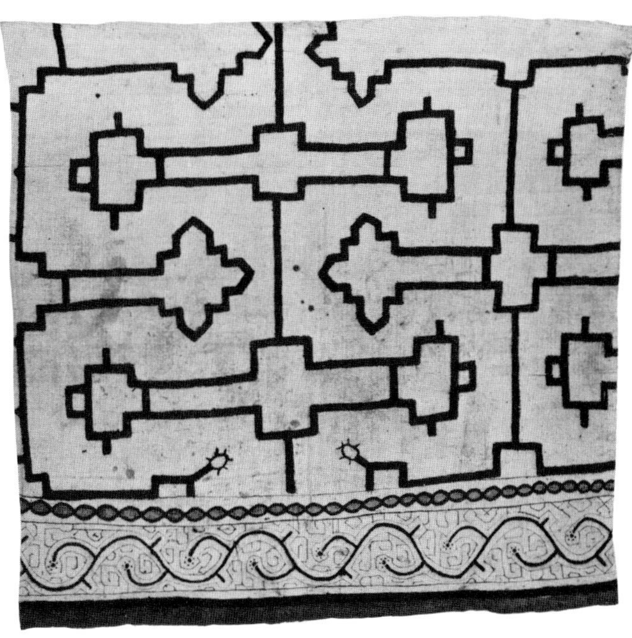

491. Painted Textile Blouse
These cotton textiles are painted in delicate geometric designs, almost identical to the patterns found on pottery from the Ucayali region. Collected by William Schaeffler. CHAMA. Ucayali, Peru. 1930-1940. 24″ x 26″. 19/5940.

492. Effigy Vessel
This anthropomorphic bowl is a fine example of the ability of the women to fashion thin-walled "varnished" pottery decorated with the geometric lines so familiar to the region. Collected by Nicole H. Maxwell. SHIPIBO. Ucayali, Peru. 1965-1966. 8½″ x 10½″. 23/9603.

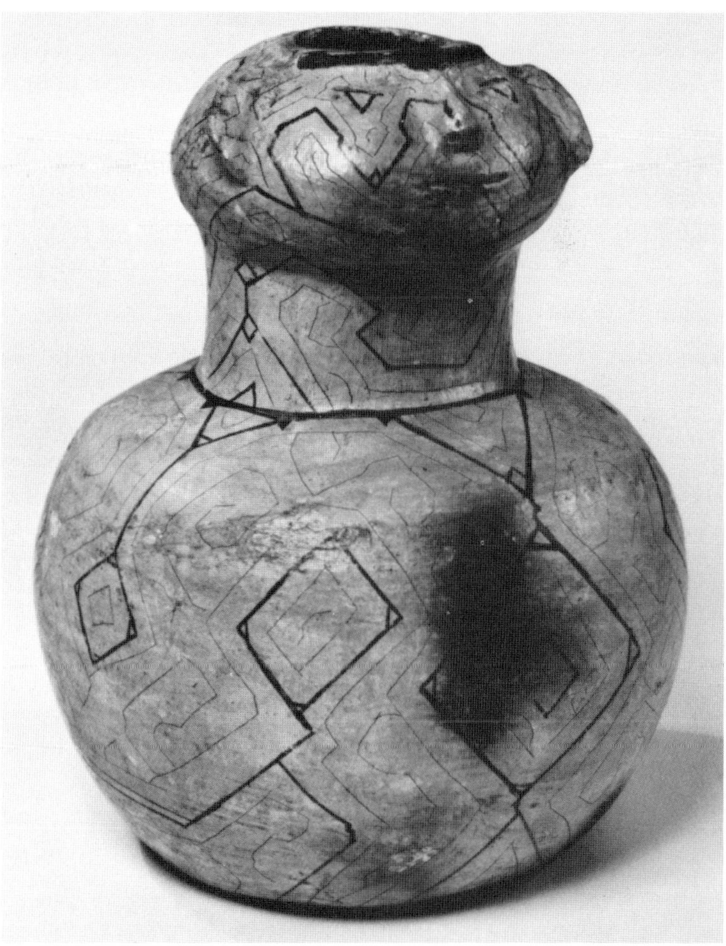

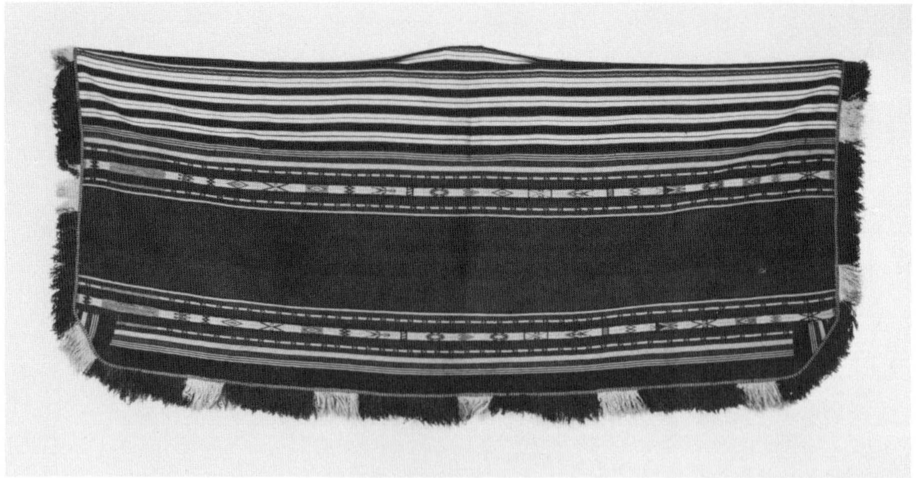

493. Woolen Poncho
The ability of the Altiplano weaver to carry on the ancient textile arts is proven by this example. The same sense of design, color pattern and technical skill makes this an attractive garment as well as an effective protection against cold weather. QUECHUA. Muñecas, Bolivia. 1900-1910. 30″ x 65″. 10/6590.

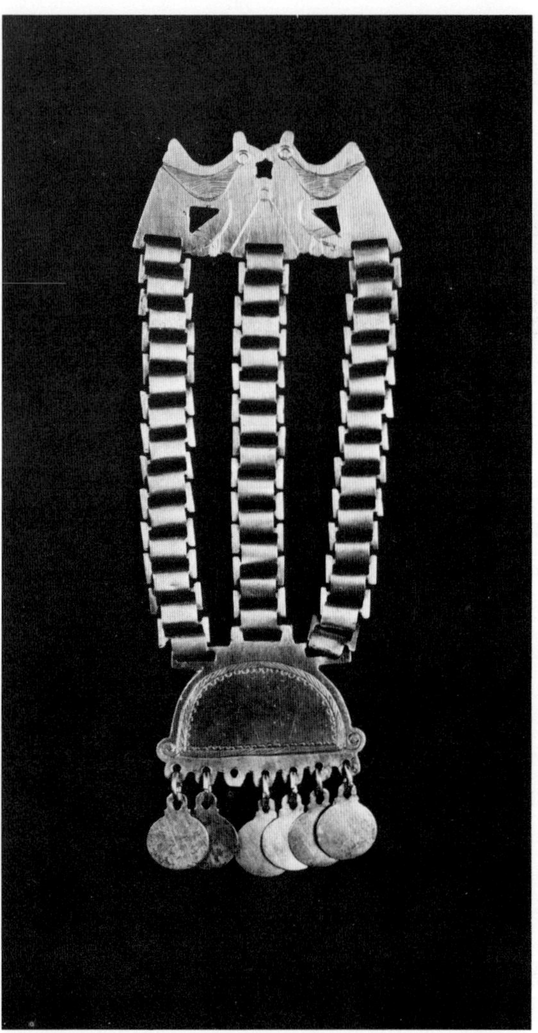

494. Silver Pendant
This heavy silver breast ornament, termed a *siquel,* is typical of the Araunaco costume, and is part of the wealth of the woman. The design is incised birds and a crescentic lower portion. Collected by J. Louis Schaefer. Presented by J. L. Schaefer, Jr., Mrs. Kathryn S. Gerdau, Mrs. Philip Sandblom, and Bernhard K. Schaefer. ARAUCANO. Santiago, Chile. 1900-1905. 3½″ x 9″. 22/5039.

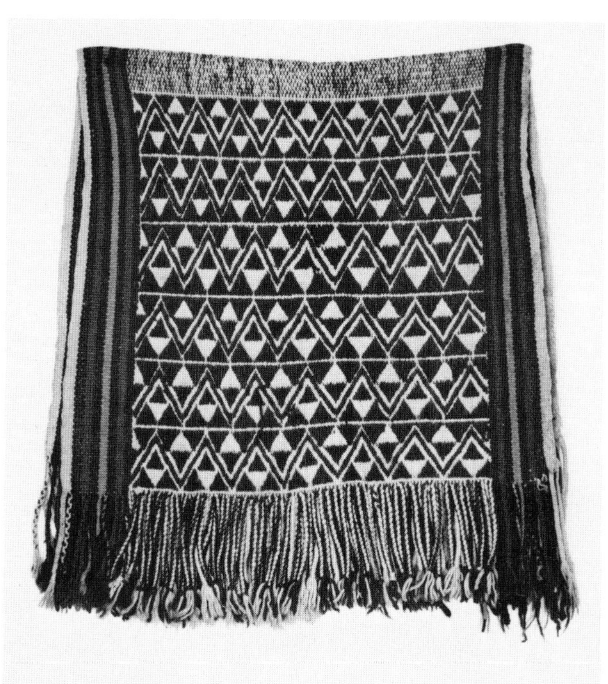

495. Woolen Textile
This red and white throw is decorated by an embroidery technique. These are employed as saddle pads, and other uses. Collected and presented by Helen Treadwell. MAPUCHE. Santiago, Chile. 1930-1935. 18″ x 21″. 22/9235.

496. Watercolor Painting
An example of the fine work produced by this master, the motion achieved in the fast-moving performers is enhanced by the brilliant color. The subject, *Komantsi Kachinas*, is by Fred Kabotie, and depicts a sequence in the public ceremony. HOPI. Arizona. 1928. 10¾″ x 14½″. 22/8645.

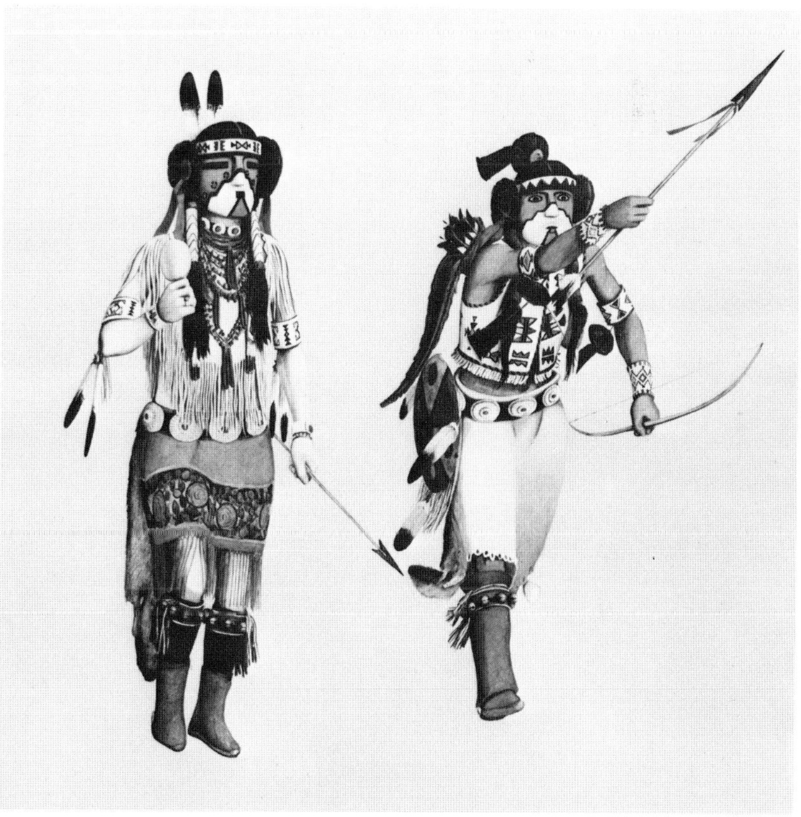

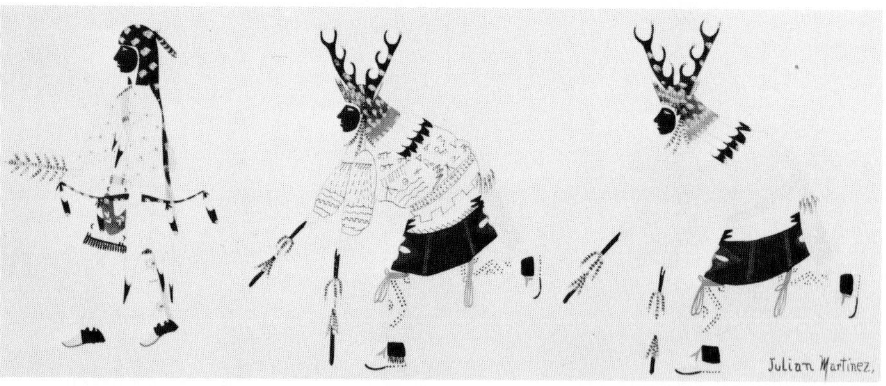

497. Watercolor Painting
A painting of two deer dancers and the hunter, this is typical of the work of the Santa Fe School earliest period. By Julián Martínez. San Ildefonso, New Mexico. 1922. 10¾″ x 26″. 24/7983.

498. Watercolor Painting
By one of the foremost Navajo painters, Harrison Begay, this is titled *Women Picking Corn,* and exemplifies the middle period of Southwestern painting. Collected by Oscar B. Jacobson. Navajo, Arizona. 1940. 11½″ x 15″. 23/6011.

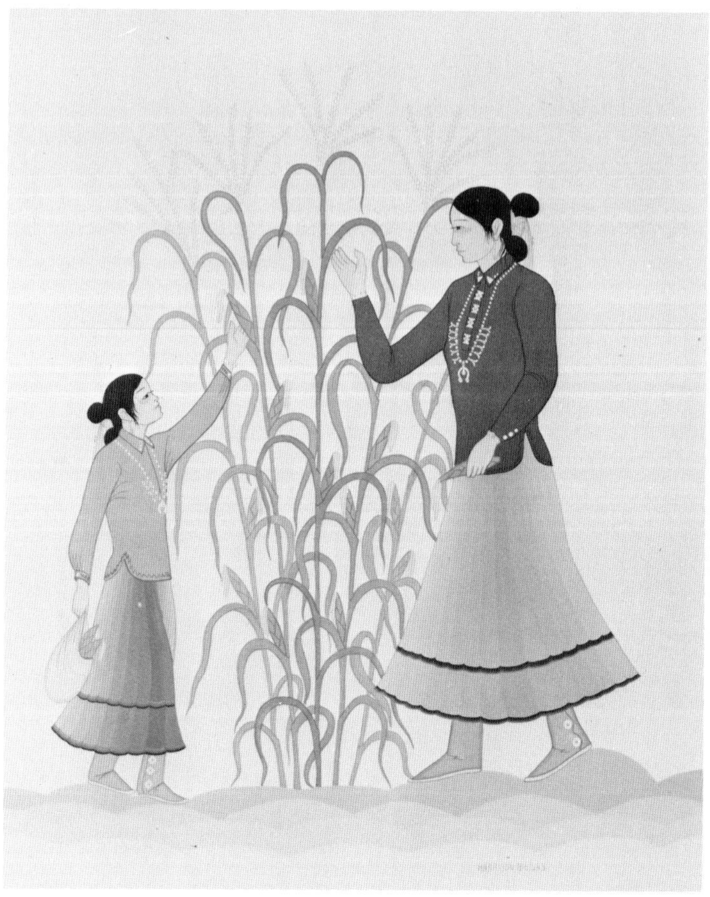

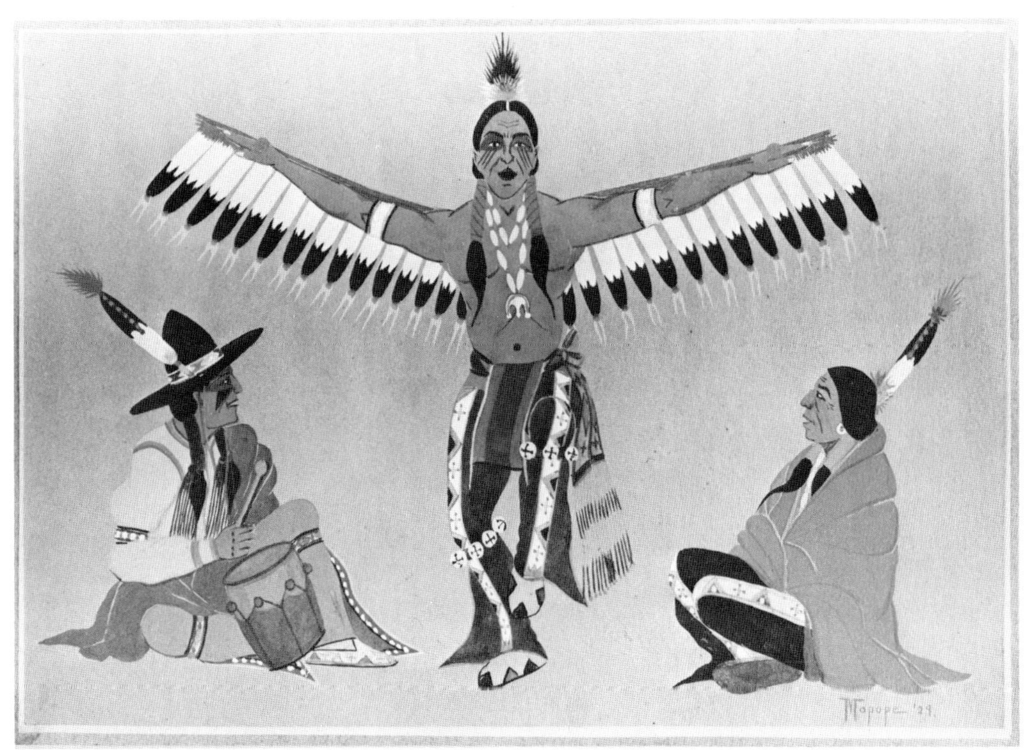

499. Watercolor Painting

From the group of young Indian painters taught by Oscar Jacobson, this painting, *The Eagle Dancer*, by Steve Mopope, characterizes the work of five men destined for considerable success in art. KIOWA. Oklahoma. 1920-1925. 7½" x 11". 22/8618.

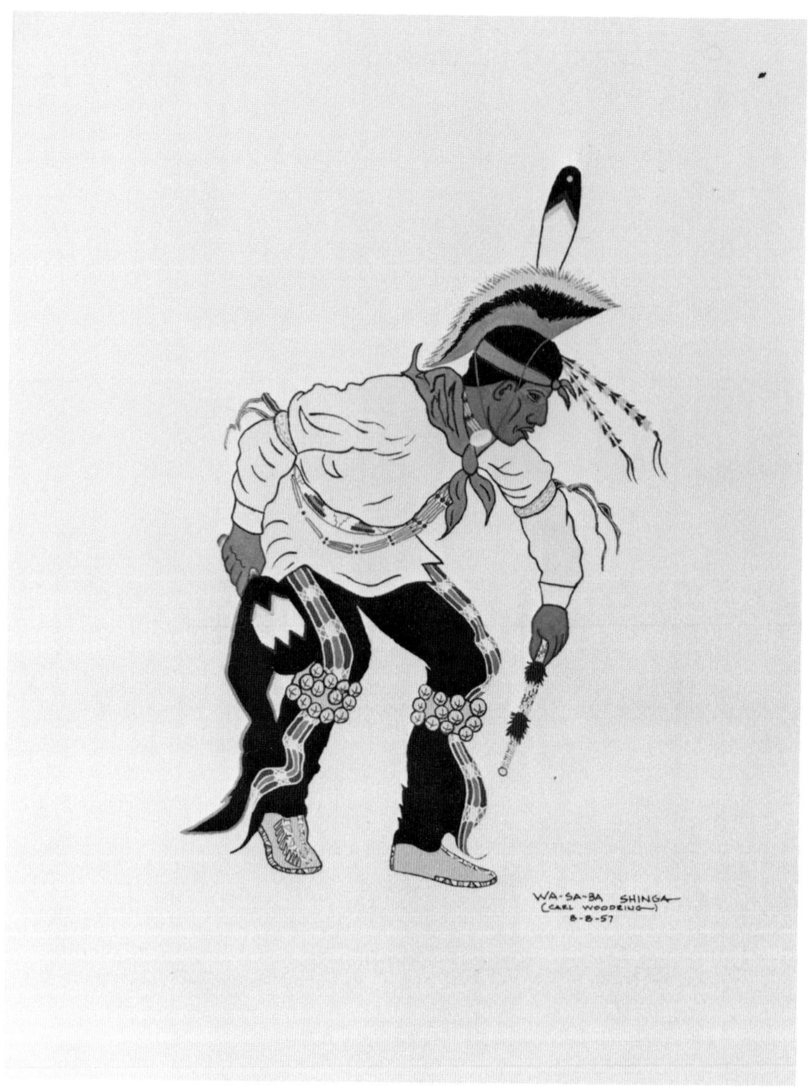

500. Watercolor Painting
A young painter who represents the post-World War II period, *Osage Straight Dancer*, by Carl Woodring, was the Grand Award Winner at Philbrook Anadarko Exposition in 1957. Collected by Jeanne O. Snodgrass. OSAGE. Oklahoma. 12¾" x 17". 23/8384.

FOR FURTHER READING

This bibliography has been compiled on the basis of general availability and thoroughness of illustrations, in the hope of introducing the reader to background resources related to the several areas and periods covered in this exhibition. Primarily, book-length works have been included; with a few exceptions, specialized academic studies have been omitted.

Since each volume includes its own individual bibliography, the total number of titles is extensive. Those works marked * will present the reader with particularly helpful or well-illustrated material.

NORTH AMERICA

ADAIR, JOHN, *The Navaho and Pueblo Silversmiths.* Norman, Oklahoma: University of Oklahoma Press (1944) 220 pp.

ALEXANDER, HARTLEY BURR, *Pueblo Indian Painting.* Nice: C. Szwedzicki (1932) 18 pp. + 50 plates.

*AMSDEN, CHARLES AVERY, *Navaho Weaving: Its Technic and History.* Santa Ana, Calif.: The Fine Arts Press (1934) 261 pp.

ASTROV, MARGOT (ed)., *The Winged Serpent; American Indian Prose and Poetry.* New York: Putnam (1962) 366 pp.

BAHTI, TOM, *Southwestern Indian Arts & Crafts.* Flagstaff: KC Publications (1966) 34 pp.

BARBEAU, MARIUS, "Haida Carvers in Argillite." Ottawa: *National Museum of Canada, Bulletin 139, Anthropological Series, No. 38* (1957) 214 pp.

*————, "Totem Poles." Ottawa: *National Museum of Canada, Bulletin 119, Anthropological Series* No. 30 (1930) 2 Vols.

BARRETT, S. A., "Pomo Indian Basketry." Berkeley, Calif.: *University of California, Publications in American Anthropology and Ethnology, VII, No. 3* (1908) p. 133-309.

BEDINGER, MARGERY, *Indian Silver; Navajo and Pueblo Jewelers.* Albuquerque: Univ. of New Mexico Press (1973) 264 pp.

BOAS, FRANZ, "Decorative Art of the Indians of the North Pacific Coast," New York: *American Museum of Natural History, Bulletin 9* (1897) pp. 123-76.

————, *Primitive Art.* Instituttet for Sammenlignende Kulturforskning, XIII Series B (1927) 373 pp. Reprint: New York, Dover Publications (1955) 378 pp.

BRODY, J. J., *Indian Painters and White Patrons.* Albuquerque: Univ. of New Mexico Press (1971) 238 pp.

BUNZEL, RUTH L., "The Pueblo Potter." New York: *Columbia University, Contributions to Anthropology,* VII (1929) 134 pp.

*BURNETT, E. K., "The Spiro Mound Collection in the Museum." New York: *Museum of the American Indian, Contributions,* Vol. XIV (1945) 68 pp. + 94 plates.

CHAPMAN, KENNETH M., "The Pottery of Santo Domingo Pueblo." Santa Fe, N.M.: *Laboratory of Anthropology, Memoir I* (1939) 192 pp.

————, *Pueblo Indian Pottery.* Nice: C. Szwedzicki (1933; 1939) 2 Vols. + 100 plates.

————, *The Pottery of San Ildefonso Pueblo.* Santa Fe: School of American Research (1970) 260 pp. + 174 plates.

COLLINS, HENRY B., "Prehistoric Art of the Alaskan Eskimo." Washington: *Smithsonian Institution, Miscellaneous Collections 81,* No. 14 (1929) 52 pp.

COSGROVE, H. S. *and* C. B., "The Swarts Ruin; A Typical Mimbres Site in Southwestern New Mexico." Cambridge, Mass.: *Peabody Museum Papers, XV,* No. 1 (1932) 178 pp. + 236 plates.

*DAVIS, ROBERT TYLER, *Native Arts of the Pacific Northwest.* Stanford, Calif.: Stanford University Press (1949) 165 pp.

DAY A. GROVE, *The Sky Clears; Poetry of the American Indian.* Lincoln: Univ. of Nebraska Press (1964) 204 pp.

DIXON, ROLAND B., "Basketry Designs of the Indians of Northern California." New York: *American Museum of Natural History, Bulletin 17, Part I* (1902) pp. 1-32.

*DOCKSTADER, FREDERICK J., *Indian Art in America.* Greenwich: New York Graphic Society (1962; 1966) 224 pp. + 250 plates. Reprint, 1972, as *Indian Art in North America.*

————, "The Kachina and the White Man." *Cranbrook Institute of Science, Bulletin No. 35* (1954) 185 pp.

*DOUGLAS, FREDERICK H., *and* RÉNE D'HARNONCOURT, *Indian Art of the United States.* New York: Museum of Modern Art (1941) 219 pp.

*DUNN, DOROTHY, *American Indian Painting of the Southwest and Plains Areas.* Albuquerque: Univ. of New Mexico Press (1968) 429 pp. + 32 plates.

*EARLE, EDWIN, *and* EDWARD KENNARD, *Hopi Kachinas.* New York: J. J. Augustin (1938) 40 pp. + 28 plates. Reprint (1970) New York: Museum of the American Indian.

EMMONS, LT. GEORGE T., "The Chilkat Blanket." New York: *American Museum of Natural History, Memoir III* (1907) pp. 329-400.

EWERS, JOHN C., *Plains Indian Painting.* Stanford, Calif.: Stanford University Press (1939) 84 pp.

———, *Blackfeet Crafts.* Washington, D.C.: Office of Indian Affairs (1945) 66 pp.

**Exposition of Indian Tribal Arts, Inc.*, JOHN SLOAN *and* OLIVER LAFARGE, eds. (1931) 2 vols., many illustrations.

*FEDER, NORMAN, *American Indian Art.* New York: Harry N. Abrams (no date) 447 pp. + 242 plates.

———, *Two Hundred Years of North American Indian Art.* New York: Praeger Publishers (1971) 128 pp. + 150 plates.

FORBES, ANNE, "A Survey of Current Pueblo Indian Paintings." Santa Fe: *El Palacio,* Vol. 57, No. 8 (1950) pp. 235-52.

*FUNDABURK, EMMA LILA, *and* MARY DOUGLASS FOREMAN, *Sun Circles and Human Hands.* Luverne, Alabama (1957) 232 pp.

———, *Southeastern Indians; Life Portraits.* Luverne, Alabama (1958) 136 pp.

GARFIELD, VIOLA, *The Tsimshian: Their Arts and Music.* New York: J. J. Augustin (1951) 290 pp.

HABERLAND, WOLFGANG, *The Art of North America.* New York: Crown Publishers (1964) 252 pp. + 60 plates.

*HARDING, ANNE, *and* PATRICIA BOLLING, *Bibliography of Articles and Papers on North American Indian Art.* Washington, D.C.: Department of the Interior, Indian Arts and Crafts Board (1938) 365 pp. Mimeographed.

HAWTHORN, AUDREY, *Art of the Kwakiutl Indians; and Other Northwest Coast Tribes.* Seattle: Univ. of Washington Press (1967) 472 pp.

HOFFMAN, WALTER JAMES, "The Graphic Art of the Eskimos." Washington, D.C.: *U.S. National Museum, Annual Report for 1895,* pp. 739-968.

HOLM, BILL, *Northwest Coast Indian Art; an Analysis of Form.* Seattle: Univ. of Washington Press (1965) 115 pp., illus.

HOLMES, WILLIAM HENRY, "Aboriginal Pottery of the Eastern United States." Washington, D.C.: *Bureau of American Ethnology, Annual Report XX* (1899) 201 pp. + 177 plates.

———, "Art in Shell of the Ancient Americans." Washington, D.C.: *Bureau of American Ethnology, Annual Report II* (1891) pp. 179-305 + 56 plates.

*———, "Origin and Development of Form and Ornament in Ceramic Art." Washington, D.C.: *Bureau of American Ethnology, Annual Report IV* (1886) pp. 437-465 + 25 plates.

*INVERARITY, ROBERT BRUCE, *Art of the Northwest Coast Indians.* Berkeley, Calif.: University of California Press (1950) 243 pp.

———, *Movable Masks and Figures of the North Pacific Coast Indians.* Bloomfield Hills, Mich.: Cranbrook Institute of Science (1941), portfolio.

JACOBSON, OSCAR B., *Kiowa Indian Art.* Nice: C. Szwedzicki (1929) 11 pp. + 30 plates.

———, *and* D'UCEL, JEANNE, *American Indian Painters.* Nice: C. Szwedzicki (1950) portfolio.

KEITHAHN, EDWARD, *Monuments in Cedar.* Ketchikan, Alaska: Roy Anderson (1945) 160 pp.

*KELEMEN, PÁL, *Mediaeval American Art.* New York: Macmillan (1943, 1956; 1969) 414 pp. + 308 plates.

KNOBLOCK, BYRON W., *Bannerstones of the North American Indians.* LaGrange, Ind.: The author (1939) 596 pp. + 266 plates.

KRAUSE, AUREL, *Die Tlinkit Indianer,* Jena (1888). English edition translated by Erna Gunther. Seattle: University of Washington Press (1956) 310 pp.

*KRIEGER, HERBERT W., "Aspects of Aboriginal Decorative Art in America. Based on Specimens in the U.S. National Museum." Washington, D.C.: *Smithsonian Institution, Annual Report for 1930,* pp. 519-56.

LYFORD, CARRIE, *Quill and Beadwork of the Western Sioux.* Washington, D.C.: Office of Indian Affairs (1940) 116 pp.

———, *Iroquois Crafts.* Washington, D.C.: Office of Indian Affairs (1942) 97 pp.

———, *Ojibwa Crafts.* Washington, D.C.: Office of Indian Affairs (1943) 216 pp.

MALLERY, GARRICK, "Pictographs of the North American Indians." Washington, D.C.: *Bureau of American Ethnology, Annual Report IV* (1886) pp. 3-256 + 88 plates.

———, "Picture-writing of the American Indians." Washington, D.C.: *Bureau of American Ethnology, Annual Report X* (1893) pp. 3-807 + 54 plates.

MARRIOTT, ALICE, *María: The Potter of San Ildefonso.* Norman, Okla.: University of Oklahoma Press (1948) 294 pp.

MASON, J. ALDEN, "Eskimo Pictorial Art." Philadelphia: *Museum Journal,* XVIII (1927) pp. 248-83.

MASON, OTIS TUFTON, "Aboriginal American Basketry." Washington, D.C.: *U.S. National Museum, Annual Report for 1902,* pp. 171-548 + 248 plates.

MERA, HARRY P., *Indian Silverwork of the Southwest, Illustrated.* Globe, Ariz.: Dale S. King (1959) 122 pp.

————, "The 'Rain Bird' A Study in Pueblo Design." Santa Fe.: *Laboratory of Anthropology, Memoir II* (1937) 113 pp.

MILLS, GEORGE, *Navaho Art and Culture.* Colorado Springs: The Taylor Museum (1959) 273 pp.

MOOREHEAD, WARREN K., *Stone Ornaments of the American Indians.* Andover, Mass.: The Andover Press (1917) 448 pp.

————, *The Stone Age in North America.* Boston: Houghton Mifflin (1910) 2 vols.

NEWCOMB, FRANC J. *and* GLADYS A. REICHARD, *Sand Paintings of the Navajo Shooting Chant.* New York: J. J. Augustin (1937) 87 pp. + 35 plates.

ORCHARD, WILLIAM C., "Beads and Beadwork of the American Indians." New York: *Museum of the American Indian, Contributions* Vol. XI (1929) 140 pp. + 31 plates.

————, "The Technique of Porcupine-quill Decoration Among the North American Indians." New York: *Museum of the American Indian, Contributions,* Vol. III, No. 1 (1916) 53 pp. Reprint (1972) New York: Museum of the American Indian.

RAY, DOROTHY JEAN, *Eskimo Masks, Art and Ceremony.* Seattle: Univ. of Washington Press (1967) 272 pp.

SHETRONE, HENRY CLYDE, *The Mound Builders.* New York: Appleton (1930) 508 pp.

*SIDES, DOROTHY, *Decorative Art of the Southwestern Indians.* Santa Ana, Calif.: The Fine Arts Press (1936) 50 plates.

SMITH, HARLAN I., "An Album of Prehistoric Canadian Art." Ottawa: *National Museum of Canada, Bulletin 37* (1923) 195 pp.

SMITH, WATSON, "Kiva Mural Decorations at Awátovi and Kawaika-a." Cambridge, Mass.: *Peabody Museum Papers,* Vol. 37 (1952) 363 pp. + 92 plates.

SNODGRASS, JEANNE O., "American Indian Painters; A Biographical Directory." New York: *Museum of the American Indian, Contributions XXI.* pt. 1 (1968) 269 pp.

SPECK, FRANK G., "The Double Curve Motive in Northeastern Algonkin Art." Ottawa: *National Museum of Canada, Memoir No. 42* (1941) 17 pp.

————, "Decorative Art and Basketry of the Cherokee." Milwaukee: *Milwaukee Public Museum, Bulletin 2* (1920) pp. 53-86.

————, "Montagnais Art in Birch-bark, a Circumpolar Trait." New York: *Museum of the American Indian, Indian Notes and Monographs,* XI No. 2 (1937) 157 pp.

STEWARD, JULIAN H., "Petroglyphs of California and Adjoining States." Berkeley, Calif.: *University of California, Publications in American Archaeology and Ethnology, Vol. 24* (1929) pp. 47-238.

————, " Petroglyphs of the United States." Washington, D.C.: *Smithsonian Institution, Annual Report for 1936,* pp. 405-426.

SWANTON, JOHN R., "Contributions to the Ethnology of the Haida." New York: *American Museum of Natural History, Memoir VIII,* Part I (1905) 300 pp.

*TANNER, CLARA LEE, *Southwest Indian Craft Arts.* Tucson: Univ. Arizona Press (1968) 206 pp., illus.

*————, *Southwest Indian Painting.* Tucson: Arizona Silhouettes (1957) 157 pp., illus.

TOWNSEND, EARL C., JR., *Birdstones of the North American Indians.* Indianapolis: The author (1959) 719 pp.

UNDERHILL, RUTH M., *Pueblo Crafts.* Washington, D.C.: Bureau of Indian Affairs (1944) 145 pp.

*VAILLANT, GEORGE C., *Indian Arts in North America.* New York: Harper & Bros (1939) 63 pp. + 96 plates.

VANDERWERTH, W. C. (ed)., *Indian Oratory.* Norman: Univ. of Oklahoma Press (1971) 300 pp.

WEST, GEORGE, "Tobacco Pipes and Smoking Customs of the American Indians." Milwaukee, Wisconsin: *Milwaukee Public Museum, Bulletin 17* (1934) 2 vols.

WILDSCHUT, WILLIAM, *and* JOHN C. EWERS, "Crow Indian Beadwork; A Descriptive and Historical Study." New York: *Museum of the American Indian, Contributions* Vol. XVI (1959) 55 pp. + 47 plates. Reprint (1973) New York: Museum of the American Indian.

WILLEY, GORDON, *An Introduction to American Archaeology.* Vol. I: *North and Middle America.* New Jersey: Prentice-Hall (1966) 526 pp.

WISSLER, CLARK," Decorative Art of the Sioux Indians." New York: *American Museum of Natural History, Bulletin XVIII,* Part 3 (1904) pp. 231-78 + 9 plates.

WOODWARD, ARTHUR, "A Brief History of Navaho Silversmithing." Flagstaff, Ariz.: *Museum of Northern Arizona, Bulletin 14* (1938) 78 pp.

MEXICO AND CENTRAL AMERICA

ANDERSON, LAWRENCE, *The Art of the Silversmith in Mexico, 1519-1936.* New York: Oxford University Press (1941) 2 vols.

*ATL., DR. [GERARDO MURILLO], *Las Artes Populares en México.* México, D.F.: Publicaciones de la Secretaria de Industria y Comercio (1922) 2 vols.

BALSER, CARLOS, *Pre-Columbian Jade in Costa Rica.* San Jose: Librería Lehmann (1958) 18 pp. + 9 plates.

BERGSØE, PAUL, *The Metallurgy and Technology of Gold and Platinum among the Pre-Columbian Indians.* Copenhagen: Danmarks naturvidenskabelige samfund (1937) 44 pp.

*BERNAL IGNACIO, "Bibliografia de Arqueología y Etnografía. Mesoamérica y Norte de México, 1514-1960." México, D.F.: *Instituto Nacional de Antropología e Historia, Memorias VII* (1962) 1634 pp.

BOVALLIUS, CARL, *Nicaraguan Antiquities.* Stockholm: P. A. Norstedt söner (1886) 50 pp. + 41 plates.

CASO, ALFONSO, *The Aztecs, People of the Sun.* Norman: University of Oklahoma Press (1958) 125 pp.

*———, "Bibliografía de las Artes Populares Plásticas en México." Mexico D.F.: *Instituto Nacional Indigenista, Memorias I* (1950) pp. 83-132.

*———, *and* IGNACIO BERNAL, "Urnas de Oaxaca." Mexico, D.F.: *Instituto Nacional de Antropología e Historia, Memorias II* (1952) 389 pp.

COE, MICHAEL D., *Mexico.* New York: Frederick A. Praeger (1962) 245 pp.

CORDRY, DONALD B., *and* DOROTHY CORDRY, "Costumes and Textiles of the Aztec Indians of the Cuetzalán Region, Puebla, Mexico." Los Angeles: *Southwest Museum, Papers No. XIV* (1940) 60 pp.

———, "Costumes and Weaving of the Zoque Indians of Chiapas, Mexico." Los Angeles: *Southwest Museum, Papers No. XV* (1941) 23 pp.

*———, *Mexican Indian Costumes.* Austin: Univ. of Texas Press (1972) 373 pp., illus.

*COVARRUBIAS, MIGUEL, *The Eagle, the Jaguar and the Serpent.* New York: Alfred A. Knopf (1954) 31 pp. + 48 plates.

*———, *Indian Art of Mexico and Central America.* New York: Alfred A. Knopf (1957) 36 pp. + 48 plates.

DAVIS, MARY L., *and* GRETA PACK, *Mexican Jewelry.* Austin: Univ. of Texas Press (1963) 262 pp. + 145 plates.

*DISSELHOFF, HANS D., *and* SIGVALD LINNÉ, *The Art of Ancient America.* New York: Crown Publishers (1960) 274 pp.

*DOCKSTADER, FREDERICK J., *Indian Art in Middle America.* Greenwich: New York Graphic Society (1964) 56 pp. + 248 plates.

DÖRNER, GERD, *Folk Art of Mexico.* New York: A. S. Barnes (1962) 68 pp. + 28 plates.

*DRUCKER, PHILIP, "La Venta, Tabasco: A Study of Olmec Ceramics and Art." Washington, D.C.: *Bureau of American Ethnology, Bulletin 153* (1952) 257 pp. + 66 plates.

*EASBY, ELIZABETH K., *and* JOHN F. SCOTT, *Before Cortés; Sculpture of Middle America.* New York: Metropolitan Museum of Art (1970) 322 pp. + 308 plates.

*EMMERICH, ANDRÉ, *Art Before Columbus: the Art of Ancient Mexico.* New York: Simon and Schuster (1963) 256 pp.

ENCISCO, JORGE, *Design Motifs of Ancient Mexico.* New York: Dover Publishers (1953) 153 pp.

FERNÁNDEZ, JUSTINO, *Arte Mexicano: de sus Orígines a Nuestros Días.* México, D.F.: Instituto de Investigaciones Estéticas (1958) 208 pp. + 224 plates.

*FEUCHTWANGER, FRANZ, *and* IRMGARD GROTH-KIMBALL, *The Art of Ancient Mexico.* New York: Thames & Hudson (1954) 125 pp. + 109 plates.

*FEWKES, JESSE W., "The Aborigines of Porto Rico and Neighboring Islands." Washington, D.C.: *Bureau of American Ethnology, 25th Annual Report* (1907) pp. 3-220 + 113 plates.

*———, "A Prehistoric Island Culture Area of America." Washington, D.C.: *Bureau of American Ethnology, 34th Annual Report* (1922) pp. 35-271 + 120 plates.

*GORDON, GEORGE B., *Examples of Mayan Pottery in the Museum and in Other Collections.* Philadelphia: University Museum (1925-1928) portfolio, in two parts.

———, "Prehistoric Ruins of Copán, Honduras." Cambridge: *Peabody Museum, Memoirs I, No. I* (1896) 48 pp. + 8 plates.

GROTH-KIMBALL, IRMGARD, *Mayan Terracottas.* New York: Frederick A. Praeger (1960) 45 plates.

D'HARCOURT, RAOUL, *Primitive Art of the Americas.* Paris: Editions du Chêne (1950) 199 pp. + 4 plates.

HOLMES, WILLIAM HENRY. "Ancient Art of the Province of Chiriquí, Colombia." Washington, D.C.: *Bureau of American Ethnology, 6th Annual Report* (1888) pp. 3-187.

*KELEMEN, PÁL, *Art of the Americas, Ancient and Hispanic.* New York: Thomas Y. Crowell (1969) 402 pp., illus.

*———, *Mediaeval American Art.* New York: Macmillan (1943; 1956; 1969) 414 pp. + 308 plates.

*KIDDER, ALFRED VINCENT, II, *and* CARLOS SAMAYOA CHINCHILLA, *The Art of the Ancient Maya.* New York: Thomas Y. Crowell (1959) 124 pp.

*KINGSBOROUGH, EDWARD KING, *The Antiquities of Mexico.* London: Lord Kingsborough (1830-1848) 9 volumes, portfolio.

KRICKEBERG, WALTER, *Altmexikanische Kulturen.* Berlin: Safari-verlag (1956) 616 pp.

KRIEGER, HERBERT W., "Aboriginal Indian Pottery of the Dominican Republic." Washington, D.C.: *United States National Museum, Bulletin 156* (1931) 65 pp.

————, "The Aborigines of the Ancient Island of Hispaniola." Washington, D.C.: *Smithsonian Institution, Annual Report for 1929,* pp. 473-506.

*KUBLER, GEORGE, *The Art and Architecture of Ancient America; The Mexican, Maya and Andean Peoples.* Baltimore: Penguin Books (1962) 396 pp. + 168 plates.

KURATH, GERTRUDE, *and* SAMUEL MARTÍ, *Dances of Anahuac; the Choreography and Music of Pre-Cortesian Dances.* Chicago: Aldine. Viking Fund Pub. No. 38 (1964) 251 pp.

LEÓN-PORTILLA, MIGUEL, *Aztec Thought and Culture; a Study of the Ancient Nahuatl.* Norman: University of Oklahoma Press (1963) 241 pp.

————, *The Broken Spears; The Aztec Account of the Conquest of Mexico.* Boston: Beacon Press (1962) 168 pp.

LONGYEAR, JOHN M., III, "Archaeological Investigations in El Salvador." Cambridge, Mass.: *Peabody Museum, Memoirs IX, No. 2* (1944) 90 pp. + 14 plates.

————, "Copán Ceramics." Washington, D.C.: *Carnegie Institution of Washington, Publication No. 597* (1952) 114 pp.

*LOTHROP, SAMUEL KIRKLAND, "Archaeology of Southern Veraguas, Panama." Cambridge, Mass.: *Peabody Museum, Memoirs IX No. 3* (1950) 116 pp.

*————, "Coclé; an Archaeological Study of Central Panama." Cambridge, Mass.: *Peabody Museum, Memoirs VII-VIII* (1937; 1942) 327 pp., 292 pp.

*————, "Pottery of Costa Rica and Nicaragua." New York: *Museum of the American Indian, Contributions VIII* (1926) 2 vols.

MACCURDY, GEORGE G., "A Study of Chiriquian Antiquities." New Haven: *Connecticut Academy of Arts and Sciences, Memoirs III* (1911) 249 pp. + 49 plates.

*MARQUINA, IGNACIO, "Arquitectura Prehispánica." México, D.F.: *Instituto Nacional de Antropología e Historia, Memorias I* (1951) 470 pp. + 291 plates.

MEDELLÍN ZENIL, ALFONSO, *Cerámicas de Totonacapán.* Xalapa: Universidad Veracruzana (1960) 220 pp.

*MORLEY, SYLVANUS G., *The Ancient Maya.* Revision by George W. Brainerd. Palo Alto: Stanford University Press (1956) 194 pp. + 102 plates.

*NORIEGA, RAUL, et al [eds.] *Esplendor del México Antiguo.* México, D.F.: Centro de Investigaciones Antropológicos de México (1959) 2 vols.

OGLESBY, CATHARINE, *Modern Primitive Arts of Mexico, Guatemala and the Southwest.* New York: Whittlesey House (1939) 226 pp. + 12 plates.

*O'NEALE, LILA M., "Textiles of Highland Guatemala." Washington, D.C.: *Carnegie Institution of Washington, Publication No. 567* (1945) 319 pp. + 130 plates.

OSBORNE, LILLY DEJONGH, *Guatemalan Textiles.* New Orleans: Middle American Research Institute (1935) 110 pp.

*PEÑAFIEL, ANTONIO, *Monumentos del Arte Mexicano Antiguo.* Berlin: A. Asher & C., (1890) 3 vols. + atlas of 317 plates.

PETERSON, FREDERICK A., *Ancient Mexico.* New York: G. P. Putnam's Sons (1959) 313 pp.

PIÑA CHAN, ROMÁN, "Mesoamérica." México, D.F.: *Instituto Nacional de Antropología e Historia, Memorias VI* (1960) 178 pp.

————, Tlatilco, México, D.F.: *Instituto Nacional de Antropología e Historia, Serie Investigaciones Nos. 1 and 2* (1958) 2 vols. + 56 plates.

PORTER, MURIEL N., "Excavations at Chupícuaro, Guanajuato, Mexico." Philadelphia: *American Philosophical Society, Transactions,* n.s., Vol. 46, part 5 (1956) pp. 513-638.

————, "Tlatilco and the Pre-Classic Cultures of the New World." New York: *Viking Fund Publications, No. 19* (1953) 104 pp.

*PROSKOURIAKOFF, TATIANA, "An Album of Maya Architecture." Washington, D.C.: *Carnegie Institution of Washington, Publication No. 558* (1946) 72 pp. + 36 plates.

*————, "A Study of Classic Maya Sculpture." Washington, D.C.: *Carnegie Institution of Washington, Publication No. 593* (1950) 209 pp.

*ROBERTSON, DONALD M. *Mexican Manuscript Painting of the Early Colonial Period.* New Haven: Yale University Press (1959) 234 pp. + 88 plates.

*ROBICSEK, FRANCIS, *Copán; Home of the Mayan Gods.* New York: Museum of the American Indian (1972) 250 pp. + 300 color plates.

*SAHAGÚN, FRAY BERNARDINO DE, *"General History of the Things of New Spain: The Florentine Codex."* Translated and annotated by Arthur J. O. Anderson and Charles E. Dibble. Santa Fe, N.M.: School of American Research (1950-). In 14 volumes.

*SAVILLE, MARSHALL H., "The Goldsmith's Art in Ancient Mexico." New York: *Museum of the American Indian. Miscellaneous No. 7* (1920) 264 pp.

————, "A Sculptured Vase from Guatemala." New York: *Museum of the American Indian, Leaflet No. 1* (1919) 5 pp.

*————, "Turquois Mosaic Art in Ancient Mexico." New York: *Museum of the American Indian, Contributions Vol. VI* (1922) 110 pp. + 40 plates.

*————, "The Woodcarver's Art in Ancient Mexico." New York: *Museum of the American Indian, Contributions Vol. IX* (1925) 120 pp. + 51 plates.

SHEPARD, ANNA O., "Plumbate: A Mesoamerican Trade Ware." Washington, D.C.: *Carnegie Institution of Washington, Publication No. 573* (1948) 176 pp.

*SOUSTELLE, JACQUES, *and* IGNACIO BERNAL, *Mexico in Prehispanic Paintings.* Greenwich, Conn.: New York Graphic Society (1958) 25 pp. + 32 plates.

*SPINDEN, HERBERT J., "A Study of Maya Art." Cambridge, Mass.: *Peabody Museum, Memoirs VI* (1913) 285 pp. + 30 plates.

STIRLING, MATTHEW W., "Stone Monuments of Southern Mexico." Washington, D.C.: *Bureau of American Ethnology, Bulletin No. 138* (1944) 84 pp. + 62 plates.

*THOMPSON, J. ERIC S., *Maya Hieroglyphic Writing; an Introduction.* Norman: University of Oklahoma Press (1960) 347 pp.

*————, *The Rise and Fall of Maya Civilization.* Norman: University of Oklahoma Press (1954) 289 pp. + 24 plates.

*TOOR, FRANCES, *A Treasury of Mexican Folkways.* New York: Crown Publishers (1947) 570 pp.

————, *Mexican Popular Arts.* México, D.F.: Frances Toor Studio (1928) 107 pp.

*TOSCANO, SALVADOR, *Arte Precolombino de México y de la América Central.* México, D.F.: Instituto de Investigaciones Estéticas (1944) 556 pp.

————, PAUL KIRCHHOFF *and* DANIEL RUBÍN DE LA BORBOLLA, *Arte Precolombino del Occidente de México.* México, D.F.: Secretaria de Educación Pública (1946) 68 pp.

VAILLANT, GEORGE C., "Artists and Craftsmen in Ancient Central America." *American Museum of Natural History. Guide Leaflet No. 88* (1935) 102 pp.

*————, *Aztecs of Mexico: Origin, Rise and Fall of the Aztec Nation.* Revised by Suzannah B. Vaillant. New York: Doubleday & Co. (1962) 312 pp. + 68 plates.

VAN DE VELDE, PAUL *and* HENRIETTE VAN DE VELDE, "The Black Pottery of Coyotepec, Oaxaca, Mexico." Los Angeles: *Southwest Museum, Papers No. XIII* (1939) 43 pp.

VILLAGRÁ CALETI, AGUSTÍN, *Bonampak, la Ciudad de los Muros Pintados.* México, D.F.: Instituto Nacional de Antropología e Historia (1949) 43 pp.

VON WINNING, HASSO, *Pre-Columbian Art of Mexico and Central America.* New York: Abrams (1969) 388 pp. + 595 plates.

*WEAVER, MURIEL PORTER, *The Aztecs, Maya, and Their Predecessors.* New York: Seminar Press (1972) 348 pp. + 16 plates.

*WESTHEIM, PAUL, *Arte Antiguo de México.* México, D.F.: Fondo de Cultura Económica (1950) 356 pp.

————, *The Sculpture of Ancient Mexico.* New York: Doubleday Anchor Books (1963) 69 pp. + 96 plates.

WOOD, JOSEPHINE, *and* LILLY DEJONGH OSBORNE, *Indian Costumes of Guatemala.* Graz: Akademische Druck (1966) 154 pp., illus.

SOUTH AMERICA

*Anton, Ferdinand, *Alt-Peru und seine Kunst.* Leipzig: E. A. Seemann Verlag (1962) 128 pp. + 163 plates.

*Baessler, Arthur, *Ancient Peruvian Art; Contributions to the Archaeology of the Empire of the Incas.* Trans. by A. H. Keane, New York: Dodd, Mead & Co. (1902-03) 4 vols.

Bennett, Wendell C., *Ancient Arts of the Andes.* New York: Museum of Modern Art (1954) 186 pp., illus.

———, "Chavín Stone Carving." New Haven: *Yale University, Anthropological Studies,* Vol. III (1942) 9 pp. + 30 plates.

Bergsøe, Paul, *The Gilding Process and the Metallurgy of Copper and Lead Among the pre-Columbian Indians.* Copenhagen: Danmarks Naturvidenskabelige Samfund (1938) 56 pp.

———, *The Metallurgy and Technology of Gold and Platinum Among the pre-Columbian Indians.* Copenhagen: Danmarks Naturvidenskabelige Samfund (1937) 44 pp.

*Bird, Junius B., *Art and Life in Old Peru: an Exhibition.* New York: American Museum of Natural History. *Curator Magazine* excerpt, Vol. V, No. 2 (1962) pp. 147-210.

*———, *and* Louisa Bellinger, *Paracas Fabrics and Nazca Needlework.* Washington: The Textile Museum (1954) 128 pp. + 127 plates.

d'Harcourt, Raoul, *Textiles of Ancient Peru and their Techniques.* Seattle: University of Washington Press (1962; orig. pub. 1934) 186 pp. + 117 plates.

*de la Vega, Garcilaso El Inca, *The Royal Commentaries of the Incas and General History of Peru.* Translated by Harold V. Livermore. Austin: University of Texas (1966) 2 vols.

*Disselhoff, H. D., *and* Sigvald Linné, *The Art of Ancient America.* New York: Crown Publishers (1960) 274 pp.

*Dockstader, Frederick J., *Indian Art in South America.* Greenwich: New York Graphic Society (1967) 222 pp. + 250 plates.

Easby, Dudley T., Jr., *Orfebrería y Orfebres Precolombinos.* Buenos Aires: Instituto de Arte Americano (1956) Vol. IX.

Emery, Irene, *The Primary Structures of Fabrics.* Washington: The Textile Museum (1966) 340 pp.

*Emmerich, André, *Sweat of the Sun and Tears of the Moon.* Seattle: University of Washington Press (1965) 216 pp.

Jones, Julie, *Art of Empire: The Inca of Peru.* New York: Museum of Primitive Art (1946) 56 pp.

Joseph, R. H. Claude, *La Platería Araucana.* Santiago: Balcells & Co. (1928) 42 pp.

———, *Los Tejidos Araucanos.* Santiago: Imprenta y Lit. La Ilustración (1929) 58 pp.

*Kelemen, Pál, *Art of the Americas, Ancient and Hispanic.* New York: Thomas Y. Crowell (1969) 402 pp., illus.

*———, *Mediaeval American Art.* New York: Macmillan (1953; 1956; 1969) 414 pp. + 308 plates.

*Kubler, George, *The Art and Architecture of Ancient America; The Mexican, Maya and Andean Peoples.* Baltimore: Penguin Books (1962) 396 pp. + 168 plates.

*Leicht, Hermann, *Pre-Inca Art and Culture.* Translated by Mervyn Savill. New York: Orion Press (1960) 253 pp.

Linné, Sigvald, *Prehistoric Peruvian Painting.* Stockholm: Ethnos, Vol. XVIII (1943).

*———, *The Techniques of South American Ceramics.* Göteborg: Elanders (1925) 199 pp.

Lothrop, Samuel Kirkland, *Essays in Pre-Columbian Art and Archaeology.* Cambridge: Harvard University Press (1961) 507 pp.

———, "Gold Ornaments of Chavín Style from Chongoyape, Peru." Menasha: *American Anthropologist.* Vol. VI, No. 3 (1941) pp. 250-262.

———, "Indians of Tierra del Fuego." New York: *Museum of the American Indian, Contributions, Vol. X* (1928) 244 pp. + 19 plates.

*———, *Treasures of Ancient America.* New York: World Publishing Co. (1964) 229 pp. + 145 plates.

*———, W. F. Foshag, *and* Joy Mahler, *Pre-Columbian Art; the Robert Woods Bliss Collection.* New York: Phaidon Publishers (1957) 288 pp. + 162 plates.

*Meggers, Betty J., *Ecuador.* New York: Frederick A. Praeger (1966) 220 pp. + 76 plates.

*Montell, Gosta, *Dress Ornaments in Ancient Peru.* Göteborg: Elanders boktryckeri (1929) 262 pp.

Moreno, Segundo L., *La Música de los Incas.* Quito: Editoral Casa de Cultura Ecuatoriana (1957) 179 pp.

Mujica Gallo, Miguel, *The Gold of Peru.* (1959) 294 pp. Many editions; published wherever this exhibit was presented.

O'Neale, Lila M., "Textile Periods in Ancient Peru." Berkeley: *University of California Publications in American Archaeology and Ethnology,* Vol. 28, No. 2 (1930); Vol. 39, No. 2 (1942).

*Palmatary, Helen C., "The Pottery of Marajó Island, Brazil." Philadelphia: *American Philosophical Society, Transactions,* n.s., Vol. 39, Part 3 (1950) pp. 261-470 + 112 plates.

Pérez de Barradas, José, *Arqueología Agustiana.* Bogotá: Banco de la República (1943) 169 pp.

*————, *Orfebrería Prehispánica de Colombia; Estilo Calima.* Bogotá: Banco de la República (1954) 2 vols.

*————, *Orfebrería Prehispánica de Colombia: Estilo Tolima y Muisca.* Bogotá: Banco de la República (1958) 2 vols.

*————, *Orfebrería Prehispánica de Colombia: Estilos Quimbaya y Otros.* Bogotá: Banco de la República (1966) 2 vols.

*PREUSS, K. THEODOR, *Arte Monumental Prehistórico.* Bogotá: Escuela Salesianas (1931) 2 vols.

*REICHEL-DOLMATOFF, GERARDO, *Colombia.* New York: Frederick A. Praeger (1965) 231 pp. + 65 plates.

ROTH, WALTER EDMUND, "Additional Studies of the Arts, Crafts, and Customs of the Guiana Indians." Washington: *Bureau of American Ethnology, Bulletin 91* (1929) 110 pp. + 34 plates.

————, "An Introductory Study of the Arts, Crafts, and Customs of the Guiana Indians." *Bureau of American Ethnology, 38th Annual Report* (1924) pp. 25-720 + 183 plates.

*ROUSE, IRVING *and* JOSÉ M. CRUXENT, *Venezuelan Archaeology.* New Haven: Yale University Press (1963) 179 pp. + 55 plates.

ROWE, JOHN H., *Chavín Art; an Inquiry into its Form and Meaning.* New York: Museum of Primitive Art (1962) 23 pp. + 55 plates.

*SAVILLE, MARSHALL HOWARD, *The Antiquities of Manabí, Ecuador: A Preliminary Report.* New York: Museum of the American Indian (1907) 135 pp. + 55 plates.

*————, *The Antiquities of Manabí, Ecuador: Final Report.* New York: Museum of American Indian (1910) 284 pp. + 114 plates.

————, "A Golden Breastplate from Cuzco, Peru." New York: *Museum of the American Indian, Miscellaneous No. 21* (1921) 8 pp.

————, "The Gold Treasure of Sigsig, Ecuador." New York: *Museum of the American Indian, Leaflet No. 3* (1924) 20 pp.

*SAWYER, ALAN R., *Ancient Peruvian Ceramics; the Nathan Cummings Collection.* New York: Metropolitan Museum of Art (1966) 144 pp. + 218 plates.

*————, *Mastercraftsmen of Ancient Peru.* New York: Solomon R. Guggenheim Museum (1968) 109 pp.

*SCHMIDT, MAX, *Kunst und Kultur von Peru.* Berlin: Propylaen Verlag (1929) 621 pp.

SERRANO, ANTONIO, *El Arte Decorativo de los Diaguitas.* Córdoba: Imprenta de la Universidad (1943) 137 pp.

*STEWARD, JULIAN H., (editor), "The Handbook of South American Indians." Washington: *Bureau of American Ethnology, Bulletin 143* (1946-1959) 7 vols.

STIRLING, MATTHEW W., "Historical and Ethnographical Material on the Jívaro Indians." Washington: *Bureau of American Ethnology, Bulletin 117* (1938) 148 pp. + 37 plates.

*UBBELOHDE-DOERING, HEINRICH, *The Art of Ancient Peru.* New York: Frederick A. Praeger (1954) 68 pp.

*VALCARCEL, LUÍS EDUARDO, *Cuadernos de Arte Antiguo del Peru.* Lima: Museo Nacional del Peru (1935-1938) 6 vols.

————, *Historia de la Cultura Antigua del Peru,* Lima: Museo Nacional del Peru (1943) 2 vols.

VON HAGEN, VICTOR W., *The Ancient Sun Kingdoms of the Americas.* Cleveland: World Book Co. (1961).

*————, *The Desert Kingdom of Peru.* Greenwich: New York Graphic Society (1965) 192 pp. + 137 plates.

*WASSERMANN-SAN BLAS, BRUNO J., *Cerámicas de Antiguo Peru.* Buenos Aires: J. Penser (1938) 367 pp.

WILLEY, GORDON R., *An Introduction to American Archaeology. Vol. II: South America.* Prentice-Hall (1971) 559 pp.

YACOVLEFF, EUGENE, *Arte Plumaría entre los Antiguos Peruanos.* Lima: Revista del Museo Nacional de Lima, Vol. 2 (1933) pp. 137-158.